W. Daniel Wilson is a professor of
German at the University of California,
Berkeley. A Ph.D. from Cornell University,
he is the author of several books including
*Geheimräte gegen Geheimbünde: Ein
unbekanntes Kapitel der klassisch-
romantischen Geschichte Weimars*.

Robert C. Holub is a professor and
chair of the Department of German at the
University of California, Berkeley. His most
recent books are *Reflections of Realism:
Paradox, Norm and Ideology in Nineteenth-
Century German Prose*, *Jürgen Habermas:
Critic in the Public Sphere*, and *Crossing
Borders: Reception Theory,
Poststructuralism, Deconstruction*. He
earned his Ph.D. from the University of
Wisconsin-Madison.

IMPURE
REASON

IMPURE
REASON

Dialectic of Enlightenment in Germany

Edited by

W. DANIEL WILSON

and

ROBERT C. HOLUB

Wayne State University Press   Detroit

Library of Congress Cataloging-in-Publication Data

Impure reason : dialectic of enlightenment in Germany / edited by W. Daniel Wilson and
    Robert C. Holub.
        p.   cm.
        Essays originally presented at the Berkeley Symposium on "Dialectic of Enlighten-
    ment and the Age of Enlightenment", held in Oct. 1991.
        Includes bibliographical references and index.
        ISBN 0-8143-2496-7 (alk. paper)
        1. Enlightenment—Germany—Congresses. I. Wilson, W. Daniel. II. Holub,
    Robert C.   III. Berkeley Symposium on "Dialectic of Enlightenment and the Age of
    Enlightenment" (1991)
        B2621.I525 1993
        193—dc20   93-30901
                                                                            CIP

Grateful acknowledgment is made to the Max Kade Foundation for financial
assistance in the publication of this volume.

CONTENTS

5

PREFACE

THIS VOLUME IS comprised of essays that were originally presented at a Berkeley Symposium on "Dialectic of Enlightenment and the Age of Enlightenment" in October of 1991. At that conference our intention was to initiate a more differentiated and historically informed discussion of the notion of enlightenment. On both sides of the Atlantic, "enlightenment" has become a hotly disputed term in intellectual circles. In Germany, where editorials in newspapers and political figures from various parties have been known to accuse adversaries of "anti-enlightenment" values, debate and commentary has reached a wide public. These debates make clear what is at stake in any debate on enlightenment: it is the enlightenment discourse that gave birth to modern concepts of democratic government, human rights, and concepts like emancipation, equality, and (self-) critique. The American Constitution and particularly its Bill of Rights, for example, are unthinkable except as products of the historical Enlightenment. The debates also make clear, however, that the concept of enlightenment can be abused and misrepresented, and that liberal democracies are easily diverted from their enlightenment origins.

In the United States and on most of the continent, the modern controversy around enlightenment and related concepts has involved many of the most important postwar intellectuals. Although the first debates on enlightenment are prefigured in the Age of Enlightenment, the most important twentieth-century contribution was undoubtedly Max Horkheimer and Theodor W. Adorno's *Dialectic of Enlightenment*. Written during the final years of World War II and published in 1947, this book has remained a classic of modern thought for the past forty-five years. Proceeding from a notion of enlightenment as domination over nature, Horkheimer and Adorno argue that the original emancipatory notion of "enlightenment" ultimately endorses repressive and oppressive behaviors. One consequence of enlightenment rationality

7

manifests itself in the brutality of fascisms and state communisms, and in the "repressive tolerance" of "liberal" societies dominated by a mindless culture industry. Although the bleakness of Horkheimer and Adorno's view was certainly influenced by the war, the Holocaust, and their experience in American exile, the thesis that enlightenment cancels itself in this radically negative fashion has remained a fruitful starting point for much critical postwar thought.

While Horkheimer and Adorno's critique of enlightenment was directed at almost all philosophical and political positions—from doctrinaire communists and fascists to conservatives of all stripes and liberal democrats—in more recent years the most significant conflicts around enlightenment have pitted progressive advocates of reason against critics who, in extending Horkheimer and Adorno's thesis, conceive of rationality itself as a reactionary vestige of Western thought. It is perhaps ironic that Jürgen Habermas, the heir to the Frankfurt School of Critical Theory with which Adorno and Horkheimer are closely identified, has been the most vociferous defender of enlightenment in postwar Germany. Against Habermas, although rarely in direct confrontation, are a group of thinkers from France who have often received the label "poststructuralist." Habermas's position, of course, is not directly antithetical to those of his forerunners in Critical Theory. He agrees that a certain type of rationality—instrumental rationality—has pernicious manifestations in the modern world. Rationality, however, is not pure and undivided in his theory. To counter the effects of a one-sided "enlightenment" rationality grounded in the domination over nature, he posits communicative reason, which has to do with reaching understanding among human beings. Habermas's French adversaries, who rarely recognize this bifurcation of reason in Habermas's thought, contend, by contrast, that the rationality associated with European enlightenment is ultimately bound to hegemonic political and philosophical systems that ignore difference and diversity. Philosophers such as Jean-François Lyotard, Michel Foucault, and Jacques Derrida argue that at the very foundation of Western notions of reason is a dangerous "metaphysical" core that has contributed to an ongoing oppression in the name of identity, sameness, and totality. While Habermas believes that his distinction between instrumental and communicative rationality has moved him beyond metaphysical thought, his detractors in Europe and the United States view his writings as simply another attempt to purge the impurities of reason.

A central motivation for the organization of our conference and the publication of the proceedings was our perception that all parties in the postwar discussions of enlightenment have neglected or simplified the

Age of Enlightenment. Although enlightenment in a broader, theoretical sense cannot be limited to the Age of Enlightenment—various thinkers, including Horkheimer and Adorno, have dated it from antiquity—the eighteenth century stands at the beginning of the *modern* discourse of enlightenment and has often provided the historical material for debates. The ongoing debates on rationality have exhibited either an insufficient theoretical reflection or a lack of historical grounding. Our contention is that the modern theoretical debate on Enlightenment must look to the historical origins of this phenomenon in order to reach a full understanding of it. Our strategy, therefore, was not to intervene directly in current controversies conducted by either historians or theoreticians, but to confront the often abstract theories of the dialectic of enlightenment with concrete studies on cultural, social, and political aspects of the Age of Enlightenment. In order to have a manageable scope we restricted our purview to the German context, from which some of the most trenchant critiques of enlightenment emerge. But within this framework we encouraged interdisciplinary approaches that would demonstrate affinities and divergences across traditional boundaries. Because gender and sexuality have been crucial in recent debates around enlightenment, we were particularly interested in contributions that focused on these issues. We were also successful in our attempt to include among the participants not only renowned scholars, but also newer names in the profession, including graduate students.

The five divisions in this volume are virtually identical to the sessions of our conference. In the first we set the stage for our confrontation of history and theory by examining the various implications of twentieth-century critiques of enlightenment. Of central interest here are not only the works of Habermas, but also writings of Christa Wolf, Manfred Frank, and Richard Rorty, whom some contributors compare to eighteenth-century (self-)critics or advocates of enlightenment. Our second division concentrates on the wide-ranging topic of philosophical aesthetics, which can be considered a product of the eighteenth century. The contributions in this section range from considerations of the aesthetics of the horrible and narratology to analyses of the writings of Schiller and Hölderlin. In our third grouping the contributions focus on the connection between patriarchal structures and enlightenment. A rich variety of essays examines those dimensions of enlightenment thought that create gender stereotypes and force men and women into conventional roles. The complex interplay of power and otherness informs, at some level, the essays in our fourth grouping. In two essays this interplay involves the historical confrontation between the European and the non-European; in the others this relationship helps elucidate the mechanisms of the absolutist state. Our final set of essays deals with issues of psychology, education, and socialization. Of particular concern here were the way in which enlightenment ideologies are disseminated and how the paths of dissemination are themselves implicated in a dialectic of enlightenment. In each division, therefore, despite the diversity of topics and approaches, and despite the widely differing degrees of sympathy toward the enlightenment project, the contributions provide complementary analyses and illustrations of the phenomenon we have called "impure reason."

An ancillary goal of this volume is to introduce readers outside the field of German Studies to various aspects of the German Enlightenment, which deserves to be more widely known than through essays on Kant or Hölderlin. With this purpose in mind, we have designed the book so that a knowledge of German is not necessary in order to follow the argument. Where published translations of the works quoted were not available, the authors provided their own translations; those familiar with German will find the original for most quotations in the endnotes. Full bibliographical references for works referred to by author's name in the text or the endnotes are listed at the end of each essay.

The conference and this volume would not have been possible without the support of many people and institutions. Most significant was a generous grant from the Max Kade Foundation in New York. The Deutsche Forschungsgemeinschaft provided indispensable travel funds for the German participants. At Berkeley, the conference was supported by the College of Letters and Science, the Graduate Division, the Center for German and European Studies, the Bonwit-Heine Fund, and the Department of German.

During the time-consuming early stages of selection of papers, Helga Slessarev and Gerd Hillen were full partners in the organization of the conference and deserve special recognition. We wish to extend our warm gratitude to those colleagues who served as respondents and stimulated very productive discussions: Margaret L. Anderson, Renate W. Holub, Helmut J. Schneider, Helga Slessarev, and Kenneth D. Weisinger. We are deeply indebted to Susanne Hoopmann-Löwenthal, who took on the heavy burden of logistical arrangements for the conference. Several graduate students—Robert Bledsoe, Bernd Estabrook, Wayne Miller, and Arnim Polster—helped with logistics during the conference.

Robert C. Holub
W. Daniel Wilson
Berkeley, June 1993

PART ONE

Twentieth-Century Critiques of Enlightenment

Verständigung and *Dialektik*:
On Consensus Theory
and the Dialectic of Enlightenment

John A. McCarthy

I

THE FORTIETH ANNIVERSARY of the publication of Max Horkheimer and Theodor W. Adorno's *Dialectic of Enlightenment* (*Dialektik
der Aufklärung*) in 1947 (1944 in mimeograph form) caused the debate
on *Verständigung* (variously translatable as consensus, agreement, or
understanding) and dialectic to heat up considerably. In this essay I
will address certain aspects of that debate.

Unfortunately, Horkheimer and Adorno's treatise was reissued in
1988 in two easily accessible paperback editions to commemorate the
occasion.[1] I say "unfortunately" not because of any desire to suppress
open debate but because I think it is time for truly critical reflection
upon the nature of the historical epoch of Enlightenment and the
applicability of its "projects" today. We must resist the impulse to
categorize the Enlightenment one-dimensionally and categorically.
Following Werner Schneiders, I will argue that enlightenment by its
very nature is an open-ended, anti-authoritarian process which resists
categorization. It cannot be totalitarian or prescriptive without betray-
ing its essential impulses. In fact, it is inaccurate to see it as a project, if
by project we mean something based on a clearly conceived plan
(Schneiders 175-86). Horkheimer and Adorno, however, misjudged
that essential character. They were not objective in their 1944 assessment (unchanged in 1947 and 1969) of the phenomenon. The reprints
threaten, therefore, to reinforce the two philosophers' jaundiced view
of the nature of the European Enlightenment and its dialectical

13

method, misleading yet another generation of scholars on the *actual* historical configuration and objectives of the epoch.

Horkheimer and Adorno's antagonistic approach is understandable against the backdrop of fascism that provoked their sharp reaction in *Dialectic of Enlightenment*. Their main purpose was to argue that the dehumanization of modern industrialized society is directly traceable to the instrumentalization of reason, i.e., to the Enlightenment's penchant for developing encompassing, rational systems to master the environment. While their undertaking is legitimate, their method is one-dimensional and reductionistic. The actual configuration of Enlightenment thought and methodologies was much more complex than they would have us believe in their interpretation of the dialectic as domination. Consequently, while overplaying the characteristics of the scientific Enlightenment, they tended to downplay that movement's views on central moral values such as humankind's calling to be self-directive and autonomous.[2]

The republication of that 1940s argument is doubly unfortunate because Adorno presented a more balanced view of the dialectics of Enlightenment elsewhere, for example, in the essay collection, *Interventions: Nine Critical Models* (*Eingriffe: Neun kritische Modelle*, 1963), or *Educating for Autonomy* (*Erziehung zur Mündigkeit*, 1969). Considerable confusion about the nature of Enlightenment and dialectics could have been avoided had the 1963 text served as a source of inspiration for critics rather than *Dialectic of Enlightenment* with its distorting view.

The continuing topicality of the *Dialectic of Enlightenment* is underscored overtly by the proceedings of a Dutch symposium on the work (Kunneman and de Vries). It contains several negative reactions to Horkheimer and Adorno's book. The debate is also continued covertly by the *Festschrift* in honor of Jürgen Habermas on the occasion of his sixtieth birthday (Honneth) as well as in the series of essays published in *New German Critique* (Spring-Summer 1987). There seems to be no end to the debate on the role of dialectics of Enlightenment and the possibility of consensus.

Fortunately, almost concurrently with the reissuing of Horkheimer and Adorno's analysis, Jürgen Habermas published a closely argued critique of *Dialectic of Enlightenment* in *The Philosophical Discourse of Modernity* (1985/1987). The work seems to him to be "the blackest book" penned by the famous writer-team; indeed, it is "an odd book," comprised of "an essay of something over fifty pages, two excursuses, and three appendixes."[3] At the same time, Habermas published his own constructive view of the uses of reason, Enlightenment, and myth in the essay collection, *Moral Consciousness and Communicative Action* (*Moralbewußtsein und kommunikatives Handeln* 1983/1990). That effort helped to focus his theory of communicative action on its ethical implications and to defuse an overemphasis of its schema of instrumental reason and rationalization (see T. McCarthy).

The key notion in Habermas's paradigm of communicative action is the free, unencumbered *participation* in a discourse which is pragmatic rather than purely logical. Communicative action designates specifically a type of interaction that transcends the speech acts themselves by means of which communicative action is coordinated. Each person has the chance to participate and reach a conclusion through interaction with others. And each must have the freedom to try to persuade the others of the validity of one's own point of view. While coercive pressures might be present, they are not dominant.

Central components of communicative action are, therefore, those of community and participation.[4] The community of interacting persons can be called an "interpretive community" for it is rooted in a shared interpretation of a life-world and it reshapes that environment through renewed, coordinated interpretation. That renewed interpretation is an ongoing process (*TCA* 1: 95, 101). The resulting normative consensus of opinion would be a free and autonomous act. The discursive structure itself must be normative in the sense that it be designed to ensure equal opportunity for all to express and shape opinion through intersubjective interaction. No view is prohibited except one that would not allow a full hearing to any other view. Decisive for Habermas is, therefore, the unwillingness to change opinion ("Unbeeinflußbarkeit . . . der Willensbildung") rather than the impartiality of judgment ("die Unparteilichkeit des Urteils") (Habermas, "Diskursethik" 81f., 86).

Habermas's theory of communicative action came under critical scrutiny almost immediately, to which he responded in several defenses. The foreword to the third German edition of *TCA* (1984) is representative of his reaction. Jean-Francois Lyotard and Manfred Frank are representative of the extreme reactions of rejection and acceptance. Those positions are summarized in Manfred Frank's imaginary dialogue between Habermas and Lyotard, *The Limits of Reaching Understanding* (*Die Grenzen der Verständigung*, 1988). While Frank is personally sympathetic to Habermas's notions of consensus and intersubjective cooperation, Lyotard would seem unsympathetic.

Siding with Habermas, Frank calls for "an ethic of intersubjective cooperation" in contrast to Lyotard's insistence that it is not possible for speakers to come to agreement on universally valid rules of meta-prescriptions for language games (Lyotard 88). Basic is Habermas's insistence that agreement ("Verständigung") is the actual objective of communicative action ("A Reply" 269). Lyotard, however, conceives of *différend* as a hindrance to common understanding ("Verständi-gung") when he defines *différend* as being rooted in a threefold incom-mensurability: (1) the impossibility of raising speech acts to a meta-discourse, (2) the incompatibility of various syntactical rules with one single discursive genre, and (3) the insuperable dissimilarity among various types of discourse (Frank 32, 65, 101). For Lyotard the goal of discourse is not consensus—which for Lyotard could never be universal, by the way, only local—but rather "paralogy," i.e., the pursuit of dis-sent. Only in that fashion can the totalizing impact of consensus be counteracted.[5] This aversion to the totalizing impact of consensus is, actually, a facet of Habermas's concept which has been given short shrift. Frank draws attention to this point when he explains that con-sensus theory does not preclude dissent and is not idealistically har-monic: "Consensus theory, therefore, is not really less inclined to con-flictual situations than is Lyotard's advocacy of agonistic discourse; rather it emphasizes the fact that every communicative act ("Mitein-ander-Sprechen") presupposes the possibility of agreement contrary to the facts presented ("kontrafaktisch")" (Frank 73f.).

Thus Habermas and Lyotard share a postmodern feature in com-mon: their recognition of the loss of a pre-established harmony which accords order to our universe. Yet Habermas does not give up on the possibility of reaching understanding, i.e., on the validity of a meta-dis-course. We must reach a consensus ("uns verständigen"), Frank argues in support of Habermas, not because universal values mandate it but precisely because there is no longer a universally recognized norm (66).

In the following I wish to argue against a facile understanding of the "dialectic of Enlightenment" as a power struggle, against the notion of information monopoly, and against the widespread disparagement of an Enlightenment which has failed to achieve a utopia by shifting the focus away from *différend* and *Verdinglichung* and toward a paradigm of the enlightenment as consensus-seeking, as "pragmatic rationalism."[6] I will advance a view of the Enlightenment as promulgating "philosophi-cally true propositions, which are neither analytic, nor factual ... but rather 'essential' " because they express essential *possibilities* of human-kind, that is, human creativity (Petrovic 227f.). I therefore posit with Thomas Nagel a "metaphysics of action" and a "metaphysics of the person" which make reaching understanding ("Verständigung"), con-sensus, and ultimately objective altruism possible. Put differently, Enlightenment will be viewed as affording the ability to understand commonalities despite the differences within a pragmatic context (see Nagel 18f., 99-109).

The shift in focus highlights what I consider to be a grievous mis-understanding of the nature of enlightenment ("Aufklärung"). Pragmatic rationalism is akin to Habermas's theory of communicative action, John Dewey's "transactive situation," and William James's concept of the *"full* fact" (Haddock Seigfried 109). An experience, we would do well to remember, "is always what it is because of a transaction taking place between an individual and what, at the same time, constitutes his[/her] environment."[7] The environment includes the speaker, the interlocutors, the mood and spirit of the occasion as well as all other physical and psychological factors impacting upon the situation. Similarly, James defines his *"full* fact" as "a conscious field *plus* its object as felt or thought of *plus* an attitude towards the object *plus* the sense of self to whom the attitude belongs" (James 393). Each of these communicative acts can be seen as an attempt to make ourselves at home in the world. They are unifying endeavors, but not *ipso facto* totalitarian because each individual continues to occupy his/her spot in time and in space; each retains his or her uniqueness (Haddock Seigfried 115).

Thus, I want to highlight a postmodern side of the Age of Enlightenment itself which has been neglected in favor of its other main feature: its modernity (i.e., technology, power structures, search for stability). The overemphasis on the movement's modernity has led to what Habermas has labelled "grandiose acts of reductionism."[8] In taking this stance I follow the lead of such thinkers as Ernst Cassirer and Michel Foucault (two very different thinkers indeed!) as well as the later Adorno, Habermas, Frank, and Schneiders. My point of departure is Cassirer's definition of "true Enlightenment" as "process," as "doubting and seeking, tearing down and building up," as "constantly fluctuating activity."[9] We should take more notice of Adorno's later definition of dialectics as "no third standpoint but the attempt, by means of immanent criticism, to help philosophical standpoints transcend their own limitations and overcome the vicariousness of thinking in terms of a point of view."[10] Moreover, I wish to emphasize Adorno's insistence that philosophy is possible today only if it stops insisting with stupid arrogance upon its point of view based on accumulated "facts." Philosophy will be possible again only when it endeavors to learn without any mental reservations what those are afraid of who are dead set against renouncing their insistence that philosophy must always produce positive results.[11] Adorno seems to call for an end to the positivistic dialectical method he himself had practiced in *Dialectic of Enlightenment*.

Different sites impart distinctiveness to the ideas and values shared; this is true whether the time and place is Enlightenment Weimar or postmodern Paris (see Hayles 292, 295). Ultimately, these communicative or transactive situations can themselves be related back to a larger

paradigm, one that transcends even the supposed incommensurability
of *le différend*, namely, that of the "postmodern" concept of chaos as
womb, as that nexus of processes "which makes order possible" but
which transcends the ordering subject (Hayles 100). An omniscient
view is not undermined by chaos theory; rather the latter reaches
beyond the realm of Newtonian mechanics, advancing into a "third territory that lies between order and disorder" (Hayles 15).

This "third territory" might be likened to the space of reconciliation
in which two separate selves can come together in a kind of agreement
which transcends each of the individual identities. Thus, for example,
Adam Müller spoke in his essay on the nature of dialogue in 1812 of
three positions in dialogic interaction: (1) the speaker, (2) the interlocutor, and (3) the notion of a higher plane of understanding shared
by both persons which transcends their individual interests, thereby
accommodating both their standpoints without creating an intractable
third standpoint. The possibility of understanding is guaranteed, then,
by a space external to the interlocutors individually but shared collectively. Habermas counteracts the thesis of total relativity by positing a
realm of knowledge which is more than the sum total of its subjective
views. He calls it a "holistically structured" concept of knowledge
which is implicit and intuitive because it is caused by participation in a
consciously or unconsciously shared life-world (*TCA* 1: 336f.). In his
"Reply to My Critics" (1982), he suggests, moreover: "Perhaps we
should speak instead of a balance among moments incomplete in
themselves, an equilibrated interplay of the cognitive with the moral
and the aesthetic-expressive" (262).

Despite their pluralism, our cosmological and biological contexts
would appear to share an encoded message that reveals itself only
gradually, partially, and perhaps unconsciously. Numerous perspectives are necessary to achieve the "right perspective" even within a
shared interpretive environment (see, for example, C. M. Wieland's
Schach Lolo 1778). The character of knowledge, anchored as it is in
polyperspectivity and dependent on *"full* facts," guarantees that
humankind has the potential for understanding the world, others, and
the self. Ultimately, therefore, humankind is confident of reaching a
consensus which preserves differences while narrowing the space separating entities and which has the potential for uniting local communities
with a universal one.

Finally, Foucault's reading of Kant's essay, *What Is Enlightenment*,
also figures dominantly in this view of consensus formation. Foucault
locates the essence of Enlightenment in its quality as a permanent critique and a permanent re-creation of ourselves as autonomous beings.
I would insist with Foucault that that creative impulse is at the heart of

the historical consciousness which the Enlightenment had of itself and which is a source of postmodernity as well as of modernity (Foucault 44, 50). In doing so, I am not alone. In his analysis of the relationship between "Truth and Pluralism," Gajo Petrovic concludes that while there is some truth in pluralism and some plurality in truth, "there is need, not for more plurality of truth, but for more tolerance and understanding for the complexities of the world and for the difficulties of searching for truth" (229). Habermas echoes this appeal for tolerance of the complexity of social existence in his *Theory of Communicative Action* with such statements as: "This conception presupposes that acting and speaking subjects can relate to more than only one world, and that when they come to an understanding with one another about something in one world, they base their communication on a commonly supposed system of worlds" (1: 278). A few lines later, he also explains: "Finally, communicative action is dependent on situational contexts, which represent in turn segments of the life-world of the participants in interaction" (1: 278-79). The purpose of philosophy—and of dialectical discourse—should be to expose the inner sense of the "multimeaningness" of the complex form of "Being" which constitutes human existence (Petrovic 213). In other words, we can argue with Petrovic that there is a deeper reality within human existence which assures a common touchstone for measuring the various meanings of the "pluriversum" in which we exist (229).

Petrovic's inner sense of multimeaningness seems related to Charles Taylor's notion of inwardness which he sees as being part and parcel of modernity, but which has been neglected in favor of an acultural theory of modernity which reduces the movement to "cultural-neutral" operations such as the growth of scientific consciousness, the secularization of religious thought or the rise of instrumental reason (Taylor 601, 606). Excessive reliance on an acultural theory of modernity locks us into an "ethnocentric prison" and causes us to project our own forms unwittingly onto others. It distorts our understanding of ourselves, causes misclassifications, and impoverishes our ability to communicate ("Verständigung") (Taylor 606). Perspectives on oneself are central to the communicative act and they are, moreover, part of the dialectic of Enlightenment if we define Enlightenment as the process of self-understanding and not just as mastery of the physical and social environment.

II

"The discontents of modernity," Habermas has argued, "are rooted not in rationalization as such but in the failure to develop and insti-

tutionalize in a balanced way all the different dimensions of reason
opened up by the modern understanding of the world" (T. McCarthy
177). The new conflicts caused by modernity arise along the seams
between system and life-world.[12] The only way to avoid the tyranny of
any one system is not to posit any one specific permanent state as the
ultimate objective of dialectical discourse. Another way of putting it is
to assert that no one interlocutor can be allowed to impose his/her
view on another since there is, in our postmodern era, no apparent legitimacy to the claim of universalism based on a transmundane absolute or on *apriori* principles of objectivity. When the dialectical method
is subverted to realize a clearly pre-defined condition it becomes
totalitarian and instrumental in Horkheimer and Adorno's sense.

Thus, the means to escape the totalitarian thrust resides in the purpose to which the method is put to use as well as in the related self-
perception of the interlocutors. "Only *that* revolution," Manfred Frank
remarks, "would be truly non-totalitarian which is permanent."[13] An
ethically based theory of communicative action seems to take into
account the necessity of intersubjective norms, the lack of universal
standards of measurement, and the dangers of according too much importance to any one individual or idea. True, it remains anthropocen-
tric, but what else is ethics?[14] Thus this essay situates consensus theory
at the center of inquiry into the dialectics of Enlightenment.

My thesis is that consensus discourse as formulated by Habermas—free of coercion, based on mutual uncertainty yet on mutual
respect, driven by a search for non-predetermined answers, and rooted
in the capacity to regard oneself as merely one individual among many
—is as much a legacy of the Enlightenment as a single-minded, goal-
specific, self-aggrandizing dialectic. The critical positions of a Lessing,
Wieland, Josef Rückert, or Christian Karl Graf von Benzel-Sternau can
be drawn upon to illustrate my point. It will be seen that the paraphrase of the Habermas-Frank position is equally descriptive of the
eighteenth-century position.[15]

Habermas's prime concern in his *Theory of Communicative Action* is
to develop a paradigm of social action that avoids the further "techni-
cizing of the life-world" (2: 281, 277). The effort requires a distancing
of the new paradigm from those based on institutional order and normative contexts. Thus he suggests a paradigmatic change from the
nineteenth-century tradition of "philosophy of consciousness" to an
"intersubjective understanding or communication" (1: 390, 399); that
move would actually take us back to an eighteenth-century model.[16]
While the former paradigm is subject oriented, the latter is group motivated. While the former posits a confrontational situation between the
subject and the objects which are manipulated and exploited to ad-

vance the subject, the latter sees the self-directive subject as one among many self-directive subjects. Yet the relationship between the subject and its environment is highly complex and diverse.

In his assessment of consensus theory, Rolf Grimminger seems reluctant to recognize the differentiated view offered by Habermas. Grimminger devotes the first chapter of his book, *Order, Chaos, and Art* (*Die Ordnung, das Chaos und die Kunst,* 1986) to Habermas's theory, which he renders against the backdrop of the eighteenth-century Enlightenment. (Actually, Grimminger cites primarily representatives of the early Enlightenment: Gottsched, Thomasius, Wolff.) While critical of Horkheimer and Adorno's position in *Dialectic of Enlightenment,* he is equally critical of Habermas's position in *Theory of Communicative Action,* which, he argues, incorporates in an ahistorical manner naive assumptions of the early Enlightenment regarding the predominant authority of reason to order human existence (Grimminger 13). He speaks repeatedly of Habermas's adoption of a "rational ordering of all of creation" (38), a "unified order of reason" (39), and Habermas's tendency to confuse "the universal unity of reason" with mere conventions (41). According to Grimminger, Habermas must exclude from his theory of consensus the contingencies of everyday life (34), thus disallowing the possibility of dissent (36f.), so that he might posit an a priori, transcendental claim to an absolute normative authority that regulates the discourse (41).

Grimminger is right to point out that rational discourse was seldom at home in the everyday world of the eighteenth century—or of any century for that matter—but his claim that reason immediately attached itself to the authority of existing institutions in order to ensure its own validity (39) is highly questionable when seen against the backdrop of the heated debate on freedom of thought and of the press which was one of the major thrusts of the Enlightenment. That debate ultimately led to the revision of codified law in the German-speaking states and, more poignantly, to the establishment of constitutional states with their potential for democratic, participatory government. (This is, of course, one of Habermas's counterarguments to the dystopian view of *Dialectic of Enlightenment.*) In his assessment of Habermas's consensus theory, Grimminger overlooks the foundation of this theory in the principle of sincerity ("Wahrhaftigkeit") in expressing one's ethical propositions (which, we need to stress, do not represent absolute, universal norms, only local ones) and not on logical propositions of pure reason (see Grimminger 35).[17] Surprisingly absent in his sharp criticism of Habermas's theory is a close reading of *Theory of Communicative Action* itself.

Habermas is careful to distinguish communicative action from "instrumental" and "strategic" forms of interaction. While "instrumental" action focuses on technical rules as a means of controlling conditions and events, and while "strategic" designates action designed to influence the rational decisions of others in order to ensure the success of a pre-arranged goal, "communicative" action is neither egocentric nor calculative in the same sense as either of these forms of interaction. Habermas clearly states:

> By contrast, I shall speak of *communicative* action whenever the actions of the agents involved are coordinated not through egocentric calculations of success but through acts of reaching understanding. In communicative action participants are not primarily oriented to their own individual successes; they pursue their individual goals under the condition that they can harmonize their plans of action on the basis of common situation definitions. (*TCA* 1: 285f.)

Such clear formulations are encountered repeatedly in Habermas's text. The goal of communicative action is (1) to bring about understanding among persons in a shared environment and (2) to transform the mere act of understanding the other person's point into agreement on the moral value and rational validity of the point. Habermas adds:

> Processes of reaching understanding [Verständigung] aim at an agreement [Einverständnis] that meets the conditions of rationally motivated assent [Zustimmung] to the content of an utterance. A communicatively achieved agreement has a rational basis; it cannot be imposed by either party, whether instrumentally through intervention in the situation directly or strategically through the decisions of opponents (1: 287).

While Habermas understands "Verständigung" to be movement toward comprehending a point, he specifically states that "Einverständnis" rests on "common *convictions*" (*TCA* 1: 387). "Verständigung," moreover, is rooted in a teleology of language and reason whose purpose is to unite individuals in an interpretive community seeking grounds for agreement without forcing them to renounce their individuality. The concept of communicative action, he clarifies, should not itself be viewed as teleological, for it "is presented in such a way that the acts of reaching understanding, which link the teleologically structured plans of action of different participants and thereby first combine individual acts into an interaction complex, cannot themselves be reduced to teleological actions" (288). In contrast to such "parasitic" attitudes of "giving something to be understood" ("Zu-verstehen-geben") and "letting something be understood" ("Verstehen-lassen"), "the use of language with an orientation to reaching understanding" ("der verständigungsorientierte Sprachgebrauch") appears as "the *original mode* of language use" (*TCA* 1: 288). The process of reaching a consensus on the validity of norms thus takes the objective world, the social realm, and the subjective experience of the individual participant into account (*TCA* 1: 99f.).

Impartial understanding occurs in multidimensional fashion as well. Habermas identifies three levels: (1) the speech act establishes a mutually acceptable basis of interpersonal action within a given normative context, (2) the content of the message is true so that the interlocutor is willing to accept the speaker's knowledge as valid, and (3) all opinions, personal views, desires, etc. are expressed sincerely, without the intent to deceive. These three levels translate into (1) normative consensus, (2) shared propositional knowledge, and (3) mutual trust (*TCA* 1: 307f.). Yet the *sine qua non* of communicative action remains "illocutionary" or "expressive." Occurring on the interpersonal level, these objectives are to be distinguished from "perlocutionary" or "cognitive" and "locutionary" or "appellative" ones (*TCA* 1: 289f., 293ff.). Consequently, communicative action is primarily of interest as a "principle of socialization" (*TCA* 1: 337).

These passages make clear that while Habermas holds to the concept of reason as an organizing principle, he does not believe in its infallibility or see it as a source of *absolute* truth, as Grimminger asserts. On the contrary, Habermas seems aware of the dangers of "Vereinseitigung" in the application of reason. Understanding ("Einverständnis" but also "Verständigung") requires a multidimensional framework in which the dimensions of reason, ethics, and aesthetics are commingled (*TCA* 2: 398) and which takes into account a threefold relationship to the world: the objective, the social, and the subjective (*TCA* 1: 86-96). There is no evidence here of a naive, uncritical belief in the infallibility of reason which Grimminger attributes to Habermas.

III

Thus Habermas's own text refutes Grimminger's conclusions about Habermas's supposed aversion to dissent in his allegedly harmonic brand of consensus. Habermas's theory is, moreover, firmly rooted in ideas of tolerance and difference in the Age of Enlightenment.[18] The heated debate on freedom of the press in the late eighteenth century makes clear that freedom of thought was premised on the right to dissent. Kant's view that public laws must be openly discussed and justified if they are to have the force of law ("Zum ewigen Frieden," *Werke* 9: 244f., 250), Wieland's notion of the "widest publication of all facts, observations, discoveries, investigations,"[19] and Lessing's insistence that each person has an inalienable right "to think aloud," communicating those thoughts to any and all who have ears to hear (*Ernst und Falk*, First 'Gespräch'), act as a leitmotif throughout the era. Each individual has the right to think for him/herself.

The only restrictions are that no one engage in open and direct character defamation, no one endeavor directly to overthrow a legitimate government or disempower the state constitution, and that no one speak against *all* religious or moral values. Doing so is a form of tyranny. The modifier "direct" is an important restriction in judging the validity of open expression, Wieland explains, for any person who works indirectly to alter concepts and expectations in the free marketplace of ideas operates within acceptable limits. Yet the judgment of what is direct or indirect is often left to those who are not open-minded. For an intolerant censor no liberal expression of ideas would be acceptable (3: 573). On the other hand, there is no stopping an idea once it has been thought. These ideas are encountered at every turn in the 1780s and 1790s.[20]

The role of freedom of the press is closely aligned with the Enlightenment's understanding of anthropology in a pragmatic sense, as Kant's essay bearing this title shows. While physiological anthropology is concerned with humankind's place within the time-space continuum, the pragmatic is concerned with "that which man as an autonomous being makes of himself or can and should make of himself" (Kant, *Anthropologie in pragmatischer Sicht, Werke* 10: 399). The essential human quality for Kant and his contemporaries is thus the ability to be self-determining. Such is the calling of humankind. In regards to this vocation, Kant sums up his theory of pragmatic anthropology by drawing the connection between humankind as a creature of reason, as a social being, and as a moral entity. In concert with others and through the application of reason humankind is destined "by means of the arts and sciences to cultivate itself, to become more civilized and morally refined."[21] The key is the need for each person to *learn* to appreciate the good. Each human being represents a bundle of potential and each has the moral obligation to develop that potential. But it cannot be done in isolation and it cannot be done passively. Others cannot do it for one; one must do it for oneself. However, ready access to information is required. It was not per happenstance that the Enlightenment occurred largely via print culture or that open sociability was raised to the status of a universal ideal (Jäger 71f.). This notion of self-development is best known as "Mündigkeit" (autonomy, self-sufficiency) in the language of the era.

The notion of self-cultivation is a far cry from that of self-preservation ("Selbsterhaltung") or self-affirmation ("Selbstbehauptung"). While the latter are forms of egoism in that an individual subject imposes its will on an other (Grimminger 42), the former connotes the release of innate capabilities which exist in an incomplete state of development, somewhat like the biological or physiological programming of the animal and plant worlds. While it is true that development always occurs as a process of accommodation ("Anpassung") and differentiation ("Abgrenzung") from one's context (*TCA* 1: 388), self-development should not be misconstrued to mean a total loss of self. This distinction proves to be decisive for Habermas's theory of communicative action. He writes:

> A subjectivity that is characterized by communicative reason resists the denaturing of the self for the sake of self-preservation. Unlike instrumental reason, communicative reason cannot be subsumed without resistance under a blind self-preservation. It refers neither to a subject that preserves itself in relating to objects via representation and action, nor to a self-maintaining system that demarcates itself from an environment, but to a symbolically struc tured life-world that is constituted in the interpretive accomplishments of its members and only reproduced through communication. Thus communicative reason does not simply encounter ready-made subjects and systems; rather, it takes part in structuring what is to be preserved. The utopian perspective of reconciliation and freedom is ingrained in the conditions for the communicative sociation of individuals; it is built into the linguistic mechanism of the reproduction of the species. (*TCA* 1: 398)

The relationship between the subject and its environment is, to be sure, a dialectical one. But the confrontation is no longer between a forming subject and a formed object; it is the interaction of subjects with one another as forming subjects as well as "formed" objects. One might want to label this encounter "communication through competition," as Grimminger does (42). Yet for Habermas and the Enlightenment tradition in which he stands, the competitive element recedes behind intersubjective cooperation, "for in cooperative processes of interpretation no participant has a monopoly on correct interpretation."[22]

Just as plants need sun, water, and nourishment to evolve, so too does humankind. The sun, water, and nourishment are provided in the social context. The individual must be exposed to the diversity of beings, opinions, and views in order to overcome his/her own bounded view. Kant sums up: "Egoism can be counteracted only by pluralism; that is, that manner of thinking which does not take the self to be the total world, but rather views itself as a mere citizen of the world and acts accordingly" (Kant 10: 411). What is required of the individual subject is that s/he continually place her/himself in the other person's shoes. The recognition of the essential freedom of the other guards against one-sidedness ("Vereinseitigung"). It is in this meta-personal sense that we are to understand Kant's fundamental moral imperative: "Act only on those maxims which you can at the same time will to become universal laws of nature" (6: 71). Pluralism, with its incumbent relativizing of individual standpoints, is simultaneously a guard against overemphasizing the self and the means towards self-fulfillment. Every human being has the need (and right) to self-fulfillment in common. Thus, Petrovic can speak of an inner reality which transcends superficial differences, uniting all human beings in a highly pragmatic fashion, and Nagel is justified in conceiving of a "metaphysics of the person" that makes objective altruism possible.

These ideas are echoed everywhere in the Age of Enlightenment. Wieland asks, for example, who has the right to encourage others toward enlightenment, and responds: anyone who feels that he or she can do it: "thus it will remain such that everyone from Socrates or Kant to the most obscure of all supernaturally enlightened tailors and shoe makers is, without exception, justified in enlightening humankind as well as he can as soon as his good or mischievous spirit moves him to do so."[23] It is always better, he adds, to allow everyone to speak his/her mind freely and openly for all the world to judge its truth than to ascribe absolute authority to those who hold office in our churches and universities.

The open and free expression of ideas is the only real guard against subjective distortions of historical fact. "An eyewitness," Wieland informs us elsewhere, "can see incorrectly without wanting to." Any witness or historian can have judged wrongly, might have overlooked important factors, or overemphasized the importance of other elements. All human beings are subject to error. Thus "the true palladium of humankind" is a free exchange of ideas.[24] "Who would dare to be so brazen," Wieland asks yet elsewhere, "to make his reason, his views not only the measure of everyone else, but also their norm and law?"[25] The only stipulation one can impose on the free exchange of ideas is that each writer or interlocutor not willfully distort facts: "His first and foremost duty is sincerity and impartiality" (*Werke* 3: 486). Truth is not a commodity to be bought and sold; once objectified it becomes part of power brokerage and loses its truth content. Not even truth itself is of value to human beings but the pursuit of truth and the uncertainty of ever knowing whether we have, finally, attained validity, so Lessing tells us metaphorically in his *Duplik* and in *Nathan* (see Bahr 43). Habermas draws on this conception of the free exchange of ideas when he cites sincerity ("Wahrhaftigkeit") and impartiality ("Unparteilichkeit") as *sine qua nons* of any interpretive community (for example, *TCA* 1: 100).

In order to differentiate between the more and less appropriate, the more or less biased, the mind must be alert. Each individual must be aware of the ways in which opinions and feelings can be manipulated. The function of the airing of all views was intended to develop that ability to discern differences. In his advice to authors in service of enlightenment, *Considerations for the Author of our Age* (*Gesichtspunkte für den Schriftsteller unsers Zeitalters*, 1796), Christian Karl Graf von Benzel-Sternau equates literature with public administration, labelling them "siblings" and characterizing their relationship as one of constant communication (Benzel-Sternau 1796: 38). According to Benzel-Sternau, the most grievous deficit of the age is the inability to think for oneself. Thus the most pressing need is for cultivation of the mind, for a "charging of energy" which is the necessary prerequisite for self-determination and the possibility of social reform. It is an encompassing kind of energy, penetrating the realms of intellect, emotion, and volition:

> The energy of soul encompasses the spirit, the heart, and the will. Independent thinking is the result of mental energy; only a heart full of energy is capable of feeling independently; independent action results from the capacity for autonomous volition.[26]

Every obstacle to achieving this independence of judgment must be removed (69). The consensus here is that each individual can only be a responsible and productive member of the group if s/he has been encouraged to think and feel for her/himself. Given the predominance of this view in the late eighteenth century, it would be amazing had Habermas not detected the emphasis on individuality and independence in devising his theory of communicative action. Like the Enlighteners, Habermas insists on the possibility of dissent since through dissent one learns to recognize the self and its potential.

Similarly, Josef Rückert addresses the dialectics of public expression in his treatise *On Reading* (*Ueber Lektüre*, 1796), viewing the dynamics of literature from the point of view of the reader rather than of the author. A passive, one-dimensional act of reading is harmful to the human spirit because it conditions the reader to react more like a machine than to act like an autonomous, self-directive agent (239). If the reader unquestionably accepts what the author writes, s/he eventually becomes enslaved by the opinions of others, having reneged on her/his obligation to cultivate one's own intellectual and emotional capacity. "Reflect and judge yourself with all your might," Rückert urges his reader, concluding: "Herein lies the secret of the highest pleasure and of the art of taking from your clever author the latent power he has over you and by means of which he abuses you. Only your own activity and its increase in energy provides genuine pleasure. To be passive is not to feel pleasure."[27] Rückert couches his exhortations in the language of pleasure because in the newly constituted literary marketplace of the turn of the century and with the rise of pulp literature (*Unterhaltungsliteratur*), reading had become largely an exercise in pleasure-seeking. Nevertheless, the underlying pragmatics of read-

ing, writing, and thinking in nurturing human potential and advancing
true understanding and tolerance among individuals is not lost. Passively absorbing information proves unproductive, even detrimental to
the human spirit. But all attempts to think for oneself, to nurture "the
energy of spirit," are simultaneously productive and enjoyable, enjoyable because productive.

In his typically laconic manner, Christoph Georg Lichtenberg commented on the value of reason in dealing with the complexities of life.
He calls for "a gulp of reason" ("ein Schluck von Vernunft," 90). Well
aware of the problematic relationship between subject and object and
thus of the need for constant critical self-reflection, Lichtenberg urged
awareness and conscious choice. A good dose of skepticism is most
useful. Lichtenberg advises: "Doubt everything at least once, even the
axiom 2 x 2 = 4" (250). "Take nothing for granted" is the dictum of the
era—except for the human potential for development and the potential
for error, we might add. Again Lichtenberg: "In order to doubt something, it is, of course, often necessary that one not understand it. Some
people would like very much to reverse this sentence, maintaining instead that one does not understand their point if one doubts it" (243).
The truth (better: validity) of this observation has not lost any of its significance for the contemporary debate on dialectics of Enlightenment
(see, for example, Améry 133).

In the final analysis, Enlightenment should be seen as an attitude[28]
which acknowledges the fallibility of the speaker, favors a pluralism of
ideas contending with one another as a counterbalance to that individual fallibility, which seeks incessantly for the "right" perspective, which
eschews a closed system of rationalization intolerant of dissent, and
which is optimistic in its belief that *Verständigung* is possible. Like
Foucault's definition of modernity, the Enlightenment is an attitude
toward the perpetual movement within which we labor and consists in
accepting the shifting moments of time for what they are, not in imposing our will on them, and not supplanting them with a presumed cosmological telos.[29] Habermas's theory of consensus acknowledges that
complexity of movement. Although he might not agree with Grimminger's extreme statements that human beings "can only communicate
when they are simultaneously competing with one another"; and "No
society can agree on a consistent unity of reason in the canon of universally valid norms; *it cannot do it; moreover, it should not even try*,"[30]
Habermas's theory of communicative action does, in fact, allow for
"the tolerance of opposing views" ("Toleranz für Widersprüche";
Grimminger 34, 43).[31] The toleration of dissent, which the Enlightenment advanced as one of its chief tenets, gives evidence that the
Enlightenment is *not* over (see Grimminger 12); the complexity of the

movement just hasn't been fully understood. It is, as Charles Taylor argues, a result of "seeing everything modern as belonging to one Enlightenment package" (605). When we learn to see the "Enlightenment package" in a differentiated way, we will appreciate the simultaneity of the modern and postmodern aspects of the phenomenon (see also Schneiders, 14-16).

We are reminded here of Lichtenberg's aphorism on the relationship between understanding and skepticism. While skepticism is often prompted by a lack of understanding, the reversal is not necessarily true: namely, that skepticism is the sign of a lack of understanding (243).

On the contrary, the Enlightenment is exemplary for that mode of reflection that Foucault labels "transdiscursivity" and which exists outside the space occupied by science ("What Is an Author?" 113-16). Wieland, Lichtenberg, and many others anticipated this stance. The egoism of the particular can be overcome through the widening perspective created by the infusion of the many which in turn fans the "energy of mind" so necessary for Enlightenment and understanding. Far from being disjointed perspectives, the pluralism of the modern and postmodern era seems ultimately rooted in the Kantian belief that humankind is its own end and purpose (see *Foundations of the Metaphysic of Morals, Grundlegung zur Metaphysik der Sitten*). Postmodernity as well as modernity each takes its cue from the Enlightenment dialectic itself. And nowhere does that dialectic serve understanding more than in a system of communicative action. I conclude with a quotation from Wieland which prefigures Habermas's notion of unity in diversity: "Can harmony and order not coexist with diversity? Does harmony not arise from diversity through the introduction of order? And is harmony not more attractive than monotony?"[32]

Notes

1. Frankfurt/M.: Fischer, 1988 (Fischer Wissenschaft 7404); Leipzig: Reclam, 1988.

2. Typical of this position is Hennig Ritter, who castigates the work for its facile equation of fascists and their opponents, totalitarian states and advanced forms of capitalism; see also J. McCarthy, *Crossing Boundaries* 66-70 and Geyer-Ryan.

3. Habermas, "Entwinement" 130; also *Theory of Communicative Action* 1: 377-83 (hereafter cited as *TCA*). Jean Améry is no less put off: "Soeben las ich nach Jahr und Tag in einem Buche wieder, das mich vor drei Dekaden begeistert hat: *Dialektik der Aufklärung* von Adorno und Horkheimer. Ohne Zaudern bekenne ich, daß Schrecken und tiefes Unbehagen mich beim Wiederlesen dieses hochgeistreichen Werkes erfaßten. In ihrem Bemühen, die klassische Aufklärung aus einer epochenbedingten Naivität zu erlösen, und dialektisch weiterzuentwickeln, haben die Autoren sich hinreißen lassen zu wahren Enormitäten, die, wörtlich

genommen, den übelsten Obskurantismen als Alibi dienen können" (131f.).

4. Habermas, *TCA* 2: 291f. See also his clarification of this point in "A Reply to My Critics" 264-65.

5. Haddock Seigfried 114; Hayles 215, 288.

6. Haddock Seigfried 108-09. This pragmatic rationalism has the potential for a "radically pragmatic aesthetic" which is of particular interest to literary critics and historians. See also Habermas, *TCA* 1: 375; 2: 585.

7. Dewey 43; see also Habermas, *TCA* 1: 307ff.).

8. "Großartige Vereinseitigungen"—which T. McCarthy translates somewhat awkwardly as "magnificent 'one-sidednesses' ": Habermas, *TCA* 2: 397.

9. Cassirer, ix. For his part, Peter Gay points out the essential heterogeneity of the European Enlighteners despite a common *style* of thinking (3-19).

10. Adorno, *Eingriffe*: "kein dritter Standpunkt, sondern der Versuch, durch immanente Kritik philosophische Standpunkte über sich und über die Willkür des Standpunktdenkens hinauszubringen" (21).

11. The foregoing is a free translation of Adorno's formulation: "mit dümmlicher Arroganz sich Informationen zu verschaffen und dann Stellung zu beziehen, sondern ungeschmälert, ohne Mentalreservat zu erfahren, wovor die ausweichen, die sich die Maxime nicht rauben lassen wollen, es müsse nun einmal bei aller Philosophie etwas Positives herausschauen" (*Eingriffe* 28).

12. *TCA* 2: 395; see also Ingram's chapter "System and Life-World" (115-34).

13. "Nur *die* Revolution wäre wahrhaft nicht-totalität, die permanent würde" (Frank, 21). Adorno arrives at a similar conclusion in *Erziehung zur Mündigkeit*.

14. See Frank's discussion of Jean-Francois Lyotard's definition of postmodernity and his critique of Lyotard's notion of "power" discourse (11-22). See also Thomas Nagel's argument for *The Possibility of Altruism*, which is based on the view that ethics is a branch of psychology and does not reduce altruism to a feeling.

15. Frank explains, e.g., "Der gewaltfreie Diskurs hat gerade das Ziel, im Interesse der begründeten Konsensbildung alle Dissense aufkommen zu lassen und niemals einzuschränken, also etwa durch nicht-argumentative Mittel zu verhindern" (64).

16. Habermas also conceives of communicative action as an alternative to the philosophy of history, which he believes has become untenable (*TCA* 2: 397).

17. Habermas ("Diskursethik" 78) speaks of a "Sollgeltung von Normen," not a "Mußgeltung" which Grimminger attributes to him.

18. See Schneiders, passim, and Karl J. Fink's two studies of sameness and difference in eighteenth-century German anthropology.

19. Wieland, *Das Geheimnis des Kosmopolitenordens*: "die möglichste Publizität aller Tatsachen, Beobachtungen, Entdeckungen, Untersuchungen" (*Werke* 3: 572).

20. These arguments are taken up variously by Jean Améry, Dagmar Barnouw, Donald L. Guss, and John A. McCarthy ("Die gefesselte Muse" and " 'Das sicherste Kennzeichen' "). Typical is the conclusion drawn by Améry: "Darum ist Aufklärung auch kein fugenloses doktrinäres Konstrukt, sondern das immerwährende erhellende Gespräch, das wir mit uns selbst und mit dem anderen zu führen gehalten sind" (134).

21. Kant, *Werke* 10: 678; such is also the thrust of his *Idea of a Universal History* . . . (*Idee zu einer allgemeinen Geschichte in weltbürgerlicher Sicht*, 1784).

22. *TCA* 1: 100. See also Alfred Schmidt: "Subjektive und objektive Vernunft haben sich wechselweitig zu korrigieren. Ihre starre Trennung ist ideologischer Schein, den es aufzulösen gilt" (102).

23. Wieland, *Was ist Aufklärung,* Bahr 27.
24. *On the Rights and Responsibilities of Writers* ... (*Über die Rechte und Pflichten der Schriftsteller* ... , *Werke* 3: 491); also in *The Secret of the Order of Cosmopolitans* (*Das Geheimnis des Kosmopolitenordens, Werke* 3: 550-75).
25. *Thoughts on the Freedom to Philosophize on Matters of Faith* (*Gedanken von der Freiheit über Gegenstände des Glaubens zu philosophieren, Werke* 3: 540).
26. "Die Energie der Seele erstreckt sich auf Geist, Herz und Wille. Selbstdenken ist das Resultat der Geisteskraft; unabhängig fühlen kann nur ein Herz voll Energie; Selbsthandeln entspringt aus dem Vermögen eines selbstständigen Willens" (67f.).
27. "Hierin liegt das Geheimniß des höchsten Genusses und der Kunst, deinem schlauen Autor die geheime Gewalt über Dich zu nehmen, wodurch er Dich mißbraucht. Nur eigene Thätigkeit und ihr Gewinn an Kraft ist wahrer Genuß; leiden ist nicht genießen" (244).
28. See Cassirer; Hampson; Schneiders.
29. See Foucault 39; T. McCarthy 190; Schneiders 178.
30. "Keine Gesellschaft kann zu einer widerspruchslosen Vernunfteinheit im Kanon universal geltender Normen finden, *sie kann es nicht, sie soll es auch nicht versuchen*" (Grimminger 42; my emphasis).
31. Grimminger's criticism of Habermas rests on a (mis)understanding of the phrase "zurechnungsfähige Personen," which is a cornerstone of Habermas's theory. Grimminger chooses to interpret the phrase as meaning only those who are already in agreement with a central concept or who are capable of being won over to it. Grimminger then attaches to this interpretation his contention that Habermas rejects toleration of dissenting views because the ability to dissent from the dominant view does not fit the neatly designed system. The key Habermasean phrase for Grimminger is the following rhetorical question: "Must we not call action orientations that can be stabilized only at the cost of suppressing contradictions irrational?" ("Müssen wir nicht Handlungsorientierungen, die nur um den Preis der Verdrängung von Widersprüchen stabilisiert werden können, irrational nennen"; *TCA* 1: 95). Grimminger interprets the passage as meaning that Habermas equates the "tolerance for dissent" with its disallowance (34). On what basis Grimminger feels justified in drawing his conclusion remains unclear to me. Moreover, Grimminger almost immediately takes back some of the conviction with which he claims that no society should even endeavor to seek universally valid norms when he grants that "islands of harmonic consensus-seeking" do, in fact, exist (43). Habermas's view of universally valid norms within society is based on the precedence of such examples of concurrence. At the very least, the universally valid norm of a society would be the right to express one's own views in the search for some common basis of interaction, even if that common basis does not advance beyond freedom of the press.
32. "Kann Eintracht, und Ordnung nicht sehr wohl mit Mannichfaltigkeit bestehen? Entspringt Harmonie nicht aus Mannichfaltigkeit mit Ordnung? und ist Harmonie nicht schöner als Monotonie?" (*Werke* 3: 514f.).

Works Cited

Adorno, Theodor W. *Eingriffe: Neun kritische Modelle.* Frankfurt/M.: Suhrkamp, 1963.

————. *Erziehung zur Mündigkeit*. Frankfurt/M.: Suhrkamp, 1969.

Bahr, Ehrhard, ed. *Was ist Aufklärung? Thesen und Definitionen*. Stuttgart: Reclam, 1974.

Améry, Jean. "Aufklärung als Philosophia perennis." *Denken als Widerspruch: Reden zum Lessing-Preis: Plädoyers gegen die Irrationalität oder ist Vernunft nicht mehr gefragt?* Ed. Volker F. W. Hasenclever. Frankfurt/M.: Eichborn 1982.

Benzel-Sternau, Christian Ernst Karl Graf von. *Gesichtspunkte für den Schriftsteller unsers Zeitalters. Neuer Teutscher Merkur* 62 (1796): 34-74.

Barnouw, Dagmar. "Modernity and Enlightenment Thought." *The Enlightenment and its Legacy. Studies in German Literature in Honor of Helga Slessarev.* Ed. Sara Friedrichsmeyer, Barbara Becker-Cantarino. Bonn: Bouvier, 1991. 1-14.

Cassirer, Ernst. *The Philosophy of the Enlightenment.* Trans. Fritz C. A. Koelln and James P. Pettegrove. Boston: Beacon, 1955.

Dewey, John. *Experience and Education.* New York: Macmillan, 1938.

Fink, Karl J. "Kant's Concept of *telos*: Reviews Shaping Anthropology." *The Form and Function of the Eighteenth-Century German Review.* Heidelberg: Winter, 1992. 249-68.

————. "Ontogeny Recapitulates Phylogeny: A Classic Formula of Organicism." *Approaches to Organic Form.* Ed. Frederick Burwick. Dordrecht: Reidel, 1987. 87-112.

[Foucault, Michel.] *The Foucault Reader.* Ed. Paul Rabinow. New York: Pantheon Books, 1984.

Frank, Manfred. *Die Grenzen der Verständigung: Ein Geistergespräch zwischen Lyotard und Habermas.* Frankfurt/M.: Suhrkamp, 1988.

Gay, Peter. *The Enlightenment: An Interpretation.* New York: Random House, 1966.

Geyer-Ryan, Helga. "Von der *Dialektik der Aufklärung* zur Dialektik der *Odyssee*: Gegen eine puristische Moderne bei Adorno und Horkheimer." *Die Aktualität der "Dialektik der Aufklärung": Zwischen Moderne und Postmoderne.* Ed. Harry Kunneman and Hent de Vries. Frankfurt/M.: Campus, 1989. 114-27.

Grimminger, Rolf. *Die Ordnung, das Chaos und die Kunst.* Frankfurt/M.: Suhrkamp, 1986.

Guss, Donald L. "Enlightenment as Process: Milton and Habermas." *PMLA* 106 (1991): 1156-69.

Habermas, Jürgen. "The Entwinement of Myth and Enlightenment: Max Horkheimer and Theodor Adorno." *The Philosophical Discourse of Modernity: Twelve Lectures.* Trans. Frederick Lawrence. Cambridge: MIT Press, 1987 (German original: Frankfurt/M.: Suhrkamp, 1985).

————. *Moral Consciousness and Communicative Action.* Trans. Christian Lenhardt, Shierry Weber Nicholsen; introd. Thomas McCarthy. Cambridge: MIT Press, 1990 (German original: Frankfurt/M.: Suhrkamp, 1983).

————. "A Reply to my Critics." *Habermas, Critical Debates.* Ed. John B. Thompson and David Held. Cambridge: MIT Press, 1982. 219-83.

————. *Theory of Communicative Action.* 2 vols. Trans. Thomas McCarthy. Boston: Beacon, 1984, 1987 (German original: Frankfurt/M.: Suhrkamp, 1983). Cited as "*TCA*."

Haddock Seigfried, Charlene. "Weaving Chaos into Order: A Radically Pragmatic Aesthetic." *Philosophy and Literature* 14.1 (1990): 108-16.

Hampson, Norman. *The Enlightenment.* Baltimore: Penquin, 1968.

Hayles, N. Katherine. *Chaos Bound: Orderly Disorder in Contemporary Literature and Science.* Ithaca: Cornell UP, 1990.

Honneth, Axel, et al., ed. *Zwischenbetrachtungen im Prozeß der Aufklärung.* Frankfurt/M.: Suhrkamp, 1989.

Horkheimer, Max and Theodor W. Adorno. *Dialectic of Enlightenment.* Tr. John Cumming. New York: Continuum, 1972.

Ingram, David. *Habermas and the Dialectics of Reason.* New Haven: Yale UP, 1987.

Jäger, Georg. "Freundschaft, Liebe und Literatur von der Empfindsamkeit bis zur Romantik: Produktion, Kommunikation und Vergesellschaftung von Individualität durch 'kommunikative Muster ästhetisch vermittelter Identifikation.' " *Spiel* 9.1 (1990): 69-87.

James, William. *The Varieties of Religious Experience.* Cambridge: Harvard UP, 1985.

Kant, Immanuel. *Werke.* Ed. Wilhelm Weischedel. 10 Vols. Darmstadt: Wissenschaftliche Buchgesellschaft, 1983.

Kunneman, Harry, and Hent de Vries, eds. *Die Aktualität der "Dialektik der Aufklärung": Zwischen Moderne und Postmoderne.* Frankfurt/M.: Campus, 1989.

Lichtenberg, Christoph Georg. *Gedankenbücher.* Ed. Franz Mautner. Frankfurt/M.: Fischer, 1963.

Lyotard, Jean-François. 1987. *After Philosophy.* Ed. K. Baynes, et al. Cambridge: MIT Press, 1987.

McCarthy, John A. *Crossing Boundaries: A Theory and History of Essay Writing in German 1680-1815.* Philadelphia: U of Pennsylvania P, 1989.

————. "Die gefesselte Muse? Wieland und die Pressefreiheit." *MLN* 99 (1984): 437-60.

————. " 'Das sicherste Kennzeichen einer gesunden, nervösen Staatsverfassung': Lessing und die Pressefreiheit." *Lessing und die Toleranz: Beiträge der vierten internationalen Konferenz der Lessing Society in Hamburg vom 27. bis 29. Juni 1985.* Ed. Peter Freimark, Franklin Kopitzsch, and Helga Slessarev. Detroit: Wayne State UP, 1986. 225-44.

McCarthy, Thomas. "Reflections on Rationalization in *The Theory of Communicative Action.*" *Habermas and Modernity.* Ed. Richard J. Bernstein. Cambridge: MIT Press, 1985. 176-91.

Müller, Adam. "Über das Gespräch." *Zwölf Reden über die Beredsamkeit und deren Zerfall in Deutschland* [Vienna 1812]. Frankfurt/M.: Insel, 1967.

Nagel, Thomas. *The Possibility of Altruism.* Princeton: Princeton UP, 1970.

Petrovic, Gajo. "Truth and Pluralism." Honneth et al. 210-30.

Ritter, Hennig. "Das feinste Organ: Zur ersten kritischen Ausgabe der *Dialektik der Aufklärung.*" *Frankfurter Allgemeine Zeitung,* Jan. 1, 1988, No. 16: 29.

[Rückert, Josef.] *Ueber Lektüre. Neuer Teutscher Merkur* 62 (July 1796): 238-63.

Schmidt, Alfred. "Aufklärung und dialektische Vernunft." *Denken als Widerspruch: Reden zum Lessing-Preis: Plädoyers gegen die Irrationalität oder ist Vernunft nicht mehr gefragt?* Ed. Volker F. W. Hasenclever. Frankfurt/M.: Eichborn, 1982.

Schneiders, Werner. *Hoffnung auf Vernunft: Aufklärungsphilosophie in Deutschland.* Hamburg: Meiners, 1990.

Taylor, Charles. "Inwardness and the Culture of Modernity." Honneth et al. 601-23.

Wieland, Christoph Martin. *Werke.* Ed. Fritz Martini and Hans Werner Seiffert. 5 vols. München: Hanser, 1964-68.

The Enlightenment of Dialectic:
Jürgen Habermas's Critique of the Frankfurt School

Robert C. Holub

THE WORK OF Jürgen Habermas can be viewed profitably as an ongoing dialogue and debate with the work of the Frankfurt School, in particular with the writings of Max Horkheimer and Theodor Adorno. Although Habermas has obviously widened his intellectual scope to incorporate many different directions in social theory, philosophy, and political science, and although many of the theories on which he has come to rely stand in putative opposition to basic tenets of Critical Theory, the Frankfurt School has nonetheless remained present in and vital for his writings. Among the works of his mentors at the Institute for Social Research perhaps no book has been more important for Habermas than the *Dialectic of Enlightenment* (1947). It is not hard to understand why. Horkheimer and Adorno's dark vision in their collectively written volume of essays and reflections is accompanied not only by a trenchant analysis of their (and to some extent our) contemporary world, but also by the implication that philosophical and social thought have no positive place from which to theorize. Adorno's subsequent insistence on a "negative dialectic" and on an aesthetic theory based on the more hermetic products of modernism is thus a logical extension of this pessimistic analysis of Western societies. Habermas's writings, from the early book *The Structural Transformation of the Public Sphere* (1962) through his more recent work on communicative action, have sought, in contrast to his predecessors, to locate a space in which and from which social theory can be articulated. In his initial period this place was conceived in empirical and sociological terms as the public sphere; later it was identified with a "quasi-transcendental" critical interest; and in his latest modifications it has been identified as the

34

arena of "discourse" and the "ideal speech situation." In each instance Habermas has proposed in effect an opening for emancipatory thought that the dialectic of enlightenment claimed was closed down. The remarkable continuity in his concerns is thus attributable not only to the relentless drive to improve and refine his theoretical apparatus. In part at least, it may be accounted for by the equal inexorability with which the dialectic of enlightenment has shadowed every turn of his speculative enterprise.

Many commentators on Habermas over the last decade have noted that his relationship to the first generation of Critical Theorists was complex, but that in the final analysis Habermas broke significantly with his predecessors. In most cases critics have viewed the rift between Habermas and the core members of the Frankfurt School in the context of two larger complexes: the development of the theory of communicative action in the seventies, and the discussions of French poststructuralist theory in the eighties. Peter Uwe Hohendahl, for example, focuses specifically on these two moments of Habermas's critique in his essay "The Dialectic of the Enlightenment Revisited." According to Hohendahl, Habermas's work from the sixties is still tied to the orbit of traditional Critical Theory. Only in the following decade, when he begins to reexamine and revamp marxist theory for the analysis of advanced capitalism, does he embark on a path that propels him away from his former mentors. The irreconcilability between Habermas and the Frankfurt School becomes apparent in the late seventies, when "friendly gestures notwithstanding, this process reaches a point from where, given the systematic development of Habermas's own theory, a return to the discourse of the old Frankfurt School is no longer possible" (4).

In contrast to Hohendahl, Dagmar Barnouw situates Habermas's critique of Adorno and Horkheimer more squarely in his comments on the issues of modernity and postmodernity. Although she recognizes, as Hohendahl does, that even *The Structural Transformation* represents a departure from the tradition of Critical Theory, her concerns are with Habermas's confrontation with postmodern thought in the eighties. Analyzing Habermas's essay "The Entwinement of Myth and Enlightenment," which was an early version of the chapter on Adorno and Horkheimer in the *Philosophical Discourse of Modernity* (1985), Barnouw even finds that Habermas and his predecessors share a "neglect of the meanings of historicity" which vitiates both his and their critique. Indeed, her overall point is that despite Habermas's separation from Adorno and Horkheimer on the issue of enlightenment, his thinking, like theirs, is "still very much dominated by a curiously abstract and narrow attitude toward modern mass culture and technology" (4). Fi-

nally, Rolf Grimminger, like Barnouw, locates Habermas's most important statements on the *Dialectic of Enlightenment* in the eighties. Grimminger, however, is less concerned about Habermas's relationship with
the Frankfurt School than about his alleged intolerance for dissent.
According to his confused and inaccurate understanding of Habermas's
project, communicative rationality is an idealist, utopian, totalized
notion that demands conformity and absolute obedience (11-43). This
type of willful ignorance about Habermas is rivaled only by the
inanities that flourish about him in the circles of poststructuralist
epigones in the United States.

In contrast to the dominant views on Habermas's relationship to
Horkheimer and Adorno's *Dialectic of Enlightenment*, what will concern
me most here are the early and initial steps—or perhaps sidesteps—
Habermas took to avoid the bleak conclusions of his predecessors.
Although critics like Hohendahl, Barnouw, and Grimminger are
undoubtedly correct in regarding Habermas's work for the past two
decade as decisive, I would maintain that there exists a considerable
and ultimately more important distancing from the Frankfurt School
—at least implicitly—in his writings from the sixties as well. Perhaps the
most important feature from these early years—one that would also
have enormous ramifications for his reworking of marxist theory—is his
break with the dialectical movement associated with the Hegelian-
marxist heritage. This break was essential because the dialectic as it
had been expounded by Adorno and Horkheimer evidenced three features which hindered an emancipatory social philosophy. The first of
these was its determinism or inevitability. From the perspective of the
mid-forties, rationality appears to lead straight to the horrors of the
Second World War and the genocide perpetrated by the Third Reich.
Humankind's hegemonic relationship to nature flows unalterably into
hegemonic social structures; the desire to control the external environment necessarily results in repressive internal and external controls on
humanity. In the scheme developed by Adorno and Horkheimer there
is no escape from this fate in the modern world: fascism may be an
extreme variant of social ordering, but liberal democracy and state
socialism are not alternatives. Each follows a path preordained by
enlightenment rationality. A second feature of the dialectic of enlightenment is its pervasiveness in history. At the very latest in the first
excursus, where Horkheimer and Adorno refer to Odysseus as a prototypical figure of the enlightenment (72-80), it becomes obvious that
their conception is meant to encompass all of recorded history. Enlightenment is thus not exclusively located in the eighteenth century, in
the history of modern philosophy since Descartes, or in scientific thinking since Bacon, but in the totality of human endeavor in our confron-

tation with nature. Progress is thus rendered illusory; we remain caught in the founding myth of Western civilization. Finally, the dialectic that Adorno and Horkheimer analyze is characterized by an aura of stasis and finality. Although they insist on process over essences, it seems that with the modern era we have arrived at the end of historical development. There is no point beyond enlightenment; it has run its course and can be carried no further by a dialectical, evolutionary/revolutionary movement. Frozen into an age where reason has manifested itself as its own perversion, we can neither return to our original point of departure nor sublate the contradictory antipodes that have become our second nature.

The application of dialectic to enlightenment undertaken by Adorno and Horkheimer in the forties was of course not the first time that enlightenment had been subjected to dialectical analysis. Indeed, their most illustrious predecessor in dialectics, Georg Wilhelm Friedrich Hegel, provided a more optimistic, if equally critical view of enlightenment in his *Phenomenology of Mind* (1805). His dialectic of enlightenment, which was likely the first, initially seems to be more attractive for Habermas in going beyond the Frankfurt School. Hegel's analysis avoids at least the stasis and finality that we find in Adorno and Horkheimer. For him enlightenment, which is merely the general diffusion of pure insight into society, comes from the sphere of culture, by which he means the world in which the spirit is alienated from itself. The result of this alienation is a split: on the one hand spirit manifests itself as faith (*Glaube*), regaining a unity with itself without, however, thinking this unity; and on the other hand, we encounter the realm of intellection or pure insight, a universalization of the individual wit found in culture. Pure insight is solely negative; it contains no content itself. It rejects all otherness and transforms every content it encounters into the self. By contrast, faith, is a positivity and a content; it is thus static and self-satisfied, although equally the one-sided product of alienated spirit. Faith and pure insight are, of course only opposites for themselves; for us or in themselves, that is from the perspective of the observer of the phenomenological process, they are really a unity. The struggle between faith and pure insight, eventually resolved in favor of the latter, provides then the basis for a further stage in the dialectical process. Unlike Adorno and Horkheimer, Hegel does not terminate the enlightenment in its negative manifestations. In his philosophy enlightenment, like belief, is left behind, transformed and preserved in a higher stage of spirit.[1]

One of the reasons that Hegel can provide such an optimistic dialectic of enlightenment is that he conceives it in a more narrow historical framework than do Adorno and Horkheimer. For him enlighten-

ment is clearly identified with the eighteenth century, and almost exclusively with the religious controversies of that age.[2] Despite his abstractness, therefore, Hegel's concept has more historical specificity. This is
most obvious in his delineation of three moments that the enlightenment opposes.   The first is the naive consciousness of the masses
trapped in unreflected belief. The second is the priesthood, "which
carries out its envious vain conceit of being alone in possession of
insight, and carries out its other selfish ends as well" (562). With this
comment Hegel is obviously rebuking the narrow religious orthodoxies
of the eighteenth century that posed as universal truth. He is even har-
sher, however, with regard to the political realm. The third manifestation that enlightenment distinguishes is despotism, which takes up the
pretense of being the unity of the real and the ideal. Hegel's attitude
toward this political institution is clearly condemnatory: "As the result
of the stupidity and confusion produced amongst the people by the
agency of priestly deception, despotism despises both and draws for
itself the advantage of undisturbed control and the fulfillment of its
lusts, its humours, and its whims" (562). This historical specificity, however, points simultaneously to the weakness of Hegel's dialectic and
suggests why, in spite of its progressive nature, it is of little use for
Habermas or other contemporary theorists. For pure insight, which
becomes enlightenment, does not bother opposing the individual
moments it recognizes as superstition and error. Enlightenment is not
conceived in political, institutional, or sociological terms, but chiefly
and most importantly as a moment of spirit. The proper opponent for
pure insight is thus belief, and even though insight emerges the victor,
it is not because it can show belief to be in error, but because it
manages to demonstrate that belief is inherently contradictory. Indeed, pure insight is ignorant of the truth of belief, and is thus itself a
variety of blindness. Enlightenment is thus actually shown to be not
pure insight, but one-sided insight: it is insight without insight into what
belief truly is and therefore insight without insight into its own true
nature as insight. It ultimately manifests itself as utilitarianism, a
reduction of all spirituality contained in belief to the world of the
senses. In this outcome of Hegel's dialectical process we find a conclusion that is therefore not so very different from the findings of
Adorno and Horkheimer a hundred and forty years later.
     The history of the dialectic of enlightenment that Habermas con-
fronted, even in his earliest work, was therefore unappealing and produced a tension or strain when dealing with related topics. This uneasiness is most noticeable in the second half of his *Structural Transformation of the Public Sphere*, where the influence of Adorno and Horkheimer's *Dialectic of Enlightenment* is most apparent. Habermas had

spent most of the initial sections of his book developing a notion of the public sphere that is consonant with basic enlightenment principles. Described as a realm in which individuals gather to participate in open discussions, the public sphere is prototypically democratic, non-hierarchical, and critical. Its most developed form occurs squarely in the middle of the European enlightenment. Habermas's "model" case is eighteenth-century Britain, where "forces endeavoring to influence the decisions of state authority appealed to the critical public in order to legitimate demands before this new forum" (57). The continental variants are also tied to enlightenment institutions, if not directly to enlightenment thought. Habermas is particularly concerned with political journalism in his discussion, and in the case of Germany, which is presented as somewhat retrograde in comparison with England, he mentions Schlözer's *Staatsanzeigen*, Wieland's *Teutscher Merkur*, Archenholz's *Minerva*, the Hamburg *Politisches Journal*, the *Journal von und für Deutschland*, Wekhrlin's *Felleisen*, and Schubart's *Deutsche Chronik*. In citing these critical and political journals, Habermas directs his enlightenment public sphere against the governmental despotism thematized in Hegel's *Phenomenology*, but left untouched by the Hegelian dialectic.

But in this early work the critical force associated initially with the public sphere succumbs to Habermas's own variant of the dialectic. The growth of the public sphere leads to its own demise; its success becomes its undoing. Significantly, Habermas portrays this process as the unfolding of an inevitable process. "Two tendencies dialectically related to each other indicated a breakdown of the public sphere. While it penetrated more *spheres* of society, it simultaneously lost its political *function*, namely: that of subjecting the affairs that it had made public to the control of a critical public" (140). The demise of the public sphere is not related to its failure, but to its expansion into arenas that necessarily change its function. The quantitative growth of the public sphere leads to a change in its quality, indeed, to a negation of its very public nature. We could say that it collapses under its own weight. This collapse occurs therefore because of a dual movement associated with the dialectical process in history: the intervention of the state into private affairs and the penetration of society into the state. Since the public sphere depended on a clear separation between the private realm and public power, their mutual interpenetration causes the demise of the public sphere. The role of the public sphere is then assumed by other institutions, for example parliament, and the free exchange of ideas among equals is transformed into less democratic communicative forms, for example public relations. Party politics and the manipulation of the mass media lead to what Habermas calls a "re-

feudalization" of the public sphere, where representation and
appearances outweigh public debate.

The result is a situation remarkably similar to what Adorno and
Horkheimer describe in *Dialectic of Enlightenment*. This similarity is
perhaps most evident in Habermas's discussion of the increasing orientation toward consumerism. The public sphere, which had once been
characterized by open debate and reason, becomes a passive recipient
for cultural commodity production as the market gradually penetrates
and reshapes the private sphere. Starting in the nineteenth century,
the institutions that had ensured a public sphere are gradually eroded
under the pressure of capitalist production. The family, which Habermas had perhaps idealized into a realm capable of critically reflecting
on both literary and political matters, degenerates into a consumer-
oriented unit controlled by the manipulations of the mass media. The
critical journals of the enlightenment are succeeded by magazines, such
as *Westermanns Monatshefte* and the *Gartenlaube*, that propagate an
idyllically narrow-minded, provincial mentality, and in more recent
times by publications designed by and for advertising and marketing
firms. The newspaper, which initially carried information and opinion
vital for public decision-making, becomes a commercialized organ for
mass consumption, devoid of genuine political and intellectual content.
And the stratum of critical intellectuals becomes integrated into the
functioning of bourgeois society, either as cultural functionaries, the
institutionalized avant-garde, or as specialists and amateurs confined to
well defined areas of expertise. The result is a decimation of the former bourgeois ideal of a public sphere based on accessibility and equality. "The sounding board of an educated stratum tutored in the public
use of reason has been shattered; the public is split apart into minori-
ties of specialists who put their reason to use nonpublicly and the great
mass of consumers whose receptiveness is public but uncritical" (*Structural Transformation* 175). With these trends the public sphere continues to exist in appearance alone.

Despite the overt similarity with regard to the state of modern
societies, Habermas's early dialectic of enlightenment differs from that
of his predecessors in its social and philosophical foundations. It does
not proceed from the confrontation between the individual human
being and a realm of nature considered external to this human being.
In anticipation of his later thematization of intersubjectivity and communication, Habermas focuses on an arena of dialogue and exchange.
Already implicit in his formulation of the problem is the beginnings of
his critique of a philosophy of consciousness and its reliance on a basic
dichotomy of subject and object. It is perhaps interesting to note in this
regard that in spite of his implicit shift from consciousness to inter-

subjectivity, he winds up with the identical critique of mass culture. Instrumental reason and communicative reason evidently follow a similar trajectory in Habermas's early thought. In his later work Habermas will separate the two more carefully, at times perhaps too neatly, and rescue the project of modernity via a consideration of the foundational nature of language competence and the derivative communicative rationality. In *The Structural Transformation*, communicative rationality, which is embodied in the public sphere, deteriorates not from the encroachment of strategic reason, which is the shorthand philosophical description for the colonization of the lifeworld, but from dynamics contained in the lifeworld itself. To be sure, the public sphere is violated by forces that originate in capitalist economic relations. But in keeping with his dialectical predecessors, Habermas attributes its demise more centrally to its own imminent unfolding over time. *Structural Transformation* thus ultimately appears to offer us a communicative version of the instrumental story told in *Dialectic of Enlightenment*, not an emancipatory alternative.

This appearance of dialectical movement, however, is constantly undermined by other features of the book. The notion that the public sphere is an entity found empirically in history and that it undergoes an inevitable demise in the course of modernization exists in an uneasy tension with the normative account of the public sphere as an ideal realm for social interaction. Of course the historical could coincide with the theoretical or normative, and Habermas at times makes an implicit case for this coincidence when he writes of the bourgeois public sphere. But the insistence on an overlap of the empirical and the normative would result in serious methodological problems for a marxist dialectic. Traditionally marxist analysis of concepts has most often followed the remarks Marx himself made in the "Introduction" to the *Grundrisse* (1857-58). Here Marx states that only the most fully developed form enables us to understand the history of a concept (6-31). Despite their differences with traditional marxist theory, Adorno and Horkheimer retain this feature of his methodology. Enlightenment for them is only fully realized in its unfolding through history; its essence is not located in the eighteenth century or any other period; it can be known only when we encounter its "highest" forms. The bourgeois norm for the public sphere, however, does not even occur in fully developed bourgeois society, but rather in its early liberal phase; some critics have even suggested that if such a sphere existed at all it should be located in the incipient phases of bourgeois society when it began to assert itself against feudalism.[3] Habermas's lack of clarity with regard to this issue stems from his desire to have it both ways. On the one hand, he wants to retain the dialectical and historical process that leads

to the condemnation of the public sphere in modern society as a deformed and distorted copy of an admirable original. On the other
hand, he wants to retain the public sphere as an ideal that can be
attained even in the modern age. In the latter case he conceives of the
bourgeois public sphere as an ideological anticipatory form that, like
ideology itself, "transcends the status quo in utopian fashion" (*Structural Transformation* 88). From this perspective Habermas implicitly
negates a dialectic that would lead inevitably to the corruption of the
public sphere, instead using it as a foil to critique modern society.
Indeed, if Habermas had included only the negatively tinged dialectical
outcome, his notion of the public sphere would be purely nostalgic and
lose its political relevance; the entire monograph would then amount
to little more than an antiquarian investigation of an obsolete institution. That Habermas does not wish this to be the case is evident not
only in his discussion of contemporary society later in the book, but
also in all of his subsequent thought.

The tension between a normativity ultimately indebted to the historical enlightenment and a historical process driven by a dialectic is a
consequence of Habermas's more differentiated view of both the enlightenment and of the modern world. In contrast to Adorno and
Horkheimer, Habermas does not conceive the seminal achievement of
the eighteenth century solely in terms of epistemological, technical, or
scientific progress, but rather in terms of social and political forms of
interaction as well. Expressed in the vocabulary of *Knowledge and
Human Interest* (1968), the achievements Habermas values would be
labeled "practical" and "critical." The enlightenment is thus not simply
a cipher for hegemony over nature or a period of bourgeois ideals and
obfuscations, but an age that develops concrete, albeit incomplete
because insufficiently realized, modes for democratic decision-making.
Power is asserted not only to control the external world of nature and
to tame the inner world of desires, as it is conceived in the *Dialectic of
Enlightenment*, but against those forces that exclude individual and collective participation in activities that affect people's livelihoods and
lives. When extended into the twentieth century these achievements
may become tarnished, but in general Habermas is still unwilling to
relinquish their viability or desirability for the modern era. We can
never return to the liberal public sphere of bourgeois society, but the
conceptual underpinnings of that ideal entity possess validity for the
contemporary world. Unlike Adorno and Horkheimer, Habermas does
not succumb to the equation of fascism, communism, and liberal democracy. As pernicious as the American cultural industry may be, the
direct and violent coercion of fascism is still qualitatively different from
the perverse manipulation of the United States. As inadequate as

Western parliamentary democracies may be as genuine participatory structures, they nonetheless retain an originary ideal and an unrealized potential that is not available under repressive forms of government. Habermas's more favorable, although hardly uncritical, views on the enlightenment sources of the Western heritage and their inherent possibilities cause him to find a ray of hope even in the stifling politics and cultural malaise of postwar Europe.

There is no resolution to the tension between enlightenment norms and the dialectical process in *Structural Transformation*, and it is quite possible that Habermas's reluctance to have the work published in English—it did not appear until 1989—or to revise the German edition was due his recognition of the antagonisms that inhere in the argumentation.[4] The model that finally emerges in his thought, however, is neither dialectical in the traditional Hegelian sense of the word, nor deterministic, as the dialectic had been implemented by Adorno and Horkheimer, but evolutionary and open. This direction in Habermas's works is most evident starting with his *Reconstruction of Historical Materialism* (*Zur Rekonstruktion des Historischen Materialismus*) in 1976, but his rejection of the dialectic, although never explicitly thematized, is over a decade older. Illustrative of this rejection are the essays Habermas contributed to the positivist dispute. Habermas entered the fray following a rather tepid exchange between Adorno and Karl Popper, in which neither philosopher appears particularly well informed about the other's theoretical leanings. Dialectics plays a role in the original contributions insofar as Adorno chose to defend a dialectical approach to the social sciences against Popper's putatively positivist methodology. Popper, it should be noted, objected to his characterization as a positivist—with good reason—and never explicitly mentioned dialectics in the twenty-seven theses he offered to initiate the debate. Adorno's characterization of Popper as a positivist and his defense of the dialectic may therefore be explained as a response to an earlier essay by Popper, "What is Dialectic," in which he denies any validity to dialectical reasoning. In this earlier piece Popper argues against a specifically dialectical logic, maintaining that contradictions must be eliminated, rather than sublated, to reach an understanding of reality. Adorno, by contrast, sees contradictions as structural necessities in societies based on hegemonic social relations; they are part of a totality that can only be resolved by changing the social order in which they are found.[5]

Habermas's first contribution to this debate occurs in the form of an essay in a Festschrift for Adorno in 1963.[6] It occasioned a reply by Hans Albert, and Habermas's rebuttal, which was more polemical in tone, was published a year later. With regard to the dialectic, the difference between the two contributions is worth noting. In the first

piece, Habermas structures his remarks around citations from Adorno's reply to Popper; he thus gives the appearance of defending his
mentor's position against attacks by adherents to Popper's critical
rationalism. Thus it is not surprising to find that the word "dialectic"
occurs frequently in either its substantive or adjectival forms; on the
average it appears about once on every page. In the second essay, after
Habermas had been attacked for the notion of a "dialectical totality," a
phrase that he had borrowed directly from Adorno's essay, not only
does he not bother to defend this concept, but he omits almost all
reference to "dialectic" as well. When he does discuss the term briefly
toward the end of the essay, it is obvious that it has lost the specifically
teleological and deterministic aspects that were so prominent in the
Dialectic of Enlightenment. The clarification that he supplies is that
dialectics "only expresses the fact that we think and are able to think
when, according to the traditional rules of logical inference [Regeln der
Schlüssigkeit], we really should not be able to do so" (*Positivist Dispute*
223). It is not an abandonment of the rules of formal logic, Habermas
continues, but an especially stringent application of them. Indeed, if
we examine his use of the term in the first contribution, we observe
that it comes closer to what Gadamer means by "effective-historical
consciousness" than to what Adorno and Horkheimer developed in the
mid-forties.[7] It entails the attempt to comprehend analysis as well as
its potentially critical self-consciousness as themselves part of the social
process. Even in his apparent defense of Adorno's theoretical position,
Habermas has recourse to a notion of dialectics that is based more in
the hermeneutic tradition than in Hegelian logic.

Habermas's critique of the *Dialectic of Enlightenment* in the
seventies and eighties is thus in part the result of his rejection of an
unenlightened dialectic. The inadequacies of Adorno and Horkheimer
are due not so much to their analysis of instrumental reason as to their
adherence to a Hegelian model in which changes are perceived in
terms of the production of antagonisms. Habermas's discussion of the
Dialectic of Enlightenment in his *Philosophical Discourse of Modernity*
emphasizes the aporia reached when the critique of enlightenment
turns back on itself. In an analysis reminiscent of the Hegelian dialectic, Habermas contends that enlightenment's original opposition to
myth, its critique of unfounded knowledge as superstition, at one point
boomerangs. "The drama of enlightenment first arrives at its climax
when ideology critique *itself* comes under suspicion of not producing
(any more) truths" (116). This "second-order reflectiveness" calls into
question the foundations of reason itself, undermining in the process
the basis for all critique. Only two choices remain for the would-be
critic: one can have recourse to an all-pervasive explanatory principle,

such as Nietzsche did in his reduction of all knowledge and values to power; or one can refuse to resolve the inherent self-contradiction (or performative contradiction) of critique and, in a sort of guerrilla warfare against totalizing systems, undertake occasional and unreinforced forays against the enemy. The latter alternative, chosen by Adorno, is equally unsatisfactory for Habermas, although it can be conceived as the dialectical alternative to a Nietzschean essentialism. In keeping with his earlier skepticism with regard to the dialectic, Habermas implies that this solution only covers some of the problems associated with modernity. Neither the *Dialectic of Enlightenment* nor Adorno's subsequent work does justice to a realm of problems and experiences that define our contemporary world:

> I am thinking here of the specific theoretical dynamic that continually pushes the sciences, and even the self-reflection of the sciences, *beyond* merely engendering technically useful knowledge; I am referring, further, to the universalistic foundations of law and morality that have *also* been incorporated (in however distorted and incomplete a fashion) into the institutions of constitutional government, into the forms of democratic will formation, and into individualist patterns of identity formation; I have in mind, finally, the productivity and explosive power of basic aesthetic experiences that a subjectivity liberated from the imperatives of purposive activity and from conventions of quotidian perception gains from its own decentering. (113)

The dialectic of enlightenment is not wrong; it is simply one-sided and incomplete. And this is because Habermas came to believe that dialectical processes account for only one strand in the progress of human history.

Habermas's theory of communicative action, as he developed it in the seventies and defended it in the eighties, is thus not only an answer to the problems implicitly raised in the *Dialectic of Enlightenment*; it is simultaneously a response to the *dialectic* of enlightenment. Initiated by his rethinking of historical materialism in the seventies, communicative action depends less on movement through antagonism and resolution than on evolutionary models from the social sciences. Piaget and Kohlberg are more important than Hegel and Marx for demonstrating a linear development in the sphere of interaction. Indeed, with increasing frequency Habermas understands and relies on non-dialectical schemes to define progress. Whether dealing with the ego development of individuals, role identities, or ethical norms, he ascribes progress to a succession of stages or models that emerge on the basis of increasingly complex or mature interaction with a human environment, not from self-contained sublations. The "pacemaker of social evolution" is shifted from the sphere of production, where Marx had located it, or from our dominance of nature, as Adorno and Horkheimer interpreting Marx still describe it, to the realm of social intercourse ("Historical Materialism," 120). What is sacrificed in this shift from labor to interaction, from the technical to the practical, from production to communication, is the dialectic that, at least in Hegelianized marxist theory, had informed the first terms in these oppositions. Perhaps more than any substantive critique of his predecessors in the Frankfurt School, Habermas's jettisoning of an exclusively dialectic method helped propel him onto a theoretical terrain where the de-dialecticized enlightenment still holds the promise of human emancipation.

Notes

1. For an excellent discussion of this section of Hegel's *Phenomenology*, see Hyppolite (376-452).
2. In the *Philosophy of History*, however, Hegel associates the enlightenment more directly with the preparation for the French Revolution.
3. For a discussion of the critics of Habermas's notion of the public sphere, see Hohendahl, "Critical Theory."
4. Although *Strukturwandel der Öffentlichkeit* had gone through more than seventeen editions by the late eighties, until very recently Habermas has shown little inclination to examine the central notion of the public sphere. Indeed the term almost disappears from his critical vocabulary after the sixties. This makes his recent turn to the notion all the more significant. See, for example, the essay "Volkssouveränität," as well as the preface to the Suhrkamp edition of *Strukturwandel* from 1990 (11-50).
5. *The Positivist Dispute in German Sociology* is essentially a translation of *Der Positivismusstreit in der deutschen Soziologie*. The English version contains two additional entries: a fine and informative introduction by David Frisby (ix-xliv) and the short commentary by Popper (288-300).
6. The essays discussed here are quoted from reprints in *The Positivist Dispute*.
7. Habermas was obviously much concerned with Gadamer's hermeneutic theory, as evidenced by the debate that he initiated with Gadamer in the late sixties. Indeed, his initial discussion of Gadamer in *Zur Logik der Sozialwissenschaften* (1970; On the Logic of the Social Sciences) shows how closely he identifies hermeneutics and the dialectic. "The concept of translation is itself dialectical; only when we lack transformation rules permitting the establishment of a deductive relation between languages through substitution and where an exact 'translation' is excluded do we need that kind of interpretation that we commonly call translation. It expresses in one language a state of affairs that cannot be literally expressed in it, but can nevertheless be rendered 'in other words.' H.-G. Gadamer calls this experience, which is at the basis of hermeneutics, the hermeneutic experience" ("A Review," 213-14). This is a rather odd way to refer to the dialectic, although it is consistent with the use Habermas employs at other points in the positivist dispute. It is obviously un-Hegelian and, as far as I can tell, departs significantly from the way in which Adorno and Horkheimer use the term. For a review of Habermas's debate with Gadamer, as well as his contributions to the positivist dispute, see chapters 2 and 3 in my *Jürgen Habermas* (20-77).

Works Cited

Adorno, Theodor, et al. *The Positivist Dispute in German Sociology*. Trans. Glyn Adey and David Frisby. London: Heinemann, 1976. (Trans. of *Der Positivismusstreit in der deutschen Soziologie*. Darmstadt: Luchterhand, 1969.)

Barnouw, Dagmar. "Modernity and Enlightenment Thought." *The Enlightenment and Its Legacy: Studies in German Literature in Honor of Helga Slessarev*. Eds. Sara Friedrichsmeyer, Barbara Becker-Cantarino. Bonn: Bouvier, 1991. 2-14.

Grimminger, Rolf. *Die Ordnung, das Chaos und die Kunst: Für eine neue Dialektik der Aufklärung*. Frankfurt: Suhrkamp, 1986.

Habermas, Jürgen. "The Entwinement of Myth and Enlightenment." *New German Critique* 26 (1982): 13-30.

————. "Historical Materialism and the Development of Normative Structures." *Communication and the Evolution of Society*. Trans. Thomas McCarthy. Boston: Beacon, 1976. 95-129.

————. *The Philosophical Discourse of Modernity*. Trans. Frederick Lawrence. Cambridge: MIT Press, 1987.

————. "A Positivistically Bisected Rationalism." Adorno et al. 198-225.

————. "A Review of Gadamer's *Truth and Method*." In *The Hermeneutic Tradition: From Ast to Ricouer*. Eds. Gayle L. Ormiston and Alan D. Schrift. Albany: SUNY Press, 1990. 213-44.

————. *The Structural Transformation of the Public Sphere: An Inquiry into a Category of Bourgeois Society*. Trans. Thomas Burger. Cambridge: MIT Press, 1989.

————. *Strukturwandel der Öffentlichkeit: Untersuchung zu einer Kategorie der bürgerlichen Gesellschaft. Mit einem Vorwort zur Neuauflage 1990*. Frankfurt: Suhrkamp, 1990.

————. "Volkssouveränität als Verfahren: Ein normativer Begriff von Öffentlichkeit." *Merkur* 43.6 (1989): 465-77.

————. *Zur Logik der Sozialwissenschaften*. Frankfurt: Suhrkamp, 1982.

————. *Zur Rekonstruktion des Historischen Materialismus*. Frankfurt: Suhrkamp, 1976.

Hegel, Georg Wilhelm Friedrich. *The Philosophy of Mind*. Trans. J. B. Baillie. New York: Harper and Row, 1967.

Hohendahl, Peter Uwe. "Critical Theory, Public Sphere and Culture: Jürgen Habermas and his Critics." *New German Critique* 16 (1979): 89-118.

————. "The Dialectic of Enlightenment Revisited: Habermas' Critique of the Frankfurt School." *New German Critique* 35 (1985): 3-26.

Holub, Robert C. *Jürgen Habermas: Critic in the Public Sphere*. London: Routledge, 1991.

Horkheimer, Max and Theodor W. Adorno. *Dialectic of Enlightenment*. Trans. John Cumming. New York: Continuum, 1972.

Hyppolite, Jean. *Genesis and Structure of Hegel's Phenomenology of Spirit*. Trans. Samuel Cherniak and John Heckman. Evanston: Northwestern UP, 1974.

Marx, Karl. *Grundrisse der Kritik der politischen Ökonomie*. Berlin: Dietz, 1974.

Popper, Karl. "What is Dialectic?" In *Conjectures and Refutations: The Growth of Scientific Knowledge*. London: Routledge, 1963. 312-35.

Patriarchy and German Enlightenment Discourse: From Goethe's *Wilhelm Meister* to Horkheimer and Adorno's *Dialectic of Enlightenment*[1]

Barbara Becker-Cantarino

PATRIARCHY IS DEEPLY ingrained in German Enlightenment discourse and in one of the most influential works in the German literary canon, Goethe's *Wilhelm Meister's Apprenticeship* (*Wilhelm Meisters Lehrjahre*). This novel depicts a (mostly) conciliatory, orderly, at times repressive, yet productive, in short a benign, image of enlightened patriarchy[2] as the *natural* order. The father/son dyad with the absent mother represents the symbolic order, while in realistic terms the Wilhelm-Felix duo moves to the center of the novel's plot and remains there throughout the sequel, *Wilhelm Meister's Travels* (*Wilhelm Meisters Wanderjahre*). The hero's trials and tribulations all happen and are resolved within this symbolic order; confrontational situations and subversive characters that threaten or question this benign, seemingly natural, patriarchal order have been relegated mostly to the past (as was the "Beautiful Soul"[3] in her confessions) and repressed; they surface only in such tales of mystery as Mignon's and the Harper's, both of whom die in somewhat inexplicable, irrational ways. After their deaths the patriarchal order as such is never seriously disturbed (nor is it problematized); patriarchy then appears as the natural order. An educative and moral force, patriarchy is not a category reflected upon within the text (nor by the vast majority of its interpreters).

My point of departure in looking at patriarchy is this enlightened (paternalistic and "humane") Goethean construct in a gendered reading of this text; then I will critically distance myself from it in theorizing patriarchy, although I will do so from a historically different vantage point, from a position within present feminist discourse and its assumptions about the sex/gender system[4] as the organizational principle of social formation, as value orientations in our lives, and meaning structures of the culture. Historicizing the sex/gender system and looking at a specific location, German enlightenment discourse and beyond, I use the term "patriarchy," which I consider expressive and historically appropriate for Germany (for reasons that I elaborate below): Germany was (still is?) a *Vaterland*, a land of fathers (and sons).

Feminists have questioned the language of patriarchy in its historical, sociological, and psychoanalytic appearance, have sought to distance us from it, have made us skeptical about it, and have attempted to rethink and to reposition mother and daughter, father and son.[5] A fundamental goal remains: to analyze patriarchy, how patriarchy is constructed (and experienced) and how we think (avoid or fail to think) about it. I will attempt to address the situation of woman in patriarchy (as manifested in Germany); the relationship of male/female; the appearance, nature, and effect of male domination; the power/knowledge /phallus juncture; and the configuration of the (engendered) subject.

Within this theoretical frame I will look at a seminal text from modern Enlightenment discourse in Germany, a text that inaugurated the comprehensive critique of Enlightenment of recent decades: Horkheimer and Adorno's *Dialectic of Enlightenment* (*Dialektik der Aufklärung*). Here my reading focuses on what has been called the "patriarchal core" of Frankfurt School thought (Benjamin 430; Benhabib, *Critique, Norm, and Utopia* 384); thus I will look at this text's relationship to patriarchal discourse as it poetically and historically manifested itself in Germany's intellectual culture rooted in the Enlightenment. I suggest that even in this text critical of Enlightenment, as in most of the German discourse on modernity that is grounded in, or directed against, Enlightenment concepts, patriarchy appears as an inarguable corollary, as an unreflected mode of thought. Until very recently, the question of patriarchy has not, or has only rarely, been raised in regard to, or by, texts of German intellectuals. But first, in the politics of signification, we need to ask the question: what is patriarchy?

I. The Poetics of Enlightened Patriarchy

During a ceremonial episode in *Wilhelm Meister's Apprenticeship*, an episode reminiscent of a Masonic initiation rite, Wilhelm is introduced to the secrets of the all-male Tower Society. Here Wilhelm meets his father's spirit and is authenticated in his paternity. Wilhelm wanders between and comes to fill both roles, father and son: this ceremonial scene plays out the ritual of patriarchy. After former strangers (now

turned friendly companions) have come forth revealing their identity as
members of the Tower Society and explaining their role in Wilhelm's
life, the old King of Denmark—we are of course immediately reminded
of Wilhelm's earlier performance of Hamlet and his fateful encounter
with the king's ghost who proclaimed to be his father's—appears before
Wilhelm:

> "I am your father's ghost," said the figure in the frame, "and I depart in peace,
> for all I wished for you has been fulfilled more than I myself could imagine. . . .
> Farewell, and remember me when you partake of what I have prepared for
> you."[6]

This meeting of son and father, a first climax in this ritualistic scene,
signals a fruitful relationship, a sort of blessing from the father, a passing on of the father's heritage to the son; the father's aspirations or desires for the son have been realized and he wishes him well, wants the
son to remember the father when enjoying what he prepared for him.
The father, though absent from the novel's representational level as a
real, active character, is symbolized by a complex theatrical image: as
Hamlet's father, as king in full armor, and with reference to a painting
(depicting a sick prince[7]). The father image seems to signify a whole
world, a world of art and life, of power (as king) and mastery (the armor). In its theatricality it is illusion, imagination and reality at once;
time appears to be suspended, with past, present and future collapsed
into this moment of passage from son to father.

Wilhelm is "dumbfounded" (303), believing that he hears his
father's voice and yet it isn't his voice; he is rescued from his confusion
by the Abbé's immediate appearance and intervention in that other
essential role in patriarchy, as the guiding, helpful mentor—a father
surrogate—who hands Wilhelm his "Certificate of Apprenticeship," a
collection of allegorical, moralistic aphorisms to guide Wilhelm, the
"true student" of art and life, to advance to the stage of "master"
("Meister"). Master and Father (with their respective corollaries of
student and son) are key concepts of patriarchy embodying power as
well as the promise of (individual) achievement, of continuity of the
bloodline and (material, artistic, intellectual) inheritance; male bonding, which overcomes generational conflicts and all other rivalries or
competitive confrontations, is celebrated in this Goethean vision of
Wilhelm's rite of passage into manhood, into the all-male Tower
Society.

And there is another important aspect of this rite of passage into
patriarchy, Wilhelm's coming into fatherhood. In a matter "that is
close to [Wilhelm's] heart and should be so"—the reference here is to

the emotional, personal, essentialist aspect of the hero's being—he asks the right question:

> "Very well, then! You strange wise men, whose sight can pierce so many mysteries, tell me if you will: is Felix really my son?"
> "Praise be to you for asking that question!" exclaimed the Abbé, clapping his hands with joy. "Felix is your son! I swear it by all our most sacred mysteries. Felix is your son, and in spirit his deceased mother was not unworthy of you. Take unto yourself this lovely child from our hands, turn around and dare to be happy."(304)

Wilhelm receives his son from the hands of the patriarchal order and he explicitly acknowledges this confirmation of his paternity. For when Felix appears this very moment on the scene,

> his father rushed towards him, folded him in his arms and pressed him to his heart. "Yes, oh yes," said Wilhelm, "you are indeed mine! What a gift this is from Heaven that I have to thank my friends for. Where have you come from at this moment, my child?"
> "Don't ask," said the Abbé. "Hail to you, young man. Your apprenticeship is completed, Nature has given you your freedom." (304)

Nature, no less, has absolved, has legitimized Wilhelm, the male order has confirmed his (biological) paternity.[8] This is indeed a curious appropriation of procreative labor by the patriarchal Tower Society, for in the politics of reproduction[9] the natural mother has (conveniently) been obliterated. We recall that Felix was born out of wedlock by the actress Mariane, Wilhelm's first great love, whom he had deserted before she bore "his" son, believing her to be unfaithful and promiscuous. Mariane, the mother, fades from the narrative and eventually dies. But "fate" would have it that Wilhelm meets the orphan Felix and befriends him *like a father*. Yet Wilhelm cannot quite bring himself to believe the old servant woman's story assuring him of his paternity—women's, especially old women's, stories appear mysterious, unreliable, and untrustworthy to the male hero. Only his male mentors of the Tower Society can speak the truth. Their ritual assures the hero of his paternity, thus making him a worthy man, a son and father.

In the initiation ritual of the Tower Society, history is made symbolic, for, as Mary Douglas has reminded us, rituals are not merely empty or hollow but inscribe and bestow meaning. As a living symbol of patriarchy, the Tower Society reconfirms and thus authorizes Wilhelm's paternity; this rite of passage signifies both a climactic fulfillment (being assured of biological progeny) and a mission for his future (raising his son). Wilhelm has become a worthy link in the eternal chain of patriarchy. The mother (who died much earlier anyway, and her story was related in a brief, unreliable tale) is absent, her procreative role taken over by the patriarchal order and bestowed upon Wilhelm. Mothers (notably Wilhelm's own) are absent from this ritual, as women are excluded from the Tower Society; women as autonomous subjects (human subjects in the way male individuals are conceived) are written out of this order, they are assigned a subordinate role in the novel's text. Women are domesticated into useful, cooperative females subordinate to the needs of males. Towards the end of the novel even the formerly untamed, alluring, erotic Philine reappears tamed: married and very unattractively pregnant.

II. Patriarchy and the Female Subject

Goethe's poetic vision of a patriarchal society speaks—to be sure, unreflected—to the heart of eighteenth-century discourse on gender, the ideology of separate spheres for the male and the female with its prescriptive features especially addressed to women and its myth-making elements for the relationship of the sexes. Wilhelm (and his male, mostly aristocratic friends) have far-reaching freedom as agents, experimenting with their lives and experiencing the world, making mistakes as well as progressing, imagining and reinventing their world as father/son. Authority, privilege, and power, especially over women, are associated with his position; hierarchy, bonding, leadership, and charisma organize the Tower Society. It (secretly) guides Wilhelm's education, it perpetuates the patriarchal order by controlling his fatherhood (by authorizing Felix as his son and heir). The world, so it would seem in *Wilhelm Meister's Apprenticeship*, is male or at least exists for the purpose of enabling the male individual to live a creative life. Women, as derivatives of the first sex, complement the male's education and support his general welfare and well-being, including his intellectual and artistic pursuits. In *Wilhelm Meister*, as in much of eighteenth-century thinking and practice, the realm of women is the private, not the political, and thus does not speak to public life, great art, powerful signification or theoretical abstraction.

Historically speaking, patriarchy signifies a biologically determined order in which the (first-born) son inherits the father's place; moreover, it regulates and controls power, ensures participation of all males and enfranchises them within this order. As a system, patriarchy can be described as "the organization and division of all practices and signification in culture in terms of gender and the privileging of one gender over the other, giving males control over female sexuality, fertility, and labor" (Ebert 19). Patriarchy thus means "the manifestation and institutionalization of male dominance over women and children in the family . . . and male dominance over women in society in general" (Lerner 239); it is "a system of social structures, and practices in which men dominate, oppress and exploit women" (Walby 214). Male power, then, with its corollaries of authority and privilege, its extremes of violence, colonization, and tyranny, its more benign aspects of responsibility, patronage, and surveillance, appears at the heart of patriarchy. How women are affected by, live with, internalize, respond to, manipulate, subvert, and (rarely) openly rebel against male power is also part of the story of patriarchy (and the female figures in *Wilhelm Meister* react in a number of different ways to the empowered male and to patriarchal power).

But woman has been conspicuously absent from the discourse of patriarchy; empirical woman was not considered to be an autonomous individual, but under male tutelage, she could not be a citizen in the patriarchal nation (*Vaterland*), did not have political rights vis-à-vis the patriarchal state (*Vater Staat*), as Fichte observed in 1796:

> [Woman's] own dignity requires that she should give herself up entirely as she is, and live to his choice and should utterly lose herself in him. The least consequence is, that she should renounce to him all her property and all her rights, and follow him. Henceforth she has life and activity only under his eyes and in his business. She has ceased to lead the life of an individual; her life has become a part of his life. (This is aptly characterized by her assuming his name.) (*The Science of Rights* 402)

Fichte's elaboration in the "Deduction of Marriage" succinctly describes the essence of order, power, and signification of the subject in patriarchy—as the "natural" order.

The family is the cornerstone of patriarchy, with the father (historical or symbolic) as the family's principal player. The *pater familias*, or *Hausvater*, seen in analogy with God the Father and the king as father to his subjects, looms large during the eighteenth century. The father possesses not only authority and control over his wife and children, other dependent relatives, and servants, but also moral and civic responsibility for his entire household.[10] While Wilhelm Meister (together with his son) prefers travelling, learning, and exploring to living as a family in a household with wife and children, the patriarchal family is celebrated in Goethe's epic *Hermann and Dorothea* (published soon after *Wilhelm Meister's Apprenticeship*). Here the father's position of power and significance, to be subsequently assumed by the son, stands out within the familial configuration.

In the patriarchal family, the father controls woman's labor, woman's procreative function, and (in psychoanalytic discourse) the psychosexual configurations within the family, which are of central importance for childrearing. In the family, and all (Western) families are intrinsically patriarchal, the individual comes to acquire "the law of the father." It is the patriarchal family under the father's domination in which women (and men) are engendered and which replicate the men who dominate and the women who submit, as feminist theorists such as Gail Rubin have pointed out. Freud described (or prescribed?) the story of "father-based" Oedipal structures (Gallop) with castration complexes and the development of the psychic structure in patriarchal social relations; Lacan essentially re-wrote the Freudian script in terms of what he calls a symbolic order which is structured by "the Law of the father" and is synonymous with the "name of the father." The subject as theorized by Lacan is doubly determined by the Other and by language; here the special role of the "phallus" as universal signifier, sexuality, and gender emerge and converge. The "phallus" (in Lacan's terminology, not as such an object, not an organ, not a fantasy, but a signifier) is the privileged signifier around which all signifying practices in patriarchy circulate.[11] Lacan retells the story of patriarchy in familiosexual terms; thus it is not surprising that "the phallus assumes the role of 'universal signifier' within Lacan's theory or that he wishes to consign women to presymbolic silence" (Flax 107).

For as long as sexual difference is construed as "feminine lack and masculine presence," and as long as "the woman as mother must always be the natural residue left behind as the speaking being enters the symbolic" (Nye 140), patriarchy is reborn in the psychoanalytic imagination, as it was in Goethe's novel. *Wilhelm Meister's Travels* closes with a significant scene: son Felix almost drowns in an accidental fall into water (a symbol of the female, the womb?); he is rescued by several men, and father Wilhelm in his capacity as a trained physician revives him. Covering his son with his coat, Wilhelm exclaims: "Again and again you are born, in the great image of god."[12] Here the father restores and authorizes the son's life (a ritual not unlike the initiation into the Tower Society), father and son are reunited and reborn; with this tribute to and affirmation of patriarchy, the novel closes, having left the female behind, just as Felix was rescued from the water.

Re-affirmation of the patriarchal order in the bonding of males, of father and son, by excluding woman from social life and displacing the female into mythic being, and by appropriating or obliterating "reproductive" (nurturing and creative) activities, such imaginary (and socially real) power lies at the heart of patriarchy in German poetic and philosophical discourse. There is still a patriarchal core even in a work as critical of the Enlightenment tradition as *Dialectic of Enlightenment*.

III. Displaced into Myth:
Woman in the Patriarchal Discourse of *Dialectic of Enlightenment*

Written in America "when the end of Nazi terror was within sight" (ix), published in Amsterdam in 1947 and reissued in Frankfurt in 1969, *Dialectic of Enlightenment*[13] faces as its "first phenomenon for investigation: the self-destruction of Enlightenment" (xiii) in its critique of modern civilization and specifically of fascism. A reflection on Enlightenment's own regressive tendency is at the center of the text, which operates within a critique of (Western) rationality, a reflection that foregrounds the productive capacity as well as the destructive aftermath of an instrumental reason. Horkheimer and Adorno maintain as their central thesis that the value of the autonomous personality and the radical separation of nature from culture are mutually incompatible, are antagonistic; the antagonism evolves into a dialectic of culture and nature, and into a dialectic of the personality that results in the self-destruction of reason and of the autonomous personality of a subject who is conceptualized as a male subject.

In a gendered reading of *Dialectic of Enlightenment*,[14] I wish to address the patriarchal core of the text (not the authors' personal attitudes or convictions expressed elsewhere) and its intertextual relationship with the patriarchal tradition of German Enlightenment discourse. While *Dialectic of Enlightenment* is an elusive, at times contradictory and elliptical text, as has often been observed (Benhabib 163), several aspects can be identified that constitute its patriarchal core: there is a lack of reflection on patriarchal power and oppression; woman is encoded in nature, placed in the position of the "Other" in the "self/ Other" dialectic constructed in the text; woman is left out as a subject in culture and history, instrumentalized without emancipatory possibility; and references to women are, in many instances, embedded in a stereotyped, if not misogynist, discourse on women current in German intellectual and cultural histories of the early twentieth century.

A global cultural critique is set forth in a number of propositions and statements in the initial essay, "Concept of Enlightenment," yet none of the assertions address gender or patriarchy in a critical fashion. On the contrary, "patriarchal"[15] is used in a cursory way, partly synonymous with "traditional," "fatherly," "old-fashioned," partly denoting "controlling" or "dominating." It is a reference to a given power, but the nature of this power is not questioned. "Patriarchal" makes its appearance in the first section of the text yoked with "marriage" in a metaphorical usage: "The happy marriage between the human mind and the nature of things, which he [Bacon] aims for, is patriarchal: reason, which conquers superstition, is to rule over disenchanted nature" (5). A happy marriage, so the *surface* language (not the argument) implies, is patriarchal; but here, as elsewhere, the thrust of the critical thought is neither on marriage nor on patriarchy. The argument at hand, taking its departure from Bacon, leads up to an exposure of the destructive union of reason and power: "Knowledge which is power knows no barriers, neither in enslaving creatures nor in its subservience towards the masters of the world" (6). This argument is then concretized in reference to bourgeois economy, to labor, capital, and technology. The critique includes class (with its Marxian economic parameters), but excludes gender; a "happy patriarchal marriage" remains a verbal ornament, yet its meaning (the institution of patriarchal marriage) is excluded from analysis, from the dialectic. Instead, "patriarchal" is used metaphorically in an otherwise totalizing cultural critique which lacks a recognition of patriarchy.

Referring to the disenchantment of the world, to the totalitarian effect of enlightenment, the "patriarchal" gods of Olympus (6) surface in the text in an almost nostalgic opposition to philosophical *logos* that demasked them; the thought is elaborated later:

> As a totality unfolded in language, whose claim to truth suppresses the older mythic belief, the national religion or patriarchal solar myth is itself an Enlightenment with which the philosophic form can compare itself on the same level. (11)

In the dialectic bracketing of myth and Enlightenment, myth is deemed "patriarchal," yet "patriarchal" remains a weightless epithet, though there is a reminiscence of (better) olden times, of a veritable "pre-patriarchal" stage (31), a stage that was extirpated from human consciousness. While the text does not play out this notion, it at least at this juncture admits to the other, something other than the patriarchal; but this "pre-patriarchal" stage, a vague and nostalgic reference (while the text mostly operates with cutting incisiveness in foregrounding important notions), is explicitly situated outside of human consciousness, as having been expunged from consciousness by the most severe of punishments. Even when allowing for Horkheimer and Adorno's "relentless pessimism" (Benhabib 166), one cannot help but notice that here the textual environs are studded with deterministic, fatalistic asides that appear to foreclose any escape from the "idea of patriarchy" (24).

The Homeric epic in particular becomes the site for an incisive reading as "the entanglement of myth, domination, and labor" (32) in which woman is displaced into the position of "other," into myth, and written out of man's story. In Odysseus' encounter with the alluring Sirens—Odysseus escapes the Sirens' song by using wax to plug the ears of his companions, who then must row with all their strength, and by having himself tied firmly to the mast—Horkheimer and Adorno tell a story of identity formation:

> Men had to do horrible things to themselves before the self, the identical, purposive, the virile nature of man, was formed, and something of that recurs in every childhood. The strain of holding the I together adheres to the I in all stages; and the temptation to lose it has always been there with the blind determination to maintain it. (33)[16]

This is a story of identity formation for a *male* subject in what has been called a "Bildungsroman" of a perverted educated hero, a "rationalistic, radicalized Wilhelm Meister."[17] Navigating between Nietzsche and Freud, Horkheimer and Adorno reinvent this episode of identity formation as a story of the breaking apart of "the enjoyment of art and manual labor . . . as the world of prehistory is left behind" (34); Odysseus' measures against the Sirens are seen as a "prescient allegory of the dialectic of enlightenment." Thus, while art and labor are written into the text, the gendering of this story is obscured and instrumentalized for the dialectic.

The patriarchal story inscribed in the Homeric epic is shaped by Horkheimer and Adorno to serve their argument, and in it autonomous female sexuality can only be rendered as potentially destructive, threatening, and as prostitution. It is the "old" story—from the Bible to Freudian psychology—of the seductive, castrating female who is nature and whose sexuality lures and threatens the male and, if he gives in, causes the fall from paradise or destroys him. In the Homeric epic, the Sirens were two creatures, half bird and half woman, who lured sailors to destruction by the sweetness of their song; the bewitching, animalistic creatures who possess the power of song are outwitted by the heroic wanderer Odysseus. It is a tale of yet another trial of the hero's wit and endurance against threatening, uncanny nature; a tale of male cunning overcoming the female spell; of reason over story, in short, an epic display of male power and knowledge. Horkheimer and Adorno spin this Homeric episode into a modern patriarchal tale interwoven with a nostalgia for unadulterated nature and pre-capitalist, pure civilization: the Sirens who "threaten the patriarchal order with their irresistible promise of pleasure" (33) are marked female, a modern-day "Loreley" or "femme fatale," in their desire for ensnaring the male in their sexuality and thus conquering him. The Sirens also become a sign for nature, woman vanishes behind nature. And nature must be and is conquered: "Men have always had to choose between their subjection to nature or the subjection of nature to the Self" (32). Horkheimer and Adorno's human beings ("Menschen") are men; the self has a "male character" (33) and it is a disciplined self with a "barrier between oneself and other life" (33); this (male) identity is "power, domination over nature" (Schulte-Sasse 68), and woman is a "representative of nature" (71). The monolithic power of determinism forces origin and telos into an iron circle, a monolithic reading imposed on the Odyssey. Thus women can appear in *Dialectic of Enlightenment* only as helpless victims or cynical accomplices of male power (Geyer-Ryan/Lethen 67).

In Horkheimer and Adorno's cultural critique, woman has been removed as a subject from history, submerged into nature, displaced into a fatalistic, demonic notion that lurks behind the demise of our culture, behind "a modernizing enlightenment doubling back on itself, reproducing the violence it intended to escape and asserting identity only by destroying it" (Berman 3). Man's (rationalistic) civilization, we are told, cannot escape from this cyclical dialectic whose first (and celebrated) victim is man (Stephan 121). This is patriarchy mesmerized by itself. As in Freud's reinvention of the Oedipal myth, man's psychosexual development as father/son is charted as a struggle against a threatening (castrating) mother/woman; in Horkheimer and Adorno's reinvention of the Odysseus myth, the course of man's civilization is charted as inevitable social domination of, and against, an enchanting, desirous nature/woman. And while this may be the story patriarchy likes to tell about itself, in *Dialectic of Enlightenment* it is a narcissistically distorted one, and as a *patriarchal* story it is neither reflected upon nor critiqued.

As the classic wanderer and explorer, Odysseus is further foregrounded in "Excursus I: Odysseus or Myth and Enlightenment," in which episodes from the epic are interwoven with flashes of modern man and his civilization. It is a compelling political account in several respects: illuminating, among other notions, the bourgeois subject, modes of production and labor, of dominance and (Western) imperialism, of rationalism and modernity. Beyond and outside of these political accounts, woman surfaces in the dialectic of the prostitute and bourgeois society conjoined by the wife. In preferring the word "hetaere" (since Friedrich Schlegel's essay *Diotima* the tasteful term for the prostitute in the discourse of German intellectuals), and in the rather listless reading of Penelope's story as a trite bourgeois marriage, an uneasiness with the complex question of sexuality/woman surfaces:

> Marriage is the middle way by which society comes to terms with itself. The woman remains the one without power, for power comes to her only by male mediation. (72)

And:

> Marriage does not signify merely the order that requites in life but also solidarity in facing death. Expiation develops in it for the price of subjection,[18] as in history to date the humane has flourished only and precisely in the savagery that is veiled by humanity. Even if the contract between the partners only calls down that age-old enmity, nevertheless, peacefully growing old together, they can vanish at the same moment like Philemon and Baucis. . . . Marriage belongs to the primal rock of myth in the basis of civilization. But its mythic hardness and fixity stand out from myth as the small island kingdom from the infinite sea. (75)

Woman's subjection (to male domination) is yoked, even seen as necessary for a reconciliation of "that age-old enmity" between the battling sexes; thus gender hierarchy, male domination and violence are reduced to a "natural" enmity between male and female. And within the somewhat nostalgic notion of "mythic firmness and solidity" of marriage (reminiscent of Schiller and Goethe, whose *Wilhelm Meister* is here quoted and footnoted [40, n 50]) an unsettling ambiguity about woman and sexuality outside such a marriage (closer to Schopenhauer and Nietzsche) is embedded in the text. As a representative of nature, woman (in bourgeois society) has become the "enigma of irresistibility and impotence" (73); woman as enigma and locus of weakness—only the male narcissistic viewpoint, his gaze, his language signifies woman in the cultural critique. While the sorceress Circe is elevated as prostitute to the "first female character" (74), female sexuality as love is revalued. At the same time, woman as mother, her reproductive labor, is devalued, if not effaced. Odysseus briefly visits (or dreams of) the underworld and encounters his mother: "But his mother's image is powerless, blind, and speechless, a mirage" (76). Odysseus meets mother "with patriarchal and expedient rigor" (75). Whatever notions of prehistoric matriarchy the text is alluding to—since Bachofen, a gesture towards a matriarchy removed to safely distant times has been part of German academic discourse on myth—the male hero has fortified himself against his own mother. Mother has become a mere illusion ("Wahngebild," 83). Horkheimer and Adorno re-inscribe a reduced and schematized gender/sex system which constitutes male subjectivity along the power/knowledge axis by banishing the female into speechless, empty images to be left behind, or into nature to be conquered in order to critique bourgeois society.[19]

Using the Odysseus myth turns out to be sterile and even regressive as a dialectic, in which woman *within* culture cannot not be worked out; rather, Romantic stereotypes are dusted off and reinforced. The section "Man and Animal" (from the appendix of notes and drafts) might have been left incomplete and omitted from the main text because Horkheimer and Adorno could not conceptualize woman as subject and as historical agent/subject. From animal to fairy tale to woman, the text drifts to this signification:

> Woman is not a being in her own right, a subject [Die Frau ist nicht Subjekt]. She produces nothing but looks after those who do; she is a living monument to a long-vanished era when the domestic economy was self-contained. (247-48)

And so goes the story of woman as non-subject and as victim and accomplice in the (uncharacteristically linear) rise of odious bourgeois society; "the suffering woman" is but a sign for the calamity, produced by the rise of capitalism, for men.[20] Even if we accept this "story" of woman thus far, it is a story frozen at around 1800, at the enlightened, patriarchal stage of *Wilhelm Meister*. And the remythologizing of woman follows in the image of the "Megäre" (Fury) who complains about woman's lot: "With her endless nagging she takes revenge in her own home for the misery inflicted upon her sex from time immemorial" (250). And woman emancipated from male domination and tutelage becomes "die böse Alte" (a cross old woman, 250), a mindless fanatic in politics, the most blood-thirsty in a pogrom; such a Fury even wants a job, publicity, culture, intrudes into the male domain of sciences, but she is unqualified, frustrated and unable to participate and ends joining Christian Science or the Humane Society. Now we are back to the animals. . . . If we had any doubts that Horkheimer and Adorno's text could not negotiate woman as subject, then this extensive and misogynist passage tells us that the text has not even begun to deal with woman as a historical and political subject, but is fighting off its own inability to deal with (or unconscious rejection of) the female with dull mockery and trite derision, with the kind of jokes that were cracked about the suffragettes around the turn of the century.

While advancing the critique of instrumental reason, of fascism, and of capitalist bourgeois society, *Dialectic of Enlightenment* also works against the traditional notions of enlightenment as a process of emancipation (Hohendahl 12); it works against and precludes any possibility of emancipation. In its totalizing argument it assumes a single, unified subject in history, encompassing all humanity and all culture(s), a patriarchal culture and stance at heart. This is not a question of "style," but goes to the core of the episteme and to the center of its historical and cultural critique. More specifically to the historical situation, *Dialectic of Enlightenment* has a blind spot vis-à-vis woman as subject, as historical and political agent. It is a blind spot still shared by many German intellectuals (of Horkheimer and Adorno's generation). In very general terms, it is the blind spot of patriarchy, which lacks a consideration of reproductive activities and which largely ignores the complex issues of childbearing and childrearing, of nurture and socialization. "Mother" is written out of the patriarchal text, internalized or obliterated by the male, as in the poetic imagination in the final scene of *Wilhelm Meister's Travels* or in the culture/nature dialectic in the totalizing discourse of *Dialectic of Enlightenment*.

Notes

1. Research for this essay was assisted by the generous support of the Alexander von Humboldt Foundation.

2. I use "humane" and "enlightened" here in the sense of the enlightened ruler or patriarch, who, like the protagonist of Lessing's *Nathan the Wise*, strives for the moral best for his subjects or family members and friends; the repressiveness of the patriarchal order (more appreciated by today's reader) surfaces in such episodes as Wilhelm's attempt to break away from his designated career as a merchant and his fascination with the theatre, and in the ironic narrative style.

3. See my article "Bekenntnisse" for a reading of this episode as representing a woman who refuses to assume her female role as lover/mother subjected to the father/husband, a role assigned to women in the patriarchal order. The novel's surface narrative accepts her, after her death, in her religious devotion only as beautiful image, while its deep structure of patriarchy eliminates her as the infertile, undomesticated, and potentially threatening/castrating female.

4. I am referring to Sandra Harding's incisive definition: "Sex/gender is a system of male dominance made possible by men's control of women's productive and reproductive labor, where 'reproduction' is broadly construed to include sexuality, family life, and kinship formations, as well as the birthing which biologically reproduces the species" (311). Harding assigns "patriarchy" (and such concepts as "misogyny," "sex-roles," "discrimination against women," and "the first division of labor—by sex") to "mere appearances of the underlying reality of the sex/gender system" (311); I would, however, upgrade patriarchy's "mere appearance" of the sex/gender system to historical (and national) specificity. "Patriarchy" is the historical and empirical form of the sex/gender system in Germany; I will attempt to show this in looking at Enlightenment discourse and beyond.

5. For an excellent summary of feminist theorizing on patriarchy in historical-philosophical, materialist-marxist, and psychoanalytic terms, see Flax, Nye, and Chodorow.

6. " 'Ich bin der Geist deines Vaters,' sagte das Bildnis, 'und scheide getrost, da meine Wünsche für dich, mehr als ich selbst begriff, erfüllt sind. . . . Lebe wohl und gedenke mein, wenn du genießest, was ich dir vorbereitet habe' " (495).

7. "A man in ordinary clothes stepped forward and greeted him, saying: 'Don't you recognize me? . . . Don't you remember the painting that especially appealed to you? Where do you think the sick prince is languishing at the moment?' Wilhelm had no difficulty in recognizing the stranger." (302). The story of the prince is of symbolic significance for the novel: The prince is love-sick, yearning for the woman (his stepmother) whom his father married; only when the father renounces is the son's illness cured and he can marry: this is a rewriting of the oedipal conflict in which father and son reconcile and merge. Young Wilhelm's close relationship to his mother (against the father's wishes she enables Wilhelm to play out his

fantasies in the puppet theater) is sublimated into a mere semblance of art (the theater), an illusion he later recognizes and abandons, helped (invisibly) by the Tower Society; this signals his patrilinear recoding, his merging into patriarchy; see my article, "Die Bekenntnisse einer Schönen Seele."

8. As the apprenticeship is often read as the discovery of self, Wilhelm here recognizes what is of his own fruition; his paternity affirms his masculinity and creativity.

9. See Mary O'Brien, who argues for serious theoretical attention to the pro-creative process and for recognizing paternity as an idea.

10. For a discussion of the literary representation of the "Hausvater" see my article, "Vom ganzen Haus zur Familienidylle."

11. See Ebert's critique and especially Flax's incisive reading (90-132) conclud-ing that in Lacan's narcissistic theory "male dominance becomes unanalyzable in theory and inescapable in practice" (101).

12. "Wirst du doch immer aufs neue hervorgebracht, herrlich Ebenbild Gottes" (460).

13. As is well known, a substantial part of the work was composed from notes taken by Gretel Adorno during discussions between Horkheimer and Adorno; the mode of production of this text then is fairly typical for German intellectuals, with woman (the wife) functioning as secretary to the male authors. For further detail on Horkheimer and Adorno's collaboration, historical circumstances, and textual differences, see the editorial commentary in vol. 5 of Horkheimer's *Schriften.*

14. I am not interested in Horkheimer's or Adorno's individual attitudes or personal relationships to women, nor do I wish to imply that they, as individuals, were anti-feminist or anti-woman. I am looking critically at the patriarchal stance in the text, not at their critique of bourgeois, capitalist culture. Looking at patriar-chy often seems to unsettle some (German male) intellectuals, is felt as somehow undermining their individual authority and as subverting the collective control of the intellectual and cultural agenda which men, by and large exclusively, control (in Germany). Two recent commemorative volumes (Bonß and van Reijen) reflect some of the intellectual and emotional impact and critical reception of the text in Germany, as does the excellent survey "Critical Theory and the Student Move-ment" in Wiggershaus (676-705).

15. August Bebel's *Woman and Socialism* (*Die Frau und der Sozialismus*, 1879), which had reached fifty editions by 1909, established the term "patriarchalisch" (patriarchal) in German cultural critique (followed by Engel's *The Origin of the Family, Private Property, and the State*; *Ursprung der Familie, des Privateigentums und des Staates*, 1884); Bebel did explain the term in his glossary (of foreign words) as "altväterlich, nach Altväterweise" (according to our forefathers; traditional, cus-tomary); it is synonymous with "vaterrechtlich" (according to the law of the father), the term popularized by Bachofen's *Matriarchal Law* (*Das Mutterrecht. Eine Unter-suchung über die Gynäkokratie der alten Welt nach ihrer religiösen und rechtlichen Natur*, 1861). Horkheimer and Adorno continue to use the word in this manner.

16. "Furchtbares hat die Menschheit sich antun müssen, bis das Selbst, der identische, zweckgerichtete, männliche Charakter des Menschen geschaffen war, und etwas davon wird noch in jeder Kindheit wiederholt. Die Anstrengung, das Ich zusammenzuhalten, haftet dem Ich auf allen Stufen an, und stets war die Lockung, es zu verlieren, mit der blinden Entschlossenheit zu seiner Erhaltung gepaart" (40).

17. Geyer-Ryan/Lethen (46), who gives an incisive "re-vision" of Horkheimer and Adorno's "Odysseus or Myth and Enlightenment" in a comparative re-reading

of the Homeric epics. Geyer-Ryan/Lethen likewise point to the fact that in *Dialectic of Enlightenment* women only appear as victims or collaborators of male violence (43) and that autonomous female sexuality in a world conceptualized by men can only be comprehended as female prostitution (47).

18. My translation for "Versöhnung wächst in ihr um Unterwerfung" (83).

19. For reasons of space I cannot even begin to discuss in this essay the other major sections of the text: "Juliette or Enlightenment and Morality," "The Culture Industry: Enlightenment and Mass Deception," and "Elements of Anti-Semitism: The Limits of Enlightenment," which I am addressing in another article; suffice it to say that they offer rich and suggestive passages on such areas as male bonding, father/son problematics, and the victim/sacrifice complex.

20. The passage, which is fairly long and cohesive compared with the discursive argumentation elsewhere in the text, outlines in a developmental, chronological way woman's lot in history; it is indebted in part to the cliched initial chapter "Woman in History" (in Bebel's *Woman and Socialism*, 1879; see 15, above.) Yet Horkheimer/Adorno totally omit any of Bebel's fine sociological and historical discussion and his copious notes (especially in the fiftieth edition of 1909 which was greatly revised and updated).

Works Cited

Becker-Cantarino, Barbara. " 'Die Bekenntnisse einer Schönen Seele.' Zur Ausgrenzung und Vereinnahmung des Weiblichen in der patriarchalen Utopie von Goethes *Wilhelm Meister.*" *Verantwortung und Utopie: Zur Literatur der Goethezeit.* Ed. Wolfgang Wittkowski. Tübingen: Niemeyer, 1988. 70-90.

———. *Der lange Weg zur Mündigkeit: Frau und Literatur in Deutschland 1500-1800.* Munich: dtv, 1989.

———. "Vom 'ganzen Haus' zur Familienidylle: Haushalt als Mikrokosmos in der Literatur der Frühen Neuzeit und seine spätere Sentimentalisierung." *Daphnis* 15 (1986): 261-85.

Benjamin, Jessica. "Die Antinomien des patriarchalischen Denkens: Kritische Theorie und Psychoanalyse." Bonß and Honneth 426-55.

Benhabib, Seyla. *Critique, Norm, and Utopia: A Study of the Foundations of Critical Theory.* New York: Columbia University Press, 1986.

———. "Die Moderne und die Aporien der Kritischen Theorie." Bonß and Honneth 127-75.

Benhabib, Seyla, and Drucilla Cornell, eds. *Feminism as Critique: On the Politics of Gender.* Minneapolis: University of Minnesota Press, 1987.

Berman, Russell A. *Modern Culture and Critical Theory: Art, Politics, and the Legacy of the Frankfurt School.* Madison: U of Wisconsin P, 1988.

Bonß, Wolfgang, and Axel Honneth, eds. *Sozialforschung als Kritik: Zum sozialkritischen Potential der Kritischen Theorie.* Frankfurt: Suhrkamp, 1982.

Chodorow, Nancy. *Feminism and Psychoanalytic Theory.* New Haven: Yale UP, 1989.

Douglas, Mary. *Natural Symbols.* Harmondsworth: Penguin, 1973.

Ebert, Teresa L. E. "The Romance of Patriarchy: Ideology, Subjectivity, and Postmodern Feminist Cultural Theory." *Cultural Critique* 10 (1988): 19-57.

Fichte, Johann Gottlieb. *The Science of Rights [Grundlage des Naturrechts nach*

Prinzipien der Wissenschaftslehre]. Trans. A. E. Kroeger. London: Routledge & Kegan Paul, 1970.

Flax, Jane. *Thinking Fragments: Psychoanalysis, Feminism, and Postmodernism in the Contemporary West.* Berkeley: University of California Press, 1990.

Gallop, Jane. "Reading the Mother Tongue: Psychoanalytic Feminist Criticism." *Critical Inquiry* (Winter, 1987): 314-29.

Geyer-Ryan, Helga and Helmuth Lethen. "Von der Dialektik der Gewalt zur *Dialektik der Aufklärung*." Reijen and Noerr 41-72.

Goethe, Johann Wolfgang von. *Wilhelm Meister's Apprenticeship* [*Wilhelm Meisters Lehrjahre*]. Trans. Eric Blackall and Victor Lange. New York: Suhrkamp, 1989.

———. *Wilhelm Meisters Wanderjahre* [*Wilhelm Meister's Travels*]. *Werke.* ["Hamburger Ausgabe."] Vol. 8. Ed. Erich Trunz et al. 14 vols. Munich: Beck, 1973 (translations in the text are mine).

Harding, Sandra, and Merrill B. Hintikka, eds. *Discovering Reality: Feminist Perspectives on Epistemology, Metaphysics, Methodology, and Philosophy of Science.* Studies in Epistemology, Logic, Methodology, and Philosophy of Science, 161. Dordrecht: Reidel, 1983.

Hohendahl, Peter. "The Dialectic of Enlightenment Revisited: Habermas' Critique of the Frankfurt School." *New German Critique* 35 (1985): 3-26.

Honneth, Axel, and Albrecht Wellmer, eds. *Die Frankfurter Schule und ihre Folgen: Referate eines Symposiums der Alexander von Humboldt-Stiftung.* Berlin: de Gruyter, 1986.

Horkheimer, Max. *Gesammelte Schriften.* Eds. Alfred Schmid and Guenzelin Schmid Noerr. Frankfurt: Fischer, 1985- .

Horkheimer, Max, and Theodor W. Adorno. *Dialectic of Enlightenment.* Trans. John Cumming. New York: Continuum, 1972.

Lacan, Jacques. *Feminine Sexuality.* Eds. Juliet Mitchell and Jacqueline Rose. New York: Norton, 1985.

Lerner, Gerda. *The Creation of Patriarchy.* Oxford: Oxford University Press, 1986.

Nye, Andrea. *Feminist Theory and the Philosophies of Man.* London: Croom Helm, 1988.

O'Brien, Mary. *The Politics of Reproduction.* Boston: Routledge, 1983.

Reijen, Willem van, and Gunzelin Schmid Noerr, eds. *Vierzig Jahre Flaschenpost: 'Dialektik der Aufklärung' 1947-1987.* Frankfurt: Fischer, 1987.

Rubin, Gail. "The Traffic in Women: Notes on the 'Political Economy' of Sex." *Toward an Anthropology of Women.* Ed. Rayna Rapp Reiter. New York: Monthly Review, 1975.

Schulte-Sasse, Jochen. "Gebrauchswerte der Literatur: Eine Kritik der ästhetischen Kategorien 'Identifikation' und 'Reflexivität,' vor allem im Hinblick auf Adorno." *Zur Dichotomisierung von hoher und niederer Literatur.* Ed. Christa Bürger et al. Frankfurt/M.: Suhrkamp, 1982. 62-107.

Stephan, Inge. " 'Das Natürliche hat es mir seit langem angetan': Zum Verhältnis von Frau und Natur in Fontane's *Cécile.*" *Natur und Natürlichkeit: Stationen des Grünen in der deutschen Literatur.* Eds. Reinhold Grimm and Jost Hermand. Königstein/Ts.: Athenäum, 1981. 118-49.

Walby, Sylvia. "Theorizing Patriarchy." *Sociology* 40 (1989): 213-34.

Wiggershaus, Rolf. *Die Frankfurter Schule: Geschichte—Theoretische Entwicklung—Politische Bedeutung.* Munich: Beck, 1986.

On Multiple Selves and Dialogics: Christa Wolf's Challenge to the "Enlightened" Faust

Sara Friedrichsmeyer

I

CHRISTA WOLF'S EXPANSIVE declaration in 1964 that in the GDR "[r]eason, we call it socialism, has penetrated into everyday life" (*RW* 26)[1] comes ironically close to marking the end of her optimism. Only a few months later, she felt compelled to admit the dangerous possibility that even in socialism, politics and economics could take precedence over human concerns (*Dim* 406),[2] and consequently to embark on an examination of the premises on which her society was built, concepts usually unquestioned in socialist discourse. Among the first to warn against the GDR's new economic model of 1963 and its resultant fetishism of rationality and technology (Emmerich 136), Wolf began to focus her criticism, especially after Biermann's expatriation in 1976, on the dangers inherent in a society which did not value difference and in which the Enlightenment legacy had degenerated into instrumental reason.[3] Her 1980 speech on accepting the Büchner Prize eloquently articulates the urgency of such a focus: "Sober to the marrow, we stand aghast before the dreams made real by instrumental thinking that still calls itself reason, although it has long since lost its enlightened impulse toward emancipation, toward maturity, and has entered the Industrial Age as barefaced utilitarian mania" (BP 4). Three years later in her Frankfurt lectures Wolf spoke out once more against what she perceived as the "one-track-minded route" of rationalism, describing it as the "route of segregation, of the renunciation of the manifoldness of phenomena, in favor of dualism and monism, . . .

65

of the renunciation of subjectivity in favor of a sealed 'objectivity' "
(*Cass* 287).

Despite misgivings, Wolf has not, however, abandoned the principles of Socialist Realism with its roots in the German Enlightenment.[4]
The centrality in her work of concepts such as progress, reason, even
Bildung, as well as her belief that literature can help in achieving them,
demonstrates in a concrete way her link to that value system. Unlike
those writers whose works began appearing in the late 70s and who
refused to speak within or even against Socialist discourse,[5] she has
remained rooted in a critical marxism. A relatively undiscriminated
German Idealist tradition and the bourgeois culture it produced are
her referents when she writes about the dangers of a world view in
which the individual subject is alienated from all other phenomena, not
only from nature, as the Romantics charged, but from other human
beings and from the self as well. In its scientific frame, she sees
rationalism as an impulse which has led to a mechanistic world view
with its mandate to control and subdue the natural world. This concern
takes her beyond the limited boundaries of what was the GDR, for
what she sees as the perversion of reason has been virtually endemic in
Western culture. As she has expressed it in a variety of forms, we live
in a world in which technology and science are out of control, no longer
pursued for human interests, and in which means and ends are confused; that is, a world which has exercised its reasoning faculties to
bring itself to the point of nuclear and ecological disaster. She is then
one of many contemporary writers and thinkers in various disciplines
and across the political spectrum who recognize the need to move
beyond the modern world view as bequeathed to us by the thinkers of
the Age of Reason. In this sense, she can be placed in the broad current of postmodernism, a term I am using not necessarily as a specific
theoretical or aesthetic practice, but as a general description for a
world view beyond that of modernity. But hers is not a *deconstructionist*
postmodernism, which in its efforts to abolish all possibilities of
totalitarian norms in fact eliminated the structures on which any position can be based: the individual meaning in history, truth, causality.
Her thinking instead bears many similarities to what has been called
constructive postmodernism (Griffin); her interest is in reshaping rather
than eliminating the structures of modernity, even in some cases combining them in purposeful fashion with elements of a premodern world
view. Although Wolf, for example, does not use the word organicism,
no doubt in part because of its troubled associations in German history,
it is an important concept in her thinking. Failing a restoration of the
connection between human beings and the natural world which "reason" has severed, the decaying moon with which *Accident / A Day's*

News (*Störfall. Nachrichten eines Tages*) concludes will be a permanent
fixture in our world, a powerful symbol for what Carolyn Merchant has
called the "death of nature."

Because she has so often emphasized the dangers associated with
the legacy of the eighteenth century, Wolf has found it necessary to defend herself against the charge of being anti-Enlightenment (for example, *Dim* 905-06). She would no doubt agree with Foucault in rejecting
the "blackmail" according to which "you either accept the Enlightenment and remain within the tradition of its rationalism ... or else you
criticize the Enlightenment and then try to escape from its principles of
rationality" (42-43). Certainly Wolf is not involved in an attempt to
declare an end to the Enlightenment project in Germany; she does not
promote an irresponsible irrationalism[6] and is not part of a neoconser-
vative resurgence, although some recent critics have been situating her
near that camp (Buruma). Far from rejecting reason, she in fact makes
very clear that the only way to achieve the kind of human community
she desires is the "narrow path of reason" (*RW* 212). Although she has
maintained that concepts we associate with our Enlightenment heritage
such as freedom, equality, brotherhood,[7] humanity, and justice—all
concepts she would define as constituents of this particular "path"—
have lost their meaning (BP 5), I would argue that her entire *oeuvre* is
an attempt to reclaim these concepts and reinvest them with meaning
for our own time. Despite changes in her attitude to the GDR and her
own development as a writer,[8] her goal has remained consistent: her
intent has been not to demolish what she calls, citing Büchner, the
"citadel of reason" (BP 6), but to gain freedom from its imprisoning
strictures.

Considering her preoccupation with the Enlightenment tradition, it
should be no surprise that Wolf, a writer well-known for her dense
intertextuality,[9] would almost inevitably be drawn to challenge the
epitome of her country's cultural icons, Goethe's 'enlightened' Faust; in
various semblances he has in fact made frequent appearances in her
works over more than twenty years. For Faust's perversions, under the
guise of heroic strivings, have provided the model for that singular
equation of reason with technological and scientific progress which she
finds so menacing. Her intertextuality in this case is not a mere
revisionist struggle for control of a text, but a fight, as it were, for the
German soul.

Faust as he emerges in Wolf's writings is the quintessential Enlightenment man whose thirst for knowledge destroys his ability to function
as a human being. In her Büchner Prize Speech she associates him
with death: he is, in his modern reincarnation, the "father of the atomic
bomb" (BP 4). Father, not mother; the connection between a Faustian

preoccupation with progress and a masculine epistemology has been a thematic in much of Wolf's writing at least since her 1973 short story "Self-Experiment: Appendix to a Report" ("Selbstversuch. Traktat zu einem Protokoll").[10] In her Büchner speech she recalls the women in literature and history who were not allowed entrance into Büchner's "citadel."   "Rosetta under her many names"—and for Wolf those names range from Büchner's Marie to Rosa Luxemburg—had pinned her hopes on the ideals of the Enlightenment; she had "[t]rusted its rationality" and yet found herself "at the mercy of the irrationality into which the Age has taken refuge" (BP 7-8). As Wolf adduces one after another of the women who had no share in determining cultural values, her emphasis goes beyond the tragedy of their individual lives to that of a society thus deprived of an antidote to the Faustian spirit.

In the *Cassandra* lectures this thematic becomes even more explicit. Here too, in an example of the subjectivity which has so indelibly marked her style,[11] Wolf articulates its importance in her own intellectual development, claiming that her recognition of the link between patriarchal culture and the Faustian spirit was as pivotal as the social analysis that led her to marxism (*Cass* 277-78). While writing *Cassandra: A Novel and Four Essays* (*Kassandra: Voraussetzung einer Erzählung*), consciously using myth itself to challenge the Enlightenment concept of ratio, she had located the roots of the Faustian malaise in the very origins of Western civilization. She had also discovered traces of a matriarchal society existing before what is traditionally recognized as the beginning of Western culture. Textual evidence in *Faust* convinces her that Goethe had intuited this facet of our past but rejected it, impressing instead its opposite into the rationalist paradigm. Faust, as Goethe created him, belongs to the world of males and a masculine view of progress so much so that, as Wolf reminds us, he could only shudder with fear at Mephisto's mention of the "Mothers" (*Cass* 285). And that, according to Wolf, is the world we have inherited, a world in which women have been subordinated to men and have served them in the name of that progress which such a division encourages.

Faust then, in *Cassandra*, is not only the prototype for the exclusionary practices of the Enlightenment, but his reification of the world is inseparable from a male form of ratio. Not only dangerous, but spurious as well, the objectivity for which both Goethe and Faust have been so admired is for Wolf more than anything else a subjective response demonstrating "a longing for unshakable, 'true' laws" (*Cass* 288). The unfortunate legacy of this fixation on objectivity is, according to Wolf, a society—and she refers as much to Enlightenment as to contemporary culture—which in the pursuit of progress has expunged itself of all the "magic" associated with the natural world and its processes. In a reworking of the Midnight scene of *Faust II*, Act 5, which at the same time recollects what Horkheimer and Adorno called the "disenchantment" of the world, she asks whether it was necessary in the course of human development that "man" (for whom Faust is the prototype) would have to "stand 'alone' before Nature—opposite Nature, not in it" (*Cass* 283).

In *Accident*, a diary-like work of 26 April 1986 when the narrator, easily identifiable as Wolf, hears the news of the Chernobyl disaster, she returns to a question she had asked in a 1968 essay on Anna Seghers. Asking why a modern Faust might possibly sell his soul, her tentative answer then had been the awareness that Mephisto's sardonic idea—everything that exists is worth destroying—had at last become technically possible (*Dim* 316-17). Now after almost twenty years, years during which the general obsession with scientific and technological progress has not abated, she refashions the question to ask whether the utopias of our time indeed by necessity breed monsters (*Acc* 30). This time her Faust has a name; he is Peter Hagelstein, a scientist at the Livermore Laboratories in California, obsessively involved in the pursuit of scientific progress, here again associated with destruction and a gendered form of reason. Through the figure of this contemporary Faust and allusions to his work ethic and personal relationships, Wolf continues her basic critique: an exclusive dedication to science, to "progress," leads to instrumental reason and leaves human beings without the capacity for love. As if to prove that women might make a difference, she provides in *Accident* a "Faust-Gretchen-variation" (65). Her modern Faust in this work finally rejects the kind of scientific progress which is separated from a knowledge of or concern about its uses; he leaves his laboratory, presumably because his "Gretchen" will not tolerate the instrumental view of science it demands.

For all her insistence on dissimilarity, Wolf does not see the sexes as irreconcilable opposites. Neither does she envision the elimination of sexual difference—despite her interest in androgyny, especially in *No Place on Earth* (*Kein Ort. Nirgends*)—as the impetus to a genuinely human society. Gender is an issue in her writing mainly because she believes that men, and again Faust is her example, have been deformed by the patterns of their socialization. As recently as 1990, in *In Dialogue* (*Im Dialog*), she foregrounds this conviction in her discussion of gender-specific socialization processes. Trained to be heroes, men, she posits, lose the ability to love. Again it is the relentless quester, but this time as Thomas Mann's Faust, Leverkühn, who provides an example of the consequences of such social practices. In her 1990 interpretation, he could conclude his pact with the devil—in this case, Nazism—only because he was incapable of love (63), a lack which, as critics agree, functions throughout her work as a metaphor for the loss of humanity. Although Wolf finds women less deformed by "reason," she is ultimately not a separatist feminist; nor does she promote an essentialist view of sexual differences. The cave community in *Cassandra*, we remember, is not exclusively female. She takes care elsewhere as well to insist that women are not better than men; having had the benefit historically of a less damaging socialization, they have, however, been less willing to pay the price demanded of such goal-oriented pursuits as those exemplified by Faust (*Dim* 846-47; *ImD* 63). Indeed, Wolf expresses in *Cassandra* her horror of an ideology which in rejecting an androcentric world view merely replaces it with an equally one-sided women-centered perspective, an ideology which requires of women that they "throw over the achievements of rational thought simply because men produced them" (*Cass* 260).[12]

For Wolf then, Faust's condition is one of the devastating consequences of the polarization of the sexes, itself an artificial division paralleling the dualism synonymous with Western rationalism. She is in agreement with postmodernists who deplore such a mode of thought because of what they regard as its inevitable result: the compulsion to perceive the world in terms of hierarchically valued oppositions. For Wolf it is this either/or thinking inherent in our rationalist heritage that has led to the "false alternatives" against which she so often inveighs and for which the Faustian spirit presents a paradigmatic example (e.g., *Cass* 267). Her counterpart to Horkheimer and Adorno's Odysseus, Faust can continue his quest only by repressing a part of his being, his ability to love. Locked into binary reasoning, he has no viable alternatives.

Clearly Wolf is aware of the implications of a negative dialectic of Enlightenment; the thrust of her writing, however, is to dissuade her readers, and perhaps herself as well, of its inevitability. Her work is thus not merely an examination of the perils of the Faustian world view, but even more a search for ways of going beyond the Enlightenment concept of ratio and the cultural impasse it has generated. If, as she has stated, such a vision is a kind of utopian "madness," she has willingly surrendered herself to it "so as not to fall victim to the dark side of reason" (BP 11).[13] Her entire *oeuvre*, with its emphasis on love, subjectivity, the fantastic, nature, dreams, the everyday, and even, as Myra Love has recently argued, the supernatural is not merely a challenge to traditional rationalist thinking; even more it is an attempt to expand our concept of reason to include many of the facets of life which the Faustian pursuit attempts to deny. By her own account Wolf has sought a *new* kind of subjectivity for a *new* kind of autonomous individual (*Dim* 773-805); she has sought a *new* language,[14] a *new* way to live in the world (*RW* 177), and a *new* goal for human life beyond participation in the production of material goods (*POC* 338). Nevertheless, as I hope to show in the following discussion, her later works have not sustained the radical break with tradition which her writings of the late 60s seemed to predict. Instead, her striving for "newness" has ultimately meant a turn to the German past, to the ideals of the Enlightenment. She has in fact devoted herself to reshaping that legacy for our contemporary world, primarily through a search for ways to overcome the borders imposed by its dualism, an endeavor generally considered central to postmodernism (Hutcheon 49; Harvey 311). This redefinition of Enlightenment ideals through the incorporation of certain postmodernist tenets has had crucial implications for both her thematics and her literary structure.

II

Scholars generally agree that one of Wolf's overarching thematic concerns is what Wolf herself has referred to as helping human beings "to become conscious subjects" (*RW* 212). Needless to say, this goal is not to be equated with solipsism or narcissism; neither is it the kind of search for self which, though fueled by revolutionary energy, has the conservative aim of successful integration into existing social structures. Simply stated, Wolf sees consciousness of self as necessary for the more important goal of knowing and then changing the world; there is for her no possibility of meaningful change without personal agency, a conviction which only intensified with the fading of her hopes for meaningful change from the GDR leadership.[15]

I would like to place this concern with subjectivity at the very core of Wolf's redefinition of eighteenth-century rationalism, for she is in all her discussions about and experimentation with subjectivity challenging the bourgeois notion of individualism with which it is associated. The self for her is neither the empiricist subject, blank and awaiting its imprinting, nor the Romantic subject who creates and gives meaning to the world. Rather, she has at least since the late 60s viewed the subject as constructed through its interaction with society, understood in its widest sense (*Dim* 199-200), a perception not inimical to rationalist philosophy with its subject/object core. In her Büchner Prize speech she makes explicit reference to her Enlightenment roots when she alludes to the " 'hellish journey of self-recognition,' without which . . . reason cannot exist, according to Kant" (BP 6). But her understanding of this journey, of *Bildung*, is, as her use of the word *Höllenfahrt* implies, not the traditional Enlightenment view of a serene knower securely separated from the known, progressing surely and safely toward inevi-

table selfhood. Rather, the route she advocates to the "maturity" or
"autonomy" with which she defines that goal—these unmistakable
Kantian echoes occur with regularity throughout her work—involves
her in a major reshaping of the idealist notion of a unified, autonomous self and the subject/object dichotomy on which it is founded. In
every one of her major works since *The Quest for Christa T.* (*Nachdenken über Christa T.*), she has presented characters with multiple selves.

The consciousness Wolf desires for the human subject is in her
early works problematized by the much discussed reluctance or
inability of her narrators to say "I." In *Christa T.*, for example, where
this thematic emerges, she is neither able nor willing to claim for her
fictional character the authority of a unified subject position, nor does
she choose one for herself as writer. In part a reflection of the political
and social views outlined in her seminal essay "The Reader and the
Writer" (TW 177-212), according to which all authority is suspect, this
reluctance also demonstrates Wolf's conscious questioning of a tradition which insists on the existence of a fixed self. True, the focus in
Christa T. is on the protagonist's goal, frequently stated and restated,
"to be completely oneself" (3), a longing in consonance with a search
for bourgeois selfhood. Yet Wolf allows her narrator the possibility of
split narration, the "secret of the third person" (170). One could in
fact argue that Christa T.'s attraction as a literary figure is precisely her
ability to let various selves coexist and her cognizance of selfhood as a
process. However, although Wolf in this work challenges the notion of
the self-identical subject, that thematic concern is outweighed by her
ambition to define a place for the autonomous individual within a collective whose claims, in her own GDR experience, have too often taken
precedence.

Patterns of Childhood (*Kindheitsmuster*) marks a more conscious
break with the rationalist tradition, for in it Wolf intensifies her
exploration of the fullness of the self which she had glimpsed but
allowed to remain in the background of *Christa T.* As I have argued
elsewhere, *Patterns* poses her most radical, most postmodern, challenge
to the Enlightenment construct of an integrated self, for in it Wolf
divides her autobiographical voice into three distinct personae: the
child in Nazi Germany, the adult visiting her birthplace, and the writing
narrator. In contrast to all her other literary works, her emphasis here
is less on the potential wholeness of the conscious subject than on its
parts; in this work each of the selves is granted a separate existence.
The separateness she stresses is, however, only in part a reaction to a
childhood in Fascist Germany which forced a separation of thoughts
and emotions "in order to continue functioning" (*POC* 387). Because
the selves she explores are shaped by memory and non-linear time and

thus not exclusively controlled by social or cultural imperatives, her challenge is to autonomous selfhood itself. Wolf's initial goal was a merging of the various voices (*FD* 45); nevertheless she maintains separate levels of narration until the last two pages and the "I" which she finally does achieve can only be described as the product of a precarious merging. The dream with which the book closes affirms a commitment to an all-inclusive, ever-evolving selfhood. For both the writer and the readers of *Patterns*, the elusive goal of self-knowledge proves then to involve more than the futile search for "true" identify. Although she makes no claims for knowing what consciousness is, her book asks the reader to contemplate the possibility that a sound human identity is composed of non-threatening, multiple selves which will emerge only with an individual's willingness to be *both* subject and shifting object.

After *Patterns*, Wolf's critique of the unified self takes different, in some ways less challenging, forms. The decentering of authority which she continues to value is increasingly achieved by means other than the postmodern challenge to autonomous selfhood. Although her later protagonists have rarely been self-identical, the fullness of the voice in *Patterns* has yielded in her later works to a more traditional fragmentation, largely, I believe, as a response to life in the GDR. The more important it seemed to offer meaningful alternatives to her country's repressive system, the more vital it became to identify the individual as the locus of reason and potential source of meaningful change. It is likely that what she discovered while writing *Patterns* led to the recognition of a major problem inherent in the postmodern, diffused subject; ultimately a position which denies agency, it is philosophically untenable to any marxist writer and especially to one dealing as she was with individual responsibility during Nazism. Wolf's concerns are shared by many feminist theoreticians, especially those writing in English, who have worked to identify a subject position which offers the benefits of a postmodern sensibility—decentering authority and exposing both the fallacy of hierarchical oppositions and the notion of "objectivity," for example—without destroying the concept of the individual as the source of responsible action (see Rabine, Alcoff, Nicholson).

Perhaps not coincidentally, Wolf's first major work after *Patterns* marks a distinct retreat from the problems of subjectivity. In *Cassandra* she positions narrative authority in an autonomous protagonist who, though the boundaries of her self are permeable, does achieve selfhood (12, 112). The portrayal of Cassandra as someone who becomes a part of all that she experiences marks an important stage in Wolf's thinking, but Cassandra's wholeness is achieved, at least in part, by overcoming an inner split, described here as the "old, forgotten malady" endured for the sake of consciousness (22). Consequently, although this work has achieved something like cult status among its readers, many scholars have reacted with suspicion precisely to what seems to be a retreat to the more traditional philosophical position represented by its self-identical protagonist.[16]

No Place on Earth, written after Biermann's expatriation and very much a response to it (Hilzinger 106-29), represents a different, but again a relatively conventional, way of dealing with individual subjectivity. To be sure, Wolf's protagonists, the Romantic-era writers Caroline von Günderrode and Heinrich von Kleist, do not fit the idealist model; they are both represented as conspicuously fragmented individuals. It is impossible, however, to overlook the ghost of an idealist subject lurking behind these splits, for the implication is that, given a saner society, both writers would flourish. We are told that an unconditional love can fuse Günderrode's three separate selves; although the possibility for Kleist's wholeness is less appealing, it too exists and can be achieved through his work (*NP* 117).

The divergent selves in Wolf's subsequent fiction seem increasingly compatible with conventional human psychology; certainly they offer no more serious threat to the concept of autonomous selfhood than did Faust's two souls within his breast. In *Accident*, as Anna Kuhn has phrased it, the narrator has finally learned to say "I" (213). That "I" is, however, a comfortable composite of subject and objects, one of which is described as a self which "tends to split off from the 'me' for purposes of contemplation" (*Acc* 31-32). It is then a controlled split within a self-conscious subject for the purpose of bringing to the conscious level facets of a personality which have always existed but which have been previously unexposed. The emphasis of the work is not on the parts but on the whole, on the "I" which has become conscious of its selves (83). *Summer Piece* (*Sommerstück*) is again a work filtered through memory in which the narrator, easily linked to the author, once more divides her literary voice, this time into a first person narrator who speaks to herself as "du" and that narrator's third person self, Ellen. The split is, however, peripheral; a masquerade, where each "acts" him/herself in a play called "Sommerstück" (144-48) recalls the idealist vision of a whole, unified individual. In *What Remains* (*Was bleibt. Erzählung*), Wolf presents us with another first person narrator, the extent of whose identity with the author has been the cause of considerable controversy. And again Wolf has her narrator pay at least lip service to the concept of divergent selves, for example in pondering "which of the multiple beings from which the 'I myself' is composed" is really the "I myself."[17] The parts, however, are again less important than the whole. They exist primarily as an excuse for probing the various components of the "I myself," as a vehicle for the self-scrutiny that is so much in the foreground of this book. The thrust in these recent works for the exploration of the various selves is their importance for the development of a healthy psyche, for free-ranging imagination, and for what Wolf sees as the consequence: increased self-awareness.

In all her longer works since *Patterns,* then, Wolf has moved closer to the Enlightenment position on subjectivity. She has, however, not completely revived the humanist subject offering stability and truth. By exploring the various components of the self while maintaining her focus on the whole—a sometimes precarious balancing act—she has maintained the space for meaningful human agency without completely jettisoning her insights into the fallibility of autonomous selfhood. As an alternative to the Enlightenment subject defined by exclusion, she has articulated an inclusive self, one not alienated from what it perceives. At the same time, she has moved away from the construction of subjectivity and its decentering as a theoretical issue; in her later works the multiplicity of the self has become a social, historical, and psychological problem rather than a philosophical or even linguistic puzzle. Although she has with this shift retained agency as well as the thrust for intense personal analysis, she has eliminated the existential urgency and curious scrutiny which she devoted to the issue in her fictionalized autobiography.

III

Wolf's position, unchanged since the 60s, that the world itself has no meaning and that "humanism" must therefore be learned (*RW* 210), is a primary impulse behind her concentration on subjectivity.[18] It is also the driving force behind her experiments with structure. Recognizing that a literature with authority concentrated in a single narrative voice is implicated in limiting alternatives and in furthering notions of dominance and submission, Wolf has long sought for her own prose an open structure capable of neutralizing these tendencies.[19] Early in her career she thought she had found an antidote to such thinking in the dialectic which Socialist Realism prescribed as the panacea for bringing about the enlightened individual of history. As she recently told Therese Hörnigk, the dialectic was important at that stage of her development because she saw it as a model for dealing openly and constructively with the contradictions of reality (11). Consequently, in various essays she rejected the theories underlying Enlightenment literature, charging them with a striving for harmony which rendered them incapable of exposing those contradictions. In *The Reader and the Writer,* for example, she repudiated linear plot lines as unnatural and too reflective of a Newtonian world view and for similar reasons dismissed the all-knowing, supposedly objective narrator embodying authority (194-96).

But she soon rejected a dialectic structure for her writing as well. If the linear pattern associated with Faustian striving and Enlightenment thought could too easily become a totalizing structure, neither had the marxian dialectic, Wolf gradually realized, proven itself capable of expressing the tolerance the earlier pattern denied. Its roots are also in a binary model. It too is based on clearly defined oppositions, on the kind of rigorous distinctions which lead almost by necessity to "invented opposites" (BP 10). Further, a dialectic can only function, if at all, given a certain balance between the thesis and antithesis; if one or the other becomes dominant, the movement toward synthesis is short-circuited. By the 70s she conceded that this had happened in her own society. Even more significant was her recognition that the contradictions she still felt in need of exposing, arising from the complexities of the contemporary world with its multiplicity of values and many "truths," were simply not compatible with a dualistic model. The dialectic may have been appropriate for Brecht's *Galileo*, written in the late 1930s, when there was a truth to speak and to remain silent was unconscionable, but the world of the late twentieth century, she has come to believe, defies such easy categorization (*Wb* 30).

I would like to suggest that Wolf's search for a new structure capable not only of tolerating contradictions, but of nurturing diversity and even encouraging an awareness of multiple "truths," led to her development of a dialogically structured literature. Although this term is sometimes applied to Enlightenment discourse, there are substantial differences between Wolf's understanding of a dialogic and the eighteenth-century variant. Reminiscent of the Platonic model, one voice within its multivocal dialogue possessed a clearer claim to general validity than the others. In contrast to the goal-directed, teleological structure preferred by rationalist thinkers, and likewise far removed from the marxian dialectical model based on a drive for harmony and a need to erase difference, the dialogic as Wolf uses it is capable of overcoming dualistic paradigms. It is a structure through which to interrupt hierarchies and one capable of accommodating diversity and raising new questions through non-authoritarian, democratic communication. Wolf's forms of dialogic discourse offer then the all-important possibility for overcoming the "false alternatives" of either/or thinking. In contrast to the isolation of the alienated Western "hero" exemplified by Faust, a dialogic encourages a kind of subjectivity that does not reify the "other," but grants it the possibility to exist as another subject; the dialogic subject shapes itself through this intersubjectivity but without destroying or incorporating the "other" into itself. Wolf's embrace of the dialogic is a reflection of her belief that meaningful change is not embedded in the patterns of history, as Enlightenment thinkers believed, and is not the result of an inevitable synthesis, a more nineteenth-century view of historical processes, but is only possible, if possible at all, through concentrated and conscious human effort.

There is no indication that Wolf knows the work of Mikhail Bakhtin, whose name is most frequently associated with dialogic writing, but it should be noted that both developed their literary theories while living in repressive societies. Wolf's own dialogic has been the product of experimentation, influenced undoubtedly by GDR communication theories of the 70s, by the general thrust of German reception theory and American reader response criticism, and no doubt reinforced by her work on Romanticism with its emphasis on dialogic communication. One could, however, argue that even *The Reader and the Writer* with its pointed references to the relativity theories of Einstein and Heisenberg (199-200) contains the germ of her dialogic structure. It should also be recognized that the dialogic is a narrative structure most compatible with the decentered subject of her fiction; or put differently, the cohesive selfhood she has denied her narrators would be the necessary premise for the authority they are granted in non-dialogic texts. In her 1977 essay "Berührung" ("Touching," in *Dim* 196-209), she suggests "unreserved subjectivity"[20] as a way of overcoming the separation, alienation, division, and inability to love inherent in dualism (Pickle). Described by Sara Lennox as an epistemological stance in which an object is regarded with sympathy and understanding (71),[21] "unreserved subjectivity" is Wolf's alternative to Idealism as well as to Logical Positivism. It is the attempt to incorporate this intersubjective impulse into her literature that has fueled her experiments with various kinds of dialogic discourse. She has, to name only some of the most obvious examples, conducted dialogues with other texts, as in her reworking of the Faust plot, with history, as in *No Place*, with historical figures, as in her essays on Günderrode and von Arnim (*Dim* 511-71; 572-610), and even with herself, as in *Patterns*. Although no thorough analysis of her dialogic form has yet been written, critics recognize its import. Kuhn, for example, has stated that the dialogic informs all of Wolf's writing since "Juninachmittag" (54), and others have begun to identify its specific forms. Anne Herrmann has analyzed *Christa T.* and Wolf's work on Romantic women, using Irigaray's concept of the specular subject, as a dialogic with "an/other woman" for the purpose of establishing female subjectivity. Thomas Fox has stressed her use of inter- and intratextuality to revise not only patriarchal but also her own previously published texts. Edith Waldstein has analyzed the dialogic communication between Kleist and Günderrode in *No Place*.

Basic to all Wolf's experiments with dialogic writing, I believe, is the attempt to diffuse the hierarchies and oppositional structures associated with a traditional narrator and, with them, all accepted models and channels of social and political authority. But within this broad spectrum, there are differences in her dialogic strategies which are significant in the context of her Enlightenment critique. If the goal of dialogic writing is the neutralization of all authority, Wolf has been most successful in *Accident* (1987), where the dialogic informs not just the relationship between reader and writer, but also the relationships, for example, between the writer and patriarchal texts, the narrator and herself, and the narrator and her brother. More importantly, the very essence of the book is shaped around the complex realities and ambiguities of life which the dialogic is uniquely positioned to express. The one-sided scientific progress which Wolf has so often decried and which led to the disaster at Chernobyl—one of the thematic lines in the work —has also made a treatment possible for the narrator's brother, who by strange coincidence is undergoing an operation for a brain tumor during the narrated time of the novel. Because the medical technology employed to save his life cannot be separated from Western notions of progress, the narrator is unable to reject categorically the thinking that has supported it. The notion of multiple truths is at work here and the writer does not know more than the reader or any of her other dialogic partners. There is the hint of a utopian moment in the final lines of the book,[22] but Wolf offers no perspectives on how such a moment can be extended. More so than in any of her other fiction, the writer is intricately involved with the reader in a mutual search for understanding.

In her earlier works, Wolf's dialogic had allowed for an authorial position. The concluding "when, if not now" (185) of *Christa T.*, for example, while exploding the dialectic between individual and society, had also involved the reader in an effort toward change, an undertaking clearly consonant with the writer's position. In *Patterns*, Wolf's own voice can be discerned in that of the first-person narrator who implicitly encourages self-exploration, even though she makes no pretense of knowing what a self should be. In *Cassandra*, although the Cassandra story itself is not dialogic because Wolf has posited narrative authority in the self-identical protagonist, Wolf engages the reader in dialogic communication in the four accompanying lectures by articulating, for example, her own skepticism toward traditional rationalist thinking patterns. In none of these works is Wolf's own position in doubt.

Even *No Place*, although it marks a more conscious embrace of dialogic communication, is not without a voice of authority. Although
Wolf has generally focused on the corruption of Enlightenment values
in her own age, in *No Place* she confronts the Enlightenment on its own
terms, examining the same phenomenon in a society without historical
distance from its premises.[23] The dialogic is a factor in the salon-like
setting, where conversation could be expected to flourish, as well as in
the blurring of the narrative voice. And it also structures the high point
of the work, the conversation between Kleist and Günderrode. While
they do not agree on all issues and in fact do not even strive for consensus, they open themselves up to one another and achieve, albeit for
a very brief time, authentic human communication (Waldstein). But
however much a dialogic is in evidence in this conversation, the notion
of an overall dialectic still fuels the work. Although Wolf is on one
level trying here to counter the kind of thinking which made of Enlightenment and Romanticism antonymous movements, the work remains
locked within a frame of the "old world" of Enlightenment culture
versus the "new world" of Romantic challenges, the latter the world to
which Günderrode belongs and clearly Wolf's preference. Thus *No
Place* is not a thoroughly dialogic work, and not only because the overall pattern is still indebted to a binary model. Because her own voice is
so closely identified with that of Günderrode, a voice of authority is
still to be heard.

Until *Accident*, then, Wolf had not created a dialogic that could
both overcome the structures of dualism *and* eliminate a voice of authority. What is of particular significance in the present discussion is
that she did not choose to remain with this structure. Although the
dialogic element in her succeeding works remains strong—even in the
elegiac *Summer Piece* Wolf invites the friends who people her recollec-
tions to write their own versions of the "Jahrhundertsommer" of 1975
("Club")—it is never again as sustained. To be sure, the later writings
do not embrace an either/or logic, but her narrators are all granted a
limited amount of authority. Although they are not self-identical, their
fragmentation is not so overpowering as to destroy the possibility of
responsible judgment and meaningful commitment. I would like to
stress, however, that this is not a criticism and is in no way meant to
imply a waning of authorial skill. For anyone sympathetic to socialist
(or rationalist) perspectives, it is in fact quite the opposite; clearly Wolf
is so widely read precisely because she *does* take positions, although
never in an apodictic way. A "pure" dialogic, on the contrary, with its
refusal to posit authority in a narrator and its commitment to multiple
truths, leads almost inevitably to relativism or a consciously chosen
position of indecision. Such a notion is of course contradictory for a

convinced marxist writer who, even having rejected the dialectical structure, theoretically at least still knows in which direction society is to move and feels obliged to convey that knowledge to a presumably less informed public.

Although by now a moot point, it is possible that, had 1989 unfolded differently, Wolf would have continued to explore the many conflicting verities of contemporary existence. But the wall *did* fall, and Wolf saw herself no longer confronted with the conundrum of how best to preserve life on this planet, but rather with the old question of the future of socialism. And for that she *did* have if not answers, at least some opinions, and felt compelled to share them. In her latest works *What Remains* and *In Dialogue*, then, she has not abandoned dialogic discourse; her multiple voices continue to provide a strong antidote to dualistic patterns. But it is not a dialogic aimed at conveying the postmodern position of indeterminacy; instead she has shaped it to be more compatible with her own earlier works and, not coincidentally, with the rationalist appreciation for pedagogical literature. Although she makes strong disclaimers in both about possessing any "truth" and does not profess in either to know the details of a socialist future, her position is not without a claim to authority. Because *In Dialogue* is a collection of speeches, interviews, essays, open letters and other pieces written between mid-1987 and March 1990 through which a reader can reconstruct events of the period leading to unification, a dialogic element is built into the very substance of the work. Yet, although Wolf does not offer any overall summation, her own subjective perspective, her own views, responses, and questions are centered; because these views are rarely questioned and never directly contradicted, it is clear that she intends some authority for her various narrators. In *What Remains*, dialogic exchange with various partners and with herself allows the narrator—hardly distinguishable from Wolf—to expose her own doubts, weaknesses, failures, and even feelings of resignation. Clearly she hopes that through such open communication, through a sharing of various ideas, some meaningful positions will crystallize, for herself as much as for her reader.[24]

The controversy surrounding the publication of *What Remains* has implications for Wolf's dialogism, and not only as proof of the effectiveness of her ability to engage her readers. Speaking for her in *Der Spiegel*, Günter Grass wished she would defend herself against her critics, attributing her refusal to do so to an aversion to conflict (143). He may in part be right, but even if so, Wolf's reluctance to engage in traditional forms of argumentation is another proof of her philosophical commitment to dialogic communication. And however we read *What Remains*, there is some evidence that Wolf is a victim of the totalizing structures which her dialogic has been intended to negate. As the barbed criticism directed against her documents, she has come to represent the voice of socialism through which the entire system can be dismissed. Christine Schoefer, writing in *The Nation*, refers to the obvious irony that Wolf's critical voice might be silenced only now after unification. We can hope Wolf's redefinition of Western rationalism continues. Certainly the conservative agenda, the attempt to completely discredit socialism, based as it is on a need for harmony and a rejection of difference, is in need of countering voices. The apparent inability of the established political system to allow for a continuing dialogic of difference is also—and not only in the former GDR, it would seem—what remains.

IV

Wolf's thematic concentration on the development of full, inclusive selfhood for the reader and the writer as well as her shaping of dialogic discourse to help both in their struggle toward that goal are, as I hope to have shown, very much part of her attempt to redefine and, more importantly, reinvigorate for our twentieth-century world those values we associate with our Enlightenment legacy. She has identified the dilemma inherent in modernity with its limited and false alternatives, but she has also recognized the dead end of a postmodernism which nullifies the very positions on which decisions must be based. Her response has not been an aesthetic affirmation of undecidability or of a kind of value-free communication, whatever that might be. On the contrary, she has created a body of literature with a thematic focus on the ethical responsibility of reader and writer, crafted to help through its very structure in developing the kind of critical consciousness necessary for meaningful and responsible action; she hopes to help in the development of subjects willing to take positions, even when faced with a panoply of competing, and from certain perspectives equally valid, "truths."

Although Wolf has clearly incorporated postmodern assumptions into her writing, her concept of openness and diversity, I hope to have demonstrated, owes more to Enlightenment "tolerance" than to postmodern *différance*. This becomes even more clear with the realization that there is nothing multicultural in her concept of diversity. Responding in 1989 to Aafke Steenhuis' urging for a discussion of international issues, Wolf emphasized the importance of regional and national problems in contrast to "something amorphously international that one does not know and that does not exist in reality."[25] Similarly, her understanding of "women" as an homogeneous group demonstrates that she is not engrossed in exploring cross-cultural differences *among* women, but has focused rather on the women who have been forced as a group to the margins of Western culture. Only by referring to "women" within this clear historical and cultural context does she avoid—if narrowly—the perils which such a reductivist view would otherwise entail. Her work then is not an attempt to replace Western notions with others, but instead is a plea for redefining those eighteenth-century ideals she values in the light of postmodern insights into the mechanisms of power and its neutralization. Despite political upheaval, she has remained a Socialist writer dedicated to working toward a society based on what she would define as reason. To what degree she has moved toward the rationalist understanding of a writer as teacher and model of responsible selfhood is a question readers will answer differently and should be the focus of future study.

We could read Wolf's reshaping of Enlightenment tenets as a narrow response to life in the former GDR with its calcified bureaucracy; the mimetic theories of art prescribed by socialist realism might lead us to this conclusion. We could read *Christa T.*, for example, as a reaction to the New Economic Plan of 1963 and its preoccupation with conformity and economic efficiency; we could read *Patterns* as Wolf's response to the GDR's attempt to obscure its citizens' complicity with Nazism; we could see *No Place* as a response to Biermann's expatriation, and so on. If that is all there is to her writing, then we could treat it as just one more literary document of socialist experimentation and failure. Clearly there is more. And that "more," I would argue, lies precisely in Wolf's willingness to take positions as she attempts to redefine our Western heritage. It is not just Faust who is faced with the false alternatives endemic in virtually all forms of dualism. We, her readers, unless we forge a way out of that philosophical stalemate, are not exempt. Her literary challenge to Faust and to the tradition to which he has given a name is ultimately an attempt to provide an antidote to the notion of cultural and social progress for which he stands, without which, as has become clear to many contemporary thinkers, there may be no alternatives at all.

Notes

1. Throughout this study I have cited published translations of Wolf's works whenever possible; in other cases the English versions are my own with the German originals in endnotes.
2. See her 1987/1988 interview with Hörnigk for Wolf's own view of her political and intellectual development (7-41). In a 1989 interview with Steenhuis she said: "Den wirklichen Schmerz habe ich 1969 empfunden, beim Einmarsch der Truppen" (*ImD* 149).
3. See her 1982 interview with Meyer-Gosau for Wolf's reflections on 1976 as

a turning point in GDR cultural politics (*FD* 90-102).

4. The GDR always saw itself as the legitimate heir to rationalist thinking and in the early years of its existence tended that legacy with special care; the most frequently performed play in GDR theaters after the war, for example, was Lessing's *Nathan* (Emmerich 47). Wolf's concern then cannot be totally divorced from the challenge issuing from Socialist Realism "to reawaken . . . the great German culture" (Emmerich 39).

5. Bathrick names young poets such as Uwe Kolbe, Fritz Hendrik Melle, Rüdiger Rosenthal, and Christa Moog as examples of such writers (5).

6. In the lectures accompanying *Cassandra*, Wolf expressed her "genuine horror at that critique of rationalism which itself ends in reckless irrationalism" (260).

7. Although her works document the author's increasing feminist consciousness, she has generally not sought gender neutral language.

8. In 1988 Kuhn saw her development as one from marxism to feminism; Marilyn Fries, writing in 1991 and using Said's terminology, sees it as one from social affiliation (associated with culture and society) to natural filiation (belonging to the realm of nature and of "life") (13).

9. Brandes and Fox, for example, have discussed intertexuality as an important and conscious focus in her writing.

10. In their introduction to the English translation, Fehevary and Lennox have argued that Wolf's feminism in this story is not an alternative to marxism, but "a prerequisite for its renewal" (112).

11. See especially her 1973 interview with Kaufmann, "Subjective Authenticity" (*FD* 17-38).

12. Although Wolf assiduously avoids the trap of essentialism, her insistence that the only hope for society lies in the acceptance of women's values, i.e., that women *teach* men to love (*Dim* 846-47), is problematic. As has been done so often in the past, she is thus making women the guardians of values and forcing upon them the ultimate responsibility for men's and society's failures.

13. Anna Seghers's role in this conscious struggle against cultural pessimism should not be overlooked; Wolf credits Seghers with having taught her that a writer must counteract the disenchantment of the world, must reawaken the charm of reality, in order to go on living (*Dim* 303). This is what Wolf elsewhere calls the enlightening impulse in Seghers's thinking and work (*Dim* 320). Kuhn has identified the utopian moment as the major unifying thread in Wolf's works. Although the intensity of the utopian current has varied with political and social events, it has remained strong enough so that even in her most despairing work, *What Remains*, Wolf continues to maintain her focus on the future (103).

14. This has been a concern at least since 1968, from in *The Reader and the Writer* (177) to *What Remains*, where it is a frequently occurring motif.

15. Wolf articulated the political rationale for her emphasis on experience as the basis of knowledge in her interview with Hörnigk: finally hearing the truth about Stalin and Berija made her realize how she had been misled by an older generation who had been in exile in Moscow but had repressed the truth (21). Recent revelations about corruption throughout the GDR leadership have presumably only reinforced this perspective. See Adelson for a discussion of Wolf's concept of individual agency in the context of the nuclear debate.

16. See, for example, Weigel, Schmidt, Quernheim (8-10); for a more positive appraisal see Wilke.

17. "[w]elches der multiplen Wesen, aus denen 'ich selbst' mich zusammensetzte" (57).

18. She has articulated the goal of her writing as "dem Menschen zu seiner Selbstverwirklichung zu verhelfen" (*Dim* 33). Her faith in the power of the written word is rooted in the concept of the GDR as a *Literaturgesellschaft* (Emmerich 19-33), an ideal itself derived from marxist and Enlightenment thinking.

19. Wolf has always believed, as she stated in the *Cassandra* lectures, that "narrative techniques . . . in their closedness or openness also transmit thought patterns" (266). This is an issue for her from *The Reader and the Writer* (193-97) through *In Dialogue* (26-27).

20. "rückhaltlose Subjektivität" (199). The Kantian dimension to this moral imperative—for Wolf it is crucial that one never make another human being a means to an end—has not been overlooked (Kuhn 242-43 n. 82).

21. In contrast to those Enlightenment critics who see epistemology as legitimizing the exploitative links between knowledge and power, see Sandra Harding on the importance of feminist theories of knowledge.

22. The final lines are: "How difficult it would be, brother, to take leave of this earth" (*Acc* 109).

23. This work is part of what various critics, among them Herminghouse and Greiner, have seen as the GDR's return to Romanticism in the 70s. Wolf stated in her interview with Meyer-Gosau that the work was a form of personal therapy (*FD* 91). She was also writing *What Remains* at this time, presumably an even deeper therapy.

24. In *In Dialogue* she in fact states that she now writes more for herself than for her readers (*ImD* 63-64).

25. "irgend etwas verschwommen Internationales, was man nicht kennt und was es als Realität nicht gibt" (*ImD* 145).

Works Cited

Adelson, Leslie. "The Bomb and I: Peter Sloterdijk, Botho Strauß, and Christa Wolf." *Monatshefte* 78 (1986): 500-13.

Alcoff, Linda. "Cultural Feminism Versus Post-Structuralism: The Identity Crisis in Feminist Theory." *Signs* 13.3 (1988): 405-36.

Bathrick, David. "Productive Mis-reading: GDR Literature in the USA." *GDR Bulletin* 16.2 (Fall 1990): 1-6.

Brandes, Ute. *Zitat und Montage in der neueren DDR-Prosa.* Frankfurt a.M.: Lang, 1984.

Buruma, Ian. "There's No Place Like Heimat." *New York Review of Books* 20 December 1990: 34-43.

"Club der einsamen Schmerzen." *Der Spiegel* 15 (1989): 229.

Emmerich, Wolfgang. *Kleine Literaturgeschichte der DDR.* Darmstadt: Luchterhand, 1981.

Foucault, Michel. "What Is Enlightenment?" Trans. Catherine Porter. *The Foucault Reader.* Ed. Paul Rabinow. New York, Pantheon, 1984. 32-50.

Fox, Thomas C. "Feminist Revisions: Christa Wolf's *Störfall.*" *German Quarterly* 63 (1990): 471-77.

Friedrichsmeyer, Sara. "Women's Writing and the Construct of an Integrated Self." *The Enlightenment and Its Legacy: Studies in German Literature in Honor of Helga Slessarev.* Ed. Sara Friedrichsmeyer and Barbara Becker-Cantarino. Bonn: Bouvier, 1991. 171-80.

Fries, Marilyn. "When the Mirror Is Broken, What Remains?: Christa Wolf's *Was bleibt.*" *GDR Bulletin* 17.1 (1991): 11-15.

Grass, Günter. "Nötige Kritik oder Hinrichtung?" *Der Spiegel* 29 (1990): 138-43.

Greiner, Bernhard. " 'Sentimentaler Stoff und fantastische Form': Zur Erneuerung frühromantischer Tradition im Roman der DDR." *DDR-Roman und Literaturgesellschaft.* Ed. Jos Hoogeveen and Gerd Labroisse. Amsterdam: Rodopi, 1981. 249-328.

Griffin, David Ray. "Introduction: The Reenchantment of Science." *The Reenchantment of Science: Postmodern Proposals.* Ed. David Ray Griffin. Albany: SUNY Press, 1988. 1-46.

Harding, Sandra. *Whose Science? Whose Knowledge? Thinking from Women's Lives.* Ithaca: Cornell UP, 1991.

Harvey, David. *The Conditions of Postmodernity.* Oxford: Blackwell, 1989.

Herrmann, Anne. *The Dialogic and Difference. "An/Other Woman" in Virginia Woolf and Christa Wolf.* New York: Columbia UP, 1989.

Herminghouse, Patricia. "The Rediscovery of Romanticism: Revisions and Reevaluations." *Studies in GDR Culture and Society 2.* Ed. Margy Gerber et al. Washington, D.C.: UP of America, 1982. 1-17.

Hilzinger, Sonja. *Christa Wolf.* Stuttgart: Metzler, 1986.

Hörnigk, Therese. *Christa Wolf.* Göttingen: Steidl, 1989.

Hutcheon, Linda. *A Poetics of Postmodernism: History, Theory, Fiction.* London: Routledge, 1988.

Kuhn, Anna. *Christa Wolf's Utopian Vision: From Marxism to Feminism.* Cambridge: Cambridge UP, 1988.

Lennox, Sara. "Trends in Literary Theory: The Female Aesthetic and German Women's Writing." *German Quarterly* 54 (1981): 63-75.

Love, Myra. " 'A Little Susceptible to the Supernatural'?: On Christa Wolf." *Women in German Yearbook* 7 (1991): 1-22.

Merchant, Carolyn. *The Death of Nature: Women, Ecology, and the Scientific Revolution.* San Francisco: Harper and Row, 1980.

Nicholson, Linda J., ed. *Feminism / Postmodernism.* New York: Routledge, 1990.

Pickle, Linda S. " 'Unreserved Subjectivity' as a Force for Social Change: Christa Wolf and Maxie Wander's *Guten Morgen, du Schöne.*" *Studies in GDR Culture and Society 2.* Ed. Margy Gerber et al. Washington, D.C.: UP of America. 217-30.

Quernheim, Mechthild. *Das moralische Ich: Kritische Studien zur Subjektwerdung in der Erzählprosa Christa Wolfs.* Würzburg: Königshausen + Neumann, 1990.

Rabine, Leslie. "A Feminist Politics of Non-Identity." *Feminist Studies* 14 (1988): 11-31.

Schmidt, Ricarda. "Über gesellschaftliche Ohnmacht und Utopie in Christa Wolfs *Kassandra.*" *Oxford German Studies* 16 (1985): 109-21.

Schoefer, Christine. "Germany Rewrites History: The Attack on Christa Wolf." *The Nation* 22 October 1990: 446-49.

Waldstein, Edith. "Christa Wolf's *Kein Ort. Nirgends*: A Dialogic Re-vision." *The Enlightenment and its Legacy: Studies in German Literature in Honor of Helga Slessarev.* Ed. Sara Friedrichsmeyer and Barbara Becker-Cantarino. Bonn: Bouvier, 1991. 181-93.

Weigel, Sigrid. "Vom Sehen zur Seherin: Christa Wolfs Umdeutung des Mythos und die Spur der Bachmann-Rezeption in ihrer Literatur." *Text und Kritik* 46 (1985): 67-92.

Wilke, Sabine. " 'Rückhaltlose Subjektivität': Subjektwerdung, Gesellschafts- und

Geschlechtsbewußtsein bei Christa Wolf." *Women in German Yearbook* 6 (1990): 27-45.

Wolf, Christa. *Accident / A Day's News.* Trans. Heike Schwarzbauer and Rick Takvorian. New York: Farrar, Straus & Giroux, 1989. Original 1987. Cited as "*Acc.*"

————. *Cassandra: A Novel and Four Essays.* Trans. Jan van Heurck. New York: Farrar, Straus & Giroux, 1984. Original 1983. Cited as "*Cass.*"

————. *Die Dimension des Autors: Essays und Aufsätze, Reden und Gespräche 1959-1985.* Darmstadt: Luchterhand, 1987. Cited as "*Dim.*"

————. *The Fourth Dimension: Interviews with Christa Wolf.* Trans. Hilary Pilkington. London and New York: Verso, 1988. Cited as "*FD.*"

————. *Im Dialog: Aktuelle Texte.* Darmstadt: Luchterhand, 1990. Cited as "*ImD.*"

————. *No Place on Earth.* Trans. Jan van Heurck. New York: Farrar, Straus & Giroux, 1982. Original 1979. Cited as "*NP.*"

————. *Patterns of Childhood.* Trans. Ursele Molinaro and Hedwig Rappolt. New York: Farrar, Straus & Giroux, 1984. Original 1976. Cited as "*POC.*"

————. *The Quest for Christa T.* Trans. Christopher Middleton. New York: Farrar, Straus & Giroux, 1970. Original 1968."

————. *The Reader and the Writer: Essays, Sketches, Memories.* Trans. Joan Becker. New York: International, 1977. Original 1972. Cited as "*RW.*"

————. "Self-Experiment: Appendix to a Report." Trans. Jeanette Clausen. Introd. Helen Fehevary and Sara Lennox. *New German Critique* 13 (1978): 109-12.

————. "Shall I Garnish a Metaphor with an Almond Blossom?: Büchner Prize Acceptance Speech." Trans. Henry J. Schmidt. *New German Critique* 23 (1981): 3-11. Cited as "BP."

————. *Sommerstück.* Darmstadt: Luchterhand, 1989.

————. *Was bleibt. Erzählung.* Darmstadt: Luchterhand, 1990. Cited as "*Wb.*"

Poeticizing the Enlightenment: The Case of Richard Rorty and Kant's Question

Volker Kaiser

It is so comfortable to be dependent. (Es ist so
bequem, unmündig zu sein.)
——Immanuel Kant

And I am resolutely in favor of a new university
Enlightenment (Aufklärung).
——Jacques Derrida

Happy is he who understands his feeling of lack!
(Wohl dem, der das Gefühl seines Mangels ver-
steht!)
——Friedrich Hölderlin

I. Beyond Epistemology: The Liberal Revolution

THE REVOLUTION OR transformation of the Enlightenment that
Richard Rorty outlined can best be described as an inversion of its
principle, as a non-dialectical turning it back on its feet so that it finally
may learn how to walk upright, without crutches, thus practicing, for
the first time, what it had urged others to attain: autonomy. More than
two hundred years after its birth in America, Rorty thinks that the time
has come for an enlightened, democratic society to liberate itself from
its ideological and metaphysical foundations. His inversion can be
illustrated by a simple comparison between the logo of my former *alma
mater*, The Johns Hopkins University, nowadays itself hardly an example of compliance with this logo, and Rorty's revolutionary slogan. The

87

Hopkins logo promises: "Veritas vos liberabit." This promise contains premises that Rorty's inversion will both expose and attack. Among those premises are: truth (and/or scientific inquiry) is the subject of our liberation, or the way to freedom leads through the detour of truth. And as free subjects we are always already subjected to truth. Above all, theory (truth) and practice (liberalism; freedom) are inextricably linked to each other. The essence and meaning of theory is: emancipation. Conversely, the essence of freedom is: to be the adequate and accurate expression of truth. The place of the convergence was democratic, bourgeois society at large, but foremost its microcosmic reflection, which only a few could enter: the institution of the university. In exchange for submission to the rules of this institution and of scientific inquiry, it promised to graduate its members as free subjects. By sheer metonymical force, a particular, specific, restrictive institution proclaimed itself as the parochial passage to universal liberation. In the age of Enlightenment, theory, practice, and the politics of institutionalization converge in that one and unique place which paradoxically professes to realize the hopes and universal aspirations of a particular class: the institution of the university, whose single purpose is to liberate mankind.

This traditional conception of the Enlightenment with its pathos of universal emancipation derives its critical power, its authority and legitimacy, from a metaphysical principle of reason and truth with which the nature of wo/man is supposedly endowed. In short, the critique and/or legitimation of social institutions was articulated in the name of some inalienable, universal, ahistorical and transcultural human rights bestowed on wo/man by nature. This ideological and ontological foundation of bourgeois liberalism has informed its entire social, political, economic and cultural sphere, and it is still, more than two hundred years after its invention, *the* "crazy-glue" of the societies in the Western hemisphere and—as the transformation of the Soviet system shows—beyond.

Richard Rorty's liberal revolution of this enlightened, democratic Western society is no less than an attack on its metaphysical strategy of the transcendental and ontological grounding of freedom in truth, a truth which, under the conditions of free inquiry, can and must be *discovered*. This attack, as I have mentioned, proceeds by way of a non-dialectical inversion. Non-dialectical, because this inversion, unlike others, entails and intends the destruction of the basis of the inverted model, thus depriving itself of the possibility, but also necessity, of a circular theoretical (that is, metaphysical) justification and (self-)legitimation. The freedom of a truly liberal society is irreducible, the society is not grounded, but free (of a ground), and only the absence of this ground opens up the possibility of a holistically and pragmatically induced political and cultural change. In the third chapter of Rorty's *Contingency, Irony, and Solidarity*[1], we read the condensed version of the liberated liberalism, freed from the constraints of legitimation and criticism:

> That would be just the sort of society which liberals are trying to avoid—one in which 'logic' ruled and 'rhetoric' was outlawed. It is central to the idea of a liberal society that, in respect to words as opposed to deeds, persuasion as opposed to force, anything goes. This openmindedness should not be fostered because, as Scripture teaches, Truth is great and will prevail, nor because, as Milton suggests, Truth will always win in a free and open encounter. It should be fostered for its own sake. A liberal society is one which is content to call 'true' whatever the upshot of such encounters turns out to be. (CIS 51f.)

If descriptions and declarations like this have raised charges that Rorty falls victim to the paradox of relativism (see, for example, Apel)—a paradox of which Rorty is well aware[2]—we should take notice of the fact that these charges only make sense on the basis of precisely those metaphysical assumptions which Rorty wants to eliminate. Unless one is willing to *posit* (!) Truth as an identifiable source of determination waiting to be discovered—and this would necessarily presuppose the suppression of the positing act—one cannot possibly come up with the idea that Rorty is in danger of hypostatizing relative truth-claims, thus opening the door for the tyranny and orthodoxy he seeks to combat. Nevertheless, the claim that Rorty "relativizes" truth is not entirely unfounded, if we understand this "relativization" in linguistic and not in ontological terms. That is: "the relativization [of truth] must appear in the language in which the relativized [truth] occurs (and hence cannot be *to* that language or *to* a theory for that language)." (Davidson 238)   This is another way of saying that the only *intelligible* and *reasonable* form of relativization is one that takes notice of the fact that there is no metalanguage that is not already caught up in the (object-) language which it describes. Or, to put it differently: that there is no nonlinguistic, ultimate, ahistorical and rational criterion which would allow us to choose between different vocabularies in terms of their degree of objectivity, adequate correspondence (to the world) and referential accuracy. "From a pragmatist point of view, to say that what is rational for us now to believe may not be *true*, is simply to say that somebody may come up with a better idea" (SO 23).   In the absence of an ultimate rational criterion, in the face of the madman's announcement in aphorism 125 of Nietzsche's *Gay Science* that "God is dead!" (181).[3] Rorty urges us to accept and affirm the finitude of our vocabularies, to embrace the inevitability of setting out from our ethnocentric condition and to be content with ethical (practical) rather

than epistemological (theoretical) "justifications" for both our
vocabulary and our ethnocentric particularity (see SO 23ff.). When
confronted with the dilemma of choosing between relativism and ethnocentrism, Rorty answers:

> I have been arguing that we pragmatists should grasp the ethnocentric horn of
> this dilemma. We should say that we must, in practice, privilege our own
> group, even though there can be no noncircular justification for doing so. We
> must insist that the fact that nothing is immune from criticism does not mean
> that we have a duty to justify everything. We Western liberal intellectuals
> should accept the fact that we have to start *from where we are*, and that this
> means that there are lots of views which we simply cannot take seriously. (SO
> 29; my emphasis)

Of course, provocative passages like these have occasionally infuriated
critics both on the right and left of Rorty's (ethno)centric position,
critics whom Rorty refuses to take seriously since they insist upon an
impossibility, namely the notion of a noncircular justification. However, and this seems to me a legitimate concern, does the dilemma of
the hermeneutic circularity of justification-processes free us from the
duty of justifying the privilege that we *must* assign to ourselves? And
this question entails another: If we do not want to fall behind the pragmatic critique of metaphysics, how do we have to conceive of this non-
metaphysical, non-reductive legitimation? Possible answers to these
questions may be the result of a closer look at the implications and the
significance of the finitude of our vocabularies. I interpret Rorty to be
saying that—within a historicist and nominalist culture—language, the
self and our societies are products of contingency (see *CIS* 20ff.). But
how do we know that? And how do we know, or how can we tell, what
we are, and where we are, and what we want to become, or that we are
what we become, if it were not for the finitude of our language? In
spite of his assertions to the contrary (*CIS* 55), I do not regard it as a
mere contingency that Rorty begins his elaborate and enticing manifes-
to of a liberal utopia with a chapter entitled "The Contingency of Language" (*CIS* 3-22). "Language," this is my point, is not only itself a
product of contingency, but it also contains the conditions (and they
need not be and are not purely linguistic!) that allow us to recognize or
view ourselves, our communities and our languages as such products of
contingency. This relationship between language, or more specifically,
its conflictual articulation of an alterity that is inscribed in and escapes
its nominalist function, and contingency as an *inherent* element of the
temporality (or historicity) of language (or rhetoric), is only indirectly
alluded to by Rorty. For example, in the following passage he indicates
the effects this relationship would have upon a description or re-
description of morality. Rejecting, as it were, the metaphysical notion

of "morality as the voice of a divinized portion of our soul" ingrained by nature, Rorty concludes:

> But if the demands of a morality are the demands of a language, and if languages are historical contingencies, rather than attempts to capture the true shape of the world or of the self, then to "stand unflinchingly for one's moral convictions" is a matter of identifying oneself with such a contingency. (CIS 60)

This sentence, followed by a paragraph in which Rorty identifies the "strong poet" and the "utopian revolutionary" as those moral members of a liberal society who are capable of this *identification* with contingency, is interesting for several reasons: First, because it demonstrates that there is an immediate connection between *our interpretation* of language, the subject and its sociohistorical context; secondly, because Rorty emphasizes that moral questions are identical with and/or arise from linguistic problems (although Rorty would probably object to this interpretation, since he stresses that they are demands of *a*, not *the* language[4]); thirdly, because it reveals Rorty's ethnocentrism as a *moral* or *ethical* consequence of his non-reductive, nominalist view of language. Here, then, we have the *raison d'être* for Rorty's often misunderstood and fiercely rejected insistence upon his assumption of the ethnocentric option: in a postmetaphysical society, so it seems, ethnocentrism is the *only moral* stance we can take! Hence Rorty's rhetoric of urgency. And since the poet and the utopian revolutionary cannot but identify with the historical contingency of language, they are the most ethnocentric, critical and moral members of the society. Indeed, the fusion of morality (ethics) and aesthetics, perhaps *the* most notorious tenet of the Enlightenment doctrine[5] and its poetological and aesthetic reflections, allows the poet and the utopian revolutionary to play the role of social critic and moral watchdog at once: "One can substitute for this idea (of a critique of alienation in the name of humanity) that the poet and the revolutionary are protesting *in the name of the society itself* against those aspects of the society which are unfaithful to its own self-image" (*CIS* 60; my emphasis). In short: ethnocentrism not only does not preclude criticism, it seems to be the very condition for its possibility *within* the ethnocentric limits of morality or—if you prefer this version—the moral limits of ethnocentrism.

In the absence of a transcendental ground of criticism, legitimation and morality, the *society itself*, that is, *its own self-image*, an *imaginary* construct, becomes the only available criterion of legitimation in a postmetaphysical epoch. To shift from a Kantian to a Rortian jargon, one could say: "Philosophy and the Mirror of Nature" has been replaced by "Society and the Mirror of History (or, in general: Narrative)." But, and this seems to be pointing to the limits of the liberal revolution that Rorty has in mind, the mirror remains, the mirror has no cracks, no alienating and distorting effects on the society that grounds itself and its criticism in the performative paradox of the reflection of its image, even if this image is structured like a narrative. This supposed identity, however, is precisely the reason for Rorty's inability to relinquish the project of modernity and to probe the political, social and moral limits imposed on us in the age of Enlightenment. Rorty interprets narrative structures in terms of imaginary constructs or institutions, and as necessary fictions for the institution of a society, the self and reality.   In an essay entitled "Unger, Castoriadis, and the Romance of a National Future" (*EHO* 177-92), he draws on Castoriadis's study, *The Imaginary Institution of Society*, in order to explicate the constellation into which morality, ethnocentrism, an anti-naturalist social theory, the imagination and the notion of final, descriptive vocabularies (or narratives) enter.   From Castoriadis's claim that "the imaginary—as the social imaginary and as the imagination of the psyche— is the logical and ontological condition of the 'real,' " Rorty infers: "Just as in the individual psyche, moral character is 'conflict interrupted or contained,' so is the moral character of a society—that is, its institutions" (*EHO* 185).   Aside from the fact that this definition of moral character is rather questionable (at least by no means sufficient), I would like to elaborate just two aspects of statements like this that have become the focal points of the controversy surrounding the writings of Richard Rorty.

II. "Kant's" Question

The attribution of a "moral character" to social institutions effectively exempts these institutions and society from any criticism that transcends them.   In fact, such "fundamental" criticism could be construed as immoral and politically dangerous, and—given his pragmatic premises—Rorty has had little choice but to follow this rather repressive road.[6]   Ironically—but we are quite familiar with this irony—liberalism and repression become indistinguishable, precisely when their collusion is denied.   What distinguishes Rorty from traditional liberalism is his affirmation of repression as a necessary element of an open, liberal society.   At the same time, he seeks to alleviate the effects of social or public repression (*nothing goes* when it comes to the protection of our liberal institutions) by allowing the removal of all moral restrictions and considerations from the formation of private narratives (or self-images).   While the distinction between the private and the public uses of language is reminiscent of Kant's distinction between the private and the public uses of reason and the famous imperative of the Enlightenment: *"Reason as much as you want and about whatever you want; but obey!",*[7] we should bear in mind that Rorty's point of reference is a democratic, liberal society, not an enlightened monarchy. However, the shift from reason to language demands an additional, important remark: whereas Kant urges political freedom for the *public* use of reason in order to advance the course of the Enlightenment in its own age (WiA 55), Rorty urges political freedom for the *private* use of language in order to create new self-images in a post-Enlightenment society (see *CIS* 73-95). What remains in spite of these shifts is the necessity for obedience or—less dramatically—loyalty to the prevailing social institutions, be they monarchic or democratic. But even here a shift from the public to the private has occurred: Kant's praise for the enlightened monarchy of Frederick the Great is wrapped in mechanical metaphors which enforce, through an "artificial unanimity" ("eine künstliche Einhelligkeit"[8]), the identity of private and public purposes. It is also here that Kant uses the attribute "gemein" (suggesting at once: common, ordinary, habitual, mean, nasty, vulgar) next to "öffentlich" (public) in order to describe the necessity and inevitability of a repressive government of the masses *as the perfect condition* for their enlightenment (WiA 55). Pivotal metaphors like these, I suppose, are constantly capable of unleashing an ironic force which they barely dissimulate. Thus, it is in the rhetorical movements of a conspicuously political and public text that the dialectic of Enlightenment is both announced and contained. But, and this is decisive for Kant as well as for Rorty: they both talk about a different *use* of either reason or language, not their intrinsic nature. At the same time, their pragmatic interpretations bear different consequences, since Kant defines Enlightenment, that is, the public use of reason (and implicitly, irony) in terms of a technique of writing, reading and interpretation,[9] whereas Rorty defines the public use of language as a technique of non-ironic argumentation and the private use of language(s), including irony, in terms of self-creation and self-invention (see *CIS* 96-121).[10] Rorty bans irony from public, political discourse, an irony that pervades Kant's essay—in spite of, or perhaps because of its "seemingly" subservient gesture toward the enlightened monarch— thus making it an example, an enactment of the very form of writing it encouraged. Or should we assume that Kant does not speak as an intellectual (rather than as a philosopher) through his multiple and heterogeneous writings (durch die *Schriften*!)? Kant's writings demand to be read as ironically enlightening examples distinct from the professional philosopher's book (WiA 53) that demands to be accepted. In Kant, whenever he writes as an intellectual and not as a professional, irony and the Enlightenment become strange bedfellows. Strange, since the effects of irony are unpredictable, and Enlighten-

ment can never be sure whether and/or when it falls victim to its
treacherous ally and intimate adversary. For Kant, Enlightenment is
neither simply a political doctrine of emancipation, liberation and
democratization nor the philosophical foundation of such a society, but
rather the continuous process of a "true reform of the mode of thinking" ("wahre Reform der Denkungsart," WiA 55) through a different,
that is, ironic, mode of writing and reading. This re-form defies any
identification with any political system or position, because it is constitutively impossible to affirm any position, any ground, any final
vocabulary without getting entangled by an Other. Which is, of course,
another way of saying that irony is truly—or at least it can be truly—
affirmative. As such an affirmative force its effects cannot possibly be
limited to the private narratives in which Rorty would allow them to
operate. The parallelism that he constructs between the moral character of the individual and the moral character of a society, between—if
you wish—conscience and institutions, also holds for the structure of
private and public thinking, writing and reading. The truce, the give
and take that Rorty seeks to negotiate between modernists and postmodernists, seems to me to be both impossible and unnecessary, at
least if we follow Kant. It is unnecessary, since Enlightenment and
irony are allies, though not entirely trustworthy ones; and it is
impossible, since irony cannot possibly honor any contract it signs. Or
it can do so only for a certain period of time. The contract that Kant
struck with Frederick the Great, a contract that Foucault called "the
contract of rational despotism and free reason" ("What Is Enlightenment?" 37) was subjected to irony, that is, the ineradicable possibility
of being broken by the public use of reason through the writings ["die
Schriften"] of intellectuals and their interpretation. This, I think, was
registered by Kant when he alluded to the following question:

> If (then) someone now posed the question: Do we presently live in an
> *enlightened* age?   then the answer is: No, but we are living in an age of
> *Enlightenment*.

> Wenn denn nun gefragt wird: Leben wir jetzt in einem *aufgeklärten* Zeitalter?
> so ist die Antwort: Nein, aber wohl in einem Zeitalter der *Aufklärung*.[11]

This distinction is crucial, since it insists on an ironic differentiation
within the doctrine of Enlightenment which Rorty's complete detachment of rational argumentation and idiosyncratic ironism, the private
and the public, intentionally collapses. It is quite ironic: the fact that
Rorty upholds the distinction leads to the collapse of an ironic differentiation. And vice versa: the fact that Kant submits to a rational,
benevolent despotism allows him to affirm an ironic force, the disruptive power of irony that can be contained neither by the political system

which it describes and into which it is inscribed, nor by the historical period to which it gave its name. The age of Enlightenment need not be identical with an enlightened age. Moreover, the mode in which "Kant's" anonymous question is formulated suggests that the enlightened age is always distinct from and may follow upon the age of Enlightenment. Does this mean that—horribile dictu—postmodernism is the enlightened age, enlightening the age of Enlightenment about its constitutively unacknowledged deficits? I doubt it, since this assumption would contradict the ironic force of the anonymity of the question as well as the referential indeterminacy of the deictic expressions "nun" and "jetzt" (which I have translated as "now" and "presently") and the personal pronoun "wir" ("we," a pronoun that Rorty uses so profusely as a provocative and affirmative indicator of the ethnocentric condition): "Wenn denn *nun* gefragt wird: Leben *wir jetzt* in einem aufgeklärten Zeitalter?"

This question, which we cannot be certain who is posing and whether it is ever actually posed at all, seems to be transcending all those oppositions (between the public and the private; autonomy and heteronomy, etc.) which Kant had previously set up in order to answer that other question in the title of his essay: "Answer to the Question: What Is Enlightenment?" ("Beantwortung der Frage: Was ist Aufklärung?"). While the first part of this title refers both to the specific formulation of this question by the pastor Johann Friedrich Zöllner,[12] in a previous issue of the *Berlinische Monatsschrift* (WiA 53), and to the general problem of the rhetorical or performative dimension of Kant's polemics, it is precisely this first part of the title which is hardly ever mentioned when Kant's essay is quoted.[13] Its suppression indicates an unwillingness to enter the polemical and ironic sphere of the text and a failure to recognize the performative, textual staging of the question "Was ist Aufklärung?" as providing the "constative" answer to this question, while at the same time indicating that providing a constative answer is to miss the question entirely. In this sense, and this is what Kant implies, to take Zöllner's question seriously is to reject it as a metaphysical question, precisely because it insists on an absolute distinction between the performative and the constative dimension of language, between rhetoric and logic.[14] However, and this is crucial both for Kant's operation and the chances or the destiny of the Enlightenment, Kant does not simply collapse the metaphysical distinction. His rejection, unlike Rorty's, is not a foreclosure, but rather a rhetorical displacement which maintains and at the same time alters the metaphysical difference, thus paving the path for the Enlightenment project without ever really entering the forest. Enlightenment has no proper place, and it is entirely misconceived if interpreted teleologically in terms of the achievement of a political, social or historical goal. In short: the goal of Enlightenment is not emancipation, and here Kant and Rorty are in full agreement.[15] To think of Enlightenment as emancipation is to lock oneself into the self-referential inconsistencies of a critique of ideology (see *CIS* 59), that is, the tacit repetition of the metaphysical and ideological assumptions it seeks to destroy. But does this entail—as Rorty suggests—the end of any critique of ideology? Can we preserve it without succumbing to metaphysics? If so, how do we have to conceive of it, and how does it have to be structured?

III. From Logo- to Ethnocentrism: Rorty's Dilemma

Kant, I believe, has hinted at a possibility for the conception of such a non-metaphysical, non-transcendental critique of ideology.[16] He locates—or rather, dislocates—it in a practice of interpretation in which both reading and writing partake. Textual strategies, that is, the strategic employment of rhetorical figures, questions and examples which themselves turn into ironic (dis-)figurations of these rhetorical moves,[17] provide an unassimilable space (not a ground!) for the articulation of such a critique, as a differential articulation of its representation.[18] Just as this space is neither completely inside nor outside such a critique, and just as such a critique announces itself "through writings" ("durch Schriften") which—like Kant's "Answer to the Question: What Is Enlightenment?"—demand to be read if they want to be "understood" as enlightening us about the conditions of (our) enlightenment and criticism, so the time and the place of these conditions remain uncertain. Kant's question—and it is uncertain whether it is really *his* question: "If (then) someone now posed the question: Do we presently live in an *enlightened* age?" ("Wenn denn nun gefragt wird: Leben wir jetzt in einem aufgeklärten Zeitalter?")—is neither empirical nor transcendental, neither his nor anybody else's, neither historical nor philosophical, neither present nor absent (past/future). And yet it is all of these at once. We could read this question, and this would provide us with a paradoxical, criterionless criterion[19] of criticism and legitimation, allegorically as an orphan ("eine Waise"; after all, orphans, deprived of parental guidance and stifling guardians ["Vormünder"], may be perfectly dis-posed toward enlightenment) and as the effect of a rhetorical mode ("eine Weise"), namely a chiasmus. This rhetorical crossing of adjective and genitive[20] (*aufgeklärtes Zeitalter/Zeitalter der Aufklärung*) introduces an infinite oscillation between the self-identity and difference of an age (a *Zeit-alter*),[21] for there is never any ultimate ground, never any ultimate, that is, rhetorically independent, criterion for deciding whether an age of enlightenment is an enlightened age or not. Thus the crossing that provides us with the possibility of a non-metaphysical, non-transcendental criterion of (self-)criticism (that is, the question itself) is also a *crux*. It is the crux of the Enlightenment that it believes in nontextual, rational criteria of legitimation and criticism, and that it inevitably destroys these assumptions and beliefs in their form(ul)ation. The crux and the chance of an enlightened criticism is the crux of its presentation (*Darstellung*). Only in and through a specific mode of presentation can the Enlightenment account for—and consequently *minimize*—the dogmatic *effects* of the process of socialization, that is, of its implication in the production of dogmatic and ideological effects, such as the assumption of authority in the fusion of criticism, reason and legitimation. Only in a specific mode of presentation can the Enlightenment account for the dogmatic effects of becoming, as it were, "mündig" (independent, mature, of age). And there is, as the German term "mündig" denotes, no way of becoming "enlightened" without the subjection to language.

The translation of "Mündigkeit" as "maturity" captures all the dogmatic aspects of a purely metaphorical reading of this term which are at the center of all Enlightenment discourse,[22] while it actively represses all of the literal connotations which retain the ironic and ambiguous connection between rhetoric and logic, discourse and reason, irony and argumentation. To insist on their absolute differentiation implicitly presupposes and inevitably entails the assumption of metaphysical positions. To insist on their identity, as Rorty's nominalism repeatedly does,[23] is to risk either the total appropriation of discourse by reason —as in the case of such Enlightenment proponents as Apel and Habermas—or to call, as Rorty does, for the *active* repression of rhetoric if it no longer serves the interests of communication, persuasion and liberal consensus-formation (see *CIS* 60-69). The political implications and consequences of this proposal are obvious: The loss of stability incurred from the lack of credibility of our untenable metaphysical foundations is fully compensated by the transfer of this stability onto and into our political *and* cultural institutions. We can also put it this way: Rorty's substitution of liberal politics for metaphysical philosophy,[24] of a pragmatic use of language (morality) for epistemology, is an attempt to maintain and preserve metaphysical effects (such as stability; conviction in one's beliefs and fictions; identification with imaginary constructs; the assumption of a connection between aesthetics and ethics; the assumption of the continuity of moral progress through reading and the expansion of freedom; etc.), while at the same time exposing the metaphysical—that is, linguistic—operations that lead to

these effects as historically and socially dependent language games
which we should embrace. In other words, Richard Rorty wants to have
his cake and eat it, too.[25]

Contrary to the colloquial wisdom, I think that there is nothing
wrong with the paradox that the proverb (of desire) expresses. In a
certain sense—with its allusion to the impossibility of a simultaneity of
possession and consumption—it repeats the paradox of "Kant's" question. If we wanted to break successfully with metaphysics and its dis-
simulated continuation in the cloak of Enlightenment, we would have
to make this paradox the hypothetical maxim of our private *and* public
conduct. But that does not mean that, as Rorty suggests with regard to
the public use of language, we have to embrace it, be "faithful" to and
identify with our nominalist and ethnocentric views. "Faithfulness"
—with all its moral *and* epistemological connotations of loyalty, humility, devotion, submissiveness, subjection, and accuracy, adequacy, correspondence—is *the* pragmatic equivalent and Rorty's trans- or re-
description of transcendental criteria in metaphysical and theoretical
discourses, including the transcendental criterion of a communicative
rationality, that is, the presupposition of an "internal relation between
truth and idealized rational acceptability that is embedded in our *practices* of truth-telling."[26] "Faithfulness" not only literally retains all
aspects of faith in metaphysics, but it also functions as an anchoring
center in and for Rorty's pragmatism and as the critical criterion of his
literary and philosophical analyses.[27] To put it even more bluntly:
Nietzsche's madman was wrong all along! God is *not* dead! Or rather:
Just as the primordial father in Freud's *Totem and Taboo* assumed his
full (social) significance and authority only as the murdered and devoured father,[28] so the power of God is more than fully resurrected in
the shape of pragmatic faithfulness. To be sure: in one way God's
power is diminished, because it is no longer universal (at least not yet!).
But within the particular ethnocentric societies and within certain
groups and congregations of these societies, his power is just as strong,
if not stronger than before. The ethnocentric pragmatist has no choice
but to have faith—not in God, but in faithfulness itself as a critical
criterion that guarantees the compliance of a society with its own self-
image, its ethnocentricity and its self-criticism. Is it inconceivable that
the pragmatist, that Richard Rorty, is—not in spite of, *but because of* his
nominalism—a deeply religious person, a metaphysician?[29] The answer
to this question depends on the degree of our comfort with the ethnocentric predicament and the degree of hypostatization of our final vocabularies. Just how much faith in nominalism should we have?[30] And
does raising doubts about this faith mean that we can only do so on

metaphysical grounds? Would this not entail the immunization of Rorty's innovative challenge to the liberal tradition against all criticism, that it is in danger of becoming aseptic?

In summarizing the thrust of my argument, I would like to emphasize that I am interested in what Rorty would call a re-description of the Enlightenment and its legacy. However, I am not interested in abandoning its philosophical project, as Rorty suggests in the following passage, where he urges us to simply "drop" the metaphysical Enlightenment for the sake of political liberalism and its poeticized culture:

> We need a re-description of liberalism as the hope that culture as a whole can be "poeticized" rather than as the Enlightenment hope that it can be "rationalized" or "scientized." That is, we need to substitute the hope that chances for fulfillment of idiosyncratic fantasies will be equalized for the hope that everyone will replace "passion" or fantasy with "reason." (CIS 53)

Rorty's liberal call for more pluralism, more tolerance, and more freedom identifies the philosophical heritage of the Enlightenment as an unnecessary obstacle to the realization of its own ends. To this extent, he acknowledges the dialectics inscribed in the Enlightenment process. Contrary to Adorno and Horkheimer, however, who have called the Enlightenment the *petitio principii* of their own critique of its dialectical nature, Rorty rejects the Enlightenment as an outdated language game and wants to replace it by another. He is thus bound to construct a dichotomy between poetics and philosophy which I find problematic. As my title indicates, and as I have tried to demonstrate in my readings of both Rorty and Kant, I think that philosophy does not have to be excluded from the poeticized culture of Rorty's liberal utopia. Philosophy and poetics are neither identical nor mutually exclusive. And poeticizing the Enlightenment has nothing to do with the replacement of "reason," the "subject," and "truth" by fiction and fantasy. It is rather an attempt and effort to read these seemingly fundamental figures of rational and scientific discourses as effects of poetic operations and productive processes which they dissimulate in the very assumption of their own originality and authority. This originality and authority collapses in the wake of Enlightenment's poeticization, which I also regard as an attempt to preserve the idea of a critique of ideology under postmodern conditions.

Notes

1. All further references to this book will appear in the text abbreviated as *CIS*.

2. See his essay "Solidarity or Objectivity?" in *Objectivity* 21-34. All further references to this essay are abbreviated as SO.

3. Nietzsche, *Werke* 2: 127. For a reading of this passage see Hamacher 129.

4. See also *CIS* 80: "we revise our moral identity by revising our final vocabulary."

5. This statement needs a certain clarification: the fusion between the different spheres which Kant attempted to keep separate (only to witness the collapse of his distinctions in the act of drawing them) is/was the prerogative of the poets, not the philosophers. For a corroboration of the view that this prerogative was not only a privilege of the enlightened poet, see Nussbaum 365-91. She concludes: "If we wish to develop a human ethical philosophy along Aristotelean lines, I suggest that we would do well to study the narrative and emotional structures of novels, viewing them as forms of Aristotelean ethical thinking." This view is entirely in line with Rorty's declaration that the novel has "replaced the sermon and the treatise as the principle vehicle of moral change and progress" (*CIS* xvi).

6. See, for example, Rorty's attacks on Foucault (*CIS* 83), and in his article, "Private Autonomy and Moral Identity," (*EHO* 193-98).

7. "*Räsonniert so viel ihr wollt, und worüber ihr wollt; nur gehorcht!*" Immanuel Kant, "Beantwortung der Frage: Was ist Aufklärung?" 61. All translations of this text (cited in the following as WiA) are mine.

8. "Einhelligkeit" is impossible to translate, since it links—via metaphor—enlightenment, art, technology, consensus and violence.

9. See Kant 55: "Ich verstehe aber unter dem öffentlichen Gebrauche seiner eigenen Vernunft denjenigen, den jemand als *Gelehrter* von ihr vor dem ganzen Publikum der *Leserwelt* macht." And 57: "Dagegen als Gelehrter, der durch Schriften zum eigentlichen Publikum, nämlich der Welt, spricht, mithin der Geistliche im *öffentlichen Gebrauche* seiner Vernunft, genießt einer uneingeschränkten Freiheit, sich seiner eigenen Vernunft zu bedienen und in seiner eigenen Person zu sprechen." The metaphor of the "proper audience" ("das eigentliche Publikum, die Leser-Welt") relates the Enlightenment project directly to notions of its theatrical staging in processes of writing and reading, i.e., it is staged as a problem of interpretation and reading. It is obvious that Kant affirms what Rorty denies: a *public* responsibility of the intellectual ("der Gelehrte") as a writer. The problem is that Rorty tends to identify the intellectual with the theorist, not with the writer.

10. See also his short piece on Foucault, "Moral identity," in *EHO* 193-98 as well as *CIS* 83: "Ironist theorists like Hegel, Nietzsche, Derrida and Foucault seem to me invaluable in our attempt to form a private self-image, but pretty much useless when it comes to politics."

11. WiA 59; my translation. Cf. Ted Humphrey's translation: "If it is now asked, "Do we presently live in an *enlightened* age?" the answer is, "No, but we do live in an age of *enlightenment*" (Kant, *Perpetual Peace* 44).

12. Kant must have gotten a kick out of this name. I would like to suggest that *this name* triggered Kant's entire polemics against the caste of the clergy, a polemics he shares with Nietzsche and Rorty, who would "welcome a Baconian culture dominated by 'the Rich Aesthete, the Manager, and the Therapist'—not necessarily as the final goal of human progress, but at least as a considerable improvement on cultures dominated by, for example, the Warrior or the Priest" (Rorty,

"Freud and Moral Reflection," *EHO* 161). The polemical thrust of irony that Kant playfully and devastatingly directs at people and professionals like Zöllner (the name means: tax collector and customs officer) is displayed in the series of examples he gives in order to describe the contract between the reasoning intellectual who is no longer "Vormund" (guardian or tutor) and the despot. These examples include the priest, the taxpayer and the military officer. All of these activities are somehow incorporated in "Zöllner": the man, the professional, the name. A thorough reading that addresses itself exclusively to Kant's article would have to elaborate further the complicity of irony, inter- and intratextual polemics, the circumvention of censorship and the contract that Kant is ready to strike (at) with the political powers. The ironic dimension of this contract is what gets lost in Rorty.

13. See, for example, an attentive reader like Foucault in his essays "What Is Enlightenment?" 32, and "The Subject and Power" 423. I agree, however, to a certain degree, with Foucault's treatment of Kant's essay as posing an entirely new and radically historical question: "In the text on *Aufklärung*, he [Kant] deals with the question of contemporary reality alone. He is not seeking to understand the present on the basis of a totality or of a future achievement. He is looking for difference: What difference does today introduce with respect to yesterday?" ("What Is Enlightenment?" 34). See also "The Subject and Power" 423: "But Kant asks something else: What are we? in a precise moment of history. Kant's question appears as an analysis of both us and our present." Yes, but not exclusively.

14. Zöllner asked: "*Was ist Aufklärung*? Diese Frage, die beinahe so wichtig ist, als: *was ist Wahrheit*, sollte doch wohl beantwortet werden, *ehe* [my emphasis] man aufzuklären anfinge" (WiA 53; "*What is Enlightenment*? This question, which is almost as important as: *what is Truth*, should be answered *before* [my emphasis] one starts the process of enlightenment"). Kant insists that to ask in this way is to remain in the dark forever. He is right.

15. See Rorty, "Postmodern Bourgeois Liberalism," in *Objectivity* 197-202, and "Cosmopolitanism Without Emancipation: A Response to Jean François Lyotard," *Objectivity* 211-22. Like Rorty, Kant emphasizes the complicity between the rhetoric of emancipation and metaphysics, i.e., the familiar dialectic of revolutionary processes, when he writes: "Durch eine Revolution wird vielleicht wohl ein Abfall von persönlichem Despotism und gewinnsüchtiger oder herrschsüchtiger Bedrükkung, aber niemals eine wahre Reform der Denkungsart zu Stande kommen; sondern neue Vorurteile werden, eben sowohl als die alten, zum Leitbande des gedankenlosen großen Haufens dienen" (WiA, 55). A good example for this type of "revolution" is the so called "November revolution" in the former GDR and its replacement by the unification of the two German states. While it is a topos that Germans are at best capable of conservative revolutions, we yet have to address the question as to whether or not all revolutions display a conservative tendency. And what exactly does Kant mean when he talks about "das zu Stande kommen einer Reform der Denkungsart"? Does he perhaps intimate the eventual professionalization (we cannot ignore the multiple meanings of "Stand": profession, class, institutionalization, etc.) of the intellectual?

16. Contrary to contemporary quasi-Kantians like Apel and Habermas, I think that Kant is in no need of being subjected to a pragmatic transformation, a transformation which, notwithstanding their opposite assertions, only affirms their hidden metaphysical premises, not Kant's. For a superb critique of Habermas' unacknowledged assumptions, see Nägele 67-90.

17. For an excellent study of these processes in the Romantic age, see Chase.

18. On this notion of space in Kant, see Sallis 82-131. On "differential articu-

lation," see Weber's elaborations in his study on Lacan and Freud.

19. I propose this paradox as an alternative to and a rejection of the choice between foundationalism and anti-foundationalism, including Rorty's proposition to conceive of rationality as a "criterionless muddling through" (SO 28).

20. Another uncertainty affects the status of this genitive: Is it a *genitivus obiectivus* or *subiectivus*?

21. How can we ignore the fact that the temporal other is inscribed and condensed in the word Zeit-alter, for *alter* is the Latin equivalent for other?

22. This purely figurative, i.e., idealizing, interpretation is not just a problem of translation between two languages, but also within a language, even a very specific theoretical jargon. See, as an example of such an interpretation and its political consequences, Habermas's transformation of Critical Theory in the name of a shift from reading and producing rhetorical effects to the proliferation and expansion of "Mündigkeit" through communication and dialogue. This can be traced in his distorting characterization of Adorno. Symptomatic of his reduction of the rhetorical dimension in Adorno is the following passage : "In this sense the truth of propositions is linked to the intention of the true life.... If the idea of reconciliation would immerse itself in the idea of maturity, of a social life in noncoercive communication, and if it could be outlined in the form of a logic of ordinary language which has yet to be developed, then this reconciliation would no longer be universal" (176; my translation).

23. "The ironist . . . is a nominalist and a historicist." Is this proposition reversible? (*CIS* 74); "For, in the ironist view I have been offering, there is no such thing as a 'natural' order of justification of beliefs or desires. Nor is there much occasion to use the distinctions between rhetoric and logic, or between philosophy and literature, or between rational and nonrational methods of changing other people's minds" (*CIS* 83). See also his response to Lyotard: "Si vous ne disposez pas d'un méta-récit racontant comment le sujet humain authentique s'émancipe de ses illusions et de ses préjugés, vous ne pouvez pas conserver la différence grecque traditionelle entre rhétorique et logique" (*Critique* 41 [1985]: 584).

24. See especially his essay, "The Priority of Democracy to Philosophy," in *Objectivity* 175-96.

25. I use this colloquial expression simply in response to a funny remark that Rorty made in his debate with Thomas McCarthy: "Notions like 'the rights of man,' 'surplus value,' 'the new class,' and the like have been indispensable for moral and political progress. But I am not convinced that we are currently in need of new notions of this sort. A lot of social theory nowadays seems to me just putting overelaborate icing on the cakes historians, journalists, economic statisticians, anthropologists, and others have baked' ("Truth and Freedom" 642).

26. McCarthy 369. From my point of view, Habermas disciples like McCarthy and Apel are needlessly worried about Rorty's pragmatic assault on their theoretical foundations since his political aims and moral concerns are—in spite of misleading appearances—identical with theirs. One wonders what all the fuss was about in this debate. However, to put it in Rorty's terms: the pragmatic version of a socialdemocratic liberalism has the edge and deserves to be called "true," because Rorty simply came up with a better idea than his realist liberal fellows. I regard it as a better idea because it gets rid of the bad conscience that has always plagued the bourgeoisie, and because it is more honest about the particularity of its interests. See also SO 31f.: "The comfort of the realist picture is the comfort of saying not simply that there is a place prepared for our race in advance, but also that we know quite a bit about what that place looks like. The inevitable ethnocentrism to which

we are all condemned is thus as much a part of the realist's comfortable view as of the pragmatist's uncomfortable one." The crucial question in light of our Kantian epigraph is: How comfortable does the pragmatist feel about his ethnocentric predicament? In Kantian terms there exists a direct proportion between the degree of discomfort and the enlightened or "mündig" state of mind.

27. How "faithfulness" assumes such a position can be seen in Rorty's pragmatic appropriation of Derrida. See, for example, the following passage: "Insofar as Derrida remains *faithful* to the nominalism he shares with Strawson, transcendental arguments will not permit him to infer the existence of such quasi entities as 'différance', 'trace' and 'archi-writing.' Insofar as he does *not remain faithful* to it, he is just one more metaphysician" (*EHO* 112). See also the passage from *CIS* (60, cited above) which limits social and political criticism "to those aspects of society which are *unfaithful* to its own self-image." Here the quasi transcendental critical criterion of "faithfulness" is explicitly described as a mimetic effect of its imaginary origin, a description which implicitly shatters the credibility of faithfulness. See also SO 33, where Rorty talks about "*the act of social faith* which is suggested [and which he faithfully accepts] by a Nietzschean view of truth." All emphases are mine.

Rorty's description of morality as acceptance and expansion of "we-intentions" and the avoidance of cruelty via "imaginative identification" (*CIS* 190) of and with the "Other" (as "one of us") is an extension of the imaginary grounding of pragmatism. See the third chapter of *CIS*, "Cruelty and Solidarity" 141-198.

28. See Freud 141-43; for a "truly enlightening" study on this issue, see Borch-Jacobson.

29. This is not a psychological question. I am drawing on Nietzsche's distinction between atheism and religion in *Beyond Good and Evil* (72):

Why atheism nowadays? "The father" in God is thoroughly refuted. . . . This is what I have made out (by questioning, and listening at a variety of conversations) to be the cause of the decline of European theism; it appears to me that though the religious instinct is in vigorous growth,—it rejects the theistic satisfaction with profound distrust.

Warum heute Atheismus?—"Der Vater" im Gott ist gründlich widerlegt. . . . Dies ist es, was ich, als Ursachen für den Niedergang des europäischen Theismus, aus vielerlei Gesprächen, fragend, hinhörend, ausfindig gemacht habe; es scheint mir, daß zwar der religiöse Instinkt mächtig im Wachsen ist—daß er aber gerade die theistische Befriedigung mit tiefem Mißtrauen ablehnt. (*Werke* 3: 615)

As the following passage shows, Nietzsche believes that the religious instinct (or perhaps better, drive) is now satisfied by Cartesian philosophy: "Modern philosophy, as epistemological scepticism, is secretly or openly *anti-Christian,* although (for keener ears, be it said) by no means anti-religious" (72; "Die neuere Philosophie, als eine erkenntnistheoretische Skepsis, ist, versteckt oder offen, *antichristlich*: obschon, für feinere Ohren gesagt, keineswegs antireligiös," *Werke* 2: 616).

I think that "finer ears" would have a hard time not hearing strong religious echoes in Rorty's ethnocentric pragmatism. See here also his interesting and revealing remarks upon pragmatism and faith in his "Pragmatism Without Method," in *Objectivity* 63-77, especially his comments on John Dewey's *A Common Faith*

VOLKER KAISER

and Paul Tillich's *Dynamics of Faith*: "'God' is understood as 'a rhetorical blemish, a misleading way to get one's point across' " (Ibid. 71). If "God" is bad rhetoric (and this is straight out of Nietzsche, see *Twilight of the Idols*: " 'Reason' in language—oh, what an old deceptive female she is! I am afraid we are not rid of God because we still have faith in grammar" (*Portable Nietzsche 483; "Die 'Vernunft' in der Sprache: o was für eine betrügerische Weibsperson. Ich fürchte, wir werden Gott nicht los, weil wir noch an die Grammatik glauben" in Werke* 2: 960) that does not mean that we can or should stop believing in rhetoric, i.e., it says nothing about the religious attributes of certain readings or interpretations of the rhetorical dimension of texts.

30. For a sound and challenging study that capitalizes and zeroes in on the problem of Rorty's notion of final vocabularies and re-description, see McCumber.

Works Cited

Apel, Karl Otto. "Zurück zur Normalität? Oder könnten wir aus der nationalen Katastrophe etwas Besonderes gelernt haben? Das Problem des (welt-)geschichtlichen Übergangs zur postkonventionellen Moral in spezifisch deutscher Sicht." *Zerstörung des moralischen Selbstbewußtseins: Chance oder Gefährdung? Praktische Philosophie in Deutschland nach dem Nationalsozialismus.* Ed. Forum für Philosophie Bad Homburg. Frankfurt/M.: Suhrkamp, 1988. 91-142.

Borch-Jacobsen, Mikkel. "The Law of Psychoanalysis." *diacritics* 15 (1985): 26-36.

Chase, Cynthia. *Decomposing Figures: Rhetorical Readings in the Romantic Tradition.* Baltimore: Johns Hopkins UP, 1986.

Davidson, Donald. "The Inscrutability of Reference." *Inquiries into Truth and Interpretation.* Oxford: Oxford UP, 1986. 227-41.

Freud, Sigmund. *Totem and Taboo.* Trans. James Strachey. New York: Norton, 1950.

Foucault, Michel. "The Subject and Power." *Art after Modernism: Rethinking Representation.* Ed. Brian Wallis. New York: New York Museum of Contemporary Art, 1984. 417-33.

———. "What Is Enlightenment?" *The Foucault Reader.* Ed. Paul Rabinow. New York: Pantheon, 1984. 32-50.

Habermas, Jürgen. "Theodor W. Adorno." *Philosophisch-politische Profile.* Frankfurt/M.: Suhrkamp, 1981. 160-79.

Hamacher, Werner. " 'Disgregation of the Will': Nietzsche on the Individual and Individuality." *Reconstructing Individualism: Autonomy, Individualism, and the Self in Western Thought.* Ed. Thomas C. Heller. Stanford: Stanford UP, 1986. 106-39.

Kant, Immanuel. "Answer to the Question: What is Enlightenment?" *Perpetual Peace and Other Essays.* Trans. Ted Humphrey. Indianapolis: Hackett, 1983. 41-46.

———. "Beantwortung der Frage: Was ist Aufklärung?" *Werke.* Vol. 9. Ed. Wilhelm Weischedel. Darmstadt: Wissenschaftliche Buchgesellschaft, 1983. 53-61. Cited as "WiA."

McCarthy, Thomas. "Private Irony and Public Decency: Richard Rorty's New Pragmatism." *Critical Inquiry* 16 (1990): 355-370.

McCumber, John. "Reconnecting Rorty: The Situation of Discourse in Richard Rorty's *Contingency, Irony, and Solidarity.*" *diacritics* 20 (1990): 2-19.

Nägele, Rainer. "Public Voice and Private Voice: Freud, Habermas, and the Dialectic of Enlightenment." *Reading after Freud*. New York: Columbia UP, 1989. 67-90.

Nietzsche, Friedrich. *Beyond Good and Evil*. Trans. Helen Zimmern. Buffalo, N.Y.: Prometheus, 1989.

―――. *The Gay Science*. Trans. Walter Kaufmann. New York: Random, 1974.

―――. *The Viking Portable Nietzsche*. Ed. and trans. Walter Kaufmann. New York: Viking, 1976.

―――. *Werke in drei Bänden*. Ed. Karl Schlechta. München: Hanser, 1966.

Nussbaum, Martha C. "Transcending Humanity." *Love's Knowledge: Essays on Philosophy and Literature*. Oxford: Oxford UP, 1989. 365-91.

Rorty, Richard. *Contingency, Irony and Solidarity*. Cambridge: Cambridge UP, 1989. Cited as "*CIS*."

―――. *Objectivity, Relativism and Truth. Philosophical Papers*, vol. 1. Cambridge: Cambridge UP, 1991.

―――. *Essays On Heidegger and Others. Philosophical Papers*, vol. 2. Cambridge: Cambridge UP, 1991. Cited as "*EHO*."

―――. "Truth and Freedom: A Reply to Thomas McCarthy." *Critical Inquiry* 16 (1990): 633-43.

Sallis, John. *Spacings of Reason and Imagination in Texts of Kant, Fichte, Hegel*. Chicago: Chicago UP, 1987.

Weber, Samuel. *Return to Freud*. Trans. Michael Levine. Cambridge: Cambridge UP, 1991.

PART TWO

Philosophy and Aesthetics

Enlightenment or Aesthetics?
The Aesthetic Boundary of the Enlightenment in Poetological Texts from the Second Half of the Eighteenth Century

Carsten Zelle

I

IN MY RESEARCH on the not so "fine arts,"[1] I have observed that a great number of eighteenth-century treatises dealing with the question of tragic delight articulate the knowledge of a dialectic of Enlightenment that transcends the awareness of their enlightening authors. The very fact that a bibliography of such texts contains more than forty sources,[2] speaks against the view that the discussion of aesthetic terror during the Enlightenment remained a peripheral topic. The numerous poetological tests in the eighteenth century that look into mixed feelings of delightful horror, not only provide evidence for a characteristic twist in the aesthetic history of the Enlightenment thus far overlooked. The aesthetics of terror signifies as well a special intensity in Enlightenment aesthetics—it represents its crisis.

The learned debates on the pleasure found in tragic and terrible subjects in art (and in life) prove to be a far-reaching reflection on the bounds of (literary) enlightenment in general and especially with regard to theodicy, the view of mankind, the operative (enlightening) function of art and the division of the ethical and aesthetic. Schiller's insight that bounds are confused "when moral effectiveness is demanded in aesthetic matters"[3] thus not only points forward to the decadence literature of the nineteenth century as a justification of art for art's sake, but, more immediately summarizes a discussion conducted in the late Enlightenment.[4]

The notion of compassion from the sentimental phase of the Enlightenment is also included in this self-criticism. We know that the
high ethical standing this term enjoyed for an art whose aim it was to
teach human solidarity—supported on the one hand by moral-sense
philosophy (Home, Hume, Smith) and Rousseau's "vertu naturelle"
(natural virtue) on the other was drawn on by Lessing, for instance, for
his conception of the poetic effect of domestic tragedy. This connection between sympathy and virtue is erased in the second half of the
eighteenth century in the discussion in which the exact reasons for a
paradoxical interest in tragic subjects are traced. The failure of the
sentimental ethics of compassion in favor of the aesthetic attractiveness
of Neronic[5] and Lucretian[6] bliss demonstrates that the Enlightenment
always reached its boundary when it came to aesthetics.

Under the evil eye of his aesthetics of terror, Karl Heinz Bohrer referred recently,[7] as he has on many previous occasions, to the "chasm"
between pragmatic and aesthetic discourse.[8] According to Bohrer, this
distinction did not first appear in 1900 with classical modernity and the
frequently cited Romantic precursors, Friedrich Schlegel, Kleist, and
Nietzsche. On the contrary, Bohrer's bold thesis maintains that the
amoral center of aesthetics operates independently of social or
historical influences and conditions as "the condition of art itself."[9] To
be sure, such an opinion is easily and even gladly overlooked, especially
in times of enlightenment. As a historical example Bohrer cites the
eighteenth-century reformulation of the physical and psychological
impact of emotions that Aristotle had prescribed for tragedy, which he
associates less with the aesthetics of tragedy than with the anthropology
of Enlightenment sentimentality.[10]

As a further example, one could take Ernst Cassirer's chapters on
the fundamental problems of Enlightenment aesthetics,[11] in which a
very one-sided picture is presented that limits aesthetics to a
philosophy of the beautiful and denies that other half that
accompanied its development in the eighteenth century like a bad conscience. For already in Boileau's theory of "justesse" an aesthetic of
the sublime appears in which all of those phenomena are brought
together for which there was no room in the Procrustean bed of classicist beauty but which were nonetheless of aesthetic interest. Thus
L'art Poétique and *Traité du Sublime* interact as dominant and marginalized discourses respectively. What had been denied in the former sur-
faced in the latter.[12] Under the mantle of the sublime, the not-
beautiful—the horrible, the ugly and the terrible—was spirited into the
aesthetic theory of the eighteenth century. While Cassirer emphasizes
Dubos's aesthetics of the pathetic and Burke's psychology of the sublime, Cassirer recognizes an entirely different affect in response to the

beautiful. The central problem of aesthetics for Cassirer revolves around the "Ideal of Humanity," to which he relates both Shaftesbury's concept of Kalokagathie ("All Beauty is Truth") and Schiller's aesthetic education ("Synthesis of 'Reason' and 'Sensuality' ").

Mid eighteenth-century dramatic theorists, by assuming that man was naturally good, understood aesthetics to be in essence a tool of enlightenment—and their most important affective device was the arousal of compassion. The credo of this sentimental education of humankind, well known since Hans-Jürgen Schings's outstanding book, was formulated by Lessing in his correspondence with Mendelssohn and Nicolai (*Briefwechsel über das Trauerspiel*), rejecting the drama of stoicism: "*The most compassionate person is the best person*, one who is most inclined to all social virtues and all kinds of generosity. Thus, whoever makes us compassionate makes us better and more virtuous, and tragedy that does the former, also accomplishes the latter, or—does the former in order to bring about the latter."[13]

However, as Horkheimer and Adorno put it, "Compassion did not hold out against philosophy" ["Das Mitleid hält vor der Philosophie nicht stand"] (102). With my thoughts on the enlightenment of the Enlightenment I would like to modify this sentence formulated by Horkheimer and Adorno with regard to de Sade and Nietzsche. In the second half of the eighteenth century, compassion did not "stand up to" popular philosophy, since this feeling, at first glance displaying solidarity and cultural refinement, was subjected to a closer examination from an aesthetic perspective. This second glance, aimed at sympathy in the context of the often asked question regarding the reasons for finding pleasure in the horrible, uncovers not the identification with one's suffering fellow person, but a "distancing structure"[14] of compassion, through which not the desired "bonte naturelle" but the "perversité naturelle" is confronted, precisely what the sentimental propagation of the ethics of compassion strived to counteract.

Positive has become negative and vice-versa. The dramaturgy of compassion with operative intentions can be erased. What remains is aesthetics instead of enlightenment.

II

As Horkheimer and Adorno note, the pre-critical Kant had already pointed out that compassion cannot be considered a virtue and emphasized this amiable state of mind as it appeared especially in women.[15] Kant takes compassion more strictly to task when it does not lead to an act of solidarity, but rather, as is often the case in art, when it is limited to observation. This kind of "passive compassion, that is, having one's feelings resonate sympathetically with those of others and allowing oneself to experience suffering only passively, is silly and childish."[16] Passive compassion is "mourning without taking action" (*tathenlose[s] Trauren*) as Friedrich von Matthisson, in his poem "Elegie,"[17] described the mixed emotions of pleasure and pain which in England came to be known as "joy of grief." The direct source of the German expression *Wonne der Thräne* (the joy of tears, Moritz)[18] or *Wonne der Wehmut* (the joy of melancholy, Goethe 1: 104) are Macpherson's Ossian poems, in which "the joy of grief" appears in many different variations.[19] The psychohistorical context of the joy of grief, spleen, ennui, boredom and leisure class, has also been emphasized on occasion particularly in reference to eighteenth-century England (Blaicher 44ff.). Even if painful, the stirring up of feelings was preferable to the emptiness of everyday life, as it gave people a *Lebensgefühl* (feeling of life, Kant), a *sentiment de l'existence* (a feeling of existence, Rousseau) or an "enjoyment of existence" (Frances "Fanny" Burney). In the thaw of Regence period, Jean-Baptiste Dubos accurately stated in his *Critical Reflections on Poetry and Painting* (*Reflexions critiques sur la poesie et sur la peinture*, 1719) the anthropological rule that a person will instinctively seek out spectacles, from executions to tragedies, that stimulate emotions to the point of agitation because a person would rather endure the accompanying pain than live without feelings (sections 1-3).

As early as the middle of the seventeenth century, Hobbes observed the mixed emotions of pleasure and pain, for which he at first had no name. Analyzing curiosity, Hobbes describes the phenomenon first presented by Lucretius: the pleasure of sitting on a cliff and watching a shipwreck or witnessing a violent battle from the safety of a castle. Because the onlookers choose to watch the shipwreck instead of avoiding it, they must derive pleasure from it. Hobbes writes: "Nevertheless there is in it both *joy* and *grief*: for as there is novelty and remembrance of our own security present, which is *delight*; so there is also *pity*, which is grief; but the delight is so far predominant, that men usually are content in such a case to be spectators of the misery of their friends" (51f.).

Hobbes' explanation of the "joy of grief" came under fire in the eighteenth century as a result of an anthropological change of paradigm. The criticism of Hobbes and Mandeville's egoistic theories led to moral sense philosophy, where sympathy became increasingly important. The concept of "good nature" became the dominant theme of this period, and the gauntlet was thrown down to Hobbes (Sühnel 62).

In his essay *Of Our Attachment to Objects of Distress* (1751), Henry Home (1696-1782) attempts to counter the belief that pain and pleasure, that is, deprivation and need, should be considered two mutually exclusive motivations for human behavior. Such a view, he maintained, is "imperfect" (10) since upon closer observation of human nature one could discover motivations "which have no aversion in their composition" (7). Home specifically addresses the feelings of distress, grief, and compassion. As part of his polemic against the psychology of self-love, Home does not hesitate to portray humans as masochistic. A human being is a "self-tormentor," who has "an appetite after pain, an inclination to render one's self miserable"; they are driven by "a direct appetite or desire . . . after pain" (9-10). Home locates the source of such self-tormenting pleasures in a "sympathetic principle" (10). "Mutual sympathy" unites people more strongly even than blood ties. Sympathy is thus "the great cement of human society" (11). This concept of sympathy put forth by the moral sense philosophers united individuals as human beings as opposed to simply grouping them together under the social contract as subjects and citizens. In so doing it added an emotive aspect to the theory of social contracts based on natural law. In essence, "utopian aspects of an emotional communication community"[20] are prefigured—an educative goal so to speak of solidarity beyond the realm of economic competition. Consider the emphatic closing of Schiller's lecture *The Stage as a Moral Institution* (*Die Schaubühne als moralische Anstalt betrachtet*, 1784) in which Schiller imagines the emotional affinity of the spectators who have been moved by a tragedy: "and his [the spectator's] heart contains only *one* feeling, that he is a *human being*."[21]

In addition to outlining how sympathy can be a strong impetus for sociability and mutual assistance, Home also formulates an explanation for the pleasure of sadness based on his theory of sympathy. While sympathy is perceived socially as "painful passions" (16), the pain that it evokes fails to produce aversion. On the contrary, the world is constructed in such a way that sympathy is directly related to pleasure: "Far from having any aversion to pain, occasioned by the social principle, we reflect upon such pain with satisfaction, and are willing to submit to it upon all occasions with chearfulness and heart-liking, just as much as if it were a real pleasure" (17). In his attempt to explain this transsubstantiation of pain into pleasure, Home employs a mechanism of self-referentiality which leads ironically back to the same kind of self-love that the teaching on sympathy was supposed to repudiate. We see a shift from altruism to *pleasure* in altruism. Home writes about sympathy for the unfortunate: "When we consider our own character and actions in a reflex view, we cannot help approving this tenderness and sympathy in our own nature. We are pleased with ourselves for being so constituted: we are conscious of inward merit; and this is a continual source of satisfaction" (11-12). As consciousness of our own virtue, pleasure at the misfortune of others is revealed to be a form of gratification with which "cunning nature" rewards sympathy and pity.

Equipped with these ambivalent anthropological tools, Home begins to explain the joy of pain emanating from sympathy, the puzzling pleasure at seeing a tragic drama and points to the social utility of this genre. For Home, tragedy is the place where all social inclinations, in particular the sensation of sympathy, can be practiced. In striking harmony with the later position taken in the *Correspondence on Tragedy* (*Briefwechsel über das Trauerspiel*) by Lessing, Mendelssohn and Nicolai, Home constructs a dramaturgy of sympathy through which our capacity to be moved can be trained: "By a good tragedy, all the social passions are excited" (12). The aesthetic or ontological distinction between art and reality is thereby removed. As in life, the figures in the drama become our best friends, "and we hope and fear for them, as if the whole were a true history, instead of a fable" (13). In developing the sentimental habit of sympathy, the question as to whether the characters are fictitious or real has become "totally insignificant" (Martino 178). Several years after his treatise on tragedy, Home described the relationship between a poetic work and its recipients as an "ideal presence"[22] whereby the spectator in seeing a tragedy on stage imagines that he/she is experiencing the actual event "as if he were a witness to it" (Strube 148).

The ambiguity of the sympathy doctrine, "that sympathetic feelings are *virtuous*, and therefore *pleasant*,"[23] is highlighted by the response to the Lucretian shipwreck topos. Lucretius proposed that it was pleasing to sit on top of a cliff and watch a shipwreck not because one derives pleasure from the misfortune of others, but rather because one senses how free one is of distress. For this he was condemned by Enlightenment writers as a misanthrope. A sentimental anti-Lucretian writer now responds to Lucretius. Mark Akenside took up the topos of the shipwreck in his then well-known didactic poem "The Pleasures of Imagination" (1744) but "turned it around" and reformulated it to demonstrate the beneficial nature of sympathy:

>   Ask the crowd
> Which flies impatient from the village walk
> To climb the neighbouring cliffs, when far below
> The cruel winds have hurl'd upon the coast
> Some helpless bark; while sacred Pity melts
> The general eye, or Terror's icy hand
> Smites their distorted limbs and horrent hair;
> While every mother closer to her breast
> Catches her child, and pointing where the waves
> Foam through the shatter'd vessel, shrieks aloud
> As one poor wretch who spreads his piteous arms
> For succour, swallow'd by the roaring surge,

As now another, dash'd against the rock,
Drops lifeless down: O! deemest thou indeed
No kind endearment here by Nature given
To mutual terror and compassion's tears?
No sweetly melting softness which attracts,
O'er all that edge of pain, the social powers,
To this their proper action and their end? (2.693-711)

The ethical value attributed to sympathy is cancelled out by the poet's avid description of the shipwreck. The poet makes claim to activity, when in reality he only provides images of a voyeuristic crowd that has run out of the villages to watch the calamity below from the security of the cliff. One would be hard put today to interpret the line of cars slowing down to stare at an accident on the other side of a freeway as a sign of human solidarity.

The alternate paradigms of moral sense philosophy and the psychology of self-love lend a dichotomous structure to Edmund Burke's analysis of the beautiful and the sublime.[24] In his dualistic system, those sympathetic instincts that pertain to social cohesion, in particular love, are considered "beautiful," while everything that has to do with the desire for self-preservation, with terror or pain is called "sublime." For our purposes it is important to note that Burke's explanation of how pleasure can be derived from sadness forces him to undermine the dichotomy upon which his argument is constructed. He thereby breaks down his treatise's division between sympathy and egoism. While the ability to empathize with the misfortune of others depends on sympathy, this sympathetic response becomes the source of the sublime due to its connection with pain. What consequences result then from this overlapping of the social and the individual? Burke begins with the observation that the degree of pleasure we derive from the misfortune and pain of our fellow human beings is not insignificant. He then transforms the concept of sympathy into its opposite. We can only experience sympathy if it rewards us with pleasure. The English Enlightenment thus returns to Hobbes.

Only after sympathy is exposed as a particularly refined form of self-love, does Burke begin to speak about the effects of tragedy in his "aesthetic of terror and pain" (Monk 235). To the previously demonstrated pleasure at real, but not threatening, terror and the direct pleasure of sympathy, Burke adds a pleasure which results from artistic imitation. But he states that it would be wrong to believe that this peripheral aesthetic pleasure is all we feel. On the contrary: "The nearer it [tragedy] approaches the reality, and the further it removes us from all idea of fiction, the more perfect is its power" (47). We derive pleasure from a purely fictitious catastrophe, as we have learned from

Home, because through it we get a glimmer of real catastrophe. Reality provides the most perfect form of tragic effect—a radical consequence of the principle of "ideal presence" in the theoretical discussion on sympathy, which Burke demonstrates by comparing tragedy with a public execution, a comparison which in this context was not unusual for the time.[25] MacDermot accurately sums up the English discussion on the sources of the pleasure of terror: "Burke does not confine the pleasure derived from tragic sources to the stage. Real distress, he thinks, is a source of still greater pleasure than the mere imitation of it; and hence he infers, that the nearer the imitation approaches the reality, the more powerful is its effect" (113).

If sympathy for the misfortune of others is sought after because of the pleasure that the experience of sympathy brings, why should misfortune be eliminated? This is the crisis in the concept of sympathy in the sentimental phase of the Enlightenment. Karl Philipp Moritz saw the significance of this crisis and tried to justify the terrors of the world by the pleasure derived from observing them in an aestheticized theodicy.[26]

III

In what was probably the first monograph on sympathy, its egoistical nature was defined in a different manner. In his work, *Saggio Analitico su la Compassione* (*Analytic Essay on Compassion*, 1772), Ubaldo Cassina (1736-1824) defines sympathy as a "modification" (XXVI) of self-love—but he says that the social usefulness of sympathy depends precisely on this painful emotion! Because we cannot endure the sight of misery, we do anything to eliminate it. With this definition of sympathy as real pain, which was diametrically opposed to the English concept, Cassina makes impossible an explanation of tragic delight where, by means of happiness, one is led to the practice of compassion upon witnessing misfortune. He was thus forced to explain the strange "pleasure associated with the sympathy felt at the imitation of misfortune" (76) through the consciousness of theatrical illusion. The spectator of a tragedy knows when he enters the theater that a fiction awaits him, according to Cassina, but as the tragedy unfolds, he begins to think that the imitation is real. Through this illusion sympathy is aroused that is identical to that experienced from real misfortune. How does it happen, then, Cassina asked himself, that this unpleasant sensation that calls forth real tears and pain is transformed into something "sweet and pleasant"? "Where does this deep pleasure spring from that we experience in the theater amidst our sadness?"[27] Pain as such is never associated with pleasure, according to Cassina. Instead, he navigates a two-phase theory in which illusion and pain alternate with disappointment and pleasure. Following the pain, one "becomes aware of the spell," perhaps when a neighbor clears his throat or when an actor misspeaks this disillusionment leads to pleasure, "just as we are happy when we awaken from a frightening dream and realize that we were only dreaming."[28]

While this explanation may seem somewhat trivial, it had catastrophic consequences for the dramaturgy of sympathy among Enlightenment thinkers. Both Lessing and Home perceived tragedy as an operative genre through which one could effect changes in social mentality and behavior. Cassina's analysis showed, however, that the concept of sympathy was insufficient to explain the reception of tragedy. Rather, sympathetic identification (see Jauß 271ff.) with the action is disrupted again and again by reflective distancing. Only this fluctuation could impart that particular pleasure for which we run to the theater (or today to the movies) and not to the hospital.[29] "The pleasure that we experience in the theater when we are moved to sympathy," Cassina concludes, "does not emanate from sociable compassion and cannot therefore be called an inner modification of it."[30] Thus, the Enlightenment's dramatic concept of sympathy collapses.

When Mendelssohn described the transformative power of aesthetic illusion in a similar fashion in the correspondence on tragedy, Lessing replied testily that the entire concept of illusion had nothing to do with the dramatic poet (76-85). Harking back, instead, to the Cartesian notion of "plaisir a se sentir emouvoir" (the pleasure of feeling moved —Descartes 146), familiar to him from the work of Wolff and Meier, Lessing supported the principle that even the most unpleasant emotions were pleasant because they expand our consciousness of reality (100ff.). In the second edition of *Rhapsody* (*Rhapsodie*, 1771), a revision of his letters *On Feelings* (*Über die Empfindungen*, 1755), Mendelssohn employs what he calls Lessing's "fine observation" (*Briefwechsel* 104) to align himself with the Western European aesthetics of terror as represented by Dubos and Burke. While Mendelssohn's initial rejection of Dubos's concept of "painful-pleasurable feelings" had forced him, based on the Leibniz/Wolff doctrine of perfection, to see admirable perfection in the "bloody enjoyments" of ancient gladiator matches and a sweet object of sympathy in the victim of an execution (1: 41-123, esp. 107ff.), the separation of objective and subjective points of view in his revised concept of mixed feelings rehabilitated his French predecessor. As evidence of the "inexpressible charm" of something frightening and terrible, Mendelssohn mentions the countless people who felt drawn to the earthquake-devastated city of Lisbon and, as a further example, the philosopher who, with "horror-filled pleasure," is

transfixed at the sight of a battlefield. With the first example, Mendelssohn takes the initial step toward the aestheticization of theodicy; with
the second he initiates an aestheticization of war.[31]

To elucidate this notion of pleasure, Mendelssohn explains that the
"not having representation" and the "absence of the object" are two
different things.[32] The sentimental observer is in a dual relationship to
the horrible event insofar as "representation . . . as the affirmation of
the soul [is] pleasant,"[33] although as "an image of the object it is
accompanied by disapproval and aversion."[34] The subjective aspect
guarantees pleasure because the objective imperfection which stimulates the faculty of cognition increases the soul's "reality . . . and this
necessarily causes pleasure and delight."[35] The pleasure of terror is
revealed to be a sensation of the self that ensures a human being of his
capacities, a process in which moral and natural worlds converge. For
while Mendelssohn uses the example of the battlefield to illustrate the
self-consciousness of subjective perfection resulting from the observation of objective imperfection in human life, Kant, too, sees in war (as
in amorphous and horrible natural phenomena) "something sublime in
itself." Through a comparable mechanism of negative or indirect representation, the sublime is made visible in the presence of war, according to Kant. Aesthetic pleasure in natural *and* human disasters con-
verges in the autonomy of the subject. The paradigm of mixed emotion
constructed by Mendelssohn corresponds to the "negative delight" in
the experience of the sublime in Kant's *Critique of Judgement*, where, in
the presence of chaos and devastation, the soul's own sublimity "can
make itself sensate" (186-87). The pleasure derived from horrible
events of nature, human life and history collapse into one system.
Schiller also describes sentimentality as a mixed feeling whereby the
mind experiences ill humor and retreats "into itself," thus finding
"sustenance" not in sensuous objects but in ideas.[36] The sublime is for
Schiller the true breakthrough experience to what remains when, amid
the horrors of history, chaotic nature around us and the diabolical
abyss within, nothing more remains.[37]

IV

Several studies have emphasized the reflexivity of feeling outlined
here for tragic delight "as the central aspect of sentimentality" (Sauder
1: 170), without taking into account either the Cartesian tradition or
the perspective of Kant and Schiller. Above all, the excess of sentimentality for which Campe coined the pejorative expression "Empfindelei,"
is inherently grounded in sentimental feeling. Calling to mind Richard
Alewyn, Lothar Pikulik says of this self-referentiality: "as a reflex of

feeling, sentimental feeling is also the feeling of feeling, insofar as consciousness that one feels expresses itself as feeling."[38] Because sentimental sympathy thus reveals itself as a feeling directed to the self or the "I," it has been rightfully characterized as an "autistic pleasure" (Wierlacher 153), and one can speak of the "fundamental egoism" (George 231) of the sentimental current of the Enlightenment.

In order to rescue Mendelssohn's analysis of mixed feeling—undoubtedly the philosophical basis of sentimentality—for the Enlightenment, Gerhard Sauder insists on the "predominance of the relationship to the object" in delightful worry, on the "connection to the object," stressing thereby the social character of sympathy (1: 171-72). This project was presented precisely from the standpoint of a sixties radical, since Sauder understood that period "as a third Enlightenment." If Sauder were correct, this relationship to the object would, indeed, predominate, and if sympathy were a social feeling, the sentimental person would sense grief and not the *joy* of grief, which he seeks in the theater and in other situations of horror. This point illuminates the pathology of pleasure in pain insofar as (from the standpoint of the self-referentiality of inner perception) real misfortune (or an artistic rendering of it) is only of interest as a feeding-ground of affectedness.

As is well known, Richard Alewyn not only addressed the topic of literary "Angst" at the end of the eighteenth century;[39] he also energetically denied the relationship between the Enlightenment and sentimentality,[40] which he saw as the turning point to a modern, though problematic mentality, presented most unambiguously in the aestheticization of the artist's existence. Alewyn saw the first expression of this phenomenon in the early Romantic prose *Phantasies on Art* (*Phantasien über die Kunst*, 1799), in which Wilhelm Heinrich Wackenroder described the aestheticized abyss of art in the sentimentalized terminology of self-reflecting feeling.[41] Like a "lascivious hermit"—that is, a brother of Lichtenberg's "pathological egoist"[42]—the artist crawls "into his own pleasure, and he loses the ability to stretch his hand out effectively to his fellow human being."[43] Published posthumously, Alewyn's sketch *From Sentimentalism to Romanticism*, shows that he had planned during his exile in the United States to discuss this critical phase in the development of modern consciousness in detail, using Wackenroder as a point of departure. The sketch demonstrates, in particular, Alewyn's far-reaching conclusions about the self-referential sensation of internal pleasure, that is, "feeling the feeling, divorced from any real object."[44] Alewyn then draws a connection to the modern aesthetics of autonomy and to aestheticism. In the outline of his "Dialectic of Sentimentality", composed in English,

Alewyn jotted down the notes: "Art declares its autonomy in Kant's aesthetics. 'The work of art is its own purpose,' the desentimentalized version of 'feeling the feeling.' . . . The fundamental tenets of 'l'art pour l'art' appear: art is not social, art is not useful."

In complete contrast to Kant's rebuke of sentimentality quoted at the beginning of this paper, Kant's own aesthetic theory is more deeply imbued with passive sentimentality than he himself realized. His subjective aesthetic is heir to a *de*sentimentalized sentimentality. What remains at the close of the century of Enlightenment is not the socially useful concept of sympathy, but rather the "autistic" one, which is the basis for the ethically indifferent pleasure in sorrow.

The breakdown in the sentimental ethics of sympathy was unequivocally recognized by the horror novelist Carl Grosse (1768-1847), who, in his book *Über das Erhabene* (*On the Sublime*, 1788), parenthetically examines the sympathetic explanation of tragic delight and rejects it. Unlike most Enlightenment thinkers, Grosse does not attribute moral significance to sympathy. With sympathy "which likes to conceal itself in a lustrous cloud" ("die sich so gern in eine glänzend Wolke hüllt," 25) it is more likely that "our own self-love is at work" ("unsere Eigenliebe hat ihre Hand zum Spiele," 25). Unmoved, Grosse thus concludes his portrayal of the Lucretian topos of the shipwreck by writing that "it is a pleasure to witness the misfortune of the shipwrecked seafarer, because it would be pleasurable to see disaster and remain unaffected by it,"[45] and concludes with the laconic remark "Lucretius is right" ("Lukrez hat Recht").

Grosse interprets the aesthetic attractiveness of "splendid vices" ("glänzende Laster," 59) with the categories "power" and "energy," borrowed from Edmund Burke. Consequently, he severs ethics from aesthetics, because Achilles' cruelty or the power, boldness and courage of Milton's Satan illustrates for Grosse the difference between "goodness" and "greatness" (58), and the Nero topos of finding delight in watching a burning city shows clearly that imagination finds enjoyment "not in the *good*, but in the *beautiful*" (26). As so often in the Enlightenment, the debate over the pleasurable terror of the sublime led Grosse to the brink of aestheticization. Do we not hear Nietzsche's voice from *Beyond Good and Evil*? And do we not align ourselves with Grosse when, in the context of the relationship between power and sublimity, he writes about animal baiting and bullfights: "Thus, one runs so eagerly to such spectacles in spite of the whimpering entreaties of feeble moralists; one follows one's heart so gladly to scenes where frightful powers are revealed; one does not thirst for the steaming blood of noble animals, but rather for their expressive features when they are attacked and after their powerful, beautiful death."[46]

The discovery of the beauty of gore in the second half of the eighteenth century marks the aesthetic boundary of the Enlightenment.

Notes

This essay was translated by Linda M. von Hoene.

1. See Zelle, "Angenehmes Grauen."
2. See Zelle, "Über den Grund des Vergnügens."
3. "wenn man moralische Zweckmäßigkeit in ästhetischen Dingen fodert" (*Ueber das Pathetische*, NA 20: 221).
4. It would be near-sighted to interpret Schiller's dictate only as a rejection of the "demand of contemporaneous popular philosophers to place art in the service of moral and national ideals," as Klaus L. Berghahn has (205).
5. See Zelle, "Ästhetischer Neronismus."
6. See Zelle, "Schiffbruch vor Zuschauer."
7. See Bohrer, "Erwartungsangst."
8. See Bohrer, "Im Namen der Wahrheit?"
9. "Erwartungsangst" 385.
10. "Erwartungsangst" 372. Bohrer is surprisingly inaccurate when he substitutes "Schrecken" (terror) and "Jammer" (lament) for Lessing's translation of Aristotle's "phobos" and "eleos" as "Furcht" (fear) and "Mitleid" (compassion). Bohrer's source, Manfred Fuhrmann, correctly uses Wolfgang Schadewald's translation "Schauder" (horror) and "Jammer" (lament). See Fuhrmann 19, 109, 163.
11. See chapter 7, 275-360.
12. See Zelle, "Schönheit und Schrecken."
13. "*Der mitleidigste Mensch ist der beste Mensch*, zu allen gesellschaftlichen Tugenden, zu allen Arten der Großmuth der aufgelegteste. Wer uns also mitleidig macht, macht uns besser und tugendhafter, und das Trauerspiel, das jenes thut, thut auch dieses, oder—es thut jenes, um dieses thun zu können" (55).
14. Hamburger 106ff.; see Kronauer.
15. *Observations on the Feeling of the Beautiful and the Sublime* (*Beobachtungen über das Gefühl des Schönen und Erhabenen*, 1764, 2: 834-35).
16. "tatleere Teilnehmung [s]eines Gefühls, sympathetisch zu anderer ihren Gefühlen das seine mittönen, und sich bloß affizieren zu lassen, [ist] läppisch und kindisch" (12: 558).
17. Pickerodt 296.
18. *Anton Reiser* 114, 221, 329-30.
19. See Richardson 377-81; Langen 132-33.
20. See Doktor and Sauder 203.
21. ."seine [des Zuschauers] Brust gibt jetzt nur *einer* Empfindung Raum—es ist diese: *ein Mensch* zu sein" (20: 100).
22. Home, *Elements of Criticism* 104ff.
23. Barnes 153 (a German translation by Christian Victor Kindesvater appeared in 1787).
24. The first German translation, by Christian Garve, was published in 1773.
25. See Zelle, "Strafen und Schrecken."
26. *Fragmente aus dem Tagebuche*, 299ff.
27. ."woher entspringt denn nun das innige Vergnügen, welches wir im Thea-

ter mitten bei unsrer Betrübniß selbst empfinden?" (86).

28. "grade so wie wir uns beim Erwachen von einem ängstlichen Traume freuen, indem wir wahrnehmen, daß wir geträumt haben" (87).

29. David Hume to Adam Smith, 28 July 1759: "It is always thought a difficult Problem to account for the Pleasure, received from the Tears & Grief & Sympathy of Tragedy; which woud [sic] not be the Case, if all Sympathy was agreeable. An Hospital woud [sic] be a more entertaining Place than a Ball" (1: 313).

30. "ist nicht in dem Wesen dieser geselligen Leidenschaft begriffen, und kann auch nicht einen innerliche Modification desselben gennant werden" (95).

31. A passage from Nohl reads like a contemporary application of Mendelssohn's philosopher example. While Nohl cannot be suspected of militarism, the Kantian experience of the sublime makes him think of the pilot during the battle of the Somme "who sings as he flies through the streams of bombs, mesmerized by the magnificence of the lines of fire in the night" (99).

32. "*Nichthaben* der Verstellung"; "*Nichtseyn* des Gegenstandes," *Rhapsodie* 383.

33. "Vorstellung . . . als Bestimmung der Seele [hat] etwas Angenehmes."

34. "[Als] Bild des Gegenstandes [wird sie] von Mißbilligung und Widerwillen begleitet."

35. "ihre Realität . . . , und dieses muß nothwendig Lust und Wohlgefallen verursachen."

36. *Über naive und sentimentalische Dichtung* [1796], NA 20: 474-75.

37. *Über das Erhabene* [1801], NA 21: 38-54.

38. "empfindsame Fühlen ist als Reflexion des Fühlens auch ein Fühlen des Fühlens, insofern das Bewußtsein, zu fühlen, sich selbst als Gefühl äußert" (79).

39. Alewyn, "Die Lust an der Angst."

40. Alewyn, "Was ist Empfindsamkeit?"

41. Alewyn, "Wackenroders Anteil," 52ff.

42. "everything becomes subjective to me and everything pertains to my sentimentality. . . . The whole world is a machine whose purpose it is to make me feel my illness and suffering. A pathological egoist." ["alles wird subjectiv bey mir und zwar bezieht sich alles auf meine Empfindsamkeit. . . . Ich sehe die gantze Welt, als eine Maschine an die da ist um mich meine Kranckheit und mein Leiden auf alle mögliche Weise fühlen zu machen. Ein pathologischer Egoist" (Lichtenberg 704).

43. "kriecht er in seinen selbsteignen Genuß hinein, und seine Hand verliert ganz die Kraft, sich einem Nebenmenschen wirkend entgegenzustrecken" (Wackenroder 177).

44. See Zelle, "Von der Empfindsamkeit."

45. "daß es süß sey, dem auf dem Meere herumirrenden Seefahrer . . . zuzusehen, weil es ein Vergnügen wäre, Übel vor Augen zu haben, von denen man frey ist" (24).

46. "Daher läuft man so gern zu solchen Schauspielen trotz dem weinerlichen Zurufe schlaffer Moralisten hin; man folgt so gern dem Zuge des Herzens nach Scenen, wo ungeheure Kräfte sich zeigen; man dürstet nicht nach dem rauchenden Blute edeler Thiere, aber man dürstet nach den ausdrucksvollen Mienen, nach ihren Anfällen und ihrem kraftvollen schönen Tode" (31).

Works Cited

Akenside, Mark. "The Pleasures of Imagination." *Poetical Works.* London 1845. 83-210.

Alewyn, Richard. "Wackenroders Anteil." *Germanic Review* 19 (1944): 48-58.

―――. "[The Changing Concepts of the Arts and the Artist between 1750 and 1850:] Plans for Work [1946]." In Carsten Zelle, "Von der Empfindsamkeit zum l'art pour l'art: Zu Richard Alewyns geplantem Sentimentalismus-Buch." *Euphorion* 87 (1993): 90-105.

―――. "Die Lust an der Angst" [1965]. R.A. *Probleme und Gestalten: Essays.* Frankfurt/M.: Insel, 1974. 307-34.

―――. "Was ist Empfindsamkeit? Gerhard Sauders Buch ist überall da vortrefflich, wo es nicht von seinem Thema handelt." *Frankfurter Allgemeine Zeitung.* Nov. 12, 1974. 3L-4L.

Aristoteles. *Poetik.* Ed. Manfred Fuhrmann. Stuttgart: Reclam, 1982.

Barnes, Thomas. "On the Pleasure which the Mind in many Cases receives from Contemplating Scenes of Distress." *Memoirs of the Literary and Philosophical Society of Manchester* 1 (1785): 144-58.

Berghahn, Klaus L. " 'Das Pathetischerhabene': Schillers Dramentheorie." *Deutsche Dramentheorien: Beiträge zu einer historischen Poetik des Dramas in Deutschland.* Vol. 1. Ed. Reinhold Grimm. Wiesbaden: Athenäum, 1980. 197-221.

Blaicher, Günther. *Freie Zeit, Langeweile, Literatur: Studien zur therapeutischen Funktion der englischen Prosaliteratur im 18. Jahrhundert.* Berlin: de Gruyter, 1977.

Bohrer, Karl Heinz. "Erwartungsangst und Erscheinungsschrecken: Die griechische Tragödie als Antizipation der modernen Epiphanie." *Merkur* 45 (1991): 372-86.

―――. "Im Namen der Wahrheit? Zu Peter Bürgers Klagen über den Zeitgeist." *Merkur* 39 (1985): 266-72.

Burke, Edmund. *A Philosophical Enquiry into the Origin of our Ideas of the Sublime and Beautiful.* Ed. J. T. Boulton. London: Routledge, 1958.

Cassina, Ubaldo. *Analytischer Versuch über das Mitleiden.* [Orig. in Italian, 1772.] Trans. Carl Friedrich Pockels. Hannover, 1790.

Cassirer, Ernst. *The Philosophy of the Enlightenment.* Trans. Fritz C. A. Koelln and James P. Pettegrove. Boston: Beacon, 1955.

Descartes, Rene. *Die Leidenschaften der Seele* [1649]. Ed. Klaus Hammacher. Hamburg: Meiner, 1984.

Doktor, Wolfgang and Gerhard Sauder. "Nachwort." *Empfindsamkeit: Theoretische und kritische Texte.* Stuttgart: Reclam, 1976. 197-216.

Dubos, Jean Baptiste. *Réflexions critiques sur la poesie et sur la peinture* [Orig. 1719/33]. 7th ed. 1770. Rpt. Geneva: Slatkine, 1967.

George, David E. R. *Deutsche Tragödientheorien vom Mittelalter bis zu Lessing: Texte und Kommentar.* Munich: Beck, 1972.

Goethe, Johann Wolfgang. *Werke.* ["Hamburger Ausgabe."] Ed. Erich Trunz et al. 14 vols. Rev. ed. Munich: Beck, 1981.

Grosse, Carl. *Über das Erhabene* [Orig. 1788]. Ed. Carsten Zelle. Kleines Archiv des achtzehnten Jahrhunderts 9. St. Ingbert: Röhrig, 1990.

Hamburger, Käte. *Das Mitleid.* Stuttgart: Klett-Cotta, 1985.

Hobbes, Thomas. *Tripos; in Three Discourses: I. Human Nature, or the Fundamental Elements of Policy.* In: *The English Works of Thomas Hobbes,* vol. 4. Ed. Sir William Molesworth. London, 1840. 1-76.

Home, Henry. *Elements of Criticism.* 3 vols. Edinburgh, 1762. Rpt. Hildesheim: Olms, 1970.

—————. *Of Our Attachement to Objects of Distress.* In: *Essays on the Principles of Morality and Natural Religion* [Orig. 1751]. 2nd ed. London, 1758. Rpt. Hildesheim: Olms, 1976. 1-21.

Hume, David. *The Letters of David Hume.* Ed. J. Y. T. Greig. Oxford: Oxford UP, 1932.

Horkheimer, Max and Theodor W. Adorno. *Dialectic of Enlightenment.* Trans. John Cumming. New York: Continuum, 1972.

Jauß, Hans Robert. *Ästhetische Erfahrung und literarische Hermeneutik.* Frankfurt/M.: Suhrkamp, 1982.

Kant, Immanuel. *Werkausgabe.* Ed. Wilhelm Weischedel. 12 vols. Frankfurt/M.: Suhrkamp, 1977.

Kronauer, Ulrich, ed. *Vom Nutzen und Nachteil des Mitleids: Eine Anthologie.* Frankfurt/M.: Keip, 1990.

Langen, August. *Der Wortschatz des deutschen Pietismus.* 2nd ed. Tübingen: Niemeyer, 1968.

Lessing, Gotthold Ephraim, Moses Mendelssohn and Friedrich Nicolai. *Briefwechsel über das Trauerspiel.* Ed. Jochen Schulte-Sasse. München: Winkler, 1972.

Lichtenberg, Georg Christoph. *Schriften und Briefe.* Vol. 1. *Sudelbücher.* Ed. Wolfgang Promies. München: Hanser, 1968.

MacDermot, Martin. *A Philosophical Inquiry into the Source of the Pleasures Derived from Tragic Representations.* London, 1824.

Martino, Alberto. *Geschichte der dramatischen Theorien in Deutschland im 18. Jahrhundert.* Vol. 1. *Die Dramaturgie der Aufklärung: 1730-1780.* Tübingen: Niemeyer, 1972.

Mendelssohn, Moses. *Gesammelte Schriften.* Jubiläumsausgabe. Ed. Ismar Elbogen et al. Berlin, 1929-1932; Breslau, 1938; Stuttgart: Frommann, 1971- .

Monk, Samuel H. *The Sublime: A Study of Critical Theories in Eighteenth-Century England.* 2nd ed. Ann Arbor: U of Michigan P, 1960.

Moritz, Karl Philipp. *Anton Reiser: Ein psychologischer Roman.* Ed. Wolfgang Martens. Stuttgart: Reclam, 1972.

—————. *Fragmente aus dem Tagebuche eines Geistersehers.* In: *Werke.* Ed. Horst Günther. Vol. 3. Frankfurt/M.: Insel, 1981. 271-322.

Nohl, Hermann. *Die ästhetische Wirklichkeit: Eine Einführung.* 3rd. ed. Frankfurt/M.: Schutte-Bulmke, 1961.

Pickerodt, Gerhardt, ed. *Epochen der deutschen Lyrik.* Vol. 6. *Gedichte 1770-1800.* Munich: dtv, 1981.

Pikulik, Lothar. *"Bürgerliches Trauerspiel" und Empfindsamkeit.* Köln: Böhlau, 1966.

Richardson, Peter. "Wonne der Wehmut/Joy of Grief." *Archiv für das Studium der neueren Sprachen und Literaturen* 126 (1974): 377-81.

Ritter, Henning. "Das feinste Organ: Zur ersten kritischen Ausgabe der *Dialektik der Aufklärung.*" *Frankfurter Allgemeine Zeitung.* Jan. 20, 1988. 29.

Sauder, Gerhard. *Empfindsamkeit.* Vol. 1. *Voraussetzungen und Elemente.* Vol. 3. *Quellen und Dokumente.* Stuttgart: Metzler, 1974, 1980.

Schiller, Friedrich. *Werke: Nationalausgabe.* Ed. Julius Petersen. Weimar: Böhlau, 1943- . Cited as "NA."

Schings, Hans-Jürgen. *Der mitleidigste Mensch ist der beste Mensch: Poetik des Mitleids von Lessing bis Büchner.* Munich: Beck, 1980.

Strube, Werner. "Ästhetische Illusion: Ein kritischer Beitrag zur Geschichte der Wirkungsästhetik des 18. Jahrhunderts." Diss. Univ. of Bochum, 1971.

Sühnel, Rudolf. "Tränen im empfindsamen Roman Englands: 'Handkerchiefly feeling' bei Richardson, Sterne, Mackenzie." *Das weinende Säkulum: Colloquium der Arbeitsstelle 18. Jahrhundert, Gesamthochschule Wuppertal, Universität Münster... 1981.* Heidelberg: Winter, 1983. 61-71.

Wackenroder, Wilhelm Heinrich. *Sämtliche Schriften.* Reinbeck: Rowohlt, 1968.

Wierlacher, Alois. *Das bürgerliche Drama: Seine theoretische Begründung im 18. Jahrhundert.* München: Fink, 1968.

Zelle, Carsten. *"Angenehmes Grauen": Literaturhistorische Beiträge zur Ästhetik des Schrecklichen im 18. Jahrhundert.* Hamburg: Meiner, 1987.

———. "Ästhetischer Neronismus: Zur Debatte über ethische oder ästhetische Legitimation der Literatur im Jahrhundert der Aufklärung." *DVLG* 63 (1989): 397-419.

———. "Schiffbruch vor Zuschauer." *JDSG* 34 (1990): 289-316.

———. "Schönheit und Schrecken: Zur Dichotomie des Schönen und Erhabenen in der Ästhetik des achtzehnten Jahrhunderts." *Literaturkritik—Anspruch und Wirklichkeit: DFG-Symposium 1989.* Ed. Wilfried Barner. Stuttgart: Metzler, 1990. 252-70.

———. "Strafen und Schrecken: Einführende Bemerkungen zur Parallele zwischen dem Schauspiel der Tragödie und der Tragödie der Hinrichtung." *JDSG* 28 (1984): 76-103.

———. "Über den Grund des Vergnügens an schrecklichen Gegenständen in der Ästhetik des achtzehnten Jahrhunderts." *Schönheit und Schrecken: Entsetzen, Gewalt und Tod in alten und neuen Medien.* Ed. Peter Gendolla and Carsten Zelle. Heidelberg: Winter, 1990. 55-91.

Paradoxes in the Narratological Foundation of the Enlightenment

Jochen Schulte-Sasse

IN HIS *Reading for the Plot,* Peter Brooks refers to a fact that most historians know but apparently haven't given much thought: "From sometime in the mid-eighteenth century through the mid-twentieth century, Western societies appear to have felt an extraordinary need or desire for plots, whether in fiction, history, philosophy, or any of the social sciences" (Brooks 5). I would like to raise a series of questions generated by Brooks's claim: What caused this need to arise in modernity? What does history, in the double sense of the German term, *Geschichte,* meaning both historiography and fictitious narrative, achieve in modernity? What is the relationship between historiography and aesthetic culture?

I

As is well known, a philosophy of history or even a concept of history in the modern sense did not exist before the eighteenth century. Thus, Thomas More's *Utopia* (1516), which is frequently seen as a precursor to the project of social planning in the Enlightenment, displays no concept of time as we conceive it today. Although More describes the "wise social planning" (More 40) of *Utopia* and says that the "regulations" applied there should be viewed as "possible methods of reforming European society," his reflections on the improvement of state organization lack a historical consciousness. As much as his thoughts appear to anticipate the social optimism of the Enlightenment, neither "time" nor "history" ever advances in his thinking to a qualitatively independent dimension of reality.

126

How can modern conceptions of "history" and "story" be characterized? For J. G. A. Pocock, who traces the development of a modern historical consciousness back to the Italian Renaissance, "history" means "successions of events taking place in time, social and public rather than private and subjective in character, which we try to organize, first into narratives and second into processes" (Pocock 5). The Middle Ages, according to Pocock, "did not offer a philosophy of history at all," if we understand the term "history" to mean a secular process oriented toward a goal. As one-sided as this explanation may be, it is worth pursuing a while longer. Pocock uses the term "Machiavellian" to describe the moment in history in which the acceptance of power as static and hierarchical, God-given and venerable, began to dissolve. At that moment, European cultures began to search in the political and technological organization of the world rather than in the afterlife for a secular universal (an oxymoron in the eyes of the Middle Ages) with the capacity to guide worldly action. The conception of power as hierarchical and God-given corresponds with an equally hierarchical conception of human faculties and discursive practices. Similarly, all taxonomies of the "worldly" like the narrative organization of earthly events was viewed as the mere repetition of a story or action and therefore did not count for much. The Middle Ages followed Aristotle

> in considering [narrative] inferior to poetry, as poetry was inferior to philosophy, because it was inferior in bringing to light the universal significance of events; and these were best arrived at by thinking which abandoned the particular event altogether and rose above it to contemplation of universal categories. (Pocock 5)

Scholastic thinking not only has difficulty legitimating the meaning of actions that are not somehow related to timeless transcendence but also imagining them as possible. For the thinking of the late Middle Ages proceeded on the assumption that "the temporal flux evaded men's conceptual control" (Pocock 114).

A *vita activa* that aims to improve political and technological conditions of the here and now, however, requires the projection of objectives into the future and the potential to realize these objectives through "rational" actions in time. Thus, a revaluation of "universality," or a new definition of the relationship of universality to particularity, must have appeared especially imperative to the intellectuals of early modernity, since every goal-oriented and morally engaged action presupposes a conceptual structure that is arranged according to norms and values and can provide philosophical legitimation for actions. As a purposive structure that could guide actions of individuals and collectives, a narrativization of history is only possible on the basis of a reconciliation of the medieval opposition of the universal and the particular. Such a reconciliation had to be achieved in the areas of historiography and politics before the widely-discussed revaluation of the particular or the sensual could occur in the history of aesthetic theory and the arts during the Enlightenment.

According to Pocock, the discussion of the opposition of *virtù* and *fortuna* in the Italian Renaissance and particularly in Machiavelli must be viewed as an attempt to rethink the "particular" and its normative validity; that is, it attempts to secularize or temporalize the medieval concept of universality by replacing its static and universal conception of reality with the dynamic conception underlying philosophies of history. *Virtù* indicates the worth of *vita activa*; it concerns "the ways in which a civic *virtus* or *virtù* ... might undergo exposure to, and rise triumphantly above, the insecurities of *fortuna*" (Pocock 86). For medieval thinking, virtue, as compared to the transcendental universality of eternal, divine norms, would always be compromised from the outset. For although *virtù* determines the character of any successful intervention in worldly affairs, it nevertheless is contaminated by the "particular" of *Fortuna* or history as soon as it interacts with the latter.

The main obstacle to "history," that is to mapping the "world" in a judicious and ordered fashion, was the radical finitude and arbitrariness of the "particular." How can the value of different political structures be compared; how can political discussions about the quality of state systems occur if the gap between the universal (norms to which everyone is committed) and the particular (history) is not bridgeable? "The problem of the particular was its finitude, its mortality, its instability in time, and once a virtue (itself universal) was embodied in a particular form of government it partook of this general instability" (Pocock 78).

II

As is well known, the Enlightenment fully overcame such fears of instability based on a conception of "time" as purely contingent and arbitrary. What happened? The period from the middle of the seventeenth century to the end of the eighteenth century is often described as an epoch in which the human worldview underwent a process of visualization and temporalization. I will disregard here the process of visualization, which includes a visualization of literary culture as well (see, for instance, the term "anschauende Erkenntnis"). The process of temporalization may be illustrated by such changes in everyday life as the increasing importance of clocks and the numerous attempts to measure time synchronically in greater geographical areas. More important, however, are new discursive practices such as biographical and historiographical writings as well as philosophies of history. Even discourses that at first glance have very little to do with temporality, such as the pedagogical and aesthetic, partake in the process of temporalization. The former discourses constitute a linguistic practice that is both cause and result of a broad displacement of the transcendent anchorage of individuals and collectives: the latter shifts from static points of reference, such as God, to temporal ones, such as the idea of a golden age or of a classless society. This temporalization of humankind's worldview needed a narratological foundation.

This process, which simultaneously changed our relationship to texts, that is, the way we read and interpret them, is reflected in changing concepts of education in handbooks written for princes and in the genre of the Bildungsroman. Thus, in a comparison between Fénelon's *Télemaque* of 1699 and a chapter of St. Augustine's *De Civitate Dei*, Tilo Schabert accentuates the fundamental differences between theories of socialization based on theological premises and those based on philosophies of history. Augustine's *imperatores felices* enter into an atemporal, loving and submissive relationship with God; Fénelon's pupil, however, enters into a temporal relationship with an ideal identity that he constructs for himself, and whose reconciliation with his actual ego he projects into the future. "The vertical tension between God and human being, out of which the Augustan *imperator* must act in order to be able to be called happy, is shifted to a horizontal forward movement from mere virtuality to obtaining immanent perfection" (Schabert 26).

The Enlightenment's concept of time and its narratological ramifications emerged, according to Michel Foucault, in an age in which the citizens of Western European nations internalized their own supervision. The "disciplinary methods" established during this age "reveal a linear time whose moments are integrated, one upon another, and which is oriented towards a terminal, stable point; in short, an 'evolutive' time." Foucault goes on to maintain that the new disciplinary techniques reveal

> the discovery of an evolution in terms of "genesis." These two great discoveries of the eighteenth century—the progress of societies and the geneses of individuals—were perhaps correlative with the new techniques of power, and more specifically, with a new way of administering time and making it useful, by segmentation, seriation, synthesis and totalization. A macro- and microphysics of power made possible, not the invention of history ... but the integration of a temporal, unitary, continuous, cumulative dimension in the exercise of controls and the practice of dominations. (Foucault 160)

This phenomenon surely can be explained, to a certain degree, economically. The enlightened citizen managing his affairs does so on the basis of temporalizing his "world" and individual life; he imagines that he designs his actions by projecting an improvement of his state of affairs into the future. Thus Thomas Henry, in an article with the telling title *On the Advantages of Literature and Philosophy in general, and especially on the Consistency of Literary and Philosophical with Commercial Pursuits*, writes in 1791 that the "Merchant and Manufacturer" must also be a "philosophical historian," since he cannot be satisfied "with the mere relation of facts." Henry sees very clearly that the predominant dimension of the analytic approach of the merchant or manufacturer is not spatial, as in the case of the scientist, but temporal. The businessman must discover "how the various interests, situations and connections of different countries should lead to different kinds of traffic" (*Twenty Essays* 10). Since he must translate his experiences not into knowledge, but into purposeful actions, Henry pleads for a new philosophical discipline that he calls "commercial philosophy."

III

Henry's narratological and educational presuppositions are still shared by most narrative theories today. The Enlightenment's narratology and its counterparts today presume, implicitly or explicitly, a mimetic capacity of narratives. Stories, whether fictitious or factual, are, according to these theories, a means of categorizing reality; they map the world or produce semiotic distinctions such as gender differences. In order to problematize the status of mimesis in narrative theories since the Enlightenment, I will briefly turn to a contemporary understanding of narrative that was clearly conceived in the tradition of the Enlightenment.

The essays collected in a 1990 volume on *Narrative in Culture* set out to investigate, as the subtitle indicates, *The Uses of Storytelling in the Sciences, Philosophy, and Literature*. They focus on diverse areas of discourse without distinguishing among different forms of narration and their contribution to knowledge in different fields or ways of thinking. I quote Jay Bernstein, who writes in his essay entitled "Self-knowledge as Praxis: Narrative and Narration in Psychoanalysis":

> One of the ways human beings assess and interpret the events of their life is through the construction of plausible narratives. Narratives represent events not as instances of general laws but rather as elements of a history where a continuing individual or collective subject suffers or brings about dramatic, i.e., meaningful, changes. A change is meaningful in virtue of its relation to past and future events.... Constructing narratives involves eliciting connections

between events by describing them in one way rather than another. . . . To describe an action correctly, then, means describing it under descriptions relevant to the story being told. Typically, we call the conceptual structure which binds the events of a story together a plot. Plots are not events, but structures of events. The meaningfulness of plot-structures is analogous to the meaning of human action in that they are governed by a teleological or purposive movement. (55)

Like other authors in this volume, Bernstein presupposes a more or less homogeneous discursive phenomenon called narrative culture; he neither distinguishes among different institutionalizations of narrative such as those found in literature and historiography, nor addresses the problematic structural relations of such institutionalizations among each other. A fundamental assumption he does make is that narratives are an appropriate medium in which human beings can cognize and represent their world.

In this theoretical context, imagination or the imaginary typically play a small part; fantasy is perceived as a threat to rational systems. If narrative theories conceived in the Enlightenment tradition thematize imagination at all, it is commonly reduced to a human faculty bridging time; that is, it projects an improved state of affairs into the future and devises ways to bring it about. The proposed guidelines for change are supposedly derived from rational norms. This imagination is a faculty that imagines, or forms images of the real; it is a disciplined planning tool, the flip-side of a chronological notion of time. Since the Renaissance, philosophers have emphasized the temporal nature of the imagination and valorized it as a faculty of planning, of instrumental reason. Thus, Pico della Mirandola said that imagination "conceives not only what now is no more, but as well what it suspects or believes is yet to be." The enlightenment heightened this aspect of the imagination. Christoph Friedrich Bährens, for example, holds that "the thought of future is already in and of itself for the imagination alone" (78). However, authors like Bährens often add that the temporalization of human fantasy, which is viewed as a social and historical phenomenon, tends to be motivated by desire, not by rationality. According to Bährens, "civilization" has witnessed the emergence of a new type of human being for whom it is more important to "desire and to hope than actually to enjoy pleasure" (108)—in modern parlance: to desire desire rather than to act. A desiring desire can not be stilled by satisfactions. Desire is a structural phenomenon that could only be sublated by the collapse of the structure.

What is at stake here? A position like Bernstein's or Henry's must presuppose the existence, first, of autonomous, independently acting individuals and nations and, second, of a human mastery over time and

its calculability. Yet one can observe a curious ambiguity in the
Enlightenment's notions of time, narration, imagination or fancy, planning, happiness: enlightened thinkers constantly shift between a "rational," chronological and teleological projection of goals and a
psychological projection of imaginary states of happiness. This vacil-
lation between "rational" and "imaginary" projections can certainly not
be explained as a mere difference between goal-oriented social and
public actions on the one hand and private and subjective projections
of "happiness" on the other. The two kinds of projections inhabit every
narrative form, including social and public narration, thus introducing
into the Enlightenment's notion of "story" and "history" two fundamentally conflicting, but structurally complementary functions of narration and history. The one aims at an understanding of time and future
as calculable, manipulable and classifiable; the other at pleasurable
imaginations of states of reconciliation, at an imaginary overcoming of
a structural—that is nontemporal, unsublatable—experience of lack. In
the following, I intend to analyze more closely the fundamental split in
the Enlightenment's concept of a narrative-aesthetic culture, namely
the split between art as an aesthetic experience of an imaginary community and as a medium of normative socialization.

Temporality is a twofold phenomenon. As a disciplined, chronological sense of time, it is in conflict with the capricious temporality of
desire. The same holds true for imagination, or fantasy. The mysterious ambiguity of temporality and desire and their debilitating effect
on a cognitive concept of narration often induce a puzzling move on
the part of "enlightened" narrative theories. Witness Bernstein, who
claims that temporality has nothing to do with narration, that time
remains external to narration. He therefore feels compelled to detemporalize the notion of narrative plot by disregarding the relationship
between present and future; he defines "plot" as a "conceptual structure," and reduces it to a static, timeless logic binding stories together.
Such an argument assumes that a rational discussion of norms and
values is possible; it simultaneously privileges, on the basis of that
assumption, the mimetic representation of socially relevant norms and
values in narratives. From this perspective, time and imagination are
rationalized as dimensions of human activity that can easily be subjected to our will to plan. This attitude towards time has determined
thought since the eighteenth century; in 1805 William Hazlitt expressed
it in the following way: "The object in which the mind is interested
may be either past or present, or future. These last alone can be the
objects of rational or voluntary pursuit; for neither the past, nor present can be altered for the better, or worse by any efforts of the will. It
is only from the interest excited in him by future objects that man

becomes a moral agent . . ." (1-2). The notion of a "moral agent," that is, of an independent and self-aware person who acts morally and is only familiar with "rational or voluntary pursuits," excludes other motivations for action in time—above all, the influence of imaginary, psychologically motivated perceptions. It also excludes the possibility that the latter are structurally *necessary*, attendant phenomena of modern subjectivity that find their equivalent in institutionalized forms of discourses such as the aesthetic. Thus, repression or suppression become moral achievements that set the stage for the return of the repressed, for example, in human beings' susceptibility to products of the culture industry.

I contend that the serialization of time, internalized as the will to plan and as a mode of mastering reality, is precisely the phenomenon parallel to and against which modern aesthetic culture as it emerged in the Enlightenment fosters a very different perception of temporality. An assessment of temporality and imagination and the function of narration in the aesthetic culture of modernity can only be made by inquiring into the institutionalization of the aesthetic. For within the functionally differentiated system of modernity the institutionalized aesthetic experience is assigned the task of momentarily sublating the requirements of agonistic and rationalistic behavior, including a disciplined management of time. This involves both a sublation of the constraints of a teleologically perceived temporality and of a cognitive mapping of the world. The functional differentiation of the aesthetic, if indeed a fact, fundamentally affects the possibility of a mimetic and normative understanding of art. Aesthetic experience would then correlate to those constraints which subjects experience subjectively and objectively in a compensatory fashion. Individuals experience such constraints subjectively when they project themselves as "self" teleologically in the future and transform their projections of an ideal-I into self-discipline in their daily lives; they experience restraints objectively when methodical, disciplined, institutionalized knowledge like "technology," "market," or "science" are demanded of them.

IV

The temporalization of the bourgeois worldview led to the attempt to institutionalize a secular narrative culture as a medium of collective socialization. In the narration of history and stories, Western cultures construct new transcendent anchors that are temporal in nature. The struggle between church functionaries and secular intellectuals that took place in all Western European countries between 1670 and 1730 and in which the morality of fiction was under discussion (question: is fiction in essence a lie?), was primarily a struggle between church functionaries and secular intellectuals over the institutionalization of individual and collective socialization. I refer in passing to Pierre Daniel Huet's *Traité de l'origine des romans* (1670), to the reformed Swiss theologian Gotthart Heidegger and his *Mythoscopia Romantica* of 1698, and—most importantly—to the Jeremy-Collier debate in England which led, between 1698 and 1727, to the publication of more than seventy pamphlets pro and con a worldly narrative culture. The revolutionary cultural break in the mode of individuals' socialization and society's cultural reproduction that occurred at the beginning of the eighteenth century was conceptualized two hundred years later in the theories of Freud and Parsons and in American ego-psychology. All of these theories assume that without an internalization of fundamentally homogeneous norms by individuals, it would be impossible to create a stable, viable social order.

Yet the effort of secular intellectuals to establish a secular narrative culture was marked from the beginning by ruptures, strains and contradictions. More importantly, the same intellectuals who propagated secular narration as a mode of socialization often felt the contradictory nature of their own project. Samuel Johnson is a good case in point. In an essay in his moral weekly *The Rambler*, Johnson, like so many other intellectuals of the first half of the century, defended fictitious narratives as "lectures of conduct and introductions into life." He claims that a secular narrative culture is necessary in order to moralize people and to create something like a consistent infrastructure of conduct: Emulating Gottsched's position, Johnson writes that fictitious narrations are necessary for readers "not fixed by principles," who would therefore "easily" follow "the current of fancy." "For this reason," he continues in the same installment, "these familiar histories may perhaps be made of greater use than the solemnities of professed morality, and convey the knowledge of vice and virtue with more efficacy than axioms and definitions" (1: 20). Here Johnson does not yet seem to perceive the contradiction between imagination and the normative or mimetic effect of narratives. He still sees imagination as a human faculty that mediates between rationality and emotion, present and future. In Johnson's words: "It seems to be the fate of man to seek all his consolations in futurity. The time present is seldom able to fill desire or imagination with immediate enjoyment, and we are forced to supply its deficiencies by recollection or anticipation" (4: 218).

Writers such as Johnson soon begin, however, to discuss the ambivalence of the aesthetic; they do this invariably in connection with their discussion of "imagination" and "time." According to Johnson, the tension between the different modalities of imagination, time, and narration is irreconcilable. In one mode, they are centered around a chronological notion of time and the rational pursuit of goals, while the reference to present and future remains purely *quantitative*. In another mode their relationship is dependent on the human desire "to seek . . . consolations in futurity"; that is, it is characterized by a *qualitative* discrepancy between the present and a future state of happiness. Johnson writes:

> Many impose upon the world, and many upon themselves, by an appearance of severe and exemplary diligence, when they, in reality, give themselves up to the luxury of fancy, please their minds with regulating the past, or planning out the future; place themselves at will in varied situations of happiness, and slumber away their days in voluntary visions. There is nothing more fatal to a man whose business is to think, than to have learned the art of regaling his mind with those airy gratifications.

Johnson sees the human desire for "airy gratifications" as a social phenomenon that is becoming more and more common—a phenomenon that must be culturally defused and controlled. He describes imaginary projections of happiness as "invisible riot of the mind" and "secret prodigality of being": "The dreamer abandons himself to his own fancy; new worlds rise up before him, one image is followed by another, and a long succession of delights dances around him" (2: 185-86).

Johnson's ambivalence toward imagination recurs in 1757-1761 in Rousseau's *Emile*, where imagination is described as a force that can fragment or dissolve a unified, satisfied I at peace with itself. Rousseau proceeds thereby from a concept of happiness that lets "true happiness" depend on a reduction of "difference between our desires and our powers" (44). What is interesting about this is how Rousseau attributes happiness not to a satisfaction, but to an elimination of desire, and how he blames the imagination for unsatisfied desire:

> It is imagination which enlarges the bounds of possibility for us, whether for good or ill, and therefore stimulates and feeds desires by the hope of satisfying them. But the object which seemed within our grasp flies quicker than we can follow; when we think we have grasped it, it transforms itself and is far ahead of us. We no longer perceive the country we have traversed, and we think nothing of it; that which lies before us becomes vaster and stretches still before us. Thus we exhaust our strength, yet never reach our goal, and the nearer we are to pleasure, the further we are from happiness. (44)

Paradoxically, Rousseau tries to remedy the negative effect of projecting an imaginary time (future happiness) by positing an imaginary origin. Nature, he claims in characterizing human desire, originally had put human beings in a state of balance:

> [T]he more nearly a man's condition approximates to this state of nature the less difference is there between his desires and his powers, and happiness is

therefore less remote. Lacking everything, he is never less miserable; for misery consists, not in the lack of things, but in the needs which they inspire. (45)

In other words, Rousseau constructs a pseudo-historical myth in order to escape from the dispersing effect of time. In a state of lacking differentiations, so he argues, imagination has no power over human beings; in this state imagination does not yet fragment presence through time, thus making it impossible, since here nature only lets such wishes arise "as are necessary for self-preservation, and such powers as are sufficient for their satisfaction." Only in this uncivilized, "primitive" state do human beings find "the equilibrium between desire and power, and then alone man is not unhappy" (44).

The fact that Rousseau projects the site of reconciliation into the past may appear to be contradictory in the context of my reasoning. For is such a site, such a time still within reach? If not—which is obvious—can the discursive construction of such a site still fulfill the function of anchoring present, negative experiences in a transcendent site? The stage of lacking differentiation that Rousseau imagined is, of course, not a stage in time at all but a timeless state, namely, an aesthetic one. Aesthetic experience is a mental state that, as such, is independent of the possibility of its political or social realization. More precisely, since it is structurally dependent on "difference," that is on the functional differentiation of society, it is, as a mental state, only of importance *within* differentiated systems. The alleged site on the chronological axis can in reality only gain importance as an imaginary site. Its realization is its "imagination" ("Einbildung") in the text (a concept that, unlike the German "Einbildungskraft" or "Phantasie," resonates with notions of an effect); its imagination is only important as a discursive embodiment in Rousseau's text, as aesthetic event. Rousseau, who could not yet have perceived this, searches for means that are sufficient and effective in limiting and taming the imagination: "The world of reality has its bounds, the world of imagination is boundless; as we cannot enlarge the one, let us restrict the other; for all the sufferings which really restrict us derive from the difference between the real and the imaginary" (45).

V

In an essay from 1818, *On the Concept of Time* (*Über den Begriff der Zeit*), the conservative, romantic political philosopher Franz von Baader expounds a critique of time that is conceived in the spirit of Rousseau's critique of civilization and that clearly distinguishes between the two modes of time mentioned earlier. I will briefly outline

Baader's critique in order to illustrate that wherever one experience of time collides with its contradictory counterpart, the result is an attempt to detemporalize culture again, that is, to convert secular narrative culture back into a religious culture.

Baader juxtaposes the experience of a "true" or eternal time that is fundamentally not time, but (timeless) presence, to the experience of "pseudo-time." He reproaches modernity for a "fundamental error," namely an "idolization or eternalization of pseudo-time." The reverberation of experiencing time as pseudo-time upon the subject is structural; it leads to a fragmentation or dissolution of the supposed self-identical essence of the soul, "so that these poor souls, hunted like the Eternal Jew, to all eternity would have to endure Tantalus' punishment, without ever being able to enjoy a complete existence and happiness" (118-19). The social and psychic structure that Baader assails here has chosen "time" as its organizing principle, namely, the temporal projection of states of reconciliation that become the force motivating individuals. According to Baader, any human being that lives in time fragments himself, loses his center. Baader's description of the fragmenting and dispersing effect of time is one of the best and most exact: it is "only self-deception when the human being who is always misused by this time believes in it, that is, when he always hopes to find in another point or part of the same time or the same space what he could not find in a first one" (121). Hence Baader sees above all the necessity of an anti-enlightenment, anti-modern attitude in political and moral matters, since actions directed toward political or moral changes cannot escape the dispersing effect of "pseudo-time." He sees the chronological nature of time and its internalization as expectation as inherently negative, since "the temporal being separated from his center" does not have being "in himself any longer," he is "no longer (internally) filled" (124). Hence Baader, as Rousseau or Schiller, sees the necessity of positing another site: experiences "in this time and in this space" lead a human being into temptation "to move out of it [time]—either to his happiness or to his damnation." For Baader the answer does not lie (as it did for other romantics) in aesthetic culture (this is his specific antimodernism), but in God. Since a human being "can never find the complete action of the center" in pseudo-time, "it follows therefore that he can never find his God completely if he *only* remains in this time" (124). It is crucial that Baader's notion of God is no longer an authority to which human beings are subjected. "God" has shifted from an external authority to an imaginary site of presence. Paradoxically, Baader argues that "true time," namely timeless presence, is only at this site and that human beings mistakenly have imagined eternity up to now as an immobile and rigid present, since they did not understand that the two other times, the past and the future, have to be comprised in this present. Thus everything in eternity, that is, everything included in a completed life, must be recognized as always being, as always having been being, and as always becoming being, and thus always resting in its movement, and always moving itself in rest, or as always new and yet always the same. (116)

Baader promotes here an aesthetic concept of infinity that had become important decades earlier in so-called Jena Romanticism, but passes it off as religious. This substitution has its consequences. For the replacement of aesthetic projections with religious ones permits a concretization of imaginary experiences. Religious experience may be functionally similar to aesthetic experience; it is, however, as church service for instance, less cerebral and more bodily.

VI

The displacement of aesthetic experience to the realm of religion has the effect that the concept of the imagination does not play a role in Baader. In this, he is an exception among his contemporaries. As long as the aesthetic site is institutionalized as art, the concept of imagination or fancy plays a central role in the discursive support of this institution. Therefore it is not surprising that the eighteenth century was witness to a radical revalorization of human imagination. From Addison, Duff, and Gerard to Friedrich Schlegel and Coleridge, the imagination was wrestled from its traditional place in the hierarchy of human cognitive faculties—that is, from the ascending line "senses, memory, imagination, understanding or nous and reason or pneuma"— and newly defined as an independent, qualitatively distinctive faculty.

In 1791, the English theologian Thomas Barnes maintained in a speech for the Literary and Philosophical Society of Manchester that the imagination plays an essential part in judgments of the understanding. This results from the temporalization of such judgments. Barnes upgrades the imagination to "the eye of the mind"; he thus ascribes to a healthy imagination precisely the ability to distance itself from its perceptions that had been tirelessly questioned just a few decades earlier: "If any person should think this appellation [i.e., "the eye of the mind"] would better belong to the understanding, let him recollect that the eye of the body can give no exact information, till rectified by the judgment" (Barnes 194). Both the understanding and the imagination must be motivated by a temporal and/or spatial goal. In the eighteenth century, a visualization of experience takes place. One reason for this process lay in the effect the functional differentiation of modernity had on subjects, namely not simply to temporalize our commerce with reality, as indicated earlier, but to counterbalance forms of mental differentiation with an intensification of desire which in turn changes the way human beings *visually* relate to objects and libidinally invest these objects. This also becomes apparent in the frequency with which women serve as illustrations in discussions of "imagination" and "time." Barnes, for instance, illustrates the visualization of the imagination with references to the female body. He uses the example of woman as object of desire when dealing with possible objections to his definition of the imagination as visual (and intellectual). For, according to Barnes, one can regard an excessively imaginative "lover, who sees in his mistress an imaginary idol, decked all over with charmes, perfect and matchless in every air, and in every attribute" as a being for whom the imagination is no longer "the eye of the mind." But, he counters, here a "due poise and degree of the imaginative quality" does not exist. In a healthy imagination, on the other hand, which arrests itself in an idealized image of an object of desire, rationality and desire are reconciled with each other:

> Suppose a person to contemplate excellence, female excellence, without imagination—just as he would a mathematical problem. Would the fairer sex consent to abide the sentence of such a judge? Would they not appeal—and who would not justify the appeal—to the decision of a mind, capable of feeling, and of fancy, and therefore rational, and alone competent to judge of that excellence which is fitted to cheer and captivate the heart? (195)

Barnes ends his considerations with the pathetic, yet figuratively precise exclamation, "let the imagination fly abroad to collect the various scattered breezes, which thus united into one strong current, may carry the vessel forward, across the ocean of life, under such a pilotage, with safety and satisfaction" (197). He presents an understanding of social behavior that is narrative and simultaneously sexually polarized, which is precisely what allows his essay to become a disguised theory of modernity. The image on which the imagination focuses does not remain a simple image; it becomes the driving force of public (male) actions and, moreover—as the imagery suggests—of acts of colonization, of the subjection of the world. The presupposition of modern, motivated male subjectivity is the temporalization and focussing of the imagination on a culturally valorized object of desire that has been coded as female even when it is called by other names, such as art.

Barnes' essay illustrates precisely that moment in history in which subjectivity is organized collectively as one that mirrors, and thus constitutes, itself in culturally accepted objects of desire. In high modernity (as the period between the middle of the eighteenth and the middle of the twentieth century may be called), a collectively, that is, publicly constituted subjectivity is coded as male whose object of desire, including textual culture, is coded as female.

Johnson's and Rousseau's criticism of imagination represents the flip-side of this development. Their critique reveals more of what this process is about than the completely affirmative revaluations of fancy in, say, Duff and Gerard. The need for a "luxurious imagination" set free by the process of civilization must, in the eyes of contemporaries, be tamed by attaching imagination to an institutionalized cultural practice, art. According to Johnson, the mind, if not culturally bound, "will break from confinement to its stated task, into sudden excursions." These "sudden excursions" are to be controlled institutionally. Johnson suggests that a mind attracted by the luxury of fancy focus on an external phenomenon such as literature; he holds that reading will bind an "unbridled fancy." For what is rejected in the critique of modern subjectivity resurfaces affirmatively in the new definition of art and the imaginary experience of texts. That is, the "luxuriant" imagination is not simply suppressed but integrated into the modern mode of social organization. This is the moment when aesthetic culture in the modern sense begins. According to Johnson, the cultural, non-integrated human spirit breaks "from confinement to its stated task, into sudden excursions." He suggests that a human being who easily succumbs to the temptations of fantasizing direct his attention to a cultural object such as literature. The cultural activity of reading is supposed to bind an "unbridled fancy"; reading is supposed to take over the function of focusing fantasy and thereby get it under control:

> In order to regain liberty, he must find the means of flying from himself; he must, in opposition to the Stoic precept, teach his desires to fix upon external things; he must adopt the joys and the pains of others, and excite in his mind the want of social pleasures and amicable communication. (186)

Although Johnson does not yet develop a concept of reading and interpretation that is characteristic of a later aesthetics of autonomy, his reasoning clearly indicates why such a concept of reading and interpretation became necessary. As soon as cultural critics had convinced themselves that temporal flights of fancy had become common in modernity, they had to be concerned about how to bind or anchor these fantasies institutionally as cultural activities. On the one hand, aesthetic culture should compensate for the one-sidedness of activities external to it; simultaneously, however, it should facilitate the integration of subjects into the general structure of differentiated societies. An important feature of this development is the binding of fantasy to discursive practices.

Imagination, time, and narration designate different aspects of desire. Desire may be a *conditio humana*. But this does not account for the fact that it must be organized historically in each case. The more extreme the differential demands upon the individual, the more extreme the longing for states of balance, of happiness. The concepts of imagination, time, and narration refer to the specific form of organization that desire has assumed in modernity. Their common vanishing point is an aesthetic one; their convergence in the aesthetic defuses the destructive power of desire. The pseudo-sublation of chronological time in aesthetic experience is the presupposition of this defusion. In reality the imaginary scene is set beyond time—a fact that renders all mimetic claims of the aesthetic uncertain. The aesthetic remains, however, related to the organization of real time in that it binds excessive human energies to cultural practices through which it facilitates a quantification of, and thus mastery over, time. In other words, it expedites purposive action precisely by playing a role in the institutional separation of libidinal energies. According to Foucault, "Time penetrates the body and with it all the meticulous controls of power" (Foucault 152). The oscillation between aesthetic representations and chronological management of one's own life, between the imaginary experience of presence and purposeful conduct, is entirely a bodily phenomenon. The temporalization of subjectivity, to which the aesthetic culture of modernity remains functionally subordinate, establishes new ways in which human beings collectively exercise power over themselves.

The aesthetic "high" culture of modernity checks the centripetal powers of longing more effectively than popular culture. Rousseau was very conscious of the possibilities that aesthetic culture offers for a management of desire. He devised Sophie in *Emile* as an allegory of aesthetic experience, as a discursively constructed imaginary model of woman that organizes and regulates (male) longing for symbiotic or, as Freud called them, "oceanic feelings." Rousseau writes: "when I supply the object of imagination, I have control over comparisons, and I am able easily to prevent illusion with regard to realities" (294). He says about the "object of imagination": "this model, will attach him none the less to everything that resembles itself, and will give him as great a distaste for all that is unlike it as if Sophy really existed. What a means to repress his senses by means of his imagination" (294). The controlled image of woman not only organizes desire but also the desire of desire that Bährens discussed. Rousseau was apparently entirely aware of the possibilities of textual, cultural praxis as a means of managing longing.

In this sense, the aesthetic culture of modernity can be viewed as an institution whose responsibility is to generate discourses, to transform the psyche's memory traces left by the primary process into symbolic representations. What counts here is the *form* of our commerce with these discourses, not their contents. As form, the aesthetic is already invested with libidinal energy. Aesthetic culture is thus functionally opposed to the complex "secondary process, reality principle, understanding." It is, however, important to see that these realms cannot be clearly delimited from each other. Indeed, a fundamental self-deception of modernity is the assumption that the realms of the normative-political, technological-material, and aesthetic-emotional reproduction of society (and subjectivity) are clearly institutionally separated. The instability of drawing these boundaries may be illustrated with the public sphere; the public sphere is not simply an institutionalized realm of normative-political reproduction of society, but is simultaneously a discourse that is structured narratively. Inherent in the notion of "public sphere" is an improved political climate for solving problems "rationally." Yet the fact that the temporal goal of the "public sphere" can only be related to the present in the form of a narrative allows it to take on an aesthetic character. The ideal of communication free of domination overlaps with the ideal of harmony among minds and bodies. In *The Ego and the Id*, Freud remarked that "Social feelings are based on identifications with others who share the same ego-ideal." The infiltration of aesthetic characteristics into the normative-moral reproduction of society reduces not only its rationality; it changes the character of normative-moral reproduction—for example, through the staging of collective-aesthetic experience not only in mass assemblies, in singing a national anthem together or in the common experience of national superiority (sport) or unity, but also in the theater as it was envisioned in the Enlightenment. As a matter of fact, Schiller's *The Stage Considered as a Moral Institution* (*Die Schaubühne als moralische Anstalt betrachtet*, 1785), which may well be considered one of the last great theater documents of the Enlightenment in the narrow, periodic sense, gives ample evidence of a constant fluctuation between normative-political and aesthetic experiences—a fluctuation that historically has never been contained within the aesthetic. The penetration of the normative-political reproduction of society by the aesthetic can be seen as the necessary return of the repressed, since institutional delimitations, as collectively organized blockages that confine the flow of energy of human instinctual life, can stem this flow of energy only temporarily. Since a desire to experience a reconciliation of "difference" seems to form the basis of aesthetic culture in modernity, the aesthetic nature of the ideal of consensus may very well be the point at which politics is penetrated by behavior that tends to suppress those differences that it cannot assimilate or appropriate.

VII

I have argued that as form and institution, art is invested with libidinal energy. Such an investment tends to mask art's institutional nature and its functional and structural interconnectedness with other segments of the social order. Art wants to be regarded not as function but as value, not as substitute or stand-in but as substance. In this sense there exists a fundamental difference between art and narration, even if a particular piece of art consists of nothing but a narrated story. Art is perceived to be timeless whereas narration always remains temporal, never reaching its ultimate goal of "presence." The objects of desire within narration are never experienced as "substance" or "value." Only art as institution achieves such an imaginary status. If art is enjoyed according to canonized rules, it sublimates and eases the dispersing effect of desire; as a mode of experience, it is assigned the task of suspending time and of turning the temporal imagination of the future into an experience of the imaginary that is outside time. That is, narration would only have the chance to serve as a medium in which "human beings assess and interpret the events of their life" if and when art as institution were not to form the framework within which stories were read (Bernstein)—which may be an impossibility. Within the institutional framework of art as social fantasy, however, the "meaningfulness of plot-structures" is not "analogous to the meaning of human action," since in narrations every action "governed by a teleological or purposive movement" is counteracted by the same medium in which the movement takes place.

But how are we to imagine the effect of normative differences, of ideology—whose presence in narrative texts cannot be denied and has been proven often enough—on the readers of stories? Doesn't the identification with ideologically charged narrative configurations also influence the readers of these narratives? Aren't they interpellated, in the sense of Althusser, as subjects by the ideology enmeshed in narrative? Zizek criticizes Althusser for never clarifying the relationship between ideological state apparatuses and the interpellation of subjects by ideology. Like the enlightenment's narratology, Althusser's notion of the interpellation of subjects assumes a successful and complete internalization of norms and values in interpellated individuals; he therefore has to neglect the traumatic nature of every submission to ideology. In contrast to Althusser, Zizek insists that "this external machine of State Apparatuses exercises its force only in so far as it is experienced, in the unconscious economy of the subject, as a traumatic, senseless injunction"(43). The internalization of ideology can therefore never be completely successful, "there is always a residue, a left-

over, a stain of traumatic irrationality and senselessness sticking to it."
The psychic trace of violent submission, however,

> far from hindering the full submission of the subject to the ideological command, is the very condition of it: it is precisely this non-integrated surplus of senseless traumatism which confers on the Law its unconditional authority: in other words, which—in so far as it escapes ideological sense—sustains what we might call the ideological jouis-sense, enjoyment-in-sense ... proper to ideology. (43-44)

The existence of this residue in the psyche has consequences for the status of ideology in narration. If it is correct to say that narration reconciles alienation by privileging the focal or end point of narration as an object of desire, then the traumatic side effect of a submission to ideology would to a certain degree be the exact opposite of the narrative effect. The trauma of the submission to ideology is analogous to the trauma that the "armored" fascist man suffers in the "feminine" experience of a mass rally. For the collective submission to political authority can also be a source of pleasure, as Klaus Theweleit has shown. At the same time, however, the decentering effect of pleasure is counterbalanced by an agonistic armoring against an Other (for example, "the Jew"). The paradox of an experience that is both decentering and delimiting is, then, less a matter of balance than a condition of the possibility of organizing enjoyment on the basis of delimitations; the decentering pleasure of a submission to ideology is complemented by aggressively drawn boundaries from ideological Others. Any balance between decentering and delimiting experiences would remain mechanical, as long as each would maintain its separate identity. In narration that projects an image of fulfillment into the future and turns it into an object of desire, precisely the separation of these experiences is suspended. Here, the opposites are reconciled in an imaginary scene. Submission to ideology merges, for instance, with submission to a narrative hero in which another is experienced as self. Exactly for that reason narration—as permanent staging of pseudo-reconciliations of alienation and symbiosis, separation and harmony—allows the I to experience itself as pseudo-unity. Fictitious narrative culture is one of several modes of integrating Freud's memory trace "A" into the symbolic order. Paradoxically, the symbolic representation of the memory trace serves as a mirror in which the I secures its unity. It does this by focusing its attention on the narrative text, thus raising it to a center that transcends all difference. In the experience of narration, the material reality of difference can be imagined as having lost its force to resist. In my view, this is the ultimate stumbling block of enlightened narratologies chasing dreams of normative mediations and consensual harmonies.

Works Cited

Baader, Franz von. *Vom Sinn der Gesellschaft: Schriften zur Social-Philosophie.* Köln: Hegner, 1966.

Bährens, Christoph Friedrich. *Ueber den Werth der Empfindsamkeit besonderns in Rücksicht auf die Romane: Nebst einer Nachschrift über den sittlichen Werth der Empfindsamkeit von Johann August Eberhard.* Halle: Gebauer,1786.

Barnes, Thomas. "On the Influence of the Imagination and the Passions upon the Understanding." *Twenty Essays on Literary and Philosophical Subjects.* Dublin: White, 1791.

Bernstein, J.M. "Self-knowledge as Praxis: Narrative and Narration in Psychoanalysis." *Narrative in Culture: The Uses of Storytelling in the Sciences, Philosophy, and Literature.* Ed. Christopher Nash. London: Routledge, 1990.

Brooks, Peter. *Reading for the Plot: Design and Intention in Narrative.* New York: Vintage, 1985.

Foucault, Michel. *Discipline and Punish: The Birth of the Prison.* Trans. Alan Sheridan. New York: Vintage, 1979.

Hazlitt, William. *An Essay on the Principles of Human Action* [1805]. Introd. John R. Nabholtz. Rpt. Gainesville, FL: Scholars' Facsimile, 1969.

Johnson, Samuel. *The Rambler.* 4 vols. London: Suttaby, 1809.

Lacan, Jacques. "Desire and the Interpretation of Desire in Hamlet." Trans. James Hulpert. *Literature and Psychoanalysis: The Question of Reading: Otherwise.* Ed. Shoshana Felman. Baltimore: Johns Hopkins UP, 1983.

More, Thomas. *Utopia.* Trans. and introd. Paul Turner. London: Penguin, 1965.

Pocock, J. G. A. *The Machiavellian Moment: Florentine Political Thought and the Atlantic Republican Tradition.* Princeton: Princeton UP, 1975.

Rousseau, Jean-Jacques. *Emile.* Trans. Barbara Foxley. London: Dent, 1974.

Schabert, Tilo. *Natur und Revolution: Untersuchungen zum politischen Denken im Frankreich des 18. Jahrhunderts.* Munich: List, 1969.

Schiller, Friedrich. *Die Schaubühne als moralische Anstalt betrachtet. Sämtliche Werke.* Vol. 5: *Erzählungen, Theoretische Schriften.* Ed. Gerhard Fricke and Herbert G. Göpfert. München: Hanser, 1984. 818-31.

Twenty Essays on Literary and Philosophical Subjects. Dublin: White, 1791.

Zizek, Slavoj. *The Sublime Object of Ideology.* London: Verso, 1989.

Of Beautiful and Dismembered Bodies:
Art as Social Discipline in Schiller's
On the Aesthetic Education of Man[1]

Andreas Gailus

THIS ESSAY IS ABOUT the grim images in a text concerned with a theory of beauty. In his letters *On the Aesthetic Education of Man (Über die Ästhetische Erziehung des Menschen)* Schiller draws on contrasting images of the mutilated and beautiful body to develop his argument about the social function of art under modern conditions. Whereas the *dismembered body* is used to represent the psychic and political fragmentation caused by modernity, the *beautiful body* stands as a symbol for a harmonious unity beyond fragmentation. This bodily image of harmony comprises the aesthetic, anthropological, and political ideal of the *Letters*. Essentially, Schiller argues that an art conceived of as organic, as a beautiful body, yields in the beholder a psychic harmony which in turn furnishes the subjective basis for an ideal society in which individual desire harmonizes with general laws. Hence the utopian, conciliatory aura that Schiller's *Letters* attribute to art. Aesthetic experience anticipates a reconciled modernity in which fragmentation and alienation will be overcome.

In what follows, however, I will argue that the meaning of the beautiful and dismembered body can be grasped only with reference to a *third* kind of imagery whose combative and belligerent character indicates the *aggressive* components in Schiller's concept of beauty. Taking the metaphors of war and combat as my guide in analyzing the conceptual framework of Schiller's aesthetics, I will show that aesthetic contemplation implies an element of mastery over both the object and the beholder's desire for this object. I argue that an art conceived of as organic, as a body, enforces the beholder's rational control over his senses by making this control itself a source of pleasure.

I. Beautiful Bodies, Dismembered Bodies

Schiller's letters *On the Aesthetic Education of Man* open with a scene of violence. Toward the end of Letter 1 Schiller writes:

> Like the analytical chemist, the philosopher can only discover how things are combined by analysing them, only lay bare the workings of spontaneous Nature by subjecting them to the torment of his own techniques (*durch die Marter der Kunst*). In order to lay hold of the fleetin phenomenon, he must first bind it in the fetters of rule, tear its beautiful body to pieces by reducing it to concepts (*ihren schönen Körper in Begriffe zerfleischen*), and preserve its living spirit in a sorry skeleton of words. Is it any wonder if natural feeling cannot find itself again in such an image, or that in the account of the analytical thinker truth should appear as paradox?[2]

Schiller's concern in this passage is with the form of Kantian rational analysis. As the context makes clear, Schiller does not question the results of Kant's philosophy. Indeed, he sees his own project in the *Letters* as building upon the notions of human freedom and morality which Kant had developed in the *Critique of Practical Reason*. On a rhetorical level, however, the image of a body torn apart by rational analysis pushes this agreement in content to the background. In Schiller's account, philosophical thinking is problematic because it can grasp its object only through a procedure that decomposes the unity of this object. Through the imagery of bodily mutilation analytical distinction is associated with the bloodstained activities of bestial laceration (*zerfleischen*) and physical torture (*Marter der Kunst*). Theoretical formalization, that most modern of human achievements, thus appears wedded to pre-modern, even archaic forms of violence. As a result of this rhetorical overcoding, the passage carries the air of an existential threat: conceptualizing human freedom becomes a matter of life and death.

To be sure, we are dealing here with *metaphors* of bodily mutilation, but from whence does a metaphor derive its rhetorical power if not from the appeal to its literal, non-figurative meaning? Before we can read the metaphor as a metaphor, we must first fall prey to its semantic potential. The emotionally charged image of the dismembered body imparts to this passage its existential, frightening tone. Uneasily balanced between argument (the truth of Kant's practical ideas) and imagery (man's dismemberment), the readers of Schiller find themselves in a predicament: They are asked to adopt for their own lives the findings of a moral theory whose mode of argument seems to imply a threat to their physical being.

The image of the dismembered body reemerges in Letter 6. This time Schiller enlarges the focus of his analysis: from a structural account of rational analysis we move to a historical account of cultural development where "progress" is measured in terms of increasing rationalization. The letter is well known for providing one of the first accounts of the historical process we have come to call modernization. Schiller describes the gulf between theoretical knowledge and everyday experience which is furnished by an increasingly formalized scientific language (6/39); division of labor in the economic, legal, and scientific spheres of society (6/41f.); the shift from stratificational differentiation to functional differentiation of society, accompanied by the emergence of a bureaucratic apparatus as the site of and means for the state's monopolization of political power (6/35f.); and, ultimately, the declining importance of religion and myth as commonly shared symbolic meta-discourses (6/33f.).[3] Since throughout the letter Schiller figures his account of historical progress in images of the *dismemberment* of social and individual *organisms*, modernization is linked to the wounding of bodies. On the societal level, progress entails the destruction of the "polypoid nature of the Greek States" (6/35*) in favor of a merely mechanical apparatus which runs with the efficiency of "clock-work" (6/33, 35). On the individual level, human beings, reduced to their functioning within the apparatus, are said to be mere "wheels" (6/35). Schiller depicts this "mechanization" of the individual with a plethora of sanguinary images whether discussing the infliction of a "wound" (6/33), man's "fragmentation" ("Zerstückelung," 6/39), or his "mutilated nature" (6/43). The figurative logic underlying Schiller's analysis of modernity is the same as in Letter 1: Culture dismembers entities understood as natural, organic wholes. However, despite the somber picture Schiller paints of modernization, he is unambiguous about its necessity. Progress is a bloody, but unavoidable thing.

I find Schiller's use of metaphors problematic. While the annihilation of entire cultures inside and outside the West leaves no doubt as to the tremendous physical destruction that has accompanied modernization, Schiller uses his cruel imagery only to highlight *mental* trammels. In doing so, he blurs the distinction between physical violence and psychic constraints while at the same time investing the political problematic with an organicist imagery. We tend to overlook this conflation of the physical with the psychic, translating almost automatically the one into the other, because we are trained in this usage of organic metaphors through a tradition that originated precisely with Schiller's *Letters*.[4] Admittedly, such a "translation" seems particularly plausible with regard to Kant's *Critique of Practical Reason*. There the subject becomes a moral being in the moment it sacrifices its affective attachment to empirical objects and human beings and makes the moral law the single determinant for its behavior. As it enters into morality, the Kantian subject is split between a dominating ethical self capable of conforming to the law, and a repressed "pathological" (Kant) self that is attracted to objects or people for the sake of the pleasure they provide. The prerequisite for moral conduct, then, is the immolation of "self-love or one's own happiness" (21).[5]

Should we then simply translate the *image* of the dismembered body into some other *concept* such as "alienation" or "ego dissolution"? To do so overlooks, I think, the rhetorical power of these figures for Schiller's theory. For one thing, the imagery of fragmentation and mutilation bestows on Schiller's cultural diagnosis an urgency and pathos that is clearly out of place: Regardless of how pressing the contemporary crisis, it is *not* a matter of life and death. Furthermore, the ugliness of the contemporary dismembered body prepares the rhetorical ground for the cathartic effect of the harmonious aesthetic body. Whatever the conceptual implications of Schiller's aesthetic ideal, I think it is safe to say that its rhetorical impact offers the reader a relief of sorts. After the wounding and tearing apart of subjects caught in the machinery of modernity, Schiller's aesthetic program—centered around art's function of displaying images of unified and organic bodies— acquires almost redemptive traits. This emphasis on *living wholeness* is evident whenever Schiller speaks of the nature of the beautiful object. Letter 15: "The beautiful is to be neither mere life, nor mere form, but living *Gestalt*, i.e., Beauty" (15/107*). This is more than a matter of simple, gratifying images disguising an otherwise ugly reality. In the contemplation of the beautiful object, the beholder experiences a narcissistic identification with it. Art's sensual fullness allows the subject to find a reflection of himself in an imaginary whole that provides him with the sense of completion and wholeness.[6] Schiller himself points to precisely this mirror-function of beautiful art: "He is to set up a world over against himself because he is Person, and he is to be Person because a world stands over against him" (14/95). Thus, at least in aesthetic contemplation, human beings can *imagine* themselves to be what modern society no longer allows them to *be*: whole, undivided subjects.

II. Combative Art

All this seems to suggest that we read the *Letters* in terms of compensation, and it is precisely this reading that has produced the scorn of many modern critics. Since Odo Marquard's seminal 1962 essay on

Kant, Schiller has been repeatedly criticized for cementing the social problems of modernity by providing a surrogate realm of aesthetic play and pleasure.[7] Yet for all of its strength, this reading is insufficient. Whether read in a critical or an affirmative light, this "compensation thesis" leaves unquestioned the core of Schiller's aesthetic theory, the ideal of an harmonious self and its representation in the image of an organic, whole body. It is not this ideal per se, but its *confinement* within the aesthetic realm that is the stumbling-block for most leftist criticism of Schiller. For my part, I would like to question the compensation thesis by interrogating the notion of harmonious aesthetic play on which it is based. Again I direct my reading through a scene of violence: Schiller on the artist. Letter 9:

> The artist is indeed the son of his age; but woe to him if he is at the same time its ward or, worse still, its minion! Let some beneficent deity snatch the suckling betimes from his mother's breast, nourish him with the milk of a better age, and suffer him to come to maturity under a distant Grecian sky. Then, when he has become a man, let him return a stranger, to his own century; not, however, to gladden it by his appearance, but rather, terrible like Agamemnon's son, to cleanse and to purify it. His matter he will, indeed, take from the present; but his form he will borrow from a nobler time, nay, from beyond time altogether, from the absolute, unchanging, unity of his being. Here, from the pure aether of his genius, the living source of beauty flows down, untainted by the corruption of the generations [Verderbnis der Geschlechter] and ages wallowing in the dark eddies below.... Humanity has lost its dignity; but Art has rescued and preserved it in significant stone. Truth lives on in the illusion of Art, and it is from this copy, or after-image, that the original image will once again be restored. Just as the nobility of Art *survived* the nobility of Nature, so now Art goes before her, a voice rousing from slumber and preparing the shape of things to come. Even before Truth's triumphant light can penetrate the recesses of the human heart, the poet's imagination will intercept its rays, and the peaks of humanity will be radiant while the dews of night still linger in the valley. (9/55f.*)

Agamemnon's son, Orestes, killed his mother Clytemnestra on his return from exile. Schiller reinscribes this story as a historical-philosophical allegory for modern art. Orestes' killing of the mother symbolizes now the modern artist's transformation of contemporary matter through Greek form. Before the artist can create beautiful art, his symbiotic and pleasurable relationship with the mother must be interrupted violently: The desire for the mother's breasts must be replaced by the desire for humanism. I shall return to this passage in detail toward the end of my essay. For now it suffices to note that the personality of the artist is the result of a socialization which is not at all harmonious. The various stages through which the artist must pass include the rejection of the first sexual object (the mother's breast), the reorganization of his relationship to time, and a matricide conceived of as being coterminous with the production of beautiful aesthetic art. Matricidal art, uncontaminated by the defilement of matters contemporary and sexual ("Verderbnis der Geschlechter"), will then prepare the ground for a thoroughly enlightened and rational social order to come.

Art as purification. Passages such as "truth lives on in the illusion of Art" have been the cherished sites for any utopian reading of Schiller.[8] But how utopian is an order that is based on matricide? To put it less metaphorically, what are we to think of a utopian totality whose genesis is figured as a series of murders? If someone must die—even metaphorically—for aesthetic truth to emerge, this truth cannot be as all-inclusive and reconciliatory as the notion of utopia would suggest. The figurative violence of the passage quoted above is in keeping with most of the essay: Time and again Schiller couches the act of aesthetic "purification" in military terms. Art itself is likened to Achilles who "with divine weapons, and through his victorious strength decides the great issue" (8/49); art is capable of "dominating a spirited and active foe" (13/91*) and "it play(s) the war against the Matter into the very territory of Matter itself, so that he may be spared having to fight this dread foe on the sacred soil of Freedom" (23/169).

How playful, then, is Schiller's aesthetic play? The militant metaphors give us our first inkling of the aggressive element in the production and reception of beautiful idealistic art. Yet unlike the scenes of bodily mutilation, this second example of violent imagery is coded positively, as an act of liberation. In an astute comparative analysis of Kant's and Schiller's prose, Herman Meyer has shown how Schiller's use of martial images imparts a *heroic pathos* to what in Kant was a more sober plea for enlightenment (345-8). In Schiller, truth, even in its aesthetic form, is portrayed as the result of a sublime, manly struggle. Perhaps it is this elevated tone that has prevented most Schiller scholars from noticing the aggressiveness inherent in aesthetic play. Yet once we bring this aggressive character to light, it becomes possible to assess the extent to which Schiller's theory of "aesthetic purification" provides a theory of socialization.

Schiller makes no bones about the identity of the "enemy" which art must overcome through aesthetic education: this enemy is human sensuality insofar as it does not conform to moral demands. Let us read the passage from Letter 23 in context:

> It is here, then, in the indifferent sphere of physical life, that man must make a start upon his moral life.... The law of the will he must apply even to his inclinations; he must, if you will permit me the expression, play the war against Matter into the very territory of Matter itself, so that he may be spared having to fight this dread foe on the sacred foil of Freedom. He must learn to desire

more nobly, so that he may not need to *will sublimely*. This is brought about by means of aesthetic education. (23/169)

Schiller's understanding of art's educational function rests clearly on Kant's sharp opposition between sensuality and morality. Subjective and contingent, sensuality unaffected by art is a perilous bedfellow for morality, because as long as the subject's behavior is determined by "raw" feelings, it follows only the imperative of "self-love" (9/89). Even where such a behavior is moral in content, as in pity, it is so only by chance (*ibid.*; also 4/17). Because of its contingent character, uneducated sensuality cannot coexist with the perfect "moral State" which Schiller defines as a social whole in which individual actions *necessarily* conform to general laws.

> The setting up of the moral State involves being able to count on the moral law as an effective force, and free will is thereby drawn into the realm of cause and effect, where everything follows from everything else in a chain of strict necessity. But we know that the modes of determination of the human will must always remain contingent, and that it is only in Absolute Being that physical necessity coincides with moral necessity. (4/17)

Thus it seems that the desultory and flighty character of human nature is structurally at odds with the requirements of a state predicated on the perfect calculability of the behavior of its citizens. Facing a similar problem, Kant adopted a tone of skepticism. In his writings on the philosophy of history, he repeatedly cautioned against a too optimistic belief in progress, "for from such crooked wood as man is made of, nothing perfectly straight can be built" (*Idea* 17-18). For Kant, morality is the rod with which people dominate their recalcitrant sensuality; Schiller, however, proposes to transform man *from within* so that domination will become superfluous: "If, therefore, we are to be able to count on man's moral behavior with as much certainty as we do on *natural effects*, it will itself have to be nature, and he will have to be led by his very impulses [Triebe] to the kind of conduct which is bound to proceed from a moral character" (4/17). And that is exactly the goal of idealistic art.

III. The Theory of Reconciliation

This passage from Letter 4 outlines the *project* of aesthetic socialization. Aesthetic education reorganizes man's affective structure in the interest of a political program that grants freedom to individuals only to the extent that this freedom implements the state's control over society. However, the passage's merely prescriptive character begs the question of *how* art performs its task. What exactly is the relationship between the aesthetic *form* of idealistic art and its socializing *function*? Furthermore, how is it possible for Schiller to impart to this rather repressive project the redemptive glimmer of "reconciliation" and "utopia"? For all their suggestiveness, the metaphors of beautiful and dismembered bodies in and of themselves cannot yield an answer to these questions. In order to answer them, we have to move to the *conceptual* framework of the *Letters*. I shall first sketch the anthropological and historical assumptions on which Schiller bases his claim for art's reconciliatory power, and then analyze how the symbol for reconciliation—the image of the beautiful body—both disguises and carries out the socializing function of Schillerian art.

Schiller's anthropology rests on the assumption that human beings are internally split.[9] The human psyche is divided into a sensual self and a rational self, each asserting itself through its respective drive. The sensuous drive seeks immediate gratification, and impels the subject towards a desired object. As its satisfaction depends on the presence of empirically-given phenomena, sensuality demands temporal change and sensory richness. While the sensuous drive strives for emotional *intensity*, the formal, that is, rational, drive seeks personal *stability*. It achieves this goal by "divesting external objects of their libidinal attraction, abstracting them from their concrete qualities, and turning them into formal entities" (von Mücke 198). In other words, the formal drive transforms concrete phenomena into objects of knowledge. In order to do so, it strips them of their transitory qualities, reduces them to instances of a rule, and fixes them in atemporal laws. According to Schiller, the formal drive's capacity to overcome, through abstraction, the sensuous drive's craving for affective intensity is also the source of human self-identity. Personal identity results, as a kind of mirror-effect, from the stable rational structure which abstraction superimposes on the world.

Using this anthropological dualism as his base, Schiller unfolds his argument concerning the necessity of art under modern conditions. The subject, split into antagonistic drives, is caught in a predicament: no matter which drive he follows, he cannot avoid subduing a part of himself. If he gives himself over to the sensuous drive, the libidinal attraction of the object threatens to overpower him, thus violating his rational demand for discretion and self-identity. On the other hand, if the subject relates to the world predominantly through the formal drive, he suffers from emotional anemia, for he achieves rational control over the world only at the expense of sensual intensity. Schiller amplifies this argument by giving it an historical dimension, claiming that in the modern period, more so than at any other point in history, people are required to behave in a one-sidedly rational manner. Schiller does not really spell out this thesis, but the little he says suggests that the increasingly rational demands on the subject are necessitated by the abstract nature of the bureaucratic state and moral law. Both frustrate the demands of the sensuous drive in that their rational structure eludes representation in a phenomenological object. The functional logic of the bureaucratic state is too complex and abstract to be represented in persons; similarly, Kantian ethics require that the subject sever all emotional bonds to phenomenal objects and make an invisible Law the single determining ground for his behavior. Consequently, for the modern individual to follow the rules prescribed by state and moral law is to dispense with his longings for sensuality and phenomenal concreteness. A modernity based exclusively on these abstract institutions is deficient in that it exacts from its citizens self-mastery and the repression of their sensuality.

Art is called upon to overcome this dilemma. Schiller argues that full individual freedom can be reconciled with the moral and rational demands of modernity only in and through art. Combining phenomenal concreteness with rational structure, matter with form, the artwork simultaneously satisfies the desires of the sensuous and formal drives. Liberated from the need to subdue one of its drives, the subject enjoys his full potential as a human being in the act of aesthetic contemplation. Schiller defines the mode of this aesthetic experience as *free play*. Psychologically, "play" designates the balanced interchange of rationality and sensuality in the act of aesthetic contemplation. Epistemologically, it describes the absence of coercion in the relationship between a perceiving subject and an aesthetic object. Only a relationship to the object characterized by play allows human beings to give full reign to their human potential. Hence Schiller's famous claim: "man only plays when he is in the fullest sense of the word a human being, and *he is only fully a human being when he plays*" (15/107). Art is reconciliation, the junction of the up-to-now painfully split, utopia.

Significantly, this is both an anthropological and a political utopia. The balance of the aesthetic object, the result of a supposedly even interplay of the parts with the whole, creates the conditions not only for the subject's unconstrained exercise of his psychic faculties; it also stands as a symbol for the ideal society in which the freedom of individuals ("the parts") harmonizes with general laws ("the whole"). Thanks to this double function, the artwork represents simultaneously the ideal human being *and* the ideal State. Art, understood as *living "Gestalt,"* is the symbolic expression of these ideals.

IV. The Coercive Structure of Art

So much for the reconciliation script. Let us summarize the three characteristics on which Schiller bases his claim for art's reconciliatory, utopian, quality: first, the *beholder's psychic faculties* are equally engaged in the contemplation of the artwork; second, the *artwork's structure* represents an order in which the whole does not exercise any coercion on the individual parts; third, the *relationship between beholder and aesthetic object* is free from elements of domination. Nevertheless, as we have seen from the combative imagery of the *Letters*, there is an aggressive element at work in Schiller's concept of beauty. Now I will show that the presence of aggression is not purely metaphorical in Schiller's aesthetics. The metaphors of war bespeak the structure of domination that pervades Schiller's very conceptual framework.

As to the harmony of aesthetic contemplation, the claim that art provokes an incessant movement *between* two psychic faculties is inconsistent with Schiller's assertion that, in the contemplation of the beautiful object, rationality and sensuality merge into a third state which bears not the slightest trace of its genealogy:

> In the second place, it was said, beauty *unites* [*verbindet*] these two opposed conditions and thus destroys [hebt auf] the opposition. Since, however, both conditions remain everlastingly opposed to each other, there is no other way of uniting them except by destroying them. Our second task, therefore, is to make this union complete; and to do it with such unmitigated thoroughness that both these conditions totally disappear in a third state without any trace of division behind in the new whole that has been made; otherwise we shall only succeed in isolating, but never in uniting them [sonst vereinzeln wir, aber vereinigen nicht]. (18/123*)

Art does not simply provide pleasure because it stimulates man's rationality and sensuality, but rather because it sublates (in a Hegelian sense) both faculties into something else. What is at stake in aesthetic contemplation, then, is not the open play between equal psychic forces, but the end of this play. Schiller, however, does not aspire to end this play by mere exclusion of one of the participants; his strategy is more refined and, as he aptly asserts in *On Grace and Dignity*, ultimately more successful than an openly repressive one: "The enemy who is merely *thrown down* can rise up again, but the *reconciled* enemy is truly overcome" (*Werke* 465). The combative metaphors indicate that the synthesis of psychic faculties in the "third state" is in truth characterized by the dominance of *one* faculty. This hierarchical aspect of aesthetic contemplation is clearly incompatible with Schiller's claim that art provokes in the beholder's psyche an *even* play between sensuality and rationality. Moreover, the Schillerian play lacks also another characteristic that is absolutely central to the notion of play: contingency. The synthesis of psychic forces in the "third state" is not just uneven, it is also completely determined:

> [Aesthetic education] has as its aim the development of the whole complex of our sensual and spiritual powers in the greatest possible harmony. Because, however, misled by false notions of taste and confirmed still further in this error by false reasoning, people are inclined to include in the notion of the aesthetic the notion of the arbitrary [des Willkürlichen] too, I add here the superfluous comment (despite the fact that these *Letters of Aesthetic Education* are concerned with virtually nothing else but the refutation of that very error) that our psyche in the aesthetic state does indeed act freely, is in the highest degree free from all compulsion, but in no wise free from laws; and that this aesthetic freedom is distinguishable from logical necessity in thinking, or moral necessity in willing, only by the fact that the laws according to which the psyche then behaves *do not become apparent as such,* and since they encounter no resistance, never appear as a constraint. (20/143)

As with the English "arbitrary," "willkürlich" has a moral and a logical meaning. In both cases "willkürlich" signifies that something (or someone) is not entirely determined by rules, and that chance (or choice) is possible. Schiller's banishment of contingency from aesthetic play contradicts not only the very notion of play; it also reveals the restrictive nature of aesthetic freedom. Far from evoking an equal play between rationality and sensuality in the beholder, Schiller's art engenders a state of mind in which feelings are well-channeled, and are ordered according to unspoken rules. Consequently, once the subject has entered the aesthetic state, objects "please him not because they meet a need [Bedürfnis] but because they satisfy a law which speaks, although softly as yet, within his breast" (27/211).

Let us turn now to the object-side of aesthetic harmony, and to the claim that in the beautiful artwork the individual parts freely merge into an harmonious whole:

> When the artisan lays hand upon the formless mass in order to shape it to his ends, he has no scruple in doing it violence; for the natural material he is working merits no respect for itself, and his concern is not with the whole for the sake of the parts, but with the parts for the sake of the whole. When the artist lays hands upon the same mass, he has *just as little scruple in doing it violence; but he avoids showing it.* For the material he is handling he has not a whit more respect than has the artisan; but *the eye* which would seek to protect the freedom of the material he will *endeavour to deceive* by a show of yielding to the latter. (4/19; my emphasis)

Once again Schiller doesn't mince words. The aesthetic relationship between parts and whole is far less "democratic" than the utopian reading of "beauty as a symbol of freedom" would imply. In beautiful art, the multiplicity of phenomena (matter) must submit to the unity of

a form. However, unlike scientific or moral laws which require a relationship of identity between the general (the rule) and the particular
(the single case), aesthetic unity is built on the "harmonious" interlock-
ing of differences. Since it weaves matter with form, aesthetic unity is
not predicated on the abstraction from singular phenomena, but
instead materializes itself in and through them. Thus it *appears* that in
the artwork the parts are as important as the whole, for there would be
no whole without the parts, no *Gestalt* without matter. In truth, however, this equilibrium is only apparent. The "freedom of the matter"
which the beholder enjoys is the illusory result of a carefully covered up
arrangement that has little to do with "reconciliation." Schiller makes
it unmistakably clear that the goal of aesthetic synthesis is to *destroy* the
autonomy of the parts by dissolving the matter into the form: "Here,
then, resides the true artistic secret of the master in any art: *that he can
wipe out the matter through the form* [*daß er den Stoff durch die Form ver-
tilgt*]" (22/155ff.).
   "To wipe out the matter through the form." Aesthetic rationality,
as far as its relationship to phenomena is concerned, is no less high-
handed than scientific rationality. It is, *pace* Adorno and Horkheimer,
instrumental rationality. Admittedly, my reference to instrumental
rationality may appear unjustified given that the *end* to which artistic
rationality is put—namely the beholder's pleasure in aesthetic illusion—
seems entirely removed from the prosaic world of instrumentality. But
this, too, is just an illusion.

V. Art and Vision

   So far we have seen that the laws governing both reception and production of the aesthetic object work to insure the dominance of the
rational over the non-rational. In the artwork, form outweighs matter;
in the beholder's psyche, rational control holds at bay emotional
intensity. Thus, as far as the subjective and objective sides of Schiller's
concept of beauty are concerned, Schiller's claim that art realizes an
order beyond coercion is refuted. What remains to be seen, however, is
how these two sides relate to each other in the act of aesthetic contemplation.   Through which mechanisms does a formally unified
artwork enhance the beholder's rational control over his sensuality?
From the passages concerning the structure of aesthetic production and
reception we can infer that art's capability to strengthen the subject's
rationality is dependent upon the *imperceptibility of laws* in aesthetic
contemplation. The question, then, is how "laws that do not become
apparent as such" (20/143) can yield in the beholder a thoroughly rule-
governed state of mind?

I believe this question can be answered fully only with reference to the *specular* character that Schiller ascribes to the act of aesthetic contemplation. Throughout the *Letters* Schiller discusses aesthetic contemplation in terms of *vision*. The reason for his preoccupation becomes evident as soon as we take into account the role of vision in Schiller's theory of identity-formation. In Letter 25 Schiller describes the act of visualization that characterizes the "aesthetic stage" as a formative moment in "the development of mankind as a whole, or of the whole development of a single individual" (25/183). Essentially, Schiller argues that to see an object is to represent it to oneself.[10] Seeing is a rational activity that subsumes a chaotic mass of sensual data under the principle of formal unification. Through the act of visual objectification the subject overcomes his dependence on external and internal stimuli and emerges as a person who is in control of his drives. Schiller describes this process in terms of the subject's self-reflective appropriation of the world: "contemplation [Betrachtung] removes its object to a distance, and makes it into a true and inalienable possession by putting it beyond the reach of passion" (25/183). Thus the beholder overcomes the lure of the object by attributing it to himself. What he sees in the object is only the form that he gives to it, which amounts to saying: He reflects himself in the object's form:

> From being a slave of nature, which he remains as long as he merely feels it, man becomes its lawgiver [Gesetzgeber] from the moment he thinks it. That which hitherto merely dominated him as *force*, now stands before his eyes as *object*. *Whatsoever is object for him has no power over him; for in order to be object at all, it must be subjected to the power that is his* [*Was ihm Objekt ist, hat keine Gewalt über ihn, denn um Objekt zu sein, muß es die seinige erfahren*]. To the extent that he imparts form to matter, and for precisely as long as he imparts it, he is immune to its effects; for spirit cannot be injured by anything except that which robs it of its freedom, and man gives evidence of his freedom precisely by giving form to that which is formless. (25/185; my emphasis)

In Schiller, the individual emerges as a self-identical person through an act of identification with his rational, ideal self. Kept at bay by an objectifying gaze, the object becomes a mirror-reflection of the subject's power to dominate those forces that could potentially threaten his identity as a *rational* person. Consequently, the subject represents himself in the object's *form* not as a concrete individual being but, rather, as a universalized subject, that is, as a *lawmaker*. This is why Schiller maintains that the aesthetic stage is a necessary moment in "all knowledge which comes to us through the senses" (25/183). In divesting the object of its sensual attraction, the act of self-reflective contemplation creates the condition for the further instrumentalization of the object in either scientific knowledge or instrumental action.

It is the function of the apparently *organic* form of the artwork to counteract the subject's tendency towards further instrumentalization of the object and to arrest the moment of specularity that characterizes the aesthetic stage. In aesthetic contemplation the subject as lawmaker confronts an object whose form resists further abstraction. According to Kant, an organic whole is distinguished from a mechanical whole in two respects: it is an end-in-itself (autonomy), and in it, the parts and the whole are interlocked in such a way that they are "the mutual causes and effects of their form."[11] For this to be possible, the object's unity must not be reducible to a single principle of unification, in which case this principle would be the cause of the whole without being itself effected by the parts. In other words: A form is organic if its structure cannot be *represented in a law*. Without a doubt this definition applies to the "living *Gestalt*" of Schillerian art in which all traces that govern the laws of production are carefully blurred. Now the ideological core of Schiller's theory is that the organicity-effect of the beautiful artwork both propels and obscures the disciplining function of Schillerian art.

VI. Beauty and Discipline

The object of discipline is beautiful. The perfectly unified, yet apparently highly differentiated artwork elicits in the beholder a state of mind that is both pleasant and rule-governed. While the apparent concreteness of the aesthetic image pleases the eye, its formal closure insures that it is perceived as an object removed from the beholder and therefore under his control. Moreover, since the form of the artwork is not just perfectly closed, but also beautiful, it provides the beholder with the pleasure of visual control and mastery while also remaining an object of desire. The disciplining effect of this double aesthetic pleasure—the pleasure of mastery and the pleasure of sexual stimulation—is dependent upon the *organic* form of the artwork. For while the artwork, thanks to its organicity-effect, can be experienced as an erotically attractive *body*, the aesthetic arrangement foregrounds this organism's *formal* character, thus allowing the beholder to contemplate in the beautiful artwork his rational power to overcome erotically attractive objects.

Let us see how the beautiful object provokes in the beholder's psyche this mixture of control and desire. The beautiful image is closed off from the spectator through a double arrangement. The first concerns the autonomous structure of the represented object; the second refers to the autonomy of aesthetic representation. In order for the beholder to reflect upon the object character of art, it is first necessary for the artwork to present itself to the eye as a formal unity. Hence

Schiller's imperative that the artist must "wipe out the matter through the form." The intended effect of this arrangement—that is, the apparent wholeness and perfection of the aesthetic object—is dependent upon the artist's blurring of all traces of the artwork's production. Thus, Schiller's second imperative: the aesthetic laws of production must be invisible.

Furthermore, the artwork's formal immaculateness removes it from both reality and the beholder. Faced with a perfectly flawless image, the recipient cannot avoid being aware of its ideal, illusionary character. Consequently, his attraction to the aesthetic image is kept at bay by his recognition of its purely aesthetic existence. Art's idealized form prompts the beholder to distance himself from the attractive qualities of the represented object by viewing it merely as a representation. This is the distancing effect derived from the autonomy of aesthetic representation.

The double illusionary character of Schillerian art—illusion as deception and as mere appearance—accounts for art's unique capacity to produce pliant subjects. Since the aesthetic image is both unattainable and beautiful, it incites the beholder's passions while simultaneously reinforcing his control over these passions. The beauty of the image offers the beholder a perceptual lure that stimulates his desire; yet the self-sufficient (illusion as deception) and representational (illusion as appearance) nature of the aesthetic image prompts him to divest the object of its erotic attraction and to treat it as an object of contemplation. The relationship between the beholder's attraction to and distancing of the aesthetic object is not harmonious, but rather combative, for the beholder's rational power of contemplation always dominates the object's erotic attraction. Ultimately, aesthetic education lets the beholder experience his power to withstand his desire and to yield to the erotic attraction of objects. In doing so, aesthetic education brings two different kinds of love into a combative relationship with each other. It entices the beholder's love for the beautiful object in order to increase his love for his ideal, rational self. The narcissistic structure of aesthetic experience, then, participates in the formation of a self that can feel itself only through the aggression that it exercises against that which threatens its autonomy as a rational self.

Through this coupling of mastery and pleasure, art can enlarge the scope of morality in at least two significant ways: first, art teaches the subject how to attach himself to "morally correct" objects. Since whatever passes into the realm of aesthetic representation must submit to the laws of formal unification and apparent autonomy, the perceiving subject learns to focus his desire on harmonious and "organic" objects. The beholder of idealistic art internalizes perceptual norms that induce him to shun objects that might arouse in him transgressive or otherwise uncontrollable feelings. Second, except for these extreme transgressive feelings, the aesthetic subject need not fear that his sensuality for art has taught him a contemplative form of perception that allows him to keep even erotic objects at bay. Moreover, whereas Kantian moral law, due to its abstract and prohibitive character, eludes representation in a phenomenal object, Schiller's aesthetic law turns the representation of phenomena into a source of morality. The sense of rational control that the beholder derives from the contemplation of the aesthetic *Gestalt* is all the stronger in that it shows its power over an object whose erotic qualities appear to threaten rationality itself.

Thus the subject that emerges as a free being through the contemplation of art is free precisely to the extent that he is "beyond the reach of passion" (25/183). Such a disciplined and educated subject can "retain his power of choice and yet, at the same time, be a reliable link in the chain of causality" (4/17); he can universalize his behavior without being disturbed by egoistic drives. Schillerian freedom, then, is as restrictive as Schillerian play is aggressive. Both freedom and play have their socializing interface in the "living *Gestalt*" of the idealistic artwork. Now when we turn to the most celebrated passage of the *Letters*, we should be able to see in the modulation between repulsion and attraction which is inherent to aesthetic contemplation, the workings of a socializing technique that brings the senses into play only in order to keep them once and for all under seal.

> It is not Grace, nor is it yet Dignity, which speaks to us from the superb countenance of *Juno Ludovisi*; it is neither the one nor is it the other because it is both at once. While the woman-like god demands our veneration, the god-like woman kindles our love; but even as we abandon ourselves in ecstasy to her heavenly grace, her celestial self-sufficiency makes us recoil in terror. The whole figure reposes and dwells in itself, a creation completely self-contained, and, as if existing beyond space, neither yielding nor resisting; here is no force to contend with force, no frailty where temporality might break in. Irresistibly moved and drawn by those former qualities, kept at a distance by these latter, we find ourselves at one and the same time in a state of utter repose and supreme agitation, and there results that wondrous stirring of the heart for which mind has no concept nor speech any name. (15/109).

VII. Female Images

Some final remarks about gender. In two crucial passages of the *Letters*, Schiller's description of beautiful art revolves around female figures. The Orestes story links the production and reception of beautiful art to the killing of the mother; the passage on Juno Ludovisi shows a goddess as the ideal subject for aesthetic contemplation. The two images relate the scope of aesthetic representation—its threshold and its center—to two contrasting female figures. The mother represents the femininity against which aesthetic creation has to be defined; for art to fulfill its educational task, every link to the maternal body must be severed off. Juno Ludovisi, on the other hand, figures the image of a woman made into the *source* of aesthetic pleasure; Ludovisi's beautiful head allows the spectator to contemplate in her sight the play of his own psychic forces.

These female images indicate that the subjectivity to be formed by aesthetic education is gendered male. This maleness, which is measured by its capacity to master the erotic attraction of the objects it encounters, asserts itself against a danger epitomized in the image of Clytemnestra's breasts. The synecdoche of the motherly breast associates sexuality (breast) with a time preceding the formation of personal identity and clear subject-object separation (mother, suckling). Taken together the two female figures suggest that, in Schiller's aesthetics, art's beautiful images serve as protective shields against forces —sensual, but above all, sexual—that threaten the male subject with the dissolution of his identity and the loss of his control over both the world and his drives.

This interpretation finds further evidence in Schiller's discussion of the aesthetic state, where Schiller relates, as we have already seen, the act of visual contemplation to a formative phase in the "whole development of a single individual" (25/183). Beautiful art, then, recasts this phase of ego-development in order to strengthen the subject against potentially transgressive feelings that would jeopardize, along with the subject's rational self-control, his reliability as a "link in the chain of causality" (4/17) called the moral state.

The proper working of the state, in Schiller's theory, is thus dependent upon a process which we may call, with Kaja Silverman, the "specularization" of the woman.[12]   The specularized woman—that is, the woman placed at a visual remove—offers a narcissistic screen for the male spectator who experiences in her sight the power of his own psychic faculties. This narcissism is of an aggressive, even sadistic nature. Its aggressiveness stems from the fact that in aesthetic contemplation the beholder identifies not so much with an object but rather with that part of himself that objectifies, through an act of form-giving representation, diffuse external stimuli. Since this ideal self is defined through its capacity to master an amorphous "matter," it is structurally dependent upon that which it holds under control. This is why aesthetic pleasure, in Schiller, is always wedded to aggressiveness. And this is also why the *imagery* of the Orestes scene, in which aesthetic education is shown to be coterminous with the killing of the mother, pinpoints the *logic* of Schiller's aesthetic theory. What the male subject enjoys in the aesthetic contemplation of the beautiful body is ultimately his power to "cast off those ghastly masks which were the anguish of his childhood" (25/185) and to transform the most forceful reminder of his heteronomy (the mother) into a symbolic confirmation of his autonomy (Juno Ludovisi).

Is it too far-fetched to assume that Schiller's insistence on the perfect closedness of the beautiful image bespeaks an anxious attempt to screen off from the beholder's sight the opening where the beholder originated? At stake in this closure is nothing less than the idea of autonomy. For the male beholder to contemplate in the beautiful image his ideal, autonomous self, every sign must be banned from the image that could interfere with the beholder's illusion that form-giving subjectivity is the transcendental origin of the beautiful aesthetic object. The arresting of time in aesthetic contemplation—"here is no force to contend with force, no frailty where temporality might break in" (15/109)—results from this effacing of all traces that would remind the subject of an origin predating his form-giving, signifying power. Undisturbed by signs of his limited power, Schiller's male subject can contemplate, in the harmonious structure of the artwork's living *Gestalt,* his ideal autonomous self.

Notes

1. I would like to thank Neil Levi and Beth Drenning for their help with the English, and Daniel Wilson, Andreas Huyssen, and especially Dorothea von Mücke for their perceptive comments on an earlier version of this paper.

2. *Aesthetic Education* 1/5*. Letter and page number of the Wilkinson/Willoughby edition will appear in the text (1/5 is letter 1, page 5); an asterisk (*) indicates that I have altered the translation.

3. In my summary of Schiller's description of modernity I draw on the conceptual framework of Niklas Luhmann's system theory.

4. Although Kant introduced the metaphor of organism into the aesthetic and political debate, Schiller was to my knowledge the first to treat the body as a metaphor for the psyche. This usage has achieved its theoretical consolidation in psychoanalysis, which from Freud to Lacan treats the ego as the projection or metaphor of the body's surface. For an excellent discussion of the political meaning attributed to the imagery of the body, see the essay by Ernst-Wolfgang Böckenförde, who stresses Kant's role in introducing the organism as a symbol for a democratic society (esp. 579ff.). Essentially, before Kant the human body represents the hierarchical organisation of society (head/body distinction); Kant and German Idealism, however, in their discussion of the natural body, emphasize the harmonious interrelationship of the parts with the whole. Kant also opposes the organic whole to the mechanical whole, thus initiating the use of the organism for a critique of rationality. The anti-mechanical and anti-hierarchical meaning of the organism in Kant is obviously in keeping with Schiller's utopian use of the beautiful body.

5. On this effect of splitting, see also Lacan (55-59) who, however, goes on to argue that the moral subject experiences a sadistic pleasure in the exercise of his duty. It may be argued that a similar, albeit not identical, splitting occurs whenever the subject is required to speak or act on behalf of a universalized subject—that is, the subject of scientific discourse or the functional subject of highly formalized bureaucratic activities, to mention the most prominent examples in Letter 6.

6. I say "himself" because I think that the Schillerian subject is gendered male. I discuss gender aspects of Schiller's aesthetics in the closing section of this essay.

7. I conflate here different versions of the compensation thesis, because I am mostly concerned with what they share in common. As to their differences: Marquard reads the slippage from the general political program of the first letters to the elitist aesthetic state in letter 27 as proof of Schiller's resignation about the possibilities for political change: "This is the expression of a decisive resignation: since the problem of history, the problem of the realization of the good state seems to be increasingly more impossible, it is given up" (372f.). According to Marquard, Schiller's resignation prepares the ground for a romantic aesthetics that abandons Kant's historical-philosophical understanding of art—art as anticipation of the good society—in favor of an art that is "removed from the context of historical-political problems and determined by its relationship to a 'far-away nature' " (373). While Janz stresses the elitist aspect of Schiller's concept of the aesthetic state (66f.), Bolten (229) and Grimminger (177) foreground its affirmative function. Grimminger writes that in the Letters, "historical praxis and aesthetic utopia are as unmediated as social critique and aesthetics are at the end. Culture becomes an illusion which covers over the deficiencies of historical existence and therefore gains a firm position within society" (177).—At the Berkeley conference, Carsten Zelle drew my attention to Riecke-Niklewski's book, which deals with the imagery of Schiller's Letters and comes to conclusions that are very similar to mine. She offers a close and careful analysis of the rhetorical and metaphorical structures of Schiller's text. She argues that there is a fundamental tension between Schiller's philosophical program of reconciliation and the violent imagery of the Letters, and that this tension testifies to a fundamental ambivalence of the Beautiful, which serves liberating and repressive functions. I disagree with Riecke-Niklewski insofar as she reads this ambivalence symptomatically, as an indication of the inability of the bourgeoisie to create a society free from repression. Rather than the symptom of a failed liberation, Schiller's Letters provide the program for an elaborate technique of repression. This difference is important even if one doubts, as I do, that art after Schiller put his program into practice. Despite this disagreement in how to interpret Schiller's repressive elements, Riecke-Niklewski's intelligent and precise reading of the Letters is highly recommended.

8. The most famous utopian interpretation of the Letters is Herbert Marcuse's. Marcuse writes in Eros and Civilization: "In other words, the rescue of culture would imply the end of all repressive forms of control which culture imposes on sensuality. . . . And that is indeed the idea behind the aesthetic education of man; it aims at basing morality upon sensuality" (165). A good overview of the utopian interpretations of Schiller is given by Klaus L. Berghahn. Berghahn's essay is to my knowledge the most recent example of this utopian line in Schiller scholarship.

9. My interpretation of Schiller's anthropology is indebted to Dorothea von Mücke (198-9).

10. My discussion of the aesthetic stage is very much indebted to von Mücke, who interprets this stage in terms of Schiller's implicit theory of the origin of human language. Von Mücke writes: "In the beginning, man is merely passive and

can make sense of external stimuli only through an act of exclusion and negation, coterminous with an act of positing. . . . In this thetic act, in self-consciously positing a single signifier (Herder's mark of the soul), man experiences the permanence of the self and its independence from the sensual realm" (200-1).

11. "On the use of teleological principles in philosophy," qtd. Böckenförde (580).

12. See *Acoustic Mirror*, ch. 1. I owe the Silverman reference to Jochen Schulte-Sasse.

Works Cited

Berghahn, Klaus L. *Schiller: Ansichten eines Idealisten.* Frankfurt/M.: Athenäum, 1986.

Böckenförde, Ernst-Wolfgang. "Organ, Organismus, Organisation, politischer Körper." *Geschichtliche Grundbegriffe.* Vol. 4. Ed. Otto Brunner et al. Stuttgart: Klett-Cotta, 1978.

Bolten, Jürgen. *Friedrich Schiller: Poesie, Reflexion und gesellschaftliche Selbstdeutung.* München: Wilhelm Fink, 1985.

Grimminger, Rolf. "Die ästhetische Versöhnung: Ideologiekritische Aspekte zum Autonomiebegriff am Beispiel Schiller." *Schillers Briefe über die ästhetische Erziehung.* Ed. Jürgen Bolten. Frankfurt/M.: Suhrkamp, 1984.

Janz, Rolf-Peter. *Autonomie und soziale Funktion der Kunst: Studie zur Ästhetik von Schiller und Novalis.* Stuttgart: Metzler, 1973.

Kant, Immanuel. *Critique of Practical Reason.* Translated by Lewis White Beck. Indianapolis: Bobbs-Merrill, 1978.

———. *Idea for a Universal History. Kant on History.* Ed. and trans. Lewis White Beck. New York, London: Macmillan, 1963.

Lacan, Jacques. "Kant with Sade." *October* 51 (1989): 55-75.

Marcuse, Herbert. *Triebstruktur und Gesellschaft.* Frankfurt/M.: Suhrkamp, 1979.

Marquard, Odo. "Kant und die Wende zur Ästhetik." *Zeitschrift für philosophische Forschung* 16 (1962): 231-43, 363-74.

Meyer, Herman. *Zarte Empirie.* Stuttgart: Metzler, 1963.

Mücke, Dorothea von. *Virtue and the Veil of Illusion.* Stanford: Stanford UP, 1991.

Riecke-Niklewski, Rose. *Die Metaphorik des Schönen.* Tübingen: Niemeyer, 1986.

Schiller, Friedrich. *On the Aesthetic Education of Man.* Ed. and trans. Elizabeth M. Wilkinson and L. A. Willoughby. Oxford: Oxford UP, 1967.

———. *Sämtliche Werke.* Vol. 5: *Erzählungen, Theoretische Schriften.* Ed. Gerhard Fricke and Herbert G. Göpfert. München: Hanser, 1984.

Silverman, Kaja. *The Acoustic Mirror.* Bloomington: Indiana UP, 1988.

How Enlightened Are Schiller's Aesthetics?

David V. Pugh

TO MOST RECENT WRITERS, the question whether Schiller should be seen as a representative of the German Enlightenment seems a simple one meriting an affirmative answer (e.g., Koopmann, Borchmeyer). Of the numerous reasons that can be given in support of that view, let us mention two. Schiller's drama *Don Carlos* (1787) and his speech *The Stage Considered as a Moral Institution* (*Die Schaubühne als moralische Anstalt betrachtet,* 1785) both build on the notion of humanity that had been formulated and applied by Lessing in opposition to the spirit of the court and courtly drama. Secondly, in his inaugural lecture at the University of Jena (1789), Schiller champions the notion of universal history in a way that shows dependency on Kant's writings on the subject, and in his *Aesthetic Letters* (*Über die ästhetische Erziehung des Menschen in einer Reihe von Briefen,* 1794; 5: 591), he echoes Kant's definition of Enlightenment as the mature use of one's own understanding.

Such palpable reliance on two canonical Enlighteners ("Aufklärer") provides strong support for a view of Schiller as one of their number. It is not difficult, however, to find facts and arguments that render the position somewhat less clear. A number of critics, for example, have discovered echoes of the Baroque style in the pathos of Schiller's plays (Rehm, Sengle, Michelsen). With his return to courts and high politics in his dramas from *Don Carlos* on, Schiller is abandoning the mid-century aspiration to substitute domestic tragedy ("bürgerliches Trauerspiel") for heroic tragedy, and his theory of the "pathetic sublime" contains a rejection of Lessing's theory of pity.[1] Schiller's attitude to Kant, too, is problematic, as is shown by his criticism of the latter's moral theory in *On Grace and Dignity* (*Über Anmut und Würde,* 1793; 5: 465-70). Indeed, the whole vexed question of Schiller's dependence on

Kant is indicative of the generally elusive and difficult nature of Schiller's thought.

The unclarity of Schiller's relation to Lessing and Kant raises further questions, full discussion of which is impossible in the present context. These questions pertain, first, to the definition of Enlightenment, a concept which is variously used to denote a general climate of opinion and a particular doctrine, and which uneasily combines descriptive and normative elements; and second, to the extent to which we can reasonably expect a poet and dramatist to hold stable opinions on socio-political questions. Instead, building on a particular analysis of eighteenth-century thought, this essay focusses on Schiller's writings on aesthetics and examines them in relation to those of his predecessors, concluding that his ideas reflect a crisis in what had until then been a fairly consistent tradition.

I

In a brilliantly economical study, Norman Hampson has summarized the premises of most Enlightened thought, and in addition described the rift in attitude between the placidity of the early decades and the anxiety and radicalism of the century's close. Common to all the *philosophes*, he writes, were the beliefs that nature is a system governed by laws, that man[2] is a part of nature and must be studied as such, and that both man and nature are the products of a beneficent providence. Underpinning these three tenets was a belief in a harmonious relation between man and nature, a belief that separates the eighteenth century from both its predecessor and its successor.[3]

As for the change in climate, this was not a simple process by which old beliefs were driven out by new ones. Instead, beliefs which in 1730 seemed uncontroversial descriptions of reality had by 1790 come to represent desiderata. The relevance of Hampson's analysis to the wider European context becomes clear if we compare two examples from England and Germany. The young Alexander Pope instructs the artist: "First follow Nature, and your judgement frame / By her just standard, which is still the same" (*An Essay on Criticism*, 1.68-69). Goethe's Werther, too, declares his intention, "to be guided by Nature alone in the future. She alone is infinitely rich, and she alone educates the great artist" (6: 15).[4] But Pope's nature is an ordering and restraining force—"The winged courser, like a generous horse, / Shows most true mettle when you check his course"—and allegiance to it leads to no disruptive inclinations, whether in art or elsewhere:

Those rules of old discover'd, not devised,
Are Nature still, but Nature methodised:

Nature, like liberty, is but restrain'd
By the same laws which first herself ordain'd. (1.86-91)

Werther, in contrast, spurns all restraint. For him, allegiance to nature means rejection of the rules of art and society alike. His aesthetic naturalism leads, not to Pope's bland conservatism, but to an uncritical admiration of the lust-crazed farm hand, whom he refuses to abandon even after sexual jealousy has led to murder.

As Werther's case illustrates, the harmony with nature, once treated as an unquestioned possession, is now felt as lost, and it has become the object of a disruptive longing that alienates man from society. In the French context, the catalyst in this change of spirit is of course Rousseau, who taught that man had alienated himself from nature by his progress in the arts and sciences. Hampson divides Rousseau's successors into two groups: first, the Romantics, who were content to "sigh ... for an impossible reintegration into an innocent Eden" (42), and secondly, the millenarian revolutionaries, who maintained that resolute steps could and should be taken to reconstitute the earlier harmony.

Though he is referring to France, Hampson's analysis is of such general validity that it can be adduced to illuminate a German writer's position relative to his century. Where, we may therefore ask, does Schiller fit into this picture? First of all, he did not believe that man could adequately be studied as part of the natural order. For Schiller, man is simultaneously a natural and a spiritual being, a being that straddles the gulf separating the phenomenal from the intelligible world. In order to avoid the perils of materialism and determinism, Schiller falls back into a dualism whose immediate source is Kant, though it of course derives ultimately from the Platonic tradition. Though Kant is generally thought of as a canonical Enlightener, and though he laid claim famously to the mantle of the Enlightenment, his work in fact represents a significant departure from the ontology that had sustained the German Enlightenment until his time. Indeed, he was referred to by Moses Mendelssohn, in most respects a Wolffian, as "the all-pulverizing Kant."[5] A concept of Enlightenment that includes both Leibniz and Kant, while accurate enough in terms of social history, is thus, in the narrower philosophical context, a very loose concept indeed.

Secondly, did Schiller believe man and nature to be part of a providential order? Posing the question in terms more appropriate to the German context, we might ask if he believed in the theodicy proposed by Leibniz in terms of a pre-established harmony between the realms of nature and of grace. This is the central question to be addressed in this essay.

Throughout the century the theodicy had formed a central part of German theories of aesthetics. In his *Critical Poetics* (*Critische Dichtkunst*, 1730), Gottsched had linked excellence in art to the excellence of the created universe:

> The beauty of a work of art does not rest upon an empty fancy but has its firm and necessary foundation in the nature of things. God has created everything according to its proper number, measure and weight. The things of nature are beautiful. If art also wishes to bring forth something of beauty, it must therefore imitate the pattern of nature. (70)[6]

Fifty years later, Karl Philipp Moritz argues similarly, though with a new emphasis. The beautiful work of art reproduces a beauty that exists in the universe but not in individual objects. Since we cannot see the whole universe, however, its beauty can only be presented to our senses by the depiction of individual objects, altered by the artist so as to reflect a transcendent orderliness. Though Moritz departs from a strictly mimetic aesthetic, therefore, the cosmological underpinning of beauty is constant: "Every beautiful whole from the hand of the fine artist is a miniature copy of the highest beauty in the great whole of nature" (599).[7] The qualification that the artist must depart from what he sees in order to hint at a higher perfection may seem harmless enough, but is in fact a crucial breach in the earlier position. The manifest perfection of the Leibnizian universe turns into a *perfectio abscondita* which it is the artist's task and privilege to reveal. In 1757, Moses Mendelssohn had likewise advocated an idealizing process of selection, such that the work of art reflect the perfection of the universe in concentrated form: "This is the most perfect ideal beauty, which can be met with nowhere in nature other than in the whole." But the Platonizing language takes Mendelssohn further:

> Nature has perhaps never been able to present a human character like Charles Grandison. But the poet endeavored to form him to correspond with the way man ought to have been created according to the prior will of God. The poet took an ideal beauty as his model and sought in nature all the traits which, when taken together, form such a perfect character. He has made nature more beautiful. (*Ästhetische Schriften* 181-82)[8]

In citing Sir Charles Grandison as an ideal fictional character, Mendelssohn echoes the question posed by Sir Philip Sidney in his *Defence of Poetry* (1595) as to "whether [Nature] have brought forth so true a lover as Theagenes, so constant a friend as Pylades, so valiant a man as Orlando, so right a prince as Xenophon's Cyrus, so excellent a man every way as Virgil's Aeneas" (24).

However, and this is the crux of the matter, Sidney's defense of idealization stands on quite different metaphysical foundations from Mendelssohn's. Where the latter merely claims that art represents the perfections of nature in a concentrated form, Sidney, truer to the Platonic tradition, is arguing that nature is actually surpassed by poetry:

> Nature never set forth the earth in so rich tapestry as divers poets have done; neither with so pleasant rivers, fruitful trees, sweet-smelling flowers, nor whatsoever else may make the too much loved earth more lovely. Her world is brazen, the poets only deliver a golden. (24)

The ultimate source for this kind of defense of the arts is Plotinus, who revealed how fruitfully Plato's thought could be applied to aesthetics:

> Still the arts are not to be slighted on the ground that they create by imitation of natural objects; for, to begin with, these natural objects are themselves imitations; then, we must recognize that they give no bare reproduction of the thing seen but go back to the Reason-Principles from which Nature itself derives, and, furthermore, that much of their work is all their own; they are holders of beauty and add where nature is lacking. Thus Pheidias wrought the Zeus upon no model among things of sense but by apprehending what form Zeus must take if he chose to become manifest to sight. (5.8.1; 422-23)[9]

Behind Sir Charles Grandison stands Pheidias' great statue of Zeus. The German providentialist justification of beauty, which is a fundamentally optimistic position, can therefore be seen to be a derivative of an older and darker view according to which art intimates a beauty of which no trace can be found in material reality. Far from resting on the harmony of the two realms, beauty is to be explained in terms of their disharmony.

The issue of a providential order is thus linked historically to the discipline of philosophical aesthetics. Schiller's stance on the issue is complex, and we shall see that it is misleading to state that he either believed or disbelieved in such an order. Indeed, the bifurcation of his thought into incompatible ontologies of the beautiful and the sublime, to be explored below, makes it difficult to make any categorical statements as to his beliefs. We should note here, however, that, in his poem "The Artists" ("Die Künstler," 1789), we find the following passage: "As the reflections of the bright banks, the sunset and the flowery field dance on the surface of the stream, in the same way poetry's cheerful shadow-world shimmers on the surface of life" (ll. 336-40).[10] Far from presenting the beauty of nature in condensed form, art is seen here as different from nature.[11] The lines show that Schiller was familiar with the pessimistic version of the argument.

Two preliminary points should be made here. First, Schiller did not believe in God in any conventional sense. Secondly, as the scathing portrayal of his society in the sixth *Aesthetic Letter* makes clear, he did not believe that he lived in the best of all possible worlds. However, it is possible to maintain a kind of providentialism without a belief in God, and Schiller often uses arguments based upon an immanent teleology in history that is leading man towards a full and harmonious development of his powers: "We were nature, and it is the task of our culture to lead us back to nature on the path of reason and freedom" (5: 695).[12] The best of all possible worlds existed once and shall exist again. This "plan of nature" ("Naturplan") resembles the one expounded by Kant in his *Idea for a Universal History from a Cosmopolitan Point of View* (*Idee zu einer allgemeinen Geschichte in weltbürgerlicher Absicht*, 1784) and it reflects the century's transformation of the static theodicy into a progressive one.[13]46). What distinguishes Schiller's arguments, however (while also making them difficult to follow), is the way in which this providential nature can suddenly turn into "mere nature" ("die bloße Natur"), an enemy of our rational self which it is our duty to overcome. The abrupt dissociation of reason and nature is of course diminished when reason is declared to be an agent of a natural teleology. It is worth examining here the aspects of Schiller's thought that pertain to the philosophy of history before we consider the metaphysical issues in a broader sense.

II

It is with reluctance that Schiller relinquishes the providential unity of reason and nature. In his attempts to save the notion by means of historical schemes we can see the effect of Rousseau's revolution. Throughout his aesthetic writings he depicts ancient Greece as the locus of a lost harmony, and he evokes a future condition in which that harmony will be not merely recovered but reconstituted at a higher level. Instead of being a present possession, harmony is banished to the beginning and end of history, and, as with Rousseau, it is the arts and sciences that have disrupted our enjoyment of it: "It was culture itself that inflicted this wound on modern man" (5: 583).[14]

Again, we must stress the central tension running through Schiller's thought. If reason and nature are absolutely antithetical, then it is inconceivable that they could ever be reconciled; their estrangement can neither have been caused by history nor can it be undone by history. But if that is so, the past and future states that Schiller evokes with such longing are not historical propositions at all but hypothetical constructs, comparable to the points at which, so mathematicians tell us, parallel lines meet. We therefore notice an ambivalence in Schiller's statements about this past and future. Discussing man's early history in the *Aesthetic Letters*, for example, he distinguishes between an actual despotic "state of compulsion, which had proceeded only from his [i.e., man's] natural purpose,"[15] and the "ideal state of nature" ("Naturstand in der Idee"; 5: 574) which, though posited as man's historical starting point, is actually a goal set by reason for our future progress. Schiller's vision of ancient Greece is thus left in an ambiguous position. Is it historical, or is it too an "ideal Greece"? This is a question that arises ineluctably from Schiller's conflicting axioms.

Similarly, when depicting the future reconstitution of harmony, Schiller's arguments become obscure. On the one hand, according to his declared program, aesthetic education is to lead, through the ennobling of the whole character, to the realization of the state of reason. But the essay ends with the postulate of an aesthetic state, in which the enlightened ideals of freedom and equality are realized solely as semblance ("Schein"), that is, they are not realized in society's institutions, but merely evoked through its aesthetic forms. The harmony of man's rational and natural parts is, moreover, confined to the element of play—"[man] *is only wholly human when he is at play*" (5: 618)[16]—and hence implicitly excluded from the serious business of state-building. Instead of being present at the end of history as a certain reward for our efforts, the ideals, whether one-sidedly rational or "anthropologically" rounded, belong to a world that is absolutely incompatible with our own, and we become aware of them solely through aesthetic contemplation. History, being part of the order of nature, will not admit of their realization.

This translation of providential history from actuality into the aesthetic mode culminates in the essay *On Naive and Sentimental Poetry* (*Über naive und sentimentalische Dichtung*, 1795), where it is subsumed under the literary genre of the idyll. Schiller's contradictory requirements emerge here with particular clarity. On the one hand, the idyll has the task of presenting to man, who is caught in the toils of culture and art, a vision of the historical telos that his reason dictates to him. This telos is a state of innocence, the ideal state of nature discussed above, and it is traditionally depicted in pastoral scenes not after but before civilization. The idyll thus embodies a synthesis of reason and nature, against which is set the artificiality of modern culture.

The instability of the theory becomes manifest when Schiller criticizes the existing examples of the genre. The naive idyll of the Greeks, he writes, depicts nature but excludes all the advantages of culture, and hence says nothing of the progress that will carry us to the ideal. Reason has now shifted away from nature to the side of culture. The sentimental idyll of Gessner, which treats the naive subject matter with an idealizing style, might seem to be the answer, but Schiller faults it for falling between two stools. His proposed solution is a wholeheartedly sentimental idyll in which all the antitheses of his thought are resolved. For, in spite of the rejection of Arcadian, that is, actual nature, a natural innocence is to be fused here with cultural refinement, feeling with thought, inclination with duty, peace with struggle, reality with ideal. The telos of history is defined by Schiller here in such an oxymoronic fashion that even its literary representation is impossible to imagine, and our doubts are strengthened by its designation as Elysium, the realm of the dead. Schiller's simultaneous commitment to the unity and to the irreconcilability of nature and reason thus causes him to take over the doctrine of providential history, but at the same time to subject it to such heavy qualification that he could only with difficulty be said to share the Enlightenment's faith in it. The case is indicative not only of the complexity of Schiller's thought, but also of the reservations that one is bound to feel vis-à-vis any simple allocation of it to the Enlightenment.

III

We can now return to the question whether, in Schiller's judgment, the beauty of art reflects or exceeds the beauty of nature. Does art demonstrate the theodicy or does it offer an aesthetic substitute for it? We recall the simplicity of Gottsched's view: art is beautiful because it imitates nature, and nature is beautiful because God created it. What was Schiller's opinion?

It should be said first that, when Schiller refers to nature, he is more usually thinking of human nature, a psychological and moral concept, than of what Lessing (2: 437) calls "the eternal and infinite coherence of all things" ("der ewige unendliche Zusammenhang aller Dinge"). In spite of this narrower focus, it is nonetheless legitimate to see his preoccupation with harmony as descended from Leibniz's, and to compare his famous "beautiful soul" ("schöne Seele") to Leibniz's pre-established harmony. Secondly, Schiller's concerns are not confined to aesthetics. The beautiful soul is a theory of morality, and we have already seen how the theory of the idyll addresses the philosophy of history. What unites all his various statements on beauty, however, is the conviction that beauty represents or is caused by some form of harmony between reason and nature. The theory can thus be described as ontological or cosmological in a broad sense.

Harmony is in Schiller's view not pre-established. Before it can harmonize with reason, nature must be subjected to a process that he describes in various ways; it must be formed, purified, refined, or ennobled. Until that takes place nature is "mere nature," which is comparable to the "brazen" world of which Sidney wrote. The implications of this position are of course not confined to aesthetics. In the quest for political reform, for instance, man's natural character, described as "selfish and violent" ("selbstsüchtig und gewalttätig"; 5: 575), will be more a hindrance than a help.

What then is the metaphysical status of the ennobled nature that harmonizes with reason? Is it still nature, or is it now wholly reason? We find no trace of the argument from concentration used by Mendelssohn and Moritz. Instead, the source of beauty is firmly placed outside the sensible world. Thus, in *On Grace and Dignity*, in a paraphrase of his theory of beauty as "freedom in appearance" ("Freiheit in der Erscheinung"; 5: 400), Schiller writes: "In grace, as in beauty generally, reason sees its requirement fulfilled in sensible form, and it is taken by surprise as one of its ideas confronts it in the phenomenal world" (5: 482).[17] It is the fundamental *disharmony* of reason and nature that causes Schiller to describe beauty as surprising. The beautiful object is now an exception within the debased world of material reality, and it acquires this status solely through its participation in the intelligible. Even in the opening pages of *On Naive and Sentimental Poetry*, where Schiller sounds better-disposed towards nature than usual, we find the typical insistence on the intelligible as the source of beauty in natural objects: "It is not these objects that we love, but rather an idea that they represent" (5: 695).[18] The idea he means is variously described —"life in silent creation, working peacefully from within itself, existence according to its own laws, inner necessity, eternal unity with itself" (5: 695)[19]—but these formulations all point clearly enough towards the freedom and autonomy of the moral will, rooted not in nature but in the intelligible. Without this reference to the intelligible, nature is worthless, and we have no legitimate interest in it: "And what possible attraction could a simple flower, a spring, a mossy stone, the twitter of birds, the buzzing of bees, etc., have for us in themselves?" (5: 695).[20]

For Schiller, therefore, beauty occupies a peculiarly awkward ontological position. Seen in one light, it represents a harmony between nature and reason which does not in fact exist, and in that sense it is misleading or even dangerous. Seen in another, beauty does man an incomparable service by presenting an—admittedly exceptional—harmony, hence providing him with a glimpse of the highest moral and spiritual values to which he can and should aspire. Moreover, since man's nature is hybrid, he shares a common metaphysical structure with beauty, and this leads Schiller to claim: "[I]t should be possible to demonstrate beauty to be a necessary condition of humanity" (5: 600).[21] Beauty is thus the sole commensurate vehicle for man to learn of the intelligible. It is this anomalous position of beauty, both ontologically untrue and uniquely precious, that makes it impossible for us either to affirm or deny categorically that Schiller accepted the theodicy. Though the pre-established harmony is denied, its optimistic spirit continues to haunt his writings as a lost paradise, a moral postulate, and a utopian hope.

Schiller's equivocal attitude to beauty has certain consequences for the manner in which he presents it, and these can be divided loosely into two categories: first, the reservations towards beauty that are implicit in the very formulations, such as play and semblance, in which the ideal is circumscribed, for these exclude beauty from the world of serious reality. Second, there is the compensating role of the sublime, a subject to which we must now turn.

IV

The sublime plays as important a role as beauty in Schiller's thought. Any account that fails to give it its proper weight is therefore misleading. Furthermore, while each concept taken separately is relatively simple to grasp, Schiller's writings receive their distinctive cast and their unique difficulty from his struggles to differentiate them, to establish their relative rank, and finally to integrate them into a single ideal.[22] For the sublime does not merely complement beauty, it negates it; where beauty represents the harmony of reason and nature, the sublime represents their disharmony, predicated on the baseness of nature and the necessity of its subjugation by reason. Since, as has been stressed, disharmony is the actual relation of the two realms, the sublime is ontologically true in a way that beauty is not.

The negation of beauty by the sublime can be illustrated from a number of texts, but nowhere is it presented more fully than in the short essay *On the Sublime (Über das Erhabene)*.[23] We have noted Schiller's gestures towards a providential history, and that view of history, as integration of nature and reason, represents an aspect of Schiller's theory of beauty. This kind of natural plan is firmly rejected in *On the Sublime*, where history is seen solely as a disorderly riot of natural forces. Among the various levels of this rejection is an epistemological one. In cognition, our minds impose a unity onto phenomena, but history—"that lawless chaos of phenomena" ("dieses gesetzlose Chaos von Erscheinungen"; 5: 802)—refuses to be subsumed in such a way. Listing the manifold absurdities of history, for example "that it sweeps the most and the least important, the high and the low into a single abyss," he concludes: "[T]his departure of nature as a whole from the cognitive rules to which, in its individual manifestations, it submits illuminates the absolute impossibility of explaining *nature itself* by *natural laws*" (5: 804).[24]

Inseparable from our need to explain nature by imposing our own rules is the desire to find moral meaning in it, or in other words a correspondence between (rational) merit and (natural) reward. But no such correspondence can be discovered in reality: "In its progress up to the present, history has far greater deeds to record of nature than of autonomous reason" (5: 803).[25] Far from guiding history towards a utopian goal, the phenomenology of reason is actually confined to the cases of heroic losers like Cato, Aristides and Phocion, and the selection of these figures reflects the somewhat Stoical tenor to Schiller's philosophy of the sublime and to his ethical thought in general. For Schiller regards it as a sign of weakness to demand the realization of moral ideals. To realize them would mean to transplant them to the phenomenal world, whereas the whole point about these ideals is that they belong in the intelligible. In his presentation of this argument, one can see Schiller turning against his earlier idea of moral beauty: "It is a mark of good and beautiful [!] but invariably weak souls that they always press impatiently for the existence of their moral ideals, and are painfully affected by the impediments to it" (5: 795).[26] In moral action, mankind steps outside the order of nature, and in *On the Sublime* Schiller portrays moral beauty as valuable but ultimately inadequate. In the passage where beauty and sublimity are compared to genii, beauty emerges as a fair-weather friend who accompanies and entertains us "as far as the dangerous places where we must act as pure spirits and must divest ourselves of everything corporeal. . . . Here he leaves us, for only the sensible world is his domain" (5: 796).[27]

Beauty is shown to be equally inadequate in the aesthetic sphere. Schiller now wants no truck with untruth, and he directly attacks the premises of beauty:

> Away then with the misconceived protectiveness and the lax, enfeebled taste that throws a veil over necessity's stern face, and that, in a desire to curry favor with the senses, counterfeits a harmony between well-doing and well-being, no trace of which can be found in the real world. Let evil destiny show itself to us face to face. (5: 806)[28]

Beauty is untrue in relation to material reality, but also untrue in a wider ontological sense, and for that reason is morally harmful: "Through beauty alone we would never learn that we are intended and are able to prove ourselves as pure intelligences" (5: 797-98).[29] The perils of entrapment in the material world are evoked in tones that hark back to Augustine or Plotinus: "In the depravity of uninterrupted enjoyment, we would forfeit our robustness of character; indissolubly fettered to this fortuitous mode of existence, we would lose sight of our immutable destination and our true fatherland" (5: 807).[30]

As for the aesthetic experience of the sublime in a narrower sense, Schiller's understanding of this, too, should be read as a reversal of his position on beauty, which we should first of all briefly recapitulate. In the "Kallias" letters he had developed the concept of beauty as freedom in appearance. This proved a difficult position to maintain, for, like all material objects, the object of beauty does not partake of the intelligible and hence cannot be free or autonomous, while freedom, like all noumena, cannot possibly be manifested to the senses. Beauty, moreover, results from the imposition of a (rational) form onto (natural) matter, and the visible result of such a process will normally evoke heteronomy rather than its opposite. Schiller's argument therefore has to rest on illusion; the object is thoroughly subjugated by its form, but it appears *per impossibile* to have brought forth that form from within itself, hence the oxymoronic formulae "nature in technique, freedom in artificiality" ("Natur in der Technik, Freiheit in der Kunstmäßigkeit"; 5: 417). In the examples he cites—a vase, a horse, and a bird—he emphasizes the effect of lightness, since the sense of a victorious struggle against gravity will evoke the requisite struggle of form against matter. At the same time, however, the victory must be so complete that all traces of the struggle are obliterated. Within the ontological framework that Schiller has adopted, such dialectical complexities are inherent in the transformation of a material object into a representation of freedom.

In *On the Sublime*, Schiller outlines an alternative theory of representation. Though he is referring here to the aesthetic effect of history, not of individual objects, the common logical foundation of the two texts makes their juxtaposition legitimate and useful. The notion of history as ordered by a providential plan is eminently knowable, for it is commensurate to the cognitive faculty of the understanding. However, the individual elements in such a history are subordinated to the unity of the concept, for that is how cognition operates, and for that reason they are unfree and can hardly represent freedom. There is an equivalent moment in the earlier argument where form is imposed on matter, thus depriving the latter of its autonomy. But where in the "Kallias" letters Schiller had resorted to the argument from illusion, he argues here that an unformed history consisting of discrete and disorderly events gives man a more adequate representation of independence, and hence of freedom, than does a providential one:

> This complete absence of purposive connection amongst the confused mass of phenomena renders the latter excessive and unusable for the understanding, which relies on that form of connection. It is this very disconnectedness, however, that makes those phenomena into such a fitting symbol of pure reason, for reason finds its own independence of natural conditions represented in this wild profligacy of nature. (5: 802-03)[31]

Instead of being grasped by the understanding into a unity of knowledge ("Einheit der Erkenntnis"), the chaotic spectacle provokes the

intervention of reason, which integrates it into a unity of thought ("Einheit des Gedankens") and thought for Schiller is an a priori faculty that
yields knowledge superior to that obtained from the senses. The observer thus receives an intimation of the superiority of reason to the
understanding, and hence of his own independence of the order of
nature. The clear implication is that, of the two representations of
freedom, the sublimely disorganized object is preferable on moral
grounds to the beautifully organized one.[32]

The conflict between the beautiful and the sublime is thus inescapable. To be sure, Schiller attempts to reduce the damage done to his
theory of beauty by presenting the sublime as its complement, not its
negation, and by arguing that the two can be integrated into a notion of
the aesthetic that is no longer vulnerable to the moral objections that
the sublime poses to beauty. Close analysis shows, however, that the
synthesis is a highly unstable one and that, the intelligible being superior to the phenomenal, the sublime is the senior partner.

Hampson characterizes the Enlightenment as "a privileged
moment" in which "Man and Nature seemed to coexist in elegant
symbiosis" (42). The century was preceded by an age in which "Nature
had appeared to provide the properties for a theatre where Man alone
was the tragic actor," and in which men "saw their terrestrial pil-
grimage through the Vale of Tears as a renunciation of the joys of one
world in favor of those of the next." Once the privileged moment had
passed, however, the eighteenth century's belief in providence "gave
way to a more Napoleonic conception of progress as a succession of
victorious battles" (42). If we can assume the acceptance, first, of the
foregoing analysis of Schiller's dialectic, and secondly, of Hampson's
account of the eighteenth century, it appears that Schiller occupies a
position at the very end of the Enlightenment, or perhaps just after its
end. He has been obliged to reject harmony, its key doctrine, on the
grounds that it is neither philosophically defensible (Kant) nor experi-
entially true (the French Revolution), but the doctrine still exercises
sufficient power over his emotions to survive in his work as a memory
and a dream. Meanwhile, the inevitability of conflict is accepted,
sometimes in the resigned and Stoical spirit of an earlier age (hence
Wallenstein and *Maria Stuart*), sometimes in the Napoleonic spirit of the
new (hence *The Maid of Orleans* [*Die Jungfrau von Orleans*] and *Wilhelm
Tell*).

V

As we saw, Hampson divides the post-Rousseauian generation into
two groups, the Romantics and the millenarian revolutionaries, and as

a final question we might ask whether Schiller falls into either of these. The answer must be that he does not. To claim that he sighed for an innocent Eden might seem correct if one were prepared to seize various passages from his poems from their context and to neglect the consistent tone of moral seriousness that runs throughout his work. Indeed, Schiller recognized the stance that Hampson describes as Romantic, criticizing it severely:

> Ask yourself, then, sentimental friend of nature, whether it is your sloth that yearns for nature's restfulness or your offended morality that yearns for nature's concord. . . . The nature for which you envy the man without reason is worthy of neither respect nor longing. It lies behind you, it must remain behind you forever. (5: 708)[33]

But this moral seriousness does not make Schiller a revolutionary, and here it is his insistence on the absolute distinctness of reason and nature that stands in his way. Only a weak character, he has said, will press for the realization of his ideals, and Schiller draws the political consequences of this stance by explicitly rejecting the millenarian option:

> How many people there are who do not even shrink from a crime if it will help to achieve a laudable goal, who pursue an *ideal of political bliss through all the horrors of anarchy, who trample laws into the dust in order to make room for better ones, and who have no qualms about consigning the present generation to misery in order to secure the happiness of the next.* (5: 692)[34]

Significantly enough, this blunt passage forms part of a warning against the perils of the sense of beauty. Moral struggle is thus obligatory, and the purity of that struggle is sullied if the moral agent fails to separate reason and nature; that is, if he expects any concrete good to come of his efforts.

The revolutionaries' utopia thus haunts Schiller's writings as does the Enlightenment's ideal of harmony.[35] Just as the latter is preserved aesthetically even as it is rejected in actuality, the social utopia leads a phantom-like existence in the aesthetic state (5: 661-69), in the Elysian idyll (5: 750-51), and in the perfect republic of *On Grace and Dignity* (5: 460), where the ruler's command coincides magically with the subjects' will. It is hinted at also in the community that emerges in *Wilhelm Tell* as the final curtain falls. But it is a mistake to see *Tell* as a play that preaches revolution. Its mode of existence is semblance ("Schein"), and, in a judgment that should give pause to many of his modern critics, Schiller has condemned as an enthusiast ("Schwärmer") anyone who mistakes semblance for reality in the political sphere (5: 669).

With his peculiar mixture of resignation and hope, of nostalgia and struggle, of aesthetic optimism and moral pessimism (or is it the other way around?), Schiller's response to the legacy of the Enlightenment is an elusive combination of acceptance and rejection.[36] It would plainly be absurd to designate him as a Romantic or as a representative of a Counter-Enlightenment, whether or not one considers the latter term to be legitimate. Simply to label him an Enlightener, however, is to shirk the challenge that his life and work continue to pose to our historical and critical understanding.

Notes

1. See especially his poem "Das Ideal und das Leben," ll. 111-30 (1: 204).
2. In preference to awkward (if well-intentioned) terms such as "humankind," "man" is used here and throughout in an inclusive sense equivalent to the German term "der Mensch."
3. We may add that, in the theological sphere, these beliefs were paralleled by a decline in the doctrine of original sin. See Cassirer 137-60, esp. 141: "The concept of original sin is the common opponent against which all the different trends of the philosophy of the Enlightenment join forces."
4. "mich künftig allein an die Natur zu halten. Sie allein ist unendlich reich, und sie allein bildet den großen Künstler."
5. "[Der] alles zermalmende Kant," "Vorbericht" to *Morgenstunden* (*Schriften über Religion* 469.) The conventional view of Kant as Enlightener is revised by Kondylis (637-49). As the dominant philosophical current of the later German Enlightenment, Kondylis identifies the monistic synthesis of ideas taken from Spinoza, Leibniz and Shaftesbury and presented most notably by Herder. Kant, with his fundamental rejection of monism, thus represents an exception to the German Enlightenment's rehabilitation of sensibility and can be designated as "the most radical opponent of the Enlightenment in the overwhelming majority of its manifestations" (639). One could add that Kant's identification of autonomy as the criterion of Enlightenment, as eloquent as it is, can be misleading if taken as a summary of the spirit of the eighteenth century. In his influential *Essay on Man*, Pope is concerned to demonstrate the opposite, namely man's need to understand his position within a cosmic system of which he is not the goal: "All are but parts of one stupendous whole, / Whose body Nature is, and God the soul." Where the slogan of autonomy fosters a spirit of self-assertion, Pope's message is different: "Know thy own point: this kind, this due degree / Of blindness, weakness, Heaven bestows on thee. / Submit, in this, or any other sphere, / Secure to be as blest as thou canst bear" (1.267-68, 283-86).
6. "Die Schönheit eines künstlichen Werkes beruht nicht auf einem leeren Dünkel, sondern hat ihren festen und notwendigen Grund in der Natur der Dinge. GOtt hat alles nach Zahl, Maß und Gewicht geschaffen. Die natürlichen Dinge sind schön; und wenn also die Kunst auch was Schönes hervorbringen will, muß sie dem Muster der Natur nachahmen."
7. "Jedes schöne Ganze aus der Hand des bildenden Künstlers ist . . . im Kleinen ein Abdruck des höchsten Schönen im großen Ganzen der Natur."
8. "Dieses ist die vollkommenste idealische Schönheit, die in der Natur nirgend anders, als im Ganzen anzutreffen, und in den Werken der Kunst vielleicht nie völlig zu erreichen ist. . . . Die Natur hat vielleicht niemals einen menschlichen Charakter, wie Carl Grandison, aufzuweisen gehabt; allein der Dichter hat sich bemüht, ihn so zu bilden, wie der Mensch nach dem vorhergehenden Willen Gottes hätte werden müssen. Er hat sich eine idealische Schönheit zum Muster vorge-

setzt, und in der Natur die Züge aufgesucht, die zusammengenommen einen so vollkommenen Charakter bilden. Er hat die Natur verschönert."

9. I have argued for a Platonic interpretation of Schiller's aesthetics in the articles cited below.

10. "Wie auf dem spiegelhellen Bach / Die bunten Ufer tanzend schweben, / Das Abendrot, das Blütenfeld, / So schimmert auf dem dürftgen Leben / Der Dichtung muntre Schattenwelt."

11. This is of course not the only view of poetry expressed in "Die Künstler."

12. "Wir waren Natur, ... und unsere Kultur soll uns, auf dem Wege der Vernunft und der Freiheit, zur Natur zurückführen."

13. The classic analysis of this transformation is Lovejoy, ch. 9. On the discrepancy between Kant's philosophy of history and the foundations of his moral philosophy, see Kondylis (642-43, here 643): "Kant inconsistently succumbed to a way of thinking the sophistic mechanisms of which he had himself exposed. In his philosophy of history, the Enlightener in him came to the fore in two respects: first, in his belief in the rational goal, and secondly, in his interweaving of reason and sensibility (or ought and is) in the concept of nature. Such a step was prohibited by his epistemological premises, but 'reason's need' triumphed in him, and he himself tasted, as philosopher of history at least, the sweet forbidden fruit, the elevation, that is, of the regulative to the constitutive." For Schiller, the role of the aesthetic derives from the same aporia; from the need, that is, to restore some substance to the Leibnizian concept of harmony after Kant's criticism had reduced it to a regulative idea. In *On Naive and Sentimental Poetry*, for example, Schiller holds out no hope that history will accomplish that "interweaving of reason and sensibility" and gives the task to poetry instead: "It is a matter of infinite concern to man in the condition of culture that he receive a sensible confirmation of that idea [of a condition of innocence], the possible reality of that condition. And since actual experience, far from nourishing this belief, in fact constantly refutes it, it is left to the poetic faculty (here as in so many other cases) to come to the aid of reason in order to provide an intuition of that idea and to realize it in a single instance." ("Dem Menschen, der in der Kultur begriffen ist, liegt ... unendlich viel daran, von der Ausführbarkeit jener Idee [eines Standes der Unschuld] in der Sinnenwelt, von der möglichen Realität jenes Zustandes eine sinnliche Bekräftigung zu erhalten, und da die wirkliche Erfahrung, weit entfernt, diesen Glauben zu nähren, ihn vielmehr beständig widerlegt, so kömmt auch hier, wie in so vielen andern Fällen, das Dichtungsvermögen der Vernunft zu Hülfe, um jene Idee zur Anschauung zu bringen und in einem einzelnen Fall zu verwirklichen," 5: 7

14. "Die Kultur selbst war es, welche der neuern Menschheit diese Wunde schlug."

15. "Notstaat, der nur aus seiner Naturbestimmung hervorgegangen ... war."

16. "[Der Mensch] *ist nur da ganz Mensch, wo er spielt.*"

17. "In der Anmut, ... wie in der Schönheit überhaupt, sieht die Vernunft ihre Forderung in der Sinnlichkeit erfüllt, und überraschend tritt ihr eine ihrer Ideen in der Erscheinung entgegen."

18. "Es sind nicht diese Gegenstände, es ist eine durch sie dargestellte Idee, was wir in ihnen lieben."

19. "das stille schaffende Leben, das ruhige Wirken aus sich selbst, das Dasein nach eignen Gesetzen, die innere Notwendigkeit, die ewige Einheit mit sich selbst."

20. "Was hätte auch eine unscheinbare Blume, eine Quelle, ein bemooster Stein, das Gezwitscher der Vögel, das Summen der Bienen usw. für sich selbst so

Gefälliges für uns?" Similarly, when he writes in the Foreword to *The Bride of Messina* (*Die Braut von Messina*, 1803) that art must depict nature and "the spirit of the universe" ("[der] Geist des Alls"; 2: 818), Schiller seems to be appealing to a cosmological justification of beauty. Like Mendelssohn and Moritz, moreover, he introduces this all-encompassing concept of nature in order to reject an over-literal understanding of mimesis: "What this entails is that the artist can use no single element of reality as he finds it, that his work must be ideal in *all* its parts if it is to have reality as a whole and if it is to conform to nature" ("Es ergibt sich daraus, . . . daß der Künstler kein einziges Element aus der Wirklichkeit brauchen kann, wie er es findet, daß sein Werk in *allen* seinen Teilen ideell sein muß, wenn es als Ganzes Realität haben und mit der Natur übereinstimmen soll"). But the impression is misleading, for Schiller understands nature in quite a different sense: "Nature itself is merely an idea of the mind, and it can never be perceived by the senses" ("Die Natur selbst ist nur eine Idee des Geistes, die nie in die Sinne fällt"). For the earlier writers, nature cannot be represented because it is too big; for Schiller, the reason is that nature is a noumenon.

21. "[D]ie Schönheit müßte sich als eine notwendige Bedingung der Menschheit aufzeigen lassen."

22. In their commentary on the aesthetic writings in *Sämtliche Werke*, Fricke and Göpfert compare the beautiful and the sublime to "electrical terminals which reciprocally imply and require each other, and whose ideal equilibrium and higher synthesis exceeds the bounds of human existence" (5: 1118), and refer to "the tension of man's dual vocation to the total harmony of the beautiful and to the deadly seriousness, the readiness for sacrifice, of the sublime" (5: 1196). These scholars rightly reject all attempts to use diachronic hypotheses to reduce the tension pervading Schiller's thought, e.g., the hypothesis that the sublime represents a stage in his development that was left behind once Schiller, under Goethe's influence, acknowledged the priority of beauty.

23. First published 1801 but date of composition uncertain. See the remarks of Göpfert and Fricke (Schiller 5: 1194-97).

24. "daß sie das Wichtige wie das Geringe, das Edle wie das Gemeine in *einem* Untergang mit sich fortreißt. . . . [D]ieser Abfall der Natur im großen von den Erkenntnisregeln, denen sie in ihren einzelnen Erscheinungen sich unterwirft, macht die absolute Unmöglichkeit sichtbar, durch *Naturgesetze* die *Natur selbst* zu erklären."

25. "So weit die Geschichte bis jetzt gekommen ist, hat sie von der Natur . . . weit größere Taten zu erzählen, als von der selbständigen Vernunft."

26. "Es ist ein Kennzeichen guter und schöner, aber jederzeit schwacher Seelen, immer ungeduldig auf Existenz ihrer moralischen Ideale zu dringen und von den Hindernissen derselben schmerzlich gerührt zu sein."

27. "bis an die gefährlichen Stellen, wo wir als reine Geister handeln und alles Körperliche ablegen müssen. . . . Hier verläßt er uns, denn nur die Sinnenwelt ist sein Gebiet."

28. "Also hinweg mit der falsch verstandenen Schonung und dem schlaffen, verzärtelten Geschmack, der über das ernste Angesicht der Notwendigkeit einen Schleier wirft und, um sich bei den Sinnen in Gunst zu setzen, eine Harmonie zwischen dem Wohlsein und Wohlverhalten *lügt*, wovon sich in der wirklichen Welt keine Spuren zeigen. Stirn gegen Stirn zeige sich uns das böse Verhängnis."

29. "Durch die Schönheit allein würden wir . . . ewig nie erfahren, daß wir bestimmt und fähig sind, uns als reine Intelligenzen zu beweisen."

30. "In der Erschlaffung eines ununterbrochenen Genusses würden wir die

Rüstigkeit des *Charakters* einbüßen und, an diese *zufällige Form des Daseins* unauf-lösbar gefesselt, unsre unveränderliche Bestimmung und unser wahres Vaterland aus den Augen verlieren."

31. "Gerade dieser gänzliche Mangel einer Zweckverbindung unter diesem Gedränge von Erscheinungen, wodurch sie für den Verstand, der sich an diese Ver-bindungsform halten muß, übersteigend und unbrauchbar werden, macht sie zu ei-nem desto treffendern Sinnbild für die reine Vernunft, die in eben dieser wilden Ungebundenheit der Natur ihre eigne Unabhängigkeit von Naturbedingungen dar-gestellt findet."

32. This passage is not cited by Heuer, who thus fails to see how Schiller's theory of representation is affected by the dialectic of the beautiful and the sub-lime. Düsing touches very briefly on the passage, presenting it merely as a comple-ment to the "Kallias" theory: "The beautiful symbolizes freedom as self-determination, the sublime freedom as independence" (206). The tension between the two notions, which is symptomatic of the aporetic character of Schiller's thought, is thus overlooked.

33. "Frage dich also wohl, empfindsamer Freund der Natur, ob deine Trägheit nach ihrer Ruhe, ob deine beleidigte Sittlichkeit nach ihrer Übereinstimmung schmachtet? ... Jene Natur, die du dem Vernunftlosen beneidest, ist keiner Ach-tung, keiner Sehnsucht wert. Sie liegt hinter dir, sie muß ewig hinter dir liegen."

34. "Wie viele gibt es nicht, die selbst vor einem Verbrechen nicht erschrecken, wenn ein löblicher Zweck dadurch zu erreichen steht, die ein *Ideal politischer Glückseligkeit durch alle Greuel der Anarchie verfolgen, Gesetze in den Staub treten, um für bessere Platz zu machen, und kein Bedenken tragen, die gegenwärtige Generation dem Elende preiszugeben, um das Glück der nächstfolgenden dadurch zu befestigen.*"

35. For two different views of the applicability of the concept of utopia to Schiller's political thought, see von Wiese and Berghahn.

36. Kondylis's comment on Kant is helpful here (640): "The greatest opponent of the Enlightenment with respect to the mixing of nature and reason was simultan-eously the most passionate Enlightener with respect to moral pathos." Schiller is a good Kantian in both respects.

Works Cited

Berghahn, Klaus L. "Ästhetische Reflexion als Utopie des Ästhetischen." *Utopie-forschung*. Ed. Wilhelm Voßkamp. Vol. 3. Frankfurt: Suhrkamp, 1985. 146-71.

Borchmeyer, Dieter. "Ästhetische und politische Autonomie: Schillers *Ästhetische Briefe* im Gegenlicht der Französischen Revolution." *Revolution und Autono-mie: Deutsche Autonomieästhetik im Zeitalter der Französischen Revolution*. Ed. Wolfgang Wittkowski. Tübingen: Niemeyer, 1990. 277-90.

Cassirer, Ernst. *The Philosophy of the Enlightenment*. Trans. Fritz C. A. Koelln and James P. Pettegrove. Boston: Beacon, 1955.

Düsing, Wolfgang. "Ästhetische Form als Darstellung der Subjektivitat. Zur Re-zeption Kantischer Begriffe in Schillers Ästhetik." *Schillers Briefe über die äs-thetische Erziehung*. Ed. Jürgen Bolten. Frankfurt: Suhrkamp, 1984. 185-228.

Goethe, Johann Wolfgang von. *Werke*. ["Hamburger Ausgabe."] Ed. Erich Trunz et al. 14 vols. Rev. ed. Munich: Beck, 1981.

Gottsched, Johann Christoph. *Schriften zur Literatur*. Ed. Horst Steinmetz. Stuttgart: Reclam, 1972.

Hampson, Norman. "The Enlightenment in France." *The Enlightenment in National Context*. Ed. Roy Porter and Mikulas Teich. Cambridge: Cambridge UP, 1981. 41-53.

Heuer, Fritz. *Darstellung der Freiheit: Schillers transzendentale Frage nach der Kunst*. Köln: Böhlau, 1970.

Kondylis, Panajotis. *Die Aufklärung im Rahmen des neuzeitlichen Rationalismus*. Munich: Deutscher Taschenbuch Verlag, 1986.

Koopmann, Helmut. *Schiller: Eine Einführung*. Munich: Artemis, 1988.

Lessing, Gotthold Ephraim. *Werke*. 3 vols. Ed. Kurt Wölfel. Frankfurt: Insel, 1967.

Lovejoy, Arthur O. *The Great Chain of Being*. Cambridge: Harvard UP, 1936.

Mendelssohn, Moses. *Ästhetische Schriften in Auswahl*. Ed. Otto F. Best. Darmstadt: Wissenschaftliche Buchgesellschaft, 1974.

————. *Schriften über Religion und Aufklärung*. Ed. Martina Thom. Darmstadt: Wissenschaftliche Buchgesellschaft, 1989.

Michelsen, Peter. "Die große Bühne." *Der Bruch mit der Vater-Welt: Studien zu Schillers Räubern*. Beihefte zum *Euphorion*. Heidelberg: Winter, 1979. 1-64.

Moritz, Karl Philipp. *Über die bildende Nachahmung des Schönen. Deutsche Dichtung im 18. Jahrhundert*. Ed. Adalbert Elschenbroich. Munich: Hanser, 1960. 588-620.

Plotinus. *The Enneads*. 2nd ed. Trans. Stephen MacKenna. London: Faber, 1956.

Pope, Alexander. *Collected Poems*. Ed. Bonamy Dobree. London: Dent, 1924.

Pugh, David. " 'Die Künstler': Schiller's Philosophical Programme." *Oxford German Studies* 18/19 (1989/1990): 13-22.

————. "Schiller as Platonist." *Colloquia Germanica* 24 (1991): 273-95.

Rehm, Walther. "Schiller und das Barockdrama." *DVLG* 19 (1941): 311-53.

Schiller, Friedrich. *Sämtliche Werke*. 5 vols. 7th ed. Ed. Gerhard Fricke and Herbert G. Göpfert. Munich: Hanser, 1984.

Sengle, Friedrich. "Die Braut von Messina." *Deutschunterricht* 12.2 (1960): 72-89.

Sidney, Sir Philip. *A Defence of Poetry*. Ed. Jan van Dorsten. Oxford: Oxford UP, 1966.

Wiese, Benno von. "Die Utopie des Ästhetischen bei Schiller." *Zwischen Utopie und Wirklichkeit*. Düsseldorf: Bagel, 1958. 146-71.

"The Higher Enlightenment that Mostly Escapes Us": Hölderlin and the Dialectic of Enlightenment

Michael T. Jones

IN CONTEMPORARY CULTURE, the Enlightenment survives in the form of its dialectic. As environmental dangers make the limits of an economic growth based on restless scientific rationalism ever more evident, the Frankfurt School critique of instrumental reason has been rehabilitated, in the recent discourse of postmodernism, as prophetic. As a critique insistent on the necessity of enlightening the Enlightenment (that is, the present) about itself, it found definitive expression in Horkheimer and Adorno's *Dialectic of Enlightenment* of 1947, a book whose title has itself become a concept and a bon mot. That "myth is already Enlightenment and Enlightenment reverts to mythology" (Horkheimer and Adorno xvi) is a dialectic rarely absent in discussions of this historical period and its ramifications. As is also well known, the book proceeds in an eccentric and unhistorical fashion, elevating certain figures and phenomena to exemplary status, ignoring others: most notably, the undeniable achievements of the period and the social developments it spawned. Their *"petitio principii*—that social freedom is inseparable from enlightened thought" (Horkheimer and Adorno xiii) —tends to be lost from view in the ensuing jeremiads.

Also lost from view in Horkheimer and Adorno's iconoclastic reconstruction of the history of the West is the immediate reception of the Enlightenment as soon as it became a concept, in Germany notably in the form of German idealist philosophy and aesthetics (Jamme, "Lieblose" 197f.). The basis of this reception was often an opposition between an analytical or dissecting reason, identified with the Enlightenment, and a faculty of synthetic reason, which could rejoin what analytical reason had put asunder (Frank, "Aufklärung"). Under the

185

powerful shadow of the Kantian system, after the 1790 appearance of
the *Critique of Judgment*, this synthetic faculty was often associated with
beauty and by extension with nature and art.

This essay treats one of these receptions of the Enlightenment legacy in early writings of the poet Friedrich Hölderlin. For him, the
Enlightenment survived in refurbished form most immediately in Schiller and Fichte. This immediacy was personal, as he spent the first six
months of 1795 in Jena before fleeing its oppressive influence. A prose
fragment and versions of his evolving novel *Hyperion* document this
encounter with the heritage of the Enlightenment and culminate in his
call for a "higher Enlightenment."

I

An immense amount of recent research, undertaken chiefly in the
wake of Dieter Henrich's ground-breaking investigations into Hölderlin's early influence on his friend Hegel (Henrich 1971), has essentially
recast the narrative of the evolution of German Idealism. One of its
findings was that "Hölderlin's work very explicitly contains a discourse
on the dialectic of Enlightenment" (Jamme, "Arbeitsgruppe" 281).
Christoph Jamme (282) finds a summation of the early Tübingen Enlightenment optimism in the poet's programmatic letter to his brother
of 1793, which adduces the "seeds of Enlightenment" he sees in a historical period "where everything is striving toward better days" (StA 6:
92-93). Yet this superficial optimism soon gives way, in the various versions of the novel *Hyperion*, to a critique of humankind's exploitation of
nature that foreshadows the classical account of Horkheimer and
Adorno; and like theirs, his critique includes a reckoning with the
Enlightenment.

The word "Aufklärung" (Enlightenment) is rare in Hölderlin's writings. Its confrontation with religious orthodoxy, and its latest and most
crucial expression in the critical philosophy of Kant, were an essential
part of the educational atmosphere of the Tübingen Stift, assuming the
status of a kind of automatic given.[1] The rarity of the word, therefore,
easily coexists with the ubiquity of the phenomenon. Naturally, the history of German literary scholarship also plays its usual nefarious role:
values of traditional German "history of ideas" (superficial "Western"
rationalism against genuine "German" irrationalism) were later repudiated by an insistence on the essential continuity of Enlightenment and
Idealism (especially Romanticism), at least in certain of its central
aspects. The duality of continuity and its accompanying criticism continues to characterize studies of Idealist philosophy and literature (representative: Jamme and Kurz). It is a duality that permeates the

theoretical text where Hölderlin most emphatically employs the word "Enlightenment." An extended argument ends: "And this, then, is the higher Enlightenment that mostly escapes us" ("die höhere Aufklärung, die uns größtenteils abgeht"; Hölderlin 92, trans. altered). Hölderlin's editors have entitled the text *On Religion*.[2]

An interlocuter, probably corresponding to the fictitious correspondent of the new letters on aesthetic education, opens the section of *On Religion* that culminates in the call for a "higher Enlightenment." The interlocutor's question presupposes that people live a "higher destiny" or "more intimate relation" with their world than "physical and moral needs" would require; the latter amount to a mere "mechanical *inter-relation*." The question is why people require an "idea or image" of this interrelation that "can neither be properly thought nor does it lie before our senses." The answer follows in short order: so that people can *remember* this destiny (Hölderlin 90). Yet it is soon evident that for this purpose, some forms both of thought and of memory are seriously deficient.

Why an idea or image that cannot be properly thought? Because "mere thought [der Gedanke], however noble, can repeat only the *necessary relation*, only the inviolable, universal, indispensable laws of life"; this deficient repetition transpires in a correspondingly insufficient mode of memory—"merely in *memory* ("bloß im Gedächtnis"; Hölderlin 91). *Gedanke* ascertains and *Gedächtnis* repeats those universal laws necessary for the mere subsistence of life, humanity's merely "mechanical interrelation" with the natural environment, or what a later section of the fragment will call "the course of a machine" ("Maschinengang"; Hölderlin 92). Whereas *Gedanke* merely repeats the universals of biological life, *Gedächtnis* repeats only the particular with no regard for the universal (Buhr 21). Genuine memory (*Erinnerung*) is the one in which "man's power repeats in the spirit [im Geiste wiederholt] the real life which afforded him the satisfaction" (Hölderlin 91).[3] Thus *Gedanke* and (rote) *Gedächtnis*, necessary as they are, remain insufficient without their higher manifestations in *Geist* and *Erinnerung*.

Hölderlin glosses humanity's interrelation with its environment in terms of desire and satisfaction; animal-like physical satisfaction is the necessary precondition for a "higher satisfaction" that requires *signifi-cation* (Nägele 42) as an idea or an image. Immediate "physical and moral needs" are addressed by "a priori deducible laws, which Kant had determined in his critique of cognition. They are comprehensible without particular examples and are valid in every case: their a priori grounding means precisely their independence from single particularities" (Thomasberger 296). As such, they are necessary but not suffi-

cient for the desirable "higher relation" of the species to its environment: necessary for the purely biological reproduction of its species
life, to employ the later term of Marx, but insufficient for consciousness
of that "higher destiny" available only through signification and
memory. Whereas physical and moral laws are immediately reproduci-
ble by rote *Gedächtnis*, access to this "higher realm," Hölderlin insists,
depends on "particular examples," because "the law, even if it was a
universal for civilized people, could never be conceived of abstractly
without a particular case [niemals ohne einen besondern Fall, niemals
abstract] unless one were to take away from it its peculiarity, its
intimate relation with the sphere in which it is enacted" (Hölderlin 91).
The insistent rhetorical repetition of "niemals," along with the unusual
comparative ("more infinite") that recurs throughout the fragment,
drives home the central point.

The argument then culminates in the evocation of a "higher Enlightenment that we are mostly lacking." The context is crucial and its
translation garbled.[4] True to his own argument, Hölderlin abandons
his own abstraction for "particular examples": abstract principles of
morality ("duty of hospitality," "duty to be generous to enemies")
without regard to particulars of age or gender would partially amount
to "vain etiquette or stale rules of taste" ("eine arrogante Moral, . . .
eine eitle Etiquette oder auch eine schaale Geschmaksregel"). The
phrase "arrogant morality," omitted in Pfau's translation, recalls Schiller's controversial characterization of Kant as the "Draco of his time"
in *Über Anmut und Würde*, an essay that impressed Hölderlin but that
he vowed to go beyond (letter to Neuffer, October 10, 1794). Naturally, the phrase would also include for Hölderlin the Christian
orthodoxy against which he and his friends had struggled mightily back
in the Tübingen *Stift*. The rejection of Kantian morality is
accompanied by reference to the now discredited normative poetics
also characteristic of an inflexible Enlightenment. In sum, after the
"differentiation" of culture into the three realms of knowledge,
morality, and taste, that great achievement of the three Kantian critiques, each realm is here chastised for our own modern arrogance when
we "consider ourselves more enlightened with those adamantine terms
[mit unsern eisernen Begriffen] than the ancients" (Hölderlin 92).
Inflexible "iron concepts," within all three cultural realms, are the
residue for *Gedanke* and *Gedächtnis* of those eternal a priori laws that
make life possible but not satisfying. "Higher Enlightenment," then,
would retain the necessary "iron concepts" of Enlightenment as such,
while complementing it with *representation* (*Vorstellung*) in the form of
ideas or images, which are not found in the realm of the sensible but
rather of the intelligible. Hölderlin characterizes humanity's higher

interrelations with the world "as religious ones, that is, as relations which one had to look at not in and of themselves but rather from [the viewpoint of] the *spirit* that ruled the sphere in which those relations existed. (Further elaboration.)" (Hölderlin 92). These relations constitute the desired "higher Enlightenment."

Here one section of the fragment breaks off and another section begins, one that clarifies the concept of "sphere." The common denominator with the first section is elevation "above physical and moral needs ["Notdurft"] so that a "more than mechanical interrelation" (Hölderlin 90) between human beings and their world is evident, or in the second section that human beings experience "more than the course of a machine," or a "spirit, a god exists in the world," making possible "a more living relation, superior to basic needs [Notdurft]" (Hölderlin 92). Some "further elaboration," then, is available here.

Talk about "spirit" or "god" cannot be the province of "helpful memory or professional considerations" ("aus einem dienstbaren Gedächtniß oder aus Profession"). Again, the translation does not convey the irony of "dienstbares Gedächtnis" as rote memory in the "professional" service of a dubious institution like the church and its orthodoxy. The poet's own escape from life as a Protestant pastor echoes here. "Sphere" is here a multi-faceted concept for a human being's interaction with the world: it is both the necessary presupposition for a communal experience of the divine and the necessary limitation of that experience (Thomasberger 294). The argument suddenly becomes one of cosmopolitan Enlightenment tolerance for other religious views, for "various representations [Vorstellungsarten] of the divine," so that there emerges "a harmonic whole of representational modes" wherein each recognizes its own necessary limitation as part of that whole (Hölderlin 93). At the same time, however, mental representations of the divinity are available only within limited, individual spheres; and "only to the extent that several men have a common sphere in which they work and suffer [wirken und leiden] humanely, that is, elevated above basic needs [Notdurft], only to that extent do they have a common divinity" (Hölderlin 92). It becomes the task of the poem, then, "based on the sensation of the sphere, to develop the determinate language ... that can name what was sensed and felt in the sphere as infinite unity" (Gaier, "Mythos" 326-27). The poem is in this sense the spiritual expression of the memory of infinite unity that can only be evoked in infinite approximation.[5]

A final section of the fragment distinguishes religion in Hölderlin's sense from two other modes of representation: physical (or physical-mechanical-historical) and moral (or intellectual-moral-legal), echoing once again Kant's first two critiques. These limited representational modes, based on the limited human faculties of *Gedanke* and *Gedächt-nis*, cannot constitute in themselves the "higher destiny" in which human beings "feel themselves" (a key verb in Hölderlin) united with their world. They are the "lower Enlightenment" that is to be *aufge-hoben* (cancelled, preserved, and elevated) in mental representations of the divinity that together constitute a harmonic, infinite whole—in myth. Religion depicted in the aesthetic mode is then "the uniting of several religions into one," a unity where "all religion would be poetic in its essence," where "each one celebrates his higher life and all together celebrate a communal higher life" (Hölderlin 94-95), a higher enlightenment. Here representation (*Vorstellung*) is rendered concrete in the course of its depiction or presentation in images (*Darstellung*): the merely mental must appear in corporeal form, become perceptible, able to be "felt" and experienced as constitutive of communal "higher life."

This call for imagery, for an aestheticized depiction of the mechanical abstractions of Enlightenment cognition and morality, was by no means original with Hölderlin. As one critic has put it: "The critique of 'iron concepts,' the call for living unity of understanding and sensuality fundamentally corresponds to the position of the late German Enlightenment, which aimed for a recognition of sensuality and the unification of understanding and sensuality" (Kurz, "Aufklärung" 273). But the emphatic evocation of this unity as religion, and moreover as myth where all religions are united, is a radical valorization both of Enlightenment cosmopolitan tolerance in religion and of the need for aesthetic depictions of those religious modes of representation (*Vorstel-lungsarten*).

The earlier dating of Hölderlin's fragment on religion, placing it in proximity with the earlier versions of the novel *Hyperion* and with the celebrated anonymous text its first editor entitled "The Oldest System-Program of German Idealism," makes a great deal of sense.[6] The famous call in that text for a "new mythology," in which poetry regains its original function as a "teacher of humanity," leads to a vision of aesthetic or mythological ideas as achieving a bridge between the people and their leading elites. "Thus the enlightened and the unenlightened finally have to shake hands; mythology must become philosophical in order to make the people reasonable, and philosophy must turn mythological in order to make the philosophers sensuous. Then there prevails eternal unity among us" (Hölderlin 155-56). Thus the ugly secret of the Enlightenment—class divisions of enlightened initiates and unenlightened masses—is to be abolished by the realiza-tion of this rhetorical chiasmus: the mythology of reason (see Jamme and Schneider). A mythology "because the communality of knowledge, feeling and action for a society here, as under conditions of myth, are guaranteed and made valid by symbolic systems of interpretation and values"; a mythology of reason "because it is not the content of a fable appealing to the holy that establishes the concord of a society's members," but rather what emerges from "the pure form of nonviolent intersubjectivity and communication—from reason" (Frank, *Gott* 169). Religious traditions are not obliterated but live on in non-mythic form, retaining their legitimizing function underlying the cohesion and solidarity of a society.

Hölderlin's ruminations on religion and myth must be seen, then, in the context of an idealism that seeks to retain the achievements of the Enlightenment while transforming them into a potent social force. They can have this effect only by assuming the legitimizing functions of myth and religion that the Enlightenment had effectively and irrevocably destroyed. This idealism emerged in the wake of Kantian philosophy, and it is an idealism with which Hölderlin perforce grappled in the texts that finally became his novel *Hyperion*.

II

As Christoph Jamme has pointed out, the immensely suggestive fragment called the "Oldest System-Program" envisions other ramifications for its postulated "new mythology" than political legitimation and social cohesion. "The 'new mythology' is not only to be understood from the background of a divided society, but also from that of the emergence of an instrumental reason and a 'reasonable' subjectivity (that constitutes human autonomy), that is, from the genesis of a subject that understands [begreift] everything outside itself as an object" (Jamme, "Aufklärung" 46-47). Thus, the fragment anticipates critical theory's account of instrumental rationality. Whereas it admittedly treats the relation of nature and science very sporadically, and its call for a future "physics on a grand scale" (Hölderlin 154) remains vague, an early fragment of Hegel with the title "Religion, founding a religion" ("Religion, eine Religion stiften") explicitly foreshadows Horkheimer and Adorno's equation of cognition and power in its terse formulation: "to grasp is to dominate" ("begreifen ist beherrschen," qtd. Jamme, "Aufklärung" 48). Etymologically, the figurative "begreifen" stems from the concrete force-laden verb "greifen," and is here identified with the domination expressly present in "beherrschen."[7]

The most explicit and detailed account of Hölderlin's reception of the Enlightenment, in its post-revolutionary and post-Kantian form, is the series of prose and poetic sketches that became his novel *Hyperion*. More than the finished novel itself, which rather presupposes the conclusions elaborated in the earlier versions, they document the poet's encounter with a tradition that celebrates the emergence of an emancipated, autonomous self, employing the weapons of "iron concepts" and of mastering science for its own continued survival and supremacy. These texts stem from a crucial period in Hölderlin's life, as his letters bear witness: he spent the months from late 1794 to mid-1795 in Jena, in the immediate vicinity of two men who were role models in his development: Schiller and Fichte. While the contemporaneous *Hyperion* texts are the clearest record of his engagement with the Fichtean philosophy then emanating from Jena, they also offer a stimulating narrative of the dialectic of Enlightenment.

Both the "metrical version" (with the accompanying "prose sketch" that parallels its first half), as well as the first chapter of the prose piece "Hyperion's Youth" record a conversation between a youthful first-person narrator (albeit mixed with his later value judgments about his youthful convictions) and an older "stranger" and "wise man," who exhibits traits of the mature Hyperion of the finished novel.[8] The youth narrates an anthropology of the self in relation to nature, employing at the outset a double concept of nature: it refers to the outer environment, to which the self is opposed, as well as to an aspect of the self deemed "divine" (Gaier, *Kalkül* 46). The youth glosses the struggle as one of self and nature, which had made him "tyrannical toward nature," as a battle ("Kampf") that reason fights with unreason (186) or "light" against "the old darkness" (187). Responsibility for this self-glorifying struggle, with its goal of "superiority" ("Überlegenheit"), lies with both the "school of fate and of the wise men," a contrast between a fatalistic view of the vicissitudes of history and a historical optimism evoked in the "wise" rational philosophers of the Enlightenment (Kondylis 330). The goal of the struggle is clear: "I wanted to dominate [beherrschen] her [i.e., nature]" (186); "I wanted to tame, to rule her" (187). The "natural" aspects of the self, "lawless forces" ("den gesezlosen Kräften," 186) associated with beauty and with the help that nature offers reason, were ignored in this struggle. The meaning of "lawless forces" remains unclear until we recall the association of "mechanical and physical laws" with the "lower enlightenment" of the fragment on religion. Likewise, the sudden reference to morality—"I judged others severely, like myself" (186)—becomes clearer by equating it with the "arrogant morality" of that text. "Lawless forces" were thus neglected in the subject's feeling of superiority over nature, with moral judgment accompanying it. Both physical and moral laws ("physical, mechanical, historical conditions" and "intellectual, moral-legal conditions" Hölderlin 94), or in other words the "lower Enlightenment," require higher "religious" or "mythical" conditions for their integration into a higher whole.

The wise stranger, in his extended homily, corrects this "eccentric path" by means of an anthropology based on fundamental human drives, an anthropology that recalls similar formulations in Fichte's *Grundlage* and in Schiller's letters on aesthetic education. The drive to mold nature for our own devices, to subjugate its material to our own "holy laws of unity" (188-90), is just and according to what is divine within us. The self must resist the temptation, in view of the bitterness of the struggle, to give up the fight, accept the reign of fate and the senses, and deny reason, for that would be to become animals (190). But equally dangerous is the other possibility, that we struggle against nature in order to destroy it, thereby making the world a desert and severing what connects us to other human beings. Therefore, to the first drive—for liberation, nobility [uns zu befreien, zu veredlen, 194], autonomy—is opposed a second drive, a drive "to be defined" [Trieb, bestimmt zu werden, 194]; whereas denial of the first drive would keep us animals, denial of the second would not be human; and it is a concept of the genuinely human that is at stake.

Hölderlin couches a similar duality, present in Schiller, in terms of action and suffering ("wirken und leiden"); his somewhat mysterious reference to "suffering" from the religion fragment becomes clearer in this context. "Let me speak humanly. When our original infinite essence suffered for the first time and our free full force felt its first limits, when poverty paired itself with surplus, there was love."[9] Suffering therefore refers to the effects of nature's limitations on a subject. In expanding on his notion of the external world as a necessary limit for a self tempted to exalt itself above all else, the wise stranger increasingly speaks the language of Fichte—but in contrast to him, he also speaks of love and beauty. Both the "metric version" and the later fragment "Hyperion's Youth" explicate this anthropological claim that is common in idealism: from an undifferentiated originary unity, for which childhood and ancient Greece function as reminders in the present, the human self emerges as characterized by consciousness and concomitant conflict with its environment: by division and alienation. In the mode of reflection, consciousness can then ruminate on the originary state of pre-consciousness. The wise stranger does this: "Pure spirit that is free of suffering does not deal with material, and is not conscious of any thing or of itself; there is no world for it, for outside itself is nothing.—Yet what I say is only a thought.—Now we do feel the limits of our essence."[10] We need these limits in order to be human, he continues; we require this resistance of the world, for without it, "we would not feel ourselves or others. Not to feel oneself is death."[11]

It "can only be a thought," this thought of pure spirit, or absolute Being, as Hölderlin calls it in the central early fragment on "Judgment and Being" (Hölderlin 37-38). As a "thought," it must be thought by a consciousness, as a judgment, employing the human language of subject and object; consciousness entails division, and at that point "began for us the poverty of life, and we exchanged consciousness for our purity and freedom."[12] The stress on "for us" in this passage, which foreshadows Hegel's use of the locution in the *Phenomenology of Spirit*, is significant: without consciousness, which entails finiteness and division, there would be no experience of limitation and thus no experience of the divine, including our own divine origins, from whence emerge our drives and our needs. We would not "feel ourselves" (Kondylis 332-33). Thus Hölderlin's "Fichte" figure, the wise stranger, attributes priority to the ego, but it is not and cannot be an absolute ego.[13] It is a human ego, an amalgam of "superfluity and poverty," a result of the reciprocal interaction of drives, the predominance of one of which would be either animal-like or divine, but not human. Pure spirit, or absolute being, or humanity's "divine origins," can be named as "only" a thought, a deficient form of thinking; it is forever inaccessible. The opposition of being and consciousness remains fundamental for these Jena fragments.

The lengthier fragment "Hyperion's Youth" goes on to address the search for self in friendship and in action, an extension of "acting" ("wirken") in the social realm, and thus bears greater similarity to the final novel. Of interest for my purposes here, however, is still the more programmatic metric version, particularly in its cryptic comments about the role of nature. The purported dismissal of nature was perceived as the great weakness of Fichte's philosophy.[14] Here, however, the Fichtean wise stranger, when he claims to speak in a human (as opposed to an animal or a divine) manner, attributes to "us" (to consciousness) a remarkable faculty in the interplay of humans and nature. Nature speaks to us in "beautiful forms."[15] In the later "preface to the penultimate version," the most programmatic of Hölderlin's fragmentary texts surrounding the novel, the poet claims: "We would have no notion of that infinite peace, of that being in the proper sense of the word [the absolute being of "Judgment and Being"], we would not strive to unite nature with us, we would not think or act, nothing would be (for us), we would be nothing (for us), if that infinite unity, that being in the proper sense of the word were not present. It is present —as beauty."[16] Undifferentiated unity (or "peace" in an echo of Paul's "peace that passeth all understanding") is the object of our "striving." In the metric version, the experience of nature in its "beautiful forms" is our "need"; *we* attribute to nature a "relation with the divine in us" and we "believe in a spirit in matter," but our need justifies this attribution ("uns dazu berechtigt," 192).

In the wise stranger's emphasis on the condition of need and lack that is equivalent to consciousness and life, but even more so in his appeal to the Platonic myth of the birth of Aphrodite and thus to the *Symposium*'s concept of love, Hölderlin places in "Fichte's" mouth his own most basic convictions. Here is an example of Hölderlin's eclectic willingness to integrate aspects of Plato, Fichte, Spinoza, and Kant into his own new aesthetics. In this passage of the metric version, however, Hölderlin has Fichte speak most strongly: *we* (human ego or consciousness) attribute spirit to matter; *we* animate ("beseelen") the world with *our* spirit. "Yet, dear stranger, tell me what there is that is not what it is through us."[17] Here, for the only time in the fragment, the stranger expects contradiction, and his hearer admits that some people might take umbrage ("ein kleines Ärgernis genommen"). As one critic notes, that claim comes dangerously near to unbelief, and is replaced in "Hyperion's Youth" by the claim that "faith is based on the limits of finitude" (Barnouw 255). And indeed, in the present context, it quickly gives way to the Schillerian doctrine of reciprocal drives—the drive to conquer and the drive to be limited—to a warning against false pride ("nicht stolz uns überheben," 195) and to an appeal to the mediating concept—love. It is love "that urges us to attribute to nature a relation with the divine in us" and to "believe in a spirit in matter."

Love as a concept, then, is to teach the youth more than the "schools of fate and the wise men" could, that is, not to be tyrannical toward nature and reduce it to a desert around him, for "you need the strengthening of nature" and that strength comes in the form of "golden clouds."[18] As in this passage, these clouds are further glossed in "Hyperion's Youth" as *phantasy*, creating a sign in the form of "golden clouds gathering around the ether of thought," so that beauty now becomes perceptible to the senses as a corporeal embodification of *truth*.[19] Yet there remains that troubling "Fichtean" assertion, that the world is what it is through ourselves. I reproduce the argument following the excellent reading of Ulrich Gaier ("Mythos" 321f.): we experience nature as appearances and seek something behind them, attributing to them a connection to the divine within us. The *need* that gives us the *right* to do this, however, is part of our "natural" drives and "creates *per se* a natural justification" of that toward which it strives (Gaier, "Mythos" 322).[20] In contrast to Fichte, for whom the non-I is nature conceived as "matter" or "stuff," as a means for setting in motion the real life of the ego, nature is for Hölderlin a metaphysical principle. While both find the justification (*Recht*) for this activity in human need, Hölderlin finds in the "beautiful forms" of nature something related to the immortal in man, and thus "assumes a substantial identity between subject and object in its hidden reality, which cannot be brought to consciousness but can nevertheless be felt" (Gaier, "Mythos" 325). The "golden clouds" of beautiful appearances, in nature and in art, make possible a relationship to nature unsullied by domination and bondage, for they remind human beings of their natural origins and their need for nature's receptivity to their striving.

III

German idealist philosophy in general, and Fichte's philosophy in particular, are often regarded as the epitome of arrogant, self-aggrandizing, dominating subjectivity, as the glorified reason of the Enlightenment run amok. While this simplistic view is a worthy replacement of the older view of the "Age of Goethe" as a reaction against the Enlightenment, it nevertheless ignores idealism's urgent grappling with the challenge of Enlightenment reason, with its liberating thrust toward secularization and demythologization and with the human cost of those tendencies. The romantic program of a "new mythology," to be reflectively produced rather than emerging "naturally," explicitly responds to the perceived dearth left behind by triumphant rationality.

In Hölderlin's program of "new letters on aesthetic education," and in the continuing work on his novel, the poet confronts contemporary philosophy and aesthetics as continuing shock-waves emanating from the emancipatory efforts of the movement called Enlightenment. To the allegorization and demonization of reason he opposes the allegorical figure of a nature that is neither dominated nor dominating, and of a human being characterized by striving toward an impossible absolute (reunification with nature). Inspired by perception of the beauty of nature, this human being can experience a love allegorized as the reconciliation of conflicting anthropological drives, and as the expression of infinite striving.

Horkheimer and Adorno's lamentation on the concept of Enlightenment contains a brief and fleeting utopia, a momentary expression of how things could be otherwise. Their own allegories of human beings and nature include the possibility of a concept that reflects upon itself; and such self-reflection "allows the distance perpetuating injustice to be measured. By virtue of this remembrance of nature in the subject, in whose fulfillment the unacknowledged truth of all culture lies hidden, enlightenment is universally opposed to domination" (Horkheimer and Adorno 40). The sentence immediately veers away from the momentary utopia, but it is a utopia they share with Hölderlin at a transitory moment in his development that also represents his salient reception of the legacy of the Enlightenment. The common element is remembrance, Platonic *anamnesis*, of what binds human beings and nature, a symbiotic relation transcending dominance and bondage: a prophetic vision.

Notes

1. For the most recent bibliography see Wegenast.
2. The translator Thomas Pfau follows Friedrich Beißner's rendition in StA 6.1: 275f. D. E. Sattler, editor of the Frankfurt edition of Hölderlin's works, presents plausible reasons for changing the order of the fragment's pieces (FA 14: 11-12). For easier orientation in the complex text, I follow Pfau. However, I am convinced by Sattler's argument for the earlier date of the fragment, which puts it into the program of "New Letters on Aesthetic Education" as outlined in the 1796 letter to Niethammer (Pfau ed. 132) and, even more importantly, places it in the vicinity of the crucial "Oldest System-Program."
3. The translation does not do justice to the two modes of memory, *Gedächtniß* and *Erinnerung*, but the distinction is essential for the argument. It is renewed by Walter Benjamin in his essay on Baudelaire.
4. Thomas Pfau struggles bravely with Hölderlin's labyrinthine, allusive prose, and he has performed a genuine service. But some locutions are difficult to comprehend: e.g., "adamantine terms" in the key sentence.
5. On the frequent idealist notion of infinite perfectibility, see Behler.
6. The fragment has been handed down in Hegel's handwriting, but his two friends Hölderlin and Schelling have also been proposed as its author. See Bubner.
7. Adorno's later *Negative Dialectics*, with its continually renewed effort to transcend the limitations of the concept by means of a potentiated concept of concept, so that it will conform and shape itself in imitation ("mimesis") to its object, the non-identical, is a continuation of the line of thought initiated in the 1790s by Hegel and Hölderlin.
8. Throughout this section, page references not otherwise identified are to StA 3, the volume of the Stuttgart edition containing the novel *Hyperion* and associated documents. For interpretations of the earlier fragments see Ryan 35f.; Gaier, *Kalkül* 40f.; Barnouw 252f.; Kondylis 330f.
9. "Laß mich menschlich sprechen. Als unser ursprünglich unendliches Wesen zum erstenmale leidend ward und die freie volle Kraft der ersten Schranken empfand, als die Armuth mit dem Überflusse sich paarte, da ward die Liebe" (192, ll. 11-14).
10. "Der leidensfreie reine Geist befaßt / Sich mit dem Stoffe nicht, ist aber auch / Sich keines Dings und seiner nicht bewußt, / Für ihn ist keine Welt, denn außer ihm / Ist nichts.—Doch, was ich sag', ist nur Gedanke.— / Nun fülen wir die Schranken unsers Wesens" (195, ll. 131-36).
11. "wir fühlten uns und andre nicht. / Sich aber nicht zu fühlen, ist der Tod" (195, ll. 143-44).
12. "Am Tage, da die schöne Welt für uns / Begann, begann für uns die Dürftigkeit / Des Lebens und wir tauschten das Bewußtsein / Für unsre Reinigkeit und Freiheit ein—" (193, l. 127-30).
13. Thus Hölderlin continues his critique of Fichte begun in the important letter to Hegel of January 1795, where he objects to the implication that Fichte's "I"

can be absolute, yet is intrigued by Fichte's notions of the reciprocal determination of "I" and "Non-I" and of "striving" (Hölderlin 125).

14. It should not be forgotten that Hölderlin's first reading of Fichte, described in the Hegel letter, occurred immediately after his reading of Spinoza as mediated by Jacobi. Spinoza's concept of "substance" provided the unitary antidote to Fichte's dualism of I and non-I. See Wegenast.

15. Already in the Tübingen "Hymn to Beauty" (StA 1: 152-56), Hölderlin had chosen a motto from Kant's *Critique of Judgment* wherein "nature in its beautiful forms speaks figuratively to us." See Kurz 66f.

16. "Wir hätten auch keine Ahndung von jenem unendlichen Frieden, von jenem Seyn, im einzigen Sinne des Worts, wir strebten gar nicht, die Natur mit uns zu vereinigen, wir dächten und wir handelten nicht, es wäre überhaupt gar nichts, (für uns) wir wären selbst nichts, (für uns) wenn nicht dennoch jene unendliche Vereinigung, jenes Seyn, im einzigen Sinne des Worts vorhanden wäre. Es ist vorhanden— als Schönheit" (236-37).

17. "Doch, lieber Fremdling, sage mir, was ist, / Das nicht durch uns so wäre, wie es ist?" (193, l. 111-12).

18. "Und wenn dem Göttlichen in dir ein Zeichen / Der gute Sinn erschafft, und goldne Wolken / Den Aether des Gedankenreichs umziehn, / Bestürme nicht die freudigen Gestalten! / Denn du bedarfst der Stärkung der Natur" (195, ll. 157-61).

19. "Wenn dem Geistigen in dir die Phantasie ein Zeichen erschafft, und goldne Wolken den Aether des Gedankenreichs umziehn, bestürme nicht die freudigen Gestalten! Wenn dir als Schönheit entgegenkömmt, was du als Wahrheit in dir trägst, so nehm' es dankbar auf, denn du bedarfst der Hülfe der Natur" (202, l. 29-34).

20. The argument is directed against Ryan's claim that Fichte's self-positing subjectivity is at stake here.

Works Cited

Barnouw, Jeffrey. " 'Der Trieb, bestimmt zu werden': Hölderlin, Schiller und Schelling als Antwort auf Fichte." *DVLG* 46 (1972): 248-293.

Behler, Ernst. *Unendliche Perfektibilität: Europäische Romantik und Französische Revolution.* Paderborn: Schöningh, 1989.

Bubner, Rüdiger, ed. *Hegel-Tage Villigst 1969: Das Älteste Systemprogramm.* Hegel-Studien, Beiheft 9. Bonn: Bouvier, 1973.

Buhr, Gerhard. *Hölderlins Mythenbegriff: Eine Untersuchung zu den Fragmenten "Über Religion" und "Das Werden im Vergehen."* Frankfurt: Athenäum, 1972.

Frank, Manfred. "Aufklärung als analytische und synthetische Vernunft. Vom französischen Materialismus über Kant zur Frühromantik." *Aufklärung und Gegenaufklärung in der europäischen Literatur, Philosophie und Politik von der Antike bis zur Gegenwart.* Ed. Jochen Schmidt. Darmstadt: Wissenschaftliche Buchgesellschaft, 1989. 377-403.

————. *Der kommende Gott: Vorlesungen über die neue Mythologie.* Frankfurt: Suhrkamp, 1982.

Gaier, Ulrich. *Der Gesetzliche Kalkül: Hölderlins Dichtungslehre.* Hermaea, Neue Folge 14. Tübingen: Niemeyer, 1962.

————. "Hölderlin und der Mythos." *Terror und Spiel: Probleme der Mythen-rezeption.* Ed. Manfred Fuhrmann. Poetik und Hermeneutik 4. München: Fink, 1971. 295-340.

Henrich, Dieter. *Hegel im Kontext.* Suhrkamp: Frankfurt, 1971.

Hölderlin, Friedrich. *Essays and Letters on Theory.* Trans. and ed. Thomas Pfau. Albany: SUNY Press, 1988. Cited as "Hölderlin."

————. *Sämtliche Werke.* Ed. Friedrich Beißner. Stuttgart: Cotta, 1943- . Cited as "StA."

————. *Sämtliche Werke. Kritische Textausgabe.* Ed. D. E. Sattler. Frankfurt: Roter Stern, 1975- . Cited as "FA."

Horkheimer, Max and Theodor W. Adorno. *Dialectic of Enlightenment.* Trans. John Cumming. New York: Continuum, 1972.

Jamme, Christoph. "Aufklärung via Mythologie: Zum Zusammenhang von Natur-beherrschung und Naturfrömmigkeit um 1800." Jamme and Kurz 35-58.

————. *"Ein ungelehrtes Buch: Die philosophische Gemeinschaft zwischen Höl-derlin und Hegel in Frankfurt 1797-1800.* Hegel-Studien, Beiheft 23. Bonn: Bouvier, 1983.

————. " 'Hölderlin und die Aufklärung.' Bericht über die von mir geleitete Arbeitsgruppe." *Hölderlin-Jahrbuch* 25 (1986-87): 281-82.

————. " 'Jedes Lieblose ist Gewalt': Der junge Hegel, Hölderlin und die Dia-lektik der Aufklärung." *Hölderlin-Jahrbuch* 23 (1982-83): 191-228.

Jamme, Christoph, and Gerhard Kurz, eds. *Idealismus und Aufklärung: Kontinuität und Kritik der Aufklärung in Philosophie und Poesie um 1800.* Deutscher Idea-lismus 14. Stuttgart: Klett-Cotta, 1988.

Jamme, Christoph, and Otto Pöggeler, eds. *Homburg von der Höhe in der deutschen Geistesgeschichte: Studien zum Freundeskreis um Hegel und Hölderlin.* Deut-scher Idealismus 4. Stuttgart: Klett-Cotta, 1981.

————. *'Frankfurt aber ist der Nabel dieser Erde': Das Schicksal einer Generation der Goethezeit.* Deutscher Idealismus 8. Stuttgart: Klett-Cotta, 1983.

Jamme, Christoph, and Helmut Schneider, eds. *Mythologie der Vernunft: Hegels "ältestes Systemprogramm" des deutschen Idealismus.* Frankfurt: Suhrkamp, 1984.

Kondylis, Panajotis. *Die Entstehung der Dialektik: Eine Analyse der geistigen Entwik-klung von Hölderlin, Schelling und Hegel bis 1802.* Stuttgart: Klett-Cotta, 1979.

Kurz, Gerhard. "Höhere Aufklärung: Aufklärung und Aufklärungskritik bei Höl-derlin." Jamme and Kurz 259-282.

————. *Mittelbarkeit und Vereinigung: Zum Verhältnis von Poesie, Reflexion und Revolution bei Hölderlin.* Stuttgart: Metzler, 1975.

Nägele, Rainer. *Text, Geschichte und Subjektivität in Hölderlins Dichtung: "Uneßba-rer Schrift gleich."* Stuttgart: Metzler, 1985.

Ryan, Lawrence. *Hölderlins "Hyperion": Exzentrische Bahn und Dichterberuf.* Stutt-gart: Metzler, 1965.

Thomasberger, Andreas. "Mythos—Religion—Mythe: Hölderlins Grundlegung ei-ner neuen Mythologie in seinem 'Fragment philosophischer Briefe.' " Jamme and Pöggeler, *Frankfurt* 284-99.

Wegenast, Margarethe. *Hölderlins Spinoza-Rezeption und ihre Bedeutung für die Konzeption des "Hyperion."* Studien zur deutschen Literatur 112. Tübingen: Niemeyer, 1990.

PART THREE

Patriarchy and Enlightenment

"I owed my diary the truth of my views": Femininity and Autobiography after 1784

Helga Meise

KANT'S ESSAY, *An Answer to the Question: "What is Enlightenment?"* challenged the individual to take responsibility for his own development. The famous "sapere aude," however, did not apply to women in the same way as it did to men. As Kant himself reiterated unequivocally in 1791, "women are not independent beings in civil affairs. . . . Young men later mature and come fully of age, something that women never achieve."[1]

While the Enlightenment challenged the individual to "transform himself" so that he could move from a state of immaturity to one of full individuation,[2] women were asked to pattern themselves after a universal model of femininity, one that limited women to the role of housewife, wife and mother. How did women react to a situation where a man was called upon to focus on his own self in his process of individuation and maturation, while women were expected to take on an externally dictated definition of self and to confine themselves to their naturally ordained role as mother, a process that would serve to justify the exclusion of women from civil society (see Honegger, *Ordnung*)?

This question can be answered by examining autobiographies written by women concurrent to the debate about women's dependent status. These autobiographies indicate that women were interested in their own sense of self. The specific contours of this self will become clear through three examples of these autobiographies: Margarethe Elisabeth Milow (1748-1794), Dorothea Friderika Baldinger (1739-1786), and Elisa von der Recke (1754-1833).

To begin, a few comments about the social situation of these three women: all three belonged to the same generation and composed their autobiographies in the 1780s at a time in their lives when they would have all received the "personal status" of matron,[3] that is, they all had been married for quite some time and had had several children. Baldinger mentions six childbirths; Milow fulfills her writing aspirations during her seventh of eight pregnancies; Recke, on the other hand, had only one child. The three women belong to different social classes. Margarethe Hudtwalcker, born in Hamburg in 1748, was the daughter of the merchant Heinrich Jacob Hudtwalcker. In 1769, Margarethe married the tutor and pastor Johann Nicolaus Milow (1738-1795), who initially held a position at the Academy for nobles in Lüneburg and later, in 1772, was appointed pastor in Wandsbek. Margarethe Milow died of breast cancer in Wandsbek in 1794. Dorothea Friderika Gutbier, the daughter of a minister, came from the Mühlehausen district in Thuringia. In 1764, she married a physician, Ernst Gottfried Baldinger (1738-1804). Dorothea died in 1786 in Marburg on the Lahn without having witnessed the conclusion of her husband's brilliant career as Privy Councillor and professor of medicine. Charlotta Elisabeth Konstantia von Medem was the daughter of the Courland landowner and later Imperial Count, Johann Friedrich von Medem. In 1771, Charlotta was married to Baron Georg Magnus von der Recke (1739-1795), consenting, like Margarethe Milow, to a marriage against her will. After their separation in 1776 and the death of their only child in 1778, the couple divorced in 1781 after ten years of marriage. Elisa lived for a time at the court of her stepsister, Duchess Dorothea of Courland. She also travelled extensively and eventually settled in Dresden in 1819, where she died in 1833.

When one compares the autobiographical writings of these three women, one finds different points of emphasis in the writers' thematization of self. The memoirs of Margarethe Milow seem to follow most closely the conventions of "family histories,"[4] which had become widespread in Europe since the sixteenth century. Her writings are structured chronologically, and after beginning with a description of her parents, she then proceeds with memories of her own life: "My earliest memories are of going to school to learn to read."[5] Although she employs the form and techniques of traditional autobiography, Milow makes clear from the outset that she is writing for her family. Throughout her writing she addresses her husband and children. Every memory that is called forth is readdressed to her "children," thus keeping in mind her intention that "these experiences will be of particular use to you, my children."[6] Following the tradition of family histories, the notion of honor (*Ehre*) plays a significant role in Milow's writing. Family honor and the respect that the family enjoys publicly determine the status of the individual in society and shape her perception of self.[7]

The notion of honor is also reflected in Milow's consciousness of social standing. In this traditional, family-oriented autobiography, however, we also hear "modern" voices that, following Rousseau's *Emile* (1762), propagate the inherent distinction between the sexes:

> My father was a good, and I am tempted to say, almost too good a husband. Through her beauty and behavior toward him, his wife had gained power over him. But it is not good, my children, for even the best of wives to rule their husbands. A lot of things would certainly have been different and indeed better at home if my father had had more authority, if he had been more of a man.[8]

While these individual perceptions of self and others are derived not from the family's reputation and respect in the public sphere, but rather from everyday family life, Margarethe tends increasingly in the course of her memoirs to address the children according to gender: episodes that pertain to the household are directed to "my daughters" (107), and everything that relates to work and travelling is addressed to "my sons" (120). Within this framework of role distribution according to gender, it is clear from the start that the young Margarethe Hudtwalcker will marry. This context determines her upbringing and the stages of education typical for bourgeois girls: reading, sewing, writing, arithmetic; school, private French lessons, private tutor; family theater productions, reading mania. From the time Margarethe is thirteen, she and her sisters concern themselves exclusively with the search for and evaluation of suitable candidates for marriage.

For eight years, until her marriage in 1768, the major theme of Margarethe's writing is her relationship to the opposite sex. She carefully lists all of the advances by men that she has successfully warded off in order to emphasize her own virtue. Thus, she marvels "even today at the strength with which I . . . rose above these situations,"[9] in reference to her first teacher, Flügge. She comments in the same manner on the kiss and declaration of love from a former theology student, Hahn: "For several days I was in a state of bliss thinking about Hahn . . . but after a couple of days this subsided and I was myself again."[10] Throughout the work Margarethe presents herself in the light of Rousseau's concept of femininity: "and so I remained as I was, nature through and through."[11] The thematization of self is unthinkable without taking into consideration the dictates of gender.

In 1768, Margarethe fell in love with Johann Octav Nolte, who was four years her elder. Nolte was an underling in her father's business and was the best friend of Margarethe's beloved older brother.[12] When her father became aware of this socially unacceptable relationship, Margarethe decided to remain true to Octav in spite of all opposition. This desire opens up new aspects of her self: "I was utterly hopeful and

feared nothing. I saw the future through rose-colored glasses."[13] In
response to the marriage proposal by the poor but nonetheless socially
compatible tutor Johann Milow, Margarethe decides

> to say no, come what may. . . . I said no [to my parents], and gave the excuse
> that I would never be able to leave Hamburg. . . . "By the way," my father said
> looking at me sternly, "I hope that Octav did not have the slightest thing to do
> with this refusal. You can turn this one down, but remember, the next time, it
> won't be that easy."[14]

When Flügge asks Margarethe's parents once again for their daughter's
hand in marriage, Margarethe feels forced to choose between him and
Milow. In order to spare her father any "scandal" (*Schande*, 68), but
also to free herself from social pressure within the family, Margarethe
agrees within a few days to marry Milow. The "torment" (*Leiden*) and
"fears" (*Ängste*) that are connected with the love affair with Octav lead
the author to a confrontation with self:

> I would have gladly changed places with any person who passed by my window,
> even the most impoverished or unfortunate.
>   I became sick with a terrible colic and was bedridden for two days. I wel-
> comed this, for I was alone with myself. I struggled, prayed and realized from
> all of this, that it was over.[15]

In depicting this experience, the author moves away from the traditional position of the daughter as defined by family histories, to a description of a love story experienced first hand. While this change in
perspective shifts the focus onto the female self, nowhere in the autobiography do we find protests, complaints or any mention of what Margarethe Milow 'really' feels or thinks. Instead, her portrayal adheres to
preexisting models. While her love for Octav reads like the plot of a
novel, it forces her to examine her own conscience:

> Did I behave correctly after all those assurances and promises that I had made
> to Octav? Did I do right by Milow, who loved me with all his heart, by not tell-
> ing him the whole story and by offering him at first only half a heart? Was it
> right of me that I didn't write to Octav about my decision to marry Milow? But
> I did indeed write him a consoling letter that evening, even though I can re-
> member nothing of its contents. Was I really unfaithful to him? Did I forget
> him too quickly, as many maintained afterward?[16]

It is beyond Margarethe's ability to answer this question:

> May God pass judgment on it all. He subjected me to a thorough examination.
> He saw within my soul, as always, let him judge my actions on that day, too.
> Let him judge me; he is the father and will do it in a fatherly fashion. He alone
> witnessed my struggle between love and parents. . . . Only God saw my true suf-
> ferings back then . . . [and the suffering of others]. Only he knew that I was the
> cause of it all.[17]

After deciding against love, traces of this experience can hardly be found in Milow's writing. The author shifts to a description of her life as housewife, wife and mother at the side of Johann Milow.

Margarethe Milow's autobiography reveals a self that follows the norms set for model female behavior. At the same time, however, her writing exposes the fissures in those norms.

The strong emotions revealed by her other self are channeled into the process of teaching her own children and her attempt to justify her actions to herself and her family. Her personal story is camouflaged by the novel-like techniques of the autobiography; nonetheless, the significance of this experience could not be completely eradicated from the autobiography.

In contrast to Margarethe Milow, Dorothea Friderika Baldinger's life story does not serve the purpose of chronicling family history or of describing her parents:

> My father died before I had a chance to get to know him. If intelligence were hereditary, I could have inherited some from this man who was, by all accounts, very wise and intelligent. Perhaps he bequeathed to me the ability to recognize the intelligence of others and to make use of it. I personally do not believe in this kind of heredity.[18]

The author writes instead a "History of My Intellect,"[19] and with that enters into the heart of the Enlightenment debate about the role of a girl's intellect in the fulfillment of woman's "natural vocation," that of housewife, spouse, and mother (see Meise 35ff.). At the same time, this portrayal of her intellectual development is not intended to defend women's claim to intellect: "As if I had so much intelligence that it would be worth the trouble of tracing its development."[20] Upon closer examination, one sees that Baldinger attributes exactly the same meaning to female intelligence as can be found in the Enlightenment's discourse on gender ideology: in addition to household skills, intelligence is also seen as indispensable for women. However, because women do not have authority over their own intellect, it always remains subordinate to that of men and does not enable women to achieve autonomy.

Only against the backdrop of this gender hierarchy (see Honegger) is a "history of my intellect" imaginable. Initially, Baldinger is enthusiastic about learning: "I even wanted to be learned and was angry that my sex prevented me from becoming so. However, if at least you want to become knowledgeable, I thought, you must read diligently, for knowledge comes from books."[21] This enthusiasm gives way, however, to the belief that "by marrying I would make any man unhappy and myself as well if I couldn't give his intellect its due respect."[22] Friderika's brother shared his studies at Schulpforta and at the university with her:

> From his letters came my first ray of knowledge. Or rather, I understood what many a learned man never has, namely *that I didn't know a thing.* How I looked forward to the return of my brother, who wanted to bring daylight into my dark mind. He finally came, and it would be impossible to describe how dearly we loved each other. We were of one heart and mind.[23]

Following her brother's advice, however, Friderika learns to accept the limits of female perfectibility. She gives up her passion for reading and learnedness, her loathing for the world and humankind, and accepts Ernst Baldinger's marriage proposal: "This proposal from a learned, intelligent and honest man was too much of a compliment to my own heart and mind for me to make his conquest difficult."[24]

While Baldinger interprets her story as portraying the development of her intellect, the autobiography reveals how her presentation of self is constantly caught in a struggle between a self she herself determines and one dictated by external norm, how Baldinger's reflections on her own self—what her self is or should be—are overlaid by others' models for self-understanding.[25] This is seen, for example, in the ideas about femininity presented by her brother and her "spiritual father" (*geistiger Vater*, 28) Kranichfeld, that force her to be critical of the level of intellectual development she has attained:

> Girl, you receive more approval than you can imagine. But if you ever want to marry, I beg of you, in God's name, not to choose anyone but a learned and very intelligent man. If you ever surpass your husband, you will be the unhappiest creature that I know.[26]

In the course of the autobiography it becomes clear that the self is defined mainly in comparison to other women and the characteristics of femininity they embody:

> My mother was in every respect *a woman* who distinguished herself through nothing else. . . . Everything she taught me could be summarized by the following sentence: You must be *pious and chaste.* . . . This woman [an aunt] could have influenced my intellectual development, if she herself had received the proper training. She had never read anything challenging, and in those days, when she was a young woman, things were not yet very advanced for women's education.[27]

While Baldinger obediently adopts these teachings, she also transcends the antiquated model of femininity they represent. In so doing, she becomes receptive to education.[28] Nevertheless, the emphasis in this thematization of self is not on the opportunities her "intellect" could open up for her (they were negligible enough), but rather simply on learning its proper use. In the "wit" that contemporaries perceived in Friderika Baldinger[29] one can detect what motivated this woman and what, at the same time, undermines the official version of her "story": "As a woman I have become acceptable. How insignificant I would be as a man."[30]

Margarethe Milow and Friderika Baldinger have different points of emphasis in their autobiographical writings. They resemble each other, however, in that they both limit themselves to that supposedly private sphere considered appropriate for women, namely the family.[31] Elisa von der Recke seems to break out of this pattern. She explicitly writes solely for herself, yet she repeatedly envisions publishing her autobiographical writings. This contradiction runs through all of these extensive writings—letters, diaries, an autobiography and a memoir.[32]

The diaries give insight into the everyday life of an unmarried woman of nobility, an endlessly repetitive routine that consists of visits, diplomatic missions, cultural trips and spa retreats. All of these activities are aimed at creating a social network that would assist Recke in achieving her political(!) goal, namely maintaining the independence of the Duchy Courland, which she refers to as "my fatherland."[33] Recke comes across in this regard as a woman who untypically moves between various social classes. Her statements about certain social problems, for example, the tensions between nobility and bourgeoisie, reveal that Recke never feels at home with either group (Träger ed. 15). Both of the autobiographical writings—the autobiography from her birth until her engagement (Rachel ed. 1: 1-154) and the memoir that prefaces a diary entry (Rachel ed. 2: 277-301)—describe the typical life of an unhappily married woman:

> At the age of fifteen I was given away to a man that I tried to love but simply couldn't, since we were of completely opposite natures. . . . I hid from everyone how unhappy my marriage was.[34]

Although Recke eventually manages to separate and get a divorce from her husband, her ideas about love, family and the role of women remain unchanged. She tends to valorize the "bourgeois family . . . as a refuge from an intellectually impoverished, superficial way of life" (Träger ed. 14). These ideas are expressed most clearly in the autobiography of her childhood and youth written in 1795 (Rachel ed. 1: vi-vii):

> Brinck [like Taube, a potential marital partner] stared at me with a look that I can still remember. He said nothing except the single word 'love', in a gentle, searching tone. He sighed, I was silent. Taube, too, looked down thoughtfully. A solemn silence enveloped us. After a while we stood up, but this was one of those moments in life one never forgets.[35]

The novelistic characteristics of this life are unmistakable and resemble those found in Margarethe Milow's work.[36] As Recke indicates in her diaries, subsequent to her divorce she turned down at least five additional, extremely interesting marriage proposals (Träger ed. 11).

In a central passage toward the end of the preface to her diaries for 1789/90, Recke describes the conception at the heart of her autobiographical writings: the diary is meant to ward off loneliness and compensate for the lack of a "female friend" (Rachel ed. 2: 298-99). This motivation puts autobiographical writing into the same context as the writing of fiction by male and female writers of the time (Meise 182ff.). The significance of this motivation becomes clear when one considers Recke's biography: if one keeps in mind that Recke has been experimenting with various types of autobiographical writing already for forty years when she writes about "keeping diaries" in 1810, one begins to suspect the existential significance of this life-long activity.[37] While autobiographical writing serves on the one hand as a means of warding off absence, at the same time it functions as a means of reproducing the self:

> I myself had to become my only female friend. I decided to keep a diary in which I was accountable for my innermost life as if to a conscience. I had to write down my thoughts and judgments, as they emerged, as a lesson to myself and as a form of self-scrutiny. There is no better way to judge oneself than to step outside of oneself and become a second "I."[38]

The diary as conscience posits the permanent relationship of the "I" to itself:[39] "As my most sacred precept I set a rule for myself to judge *myself strictly, others sparingly*: but I owed my diary the truth of my views."[40] This strict self-control transforms the diary into an instrument of libidinal surveillance.[41] As such, the diary appears as the only place where the "I" can experience itself as a subject. At the same time, the "I" delegates this experience to the diary: In the diary the "I's" "true" convictions are written down and are protected from further exposure: "it contains candid judgments about people, events and sources of information that must never become public" (Rachel ed. 2: 299-300).[42] This explicit self-consciousness and the relationship with the "second I" are coupled at the same time with the desire to publish the written reflection of these processes. Both of these aspects together distinguish this thematization of self from the modest methods of Margarethe Milow and Friderika Baldinger. Elisa von der Recke formulates these thoughts precisely when she begins to destroy extensive parts of her 1798 and 1790 diaries with the intention of publishing individual excerpts from them at a later date:

> From December 26, 1789, until 1804 I had kept a diary, in which I gave an account of myself, my feelings, my activities and my experiences.—*These* pages contain excerpts from the first diary that I kept in this manner, a diary that I

continued for a period of fifteen years and that grew to eighteen volumes. I destroyed the greater part of these volumes so that they would not be misused after my death.—I kept a diary of my journey through Germany and Italy with the intention of reading it to my friends, and this last diary I reworked for publication. 26 June 1823.[43]

"Truth" is elevated by Recke to the highest principle of self-thematization. It exists, however, only within the text. Because the "I" controls these texts as it pleases, the truth remains the secret of the "I" and cannot be found even in the published autobiographical writings. At the same time, however, the reader is introduced to the ways in which this use of truth functions: while Margarethe Milow speaks of "truth" in order to assert the factual condition of "innocence," Elisa von der Recke's concept of truth points to a "technology of the self" (see Foucault). With Milow, this concept of truth is characterized by a superimposing of gender-specific connotations of female behavior as dictated by social norms onto the religious meaning of innocence, that is, innocence before God: "If he [the father] could have looked into our heart, how pure it was, so free of all guilt!"[44] Recke's use of the concept of truth seems to me more a demonstration of her public support for the Enlightenment, whose discourse she employed for the process of saying the truth by concealing it.

I am referring to the position she took regarding the practices of the "magician" Cagliostro (1743-1795),[45] a man well-known and sought after throughout Europe (mainly from 1779 to 1789) as a miracle worker, alchemist, magician, seer, conjurer and impostor. Like many other successful practitioners of this type, Cagliostro maintained that "mythical belief and rational knowledge intertwined in the eighteenth century and that they belonged to the same stage in the history of consciousness that individuals were coming to terms with."[46] When Cagliostro and his wife visited Courland in 1779, Recke was already separated from her husband and had experienced the deaths of both her daughter and her beloved brother. She herself had returned to the family home. Recke's work, *A Report on the Sojourn of the Notorious Cagliostro in Mietau in 1779*, was published under her name by Nicolai in 1787. The report states clearly that the Cagliostro couple won favor with the Medem family and was able to gain a foothold in the Mitau elite mainly by exploiting Recke's personal situation:

He told me he had been sent as Grand Maitre by his superiors with the authority to establish a Loge d'Adoption or a Masonic lodge to which women would be granted membership. When the late Privy Councillor Schwander . . . saw that my aunt, my cousin and I were not to be stopped and that we insisted on being initiated as members of a Loge d'Adoption, he joined the group out of friendship and solicitude for me.[47]

Offering women the prospect of membership in these societies also meant making accessible to them the 'secret' centers of power where politics were supposedly determined. That women made up the majority of the regular audience for occult practices, which were very popular in this context, is documented in a contemporary Parisian report that appeared in the *Correspondance Littéraire* in November 1785. It shows how "rational knowledge" and "mythical belief" come together in such a seance.[48]

The seductive tactics used by Cagliostro in Paris, combining the spiritual with the material and the real social experiences of women with prospects for change, must also have been employed in Mitau, because Recke refers several times in her report to her virtue and explains that she initially had become suspicious of Cagliostro precisely in this regard (67, 137). Before the actual critique and unmasking of the "impostor," which is the central focus of the report, female virtue appears as a shield against the attacks of esoteric, un-Christian unbelief, an aspect that is also emphasized several times in Nicolai's foreword: "her unwavering moral principles" led her "on the right path."[49] Recke herself goes into no further detail about the disillusionment she experiences when she is not invited as a female lodge member. With the exception of a reference to the article mentioned above that had appeared in the *Correspondance Littéraire*, a reference which emphasizes the virtue of the Mitau women in contrast to that of the Parisian women (7-8), Recke follows the pattern of other writings in her criticism of this fanaticism and reproaches herself for not having been an "unbiased observer and composed investigator" (see "no mature reflection,"[50]), but rather for having given herself over to her "imagination" (97).[51] In that regard, the *Report* is part of the discourse against superstition and belief in miracles that was especially pronounced in the *Berlinische Monatsschrift* (*Berlin Monthly*), one of the central organs of Enlightenment debate. This discourse can be viewed as the counterpart of the debate on the meaning of Enlightenment that appeared in the same journal (for example, Kant's essay *What Is Enlightenment?*). In this journal further texts on Recke's response to Cagliostro and her experiences with him had been published in 1786,[52] and it was Nicolai, one of the leading representatives of the Berlin Enlightenment, who edited Recke's separately published critique a year later.

Recke's 1787 essay demonstrates the process of self-enlightenment to which she subjugated herself. Hence the autobiographical characteristics of the text whenever she comments on her 1779 report on Cagliostro's practices: in the editor's dedication and foreword (vii-xxi), in the author's address "To my male and female friends in Courland and Germany" (xxi-xxii), in her introduction (1-23), and, above all, in the extensive commentary that she added in 1787 as a result, according to Recke (8-9), of the influence of other contemporary works. Nicolai had the running commentary printed opposite the text (excerpts are now available in Binder's edition of Goethe's *Grand Cophta* 111-28).

Throughout these "metatexts" that seem to overshadow the report itself (see Genette), "truth" is the key concept under which a woman can take part in Enlightenment discourse even when her real intentions go unspoken. Truth also appears as a form of textual practice, one that does not, however, necessarily imply the articulation of truth. Recke explicitly assures her reader that she has guarded the secrets of the Freemasons (xxvii). The editor, Nicolai, emphasizes in the foreword that the process of critiquing the original report with a second, extensive text and additional commentary adds to the credibility of the author:

> The truth was enhanced when in 1779 the noble author wrote down everything Cagliostro did, as it was happening, as well as her own judgments, for her own use.[53]

> [S]eldom does one want to think about or at least make known how he has been deceived.[54]

It was precisely this process from which Elisa von der Recke was unable to free herself for the rest of her life. All of her autobiographical writings were put through the same critique: in 1793 she rearranged her letters (Rachel ed. 1: viii). Beginning in 1793, her diaries and other documents were suffused with a set of commentaries such that the texts progressively disintegrate and bury beneath them the very subjectivity that had been striving for expression. With Elisa von der Recke we can see how one woman's attempt at initiating and documenting changes in the self annuls autobiographical technique itself.

Notes

1. "sind die Frauenzimmer in bürgerlichen Angelegenheiten unmündig. . . . Die Jünglinge werden später reif, aber dann auch ganz mündig, welches die Frauenzimmer nie werden können" (Kant 35).

2. "an sich selbst . . . die Veränderung" [zu schaffen]. See Michel Foucault, "Was ist Aufklärung?" 38.

3. Heide Wunder ("Frömmigkeit") distinguishes among four different "personal statuses" ("Personenstände") for the phases of a typical female life from 1500 to 1800, those of daughter, wife, matron and widow, and designates for each of these phases the fixed social roles that were associated with them.

4. On "Familiengeschichten" see Davis 7-19 and Niggl 14-15.

5. "Von der Zeit an, da ich mich erinnern kann, ging ich in die Schule, um Lesen zu lernen" (8). According to a conversation I had in November 1991 with the editors and with the publisher, the 1987 edition contains the authentic text.

The original manuscript that has come to light since then consists of approximately 100 pages and pertains mainly to Milow's marriage and everyday life; its publication is forthcoming. An additional part is considered lost.

6. "Euch, meine Kinder besonders, diese Erfahrungen nützen können" (7).

7. On the role of honor, see both studies by Wunder.

8. "Mein Vater war ein guter, und ich möchte fast sagen, zu guter Ehemann; seine Frau hatte viele Gewalt über ihn, welche sie sich durch ihre Schönheit und ihr gutes Betragen gegen ihn sich erwarb. Aber es ist nicht gut, Kinder, daß die Frau, auch wenn sie die Beste ist, über den Mann herrscht, und vieles wäre gewiß anders und besser im Hause gewesen, wenn mein Vater mehr geherrscht, überhaupt mehr Mann gewesen wäre" (8).

9. "noch heute die Stärke, mit der ich ... mich doch immer wieder empor schlang" (20).

10. "Einige Tage vergingen nun noch im Rausch, im Andenken an Hahn ... aber nun hatte es nach ein paar Tagen ein Ende, ich ward wieder ich selbst" (39).

11. "und so blieb ich, wie ich war, ganz Natur" (18).

12. I will not go into detail in this paper about the role of the brother. One should note that Johann Michael Hudtwalcker (1747-1818) began writing an autobiography in 1795 after the death of his sister and his brother-in-law (see Hudtwalcker). To what extent Margarethe's project, begun in 1779, is done in conjunction with her brother and his twenty-year old intention to write remains unknown. The relationship to him runs through Margarethe's autobiography like a red thread: "My brother again became my dearly beloved from that time on when I was engaged, as he had been prior to my love for Octav." ["Mein Bruder, der von der Zeit an, da ich Braut war, wieder ganz mein Geliebter ward, wie er es vor der Zeit meiner Liebe zu Octav war"] (89). This relationship reflects a socialization in gender differences, something that Johann Michael himself continually thematizes (Hudtwackler 162f. Compare Milow 25). The same brother-sister relationship is found in Baldinger and Recke's writing; see Prokop. On the sister-brother-husband triangle, see Becker-Cantarino.

13. "ich hoffte alles, fürchtete nichts, mir hing der Himmer voll Geigen" (45).

14. "Nein zu sagen, es möchte daraus entstehen, was da wollte.... Ich sagte Nein [den Eltern gegenüber], machte die Entschuldigung, daß ich mich nie würde entschließen können, aus Hamburg zu gehen.... 'Übrigens', sagte Papa und sah mich scharf an, 'will ich nicht hoffen, daß Octav den geringsten Anteil an diesem Nein hat. Diesen kannst Du nun abschlagen, aber merke es Dir, beim zweiten wird dirs so leicht nicht werden'" (66).

15. "Jedes Menschen Zustand, den ich am Fenster vorbeigehen sah, auch des Aermsten, des Elendesten hätte ich mit Freuden mit dem meinigen vertauscht ... ich bekam die heftigste Kolik und mußte zu Bette gehen, war den andern Tag noch krank. Dies war mir willkommen, ich war mit mir selbst allein, kämpfte, betete, merkte aus Allem, daß es noch aus sei" (49, 71).

16. "Ob ich recht gehandelt? Nach allen Versicherungen und Schwüren, die ich Octav gethan? Ob ich recht gehandelt gegen Milow, daß ich ihm nicht meine ganze Geschichte erzählte, ihm, der mich mit ganzem Herzen liebte, nur ein halbes zu Anfang gab, ob ich recht gehandelt, daß ich Octav nichts von meinem Entschluß M. zu nehmen, schrieb? Doch schrieb ich ihm den Abend einen Trostbrief, von dem ich mir aber nichts erinnere. Ob ich wirklich treulos gegen ihn gewesen bin, ihn zu bald, wie man hernach glaubte, vergessen habe?" (73).

17. "Das Alles mag Gott beurteilen, er prüft Herz und Niere, er sah damals wie immer in das Innerste meiner Seele, er sei auch an jenem Tag Richter zwi-

schen mir und ihm ... er richte mich, er ist der Vater, er wird es väterlich thun, er allein hat auch meinen Kampf zwischen Liebe und Eltern gesehen, ... Gott hat auch eigentlich nur meine vorigen Leiden recht gesehen ... und die Leiden der anderen], wußte, daß ich an Allem Ursache war" (73-74).

18. "Mein Vater starb, eh ich ihn noch kannte. Wenn der Verstand erblich wäre, so hätte ich von diesem, nach allen Beschreibungen sehr weisen und verständigen Manne, welchen erben können. Vielleicht hat er mir die Fähigkeit hinterlassen, den Verstand anderer zu empfinden, und davon Gebrauch zu machen. Ich für mein Theil glaube aber an kein Erbtheil dieser Art" (17-18).

19. "Geschichte meines Verstandes" (15).

20. "Als ob ich so viel Verstand hätte, daß sich es der Mühe verlohnte seinen Gang nachzuspähen" (17).

21. "Ich wünschte so gar gelehrt zu werden, und ärgerte mich, daß mich mein Geschlecht davon ausschloß. Je so willst du wenigstens klug werden, dachte ich, und dies wird man aus Büchern, du willst brav lesen" (21).

22. "ich jeden Mann so gut als mich selbst durch eine Heurath unglüklich machen würde, wenn ich für seinen Verstand nicht den gehörigen Respect haben könnte" (33).

23. "Aus seinen Briefen schoß der erste Strahl von Verstand in meinen Kopf, oder vielmehr ich empfand, was mancher Gelehrte nie empfunden hat: nähmlich *daß ich noch nichts wußte*. Wie freute ich mich auf die Ankunft des Bruders, der den Tag in mein dunkles Hirn bringen wollte.—Er kam endlich, und wie sehr wir uns liebten, dies würde ich zu beschreiben vergebens unternehmen—Ein Herz und eine Seele" (24).

24. "Dieser Antrag, von einem gelehrten, verständigen und zugleich redlichen Manne, war zu viel Compliment für mein eigenes Herz und Verstand, als daß ich ihm seine Eroberung hätte sauer machen sollen" (34).

25. Here I follow Honegger's distinction in her work on "Gender-Specific Aspects of Thematization by Self and by Other."

26. "Mädchen du findest mehr Beifall als du glaubst, aber ich bitte dich um Gotteswillen, wenn du jemals heurathen solltest, so nimm ja keinen andern als einen gelehrten, und besonders sehr verständigen Mann, denn wo du einmal deinen Mann übersehen kannst, bist du die unglücklichste Creatur, die ich kenne" (26).

27. "Meine Mutter war in allem Verstand *Frau*, die sich weiter durch nichts auszeichnete. ... Aber alle ihre Lehren könnte ich unter folgende Wörter bringen: *Fromm und Keusch* mußt du seyn. ... Diese Frau [die Tante] hätte Einfluß auf meinen Verstand haben können, wenn der Ihrige selbst besser ausgebildet gewesen wäre: sie hatte aber niemals etwas kluges gelesen, und die Zeiten in welchen sie jung gewesen war, waren noch nicht die vortheilhaftesten für die weibliche Erziehung" (18, 20).

28. That the individual phases of development in "The History of My Intellect" lay claim to the principle of education needs no further emphasis. It does, however, point to the difference between Baldinger and Milow and the literature that Milow refers to in her autobiography:

One of the first books that my friend [Kranichfeld] lent me was *Der Zuschauer* [Gottsched's translation (1739-1744) of Addison and Steele's *The Spectator*]. I marveled at the book, as I had read nothing more beautiful in my entire life. Last year [ca. 25 years later] I tried to read this book again but was unable. That is the way I am now as compared to back then.

Eines der ersten Bücher, welche mir mein Freund [Kranichfeld] borgte, war der Zuschauer. Ich staunte das Buch an, denn ich hatte in meinem Leben nichts schöneres gelesen. Voriges Jahr versuchte ich dieß Buch wieder zu lesen, und konnte es nicht. So verhalte ich mich jezt gegen damals. (Baldinger 29)

See Goodman 11-12.

    29. Animated by wit, enlightened by knowledge;
    Yet being good was her even greater merit;
    True to her duty, never longing to excel:
    Now He will reward her, who sees what is concealed.

    Durch Witz belebt, durch Kenntniß aufgeklärt;
    Doch gut zu seyn, war ihr noch größerer Werth;
    Treu ihrer Pflicht, zu glänzen unbemüht:
    Nun lohnt Er ihr, der in's Verborgene sieht.

Abraham Gotthelf Kästner's epitaph to Baldinger (Kästner 81) was employed eight weeks later by Sophie von La Roche to describe Baldinger (La Roche 290).

    30. "Als Frau bin ich erträglich geworden, wie klein würde ich doch als Mann seyn?" (39). See also: "I didn't want to marry because I loathed any type of physical love. I had the constitution of a saint, was pious, a vestal virgin, and also had raptures. I couldn't perform any miracles, for then, according to the rules, I would have first had to excel at something so that people would have something to say about me.... Nevertheless, I had many opportunities to be happy through marriage, if one conceives of happiness as something other than selling one's body for life long to men one doesn't love in exchange for food and drink." ["Ich mogte nie heurathen, weil ich wider alle körperliche Liebe einen Eckel hatte. Ich hatte alle Anlage zu einer Heiligen, ich war fromm, und eine Vestalin, schwärmte auch, nur konnte ich keine Wunder thun, denn dazu hätte ich, nach allen Regeln, erst streben müssen, damit man etwas von mir hätte erzehlen können.... Demohngeachtet hatte ich oft Gelegenheit mein Glük durch Heurathen zu machen, wenn man anders sein Glük dadurch macht, daß man seinen Leib, für Essen und Trinken, zeitlebens an Männer verkauft, die man nicht lieben kann" (32-33).]

    31. Baldinger dedicates her writing to her husband at the time of his professional advancement to Privy Councillor and personal physician to the count of Hessen-Kassel: "I have him to thank for my entire personal development. He constructed my intellect and strengthened my will and heart" ("ihm habe ich alle Entwickelung meiner Seelenkräfte zu verdanken. Er hat meinen Verstand gebaut, meinen Willen und mein Herz gebessert," 36). See *Allgemeine Deutsche Biographie* 2 (1875): 4-5.

    32. On the transmission of the manuscripts, see Paul Rachel's foreword in his Recke edition. Recke's works will be cited parenthetically by the editor's name.

    33. "meines Vaterlandes." See Christina Träger's preface in Recke's *Tagebücher und Selbstzeugnisse* 9-34.

    34. "In einem Alter von fünfzehn Jahren wurd' ich einem Manne gegeben, den ich zu lieben wünschte und nicht lieben konnte, weil unsere Neigungen durchaus entgegengesetzt waren.... Ich verbarg es jedem—wie unglücklich meine Ehe war" (Rachel ed. 2: 277-78).

    35. "Brinck sah mich mit einem Blick an, der mir noch gegenwärtig ist, sagte nichts, als mit sanft forschendem Tone das einzelne Wort: Lieben! Er seufzte, ich schwieg, und auch Taube schlug die Blicke gedankenvoll nieder. Eine feierliche Stille herrschte unter uns. Wir verließen nach einer Weile unsere Plätze, aber dies

war auch so ein Moment des Lebens, der sich in der Seele nie verwischt" (Rachel ed. 2: 119). Significantly, the first of the three books concludes with the prospect of marrying Brinck, a man with whom she was in love, thus giving her autobiography an overarching structure typical of fiction.

36. See Goodman 47-48. On the relationship of the novel and the polarization of gender characteristics, see Gallas and Heuser. In contrast to the novel, the confession as a form of expression seems to lose significance in this period. See Blackwell.

37. See "Briefe Elisas von der Recke: Aus der Zeit ihrer unglücklichen Ehe 1771-1778" (Rachel 1: 155-429).

38. "mußte ich selbst meine einzige Freundin werden. Ich beschloß, ein Tagebuch zu führen, worin ich nun wie wor einem Gewissen von meinem innersten Leben Rechnung ablegte und meine Gedanken und Urtheile, so wie sie in mir aufstiegen, der Reihe nach zu meiner eigenen Belehrung und Prüfung aufstellte. Man lernt sich nicht besser beurtheilen, als wenn man aus sich selbst heraustritt und gleichsam sein zweites Ich wird" (Rachel 2: 299-300).

39. On the notion of reproducing the self ("Ich-Verdoppelung"), see Kittsteiner 274-75.

40. "Zum heiligsten Pflichtgebot hatte ich mir die Regel gemacht, *mich strenge, andre schonend* zu beurtheilen: aber meinem Tagebuche war ich Wahrheit meiner Ansicht schuldig" (Rachel 2: 299-300).

41. This idea is not new and can be found already in autobiographical texts of the early modern period; see Chartier.

42. "daher es über Menschen, über Begebenheiten und deren Quellen sehr offenherzige Urtheile enthält, welche nie zu einer öffentlichen Kunde gelangen dürfen" (Rachel 2: 299-300).

43. "Vom 26ten Dec. 1789 bis zum Jahre 1804 hatte ich ein Tagebuch geführt, in welchem ich über mich selbst, meine Gefühle, Handlungen und Erfahrungen mir Rechenschaft ablegte.—*Diese* Blätter enthalten Auszüge aus meinem ersten in dieser Art geschriebenen Tagebuche, welches ich in dem Zeitraume von 15 Jahren fortführte und welches bis zu 18 Bänden angewachsen war, die ich größtenteils vernichtet habe, auf daß nach meinem Tode kein Mißbrauch geschehe.—Das Tagebuch meiner Reise durch Teutschland und Italien hielt ich mit dem Vorsatze, es meinen Freunden mitzutheilen, und dies letzte Tagebuch überarbeitete ich zum Drucke. d. 26. Juny 1823" (Rachel 2: 300-1).

44. "Wenn er [der Vater] hätte in unser Herz blicken können, wie es so rein war, so frei von aller Schuld!" (Milow 69).

45. See the title of Oppeln-Bronikowski's book.

46. Kiefer, "Okkultismus" 289; see also Kiefer, "Definition," as well as his new Cagliostro documentation, which had not been published when I wrote this essay.

47. "Er sagte mir, er sei von seinen Oberen gesendet, mit der Vollmacht, als Grand Maitre eine Loge d'Adoption oder eine Freimauerloge, in welche Frauenzimmer zugelassen werden, zu gründen. Da nun der sel. Hofrath Schwander ... sah, daß meine Tante, meine Cousine und ich nicht zurückzuhalten waren und uns durchaus als Mitglieder einer Loge d'Adoption wollten aufnehmen lassen, so trat auch er aus Freundschaft und Vorsorge für mich zu dieser Gesellschaft" (*Nachricht* 7-8).

48. Kiefer, *Wiedergeburt* 159ff. See *Correspondance littéraire, philosophique et critique* (Paris, 1880) 14: 255ff. On the relationship of femininity and the occult, which has not been fully investigated, see Darnton and Vigni; I was unable to see the article by Ebrecht when I wrote this essay. On the relationship of Goethe and

Cagliostro, see Müller-Seidel.

49. "Indessen würde auch die vorzügliche Geisteskraft diese edle Frau nicht so geschwind auf den rechten Weg geleitet, wenn Ihr nicht Ihre unerschütterlichen moralischen Principien . . . zu Hülfe gekommen wären" (xi).

50. "unvoreingenommener Beobachter und ruhigforschend Untersucherinn" (35); "kein reifliches Nachdenken" (97).

51. Lessing's *Nathan* also had a decisive role in converting her (Rachel 2: 18).

52. *Berlinische Monatsschrift* (1786.5): 385-98. For a response to a reaction that had appeared in July, see *Berlinische Monatsschrift* (1786.9): 197-208.

53. "Sehr glücklich für die Wahrheit war es, daß die edle Verfasserinn, 1779, gleich auf frischer That, alles was Cagliostro vornahm, und zugleich Ihre damaligen Urtheile, zu Ihrem eigenen Gebrauche niederschrieb" (x).

54. "selten [will] jemand selbst nachdenken, oder wenigstens selten offenbaren, . . . auf welche Art er ist betrogen worden" (xv).

Works Cited

Baldinger, Friderika. *Lebensbeschreibung der Friderika Baldinger von ihr selbst verfaßt.* Ed. Sophie von La Roche. Offenbach, 1791.

Becker-Cantarino, Barbara. "Freundschaftsutopie: Fiktionen der Sophie La Roche." *Untersuchungen zum Roman von Frauen um 1800.* Ed. Helga Gallas and Magdalene Heuser. Tübingen: Niemeyer, 1990. 92-114.

Binder, Alwin, ed. Johann Wolfgang Goethe, *Der Groß-Cophta.* Universal-Bibliothek 8539. Stuttgart: Reclam, 1989.

Blackwell, Jeannine. "Herzensgespräche mit Gott: Bekenntnisse deutscher Pietistinnen im 17. und 18. Jahrhundert." *Deutsche Literatur von Frauen.* Vol. 1. *Vom Mittelalter bis zum Ende des 18. Jahrhunderts.* Ed. Gisela Brinker-Gabler. München: Beck, 1988. 265-93.

Chartier, Roger. "Les pratiques de l'écrit." *Histoire de la vie privée.* Vol. 3. *De la Renaissance aux Lumières.* Ed. Philippe Aries and Georges Duby. Paris: Seuil, 1986. 113-63.

Darnton, Robert. *Mesmerism and the End of the Enlightenment in France.* Cambridge: Harvard UP, 1968.

Davis, Natalie Zemon. "Bindung und Freiheit: Die Grenzen des Selbst im Frankreich des sechzehnten Jahrhunderts." N.Z.D., *Frauen und Gesellschaft am Beginn der Neuzeit.* Berlin: Wagenbach, 1986.

Ebrecht, Angelika. "Dürfen Frauen den Männern hinter ihr Geheimnis kommen? Frauen und Geheimgesellschaften im 18. Jahrhundert." *Feministische Studien* 7 (1989): 28-42.

Foucault, Michel. "Was ist Aufklärung?" *Ethos der Moderne: Foucaults Kritik der Aufklärung.* Ed. Eva Erdmann et al. Frankfurt/M.: Campus, 1990. 35-55.

————. "Technologies of the Self." *Technologies of the Self: A Seminar with Michel Foucault.* Ed. Luther H. Martin et al. Amherst: U of Massachusetts P, 1988.

Gallas, Helga and Magdalena Heuser, eds. *Untersuchungen zum Roman von Frauen um 1800.* Tübingen: Niemeyer, 1990.

Genette, Gerard. *Paratexte: Das Buch vom Beiwerk des Buches.* Trans. Dieter Hornig. Frankfurt/M.: Campus, 1989.

Goodman, Katherine. *Dis/Closures: Women's Autobiography in Germany Between*

1790 and 1914. New York: Lang, 1986.

Honegger, Claudia. "Hexenprozesse und 'Heimlichkeiten der Frauenzimmer': Geschlechtsspezifische Aspekte von Fremd- und Selbstthematisierung." *Selbstthematisierung und Selbstzeugnis: Bekenntnis und Geständnis.* Ed. Alois Hahn and Volker Kapp. Frankfurt/M.: Suhrkamp, 1987. 95-110.

————. *Die Ordnung der Geschlechter: Die Wissenschaft vom Menschen und das Weib 1750-1850.* Frankfurt/M.: Campus, 1991.

Hudtwalcker, Johann Michael. "Mittheilungen aus dem handschriftlichen Nachlaß des Senators Johann Michael Hudtwalcker, geboren 21. Sept. 1747, gestorben 14. Dec. 1818." Ed. Oscar L. Tesdorpf. *Zeitschrift für Hamburgische Geschichte* 9 (1894): 150-83.

Kant, Immanuel. "Von der Majorennität (Mündigkeit) und der Minorennität (Unmündigkeit)." *Die philosophischen Hauptvorlesungen Immanuel Kants: Nach den neu aufgefundenen Kollegheften des Grafen Heinrich von Dohna-Wundlacken.* Ed. Arnold Kowalewski. 1924. Rpt. Hildesheim: Olms, 1965. 31-35.

Kästner, Abraham Gotthelf. *Gesammelte Poetische und Prosaische Schönwissenschaftliche Werke.* Berlin, 1841.

Kiefer, Klaus H., ed. *Cagliostro: Dokumente zu Aufklärung und Okkultismus.* München: Beck, 1991.

————. "Okkultismus und Aufklärung aus medienkritischer Sicht: Zur Cagliostro-Rezeption Goethes und Schillers im zeitgenössischen Kontext." *Klassik und Moderne: Die Weimarer Klassik als historisches Ereignis und Herausforderung im kulturgeschichtlichen Prozess.* Stuttgart: Metzler, 1983. 207-28.

————. *Wiedergeburt und Neues Leben: Aspekte des Strukturwandels in Goethes "Italienischer Reise".* Abhandlungen zur Kunst-, Musik- und Literaturwissenschaft 280. Bonn: Bouvier, 1978.

————. "Zur Definition aufklärerischer Vernunft: Eine kritische Lektüre von Kants 'Beantwortung der Frage: Was ist Aufklärung?'" *Wirkendes Wort* 1 (1991): 15-27.

Kittsteiner, Heinz D. *Die Entstehung des modernen Gewissens.* Frankfurt/M.: Insel, 1991.

La Roche, Sophie von. *Ich bin mehr Herz als Kopf: Ein Lebensbild in Briefen.* Ed. Michael Maurer. Munich: Beck, 1983.

Meise, Helga. *Die Unschuld und die Schrift: Deutsche Frauenromane im 18. Jahrhundert.* Berlin: Guttandin & Hoppe, 1983.

"Memoires authentiques pour servir à l'histoire du comte de Cagliostro." *Correspondance littéraire* 14 (1880): 251-59.

Milow, Margarethe. *Ich will aber nicht murren.* Ed. Rita Bake and Birgit Kiupel. Hamburg: Dölling und Galitz, 1987.

Müller-Seidel, Walter. "Cagliostro und die Vorgeschichte der deutschen Klassik." *Literaturwissenschaft und Geistesgeschichte: Festschrift für Richard Brinkmann.* Ed. Jürgen Brummack et al. Tübingen: Niemeyer, 1981. 137-63.

Niggl, Günter. *Die Geschichte der deutschen Autobiographie im 18. Jahrhundert: Theoretische Grundlegung und literarische Entfaltung.* Stuttgart: Metzler, 1977.

Oppeln-Bronikowski, F. von. *Der Schwarzkünstler Cagliostro.* Dresden 1922.

Prokop, Ulrika. "Die Melancholie der Cornelia Goethe." *Feministische Studien* 2 (1983): 46-77.

Recke, Elisa von der. *Elisa von der Recke.* Ed. Paul Rachel. Vol. 1. *Aufzeichnungen und Briefe aus ihren Jugendtagen.* Vol. 2. *Tagebücher und Briefe aus ihren Wanderjahren.* Leipzig: Dieterich, 1900-1902.

————. *Tagebücher und Selbstzeugnisse.* Ed. Christine Träger. München: Beck,

220   HELGA MEISE

1984.

————. *Nachricht von des berüchtigten Cagliostro Aufenthalte in Mitau im Jahre 1779, und von dessen dortigen magischen Operationen.* Berlin: Nicolai, 1787.

Vigni, Francesca. "Portrait de la femme maçonne au dix-huitième siècle." *Lendemaine* 46 (1987): 35-39.

Wunder, Heide. "Frauen in den Leichenpredigten des 16. und 17. Jahrhunderts." *Leichenpredigten als Quelle historischer Wissenschaften.* Vol. 3. Ed. Rudolf Lenz. Marburg: Schwarz, 1984. 57-69.

————. "Von der 'frumkeit' zur 'Frömmigkeit': Ein Beitrag zur Genese bürgerlicher Weiblichkeit (15.-17. Jahrhundert)." *Weiblichkeit in geschichtlicher Perspektive: Fallstudien und Reflektionen zu Grundproblemen der historischen Frauenforschung.* Ed. Ursula A. J. Becker and Jörn Rüsen. Frankfurt: Suhrkamp, 1988. 174-89.

Socialization and Alienation
in the Female *Bildungsroman*

Todd Kontje

IN THE FOLLOWING essay I discuss the concept of the female *Bildungsroman* in the context of traditional male-oriented studies of the genre. Although critics have recently reminded us of the theoretical bias against female development and creativity during the late eighteenth century, they do not help us account for the women's literature that nevertheless exists. The absence of women writers from current studies of the *Bildungsroman* must be viewed in the context of the historical development of the German literary institution. I will argue that the concept of socialization recently introduced to the study of the male *Bildungsroman* can also prove fruitful for the analysis of texts by and about women. I then turn to examine depictions of female socialization in Sophie von La Roche's *The History of Lady Sternheim* (*Geschichte des Fräulein von Sternheim*) (1771), Caroline von Wolzogen's *Agnes von Lilien* (1798), Friederike Helene Unger's *Julchen Grünthal* (1784/98), and Therese Huber's *The Seldorf Family* (*Die Familie Seldorf*) (1795/96). In an effort to maintain a historical focus, I have deliberately restricted attention to novels written in the last three decades of the eighteenth century, that is, during the period in which men began to write works that have come to be called *Bildungsromane*.

In his innovative interpretation of Goethe's revision of *Wilhelm Meisters Theatrical Mission* (*theatralische Sendung*) into the *Apprenticeship* (*Lehrjahre*), Friedrich Kittler focusses on the increasing intimacy of the bond between Wilhelm and his mother in the historical context of the emerging nuclear family. Kittler then reads the *Apprenticeship* as a record of Meister's movement away from the primal maternal bond, created and sustained in their eroticized conversations, and toward the patriarchal written order represented by the Tower Society and its archive. Kittler views *Bildung* as a "game of socialization" (*Sozialisationspiel*), in which personal development occurs through entry into a "universe of discourses" that constitutes reality among the members of a given community ("Sozialisation" 7). The *Bildungsroman* becomes the meta-discourse in which we witness the process of socialization, and thus the genre within which we witness the birth of man: "'Man' becomes the ground and the material of the discourses . . . the very coming-into-being of man was tied to the alphabetization of Central Europe" (112).[1]

But evidently *not* the birth of woman. Both in this essay and in his more recent *Discourse Networks*, Kittler details the gender ideology of eighteenth-century Germany that militated against fictions of female development. Excluded from higher education and professional activity, women were to provide inspiration for male authors, and then serve as the admiring audience for the works they were not allowed to produce themselves.[2] Following the same logic, John Smith maintains that the sort of development portrayed in the *Bildungsroman* was restricted to men: "*Bildung*, and its narrativization in the *Bildungsroman*, is not an 'organic' but a social phenomenon that leads to the construction of male identity. . . . The strict gender codification at the basis of *Bildung*, taken in its historical context, makes female *Bildung* a contradiction in terms" (216; 220).

Even a cursory glance at standard surveys of the genre would seem to confirm this point of view. Jürgen Jacobs' tellingly entitled *Wilhelm Meister and his Brothers* (*Wilhelm Meister und seine Brüder*) typifies numerous studies of the *Bildungsroman* written in the last two decades.[3] Beginning with Wieland's *Agathon*, critics progress through a familiar list that always includes *Wilhelm Meister's Apprenticeship*, a romantic novel such as Novalis's *Heinrich von Ofterdingen* or Tieck's *Franz Sternbald's Wanderings* (*Franz Sternbalds Wanderungen*), Keller's *Green Henry* (*Der grüne Heinrich*) or Stifter's *Indian Summer* (*Nachsommer*) from the nineteenth century, and possibly Thomas Mann's *The Magic Mountain* (*Der Zauberberg*) and Grass's *The Tin Drum* (*Die Blechtrommel*) from the twentieth. Each of these texts is written by a man, and focusses on the development of a male protagonist. Indeed, the canon is so well established that it is easy to assume that novels by or about German women, whatever they might be called, simply did not exist. Due to the concerted efforts of scholars in recent years, we now know that this was not the case. There were in fact dozens of German women writers who produced scores of novels during the "Age of Goethe" alone.[4] In many of these works, female protagonists experience personal development in a social context, raising at least the possibility that they too might be participating in a process of *Bildung*.

Yet the notoriously controversial status of the genre requires us to pause before adding some of these forgotten novels to the list. Already in the 1950s, Kurt May questioned whether *Wilhelm Meister's Apprenticeship* was really a *Bildungsroman*, and others have since sharpened his critique.[5] Once critics had taken aim at the accepted prototype of the genre, it was perhaps inevitable that Wilhelm Meister's "brothers" would come under attack: one by one, novels formerly accepted into the family turned out to be imposters.[6] Reduced to one novel, itself of questionable status, it would seem time for the phantom genre to concede defeat and surrender (Amrine). Given this state of affairs, why would we want to add new novels to a genre that seems to be in the process of dissolution? If no one seems to be sure that the traditional male *Bildungsroman* exists, then why would we want to find its female counterpart?

We can begin by rethinking the notion of genre. As Adena Rosmarin has argued, genres do not exist as pre-existent categories in search of suitable objects already "out there" in the world, but rather as "the critic's heuristic tool, his chosen or defined way of persuading his audience to see the literary text in all its previously inexplicable and 'literary' fullness and then to relate this text to those that are similar or, more precisely, to those that may be similarly explained" (25). Seen against this understanding of genre, the search for the missing *Bildungsroman* is as futile as the inevitably frustrating pursuit of the Kantian *Ding an sich*. At the same time, the *Bildungsroman* remains a fact of contemporary critical discourse. Articles, monographs, and anthologies on the genre have continued to appear in recent decades despite, or perhaps in part because of, the controversy it provokes, and the term has long since entered the critical vocabulary. In order to understand the current absence of novels by women from studies of the *Bildungsroman*, we have to trace the historical development of the genre in its institutional context. In short: the search for an object gives way to the history of a discourse.

The exclusion of German women writers from the canon has its roots in the late eighteenth century, when the explosive growth of the literary market led certain writers, most notably Goethe and Schiller, to differentiate between autonomous works of genius and the broad spectrum of popular literature written in the tradition of the Enlightenment.[7] In their reflections on the growing dichotomization of the public sphere, Goethe and Schiller assigned the work of female "dilettantes" to an intermediary position. Their works might improve popuular taste and thereby pave the way for a broader appreciation of Weimar Classicism. Thus, although Goethe and Schiller viewed literature produced by women with a good measure of condescension, they did recognize its existence and actively encouraged a number of its authors.

It was only in the course of the nineteenth century that women writers disappeared completely from histories of German literature. German literary historiography from Gervinus to Dilthey can be seen as an attempt to create a cultural identity with increasingly nationalistic overtones (Hohendahl, *National Literature* 143). In the process the myriad productions of scores of writers were reduced to a seemingly natural teleology that led from Luther through Lessing to Goethe and Schiller. Not coincidentally, the term *Bildungsroman* entered the critical discourse during this period.[8] The selective narration of German literary history created a record of the ripening of the German spirit, which in turn served as the unifying cultural field for the educated members of the middle class (*Bildungsbürgertum*) in "the land of poets and thinkers." Thus the *Bildungsroman* itself becomes the privileged genre of German literature: the organic development of the hero toward maturation and social integration reproduces in miniature the movement of German literature toward its maturity, which in turn is to inspire the unification of the German nation. Literature by women was to play no role in this grand cultural-political construct.

The temporal gap between the writing of the novels and their generic classification helps to explain why the concept of the *Bildungsroman* has become problematic today. A poet writing in 1795 could make a conscious decision to compose a sonnet, but Goethe had no idea that he was writing a *Bildungsroman* when he composed *Wilhelm Meister's Apprenticeship*. The willingness to perceive positive development on the part of the hero and an affirmation of existing society on the part of the author is more a product of late nineteenth-century retrospection than of the writers of the "Age of Goethe"; after all, Hegel had already ridiculed the sort of popular novel in which the hero settles down to a boring life as a Philistine after a few youthful adventures. From today's perspective as well, Dilthey's affirmative understanding of the *Bildungsroman* seems better suited to characterize popular fiction than the complex novels written in the tradition of Wieland and Goethe (Selbmann 17). Contemporary responses to this problem have ranged from arguments for the abolition of the genre to its liberal redefinition.[9] Personal development need not—and rarely does—culminate in complacent maturity in these novels, and the surrounding society is more often criticized than affirmed.

Curiously enough, the ongoing debate about the *Bildungsroman* has not resulted in a significant revision of the canon. Although studies of the genre reveal an increasing hesitancy to apply the term to individual texts, the works chosen for analysis remain by and large the same. Even in negation, the genre retains the immense cultural prestige granted by its intimate association with what W. H. Bruford termed "the German tradition of self-cultivation." One unfortunate consequence of the identification of the German canon with the *Bildungsroman* has been to perpetuate the neglect of women's writing. The argument develops as a syllogism, whose seemingly inevitable conclusion is as predictable as it is flawed: the "best" German novels are (or once were considered) *Bildungsromane*; surveys of the *Bildungsroman* do not include texts by women; therefore there must be no novels (worth reading) by German women writers.

One response to this problem would be to argue that women's writing constitutes a counter public sphere that should be distinguished from the dominant male tradition. In fact, most recent discussion of German women novelists has taken place in studies that can assume interest and some knowledge on the part of the reader. For the uninitiated, however, the absence of texts by women in mainstream publications tends to keep them out of sight. Thus one pragmatic argument for including their works in discussions of the genre is that it could help render them visible to a wider reading public. Publications like the Metzler series and the Beck's *Arbeitsbücher zur Literaturgeschichte* continue to determine the canon, that is, what is read and taught at the university. Keeping novels by women out of literature on the *Bildungsroman* may be the best way to assure that students do not read them, for how can students be encouraged to explore forgotten novels if they are unaware that they exist? Moreover, the high status of the genre itself would suggest that these works deserve to be read with the attentiveness usually reserved for works by men, rather than as paradigmatic examples of "trivial" literature.

Those who are willing to speak of the female *Bildungsroman* risk encountering the pitfalls associated with the term's critical history. For example, Magdelene Heuser paraphrases Dilthey's familiar characterization of the male protagonist of the *Bildungsroman* in the following description of *Julchen Grünthal*:

> The new version of 1798 is therefore the reworking of a pedagogical story and boarding school tale into a novel that broadly depicts the education and development of a central female character, beginning with a brief sketch of her childhood, and continuing through the main phase of adolescence, with its temptations and mistakes, to the point where the heroine has found her place in society. ("Spuren" 37)[10]

Yet Julchen's "place in society" turns out to be at her father's side, cut off from the world she had once explored. Even if the novel did portray the positive development Heuser envisions, the presuppositions of the argument remain questionable. One could maintain that Dilthey's affirmative understanding of the genre takes on a critical edge when applied to a text with a female protagonist. In the long run, however, switching the gender of Dilthey's definition of the genre cannot render it immune to the original problem. If modern readers grow impatient with the aesthetic and ideological conservatism of earlier definitions of the male *Bildungsroman*, it seems likely that the same will prove true for its female counterpart. In fact, searching for positive female role models in the *Bildungsroman* threatens to play into the hands of those who would continue to marginalize women's fiction as "trivial" literature.[11]

Marianne Hirsch's study of "the beautiful soul as paradigm" offers a diametrically opposed notion of "spiritual *Bildung*" to characterize the development of female characters. Instead of stressing the possibility of the active, assertive heroine, Hirsch defines the female *Bildungsroman* as an inversion of the male prototype: "This type of female plot becomes a reversal of the conventional male plot, as female *Bildung* is no longer marked by progress or linear directions, but by circularity and dissolution" (42). Thus Hirsch avoids the search for a female Horatio Alger by acknowledging the degree of resignation and denied possibility attending female development. Yet this approach has at least two shortcomings of its own: one, personal development is not as one-sidedly negative in some of the major works by German women writers as Hirsch implies. If Heuser goes too far in emphasizing the positive development of Julchen Grünthal, Hirsch goes to the opposite extreme of viewing representation of female development solely in terms of suffering and decline. And two, this argument employs a stereotypically strong male protagonist as a straw man to define the difference of the women. The same strategy has been employed in discussions of the so-called *Antibildungsroman*, where a superficial reading of *Wilhelm Meister's Apprenticeship* serves as the starting point for the discussion of problematic works of the nineteenth century.[12] In both cases, critics enlist a phantom in their cause, for the powerfully assertive hero of the male *Bildungsroman* is a rare breed indeed; he is certainly not to be found in Goethe's influential novel.

Instead of searching for positive role models or identifying passive victims of male oppression, I suggest we explore novels that irritate existing social norms, that create friction between the narrowly prescribed women's roles and the possibilities of individual development. If fiction by and about women around 1800 is to be taken seriously on its own terms, then the works must be read in a way that brings out their often subtle subversiveness.[13] Here I would argue that the concept of socialization introduced by Kittler and Smith with regard to the development of male protagonists provides a useful starting point for the discussion of the female *Bildungsroman* as well. As they quite correctly stress, we cannot simply insert the heroine into the gender-specific model of *Bildung* during the "Age of Goethe." By the same token, however, Smith's reference to the "radical Otherness of much women's writing" (221) runs the double risk of imputing "radical Sameness" to literature written by men, and of rendering literature by women so alien as to exclude it from discussion once again.[14] The relation of novels by La Roche, Unger, Huber, Wolzogen, and others to the dominant male tradition might be better characterized in terms of productive tension rather than radical alterity.

As in the case of canonical texts by and about men, the female *Bildungsroman* can be viewed as a meta-discourse on the process of socialization for women. Here too socialization begins in the home, but in this case the primary Oedipal bond is between fathers and their daughters. In fact, mothers are often conspicuously absent in these texts. Sophie von La Roche sets the precedent with her influential *Lady Sternheim*. Her protagonist Sophie von Sternheim grows up in isolation with her father from age nine to nineteen after her mother's death. Memory of the mother is preserved in a portrait that Sophie and her father regard together in moments of tender sentimentality. Yet this absence allows Sophie to slip into the mother's role. Gradually she assumes her mother's former position as head of the household, and also as the object of her father's affections—not coincidentally, her mother's name was also Sophie.[15] As in the case of Wilhelm Meister and his mother, Sophie von Sternheim's love for her father has a strong element of only slightly suppressed eroticism, which is revealed most strikingly when she happily complies with his request that she dress up in her dead mother's clothing.

The psychological model established in the private sphere has political implications as well, for both family and state are structured on the basis of patriarchal authority. La Roche again sets the tone by situating the family romance in a specific historical and political context. Rather than beginning directly with the tale of Sophie von Sternheim, the novel opens with a detailed account of her family background. Born the son of a professor, her father is ennobled for his achievements as a soldier, not the accident of birth: "Your merit, not fortune, has lifted you up" declares the General upon granting him his patent of nobility (19).[16] He then marries into old nobility and governs his estate with the exemplary benevolence of an enlightened aristocrat. Thus, from the start of this novel, class distinctions are complex. Rather than pitting the rising middle class against a decadent aristocracy, La Roche offers a conservative compromise in which a liberal, enlightened nobility gains moral strength and political validation through its adoption of bourgeois values. The idyllic world depicted in the opening pages of *Lady Sternheim* leaves little room for female development. The young man is expected to leave the intimate sphere of the home, find a wife, develop a uniquely distinct identity, and play a productive role in society. More often than not, the male *Bildungsroman* depicts characters who fall short of this positive goal. For the woman, in contrast, any hope for *Bildung* involves escaping a constricting set of expectations set forth in such influential publications as Rousseau's *Emile* (1762) and Johann Heinrich Campe's *Fatherly Advice for My Daughter* (*Väterlicher Rath für meine Tochter*) (first of many editions in 1782), which would exclude her from the public sphere while limiting her to her "natural" roles of wife, mother, and head of the household. In theory, at least, the woman is to make a seamless transition from obedient daughter to obedient wife. Her identity, once obscured by her father, is to be subsumed under the identity of her husband. Seen from a more positive perspective, the period between adolescence and marriage offers the young woman a brief opportunity to explore otherwise denied possibilities for independent development. Not surprisingly, therefore, the works examined here focus on this stage in their protagonists' lives.

Far from seeking independence, Sophie von Sternheim finds it thrust upon her when her father dies. The nineteen-year-old Sophie, now thoroughly imbued with her father's liberal values, becomes the ward of her mother's half-sister, who lives in a world of court intrigue. Ironically enough, her father's ennoblement for his bourgeois virtue introduces his daughter to an unregenerate form of aristocratic vice.[17] As the narrator describes it, what follows is less a novel of personal development, a *Bildungsroman*, then a baroque test of innate character narrated for didactic purposes, a *Bewährungsroman*: "Now that unfortunate period begins, in which you will see this most charming young lady tangled up in difficulties and circumstances that suddenly destroyed the beautiful plan of a happy life she had made for herself. However, the resulting trial of her inner worth makes her story instructive for the best members of our sex" (61).[18]

Midway through the novel, the situation looks bleak for Sophie: she has been tricked into a false marriage with the dissolute English nobleman Lord Derby, who then rapes and abandons her. Yet unlike Richardson's Clarissa, who gradually fades and dies after having been violated by Lovelace, Sophie von Sternheim survives to marry the man she first loved, to become an ideal mother, and to help her husband govern a progressive community which mirrors that of her father. Thus

La Roche transforms the familiar eighteenth-century theme of seduced innocence into a tale of self-reliance, where the virtuous victim triumphs over her oppressor. The pattern of the novel as a whole can be seen as a deviation from and then a return to the values of family intimacy and benevolent paternal rule established in the opening pages.

Thus viewed, La Roche offers us a simple moral parable of innocence lost and virtue regained. The openly didactic intent of her first novel only increases in subsequent works, and has understandably rendered her work unpalatable to current taste (Maurer). Seen in historical context, however, Sophie's triumph signals a striking deviation from the pattern established by Richardson and continued in the drama of the Storm and Stress, where female figures are often reduced to silent victims of male aggression. Sophie von Sternheim gives voice to her sufferings, both in correspondence to her friend Emilia, and in the diary she keeps when she is forcefully abducted to the Scottish wilderness. Through her gradual recovery in the second half of the novel we witness the transformation of a test of virtue into a process of personal *Bildung* (Blackwell 88).

Yet La Roche does more than offer an uncharacteristically strong heroine who serves as a positive role model. More interesting from today's perspective is not the heroine's exemplary virtue, but rather the extent to which La Roche reveals her limitations, and the limitations of the cultural ideal she attains. Three examples must suffice: First, although Derby's rape is inexcusable, Sophie's motivations for marriage are not entirely innocent. She agrees to marry the transparently evil lord in part because of her desire to marry into a higher social class, as her father's humble birth had made her vulnerable at court (212). In doing so she momentarily betrays her father's values: like a good bourgeois, he had married for love, whereas Sophie falls back into the aristocratic desire to marry for social advancement. Second, Sophie's enlightened nobility has its shortcomings as well. Her random acts of charity help only the fortunate few and her own ego in the first half of the novel, as she is all too pleased by her own virtue. Even in her more effective charitable and pedagogical acts later on, Sophie never advocates changing the hierarchical structure of the society which is to blame for the wrongs she tentatively seeks to alleviate.[19] Finally, La Roche displaces the happy ending to England, as if to suggest that even this imperfect utopia could only be realized outside her contemporary Germany.

Caroline von Wolzogen's *Agnes von Lilien* is the most direct descendant of La Roche's novel, both in terms of the Oedipal structure of the family and its conservative political ideal. Unlike the betrayed Sophie von Sternheim, Agnes manages to preserve her chastity until the end of the novel, when she marries her first love, the Baron von Nordheim.[20] Yet her personal development also takes place under the father's spell. The presumably orphaned girl has fully accepted her stepfather, a learned pastor who has given her a model home education. The novel opens with a chance encounter that disrupts their private world, as Agnes experiences an awakening of sexual desire during Nordheim's brief visit. "I had been raised properly, in the highest purity and chastity of the senses and the imagination; this was the first man with whom I was aware of my full femininity" (1: 60).[21] In loving Nordheim, Agnes transfers her affections away from her stepfather, as she herself realizes when contemplating her sudden infatuation: "I gladly left even my father, for the first time in my life" (1: 60).[22] In fact, Nordheim is old enough to be Agnes' father: she is eighteen, while he is forty, and both comment on their age difference in the course of the evening. Nordheim's visit also awakens Agnes's curiosity about her biological parents; as it turns out, her real father was the enlightened ruler of the local community who was forced into exile because of the secret marriage in which she was conceived.

After this opening scene, Agnes embarks on a double quest: to find her parents and to be united with Nordheim. The first half of the novel culminates in a scene in which Nordheim bursts into the room of what he thinks is Agnes's seducer, but which turns out to be her father's. The potentially violent confrontation between Hohenfels and his future son-in-law ends instead in the first passionate kiss between the two lovers. Thus Wolzogen uses the standard motif of the innocent young woman rescued from seduction to produce a drama of Oedipal desire, where Agnes finds herself torn between her father and her fiancé.

By the end of the novel all conflict has been resolved. Part two contains long flashbacks which fill in the complicated series of political and family intrigues that surround Agnes' birth and help to explain the old prince's opposition to her marriage with Nordheim. The deliberate retardation of the plot contrasts with La Roche's episodic, picaresque narrative. In effect, Wolzogen sublates linear chronology into a self-reflexive structure in a way that parallels Goethe's transformation of the *Mission* into the *Apprenticeship*. The voyage out into the world turns into a process of self-discovery. Hohenfels eventually brings Agnes back to the home of her stepfather, where she meets and immediately marries Nordheim. Father, stepfather, and husband take part in a private ceremony soon to be followed by a public celebration, as Hohenfels is to resume his rightful position as leader of the community.[23]

Wolzogen thus ends her novel with a strong affirmation of the existing patriarchal order in both the private and public spheres. To be sure, the novel contains a sharp critique of the corrupt court that tries to manipulate the lives of its subjects. "That's the way these rusty old machines of the state are," exclaims Julius. "They seek to parlay each individual interest into the collective, to destroy it" (2: 32-33).[24] Nevertheless, the cure for current corruption lies in the restoration of a benevolently paternal political order, not in revolution. Here Wolzogen echoes both La Roche's conservatism of the 1770s, and also that of her contemporary Weimar classicists. In an analogous way, Agnes is willing to subordinate her own desires completely to those of her future husband: "To surrender myself to the inexpressible, lofty, and beautiful [man], who had appeared to me in the figure of a god; to live, to feel only in him, through him—all this swelled up in my heart, and my inner being dissolved in the power and the succession of these blissful images" (1: 68).[25] In the course of the novel she makes a nearly seamless transition from model adoptive child to loving daughter and adoring wife.

Nearly seamless: for between her initial love for Nordheim and their ultimate marriage Agnes undergoes a series of trials that force her to develop her self-reliance. Separated from her stepfather for the first time, Agnes resolves to be true to herself: "I encouraged my spirits solely with the attempt to remain true to myself, and to grant no external circumstance power over me" (1: 108).[26] As a vulnerable outsider in the world of the court, Agnes has to resist the pressure to marry Julius, whom she gently but firmly rejects long before she is sure that Nordheim loves her. Meanwhile she faces the threat of becoming financially dependent on the Duchess Amalie. Thus she employs her artistic talents as a portraitist (1: 149-50). Her career as a professional artist is short-lived, however, as her mother soon gives her a considerable fortune that makes her financially independent (1: 170).

We leave Agnes poised to begin life as the virtuous and appropriately cultured wife of a liberal aristocrat.[27] Her position bears a superficial resemblance to that of Wilhelm Meister at the conclusion of the *Apprenticeship* when the Tower Society has confirmed his fatherhood of Felix and grants him Natalie as a reward that marks the end of his apprenticeship.[28] However, Wilhelm's marriage signals the beginning of further activity that will include travel to Italy and studies for a career of public service as a doctor. In contrast, Agnes' journey ends where it began, in her stepfather's living room. Unlike Wilhelm Meister, who continues to wrestle with difficult experiences after his marriage, Agnes von Lilien looks back over the struggles of her youth with the serene calm of an individual who has transcended all conflict: "Nothing unsatisfied remains in our soul, and the quiet business of a higher *Bildung* continues uninterrupted, without being disturbed by the

disquieting dreams of an unfulfilled desire" (iv-v).[29] Having completed
her journey from stepfather to father and husband, Agnes rests in the
placid conviction that future *Bildung* will take care of itself.

Frederike Helene Unger offers us a much more rebellious protagonist in her *Julchen Grünthal*, as a French boarding school in Berlin
introduces the innocent country girl to a world of intrigue, seduction,
and adventure.   In the end, however, Julchen also returns to her
father's side. We last see her in a local pageant playing the same role
of harvest queen that had delighted her father when she was a child.
She has renounced her sinful past and returned to her reunited family.
In its primary intent neither version of *Julchen Grünthal* is a *Bildungsroman*; both can best be characterized as *Anti-Erziehungsromane*, that
is, didactic treatises cast in fictional form that teach their readers how
not to raise their daughters.

The first half of the novel traces Julchen's moral decline, as she falls
out of her role as Grünthal's obedient daughter, destroys her cousin's
marriage, and flees to St. Petersburg with the Russian Prince Demetrius.   Julchen bears the primary responsibility for her behavior,
although her father shares part of the blame for letting his wife convince him to send Julchen to a French boarding school in Berlin. The
corrupting influence of city life, exposure to the nobility, and too much
French literature erode the salutary effects of Julchen's early private
education in the country and make her ripe for seduction.

In the first half of Unger's continuation of the novel, a revision of
Johann Stutz's earlier second volume, Julchen virtually disappears.
Now Julchen's friend Minna Thalheim offers a rather formulaic
account of regained virtue, illustrating how hard work and piety in the
country have saved both her and her husband from a degenerated
urban life of gambling and infidelity. To underscore her didactic
intent, Unger italicizes the moral of the story: *"Where virtue and
diligence reign, there too resides happiness* (2: 171-72).[30] This lengthy narrative sets the tone for the story of Julchen's moral redemption. Far
from representing her "process of emancipation" through a
"confrontation with the authority of the father" (Heuser 34), her long
confession marks her complete submission to paternal control. As
Helga Meise has observed, Julchen's development involves the gradual
internalization of her father's voice as her own conscience.[31] By the
end of the novel Julchen has become a pathetic individual tortured by
remorse. She actually rubs her face in the dirt at her cousin's feet when
they first meet again, a sight that in retrospect seems to please her
father.[32] Her guilty conscience reaches neurotic levels, as she accepts
full responsibility not only for her own actions, but also for those over
which she has no control: "all of a sudden she starts crying and accuses

herself. I think she would blame herself if hail had destroyed my grain-fields" (2: 341).[33]

Only in the middle of the novel do we find "the beginnings of a female *Bildungsroman* or novel of development (*Entwicklungsroman*)" (Heuser 32), precisely at those moments when Julchen breaks free from the constricting influence of her father.[34] For example, her sarcastic commentary on Eiche's letter of proposal reveals an assertive woman who knows what she wants and realizes she will not find it in the dull pastor. She shares her future husband's interest in literature, theater, and society in a way that his first retiring wife does not. Even her flight to Leningrad to avoid imprisonment for her husband's debts has its positive moments. Julchen delights in the long summer nights, is intrigued by the Russian peasantry and overwhelmed by the beauty of St. Petersburg. Prince Demetrius also appears in a far more positive light in Unger's novel than he had in Stutz's version, where he plays a villain who enjoys destroying marriages (99). Now he appears as a melancholy nobleman who has found his first true love in Julchen, although he had been forced to consent to an arranged marriage. Julchen also finds herself strongly attracted to Demetrius, nearly regretting his willingness to renounce her company when she is overcome by guilt triggered by her father's memory: "The intervention of the father-figure immediately thwarts Julchen's desire" (Meise 56).

Thus although we cannot read the entire novel as a *Bildungsroman*, it does contain moments in which the heroine takes tentative steps toward self-affirmation. In other words, the novel is a *Bildungsroman* to the extent that Julchen begins to explore experiences that deviate from the rigid morality of the *Erziehungsroman*. Dagmar Grenz has quite plausibly suggested that the novel's popularity stemmed from the tension between its didactic intent and Unger's ability to elicit sympathy for her sinful protagonist (157-58). We need not consider this unresolved tension an artistic flaw. Rather, partial identification with Julchen complicates the novel's conservative message to encourage readers to reflect on the cultural stereotypes that made personal development and social integration incompatible goals for women. Susanne Zantop argues convincingly that this seemingly affirmative work contains an extremely critical subtext that undermines its authoritarian message (142). While contemporary readers may well have found masochistic pleasure in identifying with the ultimately repentant Julchen,[35] they may have also felt a trace of indignation at the delight her father takes in her grovelling self-abnegation. The smiles of the reunited family on the last page of the novel thinly conceal the price Julchen has paid for their happiness. She condemns her past and sacrifices her future to regress to the role of her father's little girl.

Therese Huber presents a still more rebellious heroine in *The Seldorf Family*.³⁶ The novel is set in France during the Revolution. Sara Seldorf, the work's bourgeois heroine, becomes involved with Duke L*, an active fighter in the Royalist cause. They have a child and she follows him to Paris. To her horror, however, L* inadvertently kills his own daughter in the chaotic events of the Revolution, and she soon learns that he is in fact already married to another woman. At this point Sara switches her allegiance and joins the revolutionaries. Whereas both La Roche and Wolzogen argued the virtues of an enlightened reform of the existing social structure, Huber's Sara Seldorf works to overthrow the patriarchal order. At her most furious moment, she exultantly clutches a rag she has soaked in the blood of the executed king. Later, disguised as a man, she joins the rebel armies, spurred on by her desire to kill the man who seduced and betrayed her. By the end of the novel, however, she undergoes a second change of heart. She dresses as a woman again, refuses to marry her childhood friend Roger, a patriotic bourgeois, and instead maintains a melancholy vigil over the grave of Duke L*.

What begins as an open assault on the aristocratic seducer and the corrupt social order he represents ends on an ambivalent note. Here again the protagonist's family background sheds some light on the conflict portrayed in the text. Like Sophie von Sternheim and Agnes von Lilien, Sara grows up without a mother. Her father teaches her that women should be sensitive, submissive companions to boldly decisive men. Sara later seems to rebel against her father's precepts when she refuses his demand that she renounce her love for the Duke L*. Yet her open revolt obscures the fact that she finds L* attractive because he seems to embody the very masculine ideal she has learned from her father. Although the married nobleman then brings her to Paris as his unwitting mistress, he actually treats her like a bourgeois husband would treat his wife. While he goes about his public business during the day, Sara remains a virtual prisoner in her apartment. At night she is to offer him a soothing refuge from the strains of his demanding life. In other words, a tale of class conflict rapidly turns into a critical portrait of expected gender roles in the bourgeois marriage, as aristocratic exploitation of the middle class gives way to male exploitation of the submissive woman.

When Sara discovers L*'s treachery, she becomes the sort of "unnatural" Amazon her father had once condemned. In doing so, she seems to adopt a far more assertive role than any of the characters examined thus far, as she enters the public sphere normally restricted to men. Yet although she fights *in* the revolutionary army, she fights *for* herself; her motivation remains personal rather than political throughout her military career.[37] As soon as she learns that L* is dead, she gives up her struggle for the Revolution. Moreover, she can only become publicly active as a soldier by disguising herself as a man. Instead of depicting an admirably assertive heroine, Huber exposes a dilemma: Sara can either be imprisoned in her role as surrogate wife, or deny her femininity to become an avenging virago. As a woman she finds no productive public career. The novel's conclusion reveals the disjuncture between revolutionary politics and the politics of the home. While the *ancien régime* has been overthrown, the patriarchal order of the family remains intact. Having renounced her role as soldier, Sara has no option but to return to the discredited stereotype of the submissive wife. She remains loyal to the memory of L*, not out of attraction to his reactionary politics as an aristocrat, but because he had assumed the role of bourgeois husband for her. The novel ends on a note of melancholy irony, as the former Amazon reenacts a pseudo-marriage with the memory of her seducer.

While both *Lady Sternheim* and *Agnes von Lilien* end happily, each protagonist sacrifices the modicum of independence she had attained before marriage. Unger inverts this pattern in *Julchen Grünthal*, as the heroine repudiates her adult life to regress to the arms of her father. Only Sara Seldorf remains independent, but at the cost of being isolated from the living and caught up in loyalty to the dead. In short, the texts fall into two broad categories: those that portray women who, after a period of trial in which they are forced to develop a certain degree of independence, eagerly conform to accepted stereotypes, and those with protagonists who actively rebel against the norms only to be drawn back into the fold. Together the works reveal the dilemma confronting women in search of *Bildung* in the late eighteenth century: to seek personal fulfillment is to risk ostracism as a fallen woman or an Amazon; to conform to cultural expectations is to practice self-denial. Socialization for women involves alienation from their own desires, while self-realization entails alienation from society. The conservative conclusions to works with even the most unorthodox protagonists reveal the insidious power of gender stereotypes in eighteenth-century German society. Like the twentieth-century consumers described by Horkheimer and Adorno in their essay on the culture industry, these women writers seem to "feel compelled to buy" into an ideology of female subservience, "even though they see through it" (167).

Yet the seeming capitulation to convention evident in these novels' conclusions does not obliterate the insights generated in the course of their unfolding. The movement through the text leaves a residue of critical awareness that escapes the jaws of a neatly negative dialectic. The writers open up a discursive space in these novels in which their primarily female readers can explore both the possibilities and limitations of the gender roles set forth in the many didactic treatises of the period. As such, these works are not mere reflections of the society in which they were written, but rather reflections on the discourses that constitute reality in the community of public opinion.[38] Despite the predominantly conservative "messages" offered at the conclusion to their novels, La Roche and the following generation of women writers produce texts with critical subtexts that challenge the authority of cultural stereotypes, while also suggesting—however tentatively—the possibility for productive change.

Notes

1. "Der 'Mensch' wird Grund und Sache der Diskurse.... An der Alphabetisierung Mitteleuropas war die Menschwerdung selber festgemacht" (112).
2. *Discourse Networks* 125. See also Bovenschen (esp. 220-56), and Köpke on the general prejudice against women writers in late eighteenth-century Germany.
3. Examples include Swales, Beddow, Selbmann, and Jacobs and Krause.
4. Touaillon's pioneering survey of *Der deutsche Frauenroman* (1919) remains valuable; her book has been rediscovered together with the authors and texts she discusses. More recent studies of eighteenth-century German novels by women include Meise and the volume edited by Gallas and Heuser. Blackwell offers the broadest study of the female *Bildungsroman* in her unfortunately unpublished dissertation.
5. See in particular Schlaffer, who refers to Goethe's novel as a *Zerstörungsroman*, as well as Schlechta's earlier study.
6. Sammons's assertion that the nineteenth-century *Bildungsroman* is a nearly non-existent genre has proven particularly influential.
7. Christa Bürger provides a useful overview of this development in her introduction to *Zur Dichotomisierung*. She has since examined how this dichotomization marginalized women writers in *Leben Schreiben*, esp. 19-31.
8. To be sure, Martini unearthed several essays by the obscure Karl Morgenstern in which the term occurs already in the first decades of the nineteenth century. Yet if Dilthey had not introduced the term to mainstream *Germanistik* some fifty years later, there would have been no need for Martini's literary detective work.
9. Swales makes a convincing case for the continued use of the term *Bildungsroman* with an undogmatical understanding of genre in his introduction.
10. "Die Neufassung von 1798 ist also die Umarbeitung einer Pensions- und Erziehungsgeschichte in einen Roman, der die Bildung und Entwicklung einer weiblichen Hauptfigur von der knapp eingebrachten Kindheit über die Hauptphase der Adoleszenz mit ihren Versuchen und Irrtümern bis zu dem Zeitpunkt ausbreitet, als die Heldin ihren Platz in der Gesellschaft gefunden hat" (37).
11. As Bovenschen points out, the novel's low status as a genre that originally made it more accessible to women writers soon worked to their disadvantage: "In dem Maße jedoch, wie sich der Roman zu einer Kunstform emanzipieren konnte, wie zwischen seinen trivialen und seinen künstlerischen Ausprägungen unterschieden wurde, waren es wiederum die Bereiche des Trivialen, des 'nur' Unterhaltsa-

men, auf die die Frauen—von wenigen Ausnahmen abgesehen—verwiesen waren" (215).

12. Mayer's otherwise excellent study of four nineteenth-century novels under the rubric of the *Antibildungsroman* falls into this trap.

13. In this spirit, Gallas and Heuser suggest that we look for "[d]ie im Kontext der erzählerischen Konventionalität angelegten, verborgenen Widerstände" in novels by German women around 1800 (7). In their discussion of English women writers in the nineteenth century, Gilbert and Gubar suggest that their texts "are in some sense palimpsestic, works whose surface designs conceal or obscure deeper, less accessible (and less socially acceptable) levels of meaning" (73).

14. The same charge could be leveled against Kittler, who ignores women writers around 1800 in his *Discourse Networks*. See Sebastian on the conservatism of Kittler's canon and a generally critical assessment of his project (esp. 585).

15. Moreover, both characters share the name of their author. As Bovenschen points out, this encouraged early readers to identify La Roche with her heroine, an identification that led to disappointed surprise when the real woman failed to conform to the expectations aroused by her fiction (190-200). As Becker-Cantarino observes, however, the use of the name Sophie is less autobiographical in intent than a reference to the model of femininity set forth in the fifth book of Rousseau's *Emile* (405).

16. "Ihr Verdienst, nicht das Glück hat Sie erhoben" (19).

17. As will be the case in *Wilhelm Meister's Apprenticeship*, La Roche depicts a society split between an enlightened nobility infused with the values of the rising middle class, and an immoral *Rokokoadel* which clings to the decadent life-style of a previous age. See Janz on this distinction in Goethe's novel.

18. "wo sich nun der fatale Zeitpunkt anfängt, worin Sie diese liebenswürdigste junge Dame in Schwierigkeiten und Umstände verwickelt sehen werden, die den schönen Plan eines glücklichen Lebens, den sie sich gemacht hatte, auf einmal zerstörten, aber durch die Probe, auf welche sie ihren innerlichen Wert setzten, ihre Geschichte für die Besten unsers Geschlechts lehrreich machen" (61).

19. On Sophie's self-centered conservatism, see both Blackwell (124ff.) and Hohendahl ("Empfindsamkeit," 198).

20. Wolzogen began writing the novel in the winter of 1793-94 (Touaillon 461). Parts of the novel appeared in Schiller's *Horen* (1796-97). Unger published the completed novel in the fall of 1797 in Berlin, but dated 1798 on the title page (Boerner 395-96).

21. "Ich war anständig erzogen, in der höchsten Reinheit und Keuschheit des Sinns und der Einbildung; dieß war der erste Mann, gegen den ich meine volle Weiblichkeit empfand" (1: 60).

22. "Selbst meinen Vater verließ ich gern, zum erstenmal in meinem Leben" (1: 66).

23. Gigli stresses the "fortschreitende Steigerung der väterlichen Instanzen" in an insightful psychoanalytical reading of the novel that nevertheless ignores the conservative political implications of its depiction of patriarchy.

24. "Ja, so sind diese alten eingerosteten Staatsmaschinen. . . . Jedes individuelle Interesse suchen sie ins Collective zu spielen, zu vernichten" (2: 32-33).

25. "Mich hinzugeben dem unaussprechlichen, hohen und schönen, der mir als eine Göttergestalt erschien; in ihm, durch ihn nur zu leben, zu empfinden,—alles dieses ging mir in der Seele auf, und mein Inneres zerfloß in der Gewalt und im Wechsel dieser seligen Bilder" (1: 68).

26. "ich ermunterte mein Gemüth nur durch das Bestreben, sich selbst gleich

zu bleiben, und keiner äußern Lage Gewalt über mich einzuräumen" (1: 108).

27. Unlike Grünthal, who sees little reason for his daughter's higher education, Nordheim approves of Agnes' ability to read Homer in the original (1: 206-7). As Touaillon points out, Wolzogen takes a moderate stance on feminist issues (473), particularly in comparison with a writer like Sophie Mereau.

28. The date of the novel's composition excludes the possibility of Goethe's direct influence, at least on Wolzogen's original conception, but its publication in both the *Horen* and with Unger invited comparison with *Wilhelm Meister* and even speculation that Goethe himself had written the anonymous work (Boerner 397).

29. "Es bleibt nichts unbefriedigtes in unserer Seele, und das stille Geschäft einer höheren Bildung nimmt seinen ununterbrochenen Fortgang, ohne von den beunruhigenden Träumen eines ungestillten Verlangens gestöhrt zu werden" (iv-v).

30. *"Wo Tugend und Arbeitsamkeit herrschen, da wohnt auch das Glück"* (2: 171-72).

31. Meise 55-56. Meise pays particular attention to the role that writing plays in the process. When Julchen first goes to Berlin her father requests that she keep a diary as a "personified conscience" that she is to send home for his periodic inspection (1: 43-44). Communication between Julchen and her father breaks off during her profligate years, but is restored through the lengthy written account she submits to him in part two (Meise 54-55). Heuser's contention that Julchen's autobiographical letter represents "eine Möglichkeit der Befreiung aus männlicher Vormundschaft und ihrer Partizipation am literarischen Diskurs" (34-35) remains wishful thinking: Julchen submits her private confession to receive her father's forgiveness. Thereafter she hopes to devote her life to his care: "so soll jeder Augenblick meines Lebens seiner Pflege und Erheiterung geweihet seyn!" (2: 337). Thus Meise refers correctly to the "ödipale Struktur der libidinösen Bindung zwischen Vater und Tochter" (57).

32. "Julchen riß sich vom Vater los, und stürzte zu den Füßen der liebreichen Frau hin, und legte angetrieben, man sah's deutlich, angetrieben von tiefer zerknirschender Demuth, ihr Gesicht in den Staub hin," reports her friend Wilhelmine to her husband (2: 196). At the time Grünthal finds this scene disturbing, and orders Julchen to stand up, but he later relates the same incident with some pride to pastor Eiche: "Aber Sie hätten sie auch sehen sollen! Schön wie ein Engel, und gebeugt von Reue und Schaam. Wie sie ihr Engelsgesichtchen vor Karolinen in den Staub legte, und kein Auge zu ihr aufzuheben vermochte!" (2: 242).

33. "ehe man sichs versieht, weint sie und klagt sich an. Ich glaube, wenn der Hagel meine Kornfelder zerschlagen hätte, würde sie sich dessen anklagen" (2: 341).

34. Heuser also lists numerous instances in which Julchen begins to act independently (36-37). However, she views these moments as steps in a process of self-realization that culminates at the end of the work; in my view, these moments of nascent self-awareness are emphatically denounced in the novel's final pages.

35. "Ja, er [der Leser] kann den negativen Ausgang des Romans in typisch empfindsam-masochistischer Weise sogar als eine Art Selbstbestrafung (für das Ausleben gesellschaftlich verbotener, sich selbst nicht eingestandener Wünsche) akzeptieren" (Grenz 158).

36. For a more detailed analysis of this novel, see Kontje.

37. Thus I would argue against Heuser's assertion that Sara progresses from private revenge to public service (377).

38. On the notion of literature as socially-constituting force rather than a mere reflection of a given reality, see both Schmidt (19-21) and Eagleton (4).

Works Cited

Amrine, Frederick. "Rethinking the *Bildungsroman*." *Michigan Germanic Studies* 13 (1987): 119-39.

Becker-Cantarino, Barbara. "Nachwort." La Roche 381-415.

Beddow, Michael. *The Fiction of Humanity: Studies in the Bildungsroman from Wieland to Thomas Mann.* Cambridge: Cambridge UP, 1982.

Blackwell, Jeannine. " 'Bildungsroman mit Dame': The Heroine in the German *Bildungsroman.*" Diss. Indiana University, 1982.

Boerner, Peter. "Nachwort." Wolzogen.

Bovenschen, Silvia. *Die imaginierte Weiblichkeit: Exemplarische Untersuchungen zu kulturgeschichtlichen und literarischen Präsentationsformen des Weiblichen.* Edition Suhrkamp 921. Frankfurt: Suhrkamp, 1979.

Bruford, W. H. *The German Tradition of Self-Cultivation: 'Bildung' from Humboldt to Thomas Mann.* Cambridge: Cambridge UP, 1975.

Bürger, Christa. "Einleitung: Die Dichotomie von hoher und niederer Literatur. Eine Problemskizze." *Zur Dichotomisierung von hoher und niederer Literatur.* Ed. Christa Bürger et al. Frankfurt: Suhrkamp, 1982. 9-39.

—————. *Leben Schreiben: Die Klassik, die Romantik und der Ort der Frauen.* Stuttgart: Metzler, 1990.

Eagleton, Terry. *The Rape of Clarissa: Writing, Sexuality and Class Struggle in Samuel Richardson.* Oxford: Blackwell, 1982.

Gallas, Helga, and Magdalene Heuser, eds. *Untersuchungen zum Roman von Frauen um 1800.* Untersuchungen zur deutschen Literaturgeschichte 55. Tübingen: Niemeyer, 1990.

Gigli, Donatella. "Die goldne Welt der Täuschung: Traum und Wirklichkeit in Karoline von Wolzogen's Roman 'Agnes von Lilien.' " Gallas/Heuser 160-71.

Gilbert, Sandra M., and Susan Gubar. *The Madwoman in the Attic: The Woman Writer and the Nineteenth-Century Literary Imagination.* New Haven: Yale UP, 1979.

Grenz, Dagmar. *Mädchenliteratur: Von den moralisch-belehrenden Schriften im 18. Jahrhundert bis zur Herausbildung der Backfischliteratur im 19. Jahrhundert.* Stuttgart: Metzler, 1981.

Heuser, Magdalene. "'Spuren trauriger Selbstvergessenheit': Möglichkeiten eines weiblichen Bildungsromans um 1800: Friederike Helene Unger.' " *Frauensprache—Frauenliteratur: Für und Wider einer Psychoanalyse literarischer Texte.* Vol. 6 of *Kontroversen, alte und neue: Akten des VI. Internationalen Germanisten-Kongresses Göttingen 1985.* Tübingen: Niemeyer, 1986. 30-42.

—————. "Nachwort." Huber 347-89.

Hirsch, Marianne. "Spiritual *Bildung*: The Beautiful Soul as Paradigm." *The Voyage In: Fictions of Female Development.* Ed. Elizabeth Abel et al. Hanover: UP of New England, 1983. 23-48.

Hohendahl, Peter Uwe. *Building a National Literature: The Case of Germany 1830-1870.* Trans. Renate Baron Franciscono. Ithaca: Cornell UP, 1989.

—————. "Empfindsamkeit und gesellschaftliches Bewußtsein: Zur Soziologie des empfindsamen Romans am Beispiel von *La Vie de Marianne, Clarissa, Fräulein von Sternheim* und *Werther.*" *JDSG* 16 (1972): 176-207.

Horkheimer, Max, and Theodor W. Adorno. *Dialectic of Enlightenment.* Trans. John Cumming. New York: Continuum, 1972.

Huber, Therese. *Die Familie Seldorf* (1795-96). Frühe Frauenliteratur in Deutschland 7. Hildesheim: Olms, 1989.

Jacobs, Jürgen. *Wilhelm Meister und seine Brüder: Untersuchungen zum deutschen Bildungsroman*. Munich: Fink, 1972.

————— and Markus Krause, eds. *Der deutsche Bildungsroman: Gattungsgeschichte vom 18. bis 20. Jahrhundert*. Munich: Beck, 1989.

Janz, Rolf-Peter. "Zum sozialen Gehalt der 'Lehrjahre.' " *Literaturwissenschaft und Geschichtsphilosophie: Festschrift für Wilhelm Emrich*. Ed. Helmut Arntzen et al. Berlin, New York: de Gruyter, 1975. 320-40.

Kittler, Friedrich A. *Discourse Networks 1800/1900*. Trans. Michael Metteer and Chris Cullens. Stanford: Stanford UP, 1990.

—————. "Über die Sozialisation Wilhelm Meisters." *Dichtung als Sozialisationsspiel: Studien zu Goethe und Gottfried Keller*. Göttingen: Vandenhoeck & Ruprecht, 1978. 13-124.

Kontje, Todd. "Under the Father's Spell: Patriarchy vs. Patriotism in Therese Huber's *Die Familie Seldorf*." *Seminar* 28 (1992): 17-32.

Köpke, Wulf. "Die emanzipierte Frau in der Goethezeit und ihre Darstellung in der Literatur." *Die Frau als Heldin und Autorin: Neue kritische Ansätze zur deutschen Literatur*. Ed. Wolfgang Paulsen. Bern: Francke, 1979. 96-110.

La Roche, Sophie von. *Geschichte des Fräuleins von Sternheim*. Ed. Barbara Becker-Cantarino. Stuttgart: Reclam, 1984.

Martini, Fritz. "Der Bildungsroman: Zur Geschichte des Wortes und der Theorie." *DVJS* 35 (1961): 44-63.

Maurer, Michael. "Das Gute und das Schöne: Sophie von La Roche (1730-1807) wiederentdecken?" *Euphorion* 79 (1985): 111-38.

May, Kurt. " 'Wilhelm Meisters Lehrjahre': ein Bildungsroman?" *DVJS* 31 (1957): 1-37.

Mayer, Gerhart. "Zum deutschen Antibildungsroman." *Jahrbuch der Raabe-Gesellschaft* (1974): 41-64.

Meise, Helga. *Die Unschuld und die Schrift: Deutsche Frauenromane im 18. Jahrhundert*. Reihe Métro 14. Berlin, Marburg: Guttandin & Hoppe, 1983.

Rosmarin, Adena. *The Power of Genre*. Minneapolis: U of Minnesota P, 1985.

Sammons, Jeffrey L. "The Mystery of the Missing *Bildungsroman*, or: What Happened to Wilhelm Meister's Legacy?" *Genre* 14 (1981): 229-46.

Schlaffer, Heinz. "Exoterik und Esoterik in Goethes Romanen." *Goethe Jahrbuch* 95 (1978): 212-26.

Schlechta, Karl. *Goethes Wilhelm Meister*. Frankfurt: Klostermann, 1953.

Schmidt, Siegfried J. *Die Selbstorganisation des Sozialsystems Literatur im 18. Jahrhundert*. Frankfurt: Suhrkamp, 1989.

Sebastian, Thomas. "Technology Romanticized: Friedrich Kittler's *Discourse Networks 1800/1900*." *MLN* 105 (1990): 583-95.

Selbmann, Rolf. *Der deutsche Bildungsroman*. Sammlung Metzler 214. Stuttgart: Metzler, 1984.

Smith, John H. "Sexual Difference, *Bildung*, and the *Bildungsroman*." *Michigan Germanic Studies* 13 (1987): 206-25.

Stutz, Johann Ernst August. *Julchen Grünthal: Eine Pensionsgeschichte. Zweiter Theil*. Berlin, Frankfurt an der Oder: Kunze, 1788.

Swales, Martin. *The German Bildungsroman from Wieland to Hesse*. Princeton: Princeton UP, 1978.

Touaillon, Christine. *Der deutsche Frauenroman des 18. Jahrhunderts*. Vienna: Braumüller, 1919.

Unger, Friederike Helene. *Julchen Grünthal: Eine Pensionsgeschichte* (1784). 2nd ed. Berlin: Unger, 1787.

————. *Julchen Grünthal*. 3rd revised ed. Berlin: Unger, 1798.

Wolzogen, Karoline von. *Agnes von Lilien* (1798). Hildesheim: Olms, 1988.

Zantop, Susanne. "Aus der Not eine Tugend . . . : Tugendgebot und Öffentlichkeit bei Friederike Helene Unger." Gallas and Heuser 132-47.

Healthy Families:
Medicine, Patriarchy, and Heterosexuality
in Eighteenth-Century German Novels

Robert Tobin

IN THE 1947 INTRODUCTION to their *Dialectic of Enlightenment* (*Dialektik der Aufklärung*, originally published in 1944), Max Horkheimer and Theodor Adorno write:

> On the one hand the growth of economic productivity furnishes the conditions for a world of greater justice; on the other hand it allows the technical apparatus and the social groups which administer it a disproportionate superiority to the rest of the population. (xiv)

The progress of medicine, the subject of a fragment in the *Dialectic* called "Contradictions" (237-40), clearly fulfills the conditions described in this passage: on the level of common sense, it has obviously positive effects of reducing human suffering due to illness and increasing the quality and length of life, but, on another level, it has also become a means of concentrating power in the hands of an elite, resulting in injustice and oppression. Increasingly, literary critics such as Schings[1] have noted the embedding of medical discourse in eighteenth-century novels, particularly in the Bildungsroman. Perhaps the same instincts that call forth ambivalent responses to medicine have provoked the radically opposed interpretations of the classical Bildungsroman, interpretations which describe the genre sometimes as a triumph of humanism and other times as a dismal portrait of society's ever-diminishing humanity. Issues of family and gender are often a focal point for these interpretations: It is said either that the protagonist heroically navigates the passage from childhood through adolescence to well-adjusted participation in an adult family, or that certain characters of the novel, particularly women, suffer at the hands of the novel's familial structures.

Usually, both in the criticism and in the novels themselves, medical testimony and metaphors of health and sickness are brought to bear on discussions of the familial structures at the center of the disputes about the Bildungsroman. Of three novels taken from the canon of eighteenth-century German literature, two—Christoph Martin Wieland's *Agathon* (first published 1766) and Karl Phillip Moritz's *Anton Reiser* (1785-90)—operate negatively, in the sense that they brand (more or less ironically) non-bourgeois family structures and expressions of sexuality as pathological. The final example, Johann Wolfgang Goethe's *Wilhelm Meister's Apprenticeship* (*Wilhelm Meisters Lehrjahre*, 1796), goes beyond the first two, which can only condemn the non-bourgeois, by providing a "healthy" solution, in the form of the newly emergent bourgeois family.

I. Medicine

The most important theoretical development in eighteenth-century German medicine was its adoption of a new approach to the mind-body problem. Physicians such as Boerhaave and Hoffmann used a Cartesian philosophy separating mind and body to articulate a mechanistic medicine, concerned only with the physical functioning of the body, delegating emotional, mental, and spiritual problems to others (Rothschuh). Starting with Stahl, however, the medical community in eighteenth-century Germany began to reject this strict separation of mind and body: Stahl wrote, "a system of healing which does not take the constitution of the soul into account and which does not know the world of feeling is useless."[2] Stahl's beliefs gradually took root in the medical community, until by the middle of the eighteenth century, the physician Nicolai was typical when he wrote that "body and soul are in the most exact harmony, and a sickness in the body produces . . . a sickness of the soul and this in return a sickness of the body in every instance."[3] By the second half of the century, this thinking on the mind-body problem spread from medicine back to philosophy, when Kant, in a pre-critical essay, supported Stahl and his disciples: "I am convinced that Stahl, who likes to explain animal changes organically, is often closer to the truth than Hofmann, Boerhaave, et al."[4] As the century drew to a close, the medical beliefs of Stahl and his disciples concerning the unity of mind and body had permeated society and become commonplaces in literature and anthropology as well as philosophy and medicine.

Calling themselves "philosophische" or "moralische Ärzte," physicians used their new belief in mind-body unity to treat problems formerly reserved for philosophers or the clergy. About philosophers and questions of the mind, the radical physician La Mettrie wrote: "experience and observation should therefore be our only guides here. Both are to be found throughout the records of the physicians who are philosophers, and not in the works of the philosophers who are not physicians" (88).[5] The same skepticism greeted religion, because most physicians agreed with Moritz, who cautioned in his "Proposal for a Magazine of Experiential Psychology" that, despite their work with problems of the soul in the past, religious figures could not adequately perform the tasks of psychologists because their outlook was too tainted by superstition (*Magazin* 1.1).

Medicine's belief in mind-body unity, with its concomitant expansion into psychological fields formerly considered philosophical or religious, allowed it new approaches to gender and sexuality. Concerning gender, Laqueur postulates that a "radical eighteenth-century reinterpretation of the female body in relation to the male" took place, largely emerging from a medical tradition (4). "In the late seventeenth and eighteenth centuries," Laqueur explains, "science fleshed out, in terms acceptable to the new epistemology, the categories 'male' and 'female' as opposite and incommensurable biological sexes" (154). In the world of pathology, the genders came to have specific illnesses. Arnold emphasized the connections between menstruation and madness, particularly hysteria (2: 180-200). Increasingly, hysteria became gender specific, applicable only to women, while men were afflicted with hypochondria (Foucault 268). In general, women were considered especially likely to go mad, partly because of biological facts such as menstruation, and partly because of social constraints which, for instance, prevented them from getting enough movement (Zimmermann, *Erfahrung* 600, 733).

If males and females were essentially different in body and mind, then their sexuality would obviously differ as well. Medical thought on male sexuality emerged from the context of a phallocentric glorification of semen. Tissot relied on Galen to show that the loss of a half an ounce of semen did more damage than the loss of forty ounces of blood,[6] while citing Aristotle to show that semen was one of the most nutritious fluids, as it contained everything necessary to reproduce the human being.[7] The view of female sexuality seems couched in much more negative terms. According to Laqueur, this was the era which saw the banishment of the female orgasm "to the borderlands of physiology, a signifier without a signified." Women were thought either to be "passionless" or in control of extraordinary powers of controlling their sex drives (150).

So powerful were these beliefs that many physicians ignored female sexuality entirely, even while they devoted increasing attention to deviations from the norm of male sexuality (Faderman 34). When physicians bothered to concern themselves with female sexuality, they severely censured those women who defied these theories by exhibiting too strong a sex drive, in the form of masturbation, homosexuality, or nymphomania. Tissot rages against female masturbation and particularly "the feminine disgrace which happens with the clitoris":[8]

> Nature tends to play sometimes, and creates female personages of a sort who, because of the size of their clitoris and out of ignorance about its proper usage, fall into an abuse and want to play the man. Stimulated, they stimulate others and attempt to create hereby for themselves the pleasure of true intercourse. This sort of female personage hates men and is their enemy; they were not unknown to the ancients, who called them "tribates" (lewd women who perform shameful acts with their own sort) and divided them into various categories; writers also did not silently ignore these appellations and they attributed the establishment of this order to the young Sappho.[9]

Women who tried to engage in too much sex with men could also become health problems—for men, because of the preciousness of semen. Typically, the issue of allegedly excessive female sexuality is seen as primarily a problem for men's health; since all of the physicians writing on the subject were men, male sexuality received more medical attention. One of the major concerns of the era was male masturbation, about which Tissot wrote an entire treatise. Hufeland (240) and Zimmermann (615) agreed with Tissot on the dangers of masturbation (see also Greenberg 364). The vice came to be seen by German physicians such as Müller as a "precursor of same-sex love" (Greenberg 367), pointing to another area of sexuality which came increasingly under medical supervision. In a survey conducted between 1791 and 1794, Wagnitz reports that insane asylums are among the institutions incarcerating sodomites (Wagnitz 2.2: 14). Wagnitz's numbers are small (0.5 percent of inmates), but they indicate medicine's rising interest in the formerly religious category of sexual deviance.

The desire to conserve semen also contributed to more general warnings against immoderation in intercourse. The English physician Thomas Arnold writes that "of all origins of madness, ... none are more efficient and stubborn than excessive intercourse."[10] Noting the particular link between brain and genitals, Hufeland states that "nothing in the world can blunt the most beautiful mental gifts so extensively and so irreparably as this [sexual] excess."[11] Zimmermann, who also sees "a strange linkage between the ideas of [religious] enthusiasts and their sexual parts,"[12] felt that excessive copulation led to melancholy and hypochondria, particularly for men (*Erfahrung* 600).

While excessive expenditures of semen were a health problem for eighteenth-century physicians, ascetic retention of semen was also dangerous. In his assessment of the medical consequences of celibacy, Zimmermann argues that the repression of the passions in the cloisters results in an explosion of irrational acts, including suicides, unnatural emissions during religious services, castration, love-madness, and pederasty (*Einsamkeit* 2: 232-33). Such beliefs resurface in Diderot's novella *La religieuse*, in which a woman forced into the convent by her family must submit to the amorous advances of a lecherous mother superior; according to Laqueur, this pattern can also be found in the writings of the English radical Richard Carlile, who saw masturbation as "born of the cloister" (229).

Most of all, however, eighteenth-century physicians concentrated on promoting a safe compromise between waste and ascetic retention of semen: the sensible, moderate usage of semen prevalent in a monogamous, heterosexual relationship. Unfailingly and tirelessly, the new philosophical and moral physicians propounded the health benefits of moderate intercourse. For Arnold, moderation in intercourse (along with eating, sleeping, and working) was the first rule for the prevention of insanity (2: 351). Zimmermann concluded his four volumes on the pros and cons of solitude with the compromise solution of living in solitude with one's spouse (*Einsamkeit* 4: 178-80). The newly emergent bourgeois family, characterized by its exclusion of distant relatives and large numbers of servants and by its removal from the workplace (Hausen), becomes in the medical writings of the time a matter of health.

Nonetheless, forms of sexuality and family that differed from this norm could be seen not only as a poison, but also as an antidote, leading toward monogamous heterosexuality in a bourgeois marriage, for, according to the medicine of the time, every disease contained its cure. In this era, and coming out of the tradition of reform physicians who emphasized the mind-body unity, Hahnemann developed the foundations of homeopathic medicine, which attempted to use the causes of disorders to cure those disorders (Hahnemann 133; Schwanitz). Especially in matters of mental health, the era's progressive physicians believed in using madness to combat madness and bring about sanity. The "pious fraud," usually some sort of deception by which a caretaker would play along with the insane ideas of his or her[13] ward and trick that person into seeing things sanely, was a frequently used form of therapy (Diener).

In his innovative *Journal of Experiential Psychology* (*Magazin für Erfahrungsseelenkunde*, 1783-92), Moritz, for instance, discusses the cure of a young man suffering from a severe case of theater-mania, which was endangering his happiness and well-being. Rather than for-bidding the patient to attend the theater, which would have backfired, Moritz encourages him to dedicate himself to the theater and visit it daily. Even when the patient began to doubt the sanity of his theatrical visits, Moritz encouraged him to persevere in his theatrical ambitions, which had the desired result that the patient decided not to attend the theater any longer and to go back to his parents, after which he was "completely cured of his fantasy."[14]

II. Literature

The mention of Moritz and his *Magazin* is appropriate here, for the authors of the canonical Bildungsromane of the eighteenth century—Wieland, Moritz, and Goethe—all use their era's new medicinal lan-guage to discuss the gender roles, sexuality, and familial structures of their characters.

Agathon contains much of the vocabulary of its era's medical de-bates—not surprisingly, as Wieland was well-versed in his age's medi-cine. He engaged in a lengthy dispute by correspondence with his friend Zimmermann, eventually coming over to the medical belief in mind-body unity (Schings, "Roman"). The mind-body problem thus receives prominent billing in *Agathon* (418, 503, 705, 830). Dealing more specifically with medicine, the first edition of the novel begins and ends with references to physicians and illness. The novel's very first paragraph points out that an archival account of an historical per-sonage would conclude by revealing the medical detail of the cause of that figure's death (375). Wieland creates a medical frame for the novel by concluding it with an allusion to another physician, *Don Quixote*'s "Doctor Peter Rezio von Aguero." As humorously ironical as this allusion turns out to be, it nonetheless helps medicine frame the novel and thereby establish the context of its questions.

As a prolific translator of classical texts, Wieland was well aware of a great variety of sexual practices. Indeed, according to Gleim, the reproach circulated in literary circles that it was from Wieland that German youth first heard about "Greek love," that is, homosexuality.[15] His verse tale *Juno and Ganymed* is filled with humorous and lascivious passages of a rococo sort, insinuating a knowledge of non-heterosexual practices. In *Agathon*, too, Wieland lets a tolerant light shine through on many forms of sexuality. The narrator refers casually to the fact that "Greeks had completely different notions of love from modern Europeans."[16] He also alludes without censure to the episode in which

Critobulus kisses Alcibiades' beautiful son, merely pointing out that it is "our" custom to kiss beautiful girls, not boys.[17]

Despite this seeming tolerance, however, Wieland's *Agathon* incorporates its era's medical anthropology, dismissing forms of sexuality outside the bourgeois family. Within the first pages of the novel, Psyche tells the story of her kidnapping by pirates while she was dressed in a boy's clothing. When the ship's captain calls her "Ganymede" and tries to seduce her, Psyche calls his passion "disgusting" and "absurd" ("ekelhaft" [395], "unsinnig" [396]). Significantly, it is not the force, but rather the homosexual desire itself which Psyche dislikes. Psyche's tale anticipates Agathon's own "Ganymedic" experience. As a youth he had dreamed of being, like Ganymede, loved by divinities (555). His neo-platonic interpretations of the myth, assuming a purely mental love, are dashed when a priest, disguised as Apollo, attempts to seduce him. The priest cynically argues that everything attributed to the gods consists merely of traps to ensare women and gullible boys.[18] Fortunately for the reader's sense of poetic justice, the priest attempts to seduce one gullible boy too many—one a relative of a superior, for which reason he disappears from Delphi (560). Once again, the passage rejects not the unethical means of satisfying this passion, but the pederastic passion itself—this time as "immoral" ("unsittlich" [559]).

It is appropriate that the priest dresses up as Apollo, for Apollo was known for his homosexual leanings, most famously because of his affair with Hyacinth, which in Ovid's version ended tragically when the god's discus fatally struck the beautiful youth. Through the name "Hyacinth," Danae is linked to the homosexuality which the novel finds disgusting, absurd, and immoral, because her lover before she meets Agathon is called "Hyacinthus" (473). Indeed, Hippias refers to "your Hyacinths" ("deine Hyacinthe") as a general category of Danae's lovers. As the lover of Hyacinths, Danae can even be equated with the bisexual Apollo, making clear that the novel posits Agathon moving from one morally dissatisfying expression of sexuality to another. Linking the aggressively heterosexual woman with the male homosexual sea-captains and priests is not as ridiculous as it may seem at first glance, for Danae differs from the healthy norm as much as they do. As tolerantly as the narrator regards the different mores of Greek society, and as positively as he portrays Danae, he nonetheless agrees with her decision to pursue a life of solitude outside of Tarentine doing penance for her lifestyle before she met Agathon. The narrator also assumes that his readers will agree that Agathon cannot remain in the love nest with Danae: "for you certainly will not want an Agathon to waste his whole life, like a veneris passerculus (let your lover translate that for you), making love on the bosom of the tender Danae?"[19] The narrator's anxieties about Danae's excessive sexuality conform perfectly with the era's medical anthropology, which saw inordinate intercourse as damaging for the man and an indication of something wrong in the woman.

Although Wieland implies that male homosexuality and excessive female heterosexuality are wrong in a number of ways, he stops short of bringing Agathon into a conventional family approximating bourgeois norms. Instead, he ironizes the process by referring to Sancho and "Doctor Peter Rezio von Aguero," "an all-too-scrupulous physician," who objects to so many forms of food that the residents of Barataria waste away, malnourished. In this case, the best thing to do would be to follow Sancho's example, and rid oneself of the doctor (852)! While the editor mentions medicine at the novel's beginning as part of an argument establishing the historical truth of his work, Doctor Rezio's story obviously lampoons medicine and reason; moreover, the allusion to *Don Quixote* removes the novel from the empirical world to the literary one. Wieland's depiction of gender roles, familial structures, and sexual identities recognizes the belief of his contemporaries that certain deviations from bourgeois norms are unhealthy—yet in the absence of a positive solution to these problems, he suggests that the reader choose his or her poison, and ignore the medical advice.

Moritz, a friend of influential physicians such as Herz (Müller 48ff.), had connections with the medical world of his time which are even better known than Wieland's. Indeed, nowadays Moritz's activities as the editor of the *Magazin* receive as much attention as his novels. Not that comparisons between his psychological and novelistic work are even necessary, for it is clear in *Anton Reiser*, subtitled a "psychological novel," that Moritz's two interests converge on the same raw material: the study of the soul and its sicknesses. Much more so than in *Agathon*, sickness is one of *Anton Reiser*'s recurrent themes (17, 30, 61, 76, 93, 225). While *Agathon* ends on an open, ironical note, *Anton Reiser* presents a much bleaker image of essentially irresolvable familial problems.

Moritz's work in medicine and psychology show his awareness of non-heterosexual feelings, particularly the remarkably sensitive letters he published in his *Magazin*.[20] He himself had a relationship with Klischnig which was so close that the latter had to deny explicitly charges of "Greek Love" (Müller 291). In *Anton Reiser*, the protagonist claims that he had only very "dark and confused concepts" about "certain things."[21] Although taught about "sodomy" and the "vice of self-abuse" in lessons on the Sixth Commandment,[22] he had no idea what these words actually meant and had to resolve to fight valiantly against all evil desires, whatever they should turn out to be.[23] Reiser's pleas of

ignorance regarding these practices reveal, however, that Moritz knew
and thought about them.

Combined with his medical knowledge, Moritz's thinking about
these "vices" inevitably resulted in the coupling of Anton Reiser's sicknesses with his love of men and his inability to establish a loving relationship with women. Hints of homoeroticism surface in Anton's exag-
gerated friendships. One of Reiser's earliest wishes, made clear to the
reader shortly after Reiser has mentioned sickness and religion as
important elements in his life, is the desire to know other youths: "He
felt most strongly the need of friendship with his own kind: and often,
when he saw a youth of his age, his whole soul hung on him, and he
would have given anything to become his friend."[24] He announces his
friendship with Phillip Reiser with extravagent, effusive declarations of
love (238-39) and suffers severe melancholy in the absence of the loved
one (271-72). His friendship with Iffland, while not as passionate, may
have meant even more to those readers looking for signs of "Greek
love" in that era, because the famous playwright was notorious for his
homosexual leanings.[25] Reiser subsequently becomes utterly infatu-
ated with a young Carthusian monk, "with pale cheeks of exceptionally
beautiful structure,"[26] especially when he discovers that the young
monk entered the order because lightning struck his (the boy's) best
friend (398). Finally, Anton develops "a real love and fondness" for
Neries.[27] On the novel's last page, Anton murmurs his new best
friend's name as he walks in tears to his ill-fated theatrical mission.[28]

Clearly, Reiser's enthusiasm for his fellow youths owes much to his
era's friendship cults (Meyer-Krentler). In particular, Reiser explicitly
refers to models from the literature of the Storm and Stress. As Foucault points out in a late interview, however, the decline, beginning in
the sixteenth century, of friendship as a non-sexual male bonding resulted in the eighteenth-century emergence of male homosexuality "as
a social/political/medical problem" (Gallagher 58). Especially in the
light of "medical problems," Reiser's friendships deserve closer scrutiny here.

These friendships differ from non-sexual male bonding in their
undisguised exclusion of women. Reiser identifies enthusiastically with
every aspect of Goethe's Storm-and-Stress classic *Werther* (1774),
except for the matter of love: "In short, Reiser believed he found himself in *Werther*, with all his thoughts and feelings, up to the point of
love."[29] Anton claims on several occasions that he cannot imagine
himself as the "object of the love of a woman."[30] The novel contains a
few striking images of women—the pale maid in black at Paulmann's
church (72), the beautiful young woman grieving for Phillip Reiser's
drowned friend (251)—and a fair number of passages concerning

Anton's mother and other women of her generation who deny or provide him care. Other than these visions of somber femininity and the confrontation with the maternal, however, Anton's main thought about women is that he could never be loved by one, a thought that distinguishes the novel from the usual rhetoric of friendship, which generally protects itself from the suspicions of even suppressed homosexuality by giving the friends a few girlfriends.

Not only does Anton Reiser exclude women from his horizon, he actually attempts to replace them. The novel further distinguishes itself from the "Storm-and-Stress" friendship novel when its hero plays female roles on the stage. In one play, Anton is Clelie, the beloved of Medon (400, see also 408). Of course, at all-male educational institutions, men had to play women's roles in student productions, but he plays the role of Clelie so well and is so satisfied with it that he "forgets himself" (403). Given his professed love of his fellow students, and his inability to identify with romantic stories involving men loving women, his ability to identify so well with female characters loving men signifies a desire to replace the woman as the object of the man's desire.

Moritz's response to this homosexual desire is to press the self-destruct button. The motif of self-loss and self-destruction is perhaps the strongest single unifier of this novel. It begins with the references to Madame de Guyon's philosophy of returning to one's "nothingness" ("Nichts"), and destroying all passion and all selfhood (9). It resurfaces with his love of another classic of the "Storm and Stress," Klinger's *The Twins* (*Die Zwillinge*, 1776) and Guelfo's "self-contempt and the drive for self-destruction."[31] The self's desire to destroy its passions and return to nothingness is especially understandable when it harbors desires that it considers pathological and immoral.

Like Wieland and Moritz, Goethe cultivated extensive connections in the medical community. According to his autobiography, he frequently socialized with medical students both in Leipzig and in Strassburg (HA 9: 259, 361).[32] In addition to knowing the medically well-informed Wieland and Moritz, he also knew personally many of the prominent physicians of his day, including Zimmermann and his own physician, Hufeland. A diary entry on July 1, 1795 lists a number of progressive physicians in whose work he was interested, including Hufeland, Brown, Weickard, and Reil.[33] Goethe even participated in a number of psychiatric cures (Diener). Goethe's interest in medicine carries over to *Wilhelm Meister*. Issues of illness and health, particularly psychosomatic sickness and psychological well-being, appear in details as trivial as Aurelie's headaches and Barbara's toothaches and in plot elements as significant as the Harper's madness and Mignon's literal heart-sickness. Indeed, the possession of medicine distinguishes the novel's haves and have-nots: Natalie and her "Oheim" keep a surgeon in their retinue, while the entire Tower Society frequently consults the physician to recommend treatment for such varied complaints as Lothario's gun wound, the Beautiful Soul's melancholia, the Harper's mania, and Mignon's heart condition. In contrast, the characters outside the orbit of the Tower Society are not only without medicine, but in fact sick and, in many instances, by the end of the novel, dead. In many ways, Wilhelm Meister's story is in part the story of his medical empowerment, as he moves from a kind of sickness at the beginning of the novel to a sort of health and, in *Wilhelm Meister's Travels* (final edition 1829), eventually to a modest position as a surgeon within the healing profession itself.

Goethe was also certainly aware of a wide variety of expressions of sexuality and possible familial constructions. His sensitive essay on Winckelmann (Derks 200-10) as well as his constant support of the historian Johannes Müller, who was embroiled in a scandal that revealed his homosexual inclination (Derks 315-22), demonstrate Goethe's sophistication on issues of sexuality. On another wavelength, Ronell has transmitted the erotics of the relationship between Goethe and his personal secretary Eckermann. The reconception of Wilhelm's family from a sprawling unit with an actively involved grandmother in *Wilhelm Meister's Theatrical Mission* (the first, uncompleted, attempt at a Wilhelm Meister novel, begun in the 1770s) to a tightly knit, self-contained bourgeois nuclear family in the *Apprenticeship* reveals Goethe's uncanny sensitivity to the sociological changes in family structures taking place in his era (Kittler 15-29).

Precisely this shift to the bourgeois family means that, regardless of Goethe's personal views on gender, sexuality, and family, in the novel, non-bourgeois familial structures and expressions of sexuality are signs of immaturity. Early in the novel, Wilhelm is only interested in Amazon women who wear men's clothes. As a child, he is fascinated by Tasso's character, Chlorinde, particularly because of her androgyny.[34] On the first page of the novel, he embraces not his beloved Marianne, but her snappy soldier's uniform: "How passionately he embraced that red uniform and the white satin vest!"[35] His glimpse of Natalie wearing men's attire fires passions that are only quenched when he marries her (S 9: 133; HA 7: 226). And before he marries Natalie, he has an affair with Therese, who wears exclusively male clothing, and is described as "a real Amazon, whereas others who go around like her in ambiguous clothing are nothing but dainty hermaphrodites."[36] In this novel, where clothing really does identify the character of a character (Neumann 51), Wilhelm's desires for women in male attire indicate a deviation from heterosexual norms.

The most obvious example of the androgyny present in Wilhelm's youth is Mignon, the dark waif he adopts while travelling. Both Wilhelm (S 9: 50; HA 7: 91) and the narrator, who only refers to her with a feminine pronoun five times in the novel (Keppel-Kriems 87), have difficulty determining her gender. Even her name, with its masculine ending, puts her gender into question, underscoring her lack of conformity to the heterosexual norms present at the novel's end. Mignon cannot take part in this end because of her fatal heart attack brought on by the bourgeois primal scene—the appearance, at least, of a nuclear family, with Therese kissing Wilhelm while Felix tugs at her skirt, saying, "Mother Therese, I'm here too!"[37]

If Mignon's lack of gender definition makes her unable to take part in the bourgeois nuclear family, Philine represents the eighteenth-century medical "problem" of excessive female sexuality. From the moment she is introduced, she exhibits strong desires, aggressively asking Wilhelm for flowers (S 9: 50; HA 7: 91). She spends intimate moments with a number of men, including Wilhelm: everything points to her as the possessor of the delicate arms and breast which he didn't have the strength to resist on the night of the successful performance of *Hamlet* (S 9: 198, 321; HA 7: 327, 523-24). Predictably, given eighteenth-century anthropology, her behavior leads to no good. Wilhelm cannot marry her, as she pales in comparison with the passionless Natalie (S 9: 134; HA 7: 228), who admits to lacking an understanding of love (S 9: 330; HA 7: 538). Mignon's death and Philine's fading charms turn out to be typical for non-normatively heterosexual behavior in *Wilhelm Meister*. Androgyny and "excessive" female sexuality are at the beginning of Wilhelm's life—not to mention the homoeroticism of the episode with the drowned fisherman's son, which is also from Wilhelm's youth, although it is first mentioned in the *Travels* (S 10: 284-94; HA 8: 268-79). Because Wilhelm's beginnings are saturated with illness, such as that eighteenth-century illness, "theater mania" (Flaherty), this non-normative behavior becomes textually linked to illness. The sexual deviance associated with Wilhelm's wounds and illnesses must presumably be cured just as much as they.

An organization called the Tower Society, similar to the Masons and bearing the standard of Enlightened thinking (including medicine), attempts to socialize Wilhelm Meister to a heterosexual "healthiness." Just as Moritz had done in his *Magazin*, they cure him of his mania for the theater by letting him act on stage until he loses interest in drama (Flaherty). The treatment for "theater mania" involves the typically homeopathic eighteenth-century tactic of using an illness to cure itself. Similarly, the Tower Society uses Wilhelm's initially strong homosexual drives to turn him into a heterosexual. First, the members of the

Society channel Wilhelm's libidinal energies toward men who desire women, arousing his lust for the objects of their desire. He thus finds himself more interested in Philine's quarreling lovers than in Philine herself, whom he doesn't even honor with a glance (S 9: 80-81; HA 7: 140-41). Subsequently, Therese, an associate of the Tower Society, teaches Wilhelm (a) a series of ideological gender distinctions based upon, to use Laqueur's terminology, a "two-sex system," and (b) the imperative of loving someone of the other gender (S 9: 217; HA 7: 452). Finally, Natalie, sister of Lothario, the leader of the Tower Society, inducts Wilhelm into a mature heterosexual relationship. She, whose eyes contain—homeopathically—poison and antidote,[38] first attracts Wilhelm by playing to his homosexual impulses when she appears in a man's coat as the Beautiful Amazon (S 9: 134; HA 7: 226). Only later does she reveal herself to be a woman in every sense of Therese's definition of the word, at which point Wilhelm can love her.

Such is the "happy end" of *Wilhelm Meister's Apprenticeship*. The Tower Society, with the help of medicine, can utilize Wilhelm's "illnesses" or "vices" to cure him; his love of the theater brings him away from the theater and into the bourgeois world, while his homosexuality brings him away from homosexuality and into a heterosexual relationship. Proponents of the bourgeois cause find the ending felicitous because it implies that such "problems" will heal themselves in the bourgeois order. Detractors, however, rely on the novel's irony to argue that Goethe was describing, rather than advocating, the changes taking place in his society. His novel portrays too clearly the dangers of the equation of health and the bourgeois family: many characters (the Harper, the Beautiful Soul, Laertes) will not be able to follow Wilhelm's journey to the position of father in the bourgeois family, and are therefore doomed, in the novel's world, to sickness (Hirsch). Thus, while the study of the medical discourse in *Wilhelm Meister's Apprenticeship* makes clear that Wilhelm develops from a state which the Tower Society calls sick (including theater and homosexuality) to one it calls healthy (including a practical career and a heterosexual relationship), this does not mean that the reader must greet such development as exemplary.

All three novels present non-normative gender roles and expressions of sexuality as phases to be outgrown, illnesses awaiting cures. Wieland's *Agathon* condemns homosexuality and active female sexuality as pathological and then laughingly suggests that one kill the doctor and ignore reason. Moritz's *Anton Reiser* links homosexuality and the need for self-destruction. Goethe's novel not only relegates androgyny and strong female sexuality to childhood, but—unlike its predecessors—can bring its protagonist into the semblance of a healthy nuclear family with Natalie and Felix. An indictment of the authors on charges of "intolerance" would demonstrate an inadequate understanding of the ironies and aporias inherent in all literature—in fact, good arguments suggest that Wieland satirizes the pathologization of forms of sexuality and gender when he refers to *Don Quixote*, that Moritz demonstrates the cheerlessness of a world in which non-heterosexual desires are proscribed, and that Goethe does not condone his era's increasing tendency to link health and heterosexuality but instead critiques the validity of the family that Wilhelm, Natalie, and Felix create. But ignoring the presence of a medical discourse which describes paternalistic families as "healthy" and pathologizes alternatives to such families would also be a grievous underestimation of the power of institutional discourses and the role in nineteenth and twentieth-century Euro-American culture of literary genres such as the Bildungsroman in propagating this power. In order to be true to the ironies of eighteenth-century literature, it is important not to blur the dialectic of Enlightenment, dialectic exemplified by the ability of medical discourses to produce both liberating improvements in human well-being and oppressive patriarchal structures.

Notes

1. Above all, in "Agathon—Anton Reiser—Wilhelm Meister."
2. "Vergeblich ist eine Heilkunde ohne Berücksichtigung der Verfassung der Seele und ohne Kenntnis der Gefühlswelt" (37).
3. "Leib und Seele stehn in der genausten Harmonie und eine Kranckheit im Körper führet ... eine Kranckheit der Seele und diese hinwiederum eine Kranckheit des Körpers jederzeit bey sich" (49).
4. "bin ich überzeugt, daß Stahl, welcher die thierischen Veränderungen gerne organisch erklärt, oftmals der Wahrheit näher sei, als Hofmann, Boerhaave u.a.m." (939).
5. "L'expérience et l'observation doivent donc seules nous guider ici. Elles se trouvent sans nombre dans les Fastes des médecins, qui ont été philosophes, et non dans les philosophes, qui n'ont été médecins" (16).
6. "Der Saamen ... ist so ädel, daß wie schon Galenus erinnert, der Verlust einer halben Unze denen Kräften mehr Schaden tut, als wenn man vierzig Unzen Blut abzapft" (8).
7. "Aristotles hat die Samenabsonderung vor eine der Nahrungsreichsten Feuchtigkeiten gehalten, weil er in sich selbst die Kraft hat, ein solches ähnliches Wesen hervorzubringen, als dasjenige ist, von welchem er ist ausgegossen worden" (46).
8. "die weibliche Schändung, welche mit dem Küzler geschieht" (39).
9. "Die Natur pflegt manchmal zu spielen, und bringt solche Weibs-Persohnen hervor, welche bei der Gröse ihres Küzlers aus Unwissenheit des rechten Gebrauchs, in einen Misbrauch verfallen, und einen Mann vorstellen wollen. Gereizet reizen sie andere und trachten sich hierdurch die Lust eines rechten Beischlafs zu verschaffen. Diese Art Weibs-Persohnen hasset die Männer und ist ihnen feind,

sie waren den Alten nicht unbekannt, welche sie tribates (geile Weiber die mit
ihres gleichen Schande treiben) nennten; und in gewisse Klassen abtheilten; auch
haben die Schriftsteller ihre verschiedenen Benennungen nicht mit Stillschweigen
übergangen und schrieben der jungen Sappho die Aufrichtung dieses Ordens zu"
(39-40). Tissot refers interested readers to a 1730 dissertation on the subject by T.
Tronchin. See Greenberg 374ff., and Laqueur 53 for more on tribades.

10. "Unter allen Ursachen des Wahnsinns ... sind keine wirksamer und hart-
näckiger, als *Uebermaß im Beyschlaf*" (Arnold, 2: 128).

11. "Nichts in der Welt kann so sehr und so unwiderbringlich die schönsten
Geistesgaben abstümpfen, als diese Ausschweifung" (241).

12. "Man kennt den sehr sonderbaren Zusammenhang zwischen den Ideen
der Schwärmer und ihren Geschlechtsteilen"(*Einsamkeit* 2: 132).

13. Although the physicians of the era were almost universally male, one of the
era's most famous cases of a "pious fraud" was Ernestine Christiane Reiske's treatment of her maid, who tortured herself with groundless self-reproaches. Reiske reported the case herself in the *Magazin* 3.3 (1785): 30; Moritz subsequently discussed it in the *Magazin* 4.1 (1786): 40, as did Mauchart in the *Allgemeines Repertorium*
2 (1792): 21, 50. For information on Dorothea Erxleben, one of the only female
physicians trained academically before the twentieth century, see Schiebinger 250ff.

14. Moritz, "Ein Unglücklicher Hang zum Theater," *Magazin* 3.1 (1785): 121-
25. See also I. D. Mauchart, "Eine Geschichte eines unglücklichen Hangs zum
Theater," *Magazin* 7.3 (1789): 115ff.

15. "[der] Vorwurf, ... daß aus seinem [Wielands] munde die deutsche Jugend
zuerst von griechischer Liebe gehört, und bald darauf sich Ganymede gehalten hätte" (Gleim to Wieland, 2 January 1774, *Briefwechsel* 5: 221; cf. Derks 234).

16. "Überhaupt ist es eine längst ausgemachte Sache, daß die Griechen von
der Liebe ganz andere Begriffe hatten als die heutigen Europäer" (683-84).

17. " 'Du Unglücklicher!' sagte er [Sokrates] zu dem jungen Xenophon, welcher nicht begreifen konnte, daß es eine gefährliche Sache sei, einen schönen Knaben, oder nach unseren Sitten zu sprechen, ein schönes Mädchen zu küssen" (665;
see also 659).

18. "Er zog die Folge daraus: Daß alles, was man von den Göttern sagte, Er-
findungen schlauer Köpfe wären, womit sie Weiber und leichtgläubige Knaben in
ihr Netz zu ziehen suchten" (559).

19. "denn sie werden doch nicht wollen, daß ein Agathon sein ganzes Leben
wie ein Veneris Passerculus (lassen Sie sich das von Ihrem Liebhaber verdeut-
schen) am Busen der zärtlichen Danae hätte hinweg buhlen sollen?" (671). For
those of you without lovers, a "veneris passerculus" is "a little sparrow of Venus."

20. "Aus einem Brief," *Magazin* 8.1 (1791), and under the rubric "Seelenhei-
lenkunde" in *Magazin* 8.2 (1791). For a less sensitive reference to "the disgusting
suspicion of pederasty" ("[der] abscheuliche Verdacht einer ... Knabenschände-
rei"), see "Auszug aus dem Leben H. Cardans," *Magazin* 6.1 (1788): 9-126, here
123.

21. "Reiser war so weit hievon entfernt, daß ihm drei Jahre nachher, da er zu-
fälligerweise ein anatomisches Buch zu sehen bekam, über gewisse Dinge ein Licht
aufging, wovon damals seine Begriffe noch sehr dunkel waren" (218).

22. "Er hatte bei seinem Religionsunterricht auf dem Seminarium zwar schon
von allerlei Sünden gehört, wovon er sich nie einen rechten Begriff machen konnte,
als von Sodomiterei, stummen Sünden und dem Laster der Selbstbefleckung, welche alle bei der Erklärung des sechsten Gebotes genannt wurden" (132).

23. "Zum Glück verstand Reiser nicht, was sie eigentlich damit meinte, und

wagte es auch nicht, sich genauer darnach zu erkundigen, sondern nahm sich nur fest vor, wenn böse Lüste in ihm erwachen sollten, sie möchten auch sein von welcher Art sie wollten, ritterlich dagegen anzukämpfen" (132).

24. "Er fühlte auf das innigste das Bedürfnis der Freundschaft von seines gleichen: und oft, wenn er einen Knaben von seinem Alter sahe, hing seine ganze Seele an ihm, und er hätte alles drum gegeben, sein Freund zu werden" (14-15).

25. The Vienese police reported in 1809: "Man sagt nämlich: Iffland sei ein Anhänger geheimer Gesellschaften und hege eine unmoralische Neigung gegen sein Geschlecht" (26 March); "man versicherte mich, er sei der Sodomie ergeben, es sei sehr zu verwundern, daß ein Mensch, welcher diesem Laster ergeben sei, solche moralische Stücke, als seine Theaterarbeiten sind, verfertigen könne" (31 March; qtd. Derks 432).

26. "mit blassen Wangen von ausnehmend schöner Bildung" (397).

27. "eine ordentliche Liebe und Anhänglichkeit" (410).

28. "im Gehen aber sprach er häufig den Namen Neries aus, den er wirklich liebte, und weinte heftig dabei" (436).

29. "Kurz, Reiser glaubte sich mit allen seinen Gedanken und Empfindungen bis auf den Punkt der Liebe im Werther wieder zu finden" (257).

30. "Die Teilnehmung an den Leiden der Liebe kostete ihm einigen Zwang, . . . weil es ihm unmöglich fiel, sich selbst jemals als einen Gegenstand der Liebe von einem Frauenzimmer zu denken" (256; see also 244, 287).

31. "Selbstverachtung und Selbstvernichtungssucht" (343).

32. The widely available "Hamburger Ausgabe" (HA) is used for most Goethe citations; passages from Goethe's oeuvre not included in the HA are cited from the "Weimarer Ausgabe" (WA). For *Wilhelm Meister's Apprenticeship*, references are to the good translation in the Suhrkamp edition (S).

33. The entry reads: "Hufeland Lebenskraft, Brandis, Darvin, Broun. Weickert Jacobs empirische Psychologie. Reil" (WA 3.2: 34).

34. S 9: 11. "Besonders fesselte mich Chlorinde mit ihrem ganzen Tun und Lassen. Die Mannweiblichkeit, die ruhige Fülle ihres Daseins taten mehr Wirkung auf den Geist, der sich zu entwickeln anfing, als die gemachten Reize Armidens" (HA 7: 26-27).

35. S 9: 2. "mit welchem Entzücken umschlang er die rote Uniform! drückte er das weiße Atlaswestchen an seine Brust!" (HA 7: 11).

36. S 9: 269. "und ich möchte sie als eine wahre Amazone nennen, wenn andere nur als artige Hermaphroditen in dieser zweideutigen Kleidung herumgehen" (HA 7: 439).

37. S 9: 333. "Felix zog sie am Rocke und rief: 'Mutter Therese, ich bin auch da!' " (HA 7: 544).

38. S 9: 371. "Gift und Gegengift" (HA 7: 606).

Works Cited

Arnold, Thomas. *Beobachtung über die Natur, Arten, Ursachen und Verhütung des Wahnsinns oder der Tollheit*. Trans. J. Chr. G. Ackermann. 2 vols. Leipzig: Jacobäer, 1784.

Derks, Paul. *"Die Schande der heiligen Päderastie": Homosexualität und Öffentlichkeit in der deutschen Literatur 1750-1850*. Homosexualität und Literatur, 3. Berlin: rosa Winkel, 1990.

258   ROBERT TOBIN

Diener, Gottfried. *Goethe's "Lila": Heilung eines "Wahnsinns" durch "psychische Kur."* Frankfurt/M.: Athenäum, 1971.

Faderman, Lillian. *Surpassing the Love of Men: Romantic Friendship and Love Between Women from the Renaissance to the Present.* New York: Morrow, 1981.

Flaherty, Gloria. "The Stage-Struck Wilhelm Meister and 18th-Century Psychiatric Medicine." *MLN* 110 (1986): 493-515.

Foucault, Michel. *Wahnsinn und Gesellschaft: Eine Geschichte des Wahns im Zeitalter der Vernunft.* Trans. Ulrich Köppen. Frankfurt/M.: Suhrkamp, 1969.

Gallagher, Bob, and Alexander Wilson. "Michel Foucault: An Interview." *Edinburgh Review* 1986: 52-59.

Goethe, Johann Wolfgang. *Werke.* ["Hamburger Ausgabe."] Ed. Erich Trunz et al. 14 vols. Rev. ed. Munich: Beck, 1981. Cited as "HA."

————. *Werke. Herausgegeben im Auftrage der Großherzogin Sophie von Sachsen.* 133 vols. Weimar: Böhlau, 1887-1914. Cited as "WA."

————. *Collected Works.* 12 vols. New York: Suhrkamp, 1989. Cited as "S."

Greenberg, David F. *The Construction of Homosexuality.* Chicago: U of Chicago P, 1988.

Hahnemann, Samuel. *Organon of Homoeopathic Medicine.* 4th American ed. New York: Radde, 1860.

Hausen, Karin. "Family and Role-Division: The Polarisation of Sexual Stereotypes in the Nineteenth Century—An Aspect of the Dissociation of Work and Family Life." *The German Family: Essays on the Social History of the Family in Nineteenth- and Twentieth-Century Germany.* Ed. Richard J. Evans and W. R. Lee. Totowa, N.J.: Barnes & Noble, 1981. 51-83.

Hirsch, Marianne. "Spiritual 'Bildung': The Beautiful Soul as Paradigm." *The Voyage In: Fictions of Female Development.* Eds. Elizabeth Abel et al. Hanover: UP of New England, 1983. 23-48.

Horkheimer, Max and Theodor W. Adorno. *Dialectic of Enlightenment.* Trans. John Cumming. New York: Continuum, 1972.

Hufeland, Christoph Wilhelm. *Die Kunst, das menschliche Leben zu verlängern.* Jena: n.p., 1797.

Kant, Immanuel. "Träume eines Geistersehers, erläutert durch Träume der Metaphysik." Vol. 2. *Werke.* 12 vols. Frankfurt/M.: Suhrkamp, 1968.

Keppel-Kriems, Karin. *Mignon und Harfner in Goethes "Wilhelm Meister": Eine geschichtsphilosophische und kunsttheoretische Untersuchung zu Begriff und Gestalt des Naiven.* Frankfurt/M.: Lang, 1986.

Kittler, Friedrich A. "Über die Sozialisation Wilhelm Meisters." *Dichtung als Sozialisationsspiel.* Eds. Friedrich A. Kittler and Gerhard Kaiser. Göttingen: Vandenhoeck & Ruprecht, 1978.

La Mettrie, Julien Offray de. *Man a Machine.* Annotated by Gertrude Carman Bussey. Chicago: Open Court, 1912.

Laqueur, Thomas. *Making Sex: Body and Gender from the Greeks to Freud.* Cambridge: Harvard UP, 1990.

Mauchart, Immanuel D., ed. *Allgemeines Repertorium für empirische Psychologie und verwandte Wissenschaften.* Nürnberg: Felsecker, 1792-98.

Meyer-Krentler, Eckhardt. *Der Bürger als Freund: Ein sozialethisches Programm und seine Kritik in der neueren deutschen Erzählliteratur.* Munich: Fink, 1984.

Moritz, Karl Phillip. *Anton Reiser: Ein psychologischer Roman.* Leipzig: Insel, 1959.

————, ed. *Gnothi sauton oder Magazin zur Erfahrungsseelenkunde.* 1783-92. 10 vols. Facs. edition. Ed. Anke Bennholdt-Thomsen and Alfredo Guzzoni.

Lindau: Antiqua, 1979.

Müller, Lothar. *Die kranke Seele und das Licht der Erkenntnis: Karl Philipp Moritz' "Anton Reiser."* Frankfurt/M.: Athenäum, 1987.

Neumann, Gerhard. " 'Ich bin gebildet genug, um zu lieben und trauern': Die Erziehung zur Liebe in Goethes 'Wilhelm Meister.' " *Liebesroman—Liebe im Roman.* Eds. Titus Heydenreich and Egert Pohlmann. Erlangen: Universitäts-bibliothek Erlangen-Nürnberg, 1987.

Nicolai, Ernst Anton. *Gedancken von den Würkungen der Einbildungskraft in den menschlichen Körper.* 2nd ed. Halle: Hemmerde, 1751.

Ronell, Avital. *Dictations: On Haunted Writing.* Bloomington: Indiana UP, 1986.

Rothschuh, Karl Eduard. "Leibniz, die prästabilierte Harmonie und die Ärzte seiner Zeit." *Akten des internationalen Leibniz-Kongresses Hannover, 14-19 November 1966.* 5 vols. Studia Leibnitiana Supplementa, 2. Wiesbaden: Franz Steiner, 1969. 2: 231-54.

Schiebinger, Londa. *The Mind Has No Sex? Women in the Origins of Modern Science.* Cambridge: Harvard UP, 1989.

Schings, Hans-Jürgen. "Agathon—Anton Reiser—Wilhelm Meister: Zur Pathogenese des modernen Subjekts im Bildungsroman." *Goethe im Kontext: Kunst und Humanität, Naturwissenschaft und Politik von der Aufklärung bis zur Restauration.* Ed. Wolfgang Wittkowski. Tübingen: Niemeyer, 1984. 42-68.

————. "Der anthropologische Roman: Seine Entstehung und Krise im Zeitalter der Spätaufklärung." *Deutschlands kulturelle Entfaltung: Die Neubestimmung des Menschen.* Eds. Bernhard Fabian et al. Studien zum 18. Jahrhundert, 2/3. Munich: Krauss, 1983. 247-75.

Schwanitz, Hans Joachim. *Homöopathie und Brownianismus: Zwei wissenschaftstheoretische Fallstudien aus der praktischen Medizin.* Medizin in Geschichte und Kultur 15. Stuttgart: Fischer, 1983.

Stahl, Georg Ernst. *Über den mannigfaltigen Einfluß von Gemütsbewegungen auf den menschlichen Körper (Halle, 1695). Über die Bedeutung des synergischen Prinzips für die Heilkunde (Halle 1695). Über den Unterschied zwischen Organismus und Mechanismus (1714). Überlegungen zum ärztlichen Hausbesuch (Halle 1703).* Trans. and introd. B. Josef Gottlieb. Sudhoffs Klassiker der Medizin, 36. Leipzig: J. A. Barth, 1961.

Tissot, Samuel. *Versuch von denen Krankheiten, welche aus der Selbstbefleckung entstehen.* Trans. from Latin. Frankfurt and Leipzig: Fleischer, 1771.

Wagnitz, H. B. *Historische Nachrichten und Bemerkungen über die merkwürdigsten Zuchthäuser in Deutschland. Nebst einem Anhange über die zweckmäßigste Einrichtung der Gefängnisse und Irrenanstalten.* 2 vols. Halle: Gebauer, 1791-94.

Wieland, Christoph Martin. *Werke.* Eds. Fritz Martini and Hans Werner Seiffert. Vol. 1. Munich: Hanser, 1964. [1st ed. of *Agathon* (1766/67).]

————. *Briefwechsel.* Vol. 5. Ed. Hans Werner Seiffert. Berlin: Akademie, 1983.

Zimmermann, Johann Georg. *Ueber die Einsamkeit.* 4 vols. Frankfurt, 1785.

————. *Von der Erfahrung in der Arzneykunst.* New ed. Zürich: Orell, Geßner, Füeßli und Co., 1777.

The "Other Subject" of History: Women in Goethe's Drama

Sigrid Lange

"ENLIGHTENMENT," UNDERSTOOD IN the eighteenth century as a category of the philosophy of history, is oriented around three concepts: "the subject," the self-consciously acting human individual; the related notion of "responsibility"; and "history" in its temporal dimension, structured as "progress" with the possibility of a future utopia. As "character" and the unfolding of a developing "plot," "subject" and "time" are simultaneously the constitutive categories of the poetics of tragedy. The category of "guilt" corresponds to "responsibility" and gives rise to the cathartic effect in the audience. In this parallel of concepts the aesthetic debate since its origins in antiquity transmits the semantic transformations that have arisen due to philosophical reflections on reality. Especially in the eighteenth century we can follow closely this connection between philosophy and aesthetics. I mean the reformulation of the Aristotelian theory of tragedy in the aesthetics of the Enlightenment and of the Storm-and-Stress period, using Shakespeare as a model, in contrast to the French, classicist poetic of rules. Shakespeare was viewed as a representative of modernity against antiquity because, in Goethe's concise formulation, he reconceived in dramatic conflicts subjective action and fate in the collision of our "pretended freedom of the will with the necessary course of the whole."[1] This definition is already based on the Copernican revolution in modern thought, whereby the individual human subject, due to his native capacity for reason, was thrust into the center of the world. The adversary of this autonomous subject is "history," whose apparent fatality is to be recognized in its regularity and thus made subservient.

The turn to the classical does not mean a rejection of this fundamental understanding, but rather a problematization and deepening of it. With regard to drama the debates around the ancients and the moderns in both their theoretical and practical dimensions continue to focus on the concepts of history, the subject, and guilt, and define the difference in the way in which the human being exists in the world. The classical authors use the forms from the ancient world of high literature in order to legitimize their own worldview and aesthetics, which differ from those of antiquity. As Rudolf Brandmeyer expressed it in connection with Goethe, the classical dramas achieve—against the foil of the notions of "fate" and "heroes" of ancient tragedy—a modern version that favors individual over representative subjectivity and history over the repetitive circularity of a divinely determined world. Against the background of rapidly enriched, eventful, temporal experience at the end of the century, consensual fixations were absent. What is tragic, when history, like blind necessity, breaks in and still does not fulfill the former divine fate of a well ordered world? What is human about a subjectivity that is set free, that no longer exhibits moral exemplarity, and that for this very reason has become "natural" and unfree again? And what kind of an aesthetic system of values can be founded on such a subjectivity?

Such questions are explicitly raised in the theoretical discussions of tragedy in the works of Goethe and Schiller, of Hölderlin and Kleist, and of A. W. Schlegel and Hegel. I maintain—and I am not alone in this assertion[2]—that implicitly in Goethe, namely in the dramatic literature itself, the very phenomenon is elucidated that we have come to call the "Dialectic of Enlightenment." Moreover, I would contend that in his dramatic working out of this problematic he generally employed a descriptive model that drew on gender-specific typology of the previous history of the Occident, as well as its patterns of thought and expression. In terms of content, Goethe calls this history masculine and opposes it to a feminine utopia; in formal terms, this trope does not break with aesthetic tradition. To be sure, after his early romantic tragedies, and the two early historical tragedies he *de facto* abandons the tragic genre; but he trivializes the objective problem of form by conceiving it as a matter of taste: he believes that he simply had no affinity for the tragic. Actually, however, I believe that the ambivalent patriarchal self-criticism and the equally ambivalent use of the category of "femininity" expresses itself indirectly in the dramatic form.

I will demonstrate my thesis with three closely related dramatic texts: the play *Iphigenie at Tauris*, the tragedy *The Natural Daughter*, and the festival play *Pandora*, but begin with the prehistory in Goethe's earlier works. In his early poetic productions, Goethe did not proceed

from abstract theoretical considerations but rather from the empirical
and biographical realm in the romantic tragedies *Clavigo, Stella*—whose
early conciliatory ending was replaced in 1806 by a morally and aesthetically "appropriate" tragic conclusion—and the Gretchen tragedy.
In each case it is a question of a subjective guilt-conflict on the part of a
young hero who uses his lover as a means to his own self-realization
and who then, by abandoning her, sacrifices her for the sake of his ego.
In comparison to other contemporary versions of the same subject,
Goethe avoids a moralizing of the character constellations: the male
and female protagonists are not dichotomized into good and evil, nor
are they distinguished in a political fashion in terms of class with the
inclusion of an aristocratic seducer and a middle-class victim. Instead,
Goethe presents a youthful lover, a social climber in the middle-class
sense, who is tragically torn between his responsibility to himself—the
internal duty to exhaust fully his human potential—and his responsibility to others. Especially with the figures Clavigo and Faust, he avoids
the kind of one-dimensional amorality that characterizes their satanic
doubles, Carlos and Mephisto. In this way Goethe explores the romantic conflict on its own terms, problematizes in the conflict the limitless
claim to autonomy in the bourgeois subject, and at the same time vali-
dates individual experience as something essential (see Brandt).

In these constellations I am concerned with significant gender-
specific patterns of characters and actions. These can be derived from
the opposition between motion and rest that appears as a leitmotif: the
male protagonists are always "on their way somewhere" in accord with
their roles as active and developing individuals. The motif of the
wanderer, frequently found in lyric poetry, appears here in the figure of
the traveler. In this group belong, besides Clavigo and Faust, Weislingen from *Götz*, Fernando from *Stella*, and even Egmont, all of whom
contrast with their female partners (who remain in one place). At the
same time this spatial tension repeats the social and psychic gender dis-
positions, according to which the male figures are active and the female
figures are passive. The characters are so strictly drawn in terms of
gender that their actions can turn into those of their counterparts: since
the women fulfill their expected roles in their deep, immutable, and
always forgiving love, in a moment of threatening catastrophe the
ability to act can grow out of their absoluteness of their feeling. With
Clavigo and Faust the initiative for action passes first—and with disastrous consequences—to their mephistophelian representatives, but
then later to the women. Weislingen's Marie rescues her unfaithful
lover, who has failed in his attempt to climb the social ladder; Clavigo's
Marie acts in a similar fashion; the most obvious inversions of the
original model of action occur with Stella and Cäcilie in the recognition

scene with Fernando and with Gretchen in the jail scene. Stella and Cäcilie turn the apparently unsolvable tragedy into the suggestion of a *ménage à trois*, while Gretchen decides—correctly, despite her insanity—against Faust's self-deceptive escape plans. This recurrent dramatic pattern assumes in the later work of Goethe—and this is the rationale for this brief digression about the early work—the function of a dramaturgical model.

I am speaking of *Iphigenie*. Essential for the exposition of the play is the mythological concreteness of the disposition of the woman for sacrifice: Iphigenie is selected by her father as a sacrificial victim in order to acquire the blessing of the gods for success in war. The goddess Diana intervenes to save her—a *dea ex machina* in the sense of ancient tragedy—and brings Iphigenie to Tauris. This exposition is critical for an understanding of Goethe's play. The same constellation is repeated in a drama conceived more than twenty years later, *The Natural Daughter*, except that the mythical abstraction is translated into the prose of contemporary political reality. The title character, Eugenie, is the victim of a modern intrigue, which is taken from the authentic memoirs of Princess Stephanie-Louise of Bourbon-Conti. The miraculous rescue of the heroine from the consequences of a deadly fall at the beginning of the play proves to be deceptive; similar to Iphigenie, Eugenie needs the full time of five acts of dramatic action to elude the planned sacrifice. Finally, Pandora, who is in a special sense the "heroine" of the festive play, is likewise a sacrificial figure. As a character symbolizing the feminine and love, she is sacrificed to the modern Promethean culture—which is another mythological symbol for the Faustian. Rejected by the "creative" Prometheus—and for Goethe in 1807, "creative" means forging weapons and ruling peoples—and driven by the person of deeds and days into the dark side of life, Pandora leaves the earthly world. In contrast to Goethe's earlier plays, the female victims become figures of redemption and in this double disposition transform these plays into parables that have implications for a philosophy of history.

Before I provide the evidence for this, I would like to call attention to the following phenomenon: in Goethe's oeuvre one finds, in addition to the early plays that are either comedies and musical plays or the romantic tragedies already mentioned, two tragedies: *Götz* and *Egmont*. Whereas the romantic tragedies with their private, individualistic conflicts place women figures in the very center of the action, in the historical plays they recede into the background and appear as part of a general ensemble of characters. For the chief conflict, the autonomous subject versus the historical course of the world, they play only a marginal role. After these early plays, Goethe abandons not only Shakespearean formal traditions, but also a content anchored in a historical milieu. With the turn to fables with historical and parabolic dimensions he again includes female protagonists. My thesis, which is based on these changes in his work, is that Goethe replaced the tragic constellation of his historical dramas and their unsuccessful male heroes with an abstractly historical and utopian project that explores in fiction the "other" subject of history, the feminine.

In the mythical context, Iphigenie's role as victim appears real from a contemporary standpoint as well: "I do not argue with the gods; however, the situation of women is lamentable."[3] This is true of any woman's dependent position at home as either daughter or wife, but she is even more defenseless in a foreign land. The long opening monologue intentionally makes this factor equal and parallel to the other central element of conflict: the curse of the race of Tantalus. Goethe himself later referred to this connection in his early writings: "Tantalus, Ixion, Sysiphus were my saints, . . . and when I show them as members of an enormous opposition in the background of my *Iphigenie*, I am indebted to them for a portion of the effect that this play had the good fortune to produce."[4] The opposition of the autonomous subject, which is represented in the mythical story as human hybris in confrontation with the omnipotence of the gods, is conjured up in the drama essentially by the growing cycle of previous human history, which has countered violence with more violence. This concept of action, according to Goethe, allows a new power relationship to arise from the originally justified indignation against arbitrariness; this duplication of power relations involves an apparently unavoidable implication in guilt that leads to the extermination of the race of Tantalus, or by implication of the human race. Within the parameters of the play this concept of action is identified as masculine, as a male logic that demands the sacrifice of the woman, in this case Iphigenie. Thus both components of the previously described constellation, which originally referred to eighteenth-century reality, are carried over into the mythical projection.

At the same time, in the detachment from its ancient subtext, the modern play *Iphigenie* orients itself along the lines of gender-specific models of action. Essential elements of the ancient fable influence the plot from the exposition of the heroine's conflict to her forced decision under the greatest moral pressure, produced by the anagnoresis in the third act. The demand that Iphigenie reach a decision involves exclusively her sacrifice: either of her own moral identity or of the bodily existence of her brother and his friend—and the latter alternative is an unreasonable demand that would destroy Iphigenie psychologically and morally just as surely as would the first. The tragic model from antiquity would at this point call for the pernicious or salutary intervention of the gods, and with this we would come full circle back to the original situation, when the goddess Diana appeared at the last moment before the tragic outcome. In fact, from the very beginning, Iphigenie does direct her gaze hopefully to the gods above. Even the monologue before the song of the Parcae appeals to the unity of the human and the divine, with the implicit demand that the order of the world be affirmed. As long as this order appears just, it legitimizes the natural and lawful fate of divine arbitrariness. Opposition to it is hybris, and hybris is avenged mercilessly, as the song of the Parcae reminds us. The modern reinterpretation of the myth begins at precisely the point where human self-understanding comprehends divine rule as lawless despotism and mobilizes autonomous human reason against this "natural power." However, in the hybris of Goethe's Tantalus and its consequences we do not find a reflection of the provocation of suprahuman arbitrariness, but a human implication in guilt. Reason, although intended and just, cannot free itself from the fetters of the myth. It is well known that Adorno himself interpreted Goethe's *Iphigenie* in accord with this understanding of the dialectic of enlightenment.

With regard to this plot-model it seems to me important that even women figures—for example, Klytemnestra—can be integrated into the role of agents, of guilt-ridden victors, to the extent that they involve themselves in the reality of power relations. At least in her thoughts, Iphigenie carries this possibility through to its logical conclusion; symbolically she thereby returns to the origin of this tale, to the hybris of Tantalus. On the one hand, Goethe thus revises his earlier understanding of history by relegating the "adulthood" of the modern age to the realm of prehistorical barbarity,[5] including the two steps of the human process of civilization symbolized in Sythian and Greek.[6] On the other hand, at the point when Iphigenie undertakes an active initiative, the utopian anticipation of another type of modernity begins. I would describe the feminine concept of action that Goethe displays with Iphigenie as a refusal to choose between false alternatives.

One line of recent research has attempted to reinterpret *Iphigenie* as a drama about Orestes and thus to examine critically or overturn the analyses that traditionally praised the female protagonist. In this respect, Wolfdietrich Rasch's interpretation agrees with the feminist reading by Irmgard Wagner. Rasch views the climax of this "drama of autonomy" within the context of a critique of religion, since Orestes *reinterprets* the oracle (rather than merely revising his earlier "misunderstanding," as the traditional interpretation has it) and concludes that it does not mean the divine sister of Apollo, but his own worldly sister. Wagner radicalizes this interpretation to the point of seeing a

cooptation of Iphigenie by a sort of male fraternity. By contrast, Hans
Robert Jauß follows the original line of *Iphigenie* commentary and
comes to the conclusion that Goethe replaces the ancient myth of the
gods with the myth of the feminine. I believe that this reading is in
accord with the text insofar as the play constructs the idea of a pure,
feminine morality, personifies it in Iphigenie, and ascribes to it a deed
that redeems humanity. However, the "regression" to the ancient
model is thwarted because Iphigenie is supposed to initiate a history
that is connected to the real sacrifice of woman in the patriarchy; this
history is socially as exact as the mythological parable permits.
Iphigenie's moral greatness lies solely in her ability to avoid the
sacrifice and with it corruption by the hegemonic culture of the per-
petrators.

The play does not stop here. The historical non-specificity of time
and space in the plot is made concrete by models of action that were
decipherable for Goethe's contemporaries. This is accomplished by
motifs and in structure. For the former, one could point to the song of
the Parcae, in which the alternation of rebellion and fall conjures up
the early Prometheus ode even in its language and thus demonstrates
the reproduction of hierarchical social relations. The motifs thus reinforce the structure of the ensemble of characters and their actions,
where we also find a clearly defined social hierarchy. If we were to
construct a pyramid from the figures involved in the play, then Thoas
would be placed at the top because of his social status. As the ruler of
the island, he has all the other figures in his hands: on the one hand
Iphigenie, his temple priestess, and Arkas, his servant; on the other
hand his two prisoners and potential victims. Both pairs of figures
would have to be seen in opposition to each other according to the original constellation. As long as Thoas as king possesses the initiative for
action—from his wooing of Iphigenie until his punishment of her for
refusing to continue with human sacrifices—this hierarchy remains in
place. However, when Iphigenie finally gains the initiative for action at
the beginning of the fifth act, which was anticipated earlier by her
threefold rejection of her sacrificial role, she ascends to the top of the
dramaturgical pyramid and at the same time dissolves it as a hierarchical constellation; the figures in the play become equal in status. They
part from each other as brother, sister, or friend—the only human relationships that, according to the understanding of that era, are non-
hierarchical and thus "purely human."

My conclusions are supported by the cult of friendship in the eighteenth century. For the important brother-sister relationship between
Iphigenie and Orestes, in which Pylades and Thoas are then included
as friends, one could cite Hegel, who sees in the family an embodiment

of divine law, a "naturally moral community," and defines the relationships within the family by reference to the degree of morality between husband and wife, or parents and children. "But the unadulterated relationship occurs between brother and sister. They have the same blood, but in them it comes to *rest* and *equilibrium*. They therefore do not desire each other; and they have neither given nor received this being-for-itself. Rather, they are free individuals with one another. As a sister, the feminine therefore possesses the highest *premonition* of moral being" (336).

The immanent problematic of this mythically stylized theory of the family and society cannot be discussed here. Important for me is the high esteem shown for the brother-sister relationship: it is not infected with the sexual desire of the "natural" relationship between men and women and is therefore not unfree; nor is it structured in an obviously authoritarian fashion as the father-daughter relationship is. We should recall once again the relevant passages in Iphigenie's opening monologue as well as the relationship of Thoas to her, which is both paternal and charged with male sexual desire. From this perspective the final constellation of *Iphigenie* takes on the function of a symbolic model. We should not forget, of course, that it exists in the absence of "natural" relationships and is thus an obvious construction.

When Goethe sketched his trilogy *The Natural Daughter* (*Die natürliche Tochter*) at the start of the nineteenth century, it appeared that reality had become what *Iphigenie* only hinted it could be: chaos had become part of the times; the world order had been demolished. "O this time of fearful signs: / The lowly swells up, the heights sink downward."[7] The French Revolution forced Goethe to look back again at its prehistory in order to fathom it and perhaps—as *Pandora*, written a few years later, suggests—to correct it poetically with utopian intent. The anticipated eruption of the revolution is, however, as Hans Rudolf Vaget has persuasively argued, accompanied in the structure of motifs by a steady up-and-down movement. After *Iphigenie*, this play—conceived as a tragedy, but no longer based on the classical model of guilt and penance—endeavors to comprehend real historical processes symbolically.

The connections between the two plays have been dealt with many times, for example by Wagner and Böschenstein. The similarity is most obvious in the motif of the woman exiled on a barbaric island, in several aspects of the brother-sister-father relationship, and in the portrayal of the heroine as a figure of salvation. With regard to my analysis of *Iphigenie*, I could add, moreover, a significant structural analogy in the doubling of the constellation of characters. The five figures in *Iphigenie* all act on the level of royalty: king, king's daughter, king's son, king's friend, and king's servant. The corresponding group in *The Natural Daughter* is the king, the duke, his daughter Eugenie, the abbess, the governor, as well as the two minor figures, the surgeon and the count, whose roles do not further the action and who therefore can be discounted in the parallel. A second grouping of five persons consists of the secretary, his wife—the tutor of Eugenie—the lay priest, the monk, and the judge. Clearly these two groups are symbolically associated with class principles, which then oppose each other in the revolution as aristocracy and bourgeoisie. The first group contains persons that belong to the aristocratic party either because of their position and profession, or, as in the case of the king, the duke, and Eugenie, because of familial relationships. This emphasizes the principle of personal relationships in the feudal system in contradistinction to the reified system of objective relations in the ascending middle-class order. This order characterizes the second group, although the individuals are only partially members of the traditional bourgeois estate. To the traditional bourgeoisie belong the secretary, the tutor, and the judge as the potential leader of the rebellion, as the plan of the trilogy suggests. The two clergymen, who technically belong to the second estate, function nonetheless in the second, "bourgeois" group: the secular priest acts out of purely material motives, and the monk prophesies the approaching revolution and advises Eugenie to seek a new life somewhere outside of this uncertain and dangerous environment. Most decisive is that the figures in this group are connected with each other essentially by a variety of exchanges: founding a household, social climbing and profit. Both groups of characters are connected by the central figure in the background of the play: Eugenie's brother, the head of the intrigue. He is the perfect representative of the bourgeois principle in that he embodies the merciless competition for profit, though he never appears in the play as a person.

The plot of the play shows us Eugenie immediately before her planned social legitimation by the king. While this is happening, the brother initiates the intrigue by allowing their father to believe that Eugenie is dead and preparing her abduction and exile. She tries to obtain protection in vain from the governor and the abbess; she considers suicide, but then accepts her tutor's solution of a bourgeois marriage with the judge. Of course, this marriage is not without preconditions: "Can you promise me that you will receive me / As a brother with purity of affection, / Granting me, the loving sister, protection / And advice and the quiet joy of life?"[8] At the end of the first part, the brother-sister relationship—the prerequisite for her salvation—places Eugenie in the same position that Iphigenie had acquired earlier: expecting salvation no longer from outside, but from herself.

Because of the doubling of the character groups, the analogy between the two dramas has yet another dimension. Eugenie finds her bourgeois counterpart in the figure of the female tutor. None of the previous interpreters of *The Natural Daughter* have devoted enough attention to her, despite the fact that, aside from Eugenie, she has by far the greatest number of lines. She is far more than the typical trusted servant who betrays her mistress reluctantly and only under duress; she is also concerned with salvation: "Eugenie, if you could renounce / The lofty happiness that appears boundless...."[9] She introduces the bourgeois notion of renunciation. In Goethe's thought this notion played a significant role from the 1790s to *Wilhelm Meister's Travels* (*Wilhelm Meisters Wanderjahre*, 1821/1829), with its subtitle "Those Who Renounce" ("Die Entsagenden"). It was conceived by Goethe as the individual's compromise vis-à-vis the earlier concept of autonomy, which insisted on the total development of individuality. When Eugenie— with the identical notion of renunciation—repudiates her claim to class privileges at the close of the play, she does not simply become a member of the bourgeoisie. As a "sister" she acquires a personal freedom that goes beyond any class or hierarchical order. In this play, the "solution" of the conflict is thus located between the social and political compromise of inter-class marriages in the *Wilhelm Meister's Apprenticeship* (*Wilhelm Meisters Lehrjahre*, 1795-1796) and the concept of redemption in *Iphigenie*. In *The Natural Daughter*, however, Goethe goes to great lengths to accomplish a synthesis of the individual figure and the abstract ideal. Both functions are conceived for this single figure; she is the only person in the play with a proper name, and she is distinguished in the title with the designation of "natural daughter" with its threefold meaning of illegitimate child, of a person raised according to Rousseauist principle far from courtly society, and of someone representing the purely human beyond any social status. When brought back into the concrete history of the times, however, the symbolic intention fails: Goethe gives up on a continuation of the project.

With regard to dramatic tension, Peter Pütz defines plot as "successive re-presentations of anticipated futures and recovered pasts" (11). This definition makes most sense where the temporal structures are simultaneously covered by the historical notion of time. In *The Natural Daughter* a turning-point in history is the theme, and in accord with historical reality the initiative for action is always given to the bourgeois estate. When Eugenie in the first act is miraculously saved from her apparently fatal accident as the duke prepares her introduction at court, the opposing party has already taken action behind the scenes. When at the end of the first act the king, the duke, and Eugenie all dream of a new Golden Age in which a peaceful, patriarchal harmony exists among the classes, the plan for Eugenie's abduction has already been worked out to the last detail. When she opens the chest filled with ostentatious clothing and regalia in anticipation of her impending elevation into courtly circles, the secretary and the tutor are already prepared to take her into exile. A preoccupation with blinding diversions, imprisonment in a world of appearances, cripple the aristocratic party, and accordingly it is progressively removed from the play. The king does not appear after the first act; the duke disappears in the third act, after Eugenie's apparent death, into his fantasy world of the Eugenie mausoleum. Only at the end of the play does Eugenie acquire the initiative for action in her symbolic role as redeemer after she has been freed from the fetters of her social existence.

Goethe finally accomplished and thematized such a structure of meaning around historical time in his play *Pandora* (1810). It is suggested in the symbolism attached to the names of Prometheus and Epimetheus as the man of forethought and the man of afterthought and is introduced in the old Epimetheus' account of his life. With the opposition of youth and old age he opens the first, biographical dimension of the temporal problematic, which is expressed in the contrast between spontaneous action and reflection. This corresponds to the opposition between the youthful dreams in sleep, which drive out the presence of the day, and the nocturnal waking dreams of his old age, which recall the day in order to pose the question of human capacity for self-determination. In the confrontation of these two stages of life, the monologue reflects this opposition in the form of a contradiction between enjoyment of life and responsibility, and then gives it an additional dimension in the polarity of the active man of forethought, Prometheus, and the nocturnal man of afterthought, Epimetheus.

This anthropological reflection leads the drama into an artistic play of interwoven action and contemplation—in which the reflection posited in the exposition is carried out in an action. The play of thought and dramatic play are joined in a synthesis whose philosophical center is the potential of the play of thought for altering reality, as it results from the interpretation of the name Epimetheus: "For my progenitors named me Epimetheus / To reflect upon the past, with laborious plays of thought / To lead back that which has occurred quickly / To the murky realm of possibility for combining forms."[10] Thus the "festival play" would consist of tracing back the regretted deed to alternative possibilities and playing it through again.

The initially abstract profundity of this reflective exposition is revealed gradually in the play. It takes up the theme of generations and begins with the youth Phileros, who is hurrying to a romantic rendezvous and reminds Epimetheus of his own past romantic bliss, causing him to utter envious blessings as well as concerned prophesies of disaster. This apparently banal occurrence takes on symbolic significance through the repetition of the intimated past experience of Epimetheus: the new generation, which here frivolously risks catastrophe in the pursuit of romance, appears not to have the chance to begin again with new possibilities. At the same time, the drastic result—Phileros almost murders his lover out of jealously and then wants to commit suicide—points to a more profound level of meaning than the mere misunderstanding that apparently occurs. This meaning is suggested by the related genre of the pastoral romance—Goethe himself had composed pastoral romances with this motif in his youth. The abrupt end of the envisioned idyll signals in an extremely parabolic abbreviation the transition from the Golden Age to a present of mistrust, guilt, and violence.

Thus, biographical time is constructed in a second dimension to elucidate differences in human epochs. The interpretive framework for the scene is given by the familial relationship between Phileros, the son of Prometheus, and Epimeleia, the daughter of Epimetheus. The social semantic of these symbolic relationships is disclosed only at the climax of the play, when these four persons are brought together. At the intersection of these levels of meaning and of the lines of dialogue and action, however, stands Pandora, or more accurately, an image of Pandora which determines the actions of the male characters in this drama. "Speak, is it Pandora? You saw her once, / Ruinous for fathers, a torture for sons,"[11] asks Phileros at the moment of the violent ending of his love affair. The projected image of Pandora in Epimeleia that he refers to encompasses both the goal and the content of the drama at the same time: Pandora, symbol of love, whose return is the implicit telos of the play, is present in clashing perceptions. Absence and contradictory images mutually reinforce each other and make the present time symbolically one of absent love combined with the image of love as happiness and peril, threat and promise. Epimetheus' fantasy of Pandora's return finds its polar opposite in Prometheus' anxiety about her; this had caused him to reject the female messenger of the gods, from whom he had emancipated himself. This constellation characterizes Promethean culture's ambivalence, arising from human self-creativity in isolation.

Phileros' tragedy is caused by the perseverance of his father's image of Pandora, which is characterized by the negative attributes of deceptive appearance and infidelity, while, for his part, Epimetheus lives with a threefold longing for Pandora. She is present for him in the waking dream that recalls their shared intimacy, in the sleeping dream of her daughter Elpore promising to return, and in the likeness of his daughter Epimeleia. The positive image is arrested in contemplation; the negative image motivates the actions of Prometheus and Phileros. Thus the dominance of the "demonic" Pandora appears to affirm the pessimistic account of life and history and to bolster Promethean culture. On the other hand, this image acts as a decisive factor in unleashing the catastrophe. This involves more than the individual relationship between Phileros and Epimeleia, in that Prometheus' son kills the shepherd who approaches with loving desires and thus provokes the rebellion of the pastoral folk. For them, Prometheus' prediction comes true: "Wander away peacefully! You do not go to find peace."[12]

At the same time, this scene of the strife between the lovers exhibits a countervailing tendency by bringing together Prometheus and Epimetheus. While Pandora had formerly separated them, as her image separates Phileros and Epimeleia, now, with the reunion of the fathers, the progressive line of Promethean culture is thwarted and led back to another possibility in the course of the dialogue. This interweaving of plays of thought with the dramatic play is realized in the temporal structure of the entire drama in that the realm of the deed is preceded by the realm of reflection, which thus calls into question the finality of the action: Epimetheus' narration of his meeting with Prometheus comes before the first scene with Prometheus, and Epimetheus' dream of the return of Pandora occurs before the scene depicting Phileros' jealousy. In this manner the chronology of factual happenings that is defined in terms of a Promethean line—according to which the rejection of Pandora coincides with the act of creating culture—is hypothetically cancelled. Similarly, the repetition of this rejection in the Phileros-Epimeleia episode precedes the possibility of understanding. A reversal seems to be possible.

A spatial symbolism corresponds to this temporal structure, and it is introduced in the scenic configuration of the surroundings of Prometheus and Epimetheus. One side suggests repose, peace, the permanence of human settlements that face the open sea. With its crude and unfinished buildings, the other side represents the restlessness of beginning, grounded on the craggy cliffs and mountain ranges. This cliff symbolism is drawn from the fragment of "Prometheus Unbound," where it designates the powerful hierarchy of the rule of the gods. It always carries within it the danger of overthrow, as the rebellion of the shepherds shows. Promethean culture, which is itself grounded on rebellion, reproduces the social hierarchy of master and slave, as well as the patriarchal relationship of father and son—"A good son honors the absence of the father."[13] Violence is an integral part of this social hierarchy, which has long since left behind the vision of the peaceful patriarchal realm from Goethe's early "Prometheus" fragment, replacing the building of huts with the forging of weapons (see Borchmeyer).

The symbolic spaces of cliffs and sea are repeatedly evoked at the end of the play and integrated into the temporal structure. The punishing father Prometheus sends his disobedient son to the cliffs at the sea so that he can condemn himself and plunge to his death. The fate of Phileros, who follows these directions just as he had followed his father's image of Pandora, represents the third sequence in the chronology of the Promethean line of the drama. Again it is preceded—in the dialogue of Prometheus and Epimetheus—by a reflective scene that aims at a reconciliation of both under Pandora's sign. The rising pathos from Pandora's rejection of Epimetheus to the bloody repudiation of Epimeleia achieves in Phileros' attempted suicide a climax and possible turning point which are condensed in the action and in the symbolism of space and time. In terms of space, the cliffs and the sea move closer together. The fall from the cliffs into the sea marks the transgression of the spatial boundary between life, death, and rebirth.

Rebirth is eventually granted to Phileros, but it does not happen because of him, just as in general the reconciliation of the strife-ridden cultures does not take place. Work, property, domination and servitude remain separated from the world of dreams, of beauty, and of love —on the border of their times of day. During the first appearance of the nocturnal Epimetheus, Phileros embarks on his romantic rendezvous under the sign of the morning star; his rescue occurs under the rising morning sun.

The dramatic conception of *Pandora* can be summarized in the following formula: not the solution of the conflict, but the redemption from the conflict. In the parabolic abstraction of the festival play, one line of the great historical process of the genesis of modern society is thematized and parried by one that runs contrary to it. This other line may be interpreted by its origins in the Olympian realm above as a utopian projection of a possible future.

Goethe's dramas with female protagonists, written over a period of thirty years, have various implications for a philosophy of history. In *Iphigenie*, with its parabolically abbreviated form, this message shows the previous development of humanity to be determined by self-destructive relations of power; *The Natural Daughter* relates the development of bourgeois modernity to the French Revolution; in *Pandora*, again fully abstracted from any concrete political reality, the theme is human cultural development as a connection between the unfolding of productivity and social relations of domination. This history is always described as masculine and one that demands sacrifice: the sacrifice of

the woman. It is only logical, therefore, that the removal of the sacrifice of the woman means the entry into a new, human history, in other
words, into a utopian dimension. The dramatic conflict, which in each
case stages the immanent and pernicious self-propelled dynamics of
this (hi)story—the dialectic of Enlightenment—is never resolved, however, through its own structure. It is "redeemed" insofar as the former
victims become figures of redemption.

It is possible to read Goethe's early dramas, taking as representative the first part of *Faust*, as critical of a male morality that can then be
expanded to include a bourgeois-male model of emancipation. In this
way, this aspect of these three plays takes on a historical significance.
Iphigenie is a parable of male history that is identified as barbaric: the
myth of the rise and fall of Tantalus and the resulting curse on his
descendants, who will destroy themselves in a chain of violence, is a
metaphor for human history. Independence, autonomy of mankind is
shown to be regression into a natural matrix of history in the sense that
these rebellious human beings, these men, are insulated from the consequences of their actions. With Adorno, who interpreted *Iphigenie* in
this sense, we can say that Enlightenment returns to myth.

The Natural Daughter refers to concrete history, namely to the
French Revolution, and in so doing postulates rebellion, individual
autonomy instead of collective responsibility as the metaphor of the
age. An order crumbles, and in its place arises the chaos of competing
subjective interests—bourgeois society, which for Goethe initially
appears as the disintegration of original values. The Revolution, present in this play only as premonition, is the extreme expression of this
process.

Finally, *Pandora* abstracts from the concrete political situation and
takes as its theme the cultural expression of bourgeois society. Unlike
the early dramatic fragment *Prometheus* (1774), *Pandora* is not concerned with the creative aspect of mankind's emancipation from divine
domination, but rather with the destructive component of this culture,
which threatens humane ideals. Goethe's new Prometheus no longer
builds huts, symbols of human dwelling and protectedness, but rather
has his servants make weapons in caves. In the play this production of
weapons leads to arson and war. The pastoral age of human innocence
is left behind; modernity makes way for itself with murder and death.
Violence is directly connected to an exploitative, destructive relationship of humankind to nature; nowhere else has Goethe so clearly
described the domination of humankind over nature as the destruction
of the foundations of human life, a destruction that is expressed in
social relations. Alienation, distrust, and violence are symbolically syn-
thesized in the inability to love. Rejecting the misogynist tradition of

the myth of "Pandora's box," Goethe portrays Pandora as the embodiment of love, but she is excluded from this culture.

To simplify matters, it could be said that at the end of all three plays an "unrealistic" conflict resolution replaces a "realistic" view of history and a resulting configuration of conflict. In a utopian way, male history is freed from its inextricable contradictions by a female character. Iphigenie cuts through the Gordian knot of violence that breeds violence when she makes the ethical decision to refuse the false alternatives of male history, that is, to sacrifice either oneself or another; in so doing, she opens the way to a new history (or herstory). This play can thus be read as an attempt to insert the woman—the "other sex," in Simone de Beauvoir's sense—as the "other subject" of failed male history, though in a poetic-utopian play. *The Natural Daughter* aims at the same goal; it was originally planned as a trilogy, of which only the first part was completed. The return of Pandora, promised at the end of the play, also promises resolution.

The re-introduction of the ancient deus ex machina as a modern dea ex machina in these plays uses the then-modern image of woman as a collection of ideal characteristics, an image that is abstracted more and more from the real existence of woman. Real woman is the victim of the new bourgeois age, as Goethe's early dramas show. But male guilt, which is connected to this age, can no longer be dependent on the morality of individual characters, if it is to represent the character of the age, and the elimination of this guilt cannot be tied to an individual female character. Beginning with Iphigenie, who merges individual character and utopian projection, Goethe's female characters become more and more abstract. They tend toward an image of the feminine. A male fantasy becomes evident, which functions as a vehicle of a worldview that is no longer cohesive. The image of redemption by the feminine takes the place of a historical telos that is no longer recognizable but only hoped for, a telos that resolves the contradictions of the modern age. Drama, which portrays these contradictions, cannot resolve them, but only furnish rescues from them. In this way we take leave of a conception of tragedy that elevates, confirms, sublimely raises up the male hero through his tragic defeat by reality. In this sense, Goethe's plays end very appropriately with the "festival play," *Pandora*. Nevertheless, classical drama finds meaning in the dramatic due to the category of the female.

Notes

1. "prätendierte Freiheit unseres Wollens mit dem notwendigen Gang des Ganzen" (12: 226).
2. See, for example, Adorno or Borchmeyer.
3. "Ich rechte mit den Göttern nicht; allein / Der Frauen Zustand ist beklagenswert" (5: 8).
4. "Tantalus, Ixion, Sysiphus waren meine Heiligen, . . . und wenn sie als Glieder einer ungeheuren Opposition im Hintergrund meiner 'Iphigenie' zeige, so bin ich ihnen wohl einen Teil der Wirkung schuldig, welche dieses Stück hervorzubringen das Glück hatte" (10: 277).
5. This thesis is also implicit in Reed, who follows the maturation ('Mündigkeit') of Iphigenie during the course of the play and thus locates the real enlightenment with the integration of the women.
6. Adorno places an emphasis on this distinction although it is canceled by his own interpretation.
7. "O diese Zeit hat fürchterliche Zeichen: / Das Niedere schwillt, das Hohe senkt sich nieder" (5: 226).
8. "Vermagst du zu versprechen, mich als Bruder / Mit reiner Neigung zu empfangen? mir, / Der liebevollen Schwester, Schutz und Rat / Und stille Lebensfreude zu gewähren?" (5: 298).
9. "Eugenie, wenn du entsagen könntest / Dem hohen Glück das unermeßlich scheint . . ." (5: 240).
10. "Denn Epimetheus nannten mich die Zeugenden, / Vergangenem nachzusinnen, Raschgeschehenes / Zurückzuführen mühsam Gedankenspiels / Zum trüben Reich gestaltenmischender Möglichkeit" (5: 333).
11. "Sag, ist es Pandora? Du sahst sie einmal, / Den Vätern verderblich, den Söhnen zur Qual" (5: 347).
12. "Entwandelt friedlich! Friede findend gehet ihr nicht" (5: 341).
13. "Abwesenheit des Vaters ehrt ein guter Sohn" (5: 346).

Works Cited

Adorno, Theodor W. "Zum Klassizismus von Goethes 'Iphigenie.'" *Noten zur Literatur*. Ed. Rolf Tiedemann. Frankfurt: Suhrkamp, 1981. 495-514
Borchmeyer, Dieter. "Goethes 'Pandora' und der Preis des Fortschritts." *Etudes germaniques* 1 (1983): 17-31.
Böschenstein, Bernhard. "Antike und moderne Tragödie um 1800 in dreifacher Kontroverse: Goethes 'Natürliche Tochter', Kleists 'Penthesilea' und Hölderlins 'Antigone.' " *Kontroversen, alte und neue: Akten des VII. Germanistenkongresses Göttingen, 1985*. Vol. 8. Tübingen: Niemeyer, 1986. 204-15.
Brandmeyer, Rudolf. *Heroik und Gegenwart: Goethes klassische Dramen*. Frankfurt: Lang, 1987.
Brandt, Helmut. "Der widersprüchliche Held: Goethes 'Faust' im Lichte der Gretchentragödie." *Ansichten der deutschen Klassik*. Ed. Helmut Brandt and Manfred Beyer. Berlin: Aufbau, 1981. 119-47.
Goethe, Johann Wolfgang. *Werke*. ["Hamburger Ausgabe."] Ed. Erich Trunz et al. 14 vols. Rev. ed. Munich: Beck, 1981.
Hegel, Georg Friedrich Wilhelm. *Phänomenologie des Geistes*. Frankfurt/M.:

Suhrkamp, 1986.

Jauß, Hans Robert. "Racines and Goethes 'Iphigenie.' " *Rezeptionsästhetik.* Ed. Rainer Warning. München: Fink, 1975. 352-98.

Pütz, Peter. *Die Zeit in Drama: Zur Technik der dramatischen Spannung.* Göttingen: Vandenhoeck & Ruprecht, 1970.

Rasch, Wolfdietrich. *Goethe's "Iphigenie auf Tauris" als Drama der Autonomie.* München: Beck, 1979.

Reed, Terence James. "Iphigenies Unmündigkeit." *Germanistik: Forschungsstand und Perspektiven: Vorträge des deutschen Germanistenverbands 1984.* Ed. Georg Stötzel. Vol. 2. Berlin: de Gruyter, 1985. 505-24.

Vaget, Hans Rudolf. "Die natürliche Tochter." *Goethes Dramen: Neue Interpretationen.* Ed. Walter Hinderer. Stuttgart: Reclam, 1980.

Wagner, Irmgard. "Vom Mythos zum Fetisch: Die Frau als Erlöserin in Goethes klassischen Dramen." *Weiblichkeit in geschichtlicher Perspektive.* Ed. Ursula A. J. Becher and Jörn Rüsen. Frankfurt: Suhrkamp, 1988. 234-58.

The Personal and the Philosophical in Fichte's Theory of Sexual Difference[1]

Karen Kenkel

THIS ESSAY WILL explore how Johann Gottlieb Fichte legitimates the political and social subordination of women within his philosophical system, but also *why* he feels the need to do so. Fichte's position on women's rights, as well as the philosophical system of which it is a part, bears the stamp of interrelated historical, social, political, and personal forces. This essay limits itself to understanding the conservative position Fichte takes on women's rights by examining the logic of his philosophical arguments in relation to his personal negotiation of tensions arising in his marriage. It does not try to prove that the personal is also the philosophical, but to demonstrate how Fichte's personal experience gave shape to his philosophical arguments for women's social and political subordination.

In the first and second introductions to his *Foundations of the Entire Science of Knowledge* (*Grundlage der gesammten Wissenschaftslehre*, 1794), Fichte reveals how both his reading of Kant and personal experience play a formative role in his philosophical system.[2] Fichte claims in the "First Introduction to the Science of Knowledge" that his system is "nothing other than the *Kantian; this means that it contains the same view of things" (SK* 4).[3] What Fichte derived from his reading of Kant's work was a focus on a rational, self-determining, free subject. Fichte hoped to elaborate on this idealist "view of things" in his own *Science of Knowledge*, expanding the reach of Kant's Copernican Revolution to the point where "the object shall be posited and determined by the cognitive faculty, and not the cognitive faculty by the object" (*SK* 4). In the "Second Introduction to the Science of Knowledge," Fichte acknowledges that the *Science of Knowledge* takes as its first principle

278

an *experience* of individual freedom that cannot be proved. This means that Fichte's theory is grounded in empirical experience presented as an *a priori*. Fichte argues that every system ultimately reduces to "something indemonstrable, on which all demonstration depends" (*SK* 77). Conviction of the truth of Fichte's "science" by means of proof, therefore, requires that "both parties are agreed at least on something," that both share the experience of its first principle (*SK* 78). However, if this empirical experience is for Fichte specifically, or even exclusively, a male one, then the universal truth of his science of knowledge transforms into an exclusionary truth for men and about men. It is this possibility I will explore.

Fichte follows Kant in rejecting traditionally grounded authority in favor of the internal authority of reason. Fichte's theoretical commitment to the equality of all human beings depends on his belief in the universality of reason: "Reason is common to all, and in all rational beings is exactly the same. A capacity inherent in one such being is present in every one" (*SK* 75). The universalization of reason makes it impossible for Fichte to directly deny women's equality without undermining the fundamental premise of his philosophy (see *SR* 440).[4] It is precisely because of this theoretical equality within his system that the social and political inequality of women in his contemporary society presents a difficulty for Fichte. He recognizes this problem in his introduction to the section of *The Science of Right* on marriage and announces the need to confront it directly:

> Has the woman the same rights in the state which the man has? This question may appear ridiculous to many. For if the only ground of qualification for legal rights is reason and freedom, how can a difference in rights exist between two sexes which both possess the same reason and the same freedom? Nevertheless, it seems that, so long as human beings have lived, this has been differently held, and the female sex seems not to have been placed on a par with the male sex in the exercise of its rights. Such a universal sentiment must have a deepset ground, to discover which was never a more urgent need than in our days. (*SR* 439)

The character of those days at the turn of the century has much to do with the urgency of the problem for thinkers such as Fichte. Ute Frevert shows how many philosophers theorized about women and sexual difference around the turn of the eighteenth century in an effort to define their "masculine selves" in the context of new bourgeois social and political formations. She argues, however, that this concern with relations between the sexes must also be seen as a specific reaction to the calls for women's emancipation that were appearing in the wake of the French Revolution (37-38). That Fichte was aware of and influenced by this historical climate is revealed in his letters, where he displays concern over the agitation in France and in his homeland for women's rights. He writes, for example, in a letter to his publisher in 1795:

> A certain aspiration of women, a dissatisfaction with their political situation, is one of the peculiarities of our age. This tendency has already been taken advantage of by writers; some have supported it (*On Improving the Status of Women*, for example[5]), others have suppressed, censured, mocked it. A thorough investigation of it is still lacking.[6]

The tone of displeasure in the letter with those, such as Theodor Gottlieb von Hippel, who have "taken advantage of" women's dissatisfaction warns us that Fichte will take a conservative stance in this debate. Fichte makes clear in addressing the issue of women's rights that his task will be not to explode the notion of inequality, but to find its "deep-set ground."

Although Fichte was not willing to relinquish the Enlightenment premise that all human beings, including women, are complete and equal as creatures of reason, he would prove more flexible when it came to questions of political and social equality. Fichte begins his discussion of women's rights by legitimizing women's lack of freedom in marriage:

> the woman is not subjected to her husband in such a manner as to give a *right of compulsion* over her; she is subjected through her own continuous necessary wish—a wish which is the condition of her morality—to be so subjected. She could take back her freedom, if she *willed* to do so; but that is the very point: she cannot rationally *will* to be free. Her relation to her husband being publicly known, she must, moreover, will to appear to all whom she knows as utterly subjected to, and utterly lost in, the man of her choice. (*SR* 441)

Fichte displaces the issue of rights onto the terrain of will: the wife "cannot rationally will to be free." He transforms the subordination of women in his society into a positive expression of their rational will, depicting concrete situations of social inequality as equally rational. By compelling women to choose self-annihilation as their mode of expression, Fichte disguises inequality. These philosophical contortions preserve the freedom of reason at the expense of the freedom of women; equality is extended to reason, but not to all rational subjects.

When Fichte transforms the issue of women's rights into a question of whether "the female sex *can desire* to exercise all its rights" (*SR* 440), he takes an important step in legitimizing women's social and political inequality. He supports this move by grounding women's rational predilection against choosing autonomy in a theory of sexual difference. For Fichte, then, sexual difference becomes the means for establishing inequality in the realm of experience.

Fichte's view of sexual difference derives from his understanding of propagation. Fichte envisions the woman as the passive agent in propagation, waiting for the "first moving principle" to "vitalize" and set the receptive principle into motion:

> The system of all the conditions for the generation of a body of the same species had to be completely united somewhere, and, when put in motion, to develop itself after its own laws. The sex which contains these complete conditions is called throughout all nature the *female* sex. Only the first moving principle could be set apart.... The sex in which this principle generates itself, apart from the substance to be vitalized by it, is called throughout all nature the *male* sex. (*SR* 393)

Fichte uses this model of a strict division of active and passive propagative labor to describe the nature of heterosexual intercourse and male and female sexual desire as well. He argues that nature gives each individual a sexual impulse to ensure the continuation of the species. However, this sexual desire exists in the individual only for its own satisfaction. In other words, for the individual, the satisfaction of the impulse exists independent of the aim of propagation. Although Fichte carefully distinguishes between sexual desire and the aims of propagation, he nevertheless uses his bifurcation of propagation into male activity and female passivity to support an argument for the different orientation of male and female sexual desire: "in the satisfaction of the [sexual] impulse, ... the one sex behaves purely actively [thätig], and the other purely passively [leidend]" (*SR* 393). Separating desire (will) from propagation (nature) only to equate them, Fichte imparts the semblance of empirical determinedness to his notion of female sexual passivity and male sexual activity. It is this notion of male action and female inertia that will ground Fichte's assertion that women subjugate themselves freely.

Fichte admits that women, like men, desire the satisfaction of their sexual impulse. But because the female impulse is passive, the woman cannot truly desire it, for to do so would represent a desire of passivity. This goes against the character of reason, which Fichte defines as "absolute self-activity": "it is absolutely against reason that the second sex should propose to itself the satisfaction of its sexual impulse as an end, because in that case it would make a pure passivity its end" (*SR* 394). How fortuitous for men, then, that the male sexual impulse corresponds to the activity of reason, such that "it is not at all against reason that the first sex should propose to itself the satisfaction of its sexual impulse as an end, since it can be satisfied through activity" (*SR* 394).

Because women cannot rationally desire the satisfaction of their own sexual impulse as an end, nature provides them with a transformed desire to please men sexually. Fichte names this sexual impulse once-removed love, and the object of this love, male pleasure. Love does not spring from women's efforts or reason, but is a natural gift: "we speak here of *nature* and of an *impulse of nature*; that is, of something which a woman will find in herself as something given, original, and not to be explained by any previous free acts of her own" (*SR* 395). Nature acts through the woman's sexual impulse, lending it the appearance of activity (pleasing the man) so that the woman can properly (rationally) desire it.

By maintaining a "separate but equal" notion of male and female sexual impulses, Fichte strives to support the female desire for male pleasure as positive and in accord with the dictates of reason. However, when Fichte considers a "feminine" role for the male, the true implications of the female sacrifice surface:

> Probably no man exists who would not feel the absurdity of turning this around and ascribing to the man a similar impulse to satisfy a need of a woman; a need, in fact, which he can neither presuppose in the woman nor consider himself as its tool without feeling himself disgraced to the innermost depths of his soul. (*SR* 400)

To take the sexual satisfaction of women as an end, Fichte argues, would make men means—"tools" of women's pleasure. Fichte conceives of the male fulfillment of female needs as degrading for men because entertaining another's pleasure entails a pause in the pursuit of one's own. The stigma of such a pause is that it would force the male to part ways with unrelentingly active reason, suggesting a yielding to nature. What is degrading for men as creatures of reason is what comprises women's sexual nature. We see, then, that Fichte constructs an elaborate libidinal detour for women via male pleasure that is irreconcilable with his notion of rational, self-determining subjective action. Instead, in the theoretically magic moment when women choose to objectify themselves to fulfill the dictates of (male) reason, the degradation of women's rational being ceases to be degrading.

One might attempt to defend Fichte's objectification of women by pointing to his belief that our distinct selves all exist as a means for the greater purposes of reason (*SK* 75). However, the point here is not that women become a means for *reason*, but that they become a means for *men*. Women's objectification in marriage is not solely theoretical, but social and political:

> The conception of marriage involves the most unlimited subjection of the wife to the will of the husband; not from legal, but from moral reasons. She must subject herself for the sake of her own honor. The wife does not belong to herself, but to the husband. The state, by recognizing marriage ... abandons all claims to consider the woman as a legal person. The husband takes her place; her marriage utterly annuls her, so far as the state is concerned.... The husband ... becomes her legal guardian. He lives in all ways her public life, and she retains for herself only a house life. (*SR* 417-18)

Despite his claims of loyalty to Kant's philosophy, Fichte's description of marriage deviates in significant ways from Kant's. Kant described sex as an act of abandoning one's body to another's pleasure, of becoming an *object* for the pleasure of the other. The central principle of Kant's moral philosophy, however, holds that it is implicit in the nature of rational beings that they can never justifiably become merely a means, but must remain ends-in-themselves. In Kant's system, the ethical law against self-objectification is not gender-specific. He resolves the apparent contradiction between self-objectification for the pleasure of another and his ethical mandate against objectification by limiting sexual activity to marriage. The reciprocal objectification of marriage "cancels out" the negativity of making oneself a means (Kant 167). Kant sees marriage as a contract for establishing rights to another's body between equal individuals with equal duties to themselves and others, duties which cannot be compromised—not even out of love. For Kant, reciprocity is essential for preserving the humanity of sexual activity.

Fichte accepts Kant's idea that sex is about being pleased. What Kant sees as a general principle of human sexuality, however, Fichte views as a male principle, insofar as for the man, sex involves pure self-satisfaction. Fichte accepts Kant's postulate of the end-in-itself and the consequent argument against human objectification, yet he applies Kant's universal principle only to males. Becoming the sexual means for another is unacceptable only for men. For women Fichte draws a distinction between sexuality and spirituality: sexual objectification produces spiritual realization. In distilling sexuality out from the whole female human being, Fichte departs from Kant, who insisted that in marriage "one devotes not only sex but the whole person; the two cannot be separated" (Kant 167). By isolating female sexuality, Fichte helps render it, and its subject, more serviceable to the needs of others. The theoretical woman who results is deprived of a sexuality, as well as a rationality, of her own: "The sexual impulse does not occupy, nor express itself at all, in an uncorrupted woman, but only love" (*SR* 399).

Karin Hausen argues that the development of a notion of "the character of the sexes" (*Geschlechtscharakter*) during the late eighteenth century coincided with the social transformation of the family. The unfolding discourse about the character of the sexes, Hausen argues,

> coincided with the transition ... from the household or "whole house" [*ganzes Haus*] to the bourgeois family, which occurred when both the aspect of domestic economy and the notion of house servants subject to the master's rule disappeared from the concept of family. There are many indications that in Ger-

many at the end of the eighteenth century this transition was experienced as a profound change in the social institution of the family. (58)

Fichte's deduction of marriage contributes to this discussion of the character of the sexes by using a theory of sexual difference to re-establish male hegemony in the new familial formation. He philosophically grounds the divisions upon which the bourgeois family is based—divisions between public and private activity, and between public and private labor—in the opposite sexual tendencies of men and women. What remains to be explored, however, is Fichte's personal experience of the conflicts arising from this new organization of public and private activity, conflicts which shape his philosophical deductions.[7]

Fichte's early letters to his betrothed, Johanne Rahn, offer insight into this issue in their attempts to define the nature of his and Johanne's developing relationship as paradigmatic. In the first of two important letters, penned within days of each other in the spring of 1790, Fichte writes to Johanne of his ambition to make his mark in the world:

> I have only one passion, only one need, only one complete feeling of myself, namely: to have an effect in the world. The more I do, the happier I appear to myself. Is this also a delusion? That may be, but there is truth in it. It is certainly not a deception that it gives me a heavenly feeling to be loved by good souls, to know people who take an interest in me, a lively, heartfelt, warm, constant interest. Since I have come to know your heart more closely, I sense this feeling in all its fullness. You judge with what emotions I close this letter ... Your grateful friend.[8]

While Fichte *wishes* to be loved, he recognizes in himself only one driving *need*: self-promotion. His passion is not for Johanne, who has to be content with his wish to be loved by her, but for his own activity in the world. So much is Fichte himself the focus of the letter to Johanne that he seems able to render Johanne's concern for him as a statement of his affection for her. His fondness for being loved appears as the source of his own reactive feeling for Johanne.

In Fichte's second letter, written after returning to Zurich from a brief trip, he emphasizes the pleasures but also the problems of his active life in the public realm:

> I ... was so completely in the sphere where I am content; in the sphere of a strong, diverse, strenuous occupation. If I could have filled the holes in these affairs with your sweet company; if I could have felt and thought out loud with you—noble, like-minded soul—that which I mostly had to lock inside my soul, these days would have been enviable.[9]

Fichte feels most himself in the strenuous environment of the public sphere, yet notices that it is not complete ("the holes in these affairs") when he is away from Johanne. One to have his cake and eat it too,

Fichte muses warmly on Johanne's role as an emotional outlet that will fuel his enjoyment of the diversity and challenge of public life. Fichte ends the letter by emphasizing the gender specificity of his activity in the public realm, thereby positioning Johanne's emotional sensitivity as a product of the private realm:

> How reluctantly I part from this paper. How gladly I would like to add yet another, or even two sheets, but I can't steal any more time away from my affairs. It is reserved for you, you, who shame me in all things (I state with heartfelt feeling that this is true, and with pain, that I can't change it, that I unfortunately! am a *masculine creature* according to your definition, who, especially now, always has his mind full, always full of projects and plans, is in a continual state of restlessness); it is reserved for you to surpass me in letter writing, too—hardly, however, in the emotions, with which I remain your warmest friend.[10]

Fichte accepts Johanne's invocation of gender difference to explain his predilection for public, career-oriented activity. His gesture to Johanne's superiority at letter writing contains an implicit reference to his inferiority in the realm of private communication. It also emphasizes his preoccupation with matters of greater portent. Johanne is naturally superior in emotional matters because she lives solely in the private world. Insofar as these letters are seen primarily as vehicles for the expression of their feelings for each other, Fichte can admit to his inadequacy and Johanne's superiority in her ability to express her emotions.

In these letters, Fichte comments on his need to be loved, but never expresses his love for Johanne (Kafka 12-15). Instead, he closes his letters with elliptical allusions to his "feelings" that allow him to express affection without ever committing himself to the exact nature of the emotion. How he relates to Johanne is less clear in the letters than how she relates to him, for this relationship he authors for the both of them, rendering Johanne's affection for him a primary theme in the letters. In fact, her love for him substitutes for his emotional self-expression. He both benefits from, and feeds off of, Johanne's emotion. Fichte's insecurity about his emotional capabilities emerges perhaps most revealingly in a letter written to Johanne during their courtship: "for I have already gotten used to making no distinction between your self and my self; to regarding all of the kindnesses and virtues that I discover in you as my possession; to rejoicing in them, as if I myself were the one who had them."[11] Fichte implies a moral and emotional lack in himself that is redressed by Johanne's love for him. Through that love, he acquires Johanne's "property": her moral character and ability to feel. Absent from the letters is any suggestion of a reverse transferal whereby Johanne might benefit from her tie to Fichte. For Fichte, Fichte remains the focus of the relationship.

In these early letters to Johanne, Fichte associates his identity with the rigors of the public sphere, and Johanne's with private, household emotion. The most important issue to emerge in these letters, however, is Fichte's prioritization of *himself* in the relationship as the most problematic. While Johanne is literally at home with herself, Fichte negotiates between emotional solace and professional challenge. In the letters, Fichte struggles to mediate the competing demands that the emerging division of public and private realms places on his energy. Fichte's letters appeal to Johanne to resolve this problematic division of public and private for the "masculine creature" by acting as caretaker of his private, emotional life so that he can withstand an emotionally impaired public life.

Fichte's personal experience of his problematic, ambitious nature in contrast to the passive stability of Johanne finds theoretical expression in the discussion of morality in *The Science of Ethics* (*Das System der Sittenlehre*, 1798). When Fichte claims in the *The Science of Right* that "The man . . . must first subordinate all his impulses to reason, through exertion and activity" in order to become rational (*SR* 449), he alludes to the gender specificity of rational activity and its impulse toward the domination of nature. Because the male sexual impulse merely *corresponds* to the active principle of reason men find themselves in a state of pleasurable but passive givenness that they must overcome to become self-determining and free.

Fichte argues in *The Science of Ethics* that the satisfaction of the natural impulse results in enjoyment, which annihilates the boundary between reason and nature by its "mere passive surrendering to nature." This kind of enjoyment "tears me away from myself, estranges me from myself, and wherein I forget myself. It is an *involuntary* enjoyment (which is, perhaps, the best characteristic for all sensuous enjoyment)" (*SE* 153-54). Because sex is naturally so pleasurable and self-focussed for men, they stand to lose their quality of absolute self-determination in it. It is for this reason that the man "must first subordinate all his impulses to reason, through exertion and activity" (*SR* 449). Men must generate resistance to nature in order to constitute themselves as self-determined, that is, free, beings. The pleasure of physical satisfaction must be sublimated into the satisfaction of experiencing speculative power: the absolute self-activity of the I. Opposition returns the ego to itself by distancing it from everything else; nurturing its self-awareness becomes the means and the end. The ego's self-determining activity allows men to avoid the danger of acting in accordance with reason without ever becoming self-determining moral beings. Self-determining activity is in accordance with morality, which requires action for action's sake, not for the satisfaction of a natural impulse:

"The objective is not merely that only what is good and in accordance with reason occurs, that only legality rules; but that it occurs with freedom, according to the moral law, such that actually true morality rules" (*SE* 291). For Fichte, the consequence of moral self-determination is gratification of a thoroughly narcissistic sort: the satisfaction of feeling one's own power. "It is not so much enjoyment as *satisfaction,* which never is the characteristic of sensuous enjoyment. It is not so turbulent, but more deeply felt, and infuses new courage and new strength" (*SE* 154). The active ego pumps up, and then admires its speculative muscles in the mirror of reflective thought. Male morality, then, refers to the principle of unlimited freedom of self-determination for its own sake. Women are naturally moral, and therefore never capable of becoming free in the male sense. But it is nevertheless their natural, "passive" morality that bears the responsibilities of a social existence.

The male activity of self-determination through the subordination of nature is the constitutive activity not only of Fichte's male reason, but of Fichte's universal subject. Indeed, the reflective ability to transcend natural impulse by controlling it is what distinguishes human beings from animals. Fichte defines the fundamental principle of the active ego as freedom, but this freedom is a negative principle: freedom from external determination, necessity, nature. Between determination and self-determination lies nature, which the self-conscious ego must control in order to be free:

> Only the reflected is nature. The reflecting is opposed to it, and hence, is no nature, but raised above all nature. The higher impulse, as the impulse of the purely spiritual, is directed upon absolute self-determination in an activity for the mere sake of the activity. Hence, it is opposed to all enjoyment which is a mere passive surrendering to nature. (*SE* 136)

When Fichte asserts that women are "already rational by nature," he not only excludes them from the activity by which the subject constitutes itself as free and moral, but as well denies them the status of self-determining beings. Fichte's Enlightenment leaves women behind in nature.

The first principle of Fichte's *Science of Ethics* is an I that is active, self-motivating, free, moral, and isolated—an embodiment of reason that Fichte systematically shapes as masculine. The ego's self-enclosure is a sign of its freedom, produced by absolute self-determination. This solipsistic subjectivity, while basking in its own self-positing, is predicated on aggressive isolation. This ego is in a continual, if not infinite, struggle to expand its control, to see itself in everything, or everything as determined by itself: "The self is infinite, but merely in respect to its striving; it strives to be infinite" (*SK* 238). Although Fichte discusses the necessity of a "you" for every "I" in his *Science of Knowledge*, the "you" is required so that the concrete "I" can define itself:

> that to which there is no *counterstriving* is not a striving at all. If the self did more than strive, if it had an infinite causality, it would not be a self: it would not posit itself, and would therefore be nothing. But if it did not endlessly strive in this fashion, again it could not posit itself, for it could oppose nothing to itself; again it would be no self, and would therefore be nothing. (*SK* 238)

The concrete individuality requires other individualities against which it can position itself. Intersubjectivity in the male sphere, then, takes an impoverished form. It is not based on communal relationships between individuals, but on the antagonism between individuals. A struggle for status is the dominant feature of this sphere, where one requires others to confirm one's own power.

Fichte argues that women must be excluded from the masculine public sphere, as the desire for "celebrity" does not suit their nature:

> A rational and virtuous wife can be proud only of her husband and children; not of herself, for she forgets herself in them. Add to this, that those women who seriously envy men their celebrity find themselves in a very easily exposed deception concerning the true object of their wish. The woman necessarily desires the love of some man, and, in order to attract it, she is anxious to attract the attention of the male sex. This is natural and very proper in an unmarried woman. But those women [who envy men their celebrity] calculate to increase the charms of their own sex—perhaps not having much confidence in them—by that which attracts the attention of men to men, and seek in celebrity merely a new means of captivating men's hearts. (*SR* 444)

Fichte stakes out the public sphere as male turf when he trivializes women's success in that sphere as misplaced sexual capital. In so doing, he delineates two types of social relationships, which are differentiated along gender lines: the public relationships of men to men, based in antagonistic posturing; and the private relationship of men to women, and of women to children, based in love.

Love originates in women as nature's attempt to reconcile female sexuality and reason, which would otherwise stand in opposition to each other. Because male sexuality conforms to the active character of reason, men do not inherit the impulse to love from nature. Men, therefore, are at first capable only of self-satisfaction in their relations with women. Self-focussed thought finds its parallel in self-focussed sex: "Originally, that is, so far as his mere natural inclination is concerned, the man, it is true, seeks to satisfy his sexual impulse" (*SR* 420). In order to move beyond this base inclination—a necessary step in the progression to the morality of total self-determination—the man needs to share in the intersubjectivity that the woman alone produces via her abnegation of self for others.

For Fichte, true communal relationships are based on the principle of sacrifice for others, but for men this is not a natural inclination. Men are not even capable of coming to love their children independently of their wives (*SR* 455). By witnessing his wife's self-sacrifice, the man acquires the ability to be loving and giving: "In the man is *originally* not love, but sexual impulse; love in him is not an original, but a *communicated, derived* impulse, first developed through connection with a loving woman. It has, moreover, quite a different form in the man to what it has in the woman" (*SR* 399). His acquired ability to love must take a different form than her love precisely because the essence of female love is self-sacrifice: "love is, to sacrifice one's self for the sake of another" (*SR* 399). A difference always remains for Fichte between the woman's self-denigrating and the man's self-affirming morality.

In marriage, it is precisely the position of mastery over his wife that the husband supposedly comes to renounce as he learns to love; he increasingly moves in the direction of mutual self-sacrifice rather than one-sided self-assertion, toward a close relationship rather than an absolute distance from everything outside of himself. Marriage suggests synthesis rather than repression or domination; it places obstacles, therefore, in the way of absolute self-determination. While Fichte claims the absolute hegemony of the ego over the empirical to be the goal of idealism, he nevertheless recognizes that this (masculine) principle must be domesticated: "The original tendency of the human being is egotistic; in marriage even Nature leads one to forget oneself in the other; and the marriage union of both sexes is the only way in which the human being can be ennobled through Nature" (*SE* 347).

The necessity of marriage in Fichte's system registers his recognition of the social limitations of his philosophical subject. However, the "solution" of marriage juxtaposes two irreconcilable notions of morality in Fichte's system. It sets up a competition of public vs. private, independent (isolated) vs. interactive, absolute distance from the empirical vs. embeddedness in empirical reality, masculine vs. feminine. These oppositions are rooted in the two antagonistic paths to morality that Fichte creates. One relies on the "feminine" principle of union with nature (love in marriage), the other on the "masculine" principle of the domination of nature (absolute self-activity). The struggle to be absolutely self-determining requires marriage so that a man might learn to rise above the desire for mere enjoyment and the satisfaction of natural urges. Men, the active agents, must become passive objects, must "be loved" before they can learn to love and thereby transform sexual impulse into rational, moral concern. However, when marriage binds men to the private realm and to women's emotional demands, it creates a problem for the self-focussed striving of the ego toward absolute independence.

Before he read Kant, Fichte's letters expressed a desire to supplement his public sphere activities with Johanne's emotional contribution. However, after studying Kant and beginning to formulate his own notions about (male) morality, Fichte experienced certain anxieties about marriage, which eventually produced a two-year break with Johanne. To his brother Gotthelf he wrote in the spring of 1791:

> it is always risky to marry without having a position; and, in the end, I feel too much power and drive in myself to cut off my wings, so to speak, with a marriage, to chain myself in a yoke, from which I can never again free myself, and so to decide obligingly to spend the rest of my life as a common human being.[12]

The clear metaphors of confinement in this letter voice Fichte's fear that marital ties and the obligations of the private realm will limit the freedom of his aspiring spirit. He sees the everyday responsibilities and commitments of marriage in opposition to his liberating and energizing speculative activity. In a letter to Johanne of a few months earlier, he makes this point clear when he offers a more personal reflection on the importance of Kant's work to him:

> Through an occasion that appeared to me to be mere accident, I gave myself over entirely to the study of Kantian philosophy, a philosophy which tames the imaginative power that was always very powerful in me, which gives superior weight to reason, and to the whole spirit an incomprehensible elevation above all earthly things. I have assumed a more noble ethics, and instead of busying myself with things outside of me, I busy myself more with myself. This has given me a tranquility which I never before felt; though in unstable external circumstances, I spent my most blissful days.[13]

Fichte depicts the attraction of the Kantian system as the tranquility it allows through distance ("elevation") from empirical existence ("earthly things"). He indicates that Kant's appeal derives at least in part from Fichte's tenuous material circumstances in Leipzig when he comments: "though in unstable external circumstances, I spent my most blissful days." The critical morality grounded in individual freedom that Fichte found so liberating from metaphysical uncertainty was bound up with the concrete relief of having escaped the pressure of a world marred by the struggle to earn a living. In a letter to his friend Achelis he explains: "Because I couldn't change what was outside of me, I decided to change what was in me. I threw myself into philosophy."[14] These letters reveal Fichte's association of marriage with empirical limitations to his freedom, which he understands both as freedom to pursue his career ambitions and to engage in self-determination through speculative thinking. For Fichte, turning inward and turning away from reality are part of the same motion. He defines the activity of speculation in the "First Introduction to the Science of Knowledge" with the command: "Attend to yourself: turn your attention away from everything that surrounds you and towards your inner life; this is the first demand that philosophy makes of its disciple. Our concern is not with anything that lies outside you, but only with yourself" (*SK* 6). Both women and marriage threaten his speculative escape from the disturbances and necessities of the private sphere, and therefore his career ambitions as well, by binding him to their empirical and emotional demands.

If we look again to his letters, we see how the conflict between the public and private, the speculative and empirical, unfolds, and how Fichte attempts to resolve it. Johann and Johanne were married in the fall of 1793, and shortly thereafter had an opportunity to correspond when Fichte accepted a job at the university in Jena and left Zurich four months before Johanne could follow. In the letters from this period, one can see Fichte and Johanne struggling to define their newly acquired marital roles and responsibilities. Not surprisingly, Johanne's persistent demand for intimacy generates antagonism when it encounters Fichte's insistence on the male prerogative of freedom. This conflict ignites around the issue of letter writing during their separation. Whereas Fichte had earlier praised Johanne's superiority in letter writing, and expressed a hope of learning from her in that regard, after marriage he finds her demands for correspondence unbearable. She continually begs for more letters, chastising Fichte by documenting in each letter (often several times) the elapsed days since she last received a letter. The following excerpts, taken from one letter, are entirely typical:

> Two unhappy mail days have passed, and I have no letter from my Fichte; I can't describe how I feel then; if you really knew, I know for certain that your good heart could not watch me suffer so: that you have been in Jena for more than eight days is certain, for today is the 26th. You, dear, will have already received two letters from me.

> I beg you dear, beloved! write me out of pity every twelve days, so that I don't have to wait a full two weeks for your letters, for you can't imagine what I suffer; and if you don't have any time, then write me only two words: I am healthy, happy, and still love you. Have compassion for me, beloved.

> Perhaps you shrug your shoulders, my dear, and think, well, that poor child, too, has little strength; but figure in how much strength it costs to endure this unbearable separation. O, I beseech you, write me once a week, as you promised in your dear letter.[15]

The pathos of Johanne's entreaties for communication underscores her difficult position. Because she is literally confined by law to the home and is legally Fichte's ward, life apart from Fichte leaves her with nothing but limitations. Fichte treats Johanne's entreaties sympathetically at times, explaining his busy circumstances to her patiently as if she were a child. At other times he responds with great irritation:

> Although I have no time, I write you in order to make it impossible for you to complain in this manner again. As you know, from the very beginning we never agreed that I should write you once a week, but as often as I could. I have written, though, more often than I promised; and this is your thanks? That isn't right or fair. It isn't unknown to you that of all possible things in the world nothing is more unwelcome to me than unfair and unnecessary complaints. What is more, you have not received a letter from me precisely because you also complained then, and I hereby prepare you once more for the fact that on the next day that the mail is delivered and you again complain, you will certainly receive no letters. It is necessary for your own fortification that I do this.[16]

Fichte conveniently interprets Johanne's unrelenting demands for reciprocity as a weakness on her part which he must punish for her own education. He clearly views her requests for letters as both an infringement on his activities and as a presumption regarding what she can rightfully demand. The days of wishing to learn from her fade into an insistence on his husbandly right to do as he pleases: "Fatigued by speculation, I turn to you, in order to chat with you a bit; I say, fatigued by speculation, for don't count on any other time. My daily work, the business of my life . . . comes first for me."[17] When Fichte informs his wife that she can expect his attention only after he is too tired for the work of "speculation," he attempts to reestablish the boundaries of the public and private, the theoretical and the empirical. Undeterred, Johanne continues to implore for a word from Fichte, and Fichte continues to insist on his right to ignore her, as well as everything else that is not part of his public activity, when he chooses. Because the two realms are directly antagonistic in Fichte's eyes, permanent resolution remains impossible. Not surprisingly, we see him a year later still insisting that his wife observe the boundaries of her private realm:

> by all means, let me hear from you about ideas concerning *my expenses, budget* —or *my ethical behavior in the world*—or the *integrity of my character*—concerning these let me hear from you, for you are my wife, and a worthy, trusty wife you are. But, concerning my *public* affairs, my *relationship to my public*, to the *university,* to *German literature*, let me hear nothing from you, for you are not a man, and on that note, matter closed.[18]

Although the struggle between the wife's demand for intimacy and attention and the husband's insistence on freedom never seems to be reconciled in Fichte's personal experience, we see how Fichte's marital power over Johanne allows him to assert his interests over hers. Johanne must take a back seat to his public obligations. This leaves her in a position of begging for attention and intimacy, which again only reinforces her position of powerlessness and his power. When Fichte grants her wishes, therefore, it takes shape as a concession, rather than a responsibility or a pleasure, to which Johanne responds in kind: "You beloved angel! how benevolent you are; on Saturday a letter, another on Wednesday; I want to kiss your feet out of joy, you good man."[19]

Johanne's response to her lack of social and political power is to exploit her emotional capital. Of necessity, this takes a form that reinforces her lack of public power. Johanne formulates her entreaties in the language of obsequious self-sacrifice and personal suffering. For example, she responds to Fichte's plans to begin a dining group upon her arrival in Jena by couching her opposition in the language of compliance:

> If the dining group can give you, beloved, the least bit of joy, rest assured that even if it really caused me much trouble, I would certainly be glad to do it; and that even though the kitchen has never been nor can become my passion, I am still happy to do everything that my Fichte likes to see; and this holds forever, not only in regard to the kitchen.[20]

She exaggerates her passivity and Fichte's power over her in order to obtain concessions. Fichte's marriage reproduces his theoretical conception of marital relations insofar as Johanne positions herself as self-sacrificing in order to exercise influence within the household. This is precisely the dynamic of female sacrifice and male generosity that Fichte describes between husband and wife in *The Science of Right*.

Fichte's theory of sexual difference grounds a philosophical system that is characterized by four important features: first, an aggressive, active subject (described as universal, but assumed to be male); second, an emotional, passive female subject; third, a prioritization of speculative activity (associated with men) over empirical activity (associated with women); and fourth, a notion of an incomplete rationality that requires domestication through female love. By opposing male activity to female passivity, Fichte clearly hopes to legitimate a patriarchal model of marriage, politics, and social order. However, his invocation of female love as a force of social reconciliation expresses more than a desire to ground the inequalities of the status quo. It also indicates Fichte's unease with a theory, and a society, based on radically self-determining, autonomous individuals. Left on their own (that is, unmarried), these individuals present a moral danger because of their inability or unwillingness to form social ties and assume social responsibility. Fichte perceives the social inadequacy of these, for him, *male* subjects and forges an ideological resolution to the problem by shifting the tensions inherent in the opposition of public and private onto the woman, relocating in her the difficulties, as well as the solution. Fichte attempts to stabilize himself and his philosophical system by introducing the domesticating influence of women. Love will prevent the hard, cold power of ego-centered activity from disintegrating social bonds, enabling men to pursue the bourgeois dream while holding its destructive dynamic in check.

Kant's model of marital relations is more consistent with the Enlightenment's universal claims regarding reason and rational subjects. It is interesting, however, that Fichte—in his project of expanding Kant's philosophical claims—interpreted the Kantian subject as a male subject (as Kant does sporadically, but not *systematically*). Fichte's explicit association of autonomous subjects with masculinity points to the gender issue that remains silent in Kant. What is fascinating about Fichte is his attempt, through a theory of sexual difference, to reconcile the principles of the Enlightenment with the *reality* of late eighteenth century bourgeois society in Germany. His theory of sexual difference not only enables Fichte to legitimate the institutional divisions of the newly emerging bourgeois society, but helps him both to understand his own experiences of gender difference in a self-affirming light, and to establish his privileges as a man in a society increasingly based on the principle of equality.

Notes

1. This essay is indebted to Isabel Hull and the participants in a seminar on the European Enlightenment in the spring of 1990 at Cornell University.

2. Fichte published three versions of *The Science of Knowledge* (Leipzig 1794-95; Tübingen 1802; Jena and Leipzig 1802). The first and second introductions were published in 1797 in the *Philosophisches Journal*. The Heath and Lachs translation that I use is of the 1794 version.

3. I use the following abbreviations: *The Science of Knowledge*: SK; *The Science of Right*: SR; *The Science of Ethics*: SE; *Gesamtausgabe*: G.

4. I have modified A. E. Kroeger's translations of *The Science of Right* and *The Science of Ethics*; most importantly, I have translated "Mensch" as "human being," avoiding Kroeger's confusing use of "man" for both "Mensch" and "Mann."

5. Fichte refers here to Theodor Gottlieb von Hippel's 1792 treatise: *Über die bürgerliche Verbesserung der Weiber*.

6. Translations from Fichte's letters are mine. "Ein gewißes Aufstreben der Weiber, eine Unzufriedenheit derselben mit ihrer politischen Lage gehört unter die Eigenheiten unsers Zeitalters. Dieser Hang ist von Schriftstellern schon benutzt worden; die einen haben ihn begünstigt (*Ueber die bürgerl. Verbeßerung der Weiber*, z.B.) die andern niedergedrükt, getadelt, persiflirt. An einer gründlichen Untersuchung fehlt es" (*G* 3.2: 280).

7. Gustav Kafka's article is the only work I know of that directly thematizes the relationship between Fichte's marital life and his philosophical speculations.

Other works have focused on one aspect of the issue: Becker-Cantarino shows how closely Fichte's depiction of marriage in the *Science of Right* follows the patriarchal legal code promulgated in Prussia two years earlier; Ilse Kammerlander documents some of the Fichtes' marital conflicts in her biography of Johanne Fichte, but she does not relate these to Fichte's developing philosophical ideas. Feminists have recently begun to explore changes in notions of sexuality in the late eighteenth century and the influence of these changes on philosophy. Perhaps most relevant to the issues raised in this paper is the volume of essays edited by Ute Frevert, particularly Isabel Hull's essay " 'Sexualität' und bürgerliche Gesellschaft," in which Hull describes how Fichte uses the idea of sexuality to exclude women from citizenship and public life.

8. "Ich habe nur eine Leidenschaft, nur ein Bedürfnis, nur ein Volles Gefühl meiner Selbst, das: außer mir zu würken. Je mehr ich thue, je glüklicher scheine ich mir. Ist das auch Täuschung? Es kann sein: aber es liegt doch Wahrheit zum Grunde. Aber das ist gewis keine, daß es mir Himmels Gefühl giebt, von guten Seelen geliebt zu werden; Personen zu wißen, die Antheil, lebhaften, innigen, warmen, steten Antheil an mir nehmen. Seit ich Ihr Herz näher kenne, empfinde ich dies Gefühl in aller seiner Fülle. Urtheilen Sie, mit welchen Empfindungen diesen Brief schließt . . . Ihr dankbarer Freund" (*G* 3.1: 27).

9. "Ich . . . bin so ganz in der Sphäre gewesen, wo mir's wohl ist; in der, einer starken, mannigfaltigen, angestrengten Beschäftigung. Hätte ich die Lüken dieser Geschäfte mit Ihrem süßen Umgange ausfüllen können; hätte ich mit Ihnen, edle, gleichgestimmte Seele, laut empfinden, und denken können, was ich gröstentheils im Innern meiner Seele verschließen muste, diese Tage wären beneidenswerth gewesen" (*G* 3.1: 29).

10. "Wie ungern trenne ich mich von diesem Papiere. Wie gern legte ich noch einen, oder auch wohl zwei Bogen an, aber ich kann nun nichts mehr meinen Geschäften abstehlen. Ihnen, die Sie mich in allem beschämen—ich sage das mit innigem Gefühl, daß es wahr ist, und mit Schmerz, daß ich's nicht ändern kann, daß ich leider! nach Ihrer Bestimmung, ein *männliches Geschöpf* bin, das, besonders jezt, den Kopf immer voll hat, immer voll Projekte, u. Pläne, in einer beständigen Unruhe ist—Ihnen ist's vorbehalten, mich auch im Briefschreiben zu übertreffen—schwerlich aber in den Empfindungen, mit denen ich bin Ihr wärmster Freund" (*G* 3.1: 29).

11. "denn ich habe mich schon gewöhnt, keinen Unterschied zwischen Ihrem, und meinem Ich zu machen; alle Liebenswürdigkeiten, und Tugenden, die ich Ihnen entdeke, als mein Eigenthum anzusehen; mich so darüber zu freuen, als ob ich selbst es sei, der sie hätte" (*G* 3.1: 34).

12. "es ist immer eine gewagte Sache, sich zu verheirathen, ohne ein Amt zu haben; und endlich fühle ich zu viel Kraft und Trieb in mir, um mir durch eine Verheirathung gleichsam die Flügel abzuschneiden, mich in ein Joch zu feßeln, von dem ich nie wieder loskommen kann, und mich nun so gutwillig zu entschließen, mein Leben, als ein Alltags Mensch vollends zu verleben" (*G* 3.1: 77).

13. "Ich hatte mich nämlich durch eine Veranlassung, die ein bloßes Ohngefähr schien, ganz dem Studium der Kantischen Philosophie hingegeben; einer Philosophie, welche die Einbildungskraft, die bei mir immer sehr mächtig war, zähmt, dem Verstande das Uebergewicht, und dem ganzen Geiste eine unbegreifliche Erhebung über alle irdische Dinge giebt. Ich habe eine edlere Moral angenommen, und anstatt mich mit Dingen außer mir zu beschäftigen, mich mehr mit mir selbst beschäftigt. Dies hat mir eine Ruhe gegeben, die ich noch nie empfunden; ich habe bei einer schwankenden äußern Lage meine seligsten Tage verlebt" (*G* 3.1: 64).

14. "Da ich das außer mir nicht ändern konnte, so beschloß ich das in mir zu ändern. Ich warf mich in die Philosophie" (*G* 3.1: 70a).

15. "Zwey unglükliche Poosttage sind wieder gewesen, und ich habe keine Briefe von meinem Fichte; wie mir dann allemahl zu Muthe wird, kann ich nicht beschreiben; wenn Du das so recht wüßtest, ich weiß gewis, Dein gutes Herz, könnte mich nicht so leiden sehn: daß Du in Jena schon seit mehr als 8: Tagen bist, ist gewis, denn heute haben wir den 26: Zwey Briefe von mir wirst Du Bester empfangen haben"; "Ich bitte Dich Bester, Theurster! schreib mir doch aus Erbarmen alle 12 Tage, damit ich doch nicht völlig 2: Wochen auf Deine Briefe harren müße, denn Du kannst Dirs nicht vorstellen was ich leide; und wenn Du keine Zeit hast, so schreib mir nur mit 2: Worten, ich bin gesund, vergnügt, und Liebe Dich noch. Habe Mitleiden mit mir Theurster"; "Du zukst vielleicht die Achseln mein Bester, und denkst, ja das arme Kind hat eben auch wenig Kräfte; aber berechne auch wie viel Kräfte es braucht, um diese unausstehliche Trennung auszuhalten. O ich beschwöre Dich, schreib mir doch alle 8: Tage, wie Dus mir in Deinem Theuren Brief versprichts" (*G* 3.2: 203).

16. "Ohnerachtet ich keine Zeit habe, so schreibe ich Dir doch, um Dir es unmöglich zu machen, wieder so zu klagen. Wir sind ja vom Anfange an, nicht so übereingekommen, daß ich Dir alle 8. Tage schreiben solle; sondern so wie ich könne. Ich habe aber öfter geschrieben, als ich versprochen hatte; und nun habe ich diesen Dank?—Das ist nicht recht, und billig. Es ist Dir gar nicht unbekannt, daß unter allen möglichen Dingen in der Welt nichts mir ungelegner ist, als unbillige, und unnöthige Klagen.—Du hast überdem keinen Brief eben darum bekommen, weil Du damals auch geklagt hattest, und ich bereite Dich hierdurch nochmals vor, den Posttag, wo Du wieder klagst, sicher keine Briefe zu bekommen. Es ist zu Deiner eignen Befestigung nöthig, daß ich es so halte" (*G* 3.2: 218).

17. "Vom Speculiren ermüdet, wende ich mich zu Dir, um ein wenig mit Dir zu plaudern.... Ich sage, vom Speculiren ermüdet; denn auf andere Zeit rechne nur nicht. Mein Tagewerk, das Geschäft meines Lebens ... ist mir das erste" (*G* 3.2: 226).

18. "laß mich ... zwar Vorstellungen über *meine Depensen, Oekonomie,*—oder über *mein sittliches Betragen in der Welt*—oder über die *Rechtschaffenheit meines Charakters*, diese laß mich von Dir hören, denn Du bist mein Weib, und ein braves biederes Weib—aber über meine *öffentlichen* Verhandlungen, über mein *Verhältniß zum Publikum*, zur *Universität*, zur *teutschen Litteratur* laß mich von Dir nichts hören; denn Du bist kein Mann, und hiermit Gott befohlen" (*G* 3.2: 306).

19. "Du theurster Engel! wie gütig bist Du; am Sonnabend ein Brief, am Mitwochen drauf einer; ich möchte Dir vor Freuden die Füße küßen, Du Guter" (*G* 3.2: 223).

20. "Wenn Dir Theurster die Tischgesellschaft, die mindeste Freude machen kann, so sey doch versichert, daß wenn sie mir auch wirklich viel Müh verursachte, ichs gewis gerne thäte; und daß wenn schon die Küche nie meine Liebhaberey gewesen ist, noch werden kann, so thu ich gern alles was mein Fichte gerne sieht; und dieses gielt für immer, nicht nur in Absicht der Küche" (*G* 3.2: 217).

Works Cited

Becker-Cantarino, Barbara. *Der lange Weg zur Mündigkeit: Frauen und Literatur in Deutschland von 1500 bis 1800.* Stuttgart: Metzler, 1987.

Fichte, Johann Gottlieb. *Gesamtausgabe der Bayerischen Akademie der Wissen-schaften.* Ed. Reinhard Lauth and Hans Jacob. 4 vols. to date. Stuttgart: Frommann, 1962- . Cited as "*G.*"

————. *The Science of Ethics as Based on the Science of Knowledge.* Trans. A. E. Kroeger. London: Trübner, 1907. Cited as "*SE.*"

————. *The Science of Knowledge.* Trans. Peter Heath and John Lachs. Cambridge: Cambridge UP, 1982. Cited as "*SK.*"

————. *The Science of Rights.* Trans. A. E. Kroeger. London: Trübner, 1889. 391-469. Cited as "*SR.*"

Frevert, Ute. "Bürgerliche Meisterdenker und das Geschlechterverhältnis." *Bürgerinnen und Bürger: Geschlechterverhältnisse im 19. Jahrhundert.* Ed. Ute Frevert. Göttingen: Vandenhoeck & Ruprecht, 1988. 17-48.

Hausen, Karin. "Family and Role-Division: The Polarisation of Sexual Stereotypes in the Nineteenth Century—An Aspect of the Dissociation of Work and Family Life." *The German Family: Essays on the Social History of the Family in Nineteenth- and Twentieth-Century Germany.* Ed. Richard J. Evans and W. R. Lee. Totowa, N.J.: Barnes & Noble, 1981. 51-83.

Jacobs, Wilhelm G. *Johann Gottlieb Fichte.* Reinbek: Rowohlt, 1984.

Kammerlander, Ilse. *Johanne Fichte: Ein Frauenschicksal der deutschen Klassik.* Stuttgart: Kohlhammer, 1969.

Kafka, Gustav. "Erlebnis und Theorie in Fichtes Lehre vom Verhältnis der Geschlechter: Eine charakterologische Studie." *Zeitschrift für angewandte Psychologie* 16 (1920): 1-24.

Kant, Immanuel. *Lectures on Ethics.* Trans. Louis Infield. New York: Harper & Row, 1963.

PART FOUR

Power and the Other

Dialectics and Colonialism:
The Underside of the Enlightenment[1]

Susanne Zantop

> The very basic antithesis between Old World and
> New World, the root of all those other single
> antitheses, has no existence outside the schemes of
> an impassioned and systematizing abstract and
> polemic mentality, directed now against the Old
> World, now against the New.
> —Antonello Gerbi, *The Dispute of
> the New World*, 1955

IN 1768, THE DUTCH CANON Cornelius de Pauw, protegé of Frederick II, published in Berlin his *Philosophical Investigations on the Americans* (*Recherches philosophiques sur les Américains, ou Mémoires intéressants pour servir à l'Histoire de l'Espèce humaine*).[2] This polemical two-volume treatise, which was immediately translated into German, generated a major intellectual controversy. Within less than three years, a barrage of philosophical position papers, of refutations and defenses, appeared in the Prussian capital: The royal librarian and abbé Antoine Pernety rebutted de Pauw passionately before the Berlin Academy (1769) and before the general public (1770) in his *Dissertation sur l'Amérique et les Américains contre les Recherches philosophiques de Mr. de P****; three months later, de Pauw countered, no less cuttingly, with a *Défense des Recherches philosophiques* (1770). Within a year, Pernety had renewed his attack—this time with a two-volume in-depth examination of all pertinent issues—while, at about the same time, a third, anonymous philosopher, "Le Philosophe la Douceur" (presumably Zacharie de Pazzi de Bonneville), entered the polemic with a small pamphlet that, somewhat tongue-in-cheek, took issue with both parties. The various treatises were re-worked and published over and over again, year after year, alone or in conjunction, while the press commented, elaborated, and took sides.[3]

The debate, which focused on the nature of the Amerindians—whether they were degenerate, weak, impotent, dumb, and thus inferior to the Europeans, as de Pauw maintained, or potent "rustic philosophers," equal if not superior to their European counterparts, as Pernety and Bonneville claimed—had a major impact on the discussion of difference, not just in Germany, but all over Europe and even beyond.[4] Although neither de Pauw nor Pernety nor, for that matter, Bonneville were Germans, in the minds of sympathizers and detractors alike their positions became identified with the locale of the debate, Berlin, or rather, with a specifically "Prussian" attempt at establishing intellectual hegemony.[5]

Significantly, neither de Pauw nor Pernety had much first-hand knowledge of the New World and its inhabitants. In fact, while Pernety could at least claim to have made some personal contacts with natives when he landed at Brazilian ports on his way to the Falkland Islands in 1763-64, de Pauw had never even set foot on the new continent. Yet despite the many learned, even impassioned refutations based on personal observation, de Pauw emerged as the winner of the controversy. The public preferred his project—the supposedly systematic, "philosophical" search for "truth"—over Pernety's lengthy presentations of "evidence." It noted with relief that rather than adding one more eyewitness report to the hundreds already inundating the book market, de Pauw was out to create order from the chaos of contradictory information on the New World.[6] Furthermore, while they might disagree on single points, most "enlightened" readers enjoyed de Pauw's "amusing violence" (Church 184), his bold asides against cruel Spaniards, fanatic Jesuits and their idealized depictions of savages. And they certainly shared his fascination with the supposed sexual "aberrations" of the natives (Gerbi 52, Honour 131). As far as a popular appeal was concerned, Pernety's pedantically erudite examinations could not compete with de Pauw's racy, at times shockingly "scabrous" (Gerbi) texts.

It is surprising, however, to note the extent of de Pauw's appeal among the intellectuals of his time, particularly in Germany, England, and France. Not only was he asked by Diderot to compose an article on the Americas for the *Supplément* to the *Encyclopédie* (1776/77), but after 1770, every philosopher, writer or even natural scientist attempting to classify or describe the indigenous peoples of the New World felt compelled to engage in de Pauw's arguments, either explicitly or implicitly—from Raynal and Robertson to Herder, Wieland, Kant, Blu-

menbach or Alexander von Humboldt, to name just the most prominent ones. As Antonello Gerbi has documented (417ff.), there are
echoes of the debate as late as 1821, in Hegel's dismissive remarks
about the New World in his lectures on universal history. Indeed, the
two positions, de Pauw's and, by implication, Pernety's, acquired the
status of paradigms in European colonial thinking. By providing both a
conceptual and linguistic framework for demarcating otherness and a
rationale and justification for colonial incorporation, they set up a
dialectics that in subtle and not so subtle ways prepared the stage for
colonial expansion in the late nineteenth century—even for those
nations that, like Germany, had hitherto refrained from claiming their
"place in the sun."

What made de Pauw's provocative, even offensive theories so attractive to Western European, and particularly to German "philosophers"? Certainly not just the fact that they were couched in skeptic
Enlightenment jargon and proposed, at least on the surface, a questioning of accepted beliefs; and certainly not because de Pauw's
"imaginary world" approximated American "reality" any more closely
than Pernety's[7]—the falseness of most of his allegations and gener-
alizations was obvious to anyone who had had a chance to travel in
America and see for him- or herself. The attractiveness of de Pauw's
system, I believe, had deeper reasons; it had to do with what has been
described as a European identity crisis in the second half of the eighteenth century, as the emerging bourgeoisie was trying to set up its own
patriarchal rule by defining itself vis-à-vis internal and external others.
As I want to propose, de Pauw selected handed-down observations and
popular (mis)conceptions about otherness and constructed them into a
seemingly coherent American reality that not only explained and
atoned for the history of conquest but also provided the parameters for
a new identity of the European male—that of "natural man" as "natural colonizer."

I. "Natural Men" and "Natural Man"

According to de Pauw, the discovery and conquest divided the
world into two parts, into the Eastern and the Western hemispheres,
into Old and New Worlds. This dichotomy—a reduction of the former
four-part division of the cosmos—forms the basis for a series of further
oppositions, and for their peculiarly alluring and threatening asym-
metry. As he writes in the Introduction to his *Recherches philosophiques*:

> No event in human history is more noteworthy than the Discovery of Amer-
> ica. If one goes back from present times to those of the remotest past, no sin-

gle event can be compared to this one;   and it is no doubt a great and awful
spectacle to see one half of the globe so much hated by nature that everything
there is degenerate or monstrous.

Which natural scientist of antiquity would have suspected that one and the
same planet might have two such different hemispheres, one of which would be
overcome, subjected, devoured by the other, as soon as it was discovered after
centuries lost in darkness and the abyss of time?

This surprising change [*révolution*], which transformed the face of the earth
and the fortune of nations, happened very fast, because, for some unbelievable
fatality, there existed no equilibrium between the attack and the defense. All
power and all injustice were on the side of the Europeans: the Americans had
nothing but weakness; and were therefore bound to be destroyed, destroyed in
one instant.

Whether it was due to an unhappy connection of our destinies, or the necessary consequence of so many vices and shortcomings [*fautes*—trans. as *Mängel*],
this infamous and unjust conquest of the New World is certainly the greatest
misfortune humanity has suffered.

After the cruel victor had quickly murdered several million savages, he was
visited by an epidemic disease, which by attacking at once the origins of life
and the sources of procreation, soon became the scourge of the inhabited
earth. Man, already weighed down with the burden of his existence, found, to
top his misfortune, the germs of death in the arms of pleasure and in the
bosom of delight: he believed that enraged nature herself had vowed his ruin.
(iii-v)[8]

In de Pauw's analysis, the Old World and the New are characterized by
the opposition of strong versus weak, healthy versus diseased;   what
looked like an imbalance and injustice at first—the conquest, subjugation, and appropriation of the New World by the Old—is, however, off-
set by "nature's revenge," syphilis, which the conquistadors supposedly
contracted in the New World and which has wrought havoc on the
Old.[9]

De Pauw clearly argues on two levels. While he overtly denounces
the brutality of the conquistadors, he covertly blames the annihilation
of the indigenous peoples on fate, or rather, on nature: because of their
physical inferiority, the "savages" *were bound* to be destroyed [devoient
donc être exterminés]. Furthermore, on a moral plane, the natives' legacy, the deadly disease with which they contaminated the foreign in-
truders, far outweighs the harm these inflicted on them: in a curious
twist, the conquerors become generic "man" who is not only weighed
down by the burden of existence but punished for indulging in innocent
pleasures. So while de Pauw strongly condemns the destruction of the
New World by the Old, he undercuts his verdict by suggesting that this
"natural" process was inevitable, and that excessive punishment has
already more than atoned for the infraction. The tropes, "les bras de
plaisir," "le sein de la juissance," reproduce the *massacre* of the native
warriors verbally as they reduce the *sauvages* to their body parts (an act

of "cannibalistic" dismemberment through language) and feminize them, eliminating indigenous males altogether from the discourse. What we end up with in this passage, and in de Pauw's American "reality," are male conquerors and female savages, locked in deadly embrace.

The links between conquest and pleasure, and disease, disease and femininity, femininity and conquest suggested in these introductory remarks circumscribe de Pauw's whole philosophical project. In fact, all of his further "investigations" are explorations of, and variations on the very same theme. His circular reasoning both prescribes the terms of the debate and frames the argument, setting up a trap from which Pernety and his other critics are unable to escape.

As de Pauw subsequently argues in his *Recherches*, the physical weakness of the "savages"—which caused their defeat—is a sign of degeneration produced by the American environment, the wet, swampy soils and moist airs of this continent that only recently emerged from the floods (1: 4-6; 23-28, 105). As proof for his theory of degeneracy (adopted from Buffon[10]), de Pauw claims that the humid, putrid habitat, this "venereal sourdough" (1: 23), not only corrupted the natives, but also contaminates and weakens foreign settlers, plants and animals, all of which lose their power to procreate after having been transplanted to the New World (1: 28). Weakness, degeneracy, corruption are, however, not just characteristics of the body; they affect the mind, the whole moral fabric as well. The natives are, as de Pauw says in one chapter devoted exclusively to the "génie abruti des Américains" (book 5, ch.1), indigent and stupid (1: 122); they are not only physically impotent, but lack intellectual force, "genius" (1: 44). And their weakness makes them resort to the typical weapons of the weak: to lies, treachery, and wanton cruelty (1: 45).

De Pauw goes on to claim that in this and all other respects the natives are not only similar to, but identical to (and occasionally worse than, 43) women. Linking women and "savages" is, of course, not new. Yet while the traditional association between natives and women had been metaphorical or metonymical—the female stood for the not-quite-human (Sepúlveda) or for the alluring territory to be possessed and exploited (Vespucci)—de Pauw now attempts to provide a solid "scientific," that is, biological foundation for the analogy.[11] Significantly, he resorts to the theory of the four humors prevalent among the ancients, a theory that although on the wane among eighteenth-century scientists, continued to serve the general public as indicator of gender difference.[12] De Pauw revives these traditional conceptual principles— according to which both "the west" and women (the female "temperament") were distinguished from the east and men by their moist, cold humors—and translates them into geographic and physiological "fact" based on "evidence": while Western nature "proves" its inferiority by its cold swampiness, he says, ultimate and conclusive proof for the native men's effeminacy and clammy, phlegmatic disposition is their lack of facial hair:

> I know very well that in the attempt to explain why there is no hair on the body of the Americans, people have resorted to all kinds of subtleties which can and never will be considered valid causes. . . . We, however, want to show that lack of hair stems from the moist constitution of their bodies, and that they are beardless for the same reasons that women in Europe and other parts of the world are beardless: their skin is bare because they have an extremely cold temperament. (1.1: 38)[13]

De Pauw's systematic emasculation/femininization of the natives forms part of his strategy of "naturalizing" the conquest. Since neither sexual organs nor anatomy can explain the profound difference between European and American natives, and validate the supposed superiority of the former, the beard becomes *the* natural sign for "virility," that is, maturity, strength, wisdom, and potency. Beardlessness makes the natives "naturally" inferior to the bearded conquerors, a hierarchy which, according to de Pauw, they immediately recognized and accepted:

> When these Americans saw for the first time the Spaniards with their long beards, they lost all courage: *for how could we resist, they cried, men who have hair in their faces and who are so strong that they lift up burdens we cannot even move?* (3: 16)[14]

It is thus not the Spaniards' superior war technology, nor their conquering drive, cunning, or brutality, nor differences in cosmologies that brought about the defeat of the natives: the Indians were overwhelmed by the mere sight of "natural superiority":

> The fashion which the Spaniards, and all Europeans in general, then had, namely to grow their beards, *would have alone sufficed to facilitate the conquest of America*: for the Indians could not stand the sight of bearded men, nor of dogs nor horses. (*Défense* 3: 48-49; my emphasis).[15]

The Conquest, in de Pauw's construct, is therefore not so much a natural takeover as a natural surrender: by law of nature, the weaker, the effeminate, the naturally inferior surrenders to the stronger, more virile, naturally superior. To affirm the native's emasculation is to assert the conqueror's superior masculinity, and vice versa.

"Natural surrender" also extends to the native women, albeit with different connotations. According to de Pauw, the Indian men's physical and spiritual impotence translated into lack of passion for the opposite sex (1: 42), with all its dire social and economic consequences:

infertility, depopulation, a surplus of female offspring, and uncommonly high incidences of homosexuality (1: 63-69). No wonder then that Indians (of both sexes, as the German translation of the *Recherches* suggests)[16] greeted the arrival of the Europeans with glee, since the potent conquistadors relieved the men of their burdensome marital duties, and provided diversion for their frustrated mates:

> Be it as it may, all narratives agree that the Indian women were exceedingly pleased at the arrival of the Europeans who—because of their sexual prowess, compared to that of the natives—resembled satyrs. If this strange paradox were not proven by a multiplicity of facts, one would not believe that they would have been able to surrender themselves willingly to the barbaric companions of the Pizarros and the Cortezes, who but marched over dead bodies, who had acquired the hearts of tigers and whose greedy hands were dripping with blood. Despite all the good reasons they had to hate those cruel people, the three hundred wives of the Inca Atabaliba [Atahualpa] who were taken prisoner with him at the battle of Caxamalca [Cajamarca], threw themselves at the feet of the victor, and the morning thereafter more than five thousand American women came to the Spaniards' camp and *surrendered voluntarily*, while the unfortunate remains of their vanquished nation escaped more than forty miles into the woods and deserts. (1: 69-70; my emphasis)[17]

Not only did the women voluntarily surrender, but, according to de Pauw's duplicitous text (which relies on Vespucci and countless other prophets of "Malinchismo"), they were more than willing to betray their men and "serve" the conquerors in whatever capacity they could:

> Thus it is certain that the Spaniards found in them an unexpected eagerness and attachment: they served as interpreters and guides in all the expeditions that were undertaken against their fatherland and rendered great services to all the Conquerors who were the first to penetrate the islands and the main land. (1: 70)[18]

In Vespucci/de Pauw's fantasy, the conquerors' violent penetration of "virgin" territory—"terre ferme," of course, associates *terra firma,* the continent, with "terre fermée," the closed land—is achieved by mutual consent. Or rather, the conquest is the result of an act of seduction: the native women, more in agreement with the Europeans' interests than the Europeans themselves ("plus portées pour les intérêts des Européens qu'ils ne l'étoient eux-mêmes," 70), surrender their bodies/ territory to the more potent male, while their de-natured mates disappear into the wilderness. De Pauw's recourse to gender to mark the difference between Old World and New is thus not only a strategy to explain the lack of resistance among native men or the surrender of the women: It provides a vocabulary for the articulation of desire—not the desire of the self for the other, as in traditional conquest narratives, but the desire of the other for the self, the irresistibly virile European, that is, the real "natural man."

II. "Natural Philosophers" as "Natural Colonizers"

As de Pauw's account stresses over and over again, the New World is a place of disorder and deviancy. Not only are the native men hairless "like eunuchs" (1: 145), impotent, and prone to homosexuality, but their "irregularity" also extends to the size of their genitals (1: 37)[19] and to the "fact" that they are lactiferous (1: 42). Not only do native women not suffer during childbirth, but they rarely menstruate, lactate excessively (1: 55), are frequently infertile, and sexually so voracious that they have to resort to "sex aids" to arouse their tepid husbands (1: 38). Indeed, in their sexual indeterminacy, that is, in their transgression of what de Pauw considers the boundaries of nature, native women and men coincide. "The more savage a people," de Pauw concludes, "the more the women resemble the men; & particularly in America, where men are beardless." And he adds, regretfully (?): "The beautiful sex thus does not exist here" ("Il n'y a donc pas là de beau sexe," 3: 19-20).

"Disorder" is not limited to human nature, it extends to nature itself. The sexual indeterminacy of the human beings corresponds to the indeterminacy of the American soil, its abundant swamps, its threatening bogs, where boundaries are lost, human traces effaced, and men who venture into the wilderness devoured and annihilated. Literally and metaphorically, then, degenerate men and women occupied an ill-defined, untidy, disorderly, and potentially dangerous space "in-between"—until the conquistadors arrived on the scene to "clean up":

> Thus was the state of affairs in America when the Spaniards, to complete the country's misfortune, landed there: they greedily exploited the *disorder of the Indians* as legitimate pretext to destroy them. (1: 66; my emphasis)[20]

In this configuration, the tasks of the conqueror and those of the colonizer are analogous, if not alike: whereas the virile conquistador had reestablished a natural, that is, phallocentric order by destroying or dispersing the effeminate men and by putting mannish women in their "natural place,"[21] the colonizer, ever since, has been creating order out of chaos by drying up swamps, cutting down jungles, and "taming an unyielding earth" ("domter une terre ingrate," 1: 113)[22]. The verbs with which de Pauw characterizes this domesticating endeavor, "éclaircir" (to open up), "purger" (to purge), "diriger" (to direct), "saigner" (to cure), "défricher" (to clear; 3: 13) belong to the material and literal as well as to the spiritual and figurative realm. Creating civilization is defined as both destructive, violent, and as constructive, healing; it implies the elimination, the cutting down of "wild growth" and the construction of a new "healthy" order by erecting clearly defined boundaries.

Despite his overt condemnation of the violence employed by the Spanish conquistadors, which places him, according to Manfred Tietz (991-93), squarely with other Enlightenment humanitarian thinkers, de Pauw is in complete agreement with the conquering/colonizing/ordering project itself. In fact, he himself partakes of it: his own treatise is an attempt to cut through popular myths, through the monstrosities associated with the New World, and to contain or tame the monsters in order to reorganize America as an orderly, rational universe. Thus, after constructing pre-colonial American reality in terms of degeneracy, disorder, and disease, he goes on to refute or explain all those New World myths that have survived the Age of Reason: the Patagon giants are figments of the mind of simple sailors (1: 281-326); the "blafards" or white negroes are not a race of monsters, but a small group of diseased individuals (2: 5-46); the existence of the so-called Florida hermaphrodites is unconfirmed and unlikely—they are probably women with oversized genitals or men wearing women's clothes as outward sign of their slave condition (2: 88-9); the famous "acéphales" or headless men whom Lafitau still included among his peoples of the Americas (*Moeurs des sauvages amériquains*, 1724) are in fact human beings deformed by the natives' monstrous habit of shaping their infants' heads or limbs (1: 152-53); cannibals, although they once existed everywhere on the globe, are far fewer now and less ferocious than purported (1: 207-23); and Amazon republics are highly improbable, since the concept of a republic run entirely by women is contrary to nature and to logic:

> Even if one had found a sufficiently large number of discontent women to form a whole republic, one would still not have more than a small part of a society able to survive on its own: the difficulty would reside in finding men stupid enough to allow themselves to be forced against their will to impregnate women who would chase them away as soon as the generative task was achieved. ... In the imagination, this is as possible as Plato's Republic or as that of Thomas More; but if one wants to use some judgment and reflection, the whole edifice collapses, and all that remains are absurdities that revolt against, or annihilate Nature. It is totally contradictory to assume that a woman would have a violent aversion against men and would still consent to become a mother; it would be monstrous if a mother smothered or abandoned her children, under pretext that these children aren't daughters. Is it so easy after this to assemble twenty or thirty thousand insane, murderous warrior women? The character of the most tender, the most compliant, and yes, if one wants, the least wicked sex, could it forget itself so much to commit regularly and by common agreement crimes that are only rarely committed by individuals moved by rage and despair? (1: 107-08)[23]

In de Pauw's logic, motherhood and violence are incompatible. It is inconceivable that a true mother could kill children of a particular sex for social or political reasons, particularly if they are male. In his eagerness to declare the undesirable impossible, de Pauw relates the myth of a powerful, independent women's republic back to actually existing women's societies, restrictive religious orders (1: 113), thus containing the fantasy of amazonic self-determination behind the walls of the convent.

All of de Pauw's "investigations" are characterized by his desire to dispel myths, to reduce them to natural causes or origins, and to domesticate them by including them into rational discourse. There are no hairy "wild men," no headless or one-breasted monsters; there is no alterity unaccounted for in the analysis and narrative of the European *philosophe*. Everything strange or unexplainable that early travellers encoded in monstrous form is reduced to the familiar. Monstrosity is no longer that which is completely "other"; rather, it is defined as the deviation from the familiar—that is, the European—norm: olive-skinned men who are exceedingly small, such as the Eskimos ("avor-tons," 1: 259), beardless, long-haired men who behave like women (2: 92), and women who refuse to be wives and mothers—these are the *monstres* of the enlightened eighteenth century.

By "conquering" and domesticating the last vestiges of monstrosity, the philosopher/armchair-conquistador incorporates and assimilates the unfamiliar. The fears and obsessions formerly exteriorized in monsters are re-internalized to become (again?) an integral part of his own culture. As icons of transgression, excess, or abnormality, cannibals, giants, amazons, and headless men (or headless bodies) make their re-entry into the European subconscious, whence they emerge to designate all that is threatening to the status quo.[24] As Antonello Gerbi, Peter Mason, and others have pointed out, the Europeanization of America thus goes hand in hand with an "Indianization" of the European imagination.

III. The Dialectics of Conquest and the "Indian Disease"

The "Indianization of Europe" (Mason 60), that is, the fear of contamination in the encounter with otherness, is at the core of the de Pauw-Pernety controversy. As de Pauw stresses the differences between Old World and New and Pernety the similarities, and as they attempt to emphasize their opposition to one another, they are thus engaged in what one might call a "double dialectics": the surface debate about the true nature of the Americans is, at the same time, a probing into the identity of the European male in his relationship to his various biological, social and political others. Since Pernety remains largely unaware of this double-layered project and multiple investment, he is unable to present a true challenge to de Pauw's seductive model of European superiority.

Despite attempts at presenting a more differentiated account of "the" native American, Pernety remains essentially caught in the dialectics de Pauw has set up. While the words with which Pernety characterizes his task—to clear up the chaos [débrouiller le cahos], to disperse the clouds of prejudice [dissiper les nuages du préjugé] in de Pauw's writings so that truth may triumph—echo de Pauw's Enlightenment project, Pernety's aim—to retain some of the "merveilleux," for example the Patagon giants—places him in the anti-enlightenment corner. De Pauw's construction of the New World as the negative in a series of binary oppositions continuously forces Pernety—who is out to prove that his New World is antithetical to de Pauw's—to adopt the positive pole. To contrast de Pauw's theory of degeneracy, Pernety must claim that nature has created its very "masterpieces" in the New World: the soils are fertile and bear abundant fruit (3: 35); the men are well-built, tall, enduring, healthy and live to an extremely old age (3: 46-48); their cultural level is in harmony with their physical needs (3: 95); their lack in so-called civilization is compensated by greater freedom and by a lack of those vices that accompany progress, such as ambition, vanity, and moral weakness (3: 95); in short, the New World is "paradise on earth" (3: 35). If de Pauw's theory of degeneracy required the absence of Patagon Giants, as Pernety suggested (3: 51), Pernety's depiction of the New World as somewhat larger than life clearly needed their presence.

The extent to which Pernety's evidence is controlled by dialectics becomes obvious when we turn to de Pauw's claim that the natives' effeminacy is evidenced by their beardlessness. As Pernety feels compelled to prove that the natives are in fact "real men," he insists that they do have facial hair—yet that they pluck it out for aesthetic reasons; and that they have secret knowledge on how to prevent beards from growing back (3: 120). De Pauw's association between beard and virility, between biological sign and cultural meaning is thus not questioned, but reaffirmed. Likewise, Pernety maintains that the native men are *not* indifferent to their wives, as de Pauw had claimed—on the contrary: Since the Indians build their relationships on free choice, there is no need for "that blind furor we call love" [cette fureur aveugle, que nous appellons amour]. Instead, the natives treat their partners with friendship and a tenderness, which, "although alive and lively, never carries them away ... to those excesses which love inspires in those who are possessed by it" (3: 82).[25] In every sense, the Indians are similar to the

Europeans, only better: more genuine, more trusting, less corrupted and oppressed.

On the surface, then, the two positions fall into the by now traditional dichotomy of the "ignoble" vs. the "noble savage," in which de Pauw assumes a Voltairean, Pernety a Rousseauian stance. Both clearly and repeatedly allude to this tradition: de Pauw when he refers to those who "pretended that . . . it is not the savages who are barbaric, but the civilized peoples" (3: 125), Pernety when he introduces his critique of de Pauw with a passionate indictment of the civilized world, "populated by men condemned to relentless work" (*Dissertation* 3: 15).[26] But beneath this purely academic exchange on distant peoples, questions on the relationship between sexuality and political power emerge that bear directly upon the situation in Europe.

In his article on de Pauw and Voltaire, Gisbert Beyerhaus called sexuality the "index fossil of [de Pauw's] folkloristic excavations" ("Leitfossil seiner folkloristischen Ausgrabungen," 476). Like other critics, he noted de Pauw's "almost Freudian" (Gerbi 52) obsession with "abnormal" sexual behavior, yet dismissed it, with no little embarrassment, as an indication of individual pathology, of interest only to the psychoanalyst, not the intellectual historian.[27] As I want to argue, however, de Pauw did not voice an individual obsession—"aberrations" were one important focus in most late eighteenth-century works of anthropology or natural history.[28] Instead, he partook of, and gave expression to what one might call an eighteenth-century social pathology that distinguished between sexuality, associated with chaos and disease, and "love," associated with order, restraint, and "normalcy."

As I have tried to show, in his attempt to define the other in the New World as inferior to the European self, de Pauw resorts to a conflation of gender, geography, and morality: natives and terrains of the New World are effeminate, treacherous, transgressive, in need of colonization (definition, demarcation, naming) by the superior male colonizer. By imposing a gender framework on the encounter between colonizer and colonized, and by grounding this gender structure in a particular biology, de Pauw renders the violent appropriation of the New World natural and inevitable, even desirable. However, the "desire" of taking possession is dampened by the association of sexual pleasure with fear of contamination: the conqueror risks contamination with syphilis; the colonizer may be infected with the disease of sloth in those infested swamps of otherness, he will degenerate and lose control, of himself and of his possessions, as happened to the Spaniards and Portuguese (3: 13). The remedy is either colonial abstention, which de Pauw at times advocates (1: vi), at times rejects, or "love:" man's exclusive libidinous fixation on one uncontaminated sexual object ("virgin territory"), which he colonizes, that is, appropriates, names, and renders productive.

By introducing heterosexual "love" as the driving force behind colonization, particularly in his response (*Défence*) to Pernety's critique (*Dissertation*), de Pauw is not celebrating sexual passion, as Beyerhaus suggests (476). Love, to de Pauw, is a means of establishing order. This function of love becomes clearer, when we link de Pauw's sexual-biological vision of conquest to his analysis of gender relations among the natives. Reiterating his main point that the "savages" are feeble in their passions and hence (pro-)creativity, de Pauw rejects Pernety's conclusion that the natives' sobriety has to do with free association of men and women and liberal "divorce" practices: "He [Pernety] obviously talked about morality when the physical was at stake" (3: 10).[29] Passion for the other sex, de Pauw claims, is "natural," it predates and is unaffected by social institutions like marriage and divorce. And since this "great principle of sociability is lacking or has been weakened in the minds of the savages, they fell only earlier into the dehumanization and disarray which entails all other possible disorders." And he exclaims: "How did he fail to see that love would have repaired all ills, and *that disorder is wherever love is not*?" (3: 19; my emphasis).[30]

Love and order, love of order, love and work, love of work go hand in hand (3: 230).[31] As de Pauw's colonizing "love" eliminates (sexual) indeterminacy by excluding sexually indifferent or "devious" native men and domesticating sexually promiscuous native women, it (re-) creates "natural order." One might say then that the matrimony between the Natural Man and the Natural Woman becomes the ultimate metaphor for the successful colonial encounter, and vice versa: the power relationship of colonizer to colonized becomes the model for a successful matrimony.

Clearly, de Pauw is not only speaking about the New World here—he is using the New to speak about the Old. Nor is he only providing a model for colonial relations within the family or within the family of nations: in their indolence, effeminacy, and their love of carefree living, the degenerate savages are but the vanguard [que plus avant] of a disease that might contaminate and corrupt individual European states at their very core—if it has not done so already.

Again, "hair," that principle indicator of "irregularity" in the body of the "savages" (Pauw, *Supplément* 345), provides the link between sexuality, power, and (social) disease within the body politic. As I have mentioned before, "hair," or rather its presence on the head and its absence on the chin, is, for de Pauw, the main evidence for the natives' effeminacy. In de Pauw's conceptual universe, hairlessness does not distinguish man from animal, as Blumenbach has argued (88), or civilized man from wild man—it is above all a sexual characteristic: the presence or absence of a beard draws a sharp line between men and women and between true masculinity and true femininity. The beard becomes thus the "natural" indicator of one's place within the social hierarchy. In the words of Karl Gottlob Schelle, the eighteenth-century cultural historian: "This beard . . . reveals to the women the intentions of nature; it teaches them humility, submission, and obedience" (50).

There is, however, a very different association between hair and power at work in de Pauw's argument. From the seventeenth century onward, European aristocrats were not only clean shaven, but wore increasingly bigger and more elaborate wigs, veritable lion's manes, depending on social status and wealth, while aristocratic women wore headdresses over two feet in height, decorated with feathers, flowers, and beads[32]—à l'Américaine, as Pernety suggested when he wrote in defense of the natives' fashions: "In all our countries we see men and women enjoying the beauty of their finery, who wear plumes on their head like the savages and, since they have to dress, approximating as much as possible the taste of the Americans" (3: 118).[33] In eighteenth-century high society, as Max von Böhn reminds us (193), beards were considered *déclassé*; only actors representing murderers or highwaymen were expected to wear a moustache. While beardlessness and voluminous head hair were thus associated with class and power in the eyes of those who had class and power, in the eyes of the emerging bourgeois public they had a different connotation: they became the symbols of the leisure, excess, luxury, degeneracy and "effeminacy" of the aristocracy.

The links between hair, power, and disease were stressed by the fact that the wig had been introduced in the sixteenth and seventeenth centuries simultaneous with the epidemic spread of syphilis, the "Indian disease" ("Indianische Krankheit"), as it was also known (Zedler 46: 1718). In fact, medical or cultural historians of the time, such as Friedrich Nicolai, associated the wig fashion with the sexual profligacy of the aristocracy, with the need to cover one's balding, spotted head with false hair to simulate health and strength despite physical decline (66-77; see also Zedler 46: 1747). As another sign of social "disease" and degeneracy in the eyes of the critical public, aristocrats not only dressed and painted their faces like women—embodied in the fashion model of the *petit maître*—they also admitted powerful women into their ranks, as *maîtresses, salonnières*, and counselors.

By focusing on beardlessness as sign of physical and moral decay, de Pauw thus attacks not only the American natives, but implicitly the European upper class, the aristocracy (see Gerbi 45). The contamination of the conquerors by syphilitic natives alludes to a widespread "disease" among Europeans, particularly women, who are infested with aristocratic values and lifestyles. In the process of redefining "virility" as opposed to "effeminacy," de Pauw proposes as the new Natural Man the bourgeois *Kraftmensch*[34]—one not modelled after the hairless savages of the New World, but one who carries his natural attributes of power, his beard and natural hair, publicly, and who reestablishes the "natural" order everywhere—not only abroad, but also, and particularly, at home.

Pernety's political vision is no less anti-aristocratic than de Pauw's. He, too, attacks the "men dressed in gold and purple, whose indolence, comfortably stretched out on the divan, scoffs at the insults of the air [the inclemencies of the weather] under gold and blue wainscoting; and who open their eyes only to be dazzled by the splendor of the luxury that surrounds them, and who stretch out their hands only to reach for dainty dishes to arouse their muted appetites or to satisfy their sensuality, at the expense of the life and work of those men who moan under the burden of their cruel tyranny" (*Dissertation* 16).[35] Yet while de Pauw's alternative of a shift of power and control away from effeminate despots to new, "natural" rulers, could and did appear at once rational, logical, historical and therefore realistic, Pernety's (and eventually "Le philosophe la Douceur's") Edenic vision of a "free," non-hierarchical people roaming the wild was all too easily relegated to distant, utopian realms—the past, the world of ideas, the world of literature.

IV. Epilogue

For today's readers, it might seem easier to dismiss de Pauw and revindicate Pernety. De Pauw's peculiar mix of salacious facts with scandalous fictions, political theory with sexual fears, humanitarian concerns with racist innuendo, is intellectually dishonest and morally odious, whereas Pernety's verbose "mystical primitivism" (Gerbi 94) appears endearing. In fact, primitivism à la Pernety is celebrating a belated comeback in Kevin Costner's *Dances with Wolves* or Kirpatrick Sale's *The Conquest of Paradise*. Yet it is important, in my view, to dedicate one's critical attention especially to de Pauw, because his colonial fantasy, since it was not recognized as such, could continue to play such a powerful role in the European subconscious. De Pauw was not the "rationalist turning against rationalism," as Gerbi characterized him in 1955 (65). Instead, he was symptomatic of Enlightenment thought, which, in Horkheimer and Adorno's critique, turned "mythic terror" ("das mythische Grauen," 29) of the other—nature, the feminine, the irrational—into theories (and practices) of subjugation and domination, overseas and at home.

Herein lies de Pauw's special attraction for the Prussian monarch and for the Germans whose contact with the New World was, except for isolated instances, purely intellectual. De Pauw's association of the foreign with the familiar/familial, the global with the domestic, and love with possession, order, and control, carried a special appeal for Prussians involved in "cleaning up" their own house. Although it has been argued that de Pauw's negative depiction of the New World was designed to discourage Prussian colonizers from leaving their country,[36] I would maintain that de Pauw's whole project can be read as an invitation to colonial activity "on all fronts." Not only does he explicitly and repeatedly exempt Germans from any participation in, and guilt for, the conquest and subjugation of the New World (3: 151, 224), but he reiterates his conviction that man is made to tame, to domesticate the wild : unless this task is taken up, physical nature will degenerate and revert to its diseased chaotic state, at home and abroad.

> Nature has given man perfectibility to prevent the horrible disasters of which I have spoken, and which would undoubtedly befall us if our globe were only inhabited by savages. *But one single civilized people can prevent all these evils*; for one civilized people expands, establishes trading posts, sends colonizers, and constructs settlements: the Savages, on the other hand, don't colonize, because they themselves are some kind of errant colony that does not take root anywhere and is in constant battle with other vagabonds. (3: 254)[37]

The message to his Prussian/German readership is clear: if colonization can and should be done by one civilized people, by a nation not burdened with past colonial guilt, in which arts and sciences flourish (3: 157), by a people that fantasizes about its love for work and love for order, there is no reason why the Germans should not have a try at it, too.

Notes

    1. I wish to thank the John Carter Brown Library at Brown University and the Paul W. McQuillen Memorial Fund for supporting the research for this paper.
    2. For de Pauw's biography and an account of the controversy, see Church and Beyerhaus.
    3. See, for example, the reviews in the *Hallische Neue Gelehrte Zeitungen* 39 (May 15, 1769): 308-310; *Göttingische Anzeigen von gelehrten Sachen* 1 (1769): 1369-72; 2 (1771): 997-98, 1035-38, 1046-48, 1067-71, 1087; *Der teutsche Merkur* 4.2 (Nov. 1773): 178-91; 5.3 (March 1774): 259-86; 6.1 (April 1774): 57-75; 7.2 (August 1774): 228-51.
    4. See Gerbi, Church, Beyerhaus, Honour, and Tietz.
    5. See Carli, who in his *Lettere americane* attacked Pauw for writing "from the depths of a German province" and for thinking that "everything outside Breslau is barbaric and savage" (quoted in Gerbi 237).
    6. See, for example, the review in the *Hallische Neue Gelehrte Zeitungen* (note

3) which considers de Pauw's text the answer for all those looking for "something that would be more than a travelogue, something that would reconcile contradictions, refute lies, and examine reports in order to provide a reliable knowledge of that continent." Likewise, Immanuel Kant praised de Pauw's intellectual effort, "even if nine-tenth of his material is unsupported or incorrect" (*Reflexionen zur Anthropologie*, qtd. Gerbi 329). See also Church's more recent assessment: "Yet for all its lack of purity and conciseness, de Pauw's style is quite readable and entertaining, being saved largely by its amusing violence" (184).

7. I borrow the concept "imaginary worlds" from Peter Mason 15ff.

8. "Il n'y a pas d'événement plus mémorable parmi les hommes, que la Découverte de l'Amérique. En remontant des temps présents aux temps les plus reculés, il n'y a point d'événement qu'on puisse comparer à celui-là; & c'est sans doute un spectacle grand & terrible de voir une moitié de ce globe, tellement disgraciée par la nature, que tout y étoit ou dégénéré, ou monstrueux.

Quel Physicien de l'Antiquité eût jamais soupçonné qu'une même Planète avoit deux Hémisphères si différents, dont l'un seroit vaincu, subjugué, & comme englouti par l'autre, dès qu'il en seroit connu, après un laps de siècles qui se perdent dans la nuit & l'abyme des temps?

Cette étonnante révolution, qui changea la face de la terre & la fortune des Nations, fut absolument momentanée, parce que par une fatalité presqu'incroyable, il n'existoit aucun équilibre entre l'attaque & la défense. Toute la force & toute l'injustice étoient du côté des Européans: les Américains n'avoient que de la foiblesse; ils devoient donc être exterminés & exterminés dans un instant.

Soit que ce fût une combinaison funeste de nos destins, ou une suite nécessaire de tant de crimes & de tant de fautes, il est certain que la conquête du Nouveau Monde, si fameuse & si unjuste, a été le plus grand des malheurs que l'humanité ait essuyé.

Après le prompt massacre de quelques millions de Sauvages, l'atroce vainqueur se sentit atteint d'un mal épidémique, qui, en attaquant à la fois les principes de la vie & les sources de la génération, devint bientôt le plus horrible féau du monde habitable. L'homme, déjà accablé du fardeau de son existence, trouva, pour comble d'infortune, les germes de la mort entre les bras du plaisir, & au sein de la juissance: il se crut perdu sans ressource: il crut que la nature irritée avoit juré sa ruine." (All translations of the French originals are mine.)

9. For an assessment of the much-debated issue of syphilis see Crosby.

10. Buffon's theory of degeneracy had related to the flora and fauna exclusively; de Pauw extends it to include human beings. See Gerbi 3-31. Buffon was re-translated into German after de Pauw had given his theories new publicity.

11. In his Introduction, de Pauw alludes to his "naturalist" approach when he compares his interest in "aberrations in human nature" with the naturalist's fascination with, for example, the procreation among bisexual snails ("Zeugungsart der Schnecken").

12. For a discussion of the history of humoral theories see Schiebinger 161-87.

13. "Je n'ignore point qu'en voulant expliquer pourquoi le corps des Américains est entiérement (sic) dégarni de poil, on a eu recours à plusieurs subtilités qui ne sont & qui ne sauroient jamais être des raisons.... Nous ferons voir au contraire, que c'est l'effet de l'humidité de leur constitution, & qu'ils sont imberbes par la même raison que les femmes le sont en Europe, & dans les autres parties du monde: leur peau est chauve, parce que leur tempérament est extrêmement froid."

14. "Quand ces Américains virent pour la premiere fois des Espagnols à longue barbe, ils perdirent dès-lors le courage: *car comment pourrions-nous résister,*

s'écrierent-ils, à des hommes qui ont des cheveux dans le visage, & qui sont si robustes qu'ils soulèvent des fardeaux que nous ne saurions seulement remuer?"
    The next sentence, paradoxically, takes back the claim that the savages were visually overwhelmed—but de Pauw "punishes" them verbally for this oversight: "Les Péruviens parurent le moins épouvantés a la vue des Espagnols: ils crurent même qu'ils étoient lâches & efféminés, *mais ils se détrompèrent bientôt.*"
    15. "La mode qu'avoient alors les Espagnols & tous les Européans en général, de laisser croître leur barbe, eût seule suffi pour faciliter la conquête car les Indiens ne pouvoient supporter la vue, ni des hommes barbus, ni des chiens, ni des chevaux."
    16. In the German translation "Les Indiennes" become "die Indianer"—to the German readers the delight of both Indian men and women at the arrival of the Spaniards must have been obvious.
    17. "Quoi qu'il en soit, toutes les Relations conviennent que les Indiennes furent tellement charmées de l'arrivée des Européans, que leur lubricité faisoit ressembler à des satyres en comparaison des naturels. Si la multiplicité des faits ne prouvoit cette espèce de paradoxe, on ne croiroit pas qu'elles auroient pu se livrer, de bon coeur, aux barbares compagnons des Pizarres & des Cortez, qui ne marchoient que sur des cadavres, qui s'étoient fait des coeurs de Tigres, & dont les mains avares dégouttoient de sang. Malgré tant de motifs pour haïr ces hommes féroces, les trois cents épouses de l'Incas Atabaliba, qui furent prises avec lui, prostituèrent au vainqueur sur le champ de bataille de Caxamalca; & le lendemain plus de cinq mille femmes Américaines vinrent se rendre volontairement au camp des Espagnols, lorsque les malheureux restes de leur nation vaincue fuyoient à plus de quarante lieues dans des forêts & des solitudes."
    18. "Aussi est-il certain que les Espagnols trouvèrent en elles, un zèle & un attachement auquel ils n'auroient pas dû s'attendre: elles servirent d'interprêtes & de guides dans toutes les expéditions qu'on entreprenoit contre leur patrie, & rendirent de grands services à tous les Conquérants qui les premiers pénétrèrent dans les Isles & la terre ferme."
    19. De Pauw repeatedly points to the smallness of the natives' penises (metaphorically alluded to as "instrument") while only once he mentions their supposedly oversized testicles.
    20. "tel étoit l'état des choses en Amérique, lorsque pour comble d'infortune, les Espagnols y débarquèrent: ils se servirent avidement du *désordre des Indiens,* comme d'un prétexte légitime pour les anéantir."
    21. A similar process is described by Bernadette Bucher in her analysis of early iconography relating to the New World.
    22. "Ingrate" has, of course, many meanings—from thankless to unproductive, barren. I tried to combine various meanings, because the anthropomorphic underpinnings in de Pauw's discourse are evident.
    23. "Quand on auroit trouvé un nombre suffisant de femmes mécontentes pour en composer une République entière, on n'auroit encore que la moindre partie d'une société en état de subsister: la difficulté seroit de prendre des hommes assez poltrons pour se laisser contraindre à faire des enfants, malgré eux, à des femmes qui les chasseroient, dès que l'ouvrage de la génération seroit achevé. ... Dans l'imagination cela est aussi possible que la République de Platon, ou celle de Thomas Morus; mais si on en veut faire quelque usage du jugement & de la réflexion, tout cet édifice s'abyme, & il n'en reste que des absurdités qui révoltent la Nature, ou qui l'anéantissent. Il seroit contradictoire qu'une femme eût une aversion violente pour les hommes, & qu'elle consentît à la fois à devenir mère: ils seroit

monstrueux qu'une mère égorgeât ou exposât ses enfants, sous prétexte que ces enfants ne sont pas de filles. Est-il si aisé après cela de rassembler vingt à trente mille femmes insensées, homicides, & guerrières? Le caractère du sexe le plus doux, le plus compatissant, & enfin, si l'on veut, le moins méchant, pourroit-il se démentir jusqu'au point de commettre régulièrement d'un commun accord, & de sang froid, des crimes qui ne se commettent que rarement par quelques individus qu'agitent la rage & le désespoir?

24. See, for example, my essay "Crossing the Boundaries" in which I analyze how the fear of cannibals and raging "amazons" informs German revolutionary and anti-revolutionary discourse.

25. "quoique vive et animée, ne les entraîne jamais dans ces emportements, & ne les portent pas à ces excès que l'amour inspire à ceux qui en sont possédés."

26. "habité par des hommes condamnés à un travail sans relâche."

27. In addition to Beyerhaus, Church, and Gerbi, see Honour, who spoke of the "salacious tidbits on sexual malpractice," 131.

28. See, for example, the appendix in Buffon's *Allgemeine Naturgeschichte:* "Zur Beschreibung der unterschiedenen Arten von Menschen"; Blumenbach's "On the natural variety of mankind," 141-43, 253ff., 272-73, 313; or Wünsch's tenth conversation on the "difference of individual humans" in his *Unterhaltungen über den Menschen.*

29. On voit bien qu'il a parlé du moral, lorsqu'il s'agissoit du physique.

30. Ce grand principe de la sociabilité ayant manqué ou s'étant affoibli dans l'âme des Sauvages, ils n'en sont tombés que plus avant dans l'abrutissement & dans un désordre qui comprend en lui tous les désordres possibles.... Comment n'a-t-il pas vu que l'amour eût réparé tous ces maux, & *que le désordre est toujours là ou l'amour n'est point*?

31. Au reste, c'est un bonheur inestimable pour la plus grande partie de l'Europe, d'avoir des terres qu'il faut sans cesse cultiver: cela entretient, pour peu que le gouvernement ne soit pas excessivement mauvais, l'amour du travail, & non l'amour de l'oisiveté, l'amour de l'ordre, & non celui du brigandage.

32. See Woodforde 66.

33. On voit des hommes & des femmes dans tous nos Pays, trouver de la beauté dans leur parure, porter sur la tête des aigrettes de plumes, comme les Sauvages, & contraints de se vêtir, se rapprocher du goût des Américains, autant qu'il est possible.

34. See, for example, Eduard Fuchs, who contrasted the "Parasitenideal" of the aristocratic "Weibmann" with the new ideal of the "Kraftmensch," as it emerged during Romanticism (141f.). See also Schelle (x), who advocates the reintroduction of the beard as a natural sign of wisdom, maturity, and distinction between men and women. Earlier attempts to return to the ideal of "natural masculinity" are, for example, the Saxon sculptor Balthasar Permoser's treatise on beards of 1714 or the anonymous *Der Stutzer nach der Mode* (1765).

35. "Ces hommes vêtus d'or & de pourpre, dont l'indolence, mollement étendue sur le duvet, nargue les injures de l'air sous des lambris d'or & d'azur; qui n'ouvrent les yeux que pour être éblouis par l'éclat de luxe dont ils sont environnées, & ne tendent les mains qu' à des mêts apprêtés pour irriter leur appétit émoussé, ou pour satisfaire leur sensualité, aux dépens de la vie & du travail de ces hommes qui gémissent sous le poids de leur cruelle tyrannie."

36. Honour 131.

37. "La Nature a donc donné à l'homme la perfectibilité pour prevenir les horribles désastres dont je viens de parler, & qui seroient infaillibles si notre globe

n'étoit habité que par des Sauvages;   mais *un seul peuple police peut prévenir tous ces maux*;   car un peuple policé s'étend, fait des établissemens, envoye des colonies, & bâtit des villes: les Sauvages au contraire n'envoyent pas des colonies;   parcequ'ils sont eux-mêmes une espèce de colonie errante, qui ne se fixe nulle part, & qui se bat sans cesse contre d'autres vagabonds."

Works Cited

Beyerhaus, Gisbert. "Abbé de Pauw und Friedrich der Grosse, eine Abrechnung mit Voltaire." *Historische Zeitschrift* 134 (1926): 465-93.

Blumenbach, Johann Friedrich. *On the Natural Variety of Mankind* (De generis humani varietate nativa, 1775; 3rd ed., 1795). *The Anthropological Treatises.* Ed. and trans. Thomas Bendyshe. London: Longman, 1865.

Böhn, Max von. *Die Mode: Menschen und Moden im 18. Jahrhundert.* München: Bruckmann, 1963.

Bucher, Bernadette. *Icon and Conquest: A Structural Analysis of the Illustrations of de Bry's Great Voyages.* Trans. Basia Miller Gulati. Chicago: U of Chicago P, 1981.

Buffon, George-Louis Leclerc, comte de. *Herrn von Buffons allgemeine Naturgeschichte: Eine freye mit einigen Zusätzen vermehrte Übersetzung nach der neuesten französischen Ausgabe von 1769.* 7 vols. Trans. Martini. Berlin: Pauli, 1771-74. Appendix: *Zur Beschreibung der unterschiedenen Arten von Menschen.*

Church, Henry Ward. "Corneille de Pauw, and the Controversy over his *Recherches Philosophiques sur les Américains.*" *PMLA* 51 (1936): 178-206.

Crosby, Alfred W. "The Early History of Syphilis, a Reappraisal." *The Columbian Exchange: Biological and Cultural Consequences of 1492.* Westport, Conn.: Greenwood Press, 1972. 122-64.

Fuchs, Eduard. *Illustrierte Sittengeschichte vom Mittelalter bis zur Gegenwart: Das bürgerliche Zeitalter.* München: Langen, 1912.

Gerbi, Antonello. *The Dispute of the New World: The History of a Polemic, 1750-1900* [orig. 1955]. Rev., enl. and trans. by Jeremy Moyle. Pittsburgh: U of Pittsburgh P, 1973.

Honour, Hugh. *The New Golden Land: European Images of the Americas from the Discoveries to the Present Times.* London: Lane, 1976.

Mason, Peter. *Deconstructing America: Representations of the Other.* London: Routledge, 1990.

Nicolai, Friedrich. *Über den Gebrauch der falschen Haare und Perrucken in alten und neuern Zeiten.* Berlin and Stettin: n. p., 1801.

Pauw, Cornelius de. *Récherches philosophiques sur les Américains, ou Mémoires intéressants pour servir à l'Histoire de l'Espèce humaine par M. de P.***.* 2 vols. Berlin: Decker, 1768-69. German trans.: *Philosophische Untersuchungen über die Amerikaner, oder wichtige Beyträge zur Geschichte des menschlichen Geschlechts.* 2 vols. Trans. Carl Gottlieb Lessing. Berlin: Decker and Winter, 1769.

————. *Défense des Recherches philosophiques sur les Américains par Mr. de P***.* Berlin: Decker, 1770.

Pauw, Cornelius de and Antoine-Josephe Pernety. *Recherches philosophiques sur les Américains, ou Mémoires intéressants pour servir à l'Histoire de l'Espèce humaine par Mr. de P. Nouvelle Edition, augmentée d'une Dissertation critique par*

Dom Pernety; & de la Défense de l'Auteur des Recherches contre cette Disserta-
tion. 3 vols. Berlin: Decker, 1770.
[Pazzi de Bonneville, Zacharie de, alias "Le Philosophe la douceur"]. *De l'Amé-*
rique et des Américains, ou Observations curieuses du Philosophe La Douceur,
qui a parcouru cet Hémisphere pendant la derniere guerre, en faisant le noble
métier de tuer des hommes sans les manger. Berlin: Pitra 1771. [New edition
1772].
Permoser, Balthasar. *Der ohne Ursach verworffene und dahero von Rechts wegen*
auff den Thron der Ehren wiederum erhabene BARTH. Frankfurt and Leipzig,
1714.
Pernety, Antoine-Josephe. *Dissertation sur l'Amérique et les Américains, contre les*
Recherches philosophiques de Mr. de P. Par Dom Pernety. Berlin: Decker, 1770.
————. *Examen des Recherches philosophiques sur l'Amérique et des Américains*
et de la défense de cet ouvrage. 2 vols. Berlin: Decker, 1771.
————. *Journal historique d'un voyage fait aux Iles Malouïnes en 1763 & 1764*
pour les reconnoître & y former un établissement; & deux voyages au Détroit de
Magellan, avec une Relation sur les Patagons. 2 vols. Berlin: Bourdeaux, 1769.
Schelle, Karl Gottlob. *Geschichte des männlichen Barts unter allen Völkern der Erde*
bis auf die neueste Zeit. . . . nach dem Französischen frei bearbeitet und mit einer
Theorie der Haare nach ihren Naturzwecken versehen. Leipzig: Weygand, 1797.
Schiebinger, Londa. *The Mind Has No Sex? Women in the Origins of Modern*
Science. Cambridge: Harvard UP, 1989.
Tietz, Manfred. "Amerika vor der spanischen Öffentlichkeit des 18. Jahrhunderts:
Zwei Repliken auf de Pauw und Raynal: die 'Reflexiones imparciales' von
Juan Nuix y Perpiñá und die 'México conquistada' von Juan de Escoiquiz."
Iberoamérica: Historia-sociedad-literatura. Ed. José Manuel López de Abiada
and Titus Heydenreich. Munich: Fink, 1983. 2: 989-1016.
Woodforde, John. *The Strange Story of False Hair.* London: Routledge, 1971.
Wünsch, Christian Ernst. *Unterhaltungen über den Menschen: Erster Theil: Über die*
Kultur und äußerliche Bildung desselben. 2nd ed. Leipzig: Breitkopf, 1796.
[*Zehnte Unterhaltung: Verschiedenheit einzelner Menschen.*]
Zantop, Susanne. "Crossing the Border: The French Revolution in the German
Literary Imagination." *Representing the French Revolution: Literature, Histor-*
iography, and Art. Ed. James Heffernan. Hanover: UP of New England, 1992.
213-33.
Zedler, Karl. *Großes vollständiges Universal-Lexikon 1732-1763.* Vol. 46. Halle
and Leipzig, 1718. Rpt. Graz: Akademische Drucks- und Verlagsanstalt, 1961.

Eräugnis:
Georg Forster on the Difficulties of Diversity

I

THE MODERN, THE ENLIGHTENMENT sense of the self in motion and in change is intimately tied to voyage, that is, experiencing, with the senses and in the imagination, the diversity of difference. Trials and risks were synonymous with voyaging: what would the travellers find in the new places they encountered moving along on roads, across oceans, in time? It is precisely such tolerance for moving toward new findings, the unauthorized, unpredictable, on which the modern phenomenon of accountability and testing has depended. Voyage, then, has meant progress, in a literal and figurative sense. It has meant critical, provisional consensus which presupposes trial as questioning, testing, accounting for—the presence of different voices recognized in their difference, the absence of unanimity.

It is arguable, then, that the idea of difference as a usefully distancing reflector of the self developed, above all, in voyaging with its growing emphasis on considering critically the findings, that is, the perspectives, of other travellers. The concept of accountability became more complex because there was more accounting. The idea of negotiation of distances in the exchange of words and objects became more flexible because in the physical overcoming of distances occasions for exchange multiplied. People from different cultures experienced each other in their goods, their gestures and their voices, in the perceived appearance, whether peacefully or adversarily, of other, then multiple, realities. Perhaps most importantly, acknowledgement of cultural multiplicity eventually led to the recognition of the emotional and cognitive difficulties confronting the person observing and documenting (representing) it.

To a remarkably high degree, the young Georg Forster was aware of these difficulties, and quite self-consciously he directed the reader's attention to them in the "Preface" to his *Voyage Round the World* (1777). The purpose of voyaging, he wrote here, was not to collect facts and objects for the sake of their novelty. Appointing his father, the naturalist Johann Reinhold Forster, to accompany Captain Cook on his second circumnavigation of the globe (1772-1775), the British legislature expected from him "a philosophical history of the voyage, free from prejudice and vulgar error, where human nature would be represented without any adherence to fallacious systems, and upon the principles of general philanthropy" (*AA* 1: 9f.). As his father was not in a situation to write such a history or "philosophical recital of facts,"[1] Georg, who had collaborated with his father before,[2] wrote it for him. He drew up a "narrative" of the voyage from his father's journals to which he had full access, "with the most scrupulous attention to historical truth" (*AA* 1: 11). His account was to be "true" to the flora, fauna, and people encountered on the voyage, that is, it was to be accurate with respect to *what, having been there (then), they had observed* ("they" being Georg in the company of his father, Captain Cook, other naturalists making the voyage, and officers on board the *Adventure* and the *Resolution*).

Why should the public read his rather than other accounts? Instructively, the reasons given here by Georg immediately qualify the goal of "truth" in observation and documentation. Appealing to his enlightened audience not to "credit marvelous histories," he points out that the incidents of the voyage were "various, and deeply interesting" and did not call for "the assistance of fiction," but rather for the activities of the "inquisitive mind" (*AA* 1: 11). A "narrative" (a recounting of) the voyage was served best by the discourse of experientiality— not of fictionality. Yet—and this is the most important point made in the preface—every observer will shape his own discourse of experientiality, his own kind of accuracy, which will focus, and be focused by, his responses. During the three years Forster spent at sea, and which were, as he later saw, to define the course of his life,[3] he acquired a sharp awareness of the great importance *and* the difficulties of observation and documentation. He learned to recognize the fallacies inherent in the attempts at presenting the event or *Eräugnis* as evidence.[4]

It was an extraordinary lesson if one considers where and how it was learned: a very young, inexperienced man on a long, exhausting, at times life-threatening voyage, his survival dependent, sometimes with

frightening immediacy, on the expert observations of Captain Cook
and other members of the crew. Reviewing the route of the second
voyage thirteen years later, it appeared to Forster like an event in a
dream, magical (*AA* 5: 219). The dream-like quality of the incidents
points to the literally extra-ordinary nature, the intense and puzzling
novelty of the *Eräugnis*. Having read the accounts of previous travellers, the young man was little prepared for what he was going to see,
smell, hear, touch and taste. And yet he emerged, in his "narrative" of
the sensations and perceptions which made up the experience of the
voyage, as a remarkably independent and shrewd observer, understanding quickly and concretely that different observers see differently because they have different motivations and reasons for observation. The
"same objects may have been seen in different points of view, and . . .
the same fact may often have given rise to different ideas. . . . In short,
the different branches of science which we have studied, our turns of
mind, our heads and hearts have made a difference in our sensations,
reflections, and expressions" (*AA* 1: 12). Forster points out here that
Cook's own report (edited by Dr. Douglas and made even more attrac-
tively authoritative by the inclusion of all the illustrations collected on
the voyage), is shaped by a different perspective: as a sailor and the
leader of an expedition, he saw and recorded differently. As the different accounts provide "narratives of interesting facts," writes Forster,
"it must be allowed that the latter will be placed in a stronger light, by
being related by different persons." Differences of perspective will not
undermine but rather strengthen the authority of the evidence (*AA* 1:
12).[5]

   For this reason, too, Forster argues in the "Preface," accuracy in
documentation is not served by too much conceptual collating and
streamlining of information or emphasis on systemicity. The "philosophers of the present age" have selected certain authors, on whose
authority they have relied, and rejected all others—in both cases
without asking any questions: "Without being competent judges of the
subject, they have assumed a few circumstances as facts; and wresting
even those to suit their own systems, have built a superstructure which
pleases at a distance, but upon nearer examination partakes of the
illusive nature of a dream" (*AA* 1: 13). Such seduction by superstruc-
tures on the basis of too few and then insufficiently examined facts
appears not far removed from accounts which just replace facts with
fictions. And it is precisely these fictions which tend to obscure the fact
that "two travellers seldom saw the same object in the same manner,
and each reported the fact differently, according to his sensations, and
his peculiar mode of thinking" (*AA* 1: 13).

There are differences not only in the acts of seeing the same object, there are differences, too, in the kinds of linkage between perception and language. It was therefore necessary, as Forster pointed out, "to be acquainted with the observer, before any use could be made of his observations." And in the case of his own account this meant that it was "necessary for every reader to know the colour of the glass through which I looked" (*AA* 1: 13f.). This is an extraordinary statement for the young, unknown author of a travel account in competition with the official account given by Cook himself; it was also encouraged by precisely this competition. Extraordinary, too, are the implications of this insight: the "color," Forster explained, is the product of the traveller's attempt at penetrating a host of confusingly new and rich impressions without prejudice, though explicitly not without certain preconceptions, or intellectual prerequisites. From experience, notably the association with other explorers, the young Forster learned that discoveries did not happen by chance alone. New facts were found on the basis of existing information to which they added, and they aided in the formation of general views which, pointing out "the proper objects of farther investigation," would in turn guide to more discoveries. But he had also become conscious of the fact that this process was inevitably filtered through a (socialized) individual temperament which, though nurtured and enlarged by it, would also, and to a considerable degree, control it (*AA* 1: 14). He had grasped the importance of the hermeneutic circle as *circulus methodicus*: it is inescapable with regard to the limitations of the observer's objectivity *and* essential in terms of the accessibility to him of the object. The very selectiveness of the observer's perspective, the "colored glass," enables and drives observation. As an observer, so to speak, of these acts of observation, the reader needs to be aware of this fact at least as much as the agent and the narrator of the observation himself. Competing with Cook's official account, Forster emphasizes his own authorship by drawing attention to its "questionable" documentary authority. As the author of what was promptly to become a classic of European travel literature, he claims the authority of his experience both for the intended accuracy of his account *and* its peculiar limitations, namely the observer's complexly acculturated perception.

II

Forster explicitly wished to exempt from such inevitable selectiveness racial and cultural prejudice, and in this, of course, he did not succeed.[6] Yet it is all too easy to underestimate, from the unreflected position of late twentieth-century Western dogmatic enthusiasm for multiculturalism, the difficulties faced two centuries ago by a voyager trying to accommodate, that is, make sense of, what had not heretofore been seen. Sublating too readily our cognitive distance to the experience of a past observer, our unreflected hindsight judgments of previous prejudice cannot be saved by the cunning of dialectic, but *eo ipso* repeat the alleged sin. Forster in contrast made explicit his position in the *Voyage*—"I have endeavoured to make my remarks with a retrospect to our general improvement and welfare" (*AA* 1: 14)—and his spontaneous reactions of delight and repulsion in the *Voyage*, most clearly so in the cases of the (almost) paradisiacally happy people of O-Taheitee and the fearfully "wretched" inhabitants of Tierra del Fuego,[7] have to be judged in the light of this statement.

In Forster's observation, the Fuegan "character" was the "strangest" and oppressing "compound of stupidity, indifference and inactivity." It was these traits which he thought uncivilized because they prevented this people from living "more comfortably and happily," that is, more humanly. Even in an environment as hostile as Tierra del Fuego they could have done so. Another people, whom Cook had encountered on his first voyage at nearby Success Bay, had managed much better in very similar natural circumstances: "Their stature was taller; they had contrived buskins which secured their feet; they appeared to be sensible of the excellence of several European goods, and to set a value upon them; lastly, they were more communicative, and had ideas of ceremony or civility" (*AA* 1: 617). Importantly, Forster linked the observed physical discomfort of "these wretched outcasts" with their inability to compare their own "necessitous situation with that of others more happy" than they. They were unable, it seemed, to make use of cultural difference, to *make choices*. This inability, more than anything else, accounted for their difficulties, and for Forster it underlined strongly the fallacies of a nostalgic European perspective on the noble savage:

> If ever the pre-eminence of a civilized life over that of the savage could have been reasonably disputed, we might, from the bare contemplation of these miserable people, draw the most striking conclusions in favour of our superior happiness. Till it can be proved, that a man in continual pain, from the rigour of climate, is happy, I shall give no credit to the eloquence of philosophers, who have either had no opportunity of contemplating human nature under all its modifications, or who have not felt what they have seen. (*AA* 1: 618)

Forster distinguishes here between two kinds of perception: the traveller, seeing human beings, the likes of whom he had never seen before, and striving for observation which would be responsible to the observed, will have to "contemplate," that is, look with close attention,[8] at them and bring to this act of looking his knowledge of humanity. He will also have to "feel," that is, empathize with, what he observes by putting himself in the place of the observed: and here Forster cannot suppress his own empathetic somatic perception, describing in confrontational detail the Fuegans' extremely harsh living conditions (*AA* 1: 619). Within the parameters of an always limited, relational objectivity, as he himself had stated them in the "Preface," he presents his observations here as facts—the people *were* shivering with cold continuously, their noses *were* runny all the time, the smell and taste of their food *was* repulsive—all facts borne out by the observations of other travellers to whom Forster refers: he and they had been there, and this was what they had seen, heard, smelled and touched. The argument will be made that the diet that offended European noses and taste buds signified cultural adjustment to a natural environment since it produced the body heat needed to survive in the unrelenting cold.[9] But that monotonous diet seemed much more a natural necessity than a cultural choice modifying such necessity. If Forster could not but react according to his own acculturated sensibilities, which made him abhor the putrid seal-flesh, why, then, did he—as did many of the sailors—adore the largely vegetarian diet of the Tahitians? The issue of choice, that is, of value judgments concerning cultural arrangements that are different in different ways cannot be circumvented that easily.

For the young Forster, though he was, on the whole, impressively judicious, such choices presented themselves, as it were, naturally: he adored the Tahitians because, for a time, he felt physically and socially at ease on their "blessed" island. He disliked the Fuegans because they were both remote and pitiable. Their, to him, disturbing "brutishness" was located in the passivity of their wretchedness, and he described it in terms intended to repel the reader. It is significant that he saw their ugliness derive from their being acted upon rather than acting, empty of thought rather than thoughtfully responding to their environment. When he refers to them as "loathsome" (*AA* 1: 616), he expresses precisely his, the European's, feeling of being weighed down by so much human misery—too much, in fact, to be human.

These reactions stated in the context of the *Voyage*, which thematizes mobility, difference, diversity, change and thus comparison, are valuable because of their spontaneity, since it brings out so clearly the underlying problems of value, that is, of comparison and choice in the experience of cultural diversity. Ostensibly choosing to avoid choices, multiculturalism, then and now, has tended simply to repress these problems. Forster was to deal with this phenomenon in his attempts at distinguishing his position from Herder's—attempts that were informed by his increasing awareness of the difficulties which cultural diversity presented to the observer. Instructively, this learning process began during the years immediately following the publication of *Voyage*, when Forster turned himself into a sought-after, overworked translator and critic of a great variety of travel literature, mediating not only between English and German, but also other European audiences. It was then that he developed his characteristic approach of combining translations with lengthy commentary and of framing his reviews with the larger epistemological questions of acculturation. These were the activities of a reader—and of a writer who took seriously the experiences articulated in the writings under review—which Forster hoped would contribute to the dissemination of knowledge by introducing *his* readers to different perspectives of observation, even where he disagreed with them. (He was also aware, as his letters to his friends indicate, of the strongly interpretive impulses of translation.) In his extensive commentary on a short account of Domingo Boenechea's stay on O-Taheitee from November 19 to December 20, 1772, which, together with the translation he published in early 1780 in the *Göttingisches Magazin der Wissenschaften und Litteratur*, Forster resumed and expanded the arguments made in the preface to the *Voyage*. He stresses the importance for the reader both of having access to the witness of an *Eräugnis*, the person who was there and saw for himself, and of being able to compare as many different viewpoints ("Gesichtspunkte") as possible, that is, having access to different witnesses of the same *Eräugnis*. Information based on hearsay ("Hörensagen") about out-of-the-way places is contrasted with information based on documented observation ("Anschauen"). However, the authority of the witness who claims the authority of observation is by no means unlimited or unquestioned.

Where, then, is truth? The reader who cannot be a traveller and see for herself, that is, be a responsible observer in the terms stated by Forster, will seek out the observations of others, which will vary. Everyone sees differently; it is the *kind* of difference that matters and which needs to be explored. The truth to be found in this activity is composite and relational, therefore shifting, but not, for this reason, less important as a goal for the reader.[10] Since the compositional nature of the observer's perspective comprises "national character, national politics, education, natural environment, etc., etc.," it is important to make accessible the texts of travellers from different nations (cultures), for instance Spain. Full information for the reader is synonymous with fairness to different viewpoints, because on it is based that (approximate) fairness to the observed which is its (approximate) truth. The ideal of a "clear pure truth" ("klare lautere Wahrheit") is in actuality comprised of many different views colored by many "incorporeal glasses" ("unkörperliche Brillen"), and the reviewer, like a refracting prism, makes accessible their differences (*AA* 5: 36). His reason for translating and commenting on the Spaniard's description of Tahiti, Forster wrote, had been to "facilitate the comparison" with other news about the island (*AA* 5: 38), that is, to enable the reader to perceive the differences. The Spanish account was valuable in spite of *and* because of its distortions, because these reflected Spanish acculturation, and little had been heard in Germany from Spanish travellers recently. Where Forster corrected what seemed to him important details, he did so explicitly from the position of the traveller who had been there himself, the eye-witness, and of the person who had continued to gather information about the subject, the expert. In his opinion, it was precisely this composite, relational position—like the composite, relational truth he tried to make accessible to his readers—that enabled or authorized him to be a more reliable, more decisive judge of information (*AA* 5: 48-51).[11]   Pointing out Domingo Boenechea's moral prejudices, Forster argued the relativity of concepts like virtue and vice, which have to be judged from case to case, that is, by the standards of the group which enacts them. Otherwise, as he noted shrewdly, the observer becomes guilty of first imposing (European) concepts and conventions on other peoples, and then judging them accordingly (*AA* 5: 64). In the attempt to dissipate some of the most notorious prejudices against the islanders, Forster explained for instance their indeed troublesome "thievery"[12] with the nature of European goods: they held an irresistible attraction for the person who could quickly comprehend, indeed grasp, their usefulness (*AA* 5: 65). Does not—so the implied suggestion—the act of stealing also signify, apart from violating the taboo of property rights, precisely that disposition of intelligent curiosity valued by Europeans?

Forster also pointed out that the observable physical, including sexual, freedom of Tahitian women did not point to their cultural domination, as the Spanish observer alleged with apprehension, but meant just a different and, compared to European habits, more sensible convention. Moreover, he did so with a witty perceptiveness reminiscent of Diderot's in his *Supplément au Voyage de Bougainville* (*AA* 5: 65f.).[13] In each case, the information provided by the Spaniard was selective and interpretive, even more so perhaps than that found in English or French accounts. It represented one perspective among others which, taken singly as authority, would be gravely distorting. Forster and his readers, then, were left with the task of gathering and collating as many different viewpoints as possible.[14] But in the process of doing so, in the process of becoming aware of the perspectivist, composite nature of the information, indeed, of being involved in its composition, the phenomenon of cultural diversity could become more palpably present, if not, thereby, less difficult to judge. More directly, it might reflect back on their own cultural assumptions and, changing them, transform in certain aspects the observing and composing acculturated self.

III

Since Forster was aware of the fact that acts of observation were shaped by the observers' cultural values, and that this was particularly true in situations that clearly involved the value judgments of the observed, his comparison of different documentations of observation was focused on the relating and comparing of such values. For this reason, he extended the anthropological frame of the Spanish account of O-Taheitee by including in his commentary the general question of human happiness. He approached this quintessential Enlightenment trope with notable caution, since his opinions in this respect were tempered by a great number of different and often contradictory experiences.[15] Here, where he tried to make accessible to his readers the Tahitians' experience, he did not find useful the argument from natural environment, since it did not explain the cultural difference between the inhabitants of O-Taheitee and, for instance, those of the environmentally very similar island of Mallicollo (New Hebrides). In order to make his case, Forster overemphasized here, in contrast to his account in the *Voyage* where he shows himself impressed by their intelligence,[16] the cultural weaknesses of the Mallicollese. Where Tahitian culture, by careful cultivation, assures comfort and sensory gratification in all aspects of daily life and has therefore developed a high degree of sociability (*AA* 5: 51), the Mallicollese, unfortunate and unhappy savages, are presented as arrested on the level of subsistence gathering. Half starved, naked, adorned only with black paint which "heightens their peculiar ugliness," they "skulk," never leaving their dilapidated huts without their poisonous arrows, having become aggressive through material deprivation (*AA* 5: 51f.).

Self-consciously an enlightened philosophical traveller, Forster was profoundly interested in that "beneficial predisposition for ongoing improvement" ("wohlthätige Anlage zur Vervollkommnung," *AA* 5: 52) so remarkably developed in the Tahitians, whose culture radiated physical and social well-being. In his *Ideas for a Philosophy of the History of Mankind* (*Ideen zur Philosophie der Geschichte der Menschheit*, 1785), Johann Gottfried Herder worked with a more comprehensive and more diffuse concept both of happiness and wretchedness, based on his views of the conventions developed in response to natural environments. The contentment of the Tahitians, such a remarkable cultural achievement in Forster's eyes, did not, in Herder's view, differ in kind from that of the "poor Fuegans" ("armselige Feuerländer").[17] His argument from natural environment, especially climate, in Book 8 of *Ideas* culminates in section V with what appears in part a Rousseauian praise of simplicity. But *Ideas* is shot through with ambivalences and ambiguities that reflect the cognitive obscurities of the bewildering and exhilarating wealth of new anthropological information. Herder's idea of earthly happiness ("Glückseligkeit") is, and is not, simply simplicity, since he presents it in terms of the individual's culturally mediated ability to respond to the accident of having been born into this or that environment.[18] Forster would of course have agreed with Herder's assertion that it would be "presumptuous and foolish to imagine that all inhabitants of the world have to be Europeans in order to live happily." Yet I suspect that he is troubled by the implications of Herder's reasons: "Would we ourselves have become what we are outside Europe? He who placed us here, and others there, gave to them as much right to happiness in this life as he gave to us" (*Social and Political Culture* 308; cf. *Ideen* 1: 324f.). For Forster, human happiness carries its own authority, being a cultural achievement rather than God-given right, and as such it presents a value established by judgment and choice: the Fuegans' human, that is, cultural, condition is different in kind from that of the Tahitians. As he pointed out in his account of the Fuegans, another people living in a very similar natural environment had done much better in terms of cultural adjustment (*AA*: 1, 617). Herder's critical attitude toward European complexity, his apprehensive view of "the restless desires driving the European from one end of the world to the other," suggested that complexity and curiosity should or might be absorbed by a peaceful, almost passive simple happiness, which to him was the true "character of mankind" (*Ideen* 1: 326, 329, 328). But Forster's "eyewitness" observation of many other peoples left him less certain in this respect. It also did not support Herder's climate theory, on which he based his assumption that European culture could have developed only in Europe. Perhaps most importantly, Forster's own "restless desire" to know more—in contradistinction to elaborating on speculations—the lively curiosity that shaped his intellectual life, demanded to be nurtured.

Happiness for Herder is "this simple, profound, irreplaceable sensation of existence, this something *sui generis*," shared by all human beings in all situations, but especially by all savages. It is rooted in "a quiet feeling rather than a brilliant thought," emotional enrichment rather than "the profound deliberations of reason" (*Social and Political Culture* 308; cf. *Ideen* 1: 327f.). Time-travelling into the late twentieth century and accused of Eurocentrism, Forster could have pointed out that this celebration of heart over mind, soul over intellect, was based

more on Herder's unquestioning acceptance, in principle, of the otherness of the other than on his own experience and understanding of it.
In contrast, an important part of Forster's experience of such otherness
was the recognition of the need to understand its meanings for that
other. He knew very well that he depended here on his own European
perception, which was by necessity distorting. Yet the questions that
had to be asked concerned not so much the fact itself of that distortion,
but, rather, its relational nature: distorted in relation to what situation?
what event? what act or actor? what observer? There is a broad spectrum of positions between unquestioning embracing and rejecting of
the observed otherness, namely different, strange modes of cultural
behavior, and these positions are defined, to varying degrees, by the
experiential involvement of the observer. Without it, no judgment is
possible; with it, the judgment is never completely fair because it is
always selective. Forster's delight in and clear preference for O-
Taheitee, the sheer loveliness of the place, and its inhabitants' physical
ease and social charms, was based on his having been there and
glückselig, happy in an earthly sense, for a time. Here, I think, is the
crux of the matter—in full recognition of the fact that judgments made
on the basis of the judging person's own experience are not necessarily
free of self-deception. But even less so are judgments without such
basis.[19]

Herder has increasingly been seen in the cultural vanguard of late
eighteenth-century modernity with his "rupturing of a Eurocentric
worldview" (Schulz 446). The most important aspect of his contribution here may have been his generally secular emphasis on the existential—in contrast to cultural—relatedness of all humans. Forster's
explicit, even emphatic, insistence on a multi-perspectivity of observation that would control, as much as humanly (culturally) possible,
preconceptions shaped by European culture, is, I submit, more useful
for twentieth-century modernity. In contrast to Herder's attempts in
this direction, Forster was there and saw with his own eyes the great
and confusing, exhilarating and troubling diversity of peoples—different kinds of happiness and unhappiness, different ways of feeling and
reasoning, and of their interdependencies. Even more importantly, he
also experienced the diversity of reactions to this situation in the observations of others. The company of explorers participating in Cook's
Voyage—for the young Forster an archetypical learning situation—was
extended, for the translator and critic of travel accounts, to include the
documented observations of a host of other explorers coming from different parts of Europe, whose responses to non-European cultures
reflected clearly the diversity of their own.

IV

O-Taheitee became a household word among late eighteenth-century German intellectuals mainly because of Forster's description in the *Voyage*. But almost without exception its admirers (and detractors) were sedentary and speculative scholars ("Gelehrte[r], der auf seinem Studierzimmer reiset," *AA* 9: 6). Forster's experience was notably different. He left that rarefied protected environment to witness with all his senses new, unforeseen phenomena whose very newness required sharing it with others. Forster checked his impressions in the presence of others—his father, Captain Cook, the artist Hodges, the naturalist Sparrman, officers serving on the *Resolution* and *Adventure*. And later, writing his account with the help of his father's notes, he checked his memories of these impressions. As a draftsman he had been trained to observe closely and to be attentive to visual clues. His faculty to reason and to judge, that is, to connect, compare, and distinguish (*AA* 9: 38), was developed in the context of a reality shared in observation, thus rooted in the particulars of experience.

When Kant polemicized against Herder's *Ideas* in his *Definition of the Concept of a Human Race* (*Bestimmung des Begriffs einer Menschenrasse*) and *Conjectural Beginning of Human History* (*Muthmasslicher Anfang der Menschengeschichte*), both of them published in the organ of Berlin Enlightenment, the *Berlinische Monatsschrift* (in November 1785 and January 1786), Forster countered with *More on the Human Races* (*Noch etwas über die Menschenrassen*) which appeared in two installments in Wieland's *Teutscher Merkur* (October and November 1786). He did so respectfully, acknowledging his opponent's philosophical stature, but in fact he argued directly against the foundations of Kant's position, namely the cognitive supremacy a priori of the conceptual over the empirical.[20] Yet sending Herder this essay as an answer to *Ideas*, a text he had found important to his own work, Forster was also apprehensive about his disagreements with Herder, which concerned a different understanding of the intellectual's function in a situation where new information highly important to cultural self-perception was accumulating rapidly. Herder, Forster said in the accompanying letter of July 21, 1786, writes in order to be like St. Paul—everything for everybody. "I only satisfy the impulse of the moment to communicate what seems *probable* to me" (*AA* 14: 512; my emphasis).[21]

Forster perceived his position to be essentially different from Herder's, since he discussed, on the basis of the particular information gathered by himself and others, the *probability* of certain hypotheses, where Herder maintained, from the position of general (a priori) assumptions, their truth. Notwithstanding his disagreements with Kant,

Herder's authority was that of the philosopher whose confrontation, in the mind's eye, with new realities of human (cultural) diversity was linguistically mediated. Forster's authority was that of the voyager who had moved into these realities with his eyes, ears, nose, hands, and feet. This distinction does not concern physical versus symbolic activity, as the explorer's observation, too, relies on symbolic organization. It concerns, rather, the *interactive*—with the environment and other observers—nature of the explorer's understanding of authority, which supported Forster's tolerance for probability as a kind of composite, relational, relative, provisional truth.

Kant had begun the argument of *Bestimmung des Begriffs einer Menschenrasse* with a challenge to the explorers whose contribution to knowledge regarding the diversity of the human species had intrigued ("gereizt") rather than satisfied reason: It is very important, he wrote, "to define clearly and in advance the concept one wishes to elucidate [aufklären] through observation, before appealing to experience: for one only finds in experience what one needs if one knows beforehand what one should look for" (VI: 65). Forster the voyager was wary of the distortions produced by this particularly rigid *circulus methodicus*. In this case, as he put it pithily, one might wish to take care not to be deceived by "the most common illusion," namely thinking that what one has been looking for has been found—in a place where it does not exist (*AA* 8: 132). Forster gives as an example the "true" color of the Tahitians' skin, which, in Kant's view, could be ascertained only once anthropologists were in a position to examine a Tahitian born in Europe, namely in a situation where the impact of the environment on the skin color would have been neutralized. Kant's doctrine that race was determined by color had made him so eager to get hold of the "true" article, that he wanted it to be examined only in the frictionless, impoverished environment of the study or the laboratory, regardless of the flawed nature of such a finding.

Forster knew from experience that observation is impossible without conceptual guidance, whether it concerned structures of reasoning or hierarchies of value—both of them acculturated. He did not think useful a sharp separation between the empiricist ("Empyriker") and the systemitizer ("Systematiker"), pointing out that, for both of them, attentiveness ("Aufmerksamkeit"), judgment ("Beurtheilungskraft") and impartiality ("Unpartheylichkeit") were of the essence.[22] "Is it asked too much," he wrote, "if I want the contribution made by *recent travellers* to our knowledge of the human species measured by the standards mentioned above?" Forster thought himself an attentive impartial observer who had seen with his own eyes the coexistence of light brown, dark brown and black peoples in the South Sea, but also color variations among the same people, and a fairly uniform light brown shared by a large number of peoples with very different physical and cultural attributes.[23]   Significantly, he had checked his impression against those of many other travellers in the South Sea who agreed in this matter, regardless of their differing perspectives on concepts of race—a situation which made the agreement more meaningful, more reliable, more binding (*AA* 8: 133f.). He suggested Kant ought to accept an observation thus confirmed and not hold to his preconceived thesis that color equals race with the excuse that it was "not possible at that time to arrive at a definite idea of the true color of the Southsea Islanders" (*AA* 8: 134).

Kant's argument from concept rather than documented observation seems easily demolished here.   But the issue of the philosopher's license to ride his speculative hobby horse on the basis of highly eclectic, often simply erroneous information remained profoundly irritating to the empiricist Forster.[24] In his view, general statements on the issue of race were not useful, especially since the term and the notion had become so fashionable and therefore too easily acceptable to late Enlightenment intellectuals.[25] As he wrote to Sömmering on July 23, 1786, he had argued against Kant's assertion that all races originated in one human couple because there was no possible proof for it (*AA* 14: 515). In *Noch etwas über die Menschenrassen,* he therefore suggested as an alternative to Kant's *Genesis*-based thesis of human origin that there might have been, in the beginning, several couples in several places instead of the one hypothetical garden of Eden, and that one might do well to examine the clearly observable differences between human beings in terms of the impact of different environments over long periods of time.

Forster did not think that proof could be found for his argument either,[26] but he wanted to counter dogmatic pronouncements on real-life situations. When he dealt with the slavery question as one important aspect of the race issue, he characteristically relied on the persuasiveness of documented experience, which made possible a concrete confrontation with the problem, rather than the consistency of speculation.[27] There *was,* he realized, the danger of being misunderstood: if, following him, one accepted the possibility of more than one human species on the grounds of physical and cultural differences evolving in different natural environments, did one not thereby weaken the moral argument in principle against slavery, which was based on unquestionable human fraternity, the bond of one species?

For Forster, the observed practice of slavery signified evidence that the Judeo-Christian belief in one human species had not prevented the cruel treatment of negroes[28] and that therefore the argument against

one (undiversified) human species could not (or should not) be misconstrued as supporting the institution of slavery. He was moved, if not
in the details of the argument, by Herder's passionately pleading in
Book 7 of *Ideas* for "one and the same human species," as human one-
ness in diversity and metamorphosis. But he did not agree with Herder's extrapolating from this ideal of an all-embracing human brotherhood and solidarity a clear and distinct separation between the human
and the animal realm. Especially troubling to him were Herder's assertions claiming absolute certainty that there was not now and never
would be any evidence to the contrary. If—so Herder's argument—the
descriptions of some of the recently discovered peoples seemed to suggest visual similarities with archaic monstrous shapes preserved in ape-
like mythical figures like satyrs or sylvans, such similarities were either
fallacious or located in the "nature of man" and not of apes. Calling
on human beings to uphold, to honor their human distinctness—"Du
aber, Mensch, ehre dich selbst"—Herder explicitly used this appeal to
frame the slavery question. The European was challenged to see that
"der Amerikaner, der Neger" was his brother and to treat him accordingly, but to deny emphatically any connection with the ape (*Ideen* 1:
247-50). In contrast, Forster's critique of racism and slavery emphasized the greater probability, based on possible evidence, of the connectedness rather than separateness of *all* terrestrial organisms. It was,
in his view, this connectedness which supported rather than undermined the plea to perceive and value human diversity, namely the pre-
eminence on our planet of "variety" ("das *Mancherley*") rather than the
"eternally same" ("das ewige *Einerley*")—an unquestioned brotherhood
or solidarity of all human beings in their distinctness from other forms
of life (*AA* 8: 141f. Forster's emphasis).[29] His argument against
defenders of racism and slavery was that they derived their pet theories
from prejudice that was impervious on principle to the presence of
other voices and other realities. In a lengthy 1789 review of the racist
writings of the Göttingen professor Christoph Meiners, Forster
attacked not so much the moral depravity of Meiners's position as its
intellectually flawed basis: Meiners had diligently collected an
enormous amount of anthropological material made available by the
voyages of exploration, driven by a trust in "absolute truth" that was
nurtured by "pious prejudice of all kinds" (*AA* 11: 237). Forster shares
the instinctive resistance to Meiners's quite extreme position in the
race (and slavery) question expressed by many of his readers. However, he thinks it important to examine in some detail its effect on
Meiners's treatment of evidence. In its forcefully selective fitting of
others' observations into a preconceived thesis of the cultural
supremacy of the Celtic (European) race, Meiners's argument is one-

sided and therefore, contradicting the evidence, contradictory in itself. His argument, then, is caught in an "artificial circle" no longer permissible in philosophy. But the real problem is not so much the fact as rather the premodern dogmatic quality of such circularity. In Forster's view, Meiners's "disconsolate" certainty that the majority of mankind is inexorably arrested in a state of subhuman immorality and thus excluded from human perfectibility undermines precisely "that probability on which is based a gay and blissful *belief*" in the *"relative"* usefulness of all observation undertaken with "pure intentions." He is referring here to an observational position that consciously attempts to control distorting prejudices, which call for one absolute truth or cultural value judgment. This kind of observation, attention to *Eräugnis*, will result in the documentation of each people's cultural achievement proportionate to its situation, recognizing its "excellence *sui generis*," not according to European concepts (*AA* 11: 243-45; Forster's emphasis).

Racism was just the most openly disturbed reaction to the proliferating news about human diversity which, in Forster's view, ought to have signified caution to philosophers rather than intensified speculation. Kant's particular Enlightenment intolerance for happiness based on "mere" pleasure also seemed to prevent understanding the cultural meanings of the modern experience of mobility and cultural diversity. In the attempt to undermine Herder's argument in *Ideas*, he asked ironically whether the Tahitians, continuing in their indolent comfort for millennia, might not as well have been happy sheep (*Rezension* 805).[30] But Herder's impassioned dogmatic embracing of all human diversity, too, obscured rather than clarified the new possibilities of cultural connections, which were predicated on a diversity of difference, a relativity of cultural achievement. As an eyewitness (*Augenzeuge*) of *Eräugnis*, who was also, if to varying degrees, a participator, Forster had encountered desires and fears, pleasures and sufferings on a very broad cultural scale and did not think appropriate Kant's Eurocentric prescriptiveness—not to mention Meiners's bigotry. But the questions he put to the evidence of diversity differed dramatically from those asked by Herder, too. The voyage he had undertaken as a young man had indeed determined the course of his intellectual life in that it had so literally impressed on him the difficulties of seeing the new and unexpected. Traversing and linking so many new human spaces in a relatively short time, it had confronted him physically and intellectually with a confusing, overwhelming wealth of cultural variety. To the repeated enigmas of arrival, shore after shore, island after island, he could not but respond in ways which would guide and accelerate the life-long process of growing up, of self-transformation. Not only did

Forster know, as a young man, that the glass through which he saw was inevitably colored by a temperament interdependent with acculturation. He would also come to realize that its color was changing in time with his ongoing confrontations of diversity in the accounts of others who had seen it differently, with *their* own colored glasses. If he upheld against the landlocked scholars and philosophers the modern authority of evidence, it was located for him in his, the observer's and critic's, self-questioning, probable, proportionate and provisional access to *Eräugnis*.

Notes

1. This is due mainly to his father's difficult temperament and his relatively poor command of English—in contrast to Georg's remarkable linguistic talent. The account Georg gives of the situation is brief and partisan, though not false (*AA* 1: 10f.). See here the detailed and thorough introduction by Robert Kahn, "The History of the Work" (*AA* 1: 676-709, 688ff.). Unless stated otherwise, all translations from the German are mine.

2. There had been earlier collaboration on translations of historical works and travel accounts, notably Bougainville's *Voyage Round the World*: into German, 1771; into English, 1772).

3. See here his remarks in *Ansichten vom Niederrhein* describing his feelings when he saw the ocean again after many years and his memory was poignantly triggered, sending up images of those fateful three years spent circumnavigating the globe ("die mein ganzes Schicksal bestimmten," *AA* 9: 236).

4. Forster always used this spelling of *Ereignis*, which stresses the etymological connection between event, occurrence and perception: Old High German *(ir)ougen* "vor Augen stellen," Middle High German *eröugen, eröugnen*. The English "event," too, developed from lat. *evenire* "to come out" and thereby become visible, suggests the link with perception.

5. The *Voyage* was well received, particularly in England. See Kahn's interesting summaries of and quotes from reviews in journals like *The Critical Review, The Monthly Review, The Lady's Magazine, The Town and Country Magazine, The Scots Magazine, The London Magazine* and *The Annual Register* (*AA* 1: 704-06). Several times Cook's own "mere sailor's journal, without interest and without sentiment" is compared unfavorably with Forster's lively style, "good sense and penetration" (*AA* 1: 706). But readers were also advised to buy both accounts because of the intrinsic interest of the subject matter. Work on the English text had been extremely rushed in order to precede Cook's publication, and the quality of the writing is extraordinary under the circumstances. Forster described his work on his father's journals to Spener, lamenting, as he would do habitually during this period, about his laboring under terrible time pressure. He was in the process of dramatically expanding his father's journal—10 pages into 70—and it was precisely this kind of conceptually structuring and reflexive composition that was so costly in terms of time (September 17, 1776, *AA* 13: 52f.). He also complained here about his health ruined by the living conditions, especially diet, during the voyage.

6. See Forster's 1778 "Antwort an die Göttingischen Rezensenten" where he argues against the "unfair prejudice" that all virtue is European and all savages are

morally inferior (*AA* 4: 49-60); and his almost Darwinian "Zu einer künftigen Geschichte der Menschheit" (published in the September 1789 issue of Heinrich Christian Boie's *Neues Deutsches Museum* (*AA* 8: 185-93). See also his incisive review of the racist writings of the Göttingen professor of philosophy Christoph Meiners in *Allgemeine Literatur-Zeitung*, 1791, No. 7, 8, 9 (*AA* 11: 236-52).

7. Abandoned, as it were, by their own absence of will or desire, to a desolate, de-humanizing environment, the Fuegans appeared to the observer dulled, stunted, neglected. Forster was especially disturbed by the fact that they seemed to be very cold all the time and that "from their nose there was a constant discharge of *mucus* into their ugly open mouth. The whole assemblage of their features formed the most loathsome picture of misery and wretchedness to which human nature can possibly be reduced" (*AA* 1: 615f). Berg *(Zwischen den Welten* 110) thinks this passage particularly indicative of the European acculturation of Forster's "aesthetic and other values," and finds the description of the open mouthed faces suggestive of (European notions of) mental debility. But his reading simplifies and distorts Forster's perspective (what if the Fuegans *did* have to breathe through their mouths because of continous colds?). If Forster was appalled by the appearance and behavior of these people, their strangeness did not prevent him from empathizing with their difficult lives. In *Reise um die Welt*, both the wretchedness and the observer's empathy are put in slightly stronger terms (920). In both *Voyage* and *Reise*, however, Forster was careful to present his evaluative descriptions of the inhabitants' behavior—in contrast to their exterior—as based on what *he* had observed: they did not give a *sign* of being pleased, they *seemed* to lack curiosity. Forster also recommended here to the reader, as he rarely did, a print to be published in Captain Cook's account, made from the "most excellent drawing of one of the men, which is extremely characteristic," by his co-traveler, the landscape painter William Hodges. He did so, of course, because the artist's representation corroborated his own impression. But, then, all efforts at description rely on the assumption that impressions can be shared, that is also, checked by other viewers who, as contemporaries, will share the same restrictions of perception.

8. Oxford English Dictionary: "Contemplate": to look at with continued attention, gaze upon, view, observe. In *Ansichten vom Niederrhein*, Foster points out that there is perhaps no other work so strenuous as the conscientious traveler's "unaufhörliche[s], mit aufmerksamer Spannung verbundene[s] Hören und Sehen" (*AA* 9: 231).

9. For a description of the effects of the extreme cold on the European explorers of Tierra del Fuego see Cook's account of his first voyage, Barrow 16-18.

10. See Georg Forster, "O-Taheiti": "in Ermanglung des eigenen Anschauens, in so viele Gesichtspunkte als möglich geführt zu werden, von wannen andere gesehen haben" (*AA* 5: 35-71, here 35).

11. See here also his letter to Herder of January 21, 1787: in the context of the differences between Kant and Herder (see below), Forster referred to Christoph Meiners's 1785 *Grundriss der Geschichte der Menschheit* (*AA* 14: 621f.). In spite of clearly articulated and, in Forster's view, untenable (racist) hypotheses, there is no order in the argument: one reason is its eclectic focus within the wealth of the collected material; another is a lack of critical judgment regarding the compilation of the materials themselves. Forster calls here for critical intelligence or eye witness experience as the source for critical judgment; Meiners, he felt, had neither: at best, he had compiled materials that could be used by those who have such judgment.

12. Cook was to lose his life on the third voyage in a disturbance on Hawaii

caused by his possible over-reaction to proliferating acts of theft on board that threatened to jeopardize the voyage. The account of the third voyage mentions the problem before the incident: "The satisfaction we derived from their [the Hawaiians'] gentleness and hospitality was, however, frequently interrupted by that propensity to stealing which they have in common with all the other islanders of these seas. This circumstance was the more distressing, as it sometimes obliged us to have recourse to acts of severity, which we should willingly have avoided, if the necessity of the case had not absolutely called for them" (Barrow 397).

13. Such comparing would affect, too, non-European views of European culture. In the question of prostitution on Tahiti, Forster points out that on their second visit they found the same women offering themselves "who had been so liberal of their favours" on the first stay. The practice, then, was not at all as general as had been assumed, but limited, rather, to a certain group. His comment on the misunderstanding: "It would be singularly absurd, if O-Mai [the islander who had gone to England in 1774 with Captain Tobias Furneaux, commander of the *Adventure*, and returned with Captain Cook on his third voyage] were to report to his countrymen, that chastity is not known in England, because he did not find the ladies cruel in the Strand" (*AA* 1: 374).

14. See here also Forster's comparison of different but equally convention-ruled tastes regarding clothes in *Ansichten von Niederrhein* (*AA* 9: 310).

15. See his disagreements with Kant and Herder below.

16. Here, too, the Mallicollese seemed to Forster alien in appearance (their "ugly" negroid features, woolly hair, skimpy costume, cumbersome nose ornaments), but he was impressed by their ability to communiate and to negotiate, which, from the European viewpoint, suggested resourcefulness, thoughtfulness and, on the whole, peaceableness: "They were the most intelligent people we had ever met with in the South Seas; they understood our signs and gestures, as if they had been long acquainted with them, and in a few minutes taught us a great number of their words" (*AA* 1: 452-72, here 457).

17. See here Herder's much quoted statement in *Ideen*, Book 8, no. III on the happily perfect cultural balance—"bis diese sich gleichsam ründet"—of the Australian's hunting and fishing activities (1: 303). See here also Schulz, "Erfahrene Welt" 445ff. See, however, the clearly negative passage in *Ideen*, Book 6, no. 6 (1: 242) on details of the Fuegans' life (Herder refers here to Forster's *Voyage*)—their small stature, their ugliness, their severely restricted diet and clothing, their intolerable odor, their suffering from the terrible winters, their inability to warm themselves despite available wood. The generosity of "nature itself" has not allowed the landmass of the planet to extend further south, thus preventing even deeper human deprivation ("tiefer hinab, welche armselige Bilder der Menschheit hätten ihr Leben im gefühlraubenden Frost dahingeträumet!").

18. Herder, *Ideen*, Book 8, no. V: "The very concept of 'happiness' implies that man is capable of neither experiencing nor creating pure and lasting bliss. He is the child of chance; it is a matter of luck where he comes to live, when and under what circumstances. The country, the time, the constellation of circumstances *happen* to decide both his capacity of enjoyment and the manner and measure of his joys and sorrows" (1: 324; translation quoted from Barnard 307).

19. See here Herder's statement in *Ideen*, Book 7, no. 4 (1: 272) on a uniformly harmonious proportionality in human bodies, which is in accordance with the overall argument of Book 7, emphasizing human sameness in the different forms developed under the influence of different climates. This argument is as speculative as the thesis developed in Book 6, no. 3 (1: 215-21)—which it contradicts—of a divi-

sion of mankind into beautifully formed ("schöngebildete") peoples closer to European taste, if, in certain cases (especially Hindus) on average more beautiful than Europeans (excepting the Greeks), and peoples not thus favored.

20. See here Forster's letter to Sömmering of July 23, 1786 (*AA* 14: 515f.) about his refuting Kant's argument in violation of Sömmering's principle to have only praise for live (famous) authors ("Lebendige blos zu loben"): he is not interested in presenting a new hypothesis but to show that Kant not only misquoted from Carteret's travel account but also drew from it false conclusions. Like Cook, Captain Philip Carteret was a traveler who wanted "to get it right"—an attitude much appreciated by Forster. His account was included in the three-volume 1773 edition by Dr. John Hawkesworth of the Admiralty's official collection *An Account of the Voyages undertaken ... by Commodore Byron, Captain Wallis, Captain Carteret, and Captain Cook.* This avidly awaited collection disappointed its readers' desire for more marvelous news, especially about the Patagonian giants: Wallis and Carteret—as well as Bougaineville's men—had measured them, and their measurements agreed that there were some individuals above six feet, but most of them were from five feet ten inches to six feet (Adams, *Travelers* 38-42).

21. Herder's response to the essay must have been friendly: see Forster's letters to Sömmering November 20, 1786, and to Herder January 21, 1787 (*AA* 14: 590, 620).

22. Here we find an explicit preference for the "open-minded observer" ("unbefangener Zuschauer") and clear-sighted and reliable empiricist ("scharfsichtiger und zuverlässiger Empyriker") over the prejudiced systematizing observer ("partheyischer Systematiker"): even if the latter finds more because he is looking for certain things, he often overlooks what turns out to be important (*AA* 8: 133).

23. The issue here was not an acculturated (see Forster's comparison, *AA* 8: 134) perception of "ugly," that is, very dark skin, smallish stature, woolly hair and (a particular kind of) negroid features vs. "handsome," namely light brown, tallish stature, "pleasant" features and curly hair. It was, rather, the (more than less) unmediated perception of different shades of skin color.

24. See Forster's insistence on an empirical approach of reflected falsificationism, particularly where it concerned the speculative subject of the history of mankind so dear to Enlightenment thought, in his 1789 "Leitfaden zu einer künftigen Geschichte der Menschheit" (*AA* 8: 185-93, here 186).

25. See Forster's letter to Sömmering of January 19/21, 1787 (*AA* 14: 618; his emphasis) stating that he does not like the term "Menschen*racen*" but uses it because Kant uses it in his desire to conform to the fashionable Berlin Enlightenment position.

26. See his letter to Herder of January 21, 1787 (*AA* 14: 620): "though, seriously, I am far from believing that there is real proof for the human race having several progenitors."

27. "Do we not thereby cut through the last strand that bound this mistreated people to us and afforded still some small protection against European cruelty? Let me ask instead whether the thought that blacks are our brothers has ever, anywhere, only once given pause to the slave driver's whip? Did he not mistreat the poor suffering creatures with gusto and devilish delight in the full conviction that they were of his own blood?" See also Forster's own comment at the end of the essay on his act of heresy: "Although an old book, which no one is allowed to criticize, does not mention the Negro with a single syllable; although the great man who is supposedly the author of the book probably never saw a Negro: yet it is an attack on this old book if one imagines the possibility of more than one tribe of

men; and this wicked act, which injures no one, is called heresy" (*AA* 8: 154, 156; translations of these passages in Saine, *Forster* 47, 164 n 11).

28. Thus Forster complained to Sömmering on September 7, 1789 that in his recent review of Johann Friedrich Ludwig's *Neueste Nachrichten von Surinam* (1789), the Göttingen philosophy professor Christoph Meiners had applauded rather than reproached the author for his approval of slave trade (which was very lively in that Dutch colony): "This wretch shamelessly states in his preface that the Bible approves of slave trade, and he writes: a man could be his brother in Christ, and, at the same time, physically ["im leiblichen Verhältnis"], *his slave*" (*AA* 15: 335; Forster's emphasis). See also Forster to Heyne, November 5-6, 1789 (*AA* 15: 366) on the ironies of politically correct tolerance—a black nurse in the Göttingen hospital!—among self-consciously and self-righteously enlightened academics.

29. See here also Forster's remarks in his critique of Christoph Meiners (*AA* 11: 236-52, here 239). One of the projects he did not live to realize was to write, together with his friend, the anatomist Sömmering, a "Pithecologie mit Rücksicht der Verwandtschaft der Thiere mit dem Menschen," a study of the evolutionary link between ape and man. See Forster's letters to Heyne of March 12 and 20, 1790, about his plan to gather materials for this study in the London natural history collections during his journey via Holland to England in the spring and early summer of 1790 (*AA* 16: 29, 33). Sömmering had originally planned to accompany Forster on that journey—Alexander von Humboldt was to take his place—and had written to Forster on August 21, 1787 about consulting the Dutch natural history collections (quoted *AA* 9: 338).

30. I will quote the passage in full in the original because of its characteristically twisted grammar and semantics—Forster referred to it as exhibiting Kant's "gewöhnliche Wortsubtilitäten" (to Herder, January 21, 1787, *AA* 14: 621): "Meint der Herr Verfasser wohl: dass, wenn die glücklichen Einwohner von Otaheite, niemals von gesittetern Nationen besucht, in ihrer ruhigen Indolenz auch tausende von Jahrhunderten durch zu leben bestimmt wären, man eine befriedigende Antwort auf die Frage geben könnte, warum sie denn gar existiren und ob es nicht eben so gut gewesen wäre, dass diese Insel mit glücklichen Schafen und Rindern, als mit im blossen Genusse glücklichen Menschen besetzt gewesen wäre?"

Works Cited

Adams, Percy G. *Travelers and Travel Liars 1660-1800*. New York: Dover, 1980 (1962).

Barrow, John, ed. *Captain Cook's Voyages of Discovery*. London, New York: Everyman's Library, 1967.

Berg, Eberhard. *Zwischen den Welten: Über die Anthropologie der Aufklärung und ihr Verhältnis zu Entdeckungsreise und Welt-Erfahrung mit besonderem Blick auf das Werk Georg Forsters*. Berlin: Reimer, 1982.

Forster, Georg. *Ansichten vom Niederrhein, von Brabant, Flandern, Holland, England und Frankreich im April, Mai und Junius 1790*. AA 9.

―――. "Cook, der Entdecker." *AA* 5: 191-302.

―――. "Noch etwas über die Menschenrassen." *AA* 8: 130-56.

―――. "O-Taheiti." *AA* 5: 35-71

―――. *Reise um die Welt*. Ed. Gerhard Steiner. Frankfurt: Suhrkamp, 1967.

―――. *A Voyage Round the World*. AA 1.

————. *Werke: Sämtliche Schriften, Tagebücher, Briefe. Herausgegeben von der Akademie der Wissenschaften der DDR.* Berlin: Akademie, 1958- . Cited as "*AA.*"

Herder, Johann Gottfried. *Ideen zur Philosophie der Geschichte der Menschheit.* 2 vols. Berlin: Aufbau, 1965.

————. *J. G. Herder on Social and Political Culture.* Tr. and Ed. M. Barnard. Cambridge: Cambridge UP, 1969.

Kant, Immanuel. *Bestimmung des Begriffs einer Menschenrasse. Werke* 6: 65-82.

————. *Conjectural Beginning of Human History. Kant on History.* Ed. Lewis White Beck. New York: Bobbs Merrill, 1963. 53-68.

————. *Rezension zu Johann Gottfried Herders Ideen. Werke* 6: 781-806.

————. *Werke in sechs Bänden.* Ed. Wilhelm Weischedel. Darmstadt: Wissenschaftliche Buchgesellschaft, 1966.

Saine, Thomas P. *Georg Forster.* New York: Twayne, 1972.

Schulz, Gerhard. "Erfahrene Welt: Berichte deutscher Weltreisender am Übergang vom 18. ins 19. Jahrhundert." *Antipodische Aufklärungen / Antipodian Enlightenment: Festschrift für Leslie Bodi.* Ed. Walter Veit. Frankfurt: Lang, 1987. 439-56.

Enlightenment and Despotism:
Two Worlds in Lessing's *Nathan the Wise*[1]

Christiane Bohnert

IN HIS FAMOUS STUDY on the "pathogenesis of the bourgeois world" in Germany, Reinhart Koselleck identifies "critique and crisis" (6-9, 84-86) as the two elements that constitute the Dialectics of Enlightenment. Enlightenment philosophy's moral critique triggers the crisis of the absolutist state by over-reaching itself and penetrating the realm of politics (115, 144-46). It thereby destroys the balance the state achieved after the religious civil wars of the sixteenth and seventeenth centuries. The Enlightenment representatives fall victim to their own "hypocrisy" (81-82, 98-103). They emphasize the moral nature of their critique and its utopian drive without comprehending that the effect of their critique could not but be political (4). The pursuit of absolute morality concerns not only each human being's "inside," or self, but also his or her "outside," the environment. The fanatic attempt to reconcile the "inside" with the "outside" (138) renews civil war, as in the War of Independence in the British colonies in America and in the French Revolution, and creates a "perpetual revolution" in any state that pursues such a utopia (135-36).

During the past ten years, Koselleck's approach has come to influence German eighteenth-century scholarship. Especially his discussion of Lessing's *Ernst and Falk: Conversations for Freemasons* (*Ernst und Falk: Gespräche für Freimäurer*)[2] made him known to scholars working on topics related to this dialogue, such as the play *Nathan the Wise* (*Nathan der Weise*). The interest Koselleck draws from literary scholars derives from an approach that permits us to think of the Age of Enlightenment as a "*collusion* between intellectuals and authority," (Wilson, "Flight" 239), an interplay rather than a "secession" of the intellectual from the state, as was previously assumed (ibid. 238-39).

As Leventhal (521) and Briegleb (261-63) have shown, Nathan too colludes with the authority, in his case, the sultan Saladin. He compromises his Enlightenment stance by employing a fairy tale to serve the sultan the truth in a manner Saladin can digest.[3] Nathan's willingness to confront authority distinguishes his approach from those of the Muslim dervish Al-Hafi (Kiesel 331-32) and the Christian lay brother with whom Nathan discovers an empathy similar to the one he had with Al-Hafi. Both the Muslim and the Christian friars, however, opt for retreat from the world. One is disgusted by Saladin, the other by the Patriarch.

This parallel would suggest despotism on Saladin's part, and is usually ignored. Instead, Saladin is regarded as a figure whose "personal integrity" puts him almost on a par with Nathan. Only his absolutist environment is severely criticized (Kiesel 322). He is shown as a "family man"; he "plays" the sultan in his first meeting with Nathan instead of "being" it (König 120-24); he is as moral as his enemies permit him to be (Wilson, "Flight" 256-59). The conflict of role and inner self, of "shell" and "core," as Nathan distinguishes it (1197-98),[4] is resolved in favor of the inner self.[5] Arguing that Saladin's appearance in the play as a private person and "family man" pre-empts his identity as a despot, König is forced to fault Lessing for introducing the Third Act as he does, by showing Sittah and Saladin baiting a trap for Nathan to relieve him of his money. If Saladin were the kind of ruler to expose a subject to a life-and-death situation, then he would have to be regarded as a despot (89-91).

Wilson in turn upholds his interpretation by declaring Al-Hafi to be an unreliable witness ("Flight" 255-56). He argues that Saladin is a moral character whose transgressions of the moral norm are forced on him by the cruelty and treachery of his Christian enemies. Morally superior and humanly equal to Saladin, Nathan arrives at a time when Saladin is left deprived of any moral advisers, and takes over for them (260). In my view, this argument is flawed because it confuses moral and pragmatic levels of reasoning. Pragmatically, Saladin is no doubt correct in his actions. He is a despot who is responsible for protecting his citizens. Morally, however, the other's evil cannot justify one's own. If there is any sense in our admiring Nathan for being able to forgive the Christians who slew his wife and children in a pogrom (3037-58), moral commitment must stand in the face of adversity if it is not to be revealed as a sham.

Of course, my counterargument leads to the question whether princes can act morally, a question Koselleck accuses the Enlightenment of having asked wrongfully, in a spirit of hypocrisy, thereby destroying the absolutist state (138). Koselleck argues within one world, the world of the present, in which two sides fight for control of human minds and souls, and in which the absolutist side appears helpless in the face of the Enlightenment onslaught (129).

While scholars analyzing *Nathan the Wise* are generally much more appreciative of the utopian character of Enlightenment thought than Koselleck, they also tend to see the play in terms of one world, as the apex of "classicist German humanism" on a par with Goethe's *Iphigenia at Tauris* (Greis 136).[6] *Nathan the Wise* is considered the climax of Lessing's life work, reaffirming the "optimism of Lessing's philosophy of history."[7] This optimism originates with his teleological view of history which makes human beings the subject of Providence. According to Kiesel, Lessing's concept of a humanocentric Providence excludes the notion of evil (Kiesel 318, 324).

By contrast, I will analyze the play in the context of two equal worlds, the worlds of Enlightenment and Despotism, each differing from the other in its historical and conceptual references. Rather than interpreting "utopia" as something like a u-word, as Koselleck does (4), I will take it seriously as the cornerstone of the World of Enlightenment that is focused on the future. My two-world model[8] restricts the utopian aspect to the World of Enlightenment, as it does the moral question of good and evil. The World of Despotism, as presented in *Nathan the Wise*, focusses on the present with the future as nothing more than the present's extrapolation. In this world, good and evil become a matter of chance, as a close look at the role of the Patriarch will show. Of course, there is no rejecting such a powerful and varied tradition as that established by the vast scholarship on *Nathan the Wise*. Rather than rejecting this tradition, I seek to uncover a level of textual structure that hitherto was too little emphasized.

Contrary to Koselleck's argument that the Enlightenment won a Pyrrhic victory, my approach will demonstrate that it is the World of Despotism that is victorious, and that at least Lessing's play *Nathan the Wise* does not predict the future winner with any certainty. In the context of Lessing's works, it would appear that *Nathan the Wise* does not reinforce the optimistic message of texts closely related to the play in time of writing and of subject matter: the dialogue *Ernst and Falk*, and the "soliloquy" *The Education of Humankind* (*Die Erziehung des Menschengeschlechts*, Altenhofer 26; see Bohnen 184-96).

The World of Enlightenment, as described in *Ernst and Falk* and *The Education of Humankind*, considers the present as historically transitory. This verdict also concerns all institutions that mark the present. On the one hand, there are particular religions, such as Christianity,

Judaism, and Islam. On the other, there are particular states and societies. On the religious and the secular levels, this present world is characterized by divisiveness. Hence, it is merely an interlude. The real
focus of the World of Enlightenment, as Lessing describes it, is the
highest stage in the development of humankind, when the religion of
reason (*Education*, § 81-82) will transcend the particular religions, and
the disappearance of states will make for unity (*Ernst and Falk* 8: 561).

For the present, states are useful because humankind has not yet
learned to live together. States protect their citizens against predators
from other states, and they guarantee their citizens social and economic security. Usefulness is no excuse for despotism, though. In their
treatment of their citizens, states must defer to the basic dignity of each
individual, a dignity derived from his or her share in humankind.
Hence, Falk defines the state morally rather than legally. Taking his
cue from Adam Smith (Heidsieck 140, 143 n 21), Falk states emphatically:

> The sum of the single happinesses of all members [of society] constitutes the
> happiness of the state. Except for this happiness, none exists. Any other hap-
> piness of the state, through which any members at all suffer, and must suffer, is
> tyranny in disguise. It cannot be otherwise! (8: 556)[9]

This Enlightenment concept of *state* is limited to the present, while cosmopolitan Freemasons—metaphorical Freemasons distinct from, and
unaffiliated with, the secret society—work for individual education that
will make the state disappear (8: 561). Its disappearance is historically
inevitable; it does not depend on revolutions (8: 556-57).[10] To say with
Koselleck that this utopia is "hypocrisy" (81-82, 98-103) overlooks Lessing's fervent belief in the fulfillment of the destiny of humankind, as
expressed in *The Education of Humankind*.

In the latter text, the concept of *God* suffers the same fate as the
concept of *state* in *Ernst and Falk*. At no stage of time is God an entity
independent from humankind. While a God is necessary as a metaphor for the pedagogue who establishes the three stages of growth for
humankind, He is superfluous once this destiny will be achieved. At
this point, the Enlightenment God, the pedagogue, will have written
Himself out of the universe.

God's expendability is emphasized by the manner in which the text
relates the individual to humankind. It does so by referring to the Far
Eastern tradition of metempsychosis. Whereas in the Far East, each
new rebirth of the human being depends on his or her past life, Lessing's Enlightenment transformation of the concept is oriented toward
the future (Altenhofer 34; Bohnen 196).

[§ 99] Remembering my former states would only allow me to make bad use of my present one.
[§ 100] And what will I miss? Is not all eternity mine?[11]

Remembering the past, or past lives, is an obstacle to the individual's development, while focusing on the future gives meaning to the individual's existence. Lessing's Enlightenment metempsychosis relates each and every commitment the individual makes toward the destiny of humankind to the process of humankind's growth. The text's metaphor implies that once humankind achieves its destiny, the individual reaches his or her state of nirvana, or in Enlightenment terms, perfection. Lessing emphasizes that it is the individual alone who is responsible for his or her rebirth. On the surface, his view is in accordance with a Far Eastern tradition that emphasizes the individual effort to attain nirvana. Lessing, however, writes within the Western tradition in which the individual's redemption depends on a God.   By fusing the Enlightenment emphasis on the individual with a religious tradition that also focusses on the individual, Lessing moves toward writing the Christian God out of the text, and the individual's life.

The means of progress is human reason rather than prayer, and reason will develop to ever greater knowledge about the actual world and about one's inner self. The individual is innately equal, his or her dignity independent of social rank or legal status. This equality is expressed in each individual's voluntary consent to being ruled. The Enlightenment individual knows that (s)he needs the state for protection against the ill effects of particularism.

By contrast, the World of Despotism exists in the present. It is the world of particularism, the world in which Jews and Christians are intense rivals. Here each group takes its own particular religion to be God's last word, to be the one and only revelation. In fact, the legitimacy of despotism derives from this very revelation, which is equivalent to divine grace. Since its legal status is independent of its relationship with its subjects, the state of Despotism in its enlightened absolutist form does not guarantee individual rights based upon a common share in humanity. The *philosophes* and physiocrats in France argue within the World of Despotism. They distinguish between a "legal despotism" that is tolerable, and an "arbitrary despotism" that is not (Mandt 678). Only the latter would be "tyranny."

In the World of Despotism, a state is characterized by legalism, and its legitimacy derives from the legal status of its ruler. The state is static, and does not evolve into something different. The state of the present equals the state of the future. Therefore, human beings are subjects whose status depends on their legal and social rank. If a despotic government undertakes "enlightened" reforms, it merely resorts to the use of pragmatic reason to achieve an enforced happiness for its subjects according to the will of the despot.

In this context, reason is a tool for governing pragmatically rather than a road to fulfilling the destiny of humankind, and human beings are the recipients of handouts rather than the creators of a new universe.[12] Depriving Enlightenment concepts of their context, of their reference to the future, the World of Despotism turns them from a matter of Providence into one of convenience.[13] "Enlightened despotism" manages to co-opt these concepts without compromising the essence of its world.[14]

If one assumes that Lessing portrays a state in *Nathan the Wise*, the state conquered by Saladin, any utopian drive in the play would seem questionable. Neither a state nor a God have a future in the World of Enlightenment. Hence, our first question would have to be whether there is any indication that despotism is depicted in the present, or judged with regard to the future. For this question, we must analyze the Patriarch and Saladin himself. Both of the most radical voices for retreat in the play, the Muslim and the Christian friars, seem to refer to them as despots. By implication, the Templar does, too. The second question to be posed concerns the question of human and moral equality between Saladin and Nathan. Does Saladin really accept Nathan as humanly equal, and does Nathan accept Saladin as morally equal? For an answer, I will take a close look at their interaction, both in their direct contacts and in their actions that concern the other indirectly.

Regarding the question of despotism, it is the Patriarch who provides us with an answer. He has the standing of a despot for his Christian flock, albeit in a spiritual, ecclesiastical sense, and in this role has managed to protect them to a certain extent. When he tells the Templar that he has documents that would oblige Saladin to help him punish any heretic, it can only mean that the Patriarch is equal enough to Saladin to have concluded some sort of treaty with the sultan that protects his Christian flock against whatever heresy the Patriarch wishes to prosecute. Such an arrangement would correspond to the relationship between ecclesiastical and secular authorities from the very beginning of Christian history when the Jewish High Priest had to ask the Roman proconsul Pilate to execute Jesus. Later, the Inquisition relied on secular authorities for executing their sentences. In the eighteenth century, the relationship between church and Protestant state was close, and the state censored writings against the church. Lessing himself became the victim of this practice when his employer, the Duke of Brunswick, forbade him to publish further "anti-Goeze" texts. In fact, this order served as an impetus for Lessing to write *Nathan the Wise* (Kiesel 312).

The Templar acknowledges the Patriarch as despot, though an ecclesiastical one. When he goes to the same man whose attempt to make him Saladin's assassin he so indignantly refused, it is not because his character is still "immature."[15] As the spiritual authority over the Christian knight Templar, the Patriarch is the logical person to whom to turn, all the more so, since the Templar's anti-Semitic prejudices are on the rise, and he feels this to be a conflict damaging to a Christian (Wilson, *Humanität* 75). The Patriarch who, as the friar confirms (2963), regards it as a sin against the Holy Spirit to raise a Christian child as a Jew, knows only one remedy: to burn the guilty Jew at the stake. His argument is legalistic in accordance with his standing as a religious leader dependent on secular justice. If he wants to convince Saladin that his prerogatives have been infringed upon, he needs a judicially watertight case.

The scene between the Patriarch and the Templar demonstrates that moral categories of good and evil are meaningless in this World of Despotism. Human beings are not rewarded for their merits. Rather they are saved by luck. When Nathan hears that a Templar paroled by Saladin saved his daughter from certain death, he is aghast at the narrowness of her escape (86-89):

<blockquote>
What?

A knight Templar whose life sultan Saladin spared?
Recha could not be saved by a lesser miracle? God![16]
</blockquote>

If the Patriarch were to learn Nathan's identity, he would do his utmost to achieve the same fate for Nathan, death from burning. Nathan, and the friar who warns him, are perfectly aware of this (2956-63, 2994-96). Again, it is the Templar who plays the pivotal role, first in endangering Nathan, then in saving him. The Templar is disgusted by the Patriarch's display of religious fanaticism, and plays on his role as the sultan's favorite, a role that defeats the Patriarch's "documents," the agreement with Saladin. The Patriarch recognizes someone more powerful than himself and, playing from a weak hand, yields to expediency.

Paradoxically, the fact that Nathan wants to show his gratitude to the Templar who saved Recha comes to endanger him, since the Templar, like his uncle Saladin, seems to think that what he wants is his to take. Even after the Templar turns away in disgust from the Patriarch, he does not acknowledge Nathan as an equal. In one line, the Templar assures Nathan that the Patriarch's treachery made him aware of himself (3418). In the very next line, his newly-found personality turns to blackmail. The Templar tries to turn the fear that Nathan should feel at the thought of the Patriarch to his advantage by arguing that the Patriarch cannot harm Nathan or Recha if Recha would become his wife (3419-27). Given these moral ambiguities, the Templar belongs to the World of Despotism in which human relationships are based on legalistic rather than moral arguments.

Given the relationship of despot and subject between Patriarch and Templar, the Templar's independent spirit, his ultimate refusal to accept the Patriarch's authority, needs explaining. Why would he argue against the Patriarch's opinion, and in the end choose to leave rather than denouncing Nathan to the Patriarch? The answer seems to be that the Templar is in the happy position of being able to choose between a spiritual and a secular despot for his allegiance, and indeed the very next scene shows him with Saladin. Given the Templar's actions so far, he seems to be less concerned with the religious side of the issue than with the question of how he can force Nathan to give Recha to him. Hence, the Patriarch's arguments fail to have an effect, and the Templar turns to Saladin. He is slow to get over his ire as a Christian (2785-86), but fundamentally his attitude tends more toward Saladin's secular perspective than toward the Patriarch's religious one. Consequently, Saladin can defuse the Templar's anger by promising to exercise his secular power, and aid the young man in obtaining Recha.

The sultan takes it upon himself to promise the girl to the Templar while at the same time sending the Templar out to find Nathan and become reconciled to him. No thought appears to enter Saladin's mind that a pre-emption of Nathan's paternal rights might be resented. Not only money, but also human beings are his to give.

> And if in very truth you've set your heart,
> Upon this maid, rest assured—she is yours.
> Also, Nathan shall learn that
> he was allowed to raise a Christian
> child without pork meat. (2817-21)[17]

He treats Nathan and Recha's rights as subject to his despotic decision, an indication of his view of them as subjects rather than fellow human beings. He does not acknowledge Nathan and Recha's rights. Saladin's attitude is less violent than that of the Patriarch, in keeping with his portrayal as an "enlightened despot." Nonetheless, he disposes of human beings with the same gesture of generosity with which, according to Al-Hafi, he gives away money to beggars (461-76).

The priority of legal status over moral excellence sharply distinguishes the World of Despotism from the World of Enlightenment, where humanity is defined in moral rather than legal terms. The absence of moral values is noticeable throughout the play, whose action does not reward good and punish evil. Instead, it just happens that good occasionally rises from evil.

Nathan recognizes this irony when he says to the Templar, "Thanks be to the Patriarch!" (3449).[18] It is the Patriarch's spy, sent out to supply information necessary to burn Nathan at the stake, who instead supplies vital information to Nathan, the missing link in Nathan's information on the Templar's parentage. Nathan can prevent an incestuous marriage and restore Recha to her rightful relatives because the Patriarch was set on burning a Jew. By following his legalistic course of action, the Patriarch has unwittingly invoked another law, that of family blood ties. This law in turn removes Recha from his jurisdiction, since she is the niece of Saladin, and it defeats the Templar's own ends. On the other hand, it also leads to Nathan's loss of Recha, the second time that his family bonds are destroyed. Hence, it sometimes also happens that evil arises from evil.

Instead of morality, it is pure chance that charts the course toward the final scene in *Nathan the Wise* and its World of Despotism. The fact that chance more than anything else brings the family together for the final tableau puts a question mark over the scene. The reunion of religions, as envisioned in *The Education of Humankind*, results from Providence, that is, it is purposeful and teleologically comprehensible. Compared to the pedagogically exact argument of the *Education*, the lack of purpose in the play is quite striking. It is, however, consistent with the World of Despotism, where individuals are subjects, and not in control of events, perhaps not even of their destiny. It is the despot who should be in control, and Saladin fails in this part of his position.

When it comes to his government, Saladin does not measure up to the same standard of prototypical despotism that he displays in treating his subjects. According to both the categories of the *philosophes* (Mandt 678), and to Falk's description (8: 556), his unwillingness to deal with his perpetual budget crisis, and his resultant dependence on a miracle—the timely arrival of the caravan from Cairo—to prepare for the war against the crusaders, mark him as a despotic failure (Kiesel 322). Given the bloodthirstiness of the Patriarch, Saladin's lack of preparation endangers every non-Christian in Jerusalem, especially the Jews.

The Jews of Jerusalem must rely on the despot, the sultan, for their protection. The reason for their lack of legal status is not so much their religion as their lack of a leader whose legal status would match that of Saladin, who rules over a state, and that of the Patriarch, who rules over a flock. The Jews' plight is worse because Saladin does not acknowledge their delicate position. Rather than taking his task to protect them seriously, Saladin follows the lead of his sister Sittah in counting on Nathan's weakness when they plot to relieve him of his money (1136).

Nathan's only defense is his wit, his knowledge (Leventhal 521), and to those who are sensitive to the accomplishments of a cosmopolitan Freemason, his superior humanity. Nathan's authority, as described by Al-Hafi and Sittah (1048, 1131), is moral rather than legal. It is the future-oriented authority from the World of Enlightenment, and therefore unequal in the World of Despotism that Saladin and the Patriarch inhabit. It is characteristic for this contempt of mere morality that Sittah plays with Nathan's position in her plot, although she is not really unaware of his moral worth (1128-29). The results of such a valorization of legal status over human worth are all the more striking, since the Christians are plotting to assassinate Saladin (660-78), whereas the Jews, if Nathan is an example, are good citizens. In the legalistic World of Despotism, however, the Christians enjoy a measure of protection regardless of their iniquities.

Nathan seems ironically aware of the discrepancy between him and the Christians when, asked to come closer "without fear," he assures the despot that only Saladin's enemy need fear him (1798; see Hildebrandt 458). When Saladin mentions his title "improver of the world and the laws" as one he hopes to deserve after their conversation, Nathan answers, "truly a pretty title" (1902-04), obliquely referring to the opposition between the World of Despotism and the World of Enlightenment. In the former, it is the despot who improves the world, whereas in the latter it is humankind and individuals who enact improvements. At the same time, this opposition indicates that religion is not the main issue here. The relationship is between ruler and subject rather than between Muslim and Jew.

The Third Act, with the ring parable, is usually regarded as the intellectual center of *Nathan the Wise*. Although both Nathan and Saladin hear about each other, they meet in person only twice. Both meetings revolve around Saladin's attempt to remove something from Nathan over which Nathan has certain rights, in one case proprietary, and in the other case, human rights. In their first meeting, Nathan faces the loss of his money; in the second, he fights for his daughter Recha. Nathan's values correspond to those of a cosmopolitan Freemason. Property is far less important to him than human relationships. Nonetheless, while able to hold on to his money, no rhetorical skill can prevent the loss of his daughter.

When Saladin asks Nathan for the "true" religion rather than for his money, as Nathan assumed he would, he juxtaposes two terms that have very different values in the worlds of Enlightenment and Despotism. A cosmopolitan Freemason does not place money high on his agenda, even if he is a merchant by profession, and indeed nothing Nathan does or says argues that he sees his riches as anything but a commodity. They protect him to a certain extent, as when Daja exchanges large gifts for her silence about Recha's origins, and when Saladin needs Nathan's money. Beyond this utilitarian aspect, the merchant Nathan is prone to couch his ethical beliefs in commercial language, and he is eager to pay even moral debts without delay.[19] Nonetheless, his reaction to the near-loss of his house and to Saladin's anticipated raid on his purse is guided by detachment, and in the latter case, even amusement. When he refuses to become Saladin's banker, and to sink his capital in the bottomless pit of the sultan's treasury, he recognizes the futility of any rescue operations as a matter of common sense rather than of greed.

His promise that Al-Hafi can dip into his cash register at any time, and his later immediate guarantee of any debts Al-Hafi may have outstanding, reveal that for Nathan money is a device to support friendship, to do good. It is not, however, related to the future, to the project of Enlightenment. As a commodity, it has strictly present-day value; it is tied to the World of Despotism.

When Nathan is uneasy about the evident trap Saladin has laid for him, he is not concerned about losing his money. Rather, he does not know what is in store for him, another indication that Saladin may indeed turn out to be the tyrant described by Al-Hafi. Instead of power, Nathan has only his intimate knowledge of the World of Despotism to protect him. In his monologue, he reflects on his awareness of the different values current in the Worlds of Enlightenment and Despotism.

> What can he want? I thought he wanted gold,
> and now it seems that he wants truth. Truth!
> And he wants it, too, so ready-made and shiny,
> as if the truth were a minted coin! (1866-69)[20]

Nathan juxtaposes the despot's truth and his own money, thereby indicating that he gauges Saladin and Sittah's interpretation of truth and money to be in direct conflict with his own. In the World of Despotism, *truth* is a commodity, that is, it is on the same plane as *money* in Nathan's World of Enlightenment. On the authority of Nathan's friend, the dervish, the despot knows that Nathan is one of those who search for truth (336-38), and he uses this drive for his plan. Using the highest value in the World of Enlightenment, *truth*, to coerce Nathan, may be comparable to the blasphemy Lessing saw in doubting human destiny.

Truth carries the highest possible value, being related to *humankind* on one plane and *knowledge* on the other. Like a cosmopolitan Freemason, Nathan spends his life finding and imparting truth, whether in regard to the origins and opinions of the Templar and Recha, or to the future of humankind. Since he is from the World of Enlightenment, Nathan knows about the deliberations and the continuous self-searching that precede the search for truth, the endeavor that makes a cosmopolitan Freemason. Saladin, however, bursts out with his question, as if such a question could elicit a straight and quick answer (see Kiesel 325):

> He blurted out his wish so bluntly too;
> Your friendly visitor is wont to knock,
> And give you warning ere he bursts in. (1881-83)[21]

The very fact that Saladin wants the truth without delay and deliberation renders Nathan suspicious, a suspicion that the course of the conversation does nothing to disperse. Saladin shows the same impatience during the narration, hurrying Nathan along and thereby demonstrating his lack of interest in the road to the true answer.

In his deliberations, Nathan also considers the difference between a ruler in the World of Despotism and a human being in the World of Enlightenment (1878-80):

> The mere suspicion that he put the case
> but as snare for me! That is too petty!—
> Too petty?—What is too petty for a great man?[22]

Nathan's monologue contrasts his own world in the first two lines with his reading of the despot's world in the next two lines. Given the interpretation of *truth* in the cosmopolitan Freemason's World of Enlightenment, Nathan's suspicion is slanderous; reminding himself that he is dealing with a despot, the suspicion scores as possible. At the same time, the opposition of *great* and *petty* ranks the two concepts of truth. Saladin is "great" as a despot, that is, in terms of power; he is "petty" as an individual. Since the fact that Nathan escapes the trap does not excuse the fact that it was set, we can assume that Nathan regards Saladin as a despot rather than a part of humankind.

There is a moment in the play when Nathan evidently hopes to establish a relationship with Saladin that would accord with Falk's description of the acceptable role of a "member" of a present-day state. This moment occurs when Nathan hears from the Templar that the latter owes his life, and thus the ability to rescue Recha, to Saladin's show of mercy (1349-54). Nathan speaks enthusiastically of being "committed" ["gefesselt"] to Saladin, awaiting Saladin's "commands." If Saladin had accepted this voluntary act of subjugation by his subject Nathan, the relationship between them would have been as equal as possible in the divided present-day world. By considering himself a subject without being pressed, and acknowledging a despot for his character, Nathan could have maintained equality with the despot in purely human, Enlightenment terms.

Saladin and Sittah destroy whatever possibility exists of such a rapport with Nathan. They are not interested in Nathan as a human being, and thus do not even remotely consider that he might be willing to cooperate freely. Instead, Saladin is about to coerce Nathan into lending him money, using his power against a powerless "small" subject. Hence, only on the surface does Nathan's offer of money at the end of their meeting (2061-73) replicate the conditions he had assumed prior to his visit. On a deeper level, Nathan acts upon the knowledge that, regardless of what Saladin may say when overcome by emotions, he is a despot, and inclined toward willfulness. The friendship Saladin presses into Nathan's hand (2056-60) lasts until it is overridden by another whim. When Nathan does not leave Saladin without leaving some of his money as well, he shows an intimate knowledge of the World of Despotism, the knowledge that in light of despotic power gifts are retractable, and that rights, legal or human, are such gifts.

König's question, as to why there is a ruse at all instead of a straightforward appeal for money, remains pertinent (887-912; König 89-91). The answer seems to be that Saladin is an enlightened despot, a "legal" rather than an "arbitrary" despot (Mandt 678). Therefore he needs a justification to relieve Nathan of his money, and even the shadow of a moral reason, such as Nathan's supposed hypocrisy, or other deficiencies in his moral character, will do. According to the social views of the World of Enlightenment as incorporated in the American and French constitutions, property is sacred. Sittah's plan to suggest moral character as a condition of fair treatment transforms the Enlightenment insistence on morality in public and private life into an area where it suits the World of Despotism.

Saladin's distaste at his role of cunning extortioner is not that of someone close to the Enlightenment, or even that of an "enlightened" prince; in his conversation with Sittah, Saladin argues as a warrior who fights square for whatever he wants, and despises backstabbing of any kind as a weakness (1737-47). He is to "fight with weapons he does not know how to use," and he is disdainful of so much ado about money. It is in this light that we must understand his desire to come to terms with the Christians. He admires Richard the Lionhearted, and wants to deal with him as knight to knight rather than ruler to ruler. The appropriate position for an enlightened despot is taken by Sittah rather than by Saladin. She sees Richard as a ruler of the Christians, subject to the intrigues current in the Christian camp, instead of as another individual knight (866-80).

Saladin's sister and adviser Sittah makes the first move in both instances when Nathan is about to lose something. Therefore, many scholars try to exonerate Saladin from any complicity by shifting the blame onto her. Koebner (167) sees Sittah as Saladin's evil spirit, while others regard her as the voice of *raison d'état* in the play (for example, Wilson, "Flight" 259). By contrast, I think that Saladin as the despot must ultimately be held responsible for the actions of his adviser, or of his own reluctant self.

Whether Sittah argues for squeezing Nathan or wants to have Nathan's daughter Recha fetched to her harem for mere "curiosity," Saladin does not interfere with her plans. In the first instance, we saw that his attitude is determined by his warrior past; in the second, his reaction is incongruent with his own prior words. He himself had pledged Recha to the Templar without any doubt of his power to make the marriage happen, while Sittah was listening in on the conversation. Now, when she draws the logical conclusion that Recha is her brother's —and hers—to give, Saladin pretends to remember Nathan's rights. As he is the sultan, he could stop Sittah with one word.

It is in the light of the World of Despotism that we must consider Saladin's reaction to Nathan's parable. It is particularism that is behind Saladin's question of which religion is the correct one, whereas the future stage is behind Nathan's answer. It is here that Nathan's choice of form becomes important. Telling the sultan a fairy tale makes it possible for him to deceive Saladin. Rather than making the future appear reachable, though not around the corner, Nathan speaks of an indefinite future, of "thousands and thousands of years," and he predicts that there will be a judge of Saladin's question, when in fact there will be another and final revelation. As a despot, Saladin cannot relate to this revelation. Thus, Nathan tailors his answer to the particularism of Saladin's World of Despotism.

Saladin sees religions as distinctly different, while being enlightened despot enough to refrain from religious persecution. Saladin is caught in Nathan's web for one moment. However, his outburst of shame is fleeting, in line with his usual impetuosity. As a reaction to the narrative, it does not invalidate our conclusions above, and Nathan is not deceived. That he speaks of money (a commodity) in the same breath that the sultan speaks of friendship (a realization of humanity) is an ironic reversal. Nathan speaks in terms of the World of Despotism, while Saladin for one moment seems to enter the World of Enlightenment. The moment is fleeting, however, and Saladin's reaction to the ring parable contains no evidence that he grasps, let alone adopts, the concept of human self-creation toward ultimate maturity to which the judge alludes when he says "let everyone pursue his incorruptible, unprejudiced love" (2041-42). Only cosmopolitan Freemasons can, in accordance with Lessing's theory of metempsychosis, relate to these words. They look forward to the future rather than, like Saladin, back to the past.

Saladin's actions within the play relate to his need for money, his interest in the Templar, and his resultant interest in the Templar's infatuation with Recha. In his private and public concerns, Saladin indicates again and again his attachment to the past rather than the future. He keeps harking back to his existence as a warrior at a time when he is faced with a severe budget crisis, insisting that one horse, one mantle, one sword, and one God are enough to make him content (990-91). He thereby demonstrates that he preserves his past identity as a warrior, even though his present situation and indeed the future of his house demand a ruler adept in the strategies of war. Once he meets the Templar, his reaction accords with his longing for the past. He wishes to relive with the Templar the times he spent with his brother Assad, indeed to repossess his brother in the Templar; he constantly compares the Templar with Assad, and thus constructs Assad as a role model for the Templar.

The conflict between Nathan and Saladin climaxes in the last scene. Enveloped in the mantle of a cosmopolitan Freemason, Nathan displays his intellectual superiority, whereas the despot, secure in his power, proves that the "weapons" of verbal battle are by no means beyond him, regardless of the coy ignorance he affects when being told of Sittah's plot against Nathan. When Nathan enters, Saladin opens the conversation by telling him that he can have his money back. This remark relates directly to the conclusion of their last meeting, when Nathan had spoken of money and Saladin had offered friendship. Then Nathan's words had put Saladin in his place as a despot. Now, when Nathan is accompanied by the Templar to what Saladin describes as a reconciliation scene, a feast for humanity, it is Saladin who puts Nathan in his place as a money-lending subject.

Nathan refuses this gambit, publicly asserting his paternity over Recha ("your father is not lost to you"), and Recha responds by acknowledging Nathan as her father and the only man who at present matters in her life. Nathan distinguishes between a spiritual father and a biological father. He wants to remain ("bleiben") the one while accepting that he cannot be called ("heißen") the other (2912-16). In terms of a human relationship, Recha will continue to accept him as her father, as she knows how much he loves her (2916, 3649-54). In terms of power, the continuation of this relationship demands Saladin's consent. His offer of himself as an *ersatz* father, after witnessing Recha's emotional breakdown at the thought of another father (3661-

71), makes one anything but hopeful that he recognizes Recha's deep attachment to Nathan as a sufficient reason to leave her to Nathan.

And indeed, Saladin professes to see Recha's avowal of Nathan as shyness and tries physically to dislocate her by leading her up to the Templar. When Nathan stops him and Sittah, he tries to take over Nathan's bailiwick by emphasizing his knowledge: Nathan is Recha's foster father. Nathan counters with a more complete knowledge that invalidates Saladin's bid for superiority, and for a moment seems to win: he embraces the Templar as another "child" (3812-14). Unfortunately, Nathan's knowledge, while driving Saladin from his position of knowledge, ensconces the despot in his seat of power. Thwarted in his original design, Saladin learns that he is Recha's senior male relative, her natural guardian, and he reacts triumphantly to Nathan's veiled attempt to keep him from exercising his power and taking Recha to him (3833-38):

> NATHAN: As yet, they know it not! It rests with you,
>   With you alone whether you tell them the truth.
> SALADIN: I—not claim my brother's children?
>   I—not claim my nephews—my children?
>   Not claim them? I? Leave them to you?[23]

In the change from "nephews" to "children," and the outraged "leave them to you?" Saladin interprets his relationship to Nathan as rivalry. His constantly repeated "I" refers to his despotic self-centeredness. To this point, he has not shown any consideration for Recha's feelings, and indeed his argument is legalistic, based on his rights as next of kin instead of private family feelings.

Rather than uniting a utopian family, or reconciling religious differences on a higher plane, Nathan unites a despotic family. Its *pater familias*, Saladin, acts on a memory from the past when drawing in the Templar, and on a despotic impulse from the present when refusing to let Recha go. Saladin's arguments are ritualistic rather than cosmopolitan or moral. At the fall of the curtain, only Saladin and Sittah are truly happy in their state, while for the rest of its "members" there is only silence.

Nathan, for one, the representative of the cosmopolitan Freemasons, stands alone, whatever embraces may arbitrarily be offered to him. His inescapable loneliness is that of a powerless subject in the present-day state. The play *Nathan the Wise* proves an important point that is neglected in *Ernst and Falk* as well as in *The Education of Humankind*. Neither of the latter texts consider the plight of the morally advanced human being, the individual who has achieved mere humanity as opposed to particularism, within the world of the present state. Instead, they dismiss this state as transitory and thus negligible.

Seen from the world of *Nathan the Wise*, the dialectics, or perhaps only the odds, favor the World of Despotism over that of Enlightenment. Nathan's experiences demonstrate that the present-day despotic state is a major obstacle on the road to the future. The conclusion of *Nathan the Wise* does not suggest that Nathan's present loss has any value with regard to humankind's future when despots will be unknown. Rather, the play shows us a happy despot. Handing out embraces, Saladin is left in possession of the stage.

Notes

1. Many thanks go to Daniel Wilson for his very helpful editorial comments, and to Ingeborg Walther for her thorough reading of this essay.

2. See Koselleck 68-74. Influenced by Koselleck are Bahr passim, Gustafson 1-6, 17 n 3, Naumann 325-27.

3. Wilson ("Flight" 260-61) argues that it enhances Nathan's standing by making him Saladin's moral adviser.

4. "Schale" and "Kern" (2: 374). Lessing's texts are quoted from vol. 2 (*Nathan the Wise*) and vol. 8 (*The Education of Humankind, Ernst and Falk*) of Rilla's edition. In the text, I give the line numbers for *Nathan the Wise*, and the paragraphs for the *Education*. Translations are mine; originals appear in notes.

5. See, e.g., Heydemann 93, 100; Koebner 150-51, 158, 205-06; Briegleb 161.

6. See also Wilson, *Humanität* 11-12.

7. Kiesel, first edition (1975), 277. Later revisions retain the general tenor of Kiesel's argument while omitting this sentence.

8. My two-world model derives from a theory of multiple worlds. Although, in this context, I stay with the dualistic view of traditional approaches, I do not consider these two worlds the only ones present in the eighteenth century.

9. "Das Totale der einzelnen Glückseligkeiten aller Glieder ist die Glückseligkeit des Staats. Außer dieser gibt es gar keine. Jede andere Glückseligkeit des Staats, bei welcher auch noch so wenig einzelne Glieder leiden, und leiden müssen, ist Bemäntelung der Tyrannei. Anders nicht!"

10. See Slessarev 52. Bahr and Naumann follow Koselleck (68-74) in failing to differentiate between the future and the present applications of Lessing's historical philosophy. Following Koselleck's thesis of the subversive nature of Enlightenment writings, Naumann argues that Lessing wants to "abolish" the state (327). By contrast, Bohnen (176-84) isolates the utopian core of Lessing's views, arguing that the individual's inner detachment from society permits him or her to develop toward full humanity (Bohnen 180-83).

11. "[§ 99] Die Erinnerung meiner vorigen Zustände würde mir nur einen schlechten Gebrauch des gegenwärtigen zu machen erlauben.

[§ 100] Und was habe ich denn zu versäumen? Ist nicht die ganze Ewigkeit mein?" (8: 615).

12. Contrary to Koselleck, who sees the baleful influence of the Enlightenment "gripping" the representatives of absolutism (4), I argue with Scholes (1-4) that the dominant discourse, that is, the World of Despotism, co-opts potentially dangerous concepts, and thus defuses them.

13. For the latest research on enlightened absolutism and its paradoxes, see

the essay collection *Enlightened Absolutism* (see De Madariaga). Beside a survey (1-36), there are articles on "Reform in the Habsburg Monarchy" (145-88), "Maria Theresa" (189-208) and "Joseph II" (209-20), "The Smaller German States" (221-44), and "Frederick the Great" (265-88). Two rulers epitomize the paradoxes of enlightened despotism, paradoxes engendered by the attempt to transform Enlightenment concepts in order to stabilize the old regime. One is the cabinet minister to José I of Portugal, the Marquess of Pombal (75-118), and the other is Catherine II of Russia (see De Madariaga)

14. Many enlighteners were willing to cooperate, moving within the parameters of enlightened despotism. They did not act in a cynical spirit but hoped that the World of Despotism might be fused with the World of Enlightenment, their enthusiasm kindled by "enlightened" despots, such as Frederick II (the Great) of Prussia and Emperor Joseph II in Austria. In France, Catherine II (the Great) of Russia influenced public opinion, and especially the *philosophes* (De Madariaga 305), in favor of enlightened despotism.

15. Wilson, *Humanität* 76, quoting Horst Peter Neumann.

16.   Wie?
Ein Tempelherr, dem Sultan Saladin
Das Leben ließ? Durch ein geringres Wunder
War Recha nicht zu retten? Gott! (2: 328)

17.   Wär' um das Mädchen dir
Im Ernst zu tun: sei ruhig. Sie ist dein!
Auch soll es Nathan schon empfinden, daß
Er ohne Schweinefleisch ein Christenkind
Erziehen dürfen. (2: 438).

18. "Dank sei dem Patriarchen" (2: 463). Kiesel takes these words as proof for his contention that Lessing's concept of Providence does not acknowledge evil (324).

19. See Wucherpfennig passim; "Lessing" 324, 327.

20.   —Was will der Sultan? was?—Ich bin
auf Geld gefaßt; und er will—Wahrheit. Wahrheit!
Und will sie so,—so bar, so blank—als ob
die Wahrheit Münze wäre! (2: 402)

21.   Gewiß, gewiß: er stürzte mit
Der Türe so ins Haus! Man pocht doch, hört
doch erst, wenn man als Freund sich naht. (2: 402)

22. Zwar der Verdacht, daß er die Wahrheit nur
Als Falle brauche, wär' auch gar zu klein!—
Zu klein?—Was ist für einen Großen denn
zu klein? (2: 402)

23. NATHAN: Noch wissen sie von nichts! Noch steht's bei dir
Allein, was sie erfahren sollen!
SALADIN: Ich meines Bruders Kinder nicht erkennen?
Ich meine Neffen—meine Kinder nicht?
Sie nicht erkennen? ich? Sie dir wohl lassen? (2: 481)

Works Cited

Altenhofer, Norbert. "Geschichtsphilosophie, Zeichentheorie und Dramaturgie in der *Erziehung des Menschengeschlechts*: Anmerkungen zur patristischen Tradition bei Lessing." *Nation und Gelehrtenrepublik: Lessing im europäischen Zusammenhang.* Ed. Wilfried Barner, Albert M. Reh. Detroit: Wayne State UP, 1984. 25-36.

Bahr, Ehrhard. "Lessing: Ein konservativer Revolutionär? Zu 'Ernst und Falk: Gespräche für Freimäurer.'" *Lessing in heutiger Sicht.* Ed. Edward P. Harris, Richard E. Schade. Bremen: Jacobi, 1977. 299-304.

Bohnen, Klaus. *Geist und Buchstabe: Zum Prinzip des kritischen Verfahrens in Lessings literarästhetischen und theologischen Schriften.* Cologne: Böhlau, 1974.

Briegleb, Klaus. " 'Sterbender Fechter' Lessing?" *Hamburg im Zeitalter der Aufklärung.* Ed. Inge Stephan, Hans-Gerd Winter. Berlin: Reimer, 1989. 251-67.

De Madariaga, Isabel. "Catherine the Great." *Enlightened Absolutism.* Ed. H. M. Scott. Ann Arbor: U of Michigan P, 1990. 289-311.

Fischer-Lichte, Erika. *Bedeutung: Probleme einer semiotischen Hermeneutik und Ästhetik.* Munich: Beck, 1979.

Greis, Jutta. *Drama Liebe: Zur Entstehungsgeschichte der modernen Liebe im Drama des 18. Jahrhunderts.* Stuttgart: Metzler, 1991.

Gustafson, Susan E. " 'Der Zustand des stummen Staunens': Language Skepticism in *Nathan der Weise* and *Ernst und Falk.*" *Lessing Yearbook* 18 (1986): 1-19.

Heidsieck, Arnold. "Adam Smith's Influence on Lessing's View of Man and Society." *Lessing Yearbook* 15 (1983): 125-43.

Heydemann, Klaus. "Gesinnung und Tat: Zu Lessings *Nathan der Weise.*" *Lessing Yearbook* 7 (1975): 69-104.

Hildebrandt, Dieter. *Lessing: Eine Biographie.* Hamburg: Rowohlt, 1990 [first publ. 1979].

Kiesel, Helmuth. "Arbeitsbereich VI, Parts B, C [*Nathan the Wise, Ernst and Falk*]." *Lessing: Epoche, Werk, Wirkung.* Ed. Wilfried Barner et al. 5th ed. Munich: Beck, 1987.

Koebner, Thomas. "*Nathan der Weise*: Ein polemisches Stück?" *Lessings Dramen: Interpretationen.* Stuttgart: Reclam, 1987. 138-207.

König, Dominik von. *Natürlichkeit und Wirklichkeit: Studien zu Lessings "Nathan der Weise."* Bonn: Bouvier, 1976.

Koselleck, Reinhart. *Kritik und Krise: Eine Studie zur Pathogenese der bürgerlichen Welt.* Suhrkamp Taschenbücher Wissenschaft, 1. Frankfurt/M.: Suhrkamp, 1973 [first publ. 1959; Engl. trans. Cambridge: MIT Press, 1987].

Lessing, Gotthold Ephraim. *Gesammelte Werke.* 10 vols. Ed. Paul Rilla. Berlin: Aufbau, 1954-58.

Leventhal, Robert S. "The Parable as Performance: Interpretation, Cultural Transmission and Political Strategy in Lessing's *Nathan der Weise.*" *German Quarterly* 61 (1988): 502-27.

Mandt, Hella. "Tyrannis, Despotie." *Geschichtliche Grundbegriffe: Historisches Lexikon zur politisch-sozialen Sprache in Deutschland.* Ed. Otto Brunner et al. Vol. 6. Stuttgart: Klett-Cotta, 1990. 651-707.

Naumann, Dietrich. *Politik und Moral: Studien zur Utopie der deutschen Aufklärung.* Heidelberg: Winter, 1977.

Scholes, Robert. *Textual Power: Literary Theory and the Teaching of English.* New Haven: Yale UP, 1985.

Slessarev, Helga. "Lessing und Hamburg: Wechselbeziehungen zweier 'Persönlich-keiten'." *Lessing Yearbook* 13 (1981): 1-67.

Wilson, W. Daniel. " 'Die Dienste der Großen': The Flight from Public Service in Lessing's Major Plays." *DVJs* 61 (1987): 238-65.

—————. *Humanität und Kreuzzugsideologie um 1780: Die Türkenoper im 18. Jahrhundert und das Rettungsmotiv in Wielands 'Oberon', Lessings 'Nathan' und Goethes 'Iphigenie.'* Kanadische Studien zur deutschen Sprache und Literatur, 30. New York: Lang, 1984.

Wucherpfennig, Wolf. "Nathan, der weise Händler." *Akten des VI. Internationalen Germanistenkongresses, Basel 1980.* Ed. Heinz Rupp and Hans-Gert Roloff. Jahrbuch für internationale Germanistik, A, 8. Bern: Peter Lang, 1980. 57-64.

Enlightenment's Alliance with Power: The Dialectic of Collusion and Opposition in the Literary Elite

W. Daniel Wilson

MARTIN HEIDEGGER, ATTEMPTING to justify his collusion with the Nazi state, spoke in a letter of his hopes to "lead the Leader" ("den Führer [zu] führen"[1]). Heidegger was not an exceptional case; many intellectuals of the day entertained the notion that they could 'guide" Hitler. Of course, most critics agree that Horkheimer and Adorno went too far when they drew ahistorical connections between Enlightenment and modern totalitarianism. At the risk of incurring similar criticism, I would argue that Horkheimer and Adorno over-looked a much more far-reaching parallel between these phenomena, one for which Heidegger gives the cue. It seems to me plausible that Heidegger's tragic delusion is not unrelated to similar tendencies in the eighteenth century: it is the very essence of Enlightened Absolutism that the intellectual can guide an autocratic leader, inject him with humanity and the passion for reform, and thus eliminate the need for revolution or democracy. Various scholars have pointed out that many of the same cultures that experienced "Enlightened Absolutism" in the eighteenth century ultimately spawned fascist or authoritarian regimes in the twentieth—Germany, Italy, Spain, Russia.[2] The Nazi regime itself laid claim to the absolutist heritage: "A straight path leads from Frederick [the Great] to Bismarck and Hitler," we read in a 1936 hand-book.[3] While we would be foolish to take the Nazi claims at face value, many historians trace the often-noted subservient attitude of many Germans to authority back to the eighteenth century; "The obedient loyal subject of the eighteenth century," wrote an observer in 1925, "is still running around in his servile crouch today and yearns for a real majesty before whom he can grovel. Princely absolutism is still in the bones of many Germans. The rough rod of the patriarchal regime softened up the backbone of these 'subjects' for too long" (Kampffmeyer 7f.). However, German deference to authority should be explained not only as a sort of masochistic yearning for a strong master, but partly also as a function of hopes for reform (reform defined in many different ways!) that would make a revolution from below unnecessary, and in this sense should be traced back not to "princely absolutism" alone, but, more fundamentally, to *"Enlightened"* Absolutism. Thus Hans-Ulrich Wehler writes in the context of late nineteenth-century German politics: "Especially since the end of the Thirty Years' War [1648], the praxis of absolutist regimes in German states led to an ever-increasing control from above"; he calls this system, which served as a "bulwark against revolutionary ferment," a "variant of 'enlightened' absolutism" (*Das Deutsche Kaiserreich* 106). Culminating in the eighteenth century, absolutism went through a drawn-out process of relinquishing its former divine legitimation ("by the grace of God") and adopting a social-contract legitimation stemming from its efforts to serve society's needs (as Frederick II made famous in his dictum: "The monarch is the first servant of the state").[4] This was a fateful moment in political history: the authoritarian state, faced with the challenge of enlightenment's demands for equality and justice, coopted and absorbed the Enlightenment by declaring itself "enlightened'. Of course, this transformation was also dictated by very mundane factors: the new, centralized and militarized state needed a new intellectual elite to populate its burgeoning bureaucracy, and this need could only be satisfied in an alliance with the representatives of Enlightenment, who were generally critical of traditional institutions (see Grimminger 79). Faced with these theoretical and practical moves of absolutism, the Enlightenment generally—though by no means unanimously —obliged by accepting absolutist rulers' claims of their intent to reform encrusted feudal society, and by entering into public service or other forms of cooperation with the authoritarian state. We could even see this paradigm at work in *every* case of authoritarian government since that time; Leonard Krieger has suggested that all modern despots are in theory enlightened despots, since they all proceed from the postulate that they alone can define and realize the common good on the basis of their higher insight into the nature of things (90f.). The danger of the theory of Enlightened Absolutism is that every autocratic ruler can employ it to legitimize any policy and to exclude others from the political process.

The parallel between enlightened absolutism and totalitarianism has remained little more than a suggestive tidbit in intellectual history.

To be sure, German historians have recognized that the Prussian reform era under Stein and Hardenberg early in the nineteenth century cemented an alliance between intellectuals and the state that had far-reaching consequences in later periods: it firmly established the principle of a "revolution from above," reform through an elite bureaucracy, which made a democratic constitution superfluous (Aretin, *Vom Deutschen Reich* 135). But historians have failed to recognize and study thoroughly the Enlightenment roots of this alliance between intellectuals and the state, because they too often view the Enlightenment exclusively as a source of opposition to absolutist power. There was certainly an oppositional element in the Enlightenment, which culminated in the radicals in the period of the French Revolution. But in their attempts to find oppositional impulses in a movement with which they empathize, scholars have tended to obscure the illusory hopes for an *alliance* between intellect and power that guided the major minds of the Enlightenment in the quest for a rational society. Referring to the 1780s, a contemporary wrote: "Almost everyone in Germany that had any learning aimed for a position in the public service."[5] Hans Rosenberg speaks of Prussian intellectuals, beginning around 1770, possessed by an "ambitious striving—fed by the self-consciousness of the elite—to take over political decision-making" (189). Another reason that historians have neglected these aspirations to alliance with the state may be that these ideals are given their most striking expression by *literary* figures, not primarily by political figures, and it is this literary discourse that I will sketch in the following pages. Equally important for subsequent German history, however, is not just the literary repertoire that expresses these hopes, but also writers' practical attempts to influence a potentially enlightened monarch. From the outset it is important to admit that economic motives were mixed in here, since the absence of a literary market that could feed German intellectuals motivated them to seek alternative forms of support (which often led to calls for new forms of state patronage) and to seek to influence public policy toward intellectuals and the arts in order to alleviate this situation. But economic self-interest of writers does not fully explain their moral and political commitment, which is essentially a child of the Enlightenment's confrontation with traditional social, political and economic institutions. Another reason that this phenomenon is overlooked is that the discourse is often conducted in very oblique terms. In examining "participation" in the absolutist state, I therefore wish to define it in a broad sense: the various shades of alliance to and symbiosis with the state, from casual "advice" to a prince in the public sphere, through plans for state-supported academies, and outright patronage in its various forms, to actual public service at court and in the state bureaucracy.

It is within these diverse parameters that eighteenth-century intellectuals sought to ally themselves with power. Reinhart Koselleck has shown that intellectuals, whose "Raisonnement" had been banished to the private sphere by seventeenth-century political theory, began in the course of the eighteenth century to reassert their right to a voice in public affairs, and their goal was basically a reformed society in the elitist Enlightenment tradition. The resulting pressure on the absolutist monarch is the impetus for the discourse I examine. My thesis is that the actual attempts at participation in governance led to the virtual collapse of the entire illusory discourse, since its inner contradictions became apparent—in other words, once the intellectuals tried to practice what they preached, the limitations of the project became apparent, and it lost its appeal. This process of dissolution began already before the French Revolution, so that the rise in the Revolutionary period of "political society" (Becher) in the form of class interests and the predecessors of interest groups and political parties merely accelerated the dissolution that had begun earlier.

Very early in the century, both Leibniz and Gottsched devised plans for an academy of arts and science to support intellectual endeavor,[6] but these projects basically served scholastic interests and did not envision critical or advisory political potential—indeed, the very fact that these were *public* institutions precluded any political impact on the absolutist state, which shunned any hint of public criticism. In the same year as Frederick the Great's ascension to the Prussian throne, Johann Michael von Loen expressed enlightened-absolutist aspirations in his novel *The Honest Man at Court* (*Der Redliche Mann am Hofe*, 1740), a typical product of the centuries-old topoi of anti-court discourse, but with the bold ideal that an honest man could actually survive at court and reform the state by reforming the monarch. In the tradition of the Mentor idea that was given life by Fénelon's extremely popular *Télémaque* (1699), Loen begins to make a tentative break with older notions of patronage, public service, and the relations of intellectuals to power. Interestingly enough, his first step is followed most influentially by the figures that literary historians have generally called the founders of the modern German lyric, novel, and drama, respectively: Klopstock, Wieland and Lessing. (In the following I will not treat Lessing, since I have done so elsewhere,[7] and since his ideas depart significantly from the shape of the discourse outlined here.) Goethe took up the discourse from all three of these predecessors.

Klopstock took the lead, but only in an effort to raise the status of the intellectual class and in particular of the religiously inspired poet. His patronage by two "enlightened" princes, King Frederick V of Denmark and Margrave Carl Frederick of Baden, while recognized in

scholarship as an important step toward a new self-consciousness
among writers, did not advance to a model of patronage or public service that would have seen the intellectual playing a role in the affairs of
state. In fact, Klopstock lapsed into the older affirmative paradigm; he
deceived himself by claiming that his poetry praising his patrons was
motivated only by their enlightened reign. He reveals characteristic
uneasiness when he says that he wants to praise his patron, the Danish
king, in such a way that even foreigners and "republicans" would be
able to say that someone whom the king had punished would have to
praise him in this way.[8] Klopstock also planned to write a history of his
patron's reign, just as later, in his plans for an academy under Emperor
Joseph II, he reserved for himself the task of writing a history of the
Hapsburg rulers; one can hardly imagine that this history would have
been a critical one. He defended his panegyric poetry as representing
the truth about his patrons, but the bald fact is that he praised only
those monarchs who gave him money.[9] Essentially, Klopstock partakes
in a straightforward exchange: he receives a handsome pension for the
rest of his life, and in return he offers to the patron prestige and a
measure of approbation by the intelligentsia rather than their scorn.
He steers clear of political themes, sticking to the *religious* sentimentalism (*Empfindsamkeit*) that proved so successful; both of his pensions
were offered to him solely on the basis of his religious work, *The Messiah* (*Der Messias*, 1748ff.), before the rulers had even met Klopstock.[10]
The Margrave of Baden, Carl Frederick, invited Klopstock to his court
as "poet of religion and the fatherland" (qtd. Pape 88). It is inconceivable to imagine Lessing or Wieland receiving such support on this
basis. The religious content of Klopstock's life's work, *The Messiah*,
served as a guarantee to absolutist rulers that Klopstock would not
become a political writer (though they turned out to be wrong during
the period of the French Revolution[11]); the quietist political nature of
this project is shown by the fact that Klopstock hoped for help from the
politically and religiously very obscurantist Prussian King Frederick
William II (Pape 63f.). When Klopstock later proposed a *public* institution for encouraging arts and science and raising the status of writers—
his famous plan, in the late 1760s, for Joseph II to establish an academy
to support arts and scholarship—the authorities reacted with automatic
rejection (see Hurlebusch/Schneider). Clearly, they would not support
intellectuals engaged in discourses in which there was any risk of public
criticism of their regime—though they had little to fear from Klopstock
himself. Critics like Helmut Pape go through all sorts of contortions of
argumentation to defend Klopstock, but he was clearly involved in
deep contradictions—and in the sort of exchange that did not essen-

tially depart from previous models except in the essential step of raising the social status of writers.

C. M. Wieland took up the discourse where Klopstock left off: for
if it was unacceptable to engage in praise of the patron who gave the
writer a pension, and unrealistic to expect the monarch to create a *public* institution that might end up criticizing him, then a logical alternative, strengthened by various strands of Enlightenment thought, was
that the intellectual would be employed to provide a *private* voice of
criticism for the monarch. Wieland tried to develop a concept of "critical" patronage, an idea portrayed ex negativo in one of the most underrated (because idiosyncratic) novels of the century, *The Dialogues of
Diogenes of Sinope* (*Die Dialogen des Diogenes von Sinope*, 1770), and
developed in the tradition of the "Fürstenspiegel" in his influential
novel *The Golden Mirror* (*Der goldne Spiegel*, 1772).[12] In his own life,
Wieland placed high hopes in his appointment as tutor to the young
prince Carl August of Weimar, but Wieland's influence on Carl August
was almost certainly much less significant than he had hoped.

The real sequel to Wieland's failure in Weimar is Goethe's failure
there, and Goethe's public service loses much of its idiosyncratic nature
when viewed as the culmination of the long discourse that I have
sketched. Goethe combined aspects of Klopstock's and Wieland's projects. In Klopstock's relationship to the Count of Baden, Goethe (and
probably his Duke Carl August) found the precedent of a close personal friendship between a prince and a non-conformist intellectual, a
friendship that might lead to political influence (though in Klopstock's
case it did *not* lead to political influence, and even in personal terms
the friendship between Carl August and Goethe was much less dignified than Klopstock had envisioned[13]). From Wieland, Goethe learned
the principle of slow formative influence on the monarch, partly
through gentle political criticism. This was, of course, a central idea of
Enlightened Absolutism, but it came to Goethe through demonstrable
personal influences of the examples of Klopstock and Wieland.[14] Various critics have recognized this reform impulse in Goethe's motivations
—what Christa Bürger calls Goethe's "wish for social efficacy" (55).
But most of these critics have overlooked the extensive discourse
before Goethe. One of the most recent pronouncements on Goethe's
public service (by Gerhard Sauder) backtracks in a different direction,
asserting that Goethe held out as long as he did in his very difficult
position as minister of state because of his friendship with Carl August.
It is difficult to imagine anyone as driven by his own self-conception as
Goethe spending ten of the best years of his life with his nose to the
grindstone of petty administration in a tiny German Duchy, sacrificing
his poetic and artistic talents, unless he was really committed to a set of

ideals. Goethe did not write or speak much about his motivations for public service in Weimar; as Helmuth Kiesel has noted, Goethe's period of most intense administrative activity in Weimar, his first decade there, is the period about which Goethe provided the least autobiographical reflection, for he was palpably uncomfortable with his role as what others contemptuously called a "prince's servant" ("Fürstendiener"). But certain documents do suggest that his motivations drew on the discourse to which I have drawn attention, the desire "to change the disharmony of the world to harmony."[15] Goethe tried to realize something of what Wieland had depicted in *The Golden Mirror*.

However, Wieland almost certainly imparted to Goethe sober doubts about the feasibility of such a project (since we find such doubts in *The Golden Mirror*), and these doubts turned out to be justified in Goethe's case. Over the years, he became more and more discouraged regarding the possibility of working for the good though his friendship with Carl August; I can only point in passing to literary works like *Torquato Tasso* and especially the poem *Ilmenau*, where he attempted to work through such problems. Influential authors of recent handbooks on classicism (Borchmeyer, Ueding) have tended to overlook the failures and contradictions in Goethe's administrative activity, bringing in through the back door the old "Modell Weimar" (Ueding) and the myth of Weimar liberality. Despite all of Goethe's successes, he was involved in contradictions because (this is Goethe's "advance" over Wieland) he made clear to the Duke from the beginning that he accepted fully the principle of absolutism (this demonstration of his qualification to serve an absolute ruler is, I think, an ancillary explanation for Goethe's early pranks with Carl August, all of which demonstrated the reach of absolutist caprice, even into the private lives of subjects). A few short examples from Goethe's (still too little-known) administrative service in the Privy Council, the governing body of Weimar, will flesh out these contradictions—not only because we are examining the *literary* discourse of collusion, but because Goethe's is one of the very best documented cases of administrative activity in Enlightened Absolutism—*and* because Goethe's collusion with the state gave as-yet under-investigated legitimation to authoritarian government in the nineteenth and twentieth centuries in Germany.

Because of the small size of the Duchy, the Council had to deal with the most mundane and the most lofty of matters—everything from diplomatic missions and wars to releasing a baker's apprentice from his journeymanship, punishing a drunken student and digging a new well in Weimar. One of the many "microcases" involving individuals concerned some Jewish businessmen travelling through the Duchy. They were arrested and fined for insulting a petty official, but the Privy Councillors accepted the Jews' version of the incident, that he had in fact first insulted them. The reports of three councillors, including Goethe, have been preserved. It is tempting to marvel at the apparent liberality of J. C. Schmidt and Goethe, who bend over backwards to take the party of the Jews. But soon the reasons become clear, beginning with Schmidt's report: "Is a Jew, *especially if he is a respected businessman*, such a despicable creature that he has to suffer any insult without being galled?"[16] Goethe echoes Schmidt's implication that it is the *merchant* that is important to the government, not the human being and his rights; the behavior of the official who insulted the Jews "is that much more striking if one substitutes other merchants for Jews. He would surely not have carried on this way if that were the case."[17] And then Goethe closes his report unmistakably: the Jews' fine must be cancelled, he says, "since this episode comes at a time when we have to be careful to make the journey through Weimar safe and pleasant for each and every passenger."[18] The reason for this concern is that a high priority for the Duchy was to attract transit travelers from other routes, thus gaining considerable profit from tolls and stimulating Weimar commerce.[19] The Jews' money gave them certain rights; it would be difficult to imagine that the highest levels of Weimar government would have cared much about them had they not served the interests of the state. And the fate of such individuals, as always in "Enlightened" Absolutism, lay entirely in the hands of the prince and governing bodies like the Privy Council, who judged the matter purely according to state interests, not according to enlightened concepts like individual rights.

This conclusion is supported by another case, which shows what could happen when state interests ran counter to those of an individual. In 1781, Christian Gottfried Gruner (1744-1815), a professor of medicine at Jena, was called before the Privy Council and mercilessly browbeaten because of a speech in which he had publicly criticized one of the Duke's favorite projects, a childbirth hospital (*Accouchir-Institut*) in Jena.[20] A protocol gives full details of the session, though without attributing the various statements to particular members of the Council; present were Fritsch, Schnauß and Goethe. Professor Gruner had criticized the hospital on professional grounds, and yet the members of the Council did not weigh the scientific arguments at all; they merely pointed out to him in the harshest terms that criticism of one of the Duke's projects was not permitted. Contemporaries as well as later historians have consistently praised the liberality of the Weimar government and its felicitous effect on freedom of thought in Jena. However, cases like this show that this academic freedom did not include the only really important freedom, to criticize government policy. Furthermore, I have shown elsewhere that a certain freedom of expression was *perceived* to exist in Jena only because liberal professors were hired with the understanding that they henceforth restrict their liberalism to non-political matters, and professors who could not conform to such restrictions were either not hired in the first place or were fired later.[21] Thus the university could attract students—an important economic resource for the Duchy—with the appearance of liberality, while satisfying the demands of parents and of other German governments for political reliability.

Professor Gruner's case is connected to another that is more well known: the affirmation of the death penalty for infanticide (Gruner's offending speech had treated the question of reducing the rate of infanticide, and he obviously felt that the childbirth hospital did not help to do so). Enlightenment discourse—and this includes the writers of the "Storm and Stress" movement—ran entirely in favor of leniency for women who felt driven by social mores and hypocrisy to kill their babies born out of wedlock (see the essay by Hans-Gerd Winter in this volume). The Privy Council's upholding of the death penalty—with Goethe's explicit concurrence[22]—is striking because it was apparently the Duke who had called for the Council's advice and wanted to eliminate the death penalty.[23] Scholars have for decades shaken their heads over Goethe's concurrence in this decision, but few of them have made clear—or known—that the deliberations were not an abstract matter, to be applied when an unusual case of infanticide occurred; rather, the life of a woman hung in the balance, one Johanna Höhne from Tannroda.[24] A previously unpublished letter by J. J. C. Bode gives some perspective on the case, since it shows how unpopular the decision probably was; Bode writes from Weimar: "Tomorrow I am going to Erfurt to avoid the beheading of a child-murderess here, since it seems to me more like state murder than punishment."[25] And the case is given a gruesome sort of plasticity when we look over the shoulder of the medicine professor in Jena who a few days later received the corpse of Johanna Höhne for his medical classes and complained that she had been allowed to get too fat in jail.[26] After Goethe had portrayed the agony of a child-murderess with sympathetic conviction in the first version of *Faust* (and the defiance of an unwed mother in an effective poem[27]) and thus had participated in the Enlightened discourse of liberalized criminal law and social justice, he went on to negate this discourse in his role as a minister of state. Hans Arens points out that Goethe did not need the now-famous execution of Susanna Margaretha Brandt in Frankfurt[28] to bring the issue of infanticide to his attention, since there were so many others;[29] Arens missed the case of Johanna Höhne, who might have haunted Goethe when in 1798 he gave Faust the following vision of a woman—apparently his lover Gretchen, who is eventually executed for murdering her baby:

> I cannot part from this sight.
> How strangely this fine throat
> Is adorned by a single red strand
> No wider than a knife blade!
>
> Ich kann von diesem Blick nicht scheiden.
> Wie sonderbar muß diesen schönen Hals
> Ein einzig rotes Schnürchen schmücken,
> Nicht breiter als ein Messerrücken! (4202-05)[30]

Beyond the poetic and personal aspects of this haunting episode and of the others mentioned, they show the intellectual's dilemma within the contradictions of Enlightened Absolutism. Goethe finally saw through the illusion of substantial reform under absolutism. His "flight" to Italy, as he later called it, was a flight from the dilemma of enlightened absolutism. On the eve of this flight Goethe wrote: "Whoever takes on administration without being a ruling prince is either a Philistine or a rascal or a fool."[31] Goethe's illusion that an enlightened adviser can effect change had been destroyed by this point. With this illusion gone, Goethe was no longer willing to sacrifice his artistic talents, and the result was the flight to Italy: the return to literature and art, a step that eventually established the concept of the autonomy of art in the core period of Weimar Classicism, and thus valorized for German cultural history the divorce between art and politics. In a political and even an aesthetic sense, then, the genesis of the central Classical project derives from the failure of "Enlightened" Absolutism.

Schiller's development corroborates this finding. *Don Carlos* (1787) reveals the bankruptcy of "Enlightened" Absolutism by portraying individuals incapable of responsibly wielding absolute power simply because of the inherent limitations of human beings and their personal interests; while Philipp and Carlos illustrate this failure from the point of view of the monarch, Marquis Posa demonstrates the same bankruptcy from the perspective of the intellectual. In Schiller we find manifest the genesis of the cultural-political program of German Classicism (*Aesthetic Letters*) in a belief in the inefficacy either of influence on a monarch (*Don Carlos*) or direct political action (the French Revolution). Schiller thus arrived independently at a position similar to Goethe's: the perceived impossibility of reforming the state either by collective pressure or by direct influence on a monarch led to a valorization of the aesthetic realm as a supposed catalyst for long-term political change.

I want to end with a look at two tendencies of the late Enlightenment that have been seen as radicalizations of the Enlightenment, as the closest approximation in Germany to a consistent political application of Enlightenment ideals: the secret society of Illuminati—with which both Goethe and Schiller were fascinated in different ways—and the movement of "popular Enlightenment" (*Volksaufklärung*). I see the Illuminati, however, not as a political radicalization of Enlightenment, but as a culmination of the illusion of the intellectual's influence within absolutism. To be sure, the Illuminati were a *potentially* oppositional group; in fact, they formulated a radical anarchist or revolutionary goal, the elimination of states and monarchs. But we very quickly find the typically German ideology emerging: the Illuminati hoped to *reform* society, not revolutionize it, relying on the century's favorite method: long-term educative influence on the monarch. The political-sounding goals of the Illuminati functioned merely as political alibis that convinced intellectuals that they were finally liberating themselves from the absolutist state and realizing Enlightenment goals by conspiratorial tactics; the political vocabulary remained abstract and never guided them in any sort of practical political program.[32]   Their inefficacy as a real political opposition derived from their tactic of "occupying" the state by recruiting their members among high bureaucrats and even princes, in order both to provide themselves with insurance against repression and to convince prospective members that they were politically harmless. This tactic, as well as the philosophical postponement of political action, guaranteed symbiosis with Enlightened Absolutism and even epitomizes its principles; the Illuminati had to *be*, in fact, as politically harmless as they *appeared*. But even aside from the overreactive government repression of the group in Bavaria (their breeding-grounds), the Illuminati got themselves into further trouble on the home turf of German Classicism by relying naively on the enlightened instincts of monarchs. They soon discovered that in case of conflict, dynastic and state interests always won out over enlightened or Illuminati goals in these princes. The result in Weimar, as I have shown by examining for the first time in detail the documents of the Illuminati group there, is that Duke Carl August—who was, together with Duke Ernst II of Gotha, the first important reigning prince to become a member of the Illuminati—and his leading adviser Goethe were from the very beginning of their membership in the society concerned with keeping it under surveillance, and finally turned to repression of their "Brothers."[33]   This was a crucial historical moment: historians have recognized that the repression of the Illuminati together with the resulting conspiracy theory (which blamed the Illuminati for the French Revolution) was a pivotal step toward the development of modern political categories, and in particular toward the polarization between Enlightenment and absolutism, between intellectuals demanding a role in political decision-making and a political authority that began reacting more and more in police categories. Goethe and Carl August were not merely bystanders in this process; they were among the very first political authorities to turn against the Illuminati (and it is merely a fascinating twist of intellectual and political history that they were themselves Illuminati). Thus Goethe's personal role in the crisis of Enlightened Absolutism is seminal on two fronts; at almost precisely the historical moment that he abandoned the Enlightenment illusion of the possibility of transforming society through working as a senior government official and "mentor" of the prince, he helped nip in the bud the only *potentially* radical political group produced by the German Enlightenment.[34] He thus contributed on two fronts to the schism between Enlightenment and absolutism, to the collapse of the ideal of Enlightened Absolutism, and in this schism we find him firmly on the side of absolutism.

An examination of the Illuminati in Weimar and Gotha, whose importance for the development of the secret society only becomes clear through these documents, confirms the impression, gained from analysis of other leading Illuminati, that the organization did not produce any political radicals.[35] Though conspiracy theorists from the period of the French Revolution and even some modern scholars have consistently claimed that the Illuminati favored violent overthrow of the government and have referred to a document for the highest members of the Order, my recent publication of this document makes clear that Weishaupt, its author, merely warns against the possibility of revolution and in fact seems to favor a cementing of the privileges of the aristocracy.[36] Even if radicalism is hinted at in other documents, neither Weishaupt nor any other Illuminati really thought of these theoretical musings as constituting a practical political program for the group. And once the French Revolution threatened to put into practice what Weishaupt had apparently demanded, Weishaupt himself drew back from a revolutionary solution; rule by the people, he said, would be worse than rule by the princes, and would threaten the world with anarchy.[37]

All of these Illuminati, as almost all liberal-minded intellectuals in Germany, were bound by the ideas of Enlightened Absolutism, not by revolutionary fervor. This can be shown most clearly in the case of one of the most prominent statesmen among the Illuminati, Carl Theodor von Dalberg, who was governor of the Mainz territory of Erfurt (it is to Erfurt that the above-mentioned Bode, the most important Illuminat in Weimar, wanted to flee to avoid the beheading of Johanna Höhne). A friend of Goethe's in nearby Weimar, Dalberg was chosen to be the designated Elector of Mainz, one of the most important political positions of the day, and later was the prince of the Rhenish Confederation under Napoleon. Dalberg's position in the Illuminati had been a puzzle for historians, but the Weimar Illuminati documents show clearly that he had one of the highest ranks in the order and actively tried to help Weishaupt when he was driven out of Bavaria.[38] Dalberg cannot be counted a radical, however. He was perhaps one of the most liberal of statesmen in his day, giving asylum to political refugees, especially the well-known revolutionary Georg Friedrich Rebmann. In the end, he was forced to crack down on Rebmann, but this was due to outside pressures. On the other hand, Dalberg clearly did not support revolution, and his enlightened attitude toward government did not have room for radicalism. He is one of the finest examples of Enlightened Absolutism, but his Illuminati connections clearly did not take him any further than that.

The Illuminati in Gotha also had an important link to the movement of "popular Enlightenment" (*Volksaufklärung*), in the person of Rudolph Zacharias Becker, who was both theoretically and practically the most significant representative of this attempt to extend the benefits of Enlightenment to the lower classes.[39] Becker's famous *Advice Manual for Peasants* (*Noth- und Hülfsbüchlein fur Bauersleute*, 1788) was one of the greatest commercial successes in the eighteenth (and nineteenth) century. This project of bringing "Enlightenment" to the lower classes would seem on first blush to be a politically charged one. However, "popular Enlightenment" in Germany never took the step to political discourse; its aim was to improve the quality of life for peasants through rational exploitation of the environment and through useful information, and to make the peasants happy with their lot rather than questioning the status quo.[40] At the beginning of the 1780s, before he had joined the Illuminati, Becker claimed that Enlightenment would prevent the peasants from revolting rather than encouraging them to do so, and he seems to have convinced those in power of this principle, since they bought his popular writings and had them distributed free to peasants. Becker did not change these views, either when he became an Illuminat or when he was confronted with the threat of rebellion in Germany. Though like many other German intellectuals he welcomed the French Revolution, he firmly rejected the prospect of any such event in Germany. He claimed that in contrast to France, no revolution was necessary in Germany, where princes were friends of the people and ruled in an enlightened, patriarchal manner (a statement that did not go unchallenged by Becker's contemporaries).[41]

Thus, both potential radicalizations of Enlightenment in Germany, the conspiratorial secret society and the efforts at "popular Enlightenment," stopped far short of the political implications of Enlightenment. The discourse of Enlightened Absolutism had taken root too firmly in Germany for political radicalization to reach any but a few intellectuals (the revolutionary Jacobins).[42] It was the discourse of collusion, of the intellectual's alliance with the state, that nourished the illusions of Enlightened Absolutism. All of these variants—public service, the Illuminati, and "popular Enlightenment"—ended a few years before the Revolution or during it: the literary discourse of collusion ended in the disillusionment of Goethe, its foremost representative, and his turn to art; the Illuminati ended in repression by the absolutist state itself (including Weimar), a repression the Illuminati had made inevitable by their collusion with power. And popular Enlightenment became too suspect during the Revolutionary period to remain viable— and any political aspirations its founders may have had were stillborn from the start. These important strands of the discourse thus collapsed even before the Revolution dealt a severe blow to the idea of Enlightened Absolutism. The discourse of Enlightened Absolutism survived in the halls of the German military state: as Hans Rosenberg has shown, the enlightened reform ethos drove the Prussian bureaucracy already under Frederick the Great, but increasingly in the Prussian reform period. Rosenberg shows that the emerging late Enlightenment and Classical concept of *Bildung* was a central enabling ideology for these young Prussian officials; however, it was not only this lofty abstraction, but also Goethe's actual service to the state that could give legitimacy and encouragement to the Prussian civil servants and to anyone seeking salvation in reform "from above." Though the differences between Enlightened Absolutism and totalitarianism are vast, the pattern I examine highlights the predilections of intellectuals in both centuries to seek to realize their goals by the non-democratic means of collusion with a strong ruler. The German break with the liberal French and English tradition thus began not only after the French Revolution, but decades earlier; though German imaginations were fired by the French examples of Diderot as adviser to Catherine the Great and Voltaire as adviser to Frederick the Great, the French Enlightenment had abandoned the ideal of Enlightened Absolutism in favor of radical democratic ideals at just the time when German fascination with the alliance with power was at its peak (see Aretin, "Einleitung" 21). My final plea is that this discourse not be used to discredit the German Enlightenment as a whole. Even within this discourse of collusion, the irony is that the self-reflective *doubts* of eighteenth-century proponents of enlightened public service were lost to later ages. And Germans seeking a progressive tradition can in any case look to the other heritage of the Enlightenment, the few predecessors of "political society" (Becher) such as the German "Jacobins" and the proponents of a free, critical press (in some cases this "other" Enlightenment is represented along with absolutist illusions in the same writer, such as Wieland). It is a thin tradition, but it will have to do.

Notes

1. Pöggeler 63. After the war, Heidegger explained that he had believed that "Hitler would, after he had taken on responsibility for the entire people in 1933, grow beyond the party and its doctrine" ("Hitler werde, nachdem er 1933 in der Verantwortung für das ganze Volk stand, über die Partei und ihre Doktrin hinauswachsen")—statement of 15 Dec. 1945, qtd. Martin 210.

2. Besides the well-known examples of Frederick II ("the Great") in Prussia, Joseph II, Leopold II and possibly Maria Theresa in Austria, and Catherine II ("the Great") in Russia, regimes dominated by the principle of Enlightened Absolutism were found in Tuscany (Peter Leopold, later Leopold II of Austria), Milan (1750s), Naples (Tanucci, from 1755, and Ferdinand IV and Maria Caroline), and Spain (and Parma: Charles III, from 1760). The "minor" German examples— especially Carl Friedrich of Baden and Carl August of Weimar—have been emphasized recently by historians, since the reputations of Frederick, Joseph and Catherine have begun to be tarnished. For a recent English-language survey of research on Enlightened Absolutism, see Scott.—It should be pointed out that Enlightened Absolutism also arose in states that did not develop totalitarianism in the twentieth century: Denmark (Frederick V) and Sweden (Gustav III). See Aretin, "Einleitung" 40f.; Lousse 100; Walder 105f.—The presence of Russia in this list may appear questionable for two reasons: first, historians have questioned whether Enlightened Absolutism ever appeared there (Vierhaus, "Absolutismus" 56), and second, the capacity of Soviet socialism for self-reform in the 1980s and 1990s marks only one of many fundamental differences between it and fascism.

3. Qtd. Lehmann 8; see Baumgart 104.

4. On the transformation from traditional to "enlightened" absolutism see, for example, Wehler, *Gesellschaftsgeschichte* 223; Schneiders 33; Hartung, "Der aufgeklärte Absolutismus" 149; Vierhaus 59; Aretin, "Der Aufgeklärte Absolutismus" 14. For Frederick's remark and similar ones by Joseph II and Leopold II see Aretin 15; Helen Liebel puts the quotation in a critical perspective: 530f., see 539f.

5. "Nach der Anstellung im Staatsdienste strebte fast alles in Deutschland, was auf Bildung Anspruch machte" (Brandes 167).

6. See van Dülmen and the essays in Hartmann/Vierhaus.

7. See Wilson, "'Die Dienste der Großen.' "

8. 18 Nov. 1750, to Moltke; *Briefe* 1: 145 ("Republicaner").

9. At various points in his life Klopstock sought the favor of a prince or nobleman against his own principles. On one such occasion he felt forced "under the pressure of his almost desperate situation" (Pape 38) to dedicate a poem to the Prince of Wales; on this occasion Klopstock wrote that he was *otherwise* such a decided enemy of dedications" ("sonst ein so großer Hasser der Zuschriften"). In

other respects, too, the contradictions in Klopstock's attitude are evident: Klopstock repeatedly denied that his plan for a Viennese academy under governmental auspices was intended to serve him personally, but rather arts and sciences generally; however, Helmut Pape has clearly refuted this claim (110-11).

10. In the preface to one of his poems praising the Danish king, Klopstock notes "that the author of the *Messiah* [i.e., Klopstock] owes his present leisure mainly to the dignified material" of that work ("daß der Verfasser des Meßias vornehmlich der würdigen Materie, seine itzige Musse zu verdanken hat," qtd. Pape 70). Against his intention, Klopstock shows here that his writings have gained him a pension because they are not dangerous to the state. For a misguided attempt to make a progressive writer out of Klopstock, see Zimmermann.

11. See, most recently, Winter.

12. See Wilson, "Wieland's *Diogenes*" and "Intellekt und Herrschaft" and, more recently, Bersier's elucidation of Rousseau's and Fénelon's influence on *The Golden Mirror*.

13. See the famous letter in which Klopstock warns Goethe that the Duke could be brought to an early death by excessive alcohol consumption; "Germans have until now justifiably criticized their princes who don't want to have anything to do with men of letters. At present they are happy to exclude the Duke of Weimar from this criticism. But imagine what other princes will be able to point to in their defense if you continue with your behavior" ("Die Deutschen haben sich bisher mit Recht über ihre Fürsten beschwert, daß diese mit ihren Gelehrten nichts zu schaffen haben wollen. Sie nehmen jetzo den Herzog von Weimar mit Vergnügen aus. Aber was werden andere Fürsten, wenn Sie in dem alten Ton fortfahren, nicht zu ihrer Rechtfertigung anzuführen haben?" 8 May 1776). Goethe responded brusquely: "Spare us in the future with such letters, dear Klopstock!" ("Verschonen Sie uns ins Künftige mit solchen Briefen, lieber Klopstock!" 21 May 1776). It should be remembered that Klopstock's concern is to attain favorable conditions for intellectuals at other courts; he does not mention a political interest—e.g., the welfare of the duke's subjects.

14. Goethe and Carl August had met for the second time in Karlsruhe, where Klopstock had lived in very close personal relationship with Margrave Carl Friedrich from October 1774 until almost the end of March 1775. Goethe visited Karlsruhe shortly after Klopstock's departure and later wrote in his autobiography that the margrave was "highly respected among German regents because of his excellent political goals" ("wegen seiner vortrefflichen Regierungszwecke unter den deutschen Regenten hoch verehrt," MA 16: 768; see Pape 97). Pape writes that "Klopstock's Karlsruhe support appears to have served as a model for Goethe's appointment in Weimar: in May 1775 Goethe and Carl August, who had become acquainted a few months earlier in Mainz, met during a visit at the Karlsruhe court; both were probably impressed by the ideal relationship between Klopstock and the Baden margrave, and each had shortly before had a conversation with Klopstock" (98). Furthermore, the relationship between Klopstock and Carl Friedrich, which contravened all courtly etiquette, was known publicly and debated vigorously. But what Goethe and Carl August learned from this model was not a political relationship, because none existed between Klopstock and Carl Friedrich. Rather, they probably gained from it the precedent of a poet who had become a close friend of a prince. However, the relationship between Goethe and Carl August was to take an entirely different form than the Klopstock model, as we shall see. And Goethe became a statesman; here I think we can see the influence of Wieland's ideas. Wieland had been invited to Weimar in 1772 as tutor to the then

underaged Carl August.

15. "die Disharmonie der Welt in Harmonie zu bringen," to Charlotte von Stein, 24 Apr. 1783, *Briefe* 1: 425; Bürger 58. Though Goethe, like Werther, inveighed against the "political subordination" that a courtly position would entail, he remembered later in life the heady legal reforms initiated in the period of his Frankfurt law practice, when he wrote *Werther*: "Here a happy field was opened up to us, the youngest men, where we could tumble around to our hearts' content" ("Hier war uns, den Jüngsten, ein heiteres Feld eröffnet, in welchem wir uns mit Lust herumtummelten," MA 16: 600). Though Goethe only took the step into public service (in Weimar) a year and a half after finishing *Werther*, letters from the *Werther* period, as well as his political conversations with the Weimar Duke Carl August only months after the novel was written (December 1774), reveal that Goethe's political enthusiasm—the "hundreds of wishes, hopes, plans" ("hunderterley Wünsche, Hoffnungen, Entwürfe") that a political work like Möser's *Patriotische Phantasien* awakened in him (28 Dec. 1774 to Jenny von Voigts née Möser, *Briefe* 1: 175)—were well established in the Werther period.

16. "Ist ein Jude, wenn er auch ein angesehener Handelsmann ist, ein so verworfenes Geschöpf, der jede Beschimpfung erdulden muß, ohne daß sich die Galle bey ihm regen darf?" between 20 and 25 Oct. 1785, Goethe: *Amtliche Schriften* 1: 397 (my emphasis).

17. "Am meisten fällt Lindners Betragen in die Augen wenn man statt der Juden andre Kaufleute substituirt. Er würde sich alsdann gewiß ein solches Betragen nicht erlaubt haben," ibid. 398.

18. "Es scheint mir daher eine Art von Satisfacktion um so nötiger als diese Geschichte in eine Zeit fällt, wo man Sorge tragen muß den Weeg über Weimar allen und ieden Passagieren sicher und angenehm zu machen," ibid. 398.

19. See Goethe's report, *Werke* 2.2: 708-12 and Hartung, *Großherzogtum Sachsen* 92.

20. Goethe, *Amtliche Schriften* 1: 140-43; see Wilson, *Geheimbünde* 239 n. 105. Schubart-Fikentscher mentions the case only in passing (47).

21. See Wilson, *Geheimbünde* 212-55.

22. Goethe, *Amtliche Schriften* 1: 251 (4 Nov. 1783).

23. Schubart-Fikentscher 54-59.

24. Goethe, *Amtliche Schriften* 1: 250; 4: 74. Two otherwise thorough and informative recent commentators who overlook this fact are Hannelore Schlaffer in the 'Munich Edition' (Goethe, *Werke* 2.2: 942f.) and Hans Arens in his excellent commentary to *Faust* (453). The only recent scholar of whom I am aware that draws due attention to this incident is Karl-Heinz Hahn (74-76).

25. "Morgen gehe ich nach Erfurth, um einer hiesigen Köpferey einer Kindermörderinn aus zu weichen, indem es mir nicht als eine Strafe, sondern als ein Staatsmord vorkommt". Bode to Adolph Freiherr von Knigge, dated in Illuminati code "Heropolis, den 27ten Aban. 1153. Jzdegd" (Weimar, 27 Nov. 1783), signed "Aemilius" (Bode's Illuminati name), Geheimes Staatsarchiv preußischer Kulturbesitz, Abteilung Merseburg, 5.2. G 39, Nr. 102, Dok. 136.

26. "Yesterday I got a new piece of work because of the body of the childmurderess; I only wish she had not been so well fed in prison so that she might have been more useful for my demonstrations" ("Gestern habe ich wieder eine neue Arbeit durch den Körper der Kindermörderin bekommen; ich wünschte aber nur, sie wäre in ihrem Gefängniß nicht so gut genährt worden, so wäre sie zu meinen Demonstrationen brauchbarer." Professor Justus Christian Loder to Jakob Friedrich von Fritsch—one of the members of the Council who had voted to retain

the death penalty for infanticide—30 Nov. 1783, Goethe- und Schiller-Archiv Weimar, 88/II, 2, 3, fol. 5).

27. "Vor Gericht" ("The Accused in Court"), *Werke* 2.1: 32; see the interpretation by Walter Müller-Seidel.

28. See Beutler.

29. Arens 453.

30. Hahn (75) also points to other Goethe poems that might have been influenced by the Höhne case.

31. "wer sich mit der Administration abgiebt, ohne regierender Herr zu seyn, der muß entweder ein Philister oder ein Schelm oder ein Narr seyn" (letter of 9 July 1786, *Briefe* 1: 514). Of course, though one illusion is broken, another remains: the illusion that if he *were* himself the prince, he could reform his state. Goethe remains unaware that even the prince is bound by the dictates of the system of feudal absolutism.

32. See Wilson, *Geheimbünde*, ch. 1.

33. Wilson, *Geheimbünde*, esp. ch. 3 and 4.

34. The only other possibility was the German Union (Deutsche Union), which was somewhat more radical than the Illuminati simply by virtue of its refusal to admit princes; however, this group had never really moved beyond initial organizing when it was suppressed.

35. For the following see Wilson, "Illuminatenideologie", and Wilson, *Geheimbünde*, ch. 1.

36. See Wilson, "Der politische Jacobinismus."

37. Wilson, *Geheimbünde*, Document No. 56 (351-52).

38. See Wilson, "Illuminatenideologie" and the literature on Dalberg listed there.

39. On Becker, see esp. Siegert.

40. See esp. Ruppert 347.

41. See Wilson, "Illuminatenideologie."

42. The connection between the Illuminati and the Jacobins—a connection claimed at every turn by the conspiracy theorists of the 1790s—is so thin as to be meaningless; the Jacobin Georg Forster's name appears on a list of Illuminati (see Fehn 238), but the only study of the subject concludes that he was not a member (Steiner 107-09, 196-98); if he was a member, his membership was not significant, in any case not as significant as his membership in the Rosicrucians, the conservative enemy of the Illuminati. For further detail on Illuminatism and Jacobinism, see Wilson, "Politik und Sozialstruktur."

Works Cited

Arens, Hans. *Kommentar zu Goethes Faust I.* Beiträge zur neueren Literaturgeschichte, ser. 3, 57. Heidelberg: Winter, 1982.

Aretin, Karl Otmar Freiherr von. "Einleitung: Der Aufgeklärte Absolutismus als europäisches Problem." Aretin (ed.) 11-51.

———. *Vom Deutschen Reich zum Deutschen Bund.* Deutsche Geschichte, 7. Göttingen: Vandenhoeck & Ruprecht, 1980.

———, ed. *Der Aufgeklärte Absolutismus.* Neue Wissenschaftliche Bibliothek, 67. Köln: Kiepenheuer & Witsch, 1974.

Baumgart, Peter. "Wie absolut war der preußische Absolutismus?" *Preußen. Politik, Kultur, Gesellschaft.* Ed. Manfred Schlenke. (Revised ed. of vols. 2-4 of

382 W. DANIEL WILSON

the catalogue of the 1981 Prussia exhibition in West Berlin.) Vol. 1. Reinbek: Rowohlt, 1986. 103-19.

Becher, Ursula A. J. *Politische Gesellschaft: Studien zur Genese bürgerlicher Öffentlichkeit in Deutschland.* Veröffentlichungen des Max-Planck-Instituts für Geschichte, 59. Göttingen: Vandenhoeck & Ruprecht, 1978.

Bersier, Gabrielle. "The Education of the Prince: Wieland and German Enlightenment at School with Fénelon and Rousseau." *Eighteenth-Century Life* 10 (1986): 1-13.

Beutler, Ernst. "Die Kindsmörderin." *Essays um Goethe.* Bremen: Carl Schünemann, 1957. 87-101.

Borchmeyer, Dieter. *Die Weimarer Klassik: Eine Einführung.* 2 vols. Königstein/Ts.: Athenäum, 1980.

Brandes, Ernst. *Betrachtungen über den Zeitgeist in Deutschland in den letzten Decennien des vorigen Jahrhunderts.* Hannover 1808.

Bürger, Christa. *Der Ursprung der bürgerlichen Institution Kunst im höfischen Weimar: Literatursoziologische Untersuchungen zum klassischen Goethe.* Frankfurt/M.: Suhrkamp, 1977.

Dülmen, Richard van. *Die Gesellschaft der Aufklärer: Zur bürgerlichen Emanzipation und aufklärerischen Kultur in Deutschland.* Frankfurt/M.: Fischer, 1986.

Fehn, Ernst-Otto. "Zur Wiederentdeckung des Illuminatenordens: Ergänzende Bemerkungen zu Richard van Dülmens Buch." *Geheime Gesellschaften.* Ed. Peter Christian Ludz. Wolfenbütteler Studien zur Aufklärung 5/1. Heidelberg 1979. 231-64.

Goethe, Johann Wolfgang. *Amtliche Schriften: Veröffentlichung des Staatsarchivs Weimar.* 4 vols. Ed. Willy Flach and Helma Dahl. Weimar: Böhlau, 1950-1987.

⸺. *Briefe.* ["Hamburger Ausgabe".] 4 vols. Ed. Karl Robert Mandelkow et al. 4th ed. München: dtv, 1988.

⸺. *Sämtliche Werke nach Epochen seines Schaffens. Münchner Ausgabe.* Ed. Karl Richter et al. 16 vols. in 22 vols. to date. München: Hanser, 1985ff.

Grimminger, Rolf. "Aufklärung, Absolutismus und bürgerliche Individuen. Über den notwendigen Zusammenhang von Literatur, Gesellschaft und Staat in der Geschichte des 18. Jahrhunderts." Grimminger (ed.) 15-99.

⸺, ed. *Deutsche Aufklärung bis zur Französischen Revolution, 1680-1789.* Hansers Sozialgeschichte der deutschen Literatur 3. München: Hanser, 1980.

Hahn, Karl-Heinz. "Politisches Amt und Landesverwaltung." *Goethe in Weimar: Ein Kapitel deutscher Kulturgeschichte.* Ed. Karl-Heinz Hahn. Zürich: Artemis, 1986. 69-113.

Hartmann, Fritz, and Rudolf Vierhaus, eds. *Der Akademiegedanke im 17. und 18. Jahrhundert.* Wolfenbütteler Forschungen 3. Bremen: Jacobi, 1977.

Hartung, Fritz. *Das Großherzogtum Sachsen[-Weimar] unter der Regierung Carl Augusts 1775-1828.* Weimar: Böhlau, 1923.

⸺. "Der aufgeklärte Absolutismus" [1955]. Hubatsch 118-51.

Hubatsch, Walther, ed. *Absolutismus.* Wege der Forschung, 314. Darmstadt: Wissenschaftliche Buchgesellschaft, 1973.

Hurlebusch, Rose-Maria, and Karl Ludwig Schneider. "Die Gelehrten und die Großen: Klopstocks 'Wiener Plan'." Hartmann and Vierhaus 63-96.

Kampffmeyer, Paul. *Deutsches Staatsleben vor 1789: Zum Verständnis deutscher Gegenwarts-Politik.* Berlin 1925.

Kiesel, Helmuth. "Legitimationsprobleme eines 'Hofpoeten': Zu den 'Versen für und gegen den Hof' in Goethes Autobiographie." *Germanisch-romanische*

Monatsschrift 60 (1979): 390-415.

Klopstock, Friedrich Gottlieb. *Werke und Briefe: Historisch-kritische Ausgabe.* Ed. Adolf Beck et al. Abt. Briefe. Berlin: de Gruyter, 1975- .

Koselleck, Reinhart. *Kritik und Krise: Eine Studie zur Pathogenese der bürgerlichen Welt.* 3rd ed. Frankfurt/M.: Suhrkamp, 1979.

Krieger, Leonard. *An Essay on the Theory of Enlightened Despotism.* Chicago: U of Chicago P, 1975.

Lehmann, Hannelore. "Zum Wandel des Absolutismusbegriffs in der Historiographie der BRD." *Zeitschrift für Geschichtswissenschaft* 22.1 (1974): 5-27.

Liebel, Helen. "Der aufgeklärte Absolutismus und die Gesellschaftskrise in Deutschland im 18. Jahrhundert" [1970]. Hubatsch 488-544.

Lousse, Emile. "Absolutismus, Gottesgnadentum, Aufgeklärter Despotismus" [1958]. Aretin (ed.) 89-102.

Martin, Bernd, ed. *Martin Heidegger und das 'Dritte Reich.' Ein Kompendium.* Darmstadt: Wissenschaftliche Buchgesellschaft, 1989.

Müller-Seidel, Walter. "Balladen und Justizkritik. Zu einem wenig bekannten Gedicht Goethes." *Aufklärung und Sturm und Drang.* Ed. Karl Richter. Gedichte und Interpretationen 2. Stuttgart: Reclam, 1983. 437-50.

Pape, Helmut. *Die gesellschaftlich-wirtschaftliche Stellung Fr. G. Klopstocks.* Diss. Bonn 1962.

Pöggeler, Otto. " 'Praktische Philosophie' als Antwort an Heidegger." Martin 62-92.

Rosenberg, Hans. "Die Überwindung der monarchischen Autokratie (Preußen)." Aretin (ed.) 182-204.

Ruppert, Wolfgang. "Volksaufklärung im späten 18. Jahrhundert." Grimminger (ed.) 341-61.

Sauder, Gerhard. "Pragmatische Verantwortung: Goethe in seinen amtlichen Schriften." *Verantwortung und Utopie: Zur Literatur der Goethezeit: Ein Symposium.* Ed. Wolfgang Wittkowski. Tübingen: Niemeyer, 1988. 34-56.

Schneiders, Werner. "Die Philosophie des aufgeklärten Absolutismus: Zum Verhältnis von Philosophie und Politik, nicht nur im 18. Jahrhundert." *Aufklärung als Politisierung—Politisierung der Aufklärung.* Ed. Hans Erich Bödeker, Ulrich Herrmann. Studien zum 18. Jahrhundert 8. Hamburg: Meiner, 1987. 32-52.

Schubert-Fikentscher, Gertrud. *Goethes amtliche Schriften: Eine rechtsgeschichtliche Untersuchung.* Sitzungsberichte der Sächsischen Akademie der Wissenschaften zu Leipzig, Phil.-hist. Klasse, vol. 119, no. 2. Berlin: Akademie, 1977.

Scott, H. M., ed. *Enlightened Absolutism: Reform and Reformers in Later Eighteenth-Century Europe.* Ann Arbor: U of Michigan P, 1990.

Siegert, Reinhart. "Aufklärung und Volkslektüre. Exemplarisch dargestellt an Rudolph Zacharias Becker und seinem 'Noth- und Hülfsbüchlein'." *Archiv für Geschichte des Buchwesens* 19 (1978), cols. 566-1347.

Steiner, Gerhard. *Freimaurer und Rosenkreuzer—Georg Forsters Weg durch Geheimbünde. Neue Forschungsergebnisse auf Grund bisher unbekannter Archivalien.* Berlin: Akademie, 1985.

Ueding, Gert. *Klassik und Romantik: Deutsche Literatur im Zeitalter der Französischen Revolution 1789-1815.* Hansers Sozialgeschichte der deutschen Literatur 4. München: Hanser, 1987.

Vierhaus, Rudolf. "Absolutismus" [1966]. *Absolutismus.* Ed. Ernst Hinrichs. Frankfurt/M.: Suhrkamp, 1986. 35-62.

Walder, Ernst. "Aufgeklärter Absolutismus und Staat. Zum Staatsbegriff der aufgeklärten Despoten" [1957]. Aretin (ed.) 123-36.

Wehler, Hans-Ulrich. *Deutsche Gesellschaftsgeschichte*. Vol. 1: *Vom Feudalismus des Alten Reiches bis zur Defensiven Modernisierung der Reformära 1700-1815*. 2nd ed. München: Beck, 1989.

————. *Das Deutsche Kaiserreich 1871-1918.* 5th ed. Deutsche Geschichte, 9. Göttingen: Vandenhoeck & Ruprecht, 1983.

Wilson, W. Daniel. "'Die Dienste der Großen': The Flight from Public Service in Lessing's Major Plays." *DVLG* 61 (1987): 238-65.

————. *Geheimräte gegen Geheimbünde: Ein unbekanntes Kapitel der klassisch-romantischen Geschichte Weimars*. Stuttgart: Metzler, 1991.

————. "Illuminatenideologie: Revolution, Anarchie, oder aufgeklärter Absolutismus? Vorläufige Ergebnisse aus der 'Schwedenkiste'." *Spätaufklärung und Revolution: Zur Ideologie und Struktur des Illuminatenordens*. Ed. Helmut Reinalter. Frankfurt/M.: Peter Lang, 1993.

————. "Intellekt und Herrschaft: Wielands *Goldner Spiegel*, Joseph II. und das Ideal eines kritischen Mäzenats im aufgeklärten Absolutismus." *MLN* 99 (1984): 479-502.

————. "Zur Politik und Sozialstruktur des Illuminatenordens, anläßlich einer Neuerscheinung von Hermann Schüttler." *Internationales Archiv für Sozialgeschichte der deutschen Literatur* (1993).

————. " 'Der politische Jacobinismus, wie er leibt und lebt'? Der Illuminatenorden und revolutionäre Ideologie: Erstveröffentlichung aus den 'Höheren Mysterien'." *Lessing Yearbook* 25 (1993): 133-84.

————. "Wieland's *Diogenes* and the Emancipation of the Critical Intellectual." *Christoph Martin Wieland: North American Scholarly Contributions on the Occasion of the 250th Anniversary of his Birth*. Ed. Hansjörg Schelle. Tübingen: Niemeyer, 1984. 149-79.

Winter, Hans-Gerd. "Klopstocks Revolutionsoden: 'O kom, du neue, / Labende . . . Sonne.' " *Die Französische Revolution und ihre Wirkung auf Norddeutschland und das Reich*. Vol. 1: *Norddeutschland*. Ed. Arno Herzig et al. Hamburg: Dölling und Galitz, 1989. 131-51.

Zimmermann, Harro. *Freiheit und Geschichte. F. G. Klopstock als historischer Dichter und Denker*. Heidelberg: Winter, 1986.

The Sweet Dream of Perpetual Peace: Kant's Peace Project

Klaus L. Berghahn

> Will not in the end every war, even if it were a just one, deserve the attribute barbaric?
> ——Theodor von Hippel, 1796

I. Preface

EVEN ACADEMIC ESSAYS can have a history, and some have more of it than others. This one is embedded in recent history, which may be the reason why my commentary on Kant's peace project is more tentative now than it was when I first conceived this study. That was in May, 1990, when the threat of nuclear war between the global superpowers had diminished. Thanks to Gorbachev's initiative, the cold war and the arms race came to an end, and consequently the economic and political collapse of the Communist Eastern Block made room for a peaceful new world order, in which the United States is the unopposed dominant military power. Kant's peace utopia, so it seemed, could become reality at the end of the twentieth century under the auspices of the United Nations.

Little did I know that my idealistic expectations would soon be shattered by an Iraqi dictator and by our president. The Gulf War reminded us that war is still the continuation of politics by brutal means and that people and truth become the victims of war. There can be no doubt that the aggression of Saddam Hussein, first against Kuwait and later against Israel, was unprovoked and barbaric. He had to be stopped. But by what means? Diplomatically, by economic sanctions

385

and a trade embargo, or by force? If we step back for a moment and forget the euphoria after the hundred-hour blitzkrieg, the yellow ribbons and the victory parades, we have to remember that the American public was deeply divided over the issue whether we should go to war. (In Madison, Wisconsin, 67% were against the war, but as soon as the fighting started 67%—not necessary the same people—supported the president's decision, and this support reached an unbelievable 91% by the end of the war.) What was surprising was this radical mood swing in so short a time; what was frightening was the muffling of the war protest and the propagandistic control of the media; what is still outrageous is the silence about the victims of the war. While the aggression of our former ally and now "dictator" Saddam Hussein, who still rules Iraq, had to be contained, more for the sake of Israel than the sovereignty of Saudi Arabia, we all know that the United States' interest was not just to "liberate" Kuwait, but to protect the uninhibited flow of oil from Saudi Arabia and Kuwait. The war protesters' slogan "no blood for oil" made this point, and yet the century-old slogan of a "just war" fueled the public imagination, which the propaganda machine of the White House resolutely used to turn the citizens into mindless followers of Bush. The war protesters were muzzled and public opinion was manipulated by the media, which followed patriotically the president's path to war. Looking back on the images of this war, I am tempted to say that we saw only the video version of the war as it was provided by the military. Except for Arnett's (CNN) and Fröhder's (ARD) reports from Baghdad, which were censored by Iraq, critical journalism, as we had known it during the Vietnam War, was severely hampered, and the public grew accustomed to newsroom briefings and cockpit videos of target bombing. All this was a disgrace to journalism and a free press; under the censorship of the military at the front and of patriotism at home, the reality of the war was antiseptically constructed for easy consumption in the living room. The terrible images of war, like the destroyed air-raid shelter in Baghdad, were repressed, or Saddam was blamed for the suffering of his people. Although President Bush declared many times that he had nothing against the Iraqi people and wanted only to tame a mad Saddam, the reality was and is that the Iraqis suffer and Saddam is still in power. We don't know how many thousand Iraqi conscripts were buried in Kuwait's desert by our carpet bombing, since we never wanted "to go into that body-count thing," or how many civilians died in the cities that were surgically destroyed. We only know from an United Nations observer team that we bombed Iraq back into a "pre-industrial age," that is, we destroyed 80% of its infrastructure. My point is simply this: Wars, even when they are labeled "just," make the world not a safer and better place;

the people and the truth suffer, when conflicts are not solved by peaceful means. What by May of 1990 looked like the dawn of a new world order of peace, had become a nightmare by the end of the Gulf War. What we have now is a fragile truce, but we have to speak about peace nevertheless.

So much for my trepidations when I wrote a paper on Kant's peace project, which I had once endowed with a utopian tinge (see Berghahn). This synchronic contextualization of my lecture also has a diachronic component, which is connected to the theme of this volume. The recently proclaimed New World Order, which President Bush called "a responsibility imposed by our success in the Cold War," has both a cosmopolitan and an imperialistic ring to it. Every time American presidents have invoked a New World Order, be it Woodrow Wilson, F. D. Roosevelt or Bush, it sounds idealistic and far-reaching. With their idea of a United Nations, Wilson and Roosevelt expressed the best tradition of the American Enlightenment, for which Kant could have been the ghostwriter. After two devastating World Wars, the world community seemed to be ready for peacefulness and orderliness of international life. As for Bush's New World Order or Pax Americana after the Cold War, it has the Janus head of a superpower that wants to dictate to the international community what permissible behavior of states should be; it instills both trust and fear. In his speech at Montgomery, Alabama, in April of 1991, Bush outlined four principles for a New World Order, which show how idealistic principles can be inflected by American self-interest: when he speaks of "peaceful settlements of disputes" and "solidarity against aggression" just one month after the Gulf War ended, this sounds high-minded and is clearly self-serving—without mentioning the American interest, namely oil. "Reduced and controlled arsenals" reflects the interest of a commercial power under duress that is eager to reduce its military spending. And finally, "just treatment of all people" pays idealistic lip-service to justice for all, meant formally, not materially. Bush's New World Order mixes idealistic impulses with legal principles and the self-interest of a capitalistic superpower. Making the world safe from aggression or defining legal principles for international relations is not the same as crusading for a free-market economy. Bush would certainly applaud each and every aspect of Kant's peace proposal, and he would even think that it belongs genuinely to the best tradition of the United States. Yet for him it would merely be an idealistic and moral maxim that he would easily discard when economic and national interests are at stake. He acts, as Kant would put it, as a political moralist and not as a moral politician. This is the crux of the matter when it comes to peace as an abstract concept—and it is the dialectic of

Enlightenment. Bush's sentimental idealism pays lip-service to peace when it doesn't cost much, but he resolutely goes to war when national interests, the flow of natural resources or, perhaps, if bad comes to worse, markets are threatened. Bourgeois or, better, capitalistic pacifism is a paradox, and that is the difference between Kant's peace project and Bush's New World Order. We can only wonder what Bush's Pax Americana would look like, and it is not very comforting to imagine how a triumphant capitalism would create peace at the expense of the exploited of the world.

With these preliminary remarks I do not want to suggest that the world community does not or never can achieve peace, nor do I join in the doomsday projections of postmodernism; I only want to point out the dialectic of enlightenment when it comes to peace in our time. In the same context, let us be reminded that Adorno and Horkheimer did not write their seminal essays in order to destroy the tradition of the Enlightenment, which is still the incomplete project of modernity. In their introduction they clearly state: "We are wholly convinced—and therein lies our petitio principii—that social freedom is inseparable from enlightened thought" (xiii). Kant's peace project is, consequently, not just another lofty idea of the Enlightenment but a duty for human-kind. If we do not succeed, Kant warns us, the result will be an eternal peace in a vast graveyard.

II. Kant's Peace Project
in the Context of the European Enlightenment

The idea of perpetual peace is one of the most important concepts of the European Enlightenment. "To dream this sweet dream," as Kant put it, became the concern of many philosophers and writers who fought with their pens against the absurdity of war and for the necessity of peace. After a century of devastating religious, civil, and dynastic wars, the longing for a lasting peace could be heard all over Europe, and even in the New World. All of these peace proposals of the Enlightenment seemed so reasonable, possible and practicable, that only the good will of the rulers and their nations were necessary to transform these projections into reality. I mention just the three most important authors whose ideas Kant conceptualized.

In France, Abbé de Saint-Pierre developed the most encompassing peace plan, which became the classical paradigm for modern Europe. Between 1713, when he participated in the peace conference of Ut-recht, which ended the Spanish Wars of Succession, and 1743, he worked on his proposal for perpetual peace, *Projet pour rendre la paix perpétuelle en Europe*, which in the end was a monument of four volumes. Although it was inspired by the peace treaty of Utrecht, St.-Pierre's peace plan transcended its origin by systematically analyzing the reasons for war and developing measures for avoiding war. These preventive proposals are worth mentioning, since they are still viable today: Disarmament, inviolability of the territorial *status quo,* non-intervention in the internal affairs of another state, and a confederation of states. This idea of a European confederation, which could mediate all disputes between its members, has become the central concept of enlightened pacifism and remains influential in the twentieth century. St.-Pierre's peace project could be characterized as a typical "Primer for Princes" (*Fürstenspiegel*) or as an advisory proposal for Enlightened Absolutism.

St.-Pierre's *opus magnum,* which is as learned as it is long-winded, only became well known through Rousseau's *Excerpts* (1756). Rousseau was skeptical, however, whether this reasonable plan would ever have a chance to be instituted. The power of despotic absolutism is stronger than the longing of the peoples for peace. "It would be a grave mistake to hope that this condition of lawlessness could be changed naturally and without artificial means" (378). Although he had great misgivings about St.-Pierre's naive optimism and rationalism, he refrained from ridiculing it, as some members of the ruling class did. He, too, longed for peace, but for him it was more than just a matter of foreign affairs. He could not imagine a universal peace without a civil republic. Social and peace Utopia were for him intertwined. In his own *Judgement of Eternal Peace,* which was published posthumously in 1782, Rousseau radically criticized the ruling despotism, whose aim it was "to expand its reign outward and to make it unlimited inward" (378). In short: despotism and war go hand in hand. Rousseau's pacifism was born out of the spirit of republicanism, and his criticism of despotic absolutism was correctly understood as propaganda for the coming revolution.

In England, Jeremy Bentham, developed a typical British peace plan, which saw world trade as the most important basis for universal peace. With his *Plan for a Universal and Perpetual Peace* (1786/89) he became the first theoretician of what is paradoxically called economic pacifism: wars are not profitable, since they disrupt world trade, harm national wealth, and make the bourgeoisie suffer. Expanding world trade will eventually make wars obsolete, and the bourgeois spirit, which uses monetary instead of military power, will make feudal war adventures appear antiquated. The capital that could be saved by avoiding wars would not only increase overall national wealth but also the wealth of all citizens, in accordance with Bentham's famous motto: The greatest happiness for the greatest number.

Kant's essay *Perpetual Peace* (*Zum ewigen Frieden*, 1795, 2nd ed. 1796) belongs to this European tradition. Kant summarizes the best ideas of enlightened pacifism and provides them with the most succinct and philosophical form. The title is reminiscent of St.-Pierre's seminal study, which Kant knew at least from Rousseau's *Excerpts*; he critically examined major concepts of Rousseau's republican pacifism: criticism of despotism, the interrelation of internal and external peace, and the idea of a league of nations; and even Bentham's influence is traceable. Kant's "philosophical sketch" can be understood as a philosophical analysis of peace in order to determine the conditions of its possibility.

Kant published his peace plan the same year the peace treaty of Basel was signed. One is therefore inclined to construct a causal relationship between Kant's essay and this treaty, which ended Prussia's interference in the internal affairs of France and gave northern Germany a brief period of peace. But even if Kant's peace proposal were inspired by the Basel peace accord and also imitated its form, his own sketch transcended the historical date and, unlike this treaty, influenced generations to come. The central idea, a league of nations, was a topos of the European Enlightenment, and he mentions it already in his notes for his anthropology lectures in the 1770s: "The last perfection: A union of nations" (*Gesammelte Schriften* 15: 783). This had been a central idea of his political philosophy and appeared in his essay "Idea for a Universal History with a Cosmopolitan Purpose" (1784). There he argued that the development of humankind will realize its purpose in a cosmopolitan constitution which would guard human rights and permanent peace. Only a "union of states" could end the sufferings that war inflicts on humankind. It is the birth of a philosophy of history from the spirit of pacifism.

Kant wrote his essay in the form of a fictitious peace treaty, with all the trimmings of an international accord: preliminary and definitive articles, guarantees, appendices, and even a secret article. This is not just a matter of form that organizes the content and makes it succinct, but also a matter of style, which uses irony to present as real what is merely hypothetically possible. By this stroke of genius Kant points out the discrepancy between his ideal of peace and political reality. He makes the reader aware of the contrast between the world as it is, namely bellicose, and a world as it could and should be. On the whole, Kant's peace proposal is more satirical in style and more realistic in content than the common view of an unworldly philosopher portrays him. His fictitious peace treaty transcends the date of its model, the Basel accord, which he would consider merely a truce, and postulates peace as a duty for humankind, which adds a utopian tinge to his project.

Most of the arguments of the six preliminary articles, which deal with preventive measures against wars, summarize the previous peace debate of the Enlightenment. Philosophically, they are as plain and intelligible as simple truth should be. They are all stated negatively and their concrete criticism can be read as directed against the arcane politics of eighteenth-century absolutism, which liked to see itself as enlightened:

1. "No conclusion of peace shall be considered valid as such if it was made with a secret reservation of the material for a future war" (93). Kant is not interested in the old peace treaties, which he considered merely as "a suspension of hostilities" or a truce. Secret reservations are the seeds for future wars, whereas genuine peace "nullifies all existing reasons for a future war" (93).

2. "No independently existing state, whether it be large or small, may be acquired by another state through inheritance, exchange, purchase or gift" (94). The territorial appetite of Europe's powers constantly endangered peace. In the idiom of contemporary political expediency the slogan was: *Tu felix Austria nube.* But these "peaceful" expansions easily led to wars. The recognition of existing borders and of the territorial integrity of states seemed to be the only guarantee for peace. Kant goes one step further by addressing the constitutional roots of the problem: For him a state is no longer the private possession of a monarch or a commodity, but a "moral personality," that is, a society of people who have come together in an "original contract." What he is aiming at is nothing less than a republican constitution.

3. "Standing armies (*miles perpetuus*) will gradually be abolished altogether" (94). They are a constant threat to peace, as Kant knew from Prussia, which burdened its people with a standing army of 180,000 soldiers and used it at will. An excessive military machine also puts pressure on other states to keep up with the military power of their neighbors and it can thereby cause wars of aggression. Kant's criticism of militarism does not stop here; he also warns against the "power of money—probably the most reliable instrument of war" (95). He has nothing against a voluntary army of citizens to defend their country. There is one more point, which appears strangely out of place in this context: In war men are hired to kill or to be killed, which means that they are used "as mere machines and instruments in the hands of someone else (the state)." Kant states that this cannot be reconciled with the dignity and rights of men. War is unethical!

4. "No national debt shall be contracted in connection with the external affairs of the state" (95). Since the power of money is one of the most dangerous instruments of war, national debts to finance wars must be prohibited. Kant had seen in his times enough European po-

tentates who suffocated their subjects with war debts or inflicted them with national bankruptcy. Kant thought, like Bentham, that the international commercial and credit system could in the long run become an effective restraint on the beast of war.

5. "No state shall forcibly interfere in the constitution and government of another state" (96). Since the counter-revolutionary coalition war against France was still being waged in order to prevent the expansion of revolutionary fever all over Europe, this article was as timely as ever. Such ideological warfare should be prohibited. Pretexts for such interferences, be they real or fictitious, could easily be construed by the great powers, and then used by them to annex or divide weaker states. This autonomy clause is the prerequisite of any international peace order, and it opened the door to discussions of international law.

6. "No state at war with another shall permit such acts of hostility as would make mutual confidence impossible during a future time of peace" (96). What sounds like a moral code for the conduct of war (no political assassination, no breaking of truces, no instigation of treasonable acts), is meant to guarantee a minimum of rationality during the brutality of war. War, which was considered as a continuation of politics by other means, shall neither degenerate into a war of extermination nor make a future peace impossible.

Although most of Kant's proposals to prevent wars are as valid today as they were then, they are merely prohibitive laws, and the prevention or suspension of hostilities between states does not necessarily bring about permanent peace. Peace must be formally instituted, if not coerced—that is, by the force of law. It is the function of Kant's three definitive articles to constitute a legal basis for peace in order to overcome the natural state of war. Since Kant assumes that all people already adhere "to some kind of civil constitution" (98), he ponders the conditions of a possible peace on the basis of civil, international, and cosmopolitan rights. Accordingly, he organizes the three definitive articles as follows:

1. "The civil constitution of every state shall be republican" (99). This postulate is not surprising at a time when this kind of civil constitution was already practiced in England, the United States, and, to a degree, in France, and when it was discussed all over Europe. Since Rousseau's critique of despotic absolutism, it had become an axiom of European pacifism that links internal and external peace. Kant followed this innovative idea, and also agreed with Rousseau, that the social contract is the basis of a republican state. It is founded on three principles: "Firstly, the principle of freedom for all members of a society (as men); secondly, the principle of dependence of everyone

upon a single common legislation (as subjects); thirdly, the principle of legal equality for everyone (as citizens)" (99). This does not exclude a constitutional monarchy; in fact it would be for Kant the ideal constitution. Under such a constitution the citizens would decide whether or not to declare war, and Kant reasons that they would be very reluctant to embark on so dangerous an enterprise, for they have to carry the burden of all miseries of war—the fighting and suffering, the costs and devastation. They would also think twice about financing a war by taxation or national debt. The citizens would act against their own self-interest if they waged war.[1]

2. "The right of nations shall be based on a federation of free states" (102). The idea of a league of nations, which all enlightened pacifists since St.-Pierre favored, was for Kant the precondition of international law in order to overcome the lawlessness of war. Analogous to the social contract, which establishes a civil society, the states should form a federation—without loss of their sovereignty. "This federation does not aim to acquire any power like that of a state, but merely to preserve and secure the freedom of each state in itself, along with that of the other confederated states" (104). Kant considers this form of federalism to be practical and lawful since it is in accordance with the idea of international law. Yet it has its difficulties, if not contradictions. What in theory could be a multinational state, should in practice merely be an association of autonomous states. In a world republic it could probably happen that one powerful state dominates the others and dictates the world order of peace according to its own self-interest. Therefore, Kant relinquishes the idea of a world republic and is satisfied with its "negative substitute," namely a loose federation whose single aim it would be to prevent wars. The ideal of a league of nations is the central idea of Kant's peace Utopia. In the twentieth century it has been tried twice already without securing a permanent peace.

3. "Cosmopolitan right shall be limited to conditions of universal hospitality" (105). The idea of a cosmopolitan right, which was in Kant's time still considered "fantastic and overstrained," was for him a necessary complement of civil and international rights. He stressed that he was not concerned with "philanthropy, but with right" (105). The right to hospitality, which applies to strangers in a foreign country, should not be confused with "the right of a guest," which would require a contract. Hospitality is only the "right of resort" (106). As long as the peoples of the earth are not united in a federation of free states governed by civil and international laws, the cosmopolitan right is limited to the natural right of hospitality. This postulate is not directed against those nations, which were then known to be hostile to strangers

(China, Japan), but more importantly against "the conduct of the civilized states of our continent, especially the commercial states" (106), Spain and England, who abuse their visiting rights by exploiting and oppressing foreign countries. They do this under the veil of piety and wish to be considered as chosen believers, "while they live on the fruits of iniquity." This incipient colonialism harms the world community, since "a violation of rights in one part of the world is felt everywhere" (107f.), a sentence whose implications were only understood in the nineteenth and twentieth centuries.

These are the conditions of the possibility of a perpetual peace, which make peace a regulative idea for humankind, albeit an infinite process of gradual approximation. What seems so reasonable, objectively possible, and even practical, is still contradicted by the state of nature, which fosters war, not peace. Humankind has to overcome this lawlessness and enter gradually into a state of peaceful mutual relations regulated by law. The idea of public rights is the leitmotif of Kant's peace project; as a postulate, however, it cannot bring about peace in reality. The supplements and appendices deal with the question of how to guarantee perpetual peace. Here he invokes the principles of nature, moral and public opinion, in order to legitimize his peace project.

The strongest argument for perpetual peace was war itself, which seemed to be the natural state among peoples and nations. Although war repudiates all rules of common sense and all principles of law, discord and self-interest appear to be stronger among people than harmony and a sense of law. War would be the permanent stumbling block for peace, if it would not—even against the will of humankind—contribute to the development of culture, rights and peace. This daring thought was already part of Kant's philosophy of history in the essay "Idea for a Universal History with a Cosmopolitan Purpose," and in the first supplement, "On the Guarantee of a Perpetual Peace" he comes back to this idea: "Perpetual peace is guaranteed by no less an authority than the great artist Nature herself. The mechanical process of nature visibly exhibits the purposive plan of producing concord among men, even against their will and by means of their very discord" (108).[2] To prove his point, Kant already in 1784 had to make two assumptions that are typical of the Enlightenment: first, that there is a purposeful plan in nature to which a teleological principle in history has to correspond; second, that a continued process of enlightenment will educate humankind toward the goal of perpetual peace. If nature follows a purposeful plan, we can also assume that a guiding principle for history can be found, for it would be contradictory to speak of the purposefulness of nature in all her parts without postulating the same for the world and its history as a whole. Although the final aim of history cannot be determined empirically, we can look at history as if it had a purposive function or as if there were an "objective goal for the human race" (108). "Yet while this idea is indeed far-fetched in theory, it does posses dogmatic validity and has a very real foundation in practice, as with the concept of perpetual peace, which makes it our duty to promote it" (109).

If perpetual peace is the final aim of history, it is not yet clear how humankind can accomplish it, since we know from experience that its history is a history of wars. But in Kant's teleological perspective even war has a positive function in world history. Time and again he makes the point that "nature has chosen war as a means of attaining this end," that is, peace (111). Nature takes care of human beings in areas where they settle; then by the means of war it drives them in all directions; and finally it compels them "by the same means to enter into more or less legal relationships" (110). War becomes the motor of all cultural developments, it forces humankind in the end to abandon lawless conditions and seek shelter under common legal institutions and in a commonwealth of nations. As we have already noticed in our comments on the definitive articles, the evolution of the philosophy of law has reached a stage where republican constitutions are implemented and the idea of international law is already discussed. That even cosmopolitan rights will be instituted, seems for Kant a necessity, "for the spirit of commerce sooner or later takes hold of every people, and it cannot exist side by side with war" (114). There is sufficient evidence in history that humankind is moving toward improvement of its political constitutions and into a more peaceful future, and for all practical purposes Kant can postulate a perpetual peace as a moral responsibility for the human race.

Nature prepares and coerces a slow but steady progress in political constitutions, and the teleology of history reveals the gradual process of enlightenment, but humankind has to accomplish the aim of perpetual peace through reason. In the first appendix to his peace plan, "On the Disagreement Between Morals and Politics in Relation to Perpetual Peace," Kant is exclusively concerned with morality in politics. Peace needs the security of law, and the law is founded on morality, as Kant defined it in his categorical imperative, which he repeats here: "Act in such a way that you can wish your maxim to become universal law" (122). And with an almost prophetic gesture he adds that the ultimate goal will result from adherence to this principle: "Seek first the kingdom of pure practical reason and its righteousness, and your object (the blessing of perpetual peace) will be added unto it" (123). Kant knew all too well that his advice to "worldly-wise statesmen" would fall on deaf ears, but as a political theorist primarily interested in the principle of public right, he hoped that human and constitutional rights would, however slowly, overcome the arcane politics of his time and become the law of a future state and of a commonwealth of nations.

Measured against the political reality of his time, Kant's political philosophy gains a radical urgency that is only rivalled by Rousseau's. His distinction between the political moralist and the moral politician is as timely as ever. Here the treatise becomes a tribunal directed against all those practical politicians who separate morals and politics in order to prevent the rule of law from becoming the principle of international politics. The political moralist arranges his maxims so that they legitimize his political actions or disguise his true intentions; he is the perfect ideologue of power. Whether he seizes a favorable opportunity to serve his self-interest and justifies violent acts later; whether he interferes in the internal affairs of another state and later denies any guilt; or whether he corrupts any peace effort by the sophistry of secret reservations: power always precedes law, and success is the best of advocates. The moral politician, on the other hand, will make it a principle that all his actions conform to natural right. He does not act upon anything "without first paying tribute to morality" (125). For him perpetual peace is a postulate of practical reason and a regulative idea for the human race. By contrasting reality with an ideal state of the world, Kant demonstrates the wide gap between politics and morality, but at the same time his pacifist Utopia gains a revolutionary momentum that appears to make peace conceivable, possible, and even necessary.

If Kant had ended with this apotheosis of morals, the logic and plausibility of his argument would not have suffered, but peace would have been merely a moral postulate. Worse yet, morality would have denounced politics, a gesture which gives idealism a utopian pathos that is easily contradicted and even ridiculed by reality. Kant must have felt that too, otherwise he would not have added a second appendix on "the transcendental concept of public right" and, in the second edition (1796), a "Secret Article," which also deals with the principle of publicity. Already in his short introduction Kant had included a "Clausula salvatoria" (a saving clause) to safeguard his essay against malicious interpretations. Since he knew all too well how St.-Pierre's and Rousseau's peace proposals had been received, he distanced himself from the worldly-wise statesmen, who could censure or ridicule him, and claimed for himself only the freedom of a theorist "to state his opinions in public" (93). As we know from Kant's essay *What Is Enlightenment?* (1784), to think freely and publicly is for him the most important instrument of the Enlightenment. What Kant called there euphemistically "the most harmless" of civil freedoms, namely "to make public use of reason in all affairs" was nothing less than the claim to the authority of public criticism, which would ultimately raise the political issue of freedom of speech. Under conditions that were anything but liberal, Kant made good use of his intellectual freedom and expanded it even into the political sphere, where he theorized about the possibility of peace.

The "Secret Article" is usually understood as merely an ironic coda of the fictitious peace plan which imitates the infamous secret reservations of peace treaties in the eighteenth century. Kant knows very well that a secret article in matters of public rights "is a contradiction," but it is the subtle irony of his secret supplement that he demands a public discussion of war and peace, which the state will tolerate as if it had "silently" invited the philosophers to assist. His secret reservation, which is directed against the arcane politics of absolutism, makes the point that peace only has a chance when war is discussed publicly. Accordingly, the article contains only the sentence: "The maxims of the philosophers on the conditions under which public peace is possible shall be consulted by states which are armed for war" (115). By this he does not mean "that kings will philosophize or that philosophers will become kings," which would not be desirable for Kant, "since the possession of power inevitably corrupts the free judgment of reason" (115). The state should only allow philosophers "to speak freely and publicly on the universal maxims of warfare and peacemaking" (115). What Kant proposes with the gesture of a petitioner and the irony of a philosopher is nothing less than the bold demand of public expression of opinion.

In the second appendix, "On the Agreement Between Politics and Morality According to the Transcendental Concept of Public Right," Kant abstracts from all material aspects of public right in order to come up with a formal principle: "All actions affecting the rights of other human beings are wrong, if their maxim is not compatible with their being made public" (126). This formula is as clear and practical as the categorical imperative: it has the quality of axiomatic simplicity, that is, it is "valid without demonstration"; it is a "purely negative test," which means that it is based on the logical principle of exclusion; and it is "easy to apply" (126). Every maxim of politics that cannot stand the light of public scrutiny or has to disguise its true intention is wrong and does not serve the common welfare. This "transcendental formula of public right" is nothing less than the moral foundation and political legitimation of public opinion formation. The principle of publicity cannot force rulers to submit to it, nor can it prevent wars, but it establishes the foundation of public right. Indirectly, Kant criticizes the secretive and corrupt politics of his times; in principle, he anticipates a bourgeois public sphere, where political actions are based on public opinion and consensus. The transcendental principle of publicity is the prerequisite of universal lawfulness and of peace.

As Kant makes quite clear in his final paragraph, perpetual peace is not "an empty idea" but a duty for humankind. There are good reasons for hope, since the idea of public right is slowly becoming a reality, "albeit by an infinite process of gradual approximation" (130). Peace is therefore a regulative idea for humankind.

III. Kant's Peace Project
and the Dialectic of Enlightenment

Kant's peace proposal, like many classical texts, still has a resonance, which bespeaks the timelessness of his idea; in light of our experiences, however, we have to examine critically whether Kant had indeed all the answers to the problems of our modern world. As has been true for all peace projects since the Enlightenment, Kant's text contains elements that make it a product of its time, that give it a utopian aura, and that are still of interest to us. Kant's treatise had its clearly defined historical context: in its radical criticism of war it was a reform proposal for European Absolutism. The idealistic component of the text is articulated in the moral postulate of the peace idea, and its utopian perspective is grounded in the aim of a cosmopolitan constitution. As to its relevance for our time, we have yet to demand internal and external security of law, the principle of publicity and the idea of a league of nations as the prerequisites of a permanent peace.

We cannot pride ourselves that we are wiser than Kant when it comes to the question of a permanent peace, but we know what has become of this noblest of dreams since the Enlightenment. Its unfulfilled promises still interest us as a future in the past, while our historical experience makes us aware of the dialectic of enlightenment. And Kant's peace project is no exception. Kant examined the theoretical conditions of a possible peace, laid the foundations of a well-grounded pacifism, and established the principles against which a future peace has to be measured. If his theory of peace is only of limited use for our time, it has not just to do with the historical gap that separates us from him, and only in part with his guarantees of peace, but most of all with the development of bourgeois society.

Kant could not have anticipated a new threat to peace that appeared with the rise of nationalism and imperialism in the nineteenth century. He thought—as did Rousseau—that wars were the vice of primitive or feudal conditions of society. Wars are the *ultima ratio* of potentates, not of peace-loving citizens who have to pay for these cabinet wars. Under despotic absolutism, where the head of state is also the owner of the state, the monarch "can decide on war, without any significant reason, as a kind of amusement, and unconcernedly leave it to the diplomatic corps (who are always ready for such purposes) to justify the war for the sake of propriety" (100). Kant believed that a republican constitution and the civility of the bourgeoisie would overcome wars that contradict the self-interest of the citizens. Little did he know that in the nineteenth and twentieth centuries nations, even republics (and not just absolute rulers), would enthusiastically go to war for ethnic, national or economic reasons. Although Kant was aware of the danger of war that arose from colonialism, he shared Bentham's cosmopolitan optimism that "the spirit of commerce sooner or later takes hold of every people, and it cannot exist side by side with war" (114).

This view, which comes close to Bentham's economic pacifism, has two flaws. First of all, it harmonizes the question of colonialism by making it just a function of world trade. It is true that Kant in his third definitive article sharply condemns the colonialism of the "civilized states," which under the mask of piety or trade subjugate the native inhabitants of America, Africa, and India, but he postpones any solution of this problem until "the concept of cosmopolitan right" is fully developed and protects them from violence. From a European perspective, peace is more important than the renunciation of colonialism. World trade will eventually take care of this nasty problem, since it will bring about world peace almost naturally. This reliance on "financial power" for the benefit of peace constitutes the second flaw of Kant's argument. In his third preliminary article he warned against the "power of money" as "probably the most reliable instrument of war" under despotic absolutism (95). The same means, however, are supposed to change the course of history and contribute to peace when they are used by republics in world trade. It was an illusion of the young Enlightenment that republican states and bourgeois capitalism would enhance peace. The irony is that the history of bourgeois society is a contradictory mixture of idealistic pacifism and calculated wars. Bentham and Kant hoped that peaceful trade would bring nations closer together and foster international right, but they didn't foresee that the spirit of capitalism would also breed imperialism, which would not be deterred by the risk of war if economic or national interests were at stake. Bloch, for whom perpetual peace is a noble dream and "almost" a Utopia, warns against the Janus face of bourgeois pacifism. He calls it "Wall Street pacifism," a capitalistic pacifism that does not exclude war, if war becomes necessary for its self-interest. Bourgeois pacifism for him is "a paradox" (1048-53).

The most frightening aspect of Kant's peace plan is his insistence on the dialectic of war. War functions as a purposeful catalyst in the development of humankind, which brings about peace even against its will. The state of nature, which is war, seems like the Mephistophelian principle of history that promotes evil and accomplishes good. This paradox is a relic of two older ideas, namely, of a "just" war to establish peace, and of a "last" war to end all wars. The idea of a "last war" belongs to St.-Pierre's peace proposal and fascinated even Rousseau. Kant used this apocalyptic logic in his first supplement, "On the Guarantee of Perpetual Peace." "The great artist Nature" will make sure that humankind reaches its final aim, since she "exhibits the purposive plan of producing accord among people, even against their will and indeed by means of their own discord" (108). Her purposefulness teaches us to see our own history teleologically as an educational and evolutionary process. Peace has to come, it will come, and Nature will make it possible. Although Nature is the antithesis of human reason, Kant tries to make her reasonable by looking at history from a Archimedean point, call it "providence." This teleological perspective, even if it is theoretically unprovable, allows Kant to postulate perpetual peace as an objective goal of the human race. As a means of attaining this end, Nature has chosen war. This is not just contradictory today, it is, with regard to peace, a paradox *par excellence*. It is here, not in Kant's legal principles of peace, that we find the dialectic of enlightenment.

Nature is not only the antithesis of reason that has to be disciplined and conquered, it is also "Reason's Other" (Böhme and Böhme), which undermines and threatens harmony and peace. Kant hopes that the wisdom of Nature will coerce peace, even behind the back of humankind, but he knows all too well that there are "dark forces" in human nature which work against this aim. "Nothing straight can be constructed from such warped wood as that which man is made of" (46). What Kant scorned in human nature and condemned as evil is also part of nature, but this dark side of nature is not as easily tamed as Kant wished. Human beings are not only guided by reason, but more often than not they follow their drives, desires, and emotions. This irrationality of human nature is the underside of the philosophy of the Enlightenment, the unconscious, of which Kant had already the foreboding that it would resist rational control. What the rationality of the enlightened peace projects try to exorcise is this Other which disturbs the harmony of their practical models and endangers peace. This dilemma can no longer be solved by accepting war as a state of nature or as a necessary evil, which will eventually lead to peace.

Kant's confidence in the wisdom of Nature and his optimistic outlook on the development of the human race have been shaken; the experience of two world wars and the fear of a third one have shattered this enlightened dream. It is this fear of a last war which we have to analyze and to understand. Then we will no longer set off the advantages of peace against the cost of war—an equation that never worked, but interpret the motives of war more carefully. For they are grounded in human drives, emotions, and aggressions that lead to hate and enmity; and between nations these deep-seated emotions are amplified by prejudices, projections and propaganda. At this point a self-critical reflection and revision of enlightened pacifism could begin, which would be a task that would transcend and transform Kant's peace project.

Looking at Freud's thoughts on war (and peace), which suggest themselves here, one is struck by how close he still is to Kant and how rational his ideas on peace are: "The ideal condition (of peace) would, of course, be a community of people who have subjugated their drives to the dictates of reason" (284).[3] Whether one should wish for that or fear it, Freud doesn't say, but the fact that he calls this subjugation to reason "a utopian hope" suggests that he tilts towards rationality and control. Like Kant, he believed that a federation of nations would be the best safeguard against war, if it also had the power to enforce its will. By 1932 the League of Nations watched powerless as the world was already sliding towards the next world war. Freud assumed that the death/destruction impulse is complementary to the life instinct. Since it is impossible to abolish the human inclination towards aggression, "one can only try to deflect it, so that it does not have to find its expression in war" (283). What Freud hoped for, as did Kant, was that the progress of civilization would eliminate wars. "Everything that advances the development of culture works against war" (286). This is what all pacifists hoped for, but it is not the answer we expected from Freud.[4] It needed the experience of World War II, with Auschwitz and Hiroshima as symbols of barbarism, to shake trust in human-kind's perfectibility. Only since then it has become possible to recognize the limits of enlightenment.

Kant's attempt to reconcile Nature with Reason in order to bring about peace has yet another aspect, which is cause for our anxieties today. The process of pacification of human nature by means of education, self-discipline and coercion has its corollary in the domination and exploitation of nature by instrumental reason. The progress of scientific and technological rationality has reached proportions that mock enlightened criticism and control. Spurred by scientific successes of the greatest order (atomic fission, space exploration, genetic technology), science and technology have almost achieved an aura of omnipotence. The seemingly unlimited possibilities of scientific progress, which imitate, mutate and magnify nature, are hardly predictable any longer in their consequences for humankind. Only occasionally, self-inflicted catastrophes (Chernobyl, Challenger, greenhouse effect) remind us of the limits of technology and cast a shadow on the endangered human race, which destroys nature and is able to destroy itself. The domination of nature turns against its masters. This situation, comparable to the sorcerer's apprentice who can no longer control the spirits he conjured up, makes us aware of the dangers of an uncontrollable instrumental reason. The atom bomb marks the limits of enlightenment. It has become the symbol of the life and peace threatening forces of our time.

Peace, as nuclear stalemate, has become a political reality that has prevented the superpowers thus far from using their arsenals. Even if the policy of deterrence appears to have lost its most dangerous edge since the end of the Cold War, the two superpowers alone still have the capability of destroying each other (and the world) many times over. We have no other choice than to come to terms with the nuclear age and its negative horizon. In contrast to Kant's teleology of nature and its positive horizon of the perfectibility of humankind we must adapt to a negative horizon of possible nuclear and ecological catastrophes. Our world, contaminated by nuclear warheads, reactors and toxic waste, is unsafe at any time. The cultural consequences, as we have observed them during the last decade, can be characterized by two dominant discourses on the end of history and on apocalypse now. One is as gloomy and stifling for the human mind as the other, and both are supposed to be signifiers of postmodernity. This seems to me the wrong anamnesis for the postmodern condition. The alternative they propose, world catastrophe or posthistoire, is in its binary negativity unacceptable, unlivable and unproductive. If the nuclear holocaust has become the final, absolute referent of every discourse, as Derrida correctly observes, the consequences do not have to be the end of all possibilities of history or a one-dimensional discourse of apocalypse. It has become so fashionable to talk about the end of the world and of history as if no alternatives were left. Not so surprisingly, it is Jacques Derrida who polemicizes against this modish tone of recent philosophy: "We cannot and should not—and this is our law and our fate—renounce the Enlightenment. In other words, we cannot relinquish what exists as a strange desire for vigilance, clear-sighted alertness, enlightenment, criticism and truth . . . in order to demystify the apocalyptic discourse and with it everything that speculates with visions of an impending end, a theophany, a parusy or a day of last judgement" (59f.). If even Derrida admonishes us to save the tradition of the Enlightenment, we should not hesitate to make use of Kant's best ideas on peace and transform his worst. The peace projects of the Enlightenment have failed, for many reasons to be sure, but that should not discourage us in our search for new solutions in a post-modern age. The limits of enlightenment have become clearly visible, but they should not be confused with an end of enlightenment. Basic concepts of the Enlightenment that relate to peace, such as human rights, international law, the United Nations and the principle of publicity, are still valid; what has become contradictory and irrelevant is Kant's teleology of nature that needs "just" or "last" wars to achieve peace. Kant's model for peace has to be revised and transformed in view of the nuclear age. Kant's warning that we will find eternal peace in a vast graveyard if we fail to accomplish a permanent peace, has become our absolute (nuclear) referent. We live no longer in a world in which we can project a *bonum optimum*, instead we have to struggle for a *malum minimum*.

Notes

1. One should note that Kant distinguishes between a republican constitution and a democratic one, rejecting the latter (100f.).
2. Kant's essay, "Idea for a Universal History with a Cosmopolitan Purpose" (1784), can be read as a commentary on this supplement.
3. Freud's essay was an answer to Albert Einstein, who had posed the question in 1932.
4. For a discussion of peace from a psychoanalytical perspective see Modena and Passett.

Works Cited

Berghahn, Klaus L. "Utopie und Verantwortung in Kants Schrift 'Zum ewigen Frieden.' " *Verantwortung und Utopie*. Ed. Wolfgang Wittkowski. Tübingen: Niemeyer, 1988. 165-89.

Bloch, Ernst. "Bürgerlicher Pazifismus und Friede." *Das Prinzip Hoffnung*. Frankfurt: Suhrkamp, 1959.

Böhme, Gernot and Hartmut Böhme. *Das Andere der Vernunft*. Frankfurt: Suhrkamp, 1985.

Derrida, Jacques. *Apokalypse*. Trans. Michael Wetzel. Graz: Böhlau, 1985.

Freud, Sigmund. "Warum Krieg?" *Kulturtheoretische Schriften*. Frankfurt: Fischer, 1974.

Horkheimer, Max, and Theodor W. Adorno. *Dialectic of Enlightenment*. Trans.

John Cumming. New York: Continuum, 1972.

Kant, Immanuel. *Kants gesammelte Schriften*. Ed. Preußische Akademie der Wissenschaften. Berlin: Reimer, 1912.

————. "Perpetual Peace, Appendix I: On the Disagreement Between Morals and Politics in Relation to Perpetual Peace." *Kant's Political Writings*. Trans. H. B. Nisbet. Ed. Hans Reiss. Cambridge: Cambridge UP, 1970. 116-25.

Modena, Emilio, and Passett, Peter. *Krieg und Frieden aus psychoanalytischer Sicht*. Munich: Beck, 1983.

Rousseau, Jean Jacques. "Urteil über den ewigen Frieden." *Ewiger Friede: Friedensrufe und Friedenspläne seit der Renaissance*. Ed. Kurt von Raumer. Munich: Alber, 1953.

Saint-Pierre, Charles Irénée Castel, abbé de. *Projet pour rendre la paix perpétuelle en Europe*. Ed. Simone Goyard-Fabre. Paris: Garnier, 1981.

PART FIVE

Marginalization and Discipline

The Demise of the Funeral Sermon in Eighteenth-Century Germany: Disturbed Mourning and the Enlightenment's Flight from the Body

Jill Anne Kowalik

> A funeral sermon that has been delivered at the burial of a person is a demonstration that the deceased has in fact died.[1]
>
> ——Chladenius

LESSING'S FATHER DIED on 22 August 1770. In a letter dated 24 August, his brother Theophilus informed Lessing of the death. On 2 October 1770, Theophilus sent him a copy of the biography that was to be published in honor of their father with the request that Lessing, as the most verbally gifted of all of the children, expand and improve the text prior to its publication. By 1770, such a biography was the vestige of the moribund genre of the funeral sermon (*Leichenpredigt*), a lengthy commemoration that was published following its oral delivery. Lessing took no action on this request, and on 5 December 1770 he received an eight-page letter from his barely literate sister Dorothea complaining bitterly that Lessing had not yet sent the biography back to the family. On 28 February 1771, Lessing's mother sent her own bitter complaint to her son Gotthold that he had not yet returned the biography. On 26 March 1771, a frustrated Theophilus wrote: "My dear brother, I beg you most urgently to tell me, however briefly, what might be the status of the biography?" On 15 May 1771, Karl Lessing mentions a letter he has just received from their mother: "She is demanding that you set forth our father's biography." On 3 July 1771, Lessing's

407

mother writes again to Gotthold imploring him to finish the biography. And on 5 March 1772, his sister tells him yet again how pained she is that he has never sent along the biography.[2]

Despite this enormous pressure from four different family members, which involved several attempts to manipulate him through guilt, Lessing never wrote a biography in honor of his father. The only extant references to this issue by Lessing himself are found in two letters to his mother, the first dated 7 July 1771: "As far as the memorial that is to be published is concerned, . . . I really don't see why we have to please the stupid and ill-willed people of Kamenz [Lessing's home town] by publishing it . . . there is plenty of time for praising him publicly. But this does not have to occur in a published biography such as is read following the funeral sermon. I definitely plan to write something. But it's going to be something that will be read outside of Kamenz and for longer than a half-year after the burial. But for this project I need time and good health, both of which I am now unfortunately lacking."[3]

Lessing's response to his mother suggests that he could not bring himself to produce a piece of occasional writing because the genre itself, the funeral sermon, was no longer an adequate or fitting way to remember the deceased. Such reasoning has also been used by historians and literary scholars to explain the demise of the funeral sermon in mid-eighteenth-century Germany. As a baroque oratorical genre intended to fulfill certain representational functions, it is said to have gradually lost its attraction in the age of Enlightenment and Sentimentality. While Lessing may well exemplify the turn away from baroque rhetorical forms and language, we must also remember that an equally compelling reason for him not to compose the biography was that he hated his father and therefore refused to mourn his death.[4] In the particular case of Lessing, the failure to produce a funeral sermon can be traced, in part, to a disturbance in the mourning process.

Proceeding on the assumption that Lessing cannot present a unique case in the social and psychohistory of the German Enlightenment, I have studied the funeral sermon in some detail in order to understand better the phenomenon of pathological mourning in this period. The relationship of this problem to the dialectic of the Enlightenment will be addressed at the end of this essay. Before beginning my analysis, I should like to explain briefly what the genre entailed.

From the time of Martin Luther to the mid-eighteenth century, the funeral sermon functioned as a Protestant ritual of mourning for members of the middle and upper classes who could afford to pay for it. It was not simply a published form of the eulogy ("Grabrede"), but had instead several parts. Although the genre displays a number of variations, the opening section was usually called the "Christian sermon" ("Christliche Leichpredigt") and consisted of a commentary on a Biblical passage relevant to the life or way of death of the deceased. It was delivered in church at a memorial service after the death. Next came the biography ("Lebens-Lauff," also called "Personalia," or, less frequently, "curriculum vitae"). Depending on the wealth and importance of the individual, it encompassed anywhere from one paragraph to dozens of pages. The third section was the leave-taking ("Abdankungsrede"), which was held at the time of interment. The published text may also contain "Epicedia," which are generally short poems composed in Latin or German in honor of the deceased. The social standing of the deceased can sometimes be gauged by the number of "Epicedia" included in the text. Finally, the most expensive examples of the genre contain a portrait as frontispiece, or perhaps engravings of the lying-in-state of an aristocrat, the funeral procession, embossments on the coffin, etc. Occasionally one finds musical scores of works performed at the funeral. All of these materials were collected and published as one text called the funeral sermon.

Such an elaborate genre had of course both secular and religious functions.[5] Its primary secular functions have been described first of all as the self-representation of the upper-middle classes and aristocracy, who increased their own status by circulating funeral sermons. The desire for prestige was sometimes so intense that families went bankrupt over the publication of a funeral sermon in a particularly elegant format. Second, the funeral sermon may have advanced the career of the minister or theologian who composed it and who thus had an interest in its dissemination. Moreover, improvements in paper production and the expansion of the book market affected the availability and popularity of the genre.

The religious function of the funeral sermon is universally treated in the secondary literature as an example of Protestant devotional literature (*Erbauungsliteratur*). Readers were supposed to be instructed in the *ars bene moriendi* or "art of dying." For this reason, the death scene described in nearly every biography of a funeral sermon is built on certain topoi: physical suffering is always borne with patience. The dying are said to be happy—even ecstatic—that they are finally passing on to a better life. They are represented as praying, reading from the Bible, or singing hymns as they die, and their death generally ensues without any visible gestures due to the great physical and mental composure with which they peacefully go to sleep ("sanfft und seelig einschlaffen"). That such descriptions could not have captured the horrors of illness and dying in the sixteenth, seventeenth, and eighteenth centuries is self-evident. But this was precisely the point. Readers were supposed to learn that dying should not be feared, that all of us will die someday, and that what counts is whether, at our death, we will display the appropriate level of piety. Here the funeral sermon was intended as an instructional manual. Its demise has therefore been correlated with the general decline in devotional literature in the eighteenth century (Mohr 323).

While the religious problem of death and redemption has received considerable attention in research on the funeral sermon, I cannot find that this genre has ever been discussed with regard to the problem of mourning, that is, the loss not of one's own life, but the loss of a loved one. When mourning is mentioned at all, it is only in statements *en passant* to the effect that readers are to be consoled knowing that their relative or friend lived and died as a good Christian and that therefore one may count on his or her salvation. Ariès has argued that mourning does not even become an issue in modern European culture until the age of secularization. The establishment, for example, of individual burial plots during this time indicates for Ariès the desire to "visit" the deceased and "the survivors' unwillingness to accept the departure of their loved one" (Ariès 70). The more or less permanent unwillingness to accept a loss may indeed exemplify a state of unfinished mourning, also called pathological or disturbed mourning. Ariès is, I believe, correct in stating that in the mid-eighteenth century mourning became a problem in Western Europe. But this does not allow us to conclude that mourning as a process did not take place prior to this time, as Ariès suggests in referring to the "great changes which occurred in the family and which in the eighteenth century ended in new relationships based on feelings and affection" (65). Ariès's approach to grief in the seventeenth century classes it as a psychic event relatively easily mastered with formulaic religious pronouncements. Although a large number of topoi do indeed appear in the funeral sermons, the biographical sections provide some crucial information on how mourning was practiced in the sixteenth and seventeenth centuries, and how it may have changed in the eighteenth century. Before we examine the texts themselves, a brief definition is useful.

Psychoanalytic, anthropological, and sociological studies have shown that mourning rituals provide a kind of infrastructure for individuals which allows them to pass through a period of grief and reestablish social and psychological relationships in the community. Grieving has been observed to be a four-step process involving: (1) disbelief that the loss has occurred; (2) subsequent searching for the lost loved one; (3) rage directed against those who are held responsible for the loss (including oneself); and (4) memories of the deceased accompanied by the realization of and acceptance of his or her death.

Should any of these phases be neglected, pathological grieving (also called "melancholy") may ensue.[6] Although the funeral sermon certainly fulfilled the religious and secular functions already mentioned, it can also be viewed as a reenactment of the grieving process. By describing the life of the deceased, the funeral sermon offers survivors an opportunity to reanimate imaginatively him or her, and thus facilitates their passage through the first two phases of grief. By describing, in some physical detail, the loved one's death, the funeral sermon would provide a means of experiencing the third and fourth phases of grief.

Here, however, the process of mourning appears to be circumvented by the topoi of death found in nearly all examples of the genre. If everyone dies the same Christian death—a death marked by patience despite enormous physical pain, and joy in anticipation of the afterlife —how can mourners locate in the text the specific quality of the death of an irreplaceable loved one? And how can rage over a loss be expressed and acknowledged within a system of topoi that casts death as the transition to a better life? While these topoi could be and have been dismissed as formulae that dictate how Christians should approach their death, they also have a psychological significance and fulfill a psychological function in that they provide the infrastructure which helps them to grieve. The religious attitude captured in these topoi reduced the possibility of disturbances in the mourning process because it had a compensatory function for survivors. Religious consolation allowed the bereaved to accept the death of the body because they could deny—explicitly and consciously—the death of the soul.[7] Thus anger or pain upon the death of a loved one was nearly always mentioned in funeral sermon texts as a natural reaction to loss—indeed this was yet another topos. But in contemplating the salvation of the soul, survivors were offered a way of resolving these feelings. In the wake of secularization, however, such a form of consolation lost its viability without an effective alternative immediately taking its place. Moreover, just as religious topoi reflect publicly agreed upon attitudes towards death, just as the public display of grief itself was accepted and encouraged, grief in the pending secular age would become increasingly problematic and private. An analysis of transformations in the funeral sermon, that is, in the topoi themselves, will indicate, as I shall attempt to show, changes in attitudes towards death.

The primary material used in my study is a collection of 936 funeral sermons from the Vogelsberg region of Germany, which includes Hesse and parts of Saxony and Thuringia.[8] The publication date of the texts ranges from the 1560s to the twentieth century (one example), with the great majority having appeared in the seventeenth and early eighteenth centuries. Because there are approximately 200,000 extant funeral sermons in German (or Latin) in central Europe today, the collection I use represents a minuscule sample of the genre. My results should therefore be viewed as preliminary and even conjectural. Moreover, because the publication of these texts was restricted to a small segment of society, the conclusions I draw about mourning in Germany in this period are class-specific as well as gender-specific—many more funeral sermons are preserved for men than for women—and hence necessarily limited in their generalizability.

Death figures in the funeral sermons not only as the immediate occasion for the text, but also as an experience of loss that the deceased was called upon to withstand during his or her lifetime. A recurring theme of the sixteenth- and seventeenth-century funeral sermons, but virtually absent in eighteenth-century examples, is the necessity of passing through a period of grief in order to continue one's life. Conversely, prior to the eighteenth century, incidents are described of unresolved mourning that was thought to contribute to or hasten the death of the mourner. In the former case, there are numerous references to men who remarried, sometimes three or four times, after losing wives, especially in childbirth. Martin Müller remarried in 1624 "after enduring the sad state of a widower."[9] Christoph Cheibler, "Magister in Philosophicus," remarried in 1633 "after his year of grieving was over."[10] Carol von Bose lost his first wife in 1637 and remarried "after having painfully mourned her for five-fourths year."[11] Johann Ulrich Zeller remarried in 1671 "after completing his full year as a widower."[12] Wolfgang Adam Lauterbach was encouraged by his "most trusted friends" ("best-vertrawten Freunden") to find another wife "after a fully completed year of mourning."[13] The wording of these examples suggests that a period of grieving for one year was specified by the church, after which the bereaved was free to seek a new partner. But this rule also reflected a social and psychological expectation that the widow or widower would eventually remarry, usually in order to have help with the care of children born in the previous marriage (whose very survival depended, quite literally, on an intact family unit).

References to problematic grief leading to death may be missing from eighteenth-century funeral sermons because in this period, contrary to the centuries preceding it, grief was not thought to be one of the possible causes of the complicated and sometimes deadly illness known as melancholia, a disease with both emotional and physical manifestations.[14] In the earlier centuries, however, considerable evidence exists that traumatic loss and/or unfinished mourning was indeed believed to be fatal. From among many possible examples, the case of Nicolai Varenbüller may be cited. In 1604, he was suffering from pains ("Leibs-Schmertzen") and exhaustion ("Mattigkeit"), and therefore decided "that he would follow his beloved departed wife, who had died the previous year."[15] The death of the minister Johannes Büttner in 1666 at the age of 54 was attributed to unresolved mourning over the death of his wife. "Grief had really taken hold of him," we are told.[16] Johann Friedrich Benckher's severe coughing ("beschwerlicher Husten") and congestion ("Engbrüstigkeit") were aggravated in 1676 by "the sad death of his son, his son's mother-in-law Mrs. Lichtstein, and then that of his son's two children . . . all of which no doubt increased his weakness considerably."[17] Sophia Dorothea Hennicke died in 1696 at the age of twenty-one following the birth of her fifth child, a daughter who survived only twenty-four hours. Her grief ("Betrübnüs") was said to have increased the "already serious exhaustion and insomnia" that preceded her death.[18]

The danger of not coming to terms with loss thus appears to have been given more attention in seventeenth-century texts than in the eighteenth-century funeral sermons. By examining further the death scene in the biography, we can observe subtle but important historical changes in the genre, hence in the practice of grieving itself. In addition to the topoi describing the form that a Christian death was supposed to take, there is the nearly universal statement that the deceased passed away "as those who were present prayed ("unter dem Gebeth der Umbstehenden"). The author making this statement is in most cases the minister ("Beicht-Vater") who was called in to hear the final confession, administer communion, and conduct the last rites—that is, someone who was in all likelihood present at the time of death, and who later would be called upon to compose and deliver the funeral sermon.[19]

Sixteenth- and seventeenth-century descriptions tend to contain more specific information about the *interaction* between the dying and those present at their deaths than eighteenth-century texts offer. For example, when the chamberlain Simon Bing died in 1581, his minister reported on the scene in a first-person narrative. Bing had not been feeling well ("unbaß gewesen") and had tried, without success, all available medicines (an assertion that forms a part of nearly every death scene). He then called in his minister and stated "I would like to die and pass on." Various Bible passages were discussed, "all of which he liked and to which he added his own pious comments." Their conversation continued "for a full half-hour, in the presence of his good wife." The minister leaves and returns two days later to check on Bing, but "because another guest was there, I quickly took my leave." When his death finally comes, it happens so quietly "that those around him were hardly aware of it."[20] The "Paroxismos Epilepticos" experienced by Catharina Moterus in 1583 was so overwhelming "that none of us thought she could have stayed alive for more than an hour,"[21] a statement suggesting conversation and consultation among those present as her condition deteriorated. Philip, Count of Hesse-Rheinfels, called in his entire household ("Hoffgesinde") before dying in 1583, an action that constitutes another topos but that probably reflects standard social behavior. He then gave instructions "on preparing the grave and on how the coffin should look."[22] When Caspar Schutzbar, councillor and officer in Giessen, died in 1588, his wife Agnes had left his side momentarily because she "wanted to get a broth to give him that might strengthen him." The dying man then requested some refreshment ("Labtründklein") from his servant. Upon returning, Agnes finds her now dead husband in a state she thinks is merely a "deep unconsciousness . . . and therefore his wife called out his name most earnestly," but to no avail.[23] Following a conversation about Christian dying, Anna Rau was asked in 1591 whether she understood all she had heard: "She always answered 'yes! yes!' and squeezed my hands and those of the others present almost too hard."[24] When Petrus Bittelbron was dying in 1609, he called together his household for a farewell. "First he thanked his beloved wife for the love and devotion she had shown him all this time, especially during this lingering illness. . . . Then he took his children by the hand [and] asked them to try to get along with one another. . . . Finally he asked his colleagues and other relatives present to forgive him for the occasions on which he may have angered or insulted them."[25] In 1662, the jurist Lucas Kupfferschmidt realizes there is nothing more to be done for him and tells his family "they shouldn't worry about him . . . then he said to his beloved son, who had wanted to tend him throughout the night, that he should go home and get some rest, it wasn't necessary to stay that night, but the next morning he should come back early."[26] In the morning his wife returns and, as her husband lays dying, she complains that she has a headache ("ihr Kopff thäte ihr so wehe") because she had spent a sleepless night worrying about him ("sie deß Nachts seinetwegen keinen Schlaff noch Ruhe gehabt"). This is apparently a family suffering the exhaustion of continuous caregiving.

Before he died in 1670, the theologian Gottfried Bose received "the best and most devoted care and attention" from his wife and many other good friends. His minister provides us here again with a first-person narrative of their final conversations, including an anecdote revealing his concern for the mental state of his dying colleague: "A week ago, when he wanted to reconcile himself with God, he let himself be dressed in his priestly vestments, even though he suffered from great weakness and exhaustion; and when he was reminded that he should take better care of himself in this dangerous condition—God, after all, looks at one's heart and not at one's clothing—he answered: I want to appear before my High Priest in Heaven in my priestly gown."[27]

After about 1680, references to interaction between the dying person and his or her relatives and friends are, with a few notable exceptions, reduced to the obligatory mention of the "tears of those present" ("Thränen der Umstehenden"). The new paradigm for the death scene is the medical report, always given as a third-person narrative and often quite detailed with an increasing amount of terminology in Latin and references to the number of doctors called in on the case.[28] This is not to say that medical discourse was absent from the funeral sermon prior to 1680. Rather, its function in the text was different. Although one occasionally finds Latin *termini* in the death descriptions, one is more likely to find terms from vernacular medicine: tumorous growth or boil ("Geschwulst"), pains of various kinds, exhaustion ("Mattigkeit"), bloody vomit ("Blut-Auswurff"), etc. This means that those hearing or reading the depiction of death were more likely to understand the experience of the dying. The death scene was represented as an agonistic process marked by the empathic intervention of family and friends at various points in the course of the disease, often to read Bible passages to the patient or to sing songs as a way of distracting him or her from the physical pain and easing the psychic stress of the final hours.

By contrast, Johann von den Birgden died in 1680 surrounded by doctors ("anwesenden Herren Medicis") who were struggling to restore his "Respiration" following several attacks, over a two-day period, of "Asthmate," "Catarrhum zu Naaß" (nasal congestion), "Coryzam," "Rheuma," and finally "Catarrhum suffocativum oder Stick-Fluß."[29] We do not know if his wife was with him when he died. Just Friedreich Hartlaub's problems began in 1700 "with an unexpected catarrho apoplectico."[30] His situation was so grave that the doctors ("die Herren Medicos") were constantly consulted. But they were unable to prevent the "cachexia scorbutica, pedum & abdominis intumescentia, icterus niger, affectio tympanitica, febris erratica aliaqve Scorbutum communiter, comitantia symptomata" and lastly the "Inflammation" that finally killed him. The doctors are omnipresent in this account and the family only enters at the end, with its tearful prayer ("thränendem Gebet").

This pattern is repeated throughout early eighteenth-century funeral sermons: cursory mention of the family members in the last lines of the death scene follows a lengthy medical narrative that includes references to all manner of symptoms not usually present in the seventeenth-century accounts, or not present to the same degree. We learn of infections ("Eiterung"), "Haemorrhoiden," bodily discharges containing blood and yellowish material ("mit Blut und gelblichter Materie

vermischte Ejections"), spasms of various kinds, daily vomiting ("täg-
licher vomitus"), chest congestion with phlegm ("conjestion des
Schleims auf der Brust"), pain upon urination, convulsions, vomit
("Auswurff") consisting of mucus and putrefied material ("schleimichte
und verderbte Materie"), diarrhea, legs that were swollen and emitting
a fluid material ("geschwollen und etwas wässeriches von sich gaben")
—perhaps a reference to gangrene, which can set in during advanced
states of gout—and many other pains and weaknesses at various points
of the body described in both German and Latin.

The precise medical nature of the death becomes so fascinating that
in some cases the author of the funeral sermon inserts the report of the
attending physician verbatim into the biography. Medical information
is in fact so detailed that a doctor's report could well have rested on the
desks of the authors of most of the later funeral sermons, although this
was of course not always acknowledged. Even more significant is the
inclusion of autopsy results in the funeral sermons for four members of
the upper aristocracy in the first half of the eighteenth century.[31] By
contrast, only one autopsy exists in all of the seventeenth-century funeral sermons preserved in this collection.[32] Autopsies may have been
included in the text in order to open the royal body to a nearly ritualistic public inspection or to display the corpse as a locus of the most
modern medical techniques, thereby enhancing the aristocrat's status
post mortem. Ironically, we receive instead a singular look at the internal corruption of these men: rotting ("Verwesung") of major organs,
foul impurities ("verfaulte Unreinigkeiten") surrounding others, pus
filling the chest wall, polyps, and infectious growths.

The representation of death in the funeral sermon undergoes a radical transformation around 1700. The physically suffering person
shown to be receiving the care and empathy of others is replaced by the
case study in the course of a disease. A social and psychological event
turns into a medical event. But where the body is represented as a re-
placeable member of a class of scientifically studied objects, rather than
as the irreplaceable embodiment of a discrete individual, grieving is
precluded because the loss of an individual cannot be psychologically
registered. This shift in the content of the death scene anticipates a
scientific shift located by Foucault in the latter part of the eighteenth
century, namely the birth of the "clinical gaze" and the view of death as
a segment on a temporal continuum of disease rather than as a cessa-
tion of life.[33] To die is to undergo a medical change-of-state. Although
the interventions of the many "Herren Medici" to retard or halt the illness are without success, their presence in the text—and their
responsibility for creating the text after the death—attests to the
enormous power with which they were invested. Consolation, in its

secularized form, derives from the wish that physical death itself, or its effects, be effaced.

An illustration of this wish can be found in an elaborate funeral sermon published in 1728 upon the death of Charlotta Sophia Alberti, who was a sickly but pious girl all her life and who finally died at the age of twenty: "After her blessed end this virtuous young woman maintained a sweet, friendly, and pleasant countenance, and became more beautiful each day she remained unburied, which lasted 5 days. It seemed as if she were enjoying a rather sweet and gentle natural sleep in her coffin."[34] Unless the body of this person was frozen (she had died in January), the description of her corpse is a glaring denial of the actual effects of death.

Such a denial was so pervasive in the German Enlightenment that it subsequently generated an important scene in one of the central novels of the eighteenth century. When the protagonist of Goethe's novel Wilhelm Meister's Apprenticeship (Wilhelm Meisters Lehrjahre) demands to see Mignon's dead body, the doctor, an artist in the reversal of death, restrains him: "Keep your distance from this sad object and allow me to impart some life to the remains of this strange being, insofar as my art can do this. I want to apply to this beloved creature the art that is meant not only to embalm a body, but also to preserve its appearance of liveliness."[35] Although this book was written at the end of the century, it documents the inability or unwillingness to confront the fact of physical destruction that had developed already in the early Enlightenment.

The causes of this modern denial of death are numerous and are doubtless related not only to changes in medicine and medical discourse, but also to real advances in the eighteenth century in areas such as nutrition and disease control. But the perceived ability to delay the onset of physical dissolution of the body seems to have been confused with the imagined ability, or wish, to defer it indefinitely or to ignore it. Pathological mourning results from the dominance of such wishful thinking in the face of human loss. Nowhere is the dialectic of the Enlightenment—its transformation from an apparently liberating movement into a force of repression—more evident than in eighteenth-century attitudes towards grief.

The Enlightenment, understood as the attempt to control nature totally with an instrumentalized reason, meets its nemesis in death, for death reminds reason of its limit. The psychodynamics of grief in the Enlightenment are informed by the failure of instrumental reason to acknowledge first, our lack of control over the ultimate fate of the body, and second, the overwhelming, that is, uncontrollable, affect, such as sadness or rage, that is aroused upon the loss of that which we thought we could control. Unresolved (unconscious) reactions to loss in this period may even be viewed as paradigmatic of the "repression of feeling" that is often mentioned in essays on the Enlightenment but rarely elaborated with concrete social-historical detail.

At no time did the funeral sermon constitute the only available means of dealing with loss. Rather, it was an aspect of, and functioned within, a religious, psychohistorical, and social-historical context. Transformations in the larger cultural system reduced the funeral sermon to obscurity. It is therefore appropriate to ask how expressions of grief may have been displaced onto other media. Internal changes in the funeral sermon itself that have already been described suggest a possible answer. In the earlier texts, death is shown not only to be the demise of an individual, but as the loss of that person for others. "Public" dying, where the individual is surrounded by extended family members, friends, and associates, was gradually replaced by "private" dying, where the individual was tended by one or two family members, or perhaps only by the doctor(s). Changes in family structure in the eighteenth century, leading to the privatization of emotional experience, may have significantly altered the grieving practices described in the death scene. The change from publicly shared emotional experience—both at the time of death and again at its discursive reproduction in the funeral sermon—to a private scene foreshadows or perhaps coincides with the decline of the published funeral sermon itself as a publicly available praxis for dealing with loss.

But the relocation of mourning to the private sphere did not ensure its divorce from instrumental reason. On the contrary, the privatization of emotional experience means that it "exists" in this period only with the permission of instrumental reason. Emotional experience is affixed with a tabu and banished to the sheltered confines of the home, the secret pages of a diary, or to the most private theater of all, the unconscious. For this reason, we must be exceedingly cautious with statements such as the following: "At the beginning of the age of Enlightenment, a changing expectation ("Erwartungswandel") manifests itself in discussions of the literary objectification of grief. Intellectual issues become emotional ones. Psychological perspectives begin to receive attention (Beetz 275). While it is certainly true that the eighteenth century produced an enormous interest in psychology, this observation is nonetheless in danger of replicating traditional literary-historical notions of periodization and over-simplifying the problem of mourning in the mid-eighteenth century.

The case of Klopstock illustrates this point; it is particularly significant because he is the German poet most often credited with the so-called rediscovery of feeling in the Enlightenment. He tells his friend

Cramer in a letter dated 5 December 1758 that he had feared his wife would die in childbirth. Meta Klopstock underwent an extraordinarily painful attempt to deliver their child by forceps, in the hope that the instrument would succeed where nature had failed. It is well known that Klopstock mourned Meta's death for decades (sometimes in quite theatrical ways), but it has not, to my knowledge, been examined why the process of mourning was disturbed or pathological in his case, and why he was never able to be done with his grief. The letter to Cramer provides further insight into this: "After some sensations of pain showed themselves in her face, it became fairly cheerful again, and this is how she died!" It is difficult to imagine that these lines convey the physical condition of a woman who had just bled to death following an operation for which no anesthetic was available. Moreover, we miss in this account Klopstock's rage that the instrument had failed, his anger towards the doctor for not having successfully applied it, or his anger towards himself for the impregnation that led to his wife's death. Instead Klopstock continues: "I don't want to complain, Cramer, I want to give thanks that God has given me so much strength during this great trial."[36]

Klopstock has been described as "*the* poet of the eighteenth century who gave the theme of death a far more profound form than it had had in the graveyard romanticism prevalent in that period."[37] Such statements confuse the issue of death as a literary topos with the actual problem of grieving in Enlightenment Germany. This assertion does not, however, represent an isolated oversight. Failure to examine the psychodynamics of mourning in the eighteenth century constitutes one of the most extraordinary lacunae both in traditional German literary studies and in our field today. Most surprising is the utter absence of this topic from the large body of work on melancholy. Hans-Jürgen Schings, for example, says nothing at all about the problem of grief in his comprehensive work *Melancholy and Enlightenment* (*Melancholie und Aufklärung*). If grief and melancholy were indeed dissociated in the eighteenth century, Schings may well be correct to exclude the topic.[38] Nonetheless, inasmuch as the association between mourning and melancholy was not invented by Freud, but stems from centuries of medical discourse which Freud merely appropriated for his own purposes, Schings might have noted the absence of the topic of grief in the Enlightenment's conception of melancholy and commented on the significance of the repression of this problem. Wolf Lepenies raises the issue of mourning in his *Melancholy and Society* (*Melancholie und Gesellschaft*), but there his aim, similar to Mitscherlich's for the post-war period, is to analyze the loss of ideals rather than grief brought about by death. This neglect of the problem of mourning is so curious because the literature of the late eighteenth century is replete with representations of grieving. It would be useful to approach these texts with respect to their function as (successful or unsuccessful) attempts at grief work. Such an investigation would not conjure up the nineteenth-century ghost of trivial biographism, but would instead shed new light on the interactive relationship between literature and experience in the Enlightenment.

Klopstock's story, retold all too briefly here with a few crucial quotations, needs to be reexamined with an eye to the compensatory function of his poetry for his life. Praising his great "insights" without an awareness of how he himself remained painfully mired in repressions of various kinds cannot explain how human loss was handled in the Enlightenment. Such a reevaluation of Klopstock's work would likely reveal that he is but one of many possible illustrations of a specific moment in the dialectical path of the Enlightenment: the inverse relation between the wish to prevent, that is, to undo, death and the psychological ability to come to terms with it when it occurs. In the name of mastery over death, mastery over nature, over the body, and over one's own emotions, survivors of loss in eighteenth-century Germany fell into states of incapacitating pathological grief.

Notes

1. "Eine Leichen-Predigt, die bei Beerdigung einer Person gehalten worden ist, ist ein Beweis, daß dieselbe verstorben sey" (Chladenius, §430: 311). All translations of German quotations in this essay are my own.

2. The letters in question, in the order of their mention, are in Lessing, Vol. 19, Nos. 316, 325, 346, and Vol. 20, Nos. 370, 377 ("Mein liebster Bruder, ich bitte Dich um alles in der Welt, antworte mir nur mit wenigen, wie es mit dem Lebenslaufe soll gehalten werden?"), 389 ("Sie verlangt, Du sollst den Lebenslauf unseres Vaters aufsetzen"), 398, and 463.

3. Lessing, Vol. 17, No. 306: "Was das zu druckende Andenken anbelangt, so ... sehe [ich] wahrlich nicht ein, warum es, den dummen und boshaften Camzern zu gefallen, gedruckt werden muß ... es ist immer noch Zeit, der Welt zu seinem Lobe etwas zu sagen. Nur muß das eben nicht in einem gedruckten Lebenslaufe seyn, wie er nach der Leichenpredigt abgelesen wird. Ich habe mir es fest vorgenommen, etwas aufzusetzen: aber es soll etwas seyn, was man weiter als in Camenz, und länger als ein Halbjahr nach dem Begräbniße lieset. Dazu aber brauche ich Zeit und Gesundheit, woran es mir leider itzt fehlet." The second letter to his mother, dated 9 April 1772, contains identical sentiments (Vol. 18, No. 354).

4. See Kowalik, "Nathan."

5. Information in the following paragraph has been drawn from Lenz, "Gedruckte Leichenpredigten" 37-42.

6. I rely here and throughout my study on the analytic and historical information provided by Bowlby and Lazare. Some readers may question the applicability of contemporary psychoanalytic studies to early modern experience. The resolu-

tion of this methodological issue lies outside the bounds of this essay. I am assuming certain "ahistorical" constants in the psychodynamics of grief that are present from at least since the sixteenth century with regard to the phenomena of bonding and loss. A more thorough argument for the presence of modern patterns of bonding since the Renaissance has been presented by Lenz, "Emotion und Affektion."

7. I leave out of consideration at this time the Pietist belief in the resurrection of the body, which begins to appear at the conclusion of the death scene in Pietist funeral sermons towards the end of the seventeenth century. Such a belief may reflect the modern denial of death dicussed below, but the entire matter is too complex to be explored in this study.

8. All quotations from the "Vogelsberg" region collection are made with the express permission of the "Forschungsstelle für Personalschriften" in Marburg. I am very much indebted to Prof. Dr. Rudolf Lenz, director of the institute, for making the microfilms of this collection available to me and for advising me on certain problems in the evaluation of the material. Citations of all funeral sermons include the catalogue number, followed by the page number where the quotations begin (e.g., "Lp. 1, 25" means catalogue number 1, page 25). Longer German quotations are given in the notes. Original orthography has been retained. The names of the deceased are included to facilite locating data in the catalogue, which is organized alphabetically.

9. Lp. 99, 37: "nach außgestandenem betrübten Witwenstandt."

10. Lp. 53, 133: "[n]ach Ablauff des Trawer-Jahrs."

11. Lp. 767, n.p.: "[n]achdeme . . . er 5. viertel Jahr dieselbe schmertzlich betrauret."

12. Lp. 795, 34: "nach hinbringung seines volljährigen Wittwerstands."

13. Lp. 26, 34: "nach völlig abgelegtem Trawr-Jahr."

14. Jackson 320. As a psychiatrist and historian of medicine, Jackson may be more attuned to this problem than literary scholars of melancholy.

15. Lp. 54, 16: "daß er seiner lieben Haußfrawen seeligen/ welche vorgehenden Jahrs Todts verfahren/ nachziehe."

16. Lp. 33, 30: "die Bekümmernus [war] zimlich bey ihm eingenistet." The entire passage reads as follows: "*Anno* 1665. den 16. *Novembris*, fast umb 4 Uhr Nachmittag/ ist seine Hertzgeliebte Haußfrau durch einen plötzlichen Schlag-Fluß/ doch in seeliger Bereitschaft/ von dieser Welt abgefordert/ und er dardurch in den betrübten Wittwenstand gesetzt worden. Weilen nun nach Absterben jetztgedachtes seines Ehe-Schatzes/ die Bekümmernus zimlich bey ihm eingenistet/ die Ampts-Last von Tag zu Tag schwerer/ die Pfleg und Wartung/ Kräffte und Vermögen deß Leibes/ je länger je schwächer worden: Ist es (GOtt erbarm es) geschehen/ daß heut vor 3 Wochen eine *dysenteria* und Durchbruch sich bey ihm vermercken lassen/ welche er aber den ersten und zweyten Tag gar wenig/ und so gar nichts geachtet/ daß er auch den folgenden Sambstag seine ordentliche Predigt selbsten verrichtet/ doch aber also schwach/ daß er gleich von der Cantzel sich nach Hauß begeben/ zu Bett zu legen/ und auff einrathen der Herren *Medicorum*/ allerhand dargegen dienliche Mittel gebrauchen müssen. Ob nun gleich die Herren *Medici* die aller-köstliche außgesonnen/ ihm *ordinire*t/ welche er auch willig zu sich genommen/ hat doch alles nichts verfangen wollen."

17. Lp. 14, 43: "die traurige Todts-Fäll seines Herrn Sohns/ Schwieger-Mutter Frauen Lichtsteinin/ so dann dessen beeder Kinder . . . welche ihm zweiffels ohn seine Schwachheit sehr vermehret."

18. Lp. 793, 63: "bereits innhafftende Mattigkeit/ und Schlafflosigkeit."

19. There were, of course, professional funeral sermon authors, and the ques-

tion of the veracity of the genre was already raised in the seventeenth century: "people spoke of the funeral sermon [Leichenpredigt] as the falsehood sermon [Lügenpredigt]. . . . There were without a doubt corrupt funeral sermons in the baroque period, that is, sermons that were only intended as empty praise [Lobhüdelei]. But one should not conclude from this that funeral sermons in general are unreliable," Lenz, "Gedruckte Leichenpredigten" 43-44.

20. Lp. 510, 38: "Ich begehre auffgelöset zu werden"; "welches jhm alles sehr wohl gefiel/ und seine Gottselige Reden auch darzu thet"; bey einer halben stund/ in beyseyn seiner tugentsamen Haußfrawen"; "weil auch ein ander frembder Gast allda war/ nam ich bald meinen abschiedt"; "daß es auch die so umb jhn gewesen/ kaum jnnen werden."

21. Lp. 511, 58: "daß niemandt dazumal unter uns vermeynet/ daß sie ein Stunde länger im Leben hette bleiben können."

22. Lp. 404, 120: "das Grab und Sarck zu machen/ auch wie dasselbige aller gestalt nach sein solle."

23. Lp. 498, 248: "jm ein Krafftbrülein holen und reychen wolte"; "starcke Ohnmacht . . . und deßwegen sehr ernstlich seine Haußfraw jhm zugeruffen."

24. Lp. 501, 347: "Gab sie jmmer darauff die antwort/ Ja Ja/ vnd truckt mir vnd andern vmbständern die Händ fast hart."

25. Lp. 657, 36: "Erstlich seinem lieben Eheschatz freundlich gedancket für die Lieb und Trew so sie jhme die zeit hero sonderlich in dieser langwirigen Kranckheit erzeigt vnd bewiesen. . . . Darnach hat er seine Kinder bey der Hand genommen/ sie zur Einigkeit vndereinander vermahnet. . . . Entlichen hat er auch seine Collegas vnd andere anwesende Verwandten/ wo er sie erzörnt vnd beleidigt vmb verzeihung gebeten."

26. Lp. 44, 25: "sie solten sich über Ihn nicht bekümmern . . . darauff zu seinem geliebten Sohn/ welcher des Nachts bey ihme wachen wollen/ gesagt: Er solte sich nur nach Hauß zur Ruhe begeben/ es hätte diese Nacht keine Noth/ den andern Morgen aber solte er gar frühe widerumb kommen."

27. Lp. 698, 568: "alle möglichste und treufleißigste Pflege und Wartung." "Als er heute 8. Tage frühe morgens sich mit GOtt versöhnen wolte/ ließ er sich bey seiner größten Mattigkeit und Schwachheit seine Kleider und Priesterlichen Habit anlegen/ und als erinnert wurde/ doch seiner selbsten bey diesem gefährlichen Zustand zu schonen/ GOtt sehe nicht das Kleid/ sondern das Hertz an/ antwortete er: Ich will in meinem Priesterlichen Kleide für meinen hohen Priester im Himmel treten."

28. Kümmel has noted (225) the rising number of references to doctors in funeral sermons towards the end of the seventeenth century, but he then immediately observes, in an apparent contradiction, that "from the early eighteenth century on it appears that the relationship of the dying person to death was not expressed in direct physical terms, but rather was described in terms of his psychological or spiritual condition [Seelenstimmung]." This latter statement appears to be true for some Pietist funeral sermons, but the collection I examined displays a trend towards medical reporting. Kümmel's conclusions may differ from my own because we used different collections, or the apparent contradiction may be a manifestation of two mutually reinforcing currents in the period; see my note 7. Döhner (459-60) finds that references to multiple doctors in a funeral sermon are only intended to demonstrate the wealth of the deceased's family. He does not discuss changes in the uses of medical information in the funeral sermons.

29. Lp. 27, 50.

30. Lp. 746, 36: "mit einem ohnvermutheten catarrho apoplectico."

31. Augustus, Duke of Saxony-Merseburg, died 1715 (Lp. 182); Carl Ludwig, Count of Nassau-Saarbrücken, died 1723 (Lp. 146); Friederich Ernst, Count of Solms-Laubach, died 1723 (Lp. 129); Johann Adolph, Duke of Saxony-Weißenfels, died 1746 (Lp. 907).

32. The seventeenth-century autopsy was performed on Christoph Ulrich, Count of Promnitz, who died in 1677 at the age of 14 (see Lp. 186, 35). The author of this funeral sermon mentions that the boy was initially not able to be treated by the best doctors available because they were busy with more important royal patients in Dresden. Thus the reference to the "absonderlichen Bericht" of his doctors following their very interesting "*Exenteration* des verstorbenen Cörpers" does indeed appear to be a compensatory gesture to correct this social snub. Autopsies were widely conducted in Europe in the seventeenth century as part of the anatomical research of that period. Gryphius, for example, learned the art of "Sectiones" during his matriculation at the university of Leiden; see Mannock 9. (I am grateful to James A. Parente for drawing my attention to the issue of vernacular medicine in the seventeenth century and Gryphius's relationship to it.) In seventeenth- and eighteenth-century England, autopsies were conducted for forensic reasons or to establish the cause of death in order to clarify familial predispositions to certain illnesses (according to Robert Frank, UCLA School of Medicine, personal communication). As far as I can determine, a *social* history of the autopsy in Germany remains a desideratum. It would be useful to know, for example, why only the funeral sermons of aristocratic males contain autopsy reports, whether or how frequently autopsies were performed on different classes, the status of the autopsy report as a legal document, etc.

33. Foucault, esp. Ch. 8: "Open Up a Few Corpses."

34. Lp. 353, 19: "Nach Ihrem Seeligen Ende behielte diese Werthe Jungfer ein liebliches, freundliches, und angenehmes Angesicht, und wurde täglich schöner, so lange Sie unbeerdiget gewesen, welches 5. Tage daurete: Es schiene als ob Sie in ihrem Sarge eines gantz süssen und sanfften natürlichen Schlafes genösse."

35. Goethe 7: 545: "Halten Sie sich von diesem traurigen Gegenstande entfernt, und erlauben Sie mir, daß ich den Resten dieses sonderbaren Wesens, soviel meine Kunst vermag, einige Dauer gebe. Ich will die schöne Kunst, einen Körper nicht allein zu balsamieren, sondern ihm auch ein lebendiges Ansehen zu erhalten, bei diesem geliebten Geschöpfe sogleich anwenden."

36. Klopstock 2.3: 108: "Nach einigen schmerzhaften Empfindungen in ihrem Gesichte, ist ihr Gesicht wieder ganz heiter geworden, und so ist Sie gestorben!" And: "Ich will nicht klagen, mein C., ich will danken, daß mich Gott bey dieser grossen Prüfung so sehr gestärkt hat."

37. Höpker-Herberg 189. I am indebted to Rehm, whose nearly 500-page standard work on the representation of death in German literature, however, never raises the issue of mourning.

38. See my note 14. Schings's earlier work on the funeral sermons composed by Gryphius (*Die Patristische . . . Tradition*) is an important philological study that was not intended to consider the psychohistorical problem of mourning.

Works Cited

Ariès, Philippe. *Western Attitudes Toward Death: From the Middle Ages to the Present*. Trans. Patricia M. Ranum. Baltimore: Johns Hopkins UP, 1974.

Beetz, Manfred. *Rhetorische Logik: Prämissen der deutschen Lyrik im Übergang vom 17. zum 18. Jahrhundert.* Tübingen: Niemeyer, 1980.

Bowlby, John. *Loss: Sadness and Depression.* Vol. 3 of *Attachment and Loss.* New York: Basic Books, 1980.

Chladenius, Johann Martin. *Einleitung zur richtigen Auslegung vernünfftiger Reden und Schrifften.* 1742. Reprint. Düsseldorf: Stern, 1969.

Döhner, Otto. "Historisch-soziologische Aspekte des Krankheitsbegriffs und des Gesundheitsverhaltens im 16. bis 18. Jahrhundert (anhand von gedruckten Leichenpredigten)." *Leichenpredigten als Quelle historischer Wissenschaften.* Ed. Rudolf Lenz. Vienna: Böhlau, 1975. 442-69.

Foucault, Michel. *The Birth of the Clinic: An Archaeology of Medical Perception.* Trans. A. M. Sheridan Smith. New York: Vintage, 1975.

Goethe, Johann Wolfgang. *Werke.* ["Hamburger Ausgabe."] Ed. Erich Trunz et al. 14 vols. Rev. ed. Munich: Beck, 1981.

Höpker-Herberg, E. "Der Tod der Meta Klopstock: Ein Versuch über des Dichters Auffassungen vom Tode." *Der Tod in Dichtung, Philosophie und Kunst.* Ed. Hans Helmut Jansen. Darmstadt: Steinkopf, 1978. 189-201.

Jackson, Stanley W. *Melancholia and Depression: From Hippocratic Times to Modern Times.* New Haven: Yale UP, 1986.

Klopstock, Friedrich Gottlieb. *Werke und Briefe: Historisch-kritische Ausgabe.* Ed. Adolf Beck et al. Abt. Briefe. Berlin: de Gruyter, 1975- .

Kowalik, Jill Anne. "*Nathan der Weise* as Lessing's Work of Mourning." *Lessing Yearbook* 21 (1989): 1-17.

Kümmel, Werner Friedrich. "Der sanfte und selige Tod: Verklärung und Wirklichkeit des Sterbens im Spiegel lutherischer Leichenpredigten des 16. bis 18. Jahrhunderts." *Leichenpredigten als Quelle historischer Wissenschaften.* Vol. 3. Ed. Rudolf Lenz. Marburg: Schwarz, 1984. 199-226.

Lazare, Aaron. "Unresolved Grief." *Outpatient Psychiatry: Diagnosis and Treatment.* Ed. Aaron Lazare. Baltimore: Williams & Wilkins, 1979. 498-512.

Lenz, Rudolf. "Emotion und Affektion in der Familie der frühen Neuzeit." *Die Familie als sozialer und historischer Verband.* Ed. Peter-Johannes Schuler. Sigmaringen: Thorbecke, 1987. 121-46.

———. "Gedruckte Leichenpredigten (1550-1750): Historischer Abriß, Quellenwert, Forschungsstand, Grenzen der Quelle." *Leichenpredigten als Quelle historischer Wissenschaften.* Ed. Rudolf Lenz. Vienna: Böhlau, 1975.

———. "Katalog der Leichenpredigten und sonstiger Trauerschriften in Bibliotheken und Archiven der Vogelsbergregion." Vol. 9 of *Marburger Personalschriften-Forschungen.* Marburg: Schwarz, 1987.

Lepenies, Wolf. *Melancholie und Gesellschaft.* Frankfurt a.M.: Suhrkamp, 1969.

Mannock, Eberhard. *Andreas Gryphius.* Stuttgart: Metzler, 1968.

Mohr, Rudolf. "Das Ende der Leichenpredigten." *Leichenpredigten als Quelle historischer Wissenschaften.* Vol. 3. Ed. Rudolf Lenz. Marburg: Schwarz, 1984. 293-330.

Rehm, Walther. *Der Todesgedanke in der deutschen Dichtung vom Mittelalter bis zur Romantik.* 2nd. ed. Tübingen: Niemeyer, 1967.

Schings, Hans-Jürgen. *Melancholie und Aufklärung: Melancholiker und ihre Kritiker in Erfahrungsseelenkunde und Literatur des 18. Jahrhunderts.* Stuttgart: Metzler, 1977.

———. *Die Patristische und Stoische Tradition bei Andreas Gryphius: Untersuchungen zu den Dissertationes funebres und Trauerspielen.* Cologne: Böhlau, 1966.

Controlling the Demonic:
Johann Salomo Semler and the Possession of
Anna Elisabeth Lohmann (1759)

Jeannine Blackwell

> Men had to do fearful things to themselves before
> the self, the identical, purposive, and virile nature
> of man, was formed, and something of that recurs
> in every childhood. The strain of holding the I
> together adheres to the I in all stages; and the
> temptation to lose it has always been there with
> the blind determination to maintain it.[1]
> ——Horkheimer and Adorno

IN 1759, IN THE VILLAGE of Kemberg near Wittenberg, a young woman of twenty-two was discovered to be possessed by one evil spirit and three angels. Anna Elisabeth Lohmann, an unmarried and very pious girl who worked in the family tavern in Schleesen, fell daily into paroxysms in her home, where soon crowds of hundreds gathered to watch and listen as the spirit of her nemesis, the huntsman Tietze, ranted and railed against authority through her. They heard in awe as the voices of three, later four, angels sang impromptu hymns and preached. They later witnessed her physical gyrations and the exorcist manipulations of the Lutheran minister who attended her bedside and published her story. Gottlieb Müller, the Lutheran prior of Kemberg, used this "patient" (*Patientin*), as he called her, as a means to bring about a religious renewal in his town.

In response to Müller's published report on her case came a series of critical, even vituperative responses from the German theological, medical, and philosophical intelligentsia. Johann Salomo Semler, professor of theology in Halle and a disciple of Wolff's, led the attack against belief in diabolic and divine possession, and against this case in particular. He was reinforced by the enlightened Reformed minister Johann Benjamin Gottlieb Bobbe of Dessau, the Berlin philosopher Georg Friedrich Meier, and Wittenberg professor of philosophy Gotthelf Friedrich Oesfeld, among others. Semler's critique lay the groundwork in Halle for historicism in biblical criticism, as his writings on the demoniacs of the New Testament grew out of his concern with the Lohmann case. His teachings and writings influenced later students such as Friedrich Schleiermacher, and through him David Friedrich Strauss.

Why did such renowned and sophisticated intellectuals weigh in against the relatively obscure Müller and the virtually unknown Lohmann? Why was their response so vigorous, so public, and so pejorative of both Lohmann and Müller? Divine possession was a red flag for Enlighteners, I maintain, because it was a very special subset of their critique and control of the management of madness. In contrast to the large sweep of insanity encompassed in Foucault's critique of the bourgeois Enlightenment, which puts a generalized kind of control, isolation, and surveillance at the center of institutionalized life based on the paradigm of the insane asylum, I focus on this specific behavior. I do so because divine/diabolic possession has traditionally offered participation for the illiterate and disenfranchised in religious institutions, and the Enlightenment critique of possession is a scientific-historical criticism of revelatory religion as well as a class criticism of those who believe in it. Thus the enlightened management of the phenomenon of possession is a trenchant combination of class bias against the gullible lower classes and scientific advancement. The Enlightenment critique attempts to "save" possession's victims from their multiplicity of selves in order to preserve the sanctity of the autonomous ego. Possession strikes at the core of Enlightenment (and Calvinistic) notions of religion as a stratified meritocracy, in which community-condoned morality and works are the path to transcendence; it questions the validity of conscious, autonomous selfhood; it threatens the Enlightenment view of the world as a symbolic order of representations that can be deciphered only by that conscious, autonomous self; it presents a threatening countermodel for the emergence from individual disenfranchisement (*Unmündigkeit*); and it jeopardizes the precarious Enlightenment truce with organized religion.

The Enlightenment response to claims of supernatural possession could be a page from *Dialectic of Enlightenment*. It is an actual case of the suppression of Odysseus' oracle, a silencing of the voice and gesture of terror. In contradiction to Foucault's analysis of insanity as the genesis of the "case study" in early modern Europe, one might say that the cases of religious possession lay far better claim to the origins of the genre. Cases of possession forge a direct link between the medieval *Nonnenvitae*, the lives of the saints, and the charismatic leaders of the post-Reformation splinter groups which took written (and often published) spiritual autobiography as their outlet. They were the ground on which the battles of "heutige Offenbarung" (present-day revelation) were fought between fundamentalist charismatics and orthodox Lutheranism on the one hand and Enlightenment scientific thought on the other. The refutation of divine possession and oracular power of the non-ordained (after the apostolic era) is one of the few absolute victories of the Enlightenment over Western religion: Enlightenment-inspired biblical historicism reached a consensus with orthodox Protestant theology about that impossibility, and Catholicism set up a hierarchical process for the determination of sainthood. But not without a struggle by both orthodoxies to suppress those who felt God speaking through them.

The Lohmann case is possibly the last major Protestant European case of a female oracle who gained credence and response from within the theological and intellectual hierarchies. In earlier cases, as in this one, the oracle had visions, spoke in voices, performed biblical and political exegesis in God's name, and was often supported and publicized by a man of God. During and after the Thirty Years War, Europe was awash in movements beyond the control of the church hierarchies. Many of these splinter groups were led by women and lower-class men who based their spiritual authority on signs and wonders. Jansenism and Quietism had their share: in the wake of the possessions at Loudun came Madame de Guyon and Antoinette Bourignon, Anna Vetter, Jane Leade, the Camisards, and their Berlin counterparts, the "Inspired." In early radical Pietism these charismatic women inspired nascent leaders: August Hermann Francke was strongly influenced by the infamous three inspired maids in the Quedlinburg-Erfurt area, as Gottfried Arnold was by Rosamunde von Asseburg, and Philipp Spener by Johanna Eleonore Petersen. These charismatics exhibit the same threat to a hierarchy of educated interpreter-priests: they insisted on the possibility of present-day revelation through possession or vision; they rejected the traditional concept of a priesthood; they insisted on a physical, literal understanding of biblical and inspirational language. Interpretation for them comes through visionary experience, and vision enters their lives via a multiplicity of selves over which they have, and want, no control.

Orthodoxy's struggle against these charismatic, primarily female, oracles took a variety of forms, among them charges of witchcraft and other types of intercourse with the devil. Occasionally they became "cases" in legal or ecclesiastical courts, in which the male priests or pastors associated with these women were severely punished for consorting with them; the sexual implications in such cases were frequently a source of their notoriety. Charges of lewdness or promiscuity were enough, in the minds of their critics, to discount any and all visionary power. The cases of the possessions at Loudun, at Madame Guyon's orphanage in Horn, the possession trial of Jeanne Fery, the bewitchment case of Mary Catherine Cadiere against the Jesuit priest Jean Baptist Girard, and the anti-pietist investigation of Anna Marie Schuchartin (one of Francke's three inspired maids) were all argued in part on this basis. Orthodoxy refuted divine possession by using traditional theological arguments about women as vessels of sin susceptible to the devil. Gradually, the established churches and most of the newer sects as well rejected chiliastic inspiration and claims of present-day revelation except when practiced by an acknowledged member of the church hierarchy; by the advent of institutionalized Pietism in the early eighteenth century, inspiration, miraculous healings, and "speaking in tongues," even when practiced by the ordained, were all called into question.

It is not surprising, then, to find Enlightenment theologians and philosophers dealing the death blow to divine possession in the eighteenth century. In the tradition of Thomasius, the critics Semler, Meier, Bobbe, and Oesfeld are at pains to distance themselves from charging any possessed person with witchcraft. Yet they take the older theological arguments about the dissemblance of woman, her alleged vulnerability to sexual sin, and woman as the devil's tool in arguing a case against Anna Elisabeth Lohmann. Undergirding their argument is the notion that the self is a consciously chosen, moral, and integrated construct of a religious nature, and that those who refuse to acknowledge this controlled and controlling self are foolish, if not sinful.

It is difficult to describe the Lohmann case without reverting to the language of psychoanalysis, medical pathology, or religious demonology, because even the discourse we use today about such historical cases is colored by Enlightenment and post-Enlightenment thought. I attempt to make this description as value-free as possible.

Lohmann's behavior began to change around Easter of 1756 after a confrontation with the young huntsman Johann Christian Tietze, who frequented her brother-in-law's tavern in Schleesen near Horsdorf in Anhalt-Dessau. Lohmann, who helped out in the family tavern, rejected Tietze in spite of contact with him there, and alleged that he tried to hex her by circling her three times on horseback, proclaiming she would go lame. By day's end, she was unable to undertake a planned journey because of lameness, and became an invalid. Shortly thereafter, she began to have paroxysms (uncontrolled flailing of arms, rigidity of limbs, convulsive movements including rolling of eyes, facial contortions, thrashing head, breast, and the "hysterical arch," the convulsively arched back of women in hysteria), stammering or dumbness, and insensibility. At Easter of 1757, a voice emerged from her that identified itself as Tietze himself, gave witness against himself about the bewitchment, and spoke threateningly against Lohmann, whistling, shouting, and singing. While this voice dominated her body, she repeated gestures such as drinking, taking snuff, putting on a dagger, and fighting, but did not curse or blaspheme, as Tietze was known to do. Her family kept her behavior a secret, and she was secluded at home under the care of her sister. At the beginning of Lent in 1759, there emerged a second voice, identifying itself as that of an angel, which spoke consolation to her about her maladies. From June until August of 1759, three other angelic voices identified themselves, accompanying the first in soprano, alto, and tenor parts. They were named Gabriel, Goel, Elisy, and Eli.

After two years of invalidism, her behavior gradually became public knowledge and achieved notoriety. Tietze, her alleged hexer ("Teufelsbanner"), had a long-term feud with Lohmann's brother-in-law, who had brought three civil cases against him (Tietze did not show up for trials out of fear of forced Prussian conscription). Tietze maintained that he had not bewitched Lohmann; rather, her father had sold her to the devil as a child, since she was the seventh daughter, and as in the case of Sleeping Beauty, the effect of that bewitchment began only when she turned eighteen. (Lohmann was actually born in July, 1737, and thus was eighteen when the first event began.) After medical cures of bloodletting and various potions, and partial attempts at disenchantment by the hunter's friends (smoking the house on three consecutive Fridays, dehexing by sympathetic magic, and an exorcism by the local hangman), she refused all further medical treatment. The angelic voice directed her to go to the village of Kemberg to seek help from three ministers there. The local judge in Schleesen agreed to this, and facilitated her approach to Dr. Müller in April of 1759.

After initial skepticism, Müller accepted the pleas of Lohmann and her family to have daily prayer with her; he held public prayer meetings for her, and hundreds attended to watch his ministrations over her and her speaking in voices. Three months later he insisted on a confrontation with Tietze, which took place while Lohmann was "herself." Tietze came to Kemberg accompanied by his fellow huntsmen, refuted all charges, yet bragged on their traditional huntsmen's magic tricks and spoke of the long-standing vendetta between the huntsmen and the innkeeper. Lohmann's paroxysms were heightened after this encounter, and she began to have prayer meetings in her own home which were attended by hundreds to watch her on her couch, to hear her songs and pronouncements. The pronouncements of the voices are extemporized versions of hunting songs and chants in the case of her "evil" voice, hymns and devotional poems in the angelic examples.[2]

Given the conflict between notions of the self for charismatic religious women and educated male Enlighteners, it is not surprising to hear the following terms in which Lohmann's condition and activities were described by her analysts or to see the sort of cures that were suggested and in part carried out on her.

In his description of her possession, the believer Müller calls her the patient ("die Patientin") in the sense of "the suffering one" or "the long-suffering one." As such, the term had been in use in German discourse at least since the sixteenth century to describe those bearing some sort of religiously inspired tribulation; Müller, for example, uses the term almost interchangeably with the descriptor "aggrieved/afflicted woman" ("angefochtete Weibesperson"). Semler and his cohort use the term "patient" differently; not to indicate the woman actively bearing a burden, but rather as an example of involuntary or purposeful dysfunction of a medical-psychological nature. Müller also appropriates medical terms in his effort to preempt academic criticism when he stresses that he first considered her to be a "Fall" (a "case") and her problem to be "eine besondere Art Nerven-Krankheit" (a special kind of nerve illness) or a "corruptio sanguinis" (corruption of the blood), and asks for an investigation by the medical faculty at Wittenberg. Yet in spite of these prefatory remarks, he continues to refer to her activities and symptoms in terms of inspiration and multiple souls, as did charismatic early Pietism: "es habe aus ihr und zu ihr geredet" or "die singende Begeisterung" (it spoke from her and to her, the singing enthusiasm). He stresses the literary quality of her impromptu verse-making; he compares her both to an authorial voice like those of Klopstock and others (125) and to a sympathetic heroine (Richardson's Pamela), and thus gives us a direct contemporary connection between Pietistic poetry of enthusiasm and the sentimental heroine; he praises Lohmann's "poetic imagination" ("poetische Einbildungskraft," 125). He adamantly refutes explanations of her condition as *furor uterinus* (an early medical designation of hysteria/nymphomania) or witchcraft.

Semler's criticism of Lohmann (and of Müller's interpretation of her state) is not based on personal observation; in fact, he refuses point-blank the invitation of Müller to visit and observe Lohmann. He claims that any rational analyst can use the full description provided by Müller to judge the case for himself. His real intent in absenting himself is, however, the withdrawal of audience and encouragement from what he sees as a spectacle of dissemblance. Semler's epithets for Lohmann emphasize her low class status, ignorance, sanctimonious prudery, and intended fraud: he calls her "a master of farces" ("eine Pritschmeisterin," 26), "this very questionable character" ("diese sehr verdächtige Person," 35), and a propagator of "stupid peasant nonsense" ("dummes Dorfgewäsche," 39). He finds her symptoms to be of natural origin and "hysterical" ("hysterisch"), and easily cured by marriage; the religious side of her behavior and the voices are a product of "sick imagination" ("kranke Einbildung") and the sanctimonious wish to make her symptoms and herself more important. She has, according to him and to the two medical experts who examined her and reported on her case, the secondary signs of possession (physical aspects) but not the primary, biblically acknowledged behavioral ones: knowledge of hidden things, ability to speak unknown foreign tongues, and supernatural strength. He cites the questions about her dancing with Tietze, the time-consuming laying on of hands, Müller's application of his finger to her tongue as her need for kisses and embraces. Semler quotes Bobbe approvingly on the surmisal that she is erotically obsessed ("verliebt"), and cannot stand to be around women of good repute during her enforced cure. He thus combines received Christian thinking about possession with the terminology of sexual obsession and dissemblance ("Verliebtheit") and of its latinate medical counterparts ("hysterisch").

Semler's second strategy treats her poetic statements. He ridicules the *very* low class of these spirits (20), and attacks her speeches as "nothing but a few proverbs, fragments of hymns, emulated but clumsy and crude ideas on one and the same subject." He doubts if any men of discriminating taste would find this to be the word of angels, or comparable to Mosheim, Saurin, Marino, or Klopstock.

Semler suggests curing her through force: she should have been tied down, then bound and gagged in order to interrupt her delusions by fear; she should have been beaten whenever the evil spirit came (78). He asserts that similar cases have always been proven to be a result of intentional fraud or a disordered imagination, and therefore they are not curable through religious consolation. He recommends that she be handed over to the authorities.

Semler, following the lead of British rationalists of the 1740s such as Twell, Pegge, and Whiston, uses critical biblical historicism to refute Müller's arguments by interpreting demoniacs in the New Testament and early Christianity as a God-chosen *parable* or metaphor for teaching important notions to those of little understanding. With increased insight, present-day believers can reinterpret that demonic possession, as well as divine possession, as a metaphor for certain eternal concepts. Thus biblical passages can be subject to educated interpretation, but only by those who have rigorous historical training and religious authority; not by the unlettered and charismatic Lohmann. More importantly, Semler uses natural law to refute the notion of a substantial devil and insists on a *metaphorical* meaning of any physical experience for the Christian community. That is, any apparently magical or demonically/ divinely inspired phenomenon is merely the attempt of non-substantial Evil to test the gullibility and superstition of Christians, to divide them from their Church Fathers and each other, and to encourage vanity and ignorance among the untutored, particularly women. Semler's historical argument is based on the impossibility of true divine visionary experience after the apostolic age. He agrees with orthodoxy that Lohmann should not try to assume authority in a church hierarchy, and thus gain access to interpretive activities: he criticizes the decision to hold the public prayer meetings at her home rather than praying silently in a church, as well as her physical presence at prayer sessions held for her own benefit—she should have modestly withdrawn, as St. Paul prescribes.

Semler criticizes Müller's "treatment," that is, his exorcist activities, in handling Lohmann during her paroxysms: Müller puts his finger in her mouth, passes his hands over her body, attempts exorcism through prayer and speaking directly to the demon and angels. Semler stresses how unseemly this could appear in others' eyes for a man of God; he underlines how much Lohmann seems to enjoy it.

Semler maintains that if God were to choose a vessel for divine revelation in this day, it would not be a poorly educated and ungifted peasant girl. He ridicules an oracle that speaks in a language of bad hymns of the previous century, and makes the claim that at least one criterion for the true inspirational voice is its literary quality. He thus undergirds the notion of inspiration as a *metaphorical* and literary concept, rather than a concrete and sensate public religious event. By stressing aesthetic quality as a criterion for judging inspiration, he both reinforces the notion of the educated interpreter-priest as the arbiter of inspired ideas on the one hand, and he secularizes inspiration on the other.

The philosophical grounding for this metaphorical reading of all immediate religious experience is rooted in Semler's very eclectic definition of cognition and experience ("Erkenntnis" and "Erfahrung"). Actual observation of present-day phenomena was certainly a tenet of Enlightenment science, and Semler was confronted with a report on the observation of hundreds of people. Since he is at pains to explain a rationalist Enlightened view of religion, he must explain why phenomena that were obviously seen and experienced in Kemberg, and used for devotional purposes, do *not* count as experience to the

Enlightenment way of thinking. What constitutes true experience for Semler is "experience" combined with "reason" ("Erfahrung" und "Vernunft"), and only "reasonable" ("vernünftige") witnesses are credible ones; they earn credibility by their disinterest in the phenomena, and by having a basis in "Christian cognition/knowledge" ("christliche Erkenntnis"). Experience without such a religious cognitive basis is not possible in Christian morality. These kinds of fantasies (as in the cases of Lohmann, Rosamunde von Asseburg, and Francke's three inspired maids, whom Semler takes as examples) can become accepted only when the people who *should* be exhibiting reason and cognition do not: that is, when ministers such as Müller acknowledge them. The poor ignorant masses then follow these unfortunately chosen models of religious edification ("Erbauung"), and become ever more enmeshed in error. Thus Semler, in this actual confrontation with a case of unenlightened behavior, has to limit his definition of experience by education and vocation, and implicitly by sex and class, in order to make it operable. He does not define Christian cognition, but it is clear from his approaches to New Testament exegesis that he means a process of filtering religious-ethical beliefs through the sieve of verifiable natural law, a kind of self-censorship of traditional religious belief, while never questioning the divine per se.

Semler finds that in these cases feminine weakness is often at the root of the misuse of experience, and that women's ignorance and dissemblance create experience unfettered by Christian cognition—experience which opened doors that should remained closed:

> people do not consider the horrid damage and spiritual murder they instigate against God's clear Word with such carelessness and false sources of piety; through which the whole Christian religion almost by necessity is robbed of its real and true fundament, and a perspective is opened to serious people who cannot be charged with having evil intent as their goal—a perspective which for most of them can never be closed in and limited again, at least not by these perpetrators and patrons of untrue revelations. They call themselves the messengers of the more magnificent kingdom of Jesus Christ; for the previously known kingdom of God is much too poor, it has to be raised a few levels by these female preachers and made totally spiritual (that is, sensual and fantastic). (90)[3]

Semler's definition of experience confined and controlled by Christian cognition demarcates the range of knowledge for the autonomous ego, while at the same time it denotes its sex and class. This narrowed definition of experience is mirrored in the controlling self, and other voices and "mere" experiences are to be subordinated to it.

Established institutions of church and state prevailed in the case of Anna Elizabeth Lohmann. A warrant for her arrest was issued by the Prussian state on 27 March, 1760; she was to be put into the penitentiary/poorhouse in Waldheim for cure and surveillance, but she had already been sent back home to Horsdorf in Anhalt-Dessau by the magistrate of Kemberg, and so evaded arrest. She was then taken to Dessau at the behest of the state of Anhalt-Dessau, where she was incarcerated and "cured." The Reformed minister Bobbe reported on her condition in letters to Semler and in publications, and participated in decisions on her treatments. In Dessau she was isolated from religious believers in her visions and voices, and letters to her from the Kemberg congregation were confiscated (May, 1760). Measures for treatment of her illness, diagnosed as "morbus spasmodico-convulsius cum corrupta phantasia" (Semler 50), included sensory deprivation, physical blows to overcome her partial paralysis and paroxysms, and exposure to moral models. Semler chastises the authorities in Kemberg for letting her see so many women and commonfolk, and he reports from Bobbe that she is really a nymphomaniac, because when she sees men, she has convulsions. The five divine and demonic voices stopped within a few months (by July, 1760), and Semler and Bobbe claimed a successful cure and a vindication of their analysis of "nymphomania" ("Verliebtheit") as the source of her problems. She is said to be grateful for the end of her possession, and to be embarrassed about her earlier behavior. I have not been able to trace her life after Bobbe's report.

Looking at this cure from today's perspective, we see a series of actions by the state and Enlightenment intellectuals to isolate Lohmann physically and thus cut her off from public discourse. Next was an attempt to control physical symptoms that did not correspond to Enlightenment notions of discrete and refined womanly behavior, such as body and facial contortions. Third was an explanatory model that stressed her personal guilt and collusion in duping the public: her nymphomania and interest in men, and her deliberate manipulation of symptoms to make herself interesting to them. Fourth was an emphasis on her ineptness at "inspirational" discourse: an aesthetic judgment on the crudeness of her "literary" utterances.

Semler allows inspiration to be understood only on the metaphorical level. In so doing, he defines an economy of inspiration that necessitates three groups of Enlightened elites who facilitate its production: the authors of inspirational work who can create metaphor from experience, the arbiters of that metaphorically inspired work, and the institutions of education and church that canonize and propagate it. This tripartite edifice rests on a narrowed definition of "experience," limited to those who can properly observe it through Christian cognition. Only certain kinds of people were trained in the cognitive powers necessary to evaluate experience truly; others, common and ignorant people, thought they were having experience, but they actually needed to have others interpret it for them. The touchstone for telling false inspiration from true is, for Semler, aesthetic quality in metaphor manipulation: that is what separates Lohmann from Klopstock.

The uneasy truce of the Enlightenment with organized religion was maintained only if religious tenets of the miraculous were not in contradiction to natural law and were metaphorically understood. Thus if any and all charismatic and miracle-based movements were shunned by the church fathers as superstition and not exploited for enhancement of belief, Enlighteners were placated, and were again comfortable with religious belief. In turn, religious authority helped Enlighteners define the limits of the self, to truncate the multiplicity of selves and experiences into a narrower and more hierarchically organized ego.

The key to this controlled and channeled, metaphorically understood inspiration is a rejection of multiple selves, divine and demonic, within the individual. When I claim that cases of possession posed a threat to the model of institutionalized religion as a stratified meritocracy, I mean that this kind of possession case undoes the notion of one censored and decorous voice, that of the autonomous self, as the source of all thought in a person. As a countermodel for the emergence from voicelessness (my folk-etymology translation of "Unmündigkeit"), I mean that this multiplicity of voices allowed a few members of the non-elite to issue criticisms and approach religious experience directly through voices that were seditious, immoral, and anti-institutional, long before such criticisms found an allowed constituency. Above all, divine possession questioned the idea of interpreted symbol rather than immediate sensual experience as the source of knowledge. It therefore disperses the basis of the Enlightenment truce with organized religion: the idea that knowledge, and also religious knowledge, must be a mediated interchange of ideas interpretable only by an educated elite. The battle, as so often within the Enlightenment, is a competition for hearts and minds: who is to control public discourse, and the Enlightenment's answer was a compromise with the very institutions it purported to criticize: church and state. In Lohmann's case, it was a very straightforward collusion to incarcerate and retrain her by both institutions, affirmed by all the Enlighteners familiar with the case.

In the later eighteenth and nineteenth centuries, we see a gradual imposition of the rationalist model for religion, as the charismatic female voice is ideologically showcased and rendered metaphorical by a controlling male minister, who alone can interpret the image. We find isolated fads, such as Mesmerism, that present a secularized usage of the trance and multiple voices; there is no institutional counterweight to Enlightened thought about personality constructs. By the

1780s it is understood, in such influential journals as the *Berlinische Monatsschrift*, that such cases are ludicrous and that the young woman involved is medically "hysterical." But constant tensions about spiritual immediacy recur, as the fundamentalist readings of the Bible engender new movements and leaders: Quakers, Camisards, Shakers, and Herrnhuter were followed by Wesleyan Methodism, the Great Awakening in America, and a plethora of smaller charismatic sects.   All these groups in their early years were based on a rejection of the old scholasticism and religious authority; all search for a new voice, a new form of "Mündigkeit," very often through sensual and emotional catharsis and a literal understanding of the text and of such sacraments as baptism. This new "fundamentalism" of a literal understanding of biblical language and text, open for individual inspirational interpretation, is consequently criticized by post-Enlightenment thinkers.

Ironically enough we find the Enlightenment's tendency toward self-destruction alive in its collusion to suppress the multiple voices of charismatic possession and fundamentalism in direct and literal religious interpretation. Today that same charismatic impulse, without its political and social radicalism, is coming back to haunt the Enlightenment in a criticism of a "secular humanist" elite that arbitrates power and knowledge in educational and governmental institutions. One of the reasons that Semler's criticisms of the Lohmann case sound so reasonable and believable to us as academics is that we are still operating in that explanatory mode of the autonomous self whose morality and behavior are consciously chosen and, if bad or asocial, are motivated by sexual pathology. The reassertion of charismatic religion as a proclaimed enemy of the Enlightenment (read secular humanism) today is in part a reaction to the heavy-handed dismissal of other people's experience by our intellectual forefathers. All the scientific evidence garnered in three centuries to refute literal biblical fundamentalism has not suppressed charismatic thought yet, and will not likely do so, since the social stratification behind the animosity remains intact. But that is another paper, on the dark side of the Enlightenment's dialectic with the New Right.

If the struggle against belief in supernatural possession reached a plateau, struck a truce with organized religion, and became dormant except as a literary metaphor in the later eighteenth and nineteenth centuries, it came back with a vengeance in the Freudian era. Insofar as the Enlightenment response to cases of diabolic or divine possession was one of denial, trivialization, and assignment of blame to the patient's sexuality or to her medical pathology, it prefigures the apparently different response of the elite corps of psychoanalysis in the early years, 1880-1900. I need not rehearse here Charcot's and Freud's interpretation of hysteria (which many assume to be the present-day equivalent of possession); it has become part of the post-Enlightenment understanding of compulsive behaviors by women. Indeed, it is almost impossible to hear the details of Lohmann's case *without* assuming a Freudian interpretation of repressed sexuality (read "Verliebtheit") which would be cured by romantic commitment of an appropriate and fulfilling nature. So Semler's arguments make sense to us as academics, even though we recognize that an abuse of control and punishment played too great a role in her "cure."

I bring up Charcot and Freud, however, to highlight the insistence of Enlighteners and their heirs on explaining and answering a system of ego organization that stands in contradiction to the Enlightenment—the fluid multiple personality whose boundaries are not permeated with intent, subordination to authority, and self-imposed morality.

Jean-Martin Charcot, Freud's teacher and a founder of psychoanalysis, insisted on a return to historical cases of religious possession in his search for cause of neuroses, and in so doing, he made the first major attempt since the Enlightenment to reintegrate demonic possession/ hysteria back into a philosophy of culture.[4] He mentions these cases frequently in the Tuesday lectures, and one of his students, Desiré Magloire Bourneville, edited the *Bibliothèque diabolique*, an edition of historical documents relating to such cases in France. The series was designed by Bourneville to illustrate Charcot's theory that autosuggestion, rather than organic cause, motivated certain cases of neuroses. Charcot's contribution to the series, *La foi qui guérit* (*Faith that heals*), dealt with religious healing miracles as fact; he assumes the breakup of the personality into fragments of selves in heightened or hypnotic states, and discusses the specific kinds of symptoms (paralysis, convulsions, blindness, muteness, deafness) that can actually be cured by faith healing or the laying on of hands by a doctor or minister. Indeed, he draws parallels between his own treatments of hysterics and that of miracle healers. Seemingly miraculous cures come about when a "teacher" or other authority figure directs the hypnotic-state self to overcome the symptom—not unlike the kind of cure attempted by both Gottlieb Müller and Johann Bobbe with Anna Elisabeth Lohmann.

Although Charcot was preoccupied with the famous historical cases of possession, the overwhelming number of which were females involved in public sectarian life, his disciple Freud virtually ignored them, even in his early studies of hysteria. In spite of his frequent use of historical or legendary persons to illustrate his points about culture and character (from Oedipus to Moses and Rembrandt), and in the face of Charcot's and Bourneville's publishing activities in the 1880s and 1890s, Freud never discusses the cases of multiple personality, religious possession, or visionary experience by women in religious groups—he has one brief anecdote about an unnamed elderly woman with a religious obsession.   One thinks here of how interesting a Freudian analysis of Joan of Arc, Jane Leade, Catherine Cadiere, one of the possessed nuns of Loudun, or even of a German witch trial would have been. Freud's care to listen to the words and explanations of the early cases of hysteria ("the talking cure") is not carried over into the later periods in which he is concerned with historical types. The significance of his exclusion of these kind of cases, on which there was extensive documentation and very often autobiographical writings by the individuals involved, is heightened when we examine the one case of demonic possession on which Freud did write.

This case is taken from obscure unpublished documents sent to Freud from a monastery library about a case of possession by the devil from the seventeenth century. It is uncharacteristic of a possession case, for it is an isolated instance of a lower-class male, Christian Haitzmann, who in 1677 claimed he sold his soul to the devil in a Faustian manner, complete with pact written in blood, and entered into this pact after the death of his father.[5] He has no religious following and makes no pronouncements, has no publicly declared visions, and does not associate himself with a religion or sect, other than to perform certain acts in a Catholic church.

It is clear that Freud has chosen to write about this case because it illustrates his Oedipal complex so well and can serve as a companion piece to his "Wolfman" analysis of multiple personality; Freud analyzes it, in convenient shorthand, as "the devil as surrogate father" (*Der Teufel als Vaterersatz*). Freud explains Haitzmann's mania as a flight to the mother church to avoid fear of castration by the absent and all-powerful father. Freud's choice of a case not only allows him to do a brief, veiled analysis of the Faustian pact as an Oedipal event; it also conveniently allows him to ignore the issues of competing public discourse that one must address in dealing with religious charismatics.   One would be hard put to use the Oedipal complex as an explanation for Joan of Arc or Anna Elisabeth Lohmann; one would have to use methods that explained the social movements that surrounded them as well. Nor does his analysis of this "Teufelsneurose" explain the angelic, rather than demonic, visions that a substantial number of the possessed have.

In Freud's case of demonic possession, I think we can see the parameters of what constitutes experience again being limited to the kind of ego that is reminiscent of the old-fashioned Enlightenment autonomous self. By excluding and ignoring the majority of historical possession cases, Freud can indeed define an ego that is determined by its

revolt against the fathers, while taking them as institutionally authorized models of church and state; he can cast possession as a masculine,
individual struggle against paternal authority, rather than a mass movement with its own agenda. As with so many other Enlighteners, Freud
explains much about the world by excluding even more from consideration. Freud revises the Enlightenment structure of the self, to be sure;
but the notion of *real* life and experience being determined by the
struggle of a (somewhat) autonomous self against and within experience colored by reason on the one hand, and moral/religious cognition
on the other is still at the base of the ego/superego construct. While
Freud certainly does not deny the existence of a multiple or split personality, he definitely considers it to be a pathological one. Most
importantly, he agrees with Bolz's paraphrase of *Dialectic of Enlightenment*: "Whoever does not want to be powerless must dominate" ("Wer
nicht unmündig sein will, muß herrschen," 113); one dominant personality must emerge for a cured to be enacted.

The reworking of the meaning of diabolical and divine possession
into purely medical and psychological phenomena (epilepsy, dissemblance and "Verliebtheit") in the Enlightenment period prepares the
ground for Charcot and Freud to redefine the old possession as epilepsy on the one hand, and "la chose genitale," hysteria, on the other.
The Enlightenment attempt to remove divine possession from religious
life to personal guilt of the possessed individual and her public is the
foundation on which the Charcot/Freud reading is built.

The feminist critique of the diagnosis, description, and treatment of
hysteria by psychiatrists is a refutation of the model of control and indi-
vidualized psycho-pathology. Frequently the feminist argument against
Freud takes the form of a call for a return to Enlightenment values: a
call for an autonomous self-improving (female) ego, and a rejection of
cultural pessimism and social Darwinism in sexual-social relations. An
examination of the Lohmann case shows, however, that feminist critiques of psychiatric control are actually critiques of Enlightenment
thought: a critique of domination/control by the "scientist," another
form of the interpreter-priest who defines true experience for the
untutored masses.[6] In the "case" of Lohmann we see the struggle for
hegemony over the "patient" between church, state, and intellectual
community; we find the surgical removal of the possessed woman from
her public and the elimination of vital parts of her case from view;
above all, we observe how her own religious analysis and social criticism through the voices, her interaction with her public, and her own
reading of her possession are lost, since they are discounted as invalid
experience.

Notes

1. Horkheimer and Adorno 33.
2. Examples of Lohmann's voices, taken from Müller: Tietze's voice: "ich will sie wacker quälen! zum Ehestande will ich sie untüchtig machen! warum hat sie mich nicht haben wollen! . . . zu wiederholten mahlen hönisch lachte; ha, ha, ha, ha! nu habe ich sie wacker gequält! nu habe ich sie rechte Schande gemacht! sie darfs nicht einmahl sagen, wo ich sie alle gequälet habe! sie darfs nicht sagen! sie darfs nicht sagen! ha, ha, ha, ha!" (116)
   First Angel: "Dein Leiden liebe Tochter! haenget nur noch an einer Spinnewebe, welche von einem geringen Winde kann zerrissen werden. . . .
   Wie es ein Richter machet, dass er die alten Briefe aufsuchet, um zu sehen, wer Recht, und wer Unrecht hat: so wird es auch Gott an jenem Tage machen, dass er das Schuldregister aufschlaegt, und die laengst verflossenen Thaten der Menschen untersuchet. . . . Deine Krankheit ist zwar wie ein Ungewitter. Dieses scheint zwar fuerchterlich: aber es ist doch sehr nuetzlich, und befoerdert einen sanften Regen, der hernach die Felder erquicket: und wenn es vorueber ist, so wird man froh. Hernach gehet die Sonne wieder auf, wie ein Braeutigam in seiner Herrlichkeit. . . . Gleichwie eine Mutter ihrem Kinde ein Fruehstueck giebet, und spricht: Da hast du eine Bamme, bis zur Mahlzeit: so giebt auch dein himmlischer Vater dir von Zeit zu Zeit suessen Trost, bis er dereinst dir die vollendete Huelfe schaffen wird, und dir endlich die himmlische Freuden-Mahlzeit geben wird, da du satt werden wirst von den reichen Guetern seines Hauses. . . . Es beschaeftigen sich mit den Menschen zwey Engel: ein guter und ein boeser. . . . Der Satan ist wie eine Bremse, welche zwar stechen, aber nicht toedten kann. . . . Das juengste Gericht ist wie ein grosser Jahrmarkt, auf welchem ein jeder seine Waaren zu Marckte bringen wird. Glueckselig, wer alsdenn das rechte Loesegeld mit bringen wird." (Anhang 20-21)
3. "[man] bedenkt nicht den greulichen Schaden und Seelenmord, den man mit solcher Unvorsichtigkeit und falschen Quellen der Erbauung, wider Gottes klares Wort, anrichtet; wodurch fast notwendig die ganze Christliche Religion ihres ächten und wirklichen Grundes beraubet, und nachdenkenden Menschen, ohne daß man nun ihre böse Vernunft zur Hauptursache machen könne, ein Gesichtskreis eröfnet wird, der bey den meisten, wenigstens durch diese Aufsteller und Gönner solcher unächten Offenbarungen, nicht wieder kan verengert und eingeschränkt werden. Das heissen aber so gar die Vorboten von dem herrlichern Reich Jesu Christi; denn das bekante Reich Gottes ist viel zu schlecht, es mus durch solche weibliche Predigten erst etliche Stufen höher gesetzt und ganz geistlich, (eigentlich, sinlich und fantastisch) gemacht werden" (90).
4. For a contrasting feminist analysis of the contribution of Charcot and the early Freud to the clinical study of hysteria, see de Marneffe.
5. For a recent analysis of this case as a reading of Faust, see Calhoun. Calhoun does not note that Freud's case excludes the context of religious social movements surrounding cases of possession.
6. See de Marneffe 104-11, for a listing of current feminist analysis of Charcot, Freud, and the critique of scientific objectivity.

Works Cited

Works on the case of Anna Elisabeth Lohmann:

Das bezauberte Bauermädgen: oder Geschichte von dem jetzt in Kemberg bei Wittemberg sich aufhaltenden Landmädgen Johannen [sic] Elisabethen Lohmännin. Aufgesetzt von einem vom Urtheil Befreyeten, und mit Anmerkungen eines Rechtsgelehrten versehen. Breslau: J. E. Meyer, 1760.

[Bobbe, Johann Benjamin Gottlob.] *Vermischte Anmerkungen über Sr. Hochehrwürden des Herrn Probstes und Superintendentens in Kemberg Herrn Gottlieb Müllers Gründlichen Nachricht und deren Anhang von einer begeisterten Weibesperson Annen Elisabeth Lohmännin, mitgetheilet von Antidämoniacus.* Bernburg: Christoph Gottfried Coerner, 1760.

Meier, Georg Friedrich. *Georg Friedrich Meiers, der Weltweisheit ordentlichen Lehrers, der königlichen Academie der Wissenschaften zu Berlin Mitglieds, und d. Z. Prorectors, philosophische Gedanken von der Würkungen des Teufels auf dem Erdboden.* Halle: Carl Herman Hemmerde, 1760.

Müller, Gottlieb. *Gründliche Nachricht von einer begeisterten Weibesperson Annen Elisabeth Lohmännin von Horsdorf [sic] in Anhalt-Dessau aus eigener Erfahrung und Untersuchung mitgethilet von Gottlieb Müllern, Probst und Superintendenten in Kemberg, auch Ehrengliede der Gesellschaft der freyen Künste in Leipzig.* Wittenberg: Johann Joachim Ahlfeld, 1759. Second edition with Anhang, 1760.

Oesfeld, Gotthelf Friedrich. *Gedanken von der Einwirkung guter und böser Geister in die Menschen. Nebst beygefügter Beurtheilung eines neuern Beyspiels einer vermeynten leiblichen Besitzung.* Wittenberg: Johann Joachim Ahlfeldt, 1760.

Semler, Johann Salomo. *Abfertigung der neuen Geister und alten Irrtümer in der Lohmannischen Begeisterung zu Kemberg nebst theologischem Unterricht von dem Ungrunde der gemeinen Meinung von leiblichen Besitzungen des Teufels und Bezauberungen der Christen. Mit einem Anhang von den weitern historischen Umständen vermehrt.* Halle: Johann Justinus Gebauer, 1760.

Versuch einer unpartheyischen Widerlegung S. T. Sr. Hochehrwürd. Herrn Gottlieb Müllers, Probsts und Superintendentens in Kemberg Gründlichen Nachricht von einer begeisterten Weibesperson Annen Elisab. Lohmannin etc. etc. aus philosophisch und physicalischen Gründen hergeleitet, von Alethaeo Adeisidaemone. Leipzig: Lanischens Buchhandlung, 1759.

Other Works consulted or cited:

Andersson, Ola. *Studies in the Prehistory of Psychoanlysis: The Etiology of Psychoneuroses and Some Related Themes in Sigmund Freud's Scientific Writings and Letters 1886-1896.* Stockholm: Norstedts, 1962.

Belgrad, Jürgen. "Verdichtete Welten: Annäherungen an die Aufklärung der Lebensgeschichte." Reijen and Nörr 210-32.

Bolz, Norbert. "Das Selbst und sein Preis." Reijen and Nörr 111-28.

Calhoun, Kenneth S. "The Education of the Human Race: Lessing, Freud, and the Savage Mind." *German Quarterly* 64 (1991): 178-89.

The Case of Mrs. Mary Catharine Cadiere Against the Jesuit Father John Baptist Girard In a Memroial presented to the Parliament of Aix. Wherein He is accused of seducing her, by the abominable doctrines of Quietism, into the most criminal excesses of Lewdness, and under an appearance of the highest mystical Devotion, deluding into the same Vices six other Females, who had put their consciences under his direction. 10th ed. London: J. Roberts, 1732.

Charcot, Jean-Martin. *La Foi qui guérit: Bibliothèque Diabolique (Collection Bourneville).* Paris: Progrès Medical, 1897.

de Marneffe, Daphne. "Looking and Listening: The Construction of Clinical Knowledge in Charcot and Freud." *Signs* 17 (1991): 71-111.

Foucault, Michel. *Madness and Civilization: A History of Insanity in the Age of Reason.* New York: Random House, 1965.

Frei, Hans. *The Eclipse of Biblical Narrative: A Study in Eighteenth and Nineteenth Century Hermeneutics.* New Haven: Yale UP, 1974.

Freud, Sigmund. *Eine Teufelsneurose im siebzehnten Jahrhundert.* Leipzig: Internationaler Psychoanalytischer Verlag, 1924. First publ. in *Imago* 9.1 (1923).

Horkheimer, Max, and Theodor W. Adorno. *Dialectic of Enlightenment.* Trans. John Cumming. New York: Continuum, 1972.

"Nachricht von einer hysterischen Jungfer in Lengerich in der Grafschaft Tecklenburg, die es mit dem Teufel zu tun haben will." *Berlinische Monatsschrift* (June, 1783): 595-604.

Oesterreich, Traugott Konstantin. *Die Besessenheit.* Langensalza: Wendt & Klauwell, 1921.

Owen, A. R. G. *Hysteria, Hypnosis and Healing: The Work of J.-M. Charcot.* New York: Garrett, 1971.

Reijen, Willem van and Gunzelin Schmid Nörr, eds. *Vierzig Jahre Flaschenpost: 'Dialektik der Aufklärung' 1947-1987.* Frankfurt: Fischer, 1987.

Scherer, Georg. *Christliche Erinnerung, bey der Historien von jüngst beschehener Erledigung einer Junckfrawen, die mit 12652 Teufel besessen gewesen. Gepredigt zu Wien . . . 1583.* Ingolstadt: David Sartorium, 1584.

Semler, Johann Salomo. *Commentatio de daemoniacis quorum in novo testamento fit mentio.* 4th ed. Halle, 1779.

———. *Umständliche Untersuchung der daemonischen Leute oder sogenannten Besessenen Nebst Beantwortung einiger Angriffe.* Halle, 1762.

———. *Versuch einiger Moralischen Betrachtungen über die vielen Wunderkuren und Mirakel in den älteren Zeiten, zur Beförderung des immer besseren Gebrauchs der Kirchenhistorie.* Halle, 1762.

J. M. R. Lenz as Adherent and Critic of Enlightenment in *Zerbin; or, Modern Philosophy* and *The Most Sentimental of All Novels*

Hans-Gerd Winter

I.

Song of a Shipwrecked European . . .

When I think back
On the long sea journey—everywhere—
Where the air was so moist, it gave wine
At Madera, at the happy Cape—
Where the air was sharp, coconuts grew—
Wherever it was cold, the wind floated wood to us.
We saw giants, like David,
And defeated them with little pebbles;
We saw wild devils, they sang
Mumbo-jumbo peace songs to us
So that we laughed at their good naturedness—
Oh! beneficial Nature!
Look! this last piece of wood
I now lay onto the fire—Its smoke disappears
In the air—And no one answers——
Nature, who thinks of everything!
Have you forgotten me?[1]

Henning Boëtius and Gert Vonhoff have recently drawn attention to this poem, which was not contained in the standard modern Lenz editions of Titel/Haug and Damm. In a century that was not only the age of Enlightenment, but also of exploration, merchant journeys and of forced colonialization, the poem elucidates an unreflected, utilitarian relationship to nature, a relationship that was intensified by the development of bourgeois economy and of seafaring technology. Nature and its products are transformed into objects of human exploitation. The poetic persona combines this basic stance with an unexamined consciousness of the European's superiority over non-European, unenlightened savages (beginning with "We saw giants . . ."). A rupture in the perspective and the consciousness of the speaking "I" occurs when it is banished to an island, and the smoke of the last firewood disappears without summoning help. In our century, Brecht, too, uses smoke to represent a consolatory landscape in contrast to a desolate one from which the human being has disappeared (10: 1012). The shipwrecked narrator of Lenz's poem is no longer harbored in this kind of purposeful nature, as the last line shows. While the Storm and Stress movement of the 1770s—and particularly Goethe—posits a Rousseauist opposition between nature and alienated society, the isolated poetic persona in Lenz's poem is exposed to a savage nature.

The poem can be read as an early document of a fantasized "dialectic of Enlightenment." For Horkheimer and Adorno, the suppression of external nature, which accelerated in the age of Enlightenment, the reduction of nature to "charity," are related to the suppression of inner nature, the repression of the natural environment to which the human being belongs. The compulsion to identity, including the compulsion to say "I," implies on the one hand a radical isolation of humankind, on the other hand its socialization by means of anonymous, abstract goals —for example, through economic exploitation, which is concretely expressed in expanding seafaring. The "I" of the poem has isolated itself; it is alienated from its connection to nature, which it sees as an object of exploitation. When the "I" is alone and confronted with nature, its previously optimistic self-assuredness is useless. The specific significance of the poem is that Lenz closes it with this contradiction rather than making the shipwrecked man into a Robinson Crusoe who begins to colonialize nature.

In this essay, I wish to illuminate other aspects of Lenz's work that can be understood as a dialectic of Enlightenment; I will examine the two prose texts listed in my title. We shall see that Lenz must be seen both as a proponent and as a critic of Enlightenment, though this critique is only partially coextensive with a dialectic of Enlightenment in the sense that the texts register a destructive potential of the process of civilization that is powerfully advanced in the eighteenth century.

This project must confront the stubborn prejudice that sees the Storm and Stress movement, to which Lenz belongs, as a simple championing of feeling and subjectivity against the one-sided domination of rationality in the Enlightenment. Lenz was decisively influenced by Enlightenment philosophy, which he nevertheless experiences as contradictory. He grappled with pre-critical Kant, German rationalism (Leibniz, Wolff), "enlightened" neological theology (Spalding), English empiricism, French materialism (Helvétius, La Mettrie) and especially Rousseau. The influence of the Enlightenment—at the latest during Lenz's study with Kant in Königsberg (1768-1772)—was a key factor in his emancipation from his parents' way of thinking, which combined pietist and orthodox Lutheran elements into a legacy of strict religiosity, rigid moralism and patriarchal authoritarianism. Particularly his discovery of Rousseau (perhaps before his study in Königsberg, but in any case through Kant's mediation) was a revelation for Lenz. The influence is documented in more than twenty references in letters and works of the Strasbourg period (1772-1776). Since there was no unified concept of *the* Enlightenment at the beginning of the 1770s, Lenz feels no need to set himself outside this diverse intellectual movement.[2] Undoubtedly, Lenz embraces the emancipatory potential of Enlightenment, which was primarily driven by interests of the rising bourgeoisie; however, in his texts, Lenz's own experience of limited chances for self-realization contours the shadows that the light of reason gives rise to, even produces. For example, Lenz recognizes that liberation from authority through independent thinking ("Selbstdenken") can lead to new hierarchies and subordination. And independent thinking can also be deployed to legitimize existing injustice in new and different ways. Lenz is especially sensitive to the compromises of the German Enlightenment, which because of the weakness of the bourgeoisie was coopted by the status quo even as it hoped to humanize it. Here we find the preconditions for a critique of Enlightenment that simultaneously subscribes to its principles. Because the opposition of individual and society is radicalized to the point of alienation for Lenz, his critique sometimes even questions instrumental reason. In contrast to other Storm and Stress authors, Lenz has difficulty reaching or envisioning a utopian horizon beyond his experience of the present. He cannot simply jump across the real boundaries of the free individual who wishes to imitate God the creator.[3]

Lenz is less appreciated for his prose than for his plays, and he wrote less about them than about his plays; in contemporary literary theory, too, prose plays a subordinate role. On the other hand, Lenz's prose texts, including the two discussed here, show that he masters the usual genres of his day, but also uses them for very idiosyncratic purposes. The first of these two texts clearly draws on reality and even pretends to be a historical document by means of the usual fiction of an "editor"; the second text is openly irreal and fictional.

II.

The story *Zerbin; or, Modern Philosophy* was written at the end of 1775 in Strasbourg. In December, Lenz sent it to the publisher Christian Boie, who published it in his periodical *Deutsches Museum* in February 1776.[4] Lenz's remark to Boie that the tale is written "in Marmontel's manner, but I hope not with his brush" (D 3: 358), contains a connection as well as a demarcation. Marmontel's *Moral Tales* (*Contes moraux*) had first appeared as a collection in 1761 and in a multivolume German translation in 1762-1770.[5] In these stories, a moral message is exemplified in a concrete, usually simple plot with rather typical characters. Frequently the tales merely correct human weaknesses, attitudes that depart from the "reasonable" norm. Enlightened optimism, which sees evil contributing to good and justice ultimately triumphant, is characteristic of this collection, which had considerable success in many European countries, since it satisfied the need for entertainment of a growing bourgeois readership.

Lenz holds to the construction of an exemplary case that is subjected to the enlightened and critical ruminations of the narrator. In contrast to Marmontel, however, Lenz presents a sociopsychological case study, whose complexity transcends simple moral judgment. Enlightened optimism is ruptured right from the beginning by a critique that nevertheless bespeaks an enlightened intention. The motto from Shakespeare ("O let those cities ... hear these tears") and the narrator's first two exclamations appeal to the sympathy of the reader for the manifold "kinds of misery" that "fashionable philosophy" dismisses with abstract formulae. The narrator asks questions that reveal the ambivalence of enlightened "philanthropy" and simultaneously distance his text from Marmontel's intentions. The appeal to sympathy invokes the Enlightenment's—especially Lessing's—demand that feeling be transformed into "virtuous capabilities" ("tugendhafte Fertigkeiten"). The narrator asks why there are so many "miserable people" in the century of "philanthropy and sensibility" ("Menschenliebe und Empfindsamkeit"): "Are they always unworthy, when our rationality (which is enriched by clearer views of morality) depicts them that way?"[6] Morality had never been discussed so intensively as in the eighteenth century, nor literature placed so strictly in the service of ethical training. The narrator's explanation of so much unhappiness is that the moralists are frequently egocentrics who "will ultimately never be able to discover the slightest moral beauty outside of themselves" (354). Lenz's narrator (representing the author's views here) sees misery as conditional on the abstractness of moral philosophy that causes the individual to "love only the human race, not individuals."

He thus sees a "dialectic of Enlightenment" at work, which leads to "all-too-lofty philanthropy" and from there to a misanthropy "that is that much more inflexible."[7]

The initial reflections in *Zerbin* are decisively influenced by Herder's critique of the "enlightened" century in *Another Philosophy of History for the Education of Mankind* (*Auch eine Philosophie der Geschichte zur Bildung der Menschheit*, 1774), which was directed against the historical optimism of the likes of Iselin (*Philosophical Conjectures on the History of Mankind*; *Philosophische Mutmaßungen über die Geschichte der Menschheit*) and Schlözer (*Proposals for a Universal History*; *Vorstellungen einer Universalgeschichte*). In 1775, Lenz enthusiastically welcomes Herder's decision "to oppose his voice to the voice of the whole universe."[8] Herder, too, criticizes the postulate of "progress toward increasing virtue and happiness of single people" as well as the equation of "Enlightenment" with "happiness," which diminishes and ignores the "contrary facts" ("Gegenfakta"; Herder 619). He attacks a scholarship and morality that, because of their high degree of abstraction, ignore "everything individual, in which alone species facti consists" (640), and thus allow themselves to be coopted by social hierarchy and despotic authority.

Thus the following case history valorizes individual specificity against general rules and judgments. Here Lenz takes up a tendency of other Storm and Stress authors against a narrow understanding of Enlightenment. Zerbin is a "novice in life," who wants to have "himself to thank for everything" (355). But this "chimera of all his wishes" (355) is dashed in the course of his integration into existing society, an integration that is associated with a difficult social climb. Rather, he becomes an adherent of "modern philosophy," which pretends to be philanthropic but is actually misanthropic.

Zerbin radically breaks with his father, a rich merchant who has accumulated money through usury; he moves and changes his name and identity. The narrator interprets this decision, which is based on genuine human outrage, as not entirely free of ambition and hunger for fame. Zerbin studies ethics in Leipzig with the famous and popular philosopher and writer Christian Fürchtegott Gellert; he impresses Gellert's moral teachings on his mind by "repeated reading" (356) of his lecture notes, i.e., by means of rationality and memory, not by practical experience. He gains the right to deliver private lectures by earning a diploma in mathematics. As in many texts of Lenz, the discourse on morality is bound up with sexuality. For a long time, Lenz believed that the Enlightenment goal of developing the individual's capabilities and of autonomous thought and will was only possible through repression of sexual needs. To be sure, he later weakened this conception (which is grounded in a rigid mind/body dualism), for example in his essay *On the Nature of our Mind* (*Über die Natur unsers Geistes*), where he calls for accepting one's own feelings, for examining them while letting them rage and thus overcoming them (D 2: 621). However, in most of his texts sexuality remains an unreliable, even resistant force that can be easily integrated neither into an Enlightenment program nor into a pragmatism that accepts the given.

Lenz equips Zerbin with an "excitable heart" ("reizbares ... Herz," 357). His lack of experience with galant erotic dallying, but also his image of women—"purely heavenly beings" ("lauter überirdische Wesen," 361)—make him an easy victim of a female intrigue. Renate Freundlach, the sister of a young and rich banker, wins his heart. But she uses it only as a means to win Zerbin's patron and friend, Baron Altheim. For Renate is in her "unfriendly twenty-second year" (358) and hopes for a profitable match, especially since her previous admirer, the noble officer Hohendorf, shies away from commitment. Zerbin's image of "saintly" women is shattered by the bitter experience of having his feelings exploited as an instrument. At the same time, he experiences with bitterness the social humiliation of being rejected in favor of his noble and rich friends. The abstract moral categories gleaned from Gellert do not help Zerbin resolve these conflicts. "Virtue," the narrator once notes, "is never a plan, but rather carrying out difficult plans"; now "the last kernel of virtue" in Zerbin's heart is "poisoned."[9]

A realist because of his own bitter experiences, Lenz intertwines problems of morality and love in many of his texts with economy, with access to money and capital. Zerbin, who has little income, has relied on monthly gifts from Count Altheim, who forgets all about his friend after replacing him in Renate's heart. His pride insulted, Zerbin makes no further claim to the money and gets into debt to his female servant. An affair develops with her—she is of a lower class, but is the daughter of a prosperous village official—when she shows him genuine feelings, but Zerbin draws the consequences from Renate's destruction of his image of "saintly" woman. In the course of efforts to conform and to better his condition, he develops a "new philosophy." Apparently this is a process of self-insight, of "enlightenment," which gives him a new beginning. "His eyes began to open, like Adam and Eve; he saw everything in its proper relationship."[10] Now Zerbin has become "reasonable" ("vernünftig," 369) and recognizes that love is very earthly and must be subordinated to rationalistic considerations, as he also learns from Renate and from Hortensie (his landlord's daughter, who also has her eyes on him). Logically, he distinguishes between a love relationship and marriage of convenience. This marriage is an imitation of

Count Altheim, who is engaged elsewhere and sees the affair only as entertainment. Lenz radicalizes the conflict for Zerbin when he has the character impregnate the servant, who has the allusive name Marie. The "philosopher, for whom the torch of truth only now began to shine,"[11] tries to behave in a conformist manner, that is, he is interested only in his status and his career. He becomes a professor and holds well-attended lectures on—of all things—ethics, as well as on natural law. Significantly, he becomes famous because of a compendium that he publishes. Of course, the relationship to Marie is now an obstacle. He therefore wants to have Marie bear the child in another town. Her love, which he has "harvested in advance," will not prevent him from making a "rich match" (370). Zerbin's moral "philosophy," which allows the "natural right" of individual (including bodily) satisfaction of needs, has been interpreted variously in scholarship, as satiric critique of Gellert, or of Wieland's (in Lenz's eyes) lascivious morality.[12] Essentially, however, it is "rational" behavior appropriate to existing society and legitimized by an edifice of abstract propositions. Herder had already attacked bitterly just such a "modern philosophy."[13] For Herder, it rests on an understanding of "education" ("Bildung") as "machinery" ("Mechanistik") and as a "handicraft" ("Handwerk") that can be integrated into any unjust social order. "They anguish ... and refresh themselves with freethinking. Dear, flat, useless freethinking, substitute for everything they need much more: heart! warmth! blood! life!"[14] Zerbin, too, has repressed his originally much less egotistical motives. Herder polemicizes against French materialism, whose proponents (such as La Mettrie) were, not coincidentally, coopted by German courts, especially Frederick the Great. Herder strikes out at a truncated Enlightenment in the pathos of Rousseauistic critique of civilization; however, he is not as concerned as Lenz with a critique of his time, but with an elucidation of the factors that influence the course of history. Lenz gives a critique of Enlightenment essentially the same as Herder's, but more concrete and differentiated, using an individual case. He is thus more exact than Herder but less comprehensive.

In the literature of the eighteenth century, the strict code of virtue in the bourgeois domestic sphere is often contrasted with the dissipation of the nobility. Lenz shows how easily the bourgeois can adopt aristocratic behavior patterns (even the keeping of a mistress), patterns that do not even necessarily contradict the instrumental rationality of bourgeois economic behavior. Zerbin thus begins to resemble his father, whom he had indignantly rejected. Lenz shows this assimilation by having the young social climber ask for help from his father—though in vain. "In the world of commercial exchange, he who gives over the measure is in the wrong," write Horkheimer and Adorno in *Dialectic of*

Enlightenment (73). Zerbin tries to give Renate more, turns out to be "wrong," and must suffer the consequences.

Lenz, who remains committed to genuine emancipation, mobilizes all his narrative energy against this sort of dialectic of enlightenment, which transforms emancipation into suppression of others and self. He radicalizes Zerbin's situation by having all the hero's cautionary measures fail; the "fruit of their forbidden intimacy"[15] is born dead by Marie (Lenz thus avoids the infanticide so popular in Storm and Stress literature). Marie is arrested for concealing pregnancy out of wedlock; however, she does not betray Zerbin's name and is thus sentenced to death in accordance with eighteenth-century law (see Rameckers, Wächtershäuser). This sacrifice finally brings Zerbin to his senses. He commits himself to a "marriage" with Marie, which is "not sanctioned by a priest's hand" but rather by genuine affection (378). He follows her in death. Renate and Hortensie, who have used Zerbin for their own social purposes, are punished by Lenz with banishment to cloisters and melancholy, respectively.

Lenz concentrates the main resistance to an incipient dialectic of enlightenment in the character of Marie. In the poem cited at the beginning, Lenz avoids playing off originary nature against alienated civilization. In *Zerbin*, however, he deploys this pattern of thought, which had been popularized by Rousseau. Marie is a wish-fantasy, the woman from the "people" in the imagination of the bourgeois intellectual. She lacks the sharp contours of the character of the same name in Lenz's play *The Soldiers* (that Marie, however, comes from a petit bourgeois milieu). Marie lacks Hortensie's book-learning and Renate's urbane flirtatiousness, but she is superior to them because of her self-assured inner harmony. Double standards and deception are unimaginable to her. Instinctively, she fulfills the laws of "general harmony" ("allgemeine Harmonie") that Lenz appeals to in his essay *On the Nature of our Mind* (D 2: 622), following Leibniz. The intellectual can achieve this equilibrium only after a difficult recognition of and reflection on his own feelings and experiences; this process leads to truly autonomous thinking and action, which are nevertheless subject to general harmony. However, Marie's simple humanity predestines her to be a victim of Zerbin's machinations. She lacks the "reason" to enable her to recognize that her attitude of "sacrifice" ("Aufopferung," 368) inevitably condemns her to be a "poor sacrificial animal" ("unglückliches Schlachtopfer," 375). Lenz also has Marie find guilt only in herself when she sees her fate "as a punishment for her frivolity." She embraces death: "no one dies as gladly as I."[16] The narrator stylizes her as one of the female martyrs who suffer degradation for their faith (377). Lenz demonstrates in Marie the power of love that overcomes every obstacle and *refutes* "modern philosophy." For this purpose, he uses female sacrifice—and of course he is not the first or last writer in the eighteenth century to do so. Just as Christ must die for the salvation of mankind, Marie must die in order to express her love in its highest form.

On the imagining of woman as "nature," Horkheimer and Adorno write: "As a representative of nature, woman in bourgeois society has become the enigmatic image of irresistibility and powerlessness. In this way, she reflects for domination the pure lie that posits the subjection instead of the redemption of nature" (71f.). It is striking how often Lenz uses military imagery for the (usually female) intrigues. Renate wants to "undermine" Altheim's "fortress," whose "commandant" she thinks is Zerbin, and therefore directs her "attack" against him (360). His knowledge of "military engineering" ("Kriegsbaukunst") does not help him, so that he ends up "the first sacrificial victim of this female Alexandrine spirit" ("erste[s] Schlachtopfer dieses weiblichen Alexandergeistes," 389; later he, in turn, makes Marie into a "Schlachtopfer"). However, if we reflect on the role of woman, as Lenz does much more empathically in *The Soldiers*, then we see that Renate is only taking advantage of the marginal space for action offered to a woman of the well-to-do bourgoisie of Lenz's day: she uses the few free years before her marriage and the freedom of living with her brother rather than with her parents, to amuse herself and look for the most profitable possible match. Though Hortensie prefers bookish pursuits, she acts no differently. Apparently, taking advantage of the few freedoms available, not fitting into society's mold, is to be seen as an aggressive act. For Zerbin, Renate becomes a destructive, irresistible woman, a perspective that is taken over by the narrator. One of her aristocratic lovers is killed in a duel over her; the other has to leave the city in haste. She is intimately involved with Zerbin's behavior toward Marie and his later misfortune. Marie, on the other hand, incorporates powerlessness, precisely because of her positively portrayed "nature." She is conceived as a corrective to Zerbin's destructive civilized qualities; at the same time, the whole history of her relationship that Zerbin terms "marriage" illustrates what Horkheimer and Adorno say about bourgeois marriage: "Marriage is the middle way by which society comes to terms with itself. The woman remains the one without power, for power comes to her only by male mediation" (72).

Precisely because Marie is a victim of Zerbin, her fall becomes a critique of legal proscriptions that gauge punishment solely by the crime. Just as the extensive, sentimental portrayal of female sacrifice draws the reader over to Marie's side, Lenz also gives the public in the story hope for her pardon: "no one could comprehend that such a dear figure was to die at the hands of the executioner; the pastor was not capable of giving her a single word of consolation— —in vain! The laws were too strict, the case was too clear-cut."[17] Lenz confronts the "beautiful soul" ("schöne Seele") against earthly justice; in her, despite her infraction, "general harmony" is visible.

The sentimental, poetic depiction conceals a very real demand of the Enlightenment, as it was expressed, for example, in Cesare Beccaria's treatise *On Crimes and Punishments* (*Dei delitti e delle pene*, 1764): moderate punishment that stood in an appropriate relation to the crime to be atoned for, especially after due consideration of circumstances and motivations. Beccaria treats infanticide in the chapter on "crimes difficult to prove"; for him it is the "effect of an unavoidable contradiction, one in which a woman is placed when she has either submitted out of weakness or been overpowered by violence. Faced with a choice between disgrace and the death of a creature incapable of feeling pain, who would not prefer the latter to the unavoidable misery to which the woman and her unfortunate offspring would be exposed?" (60). Beccaria also argues for the complete elimination of the death penalty, which he considers neither just nor beneficial to society. These arguments can be applied to the case portrayed by Lenz.[18] Beccaria writes:

> The death penalty becomes an entertainment for the majority and, for a few people, the object of pity mixed with scorn.... The limit that the legislator should assign to the rigor of punishment ... seems to be the point at which the feeling of compassion begins to outweigh every other emotion in the hearts of those who witness a chastisement that is really carried out for their benefit rather than for the sake of the criminal. (49)

In Germany, the Leipzig jurist Karl Ferdinand Hommel propagated Beccaria's ideas. He published a German translation of Beccaria's essay with "extensive notes" in 1778, following three earlier translations (1765, 1766, 1767). Voltaire published a commentary on Beccaria in 1766,[19] in which he generally rejected the death penalty, especially for infanticide, which he interprets as the desperate efforts of unmarried mothers to avoid public condemnation, legal punishment, and church atonement for extramarital sexuality, sanctions that still existed in most German states (Wächtershäuser 132ff., 139ff.). Since Marie's child is stillborn—a common case for "infanticides"—she could have avoided the death penalty if a medical practitioner had confirmed this cause of death and if she had named the father of the child. The criminal law in the second half of the eighteenth century shows the tendency to widen the possibilities of avoiding the death penalty (Wächtershäuser 79ff.). Lenz does not directly take part in this legal discourse, but follows Herder's arguments in *Another Philosophy* and confronts the individual case with an abstract and unrealistic proscription, just as the narrator had criticized the abstractness of moral proscriptions. Lenz also clearly distinguishes crime from sin; otherwise, it would not be possible to lay claim to the reader's empathy with Marie. This is an attitude that is revolutionary for judicial practice of the eighteenth century, one that Beccaria had also fought for.

III.

Lenz published the story *The Most Sentimental of All Novels* in the February, 1781, issue of the Mitau periodical *For Male and Female Readers (Für Leser und Leserinnen)*. Until the manuscript recently came to light in Kraków, Poland, the attribution of this work to Lenz was unsure, and the text was not included in some of the important editions. The date of composition is unknown; the mention of Hessian mercenary soldiers in America is reminiscent of the story *Forest Brother (Der Waldbruder)*, written in 1776, and the name of the magician Koromandel points to another undated piece, *On the Delicacy of Feeling (Über die Delikatesse der Empfindungen)*. The *Novel* was probably written after Lenz's first arrival in St. Petersburg (1780) or just before that.

Until now, scholars have dismissed this work without analyzing it very carefully. Friedrich Voit (who does not include the text in his edition of Lenz's tales) speaks for many when he calls the late prose texts products of a "psychically broken" author, and says that they demonstrate "more the destruction than the power of his talent. . . . None of them attains the level of his earlier stories" (147). Even Henning Boëtius, who rediscovered this "miniature novel" in his unconventional study, ultimately remains bound by traditional perspectives when he points to the bounty of "psychoanalytic and biographical material" in it (168).[20] The novel does contain a few rather unsuccessful passages, but also some very profound ones that can be related to the central issues of Enlightenment. In Livonia and Russia, Lenz held to his interest in Enlightenment, though he was forced by undignified circumstances to make compromises and thus to adopt a contradictory attitude to Enlightenment.

Because of the lowly status of novels in Germany into the 1770s, Lenz's characterization of the work as a novel refers to the love motif and to the fictionality and improbability of the story. It is also possible that Lenz was referring to the Richardsonian tradition of sentimental novels still popular in this period, though he distances himself from a sentimental, empathic reading of his text, as we shall see. In the "novel," Lenz takes up a genre that was very popular with women, the fairy tale, which had seen its glory days in France after the publication of

Perrault's *Stories or Tales from Times Past* (*Histoires ou Contes du Temps passé*, 1697). German translations were published beginning in the 1760s. In 1764, Christoph Martin Wieland's novel *Don Sylvio von Rosalva* appeared, containing the fairy tale *History of Prince Biribinker* (*Geschichte des Prinzen Biribinker*), which was published separately in 1769. Lenz does not imitate Wieland's stylistic lightness; his text is more serious and tends to the satiric. As in Caylus', Voltaire's or Rousseau's fairy tales, Lenz pursues philosophical and critical goals. Through this genre, he is able to dispense with narrow realism and can instead cultivate a satiric and grotesque play with transformations. His fairy, though she makes moral demands of Truella, is not a moralistic fairy like the majority of her species. Rather, she is an erotic creature who, however, lacks erotic opportunities because she is aging. She therefore does not use her power to produce erotic scenes, but rather her revenge for being spurned sets the play of metamorphoses in motion. While many fairy tales—including German ones—appeal to the sensibilities of the reader, Lenz raises this expectation but then disappoints it. Excessive sentimentalism has horrible consequences for the story's characters; for example, the prince who has been transformed into a mouse is killed by a very ordinary footstep just when he is able to adore his beloved Truella. The quick pace of the metamorphoses, the revelation of only the surface of the characters (more on this aspect later), and the satiric style prevent empathy, although the "dedication" of the story indicates that it is supposed to be taken in by "the heart" (which reminds the reader of the short preface to Goethe's *Werther*).

The fairy tale is a genre of the Age of Enlightenment that develops an increasingly intensive sense for the miraculous and improbable, in spite of or because of the emphasis on rationality. Many fairy tales serve only to embody a didactic teaching. Lenz avoids this technique. The *Novel* can be understood as an attempt to play through in an "unserious," entertaining, and underrated genre the conditions that would destroy a program of Enlightenment.

Since Lenz produces a confusing series of metamorphoses and accidents, it is almost impossible to summarize the plot. Two turtles are the main figures of the frame narrative, which contains the first of nine fairy tales and is briefly taken up again in the following tales. The turtles take fifty years to travel from Poland to Paris. As a result, other characters ridicule their outdated bits of news, and they can neither give their caps to the queen of France (whom they think is still a Polish princess) nor meet Count Moritz of Saxony, after whom an inn is named. On their return trip they use a mail coach and meet a mouse who is following its fiancé to Astrachan and narrates to a publisher eight tales, which have plots and characters in common. The fairy Aglaura is jealous of a prince's wife and cannot lure him away from her. In revenge, she transforms their son, Prince Torus, into a mouse. She is able to rob him of his identity and his consciousness of his status, but not his reason, and cannot prevent his "good nature" from finding expression. The son's affinity with his father keeps the fairy from further revenge. At this point, the fairy tries an experiment. She causes his beloved Truella to sense that the mouse (who is now called Thomson) is really an attractive human being. At the same time, she puts Truella's heart to the test by causing Count Aranda (the magically transformed husband of the fairy) to fall in love with her. Truella does become temporarily untrue and finds her way back to Thomson too late, after he has been killed by a chambermaid's footstep. The chambermaid vents her rage on him after a servant seems to spurn her. Briefly and remorsefully, she senses that the mouse was this lover, and in that moment he walks in the door but is immediately transformed into a turtle by the furious Aglaura. After she discovers whom she has killed, the chambermaid wants to marry the turtle and obtains the blessing of the confessor father who appears at that moment (and who is the secret lover of Aglaura). Shortly after the priest's question where "the ram" is (341), the mail coach turns over, ending the story abruptly.

The frame, in which the mouse narrates, the mail coach journey, and the accident that cuts off the tale point to the entertainment aspect of the genre—the story obviously is meant to pass the time. The subtitle, in fact, indicates that the story is "instructive and pleasant reading for women,"[21] with which Lenz merely quotes a common claim of authors of fairy tales. But a closer look reveals that the text is enigmatic and far from merely "pleasant." Kant, of course, retrospectively defined the Enlightenment in 1784 as "the human being's emergence from self-imposed immaturity";[22] the human being should attempt to take his own fate into his hands though the exercise of reason. Lenz clearly emphasizes self-realization and the activity of the individual. He points out that "action, action is the soul of the world, not enjoyment, not sentiment, not hairsplitting" and "our active force cannot rest . . . until it creates freedom around us, room to act."[23] This activist postulate corresponds, on the one hand, to the author's experiences. Ever since his determined act of independence, namely his decision to accompany two aristocrats to Strasbourg against the will of his father, and then to embrace the penniless life of an artist, Lenz saw himself as determined by circumstances and degrading dependencies. In his theological essays, he derives the freedom of the human being from his status as God's creature (following the Wolff/Leibniz tradition), but this also means that the human being is only truly free when he lives according to his divinely ordained fate. This configuration calls forth a

central problem of human freedom: his capability and willingness to
live according to God's commandments, including moral ones. This
Novel can be read as a formulation directed against this kind of optimistic and emancipatory vision of mankind. Boëtius writes of Lenz and
of this text in particular: "Everything Lenz writes indicts the deforma-
tion of the self through circumstances" (169). His postulate of action
provokes conflict with the still largely unshaken structures of class
society, which cannot be broken by the individual. The disciplining of
the individual so that he or she can "function" in society thus becomes
the central theme in Lenz's work—we need only think of central characters in his most significant plays, for example, the self-castrating tutor
Läuffer (*The Tutor*; *Der Hofmeister*, 1774). Accordingly, most of Lenz's
characters suffer from the conflict between their own claim to self-
realization and the forces of circumstance.

The astonishing aspect of the *Novel* is that this consciousness of suffering is absent. However, the characters are completely subject to circumstance. For example, the turtles reach their destination, Paris, but
there they just make themselves ridiculous. And one of them gets an
"ugly contusion" when "four coaches in succession" drive over its shell
(316). Whoever cannot adapt to traffic because of slowness and cannot
be seen because of smallness is ruthlessly run over. It makes sense to
see Lenz's repeated experience of defeat mirrored in this detail, just as
the turtles are toward the bottom end of the hierarchy of Parisian life-
forms. Even the journey in the mail coach is dangerous; for example,
the French woman feels insulted by the gaze of one of the turtles and
stabs its fleshy part. With the exception of the churchman, the characters in the tales narrated by the mouse function as mere marionettes in
the hand of the fairy.

It is striking that because of the priority of circumstances, coinci-
dences, and metamorphoses, no character is fully developed, not even
Torus or the fairy. Present only for their actions, the characters present
only their surface, though it remains unclear whether they even have an
"inside." This world corresponds to the image presented in a poem
presumably from 1772: a world far from God, an image which, however, is countered at the end of the poem by the "ecstasy of similarity"
with God and the bond of "sympathy." In the Rousseauian tradition,
"fear" and "desire" are "the great wheels" or "means" in a civilization
estranged from God.

> Behold the eternal miracles of fear.
> Every one shows the others the worst
> Side of himself.—...
> So that the small outsides
> Will find room with each other in the whole,

> They have found a means
> Of exchanging their desires,
> And they call that means money. . . .
> Either they slumber in the ice of fear
> Or they produce in the fire of love
> Eternal divine difference.[24]

Most of Lenz's texts are centered around money and sexuality. "Whoever has it long, lets it hang long" ("Wer lang hat, läßt lang hängen"): this "old German proverb," which is quoted in the second line of the *Novel*, originally referred to the devil's tail (see Düringsfeld, col. 5b), but was later used for rich people who can let their watch-chains and jewelry "hang long." In the fairy tale portrayed in the novel, money for once does not play a role; the exchange of desires is limited to feelings of love. The proverb quoted above has mainly sexual connotations in the context of the work (Boëtius 168). The turtles cannot "let hang long"; they know "no other sin than promiscuity." Of course, this gives them a disadvantage in the "frivolous world" of the fairy tales. In *My Precepts* (*Meine Lebensregeln*), Lenz describes bodily "needs" ("Bedürfnisse") and "titillation of the senses" ("sinnliche Kützelungen") as "the invisible cords with which we noble and free people are dragged around like slaves and chained dogs."[25] In the *Draft of a Letter to a Friend* (*Entwurf eines Briefes an einen Freund . . .*) he writes: "Whoever denies that human beings are dependent on nature has never really looked at them closely. . . . Nature strides on without any thought of us and our morality, that is our own concern."[26] The *Novel* demonstrates these insights. Nature has equipped the turtles, too, with "very limited" "virtue"; they tremble "with zeal and fear" of losing their virtue when they observe the French woman (who is travelling to join her fiancé) making advances to the publisher, who knows "no other virtue" "than promiscuity" (318). When the woman sits down between the turtles, they faint from excitement. Shortly thereafter, the woman takes advantage of her fright at the mouse's sudden appearance to fall into the publisher's arms "with a . . . horrible trembling" (319). Already it is evident that the text does not portray love as "one heart attaching, connecting itself to another," as Zerbin once strives for,[27] but as a sort of subterranean sexual obsessiveness that almost automatically takes advantage of every available opportunity. The power of love is active in the mouse's fairy tales, too. The father confessor warns at the end, after Torus' death, of the "consequences of a dissolute [unordentlich] love" (340). This is pure hypocrisy, since he is dallying with the fairy but is supposed to live only for virtue. One could apply the father confessor's warning to the fairy—though he was not referring to her—since she had tried to destroy another marriage and when she failed she took revenge on the couple's son. In the *Novel* we simply do not find a normal ("ordentlich") love, which according to Lenz's values can only take place in marriage, at least with respect to bodily needs. Morality is a thin veneer that does not really change the nature of human drives.

It can be said that Lenz has his characters lose their reason. This happens first of all with respect to the rigid precept that reason as a sort of disciplinarian represses all bodily needs in order to develop a truly free will. But it also happens with respect to Lenz's later, more moderate maxim of letting one's own feelings "rage with all their force" and "feel strength enough in oneself to examine the nature of these feelings and in this way to move beyond them."[28] According to Lenz, human beings must not lose their reason if they want to live free and according to their purpose. Following Freud, Horkheimer and Adorno pointed out that Enlightenment and reason bring forth reason's Other—the immoral, the body, feelings—to the extent that reason cannot accommodate these aspects. The process of civilization, which internalizes direct violent conflicts between human beings, lowers the tolerance level so that much more is prohibited than before, as Norbert Elias has shown. Lenz's essay, *My Precepts*, is an example of this development. In the fairy tale, with its generic conventions that accommodate disharmony, metamorphosis, and the erotic, Lenz (who in his own life tended to be a "dissolute" lover) finds a form that enables him to thematize this Other of reason.

The characters of the *Novel* can be described in the often-quoted words of Lenz's review of Goethe's *Götz*: they are "machines" whose "wheels" "grind and drive" against the gears of others (D 2: 637). The characters work against each other but together produce a narrated world in which they function as a whole. For machines, there is no other criterion but their ability to function. Martin Rector has shown that the machine metaphor in the *Götz* review points to Lenz's confrontation with French materialism. For La Mettrie, for example, human beings are machines, composed of bodily "drives," and therefore neither good nor evil. Their highest precept is egotism. Lenz always objected to this image of mankind, because he saw in it a rejection of free will, responsibility of the individual, and freedom of action.[29] In the *Novel* he portrays a world that is extensively determined by the egotism of individuals, though it is clothed in unrealistic structures of a fairy tale.

"The human being is the most noble and excellent of all creatures" says a mouse in the "Fairy Tale of the Mice," echoing the optimistic thinking of the Enlightenment, but he continues by qualifying this statement: "as long as he prepares our meals; but if another can be found who can do this better or at least equally well, then the welfare of the state and our conscience demand that we eat up man."[30] Here Lenz turns to the story of Bishop Hatto, who was imprisoned in the Mouse Tower of Bingen because of his un-Christian attitude. Lenz varies the story, however, by having the mice's attack on the plump gentleman fail because the cook diverts them with a piece of bacon. A bloody battle breaks out among the mice while they are consuming the bacon. The ones who succeed in eating are then caught in traps set by the cook, and then others fall victim to these "torture racks" of the "inquisition" (321). The egotism of the mice, which leads to aggression, is thus horribly punished, but the maxim is not disproven, since all the characters are marked by narrow egocentrism.

The Most Sentimental of All Novels is a fantasy about the mammoth chasm between reality and the Enlightenment's optimistic program of education and reform. Lenz is unable to interpret social determination —unlike individual purpose—as a manifestation of the Leibnizian doctrine of pre-established harmony. He experiences this determination as so oppressive and senseless that he does not transfigure it ideologically, as do many authors of his generation (see Winter 73-74).   In addition, Lenz repeatedly despairs of balancing within himself body and mind, moral law and drives—a central theme of works like *The Tutor* and *Zerbin*. The *Novel* can be seen as evidence that the precept of rational self-discipline, to which Enlightenment is allied, gives rise to a threatening sphere of the Other that continually foils the interest in autonomy and moral responsibility. The darkness in which this sphere is left in the Age of En*light*enment makes it even more dangerous, even though so much was written about this sphere (for which Lenz is an example). The *Novel* portrays characters driven by circumstances and their own desires, characters that are neither capable of nor want to be capable of action that corresponds to the program of Enlightenment.

> There are polished goblets
> That reflect even the most beautiful things
> So distorted and warped that we never
> Imagine that this image is purposely deceptive
> In order to lighten our gall and spleen a bit
> Through a hearty, honest laugh
> After sorrow, tears and sleeplessness.[31]

This is how Lenz defines the goal of satire in a poem written in his late years in Moscow, *What Is Satire?* He describes satire's starting-point in reality:

> In the pile of contradictions
> Of positions and frictions
> There are a thousand exaggerations
> And a thousand topics for the ridiculous.[32]

Satire is thus anchored in life but also serves to distort elements of life beyond recognition. "The programmatic harmony between individual and society in Enlightenment philosophy is followed by alienation," writes Jörg Schönert (51), and he derives from this phenomenon the new functions of satire beginning with the Storm and Stress, as it enters "the service of the individual." It serves to portray the contradictions between individual and society, but also between the individual's striving for independence and his natural drives. We have seen that the characters of the *Novel*—in contrast to their creator—no longer insist on achieving "freedom," "room to act" (D 2: 638). From the perspective of the Enlightenment's image of mankind, they are driven, alienated creatures, without consciousness of their alienation. In *Zerbin*, the narrator explicitly mentions his satiric intention, for example, toward middle-class women. The *Novel*'s narrator, by contrast, abstains from explicitly portraying the norm from which he judges the narrated world, so that satiric distancing becomes the "structural law" of the "fictional space" (Schönert 28ff.). The satiric intention therefore lies in the (actually only apparent) objectivity of the events and forms their organizing principle. In a variation of Kurt Tucholsky's characterization of the satirist as a "hurt idealist,"[33] the Lenz of the *Novel* can be called a "hurt Enlightener." With this text he aims to "lighten his gall a bit," that is, compensate for his experience of "sorrow."[34] In the guise of a fairy tale, Lenz arranges light-hearted play that is actually not lighthearted at all.

Writing—especially satiric writing—presupposes a stance as intellectual observer of oneself and one's surroundings, it is a medium and a forum for disciplining one's own bodily sensations, feelings and experiences; as such, it becomes a sort of protection against these things (as the passage shows) at the same time as it articulates them. "Thinking does not mean becoming deaf";[35] only when the human being has let his or her "feelings" "rage" and has simultaneously moved beyond them through analysis that for Lenz includes making them present through writing, can he or she achieve a measure of "firmness" ("Festigkeit," D 2: 621). This achievement of identity is for Lenz the prerequisite for the Enlightenment's goal of autonomy, which in turn is understood as a part of the "general harmony."

IV.

"And even if centuries stride over my poor skull with scorn," Lenz writes about one of his texts, it is "true" and will "remain."[36] We see here not only a radical isolation, but also an extreme demand, even an exaltation of himself. Sigrid Damm has written of Lenz: "He writes about his present and its contradictions, only about that. The gate to Utopia is closed to him" (689). It is well known that the Enlightenment by and large accepted the existing class order and the system of absolutism. Within this framework, it tried to guide the individual to independent thinking and to free him or her from "irrational" outer and inner forces. In his own way, Lenz partakes of this program of emancipation, but he experiences the contradictions it gives rise to more harshly than many others. As a result, he resists the "extortion of Enlightenment," the compulsion either to remain within its "rationalism" or to escape its principles (see Foucault). In this way, *Zerbin* and *The Most Sentimental of All Novels* sensitively draw attention to the destructive potential of a civilizing process that the Enlightenment has bought into.

Notes

This essay was translated by W. Daniel Wilson.

1. Qtd. Vonhoff 222f.
2. In this respect, my essay's conceptual framework is derived from a later period; Lenz himself never posed the alternative Enlightenment or critique of Enlightenment.
3. See the essay *On the Nature of Our Mind* (*Über die Natur unsers Geistes*), in *Werke und Briefe* 2: 621f.
4. The text will be cited in the following with page references from vol. 2 of Damm's edition (which will be abbreviated "D" when other texts are cited). Besides the criticism listed in Winter (52), see Herbst 102-09 and Dedert 39-60.
5. On these stories, see Schmid and Buchanan.
6. "Sind das immer Unwürdige, die uns unsere durch hellere Aussichten in die Moral bereicherten Verstandesfähigkeiten als solche darstellen?" (354).
7. "Ach! ich fürchte, wir werden uns oft nicht Zeit zur Untersuchung lassen, und, weil wir unsere Ungerechtigkeiten desto schöner bemänteln gelernt haben, aus allzugroßer Menschenfreundschaft desto unbiegsamere Menschenfeinde werden, die zuletzt an keinem Dinge außer sich mehr die geringste moralische Schönheit werden entdecken können, und folglich auch sich berechtigt glauben, an dem menschlichen Geschlecht nur die Gattung, nicht die Individuen zu lieben" (354).
8. "seine einzelne Stimme der Stimme des ganzen Universi entgegen zu setzen" (D 2: 671).
9. "Tugend ist nie Plan, sondern Ausführung schwieriger Plane" (356): "den letzten Keim der Tugend in seinem Herzen vergiften" (366).
10. "Die Augen fingen ihm, wie unsern ersten Eltern, an aufzugehen, er sah alle Dinge in ihrem rechten Verhältnis" (369).
11. "einen Philosophen, dem itzt erst die Fackel der Wahrheit zu leuchten anfing" (369).
12. Kindermann 304; Rameckers 187.
13. In *Auch eine Philosophie der Geschichte* ... ; the title *Zerbin; or, Modern Philosophy* could be seen as a link to Herder's viewpoint, so that a critique of Gel-

lert or Wieland must be seen as secondary (especially since Ramecker means not Wieland himself, but the character Hippias in the novel *Agathon*, who cannot be completely identified with Wieland).

14. "Sie knirschen ... und laben sich mit Freidenken. Das liebe, matte, unnütze Freidenken, Ersatz für alles, was sie viel mehr brauchten—Herz! Wärme! Blut! Leben!" (Herder 638, 639, 677).

15. "Frucht ihrer verbotenen Vertraulichkeit" (375).

16. "als eine Strafe für ihren Leichtsinn"; "es stirbt kein Mensch so gern als ich" (377).

17. "man konnte es nicht begreifen, nicht fassen, daß eine so liebenswürdige Gestalt unter Henkershand umkommen sollte; der Prediger war nicht im Stande, ihr ein einziges Trostwort zuzusprechen— —vergeblich! Die Gesetze waren zu streng, der Fall zu deutlich" (377).

18. In Germany, the elimination of the death penalty was proposed as early as 1764 by the later adviser of Joseph II, Joseph von Sonnenfels (*Grundsätze der Polizey-, Handlungs- und Finanzwissenschaft*). Significantly, Viktor Barkhausen's essay, *On the Elimination of the Death Penalty* (*Über die Abschaffung der Todesstrafe*), appeared in the August, 1776, issue of *Deutsches Museum* shortly after the publication of *Zerbin* there. Barkhhausen points out that infanticides are not deterred by the death penalty. Marie's behavior in *Zerbin* exemplifies these principles. In the October issue of the *Museum*, Helferich Peter Sturz's essay *On Linguet's Defense of the Death Penalty* (*Über Linguets Verteidigung der Todesstrafen*) was published, which contains the speech of an accused child-murderess in court.

19. See Rameckers 74-76, Wächtershäuser 28.

20. The short evaluation of the work in Preuß (71-72) seems to me to clash with the wording of the text.

21. "lehrreiche und angenehme Lektüre für Frauenzimmer".

22. "der Ausgang des Menschen aus seiner selbstverschuldeten Unmündigkeit" (481).

23. "daß handeln, handeln die Seele der Welt sei, nicht genießen, nicht empfindeln, nicht spitzfündeln"; "daß diese unsre handelnde Kraft nicht eher ruhe, ... als bis sie uns Freiheit um uns her verschafft, Platz zu handeln" (*Über Götz von Berlichingen*, D 2: 638).

24. Schaut die ewigen Wunder der Furcht.
Jeder weist dem andern die schlechteste
Seite von sich selbst—...
Daß die kleinen Außenseiten
Platz bei einander im Ganzen finden,
Haben sie sich ein Mittel erfunden,
Ihre Begierden auszutauschen,
Und das Mittel nennen sie Geld....
Entweder sie schlummern im Eise der Furcht,
Oder sie wirken im Feuer der Liebe
Ewige Gottesverschiedenheit. (D 3: 219f.)

25. "Just diese kleinen gering scheinenden Bedürfnisse sind die unsichtbaren Seile an welchen wir edle und freie Menschen ... wie Sklaven und Kettenhunde herumgeschleppt werden" (D 2: 496).

26. "Wer dem Menschen die Dependenz von der Natur abspricht, der hat ihn noch nie recht angesehen. ... Die Natur geht und wirkt ihren Gang fort, ohne sich um uns und unsere Moralität zu bekümmern, das ist unsere Sorge" (D 2: 485).

27. Das "Anheften, Anschließen eines Herzens an das andere" (D 2: 366-67).

28. "seine unangenehmen Empfindungen mit aller ihrer Gewalt wüten lassen und Stärke genug in sich fühlen, die Natur dieser Empfindungen zu untersuchen und *sich so* über sie hinauszusetzen" (*Über die Natur unsers Geistes*, D 2: 621).

29. See Rector 33ff. Lenz finds an ally for this point of view in Herder, who also uses the machine metaphor in *Auch eine Philosophie* mostly negatively, for example, when he accuses scholarship and morality of ultimately being part of a "machine", "and the machine is run by only one person", i.e., the despot (Herder 638).

30. "Der Mensch ist das edelste und vorzüglichste aller Geschöpfe, solang er uns die Speisen zubereitet; findet sich aber ein anderer, der dies besser oder wenigstens ebenso gut kann, so erfordert es das Wohl des Staates und unser Gewissen, den ersten aufzuessen" (320).

31. Man hat geschliffne Gläser die
Uns selbst das Schönste so verzogen
Verzerret weisen, daß wir nie
Dran denken, dieses Bild ist vorsätzlich gelogen
Um uns nach Kummer, Tränen, Wachen
Durch ein recht herzlich biedres Lachen
Die Galle und die Milz ein wenig leicht zu machen. (*Was ist Satire?* Vonhoff 249, see D 3: 234.)

32. Bei den gehäuften Widersprüchen
Von Stellungen und Reibungen
Giebts tausend Übertreibungen
Und tausend Stoff zum Lächerlichen. (Vonhoff 250, first version; see D 3: 235).

33. "gekränkter Idealist", in the essay *Was darf die Satire*, 1: 363.

34. (See the poem quoted above.) This text therefore does not mean a general break with the program of the Enlightenment. This conclusion is also supported by Lenz's further biography; in the summer of 1780 he joined the Russian Freemason movement, which was guided by Enlightenment values, and outlined far-reaching reform projects for Russia (see Winter 105-06).

35. "Denken heißt nicht vertauben" (*Über die Natur unsers Geistes*, D 2: 621).

36. On *Die Soldaten*: "Es ist wahr und wird bleiben, mögen auch Jahrhunderte über meinen armen Schädel verachtungsvoll fortschreiten" (D 3: 329).

Works Cited

Beccaria, Cesare. *On Crimes and Punishments.* Trans. David Young. Indianapolis: Hackett, 1986.

Boëtius, Henning. *Der verlorene Lenz: Auf der Suche nach dem inneren Kontinent.* Frankfurt/M.: Eichborn, 1985.

Brecht, Bertolt. *Gesammelte Werke.* Ed. Elisabeth Hauptmann. Frankfurt/M.: Suhrkamp, 1967.

Buchanan, Michelle. "Les 'Contes moraux' de Marmontel." *French Review* 41 (1967): 201-12.

Damm, Sigrid. "Jakob Michael Reinhold Lenz: Ein Essay." Lenz, *Werke und Briefe* 3: 687-768.

Dedert, Hartmut. *Die Erzählung im Sturm und Drang: Studien zur Prosa des achtzehnten Jahrhunderts.* Germanistische Abhandlungen, 66. Stuttgart: Metzler, 1990.

Düringsfeld, Ida von, and Otto von Reineberg-Düringsfeld. *Sprichwörter der germanischen und romanischen Sprachen.* Vol. 2. Leipzig 1873.

Elias, Norbert. *The Civilizing Process.* Trans. Edmund Jephcott. New York: Pantheon, 1982.

Foucault, Michel. "What Is Enlightenment?" *The Foucault Reader.* Ed. Paul Rabinow. New York: Pantheon, 1984. 32-50.

Herbst, Hildburg. *Frühe Formen der deutschen Novelle im 18. Jahrhundert.* Berlin: Erich Schmidt, 1985.

Herder, Johann Gottfried. *Werke.* Ed. Wolfgang Pross. Vol. 1. München: Hanser, 1984.

Horkheimer, Max, and Theodor W. Adorno. *Dialectic of Enlightenment.* Trans. John Cumming. New York: Continuum, 1972.

Kant, Immanuel. "Beantwortung der Frage: Was ist Aufklärung?" *Berlinische Monatsschrift* 1784: 481-94.

Kindermann, Heinz. *J. M. R. Lenz und die deutsche Romantik.* Wien: Braumüller, 1925.

Lenz, Jakob Michael Reinhold. *Werke und Briefe in drei Bänden.* Ed. Sigrid Damm. 3 vols. Leipzig: Insel; München: Hanser, 1987. Cited as "D".

————. *Werke und Schriften.* Ed. Britta Titel and Helmut Haug. 2 vols. Stuttgart: Goverts, 1966.

Preuß, Werner Hermann. *Selbstkastration oder Zeugung neuer Kreatur: Zum Problem der menschlichen Freiheit in Leben und Werk von J. M. R. Lenz.* Bonn: Bouvier, 1983.

Rameckers, Jan Matthias. *Der Kindesmord in der Literatur der Sturm und Drang-Periode.* Diss. Rotterdam 1927.

Rector, Martin. "La Mettrie und die Folgen: Zur Ambivalenz der Maschinen-Metapher bei Jakob Michael Reinhold Lenz." *Willkommen und Abschied der Maschinen: Literatur und Technik—Bestandsaufnahme eines Themas.* Ed. Erhard Schütz. Essen: Klartext, 1988.

Schmid, Gotthold Otto. *Marmontel: Seine Moralischen Erzählungen und die deutsche Literatur.* Diss. Strassburg 1935.

Schönert, Jörg. *Roman und Satire im 18. Jahrhundert: Ein Beitrag zur Poetik.* Germanistische Abhandlungen, 27. Stuttgart: Metzler, 1969.

Tucholsky, Kurt. *Gesammelte Werke.* 4 vols. Ed. Mary Gerold-Tucholsky and Fritz J. Raddatz. Hamburg: Rowohlt, 1960.

Voit, Friedrich. "Nachwort." Jakob Michael Reinhold Lenz, *Erzählungen.* Stuttgart: Reclam, 1988.

Vonhoff, Gert. *Subjektkonstitution in der Lyrik von J.M.R. Lenz: Mit einer Auswahl neu herausgegebener Gedichte.* Historisch-kritische Arbeiten zur deutschen Literatur, 9. Frankfurt: Peter Lang, 1990.

Wächtershäuser, Wilhelm. *Das Verbrechen des Kindesmords im Zeitalter der Aufklärung: Eine rechtsgeschichtliche Untersuchung der dogmatischen, prozessualen und rechtssoziologischen Aspekte.* Quellen und Forschungen zur Strafrechtsgeschichte, 3. Berlin: Erich Schmidt, 1973.

Winter, Hans-Gerd. *J. M. R. Lenz.* Sammlung Metzler, 233. Stuttgart: Metzler, 1987.

On the Use and Abuse of Reading: Karl Philipp Moritz and the Dialectic of Pedagogy in Late-Enlightenment Germany

A book is a great and noble thing. It is a human invention that surpasses all else—everything that the human mind contains can be contained in the book. ... What a service was done for the human race by the one who first invented these twenty-four little characters, by means of which all the sciences, all human events, all things in heaven and on earth can speak from within the narrow confines of a book! ... And the souls of human beings can communicate with one another at any distance by means of books, and edify one another.[1]

Reading had now become as much a necessity for him as opium might be for the people of the Orient, by means of which they pleasantly dull their senses. When he was lacking a book, he would have exchanged his coat for a beggar's frock in order to get one.[2]

THESE TWO PASSAGES indicate both the great significance and the ambivalence with which books and reading are invested in the culture of the late Enlightenment in Germany. The first, from Karl Philipp Moritz's *Tentative Small Practical Logic Text for Children* (a work not only for children, but, as the subtitle states, "also in part for teachers and thinkers"), exemplifies an optimistic view of the role of printed matter in the dissemination of information, an essential tool of enlightenment. Moritz is probably better known, however, for his account of pathological compulsive reading in the autobiographical "psychological novel" *Anton Reiser,* from which the second (frequently-quoted) passage is taken, than as the author of children's books extolling the virtues of books and the benefits of reading.[3] While the profound significance attributed to books in the passage from the *Logic for Children* may in and of itself come as no surprise to a reader of

465

Anton Reiser, the lack of concern with which the subject is broached by the same author in a work at least nominally addressed to children might seem incongruous, given Moritz's own history of pathological compulsive reading.[4] The critical focus on reading as addiction and compulsion in *Anton Reiser*—unlike the laudatory attitude Moritz exhibits toward books in his *Logic for Children*—seems to accord well with the concern of many late-Enlightenment pedagogues regarding the dangers inherent in the encounter between children and books. For by the 1780s, the phenomenon of children reading had come to be viewed by many German pedagogues with anxiety, if not outright alarm. The following passage from Johann Gottfried Hoche's *Intimate Letters* (*Vertraute Briefe*) is one of many examples in which pedagogues of the late eighteenth century invoke the metaphors of disease to express their consternation over the uncontrolled spread of pathological reading habits:

> Compulsive reading is a foolish and harmful abuse of an otherwise good thing, truly a great evil, as contagious as the yellow fever in Philadelphia. It is the source of all moral corruption in our children and grandchildren. Through it, follies and errors are established and maintained in social life; . . . as a result, the human spirit is not ennobled, but grows savage.[5]

The general attitude toward children reading among late Enlightenment pedagogues (Hoche, Joachim Heinrich Campe, Christian Felix Weisse, Johann Karl Wezel, to name a few) ranges from anxious concern to profound alarm.[6] By and large, these commentators recognize that reading is a necessary skill and a powerful tool, but only with the proper reading material and the proper *mode* of reading, which can only be insured through close supervision of the child's reading habits; unsupervised, uncontrolled reading leads all too easily to destructive vices such as the much-feared "compulsive" reading (*Lesewut* or *Lesesucht*).

Though it is usually novels that are condemned as hazardous reading material (frequently because of the overstimulation resulting from the vicarious emotional experiences they provide), the concern over reading can extend to the seemingly innocuous activity of journal reading undertaken for the purpose of educating and informing oneself. In a 1790 article, an author identified as Wigand[7] addresses the issue: "Is the reading of journals to be recommended to beginning students?" ("Ist angehenden Studirenden das Lesen der Zeitschriften zu empfehlen?"). He supports his conclusion—that students should in fact *wholly* refrain from reading journals—with the argument that journals do not provide any orientation in the subject matter dealt with; if they are worth reading at all, then only by those who have already received a proper initiation into the subject matter and are able to discern the relevant issues and differentiate between what, in a given journal, might be worth reading, and what would be a frivolous or tedious waste of time. In other words, only those who have been brought to a certain level of intellectual autonomy can be trusted to choose freely their own readings. For anyone else to occupy themselves with journal reading is at best an ineffective use of time that could be better spent gaining a guided orientation and overview in the particular discipline and its issues at the hands of an accepted authority:

> [W]ould not your time be ten times more productively employed, if, instead of the scattered, randomly assembled, perhaps insignificant collections, reports, and observations of this or that traveller or dilettante, you were to read a work that treated of art or its history in their entirety, a work in which all or much of that which you find scattered in such pages is arranged in a meaningful order, so that you can view it in context.[8]

It is expressly not reading per se that is discouraged here, only an improper choice of reading material. But even in the course of this rather straightforward and matter-of-fact argument against journal reading, one encounters a charged rhetoric that associates reading with disease. Wigand describes the "immense flood of journals" as one of the greatest plagues of his age, and the spreading habit of reading them as a pestilence ("Seuche," 398). Such an association establishes a relation between reading and issues of both mental and physical health. Although it has potential benefits and is not to be altogether discouraged, reading is dangerous; to practice it uncritically and excessively threatens the health of the individual, and its uncontrolled proliferation threatens the health of the whole society.

Among the most serious consequences of an improper choice of reading material, in Wigand's view, is simply the ineffective use of time. The injunction to put one's time to the best possible use carries with it the suggestion that anything short of maximum usefulness or productivity is unacceptable: "even just in choosing the useful over the more useful I do myself harm."[9] This is clearly a utilitarian ethic, in which reading for pleasure, or for aesthetic enrichment, more likely than not has no place. The attitude expressed here is sharply at odds with the haphazard reading habits of the protagonist of *Anton Reiser*. But while the narrator of *Anton Reiser* often appears critical of Anton's reading habits, his concerns do not have much in common with Wigand's critique of reading. Although Anton's reading, especially early on, is rather indiscriminate, he also begins, almost from the outset of his reading career, to develop *on his own* a sense of judgment and aesthetics. This development continues throughout the novel:

> Through the often repeated reading of this one book [Ramler's *Death of Christ*] his taste in poetry acquired a certain sophistication and firmness, which from

that time on remained with him, just as his taste in prose had developed through reading [Fénelon's] *Telemach*; for in the case of [Zigler und Kliphausen's] beautiful *Banise* and [Schnabel's] *Isle of Felsenburg*, he had, in spite of the pleasure he experienced in these works, a very strong sense of the crudity and the coarseness of their style.[10]

Reading plays an important role in the development of Anton's aesthetic judgment; the implications of this development for his sense of identity and autonomy will be taken up later.

The motive behind Anton's reading is frequently his need to escape from an awareness of his intolerable surroundings. In fact, where the narrator expresses his disapproval, it is more toward the conditions of Anton's upbringing, which are beyond his control, than toward his response to these conditions:

> When all around him nothing but loud noise and scolding and domestic discord reigned, or he looked around in vain for a playmate, then he hurried off to his book.
> Thus, at an early age he was forced out of the natural world of the child and into an unnatural conceptual world, where his capacity to experience a myriad of life's pleasures was impaired.[11]

The misguided upbringing Anton receives at the hands of his parents has long-term detrimental consequences. The importance of these early childhood experiences is repeatedly emphasized. Later in the novel, for instance, in describing the difficulties Anton experiences in social interactions owing to his feelings of inferiority, the narrator speaks of "the emotional paralysis that had inexcusably been brought about by the negligent behavior of his parents towards him, and which from his childhood on he had not been able to diminish."[12] In presenting the world of adults—particularly parents and teachers—from the perspective of the (abused) child, and drawing attention to the detrimental effects of careless and unsympathetic treatment of the child, the narrator of *Anton Reiser* tends to undermine the authority of the adult world. This attitude stands in contrast to Wigand (and others like him), who, in suggesting that the child or student should refrain from making his own choices and always defer to the judgment of "authorities"—presumably parents and teachers—for proper guidance, seems not to consider the possibility that the judgment of these authorities might be faulty, or that the social conditions of a child's upbringing might be less than ideal. He represents in this regard a pedagogical tendency simply to assume for adults the authority to issue prescriptions to youth.[13] In his view, only reading with a clearly defined purpose is appropriate, and this purpose must be prescribed by an adult authority: "it seems to me that one should at no age choose one's readings more carefully, or rather *be led to a good choice*, than in this one"

(406; my emphasis). While the man of mature judgment will be able to choose his readings wisely, "discriminating between the more important and the less important, skipping over much that is inconsequential," the intellectual autonomy that is the presumed end of any enlightened pedagogical program cannot be presupposed; it must first be produced. However, the issue of how to teach or impart independent judgment, without simply imposing one's own judgment (who decides what is "important"?), is a dilemma not frequently dealt with in the practical pedagogy of this period; on the contrary, the problems inherent in the production of autonomy are overshadowed by an obsession with *control* over the life of the child discernible in much of the pedagogical writing of the time.[14] In this respect, Germany's pedagogues may have taken their cue from Rousseau, whose rather enigmatic formulation: "to make a young man judicious, we must form his judgments well instead of dictating ours to him" does not resolve the issue, since he leaves unclear the distinction between "forming his judgments well" and "dictating ours to him" (*Emile* 187). The preoccupation with children's reading habits paradigmatically illustrates the obsession with control, particularly in regard to the issue of compulsive reading.

The fear of compulsive reading and its concomitant ills gains steady momentum through the 1780s and 1790s,[15] but the compulsion to control the child's reading can be traced back to the pedagogue of control *par excellence*. Rousseau suggests something approaching total isolation and continuous round-the-clock supervision for his imaginary charge Emile: "you ought to be wholly involved with the child—observing him, spying on him without letup and without appearing to do so, sensing ahead of time all his sentiments and forestalling those he ought not to have" (189). The stated purpose behind Emile's isolation is to protect him from the corrupting influence of a corrupt and decadent society; if Emile's development is to be "natural," the mentor must be able to determine to the greatest extent possible the conditions of this development. It is no accident that Rousseau feels *Robinson Crusoe*, a novel relatively short on social relations, to be the only suitable reading for his charge; he even wishes to pare it down to just that segment of the novel dealing with Robinson's sojourn on the island.[16] Moreover, the interpretive model Rousseau suggests for Emile is clearly identificatory: "I want him to think that he is Robinson himself, to see himself dressed in skins" (185); Emile is to emulate Crusoe's actions rather than reflect on his condition.[17] While Wigand displays little faith in the critical judgment of minors, he at least does not suggest limiting their reading to a single book. That Rousseau is taken seriously in Germany is evidenced by the fact that two prominent pedagogues—Campe and

Johann Karl Wezel—write revisions of *Robinson Crusoe* intended specifically as children's literature. The necessity of controlling and
determining every aspect of Emile's development—in particular, insur-
ing that no corrupting influence of literature breaks through the social
barricade—suggests that Rousseau is operating under the assumption
of a rather extreme susceptibility on the part of the child to corrupting
influences; this assumption would seem inconsistent with Rousseau's
professed belief in the innocence and innate purity of the child. For it
appears that extreme care must be taken to *manipulate* the child's
development toward the direction it supposedly should "naturally"
take. Rousseau's program of manipulation of the model charge Emile
suggests more the pursuit of an agenda than a genuine faith in nature
or in the child's nature.[18] Insofar as the posited "naturalness" of the
child provides a standpoint from which to denounce the "corruption"
of society, one might suspect that Rousseau has not so much
"discovered" the unique qualities of the child, as he has discovered an
instrumentalization of the child: he conceives of uncorrupted
"childhood" as an ideological weapon against a society whose corruption he denounces. German pedagogues, such as those associated with
the *Philanthropin* (the school founded by Basedow in Dessau to imple-
ment his ideas on educational reform), seem to some extent to have
taken their cue from Rousseau in this regard as well. But while Rousseau limits his concerns to the "natural" development of a single individual and contrasts this individual with society, the German version of
this instrumentalization emphasizes a reform, through education, of all
humanity.[19] The contrast with Rousseau is evident, for example, in
Kant's lectures "On Education," which over long stretches read like a
point-by-point commentary on *Emile*: "for in the question of education
is hidden the great secret of the perfection of human nature";
"individuals, however they might raise their charges, cannot bring
about in them the attainment of their destiny. It is not for individual
human beings, but rather for the human race as a whole to attain this
goal."[20]

An example of the distrust felt by Enlightenment pedagogues toward expressions of the child's intrinsic nature, and, by implication,
toward this nature itself, is provided by the following passage from
Christian Felix Weisse's *The Children's Friend* (*Der Kinderfreund*):

> In this matter as well, my children, . . . a comparison between the raising of
> children and the cultivation of trees proves helpful. Your urges and desires,
> were one simply to allow them to grow unchecked rather than cutting them
> back or suppressing them, would often become the largest growths, would spoil
> your moral beauty and bring forth only bad fruit, or none at all. If, however,

one prevents their voluptuous growth, and holds them in check, they often turn into the most excellent virtues.[21]

While it is obvious that, in raising children, some measure of control must be imposed, one needn't be a Freudian to feel uneasy at the idea of "cutting back the voluptuous growth [of urges and desires]." If not brought under control, the child's "natural" urges and desires can became a source of spontaneous moral corruption. The tendency of reading, if uncontrolled by an adult, to develop into the vice of compulsive reading could doubtless serve Weisse as an example of such a corrupting urge. Indeed, the fear of child sexuality expressed here by Weisse is frequently projected by eighteenth-century pedagogues onto an eroticized interpretation of children's reading. Particular cause for alarm is the solitary, self-indulgent compulsive reading of sentimental novels, a practice which over-develops the passions at the expense of the rational faculties of the child.[22]

The narrator of *Anton Reiser* employs a different approach to the child's behavior. Anton's pathological and self-destructive behavior is not judged to be evidence of a corrupt nature, nor treated simply as an aberration to be brought under control; rather, an effort is made to analyze rationally and to explain this behavior. The focus in this psychological novel is as much on the motivation behind Anton's pathological behavior as it is on this behavior itself. Rather than simply point out the detrimental consequences of his behavior, the narrator is consistently at pains to point to the detrimental conditions that gave rise to it. It is thus made clear that Anton's pathological behavior does not spontaneously well up from within him but is provoked by the peculiarly inhospitable conditions of his upbringing and education. What manifests itself outwardly as apathy and withdrawal is revealed to be the result of a critically low self-esteem; this low self-esteem, however, whose roots can be found in the misguided upbringing he experiences at the hands of his parents, is only reinforced by the manner in which Anton's teachers and fellow students react to it:

As he showed no interest in anything, it was no wonder that people in turn showed no interest in him, but rather despised him, slighted him and forgot him.
But people did not consider that this very behavior, on account of which he was neglected, was itself the result of previous neglect. This scorn, which was rooted in a series of accidental conditions, had given rise to his behavior, and not, as people thought, been the result of it.
It is to be hoped that this example might cause all teachers and pedagogues to be more attentive and pass judgment more carefully on the character development of young people, that they might take into account the effects of countless arbitrary circumstances, and first attempt to undertake the most exact inquiry, before presuming to pass judgments that decide the fate of a human being who

perhaps would require no more than an encouraging look to suddenly turn him around, because a peculiar chain of circumstances, and not the foundation of his character, had been responsible for his unseemly behavior.[23]

From the perspective of an adult, an enlightened pedagogue such as Hoche, Wigand or Campe (the sort of "teachers and pedagogues" whom the narrator criticizes), Anton's apathetic behavior alluded to in the above passage might be seen as resulting from an indolent disposition and an unhealthy self-absorption. When an effort is made to appreciate and understand the child's perspective, however, it is the adult world that comes under indictment. The presentation of the child's perspective and the effort to understand the child's motives is, for its time, an innovative if not radical feature of the novel. It is to be distinguished from Rousseau's effort to understand the child's perspective, which is undertaken mainly for the purpose of better manipulating it toward the desired end. Rather than judging Anton's behavior, the narrator turns his critical eye on those who pass premature judgments, arguing that it is precisely such judgments on the child's nature and character that tend to reinforce the behavior they address, rather than correct it. A complicated cycle of reciprocal cause and effect is revealed, which contrasts markedly with Hoche's derivation of all evil from the aberrant behavior of the child ("[compulsive reading] is the *source* of all moral corruption in children and grandchildren," my emphasis).[24] By judging not whether the child's behavior accords with the adult standards set for it, but rather whether these adult standards are adequate to the *child's* psychological needs, whether they support or undermine the child's feeling of self-worth, *Anton Reiser* moves in the direction of an appreciation of childhood experience for its own sake and represents, perhaps, a development from an Enlightenment view of childhood towards a romantic view. The concept of self-worth and of the *intrinsic* value of the child's experience is often attributed to Rousseau's *Emile,* though this work is in fact concerned more with promoting autonomy, self-reliance and self-respect in the adult Emile is to become.

In the contrast between a concern with the child's behavior on the one hand, and a concern with the child's underlying state of mind on the other, one discerns a contrasting concern or lack of concern for the child's intrinsic worth, for who the child is. To a great extent *Anton Reiser* is concerned with issues centered around the protagonist's identity and his sense of this identity. Anton's compulsive reading is one of several behavioral disorders that derive from a feeling of inferiority and an ensuing need to *forget* himself. It can thus be traced back to a damaged sense of identity on his part, the roots of which lie in his early childhood. The narrator gives the following characterization of the attitude of Anton's parents toward him at the age of seven: "now he was almost completely neglected, and every time he was referred to, he heard himself spoken of with a kind of scorn and contempt that pierced his soul."[25] Echoes of his parents' contempt, which he has by then fully internalized, can be seen in the previously quoted passage describing Anton's experiences at the Hannover school.

In particular, Anton's reading habits are a response to his damaged sense of identity. From the very beginning his reading has been of a compensatory nature, an escape from the unpleasantness of his immediate surroundings: "Reading had opened up a whole new world for him, in whose enjoyment he could to some extent compensate himself for all that was unpleasant in his real world."[26] At this point, the reading itself is not yet characterized as pathological, only the conditions that drive him to it. The period of compulsive reading, in which the narrator describes Anton's need for books as an addiction, coincides with a deterioration in his external circumstances, after he has been rapidly promoted to the first class at the Hannover school and becomes subject to the constant ridicule of his older classmates. That his reading habits have become a function of a problem with his identity is made clear in the following passage:

> The tears he frequently shed in reading and at the theater flowed, in essence, as much for his own fate as for that of the characters with whom he was concerned; to a greater or lesser degree he identified with the innocent victim, the character malcontent with himself and the world, the melancholic and the self-hater.[27]

Anton's preoccupation with the theater, his compulsion to read, and his practice of identifying with what he reads are all symptoms of a need to *displace* his identity, his inability to experience his own emotions directly and the ensuing need to project them into a literary work where they can be less threateningly experienced:

> for he had become so indifferent towards his own person, and had retained so little regard or sympathy for himself, that if his regard and his feeling of sympathy, and all the other emotions with which his heart overflowed, had not fallen on characters from a fictional world, they necessarily would have turned back in on him and destroyed his own being.[28]

The emotions he experiences through reading and theater visits emphatically do not represent an attempt to fill vicariously an empty emotional life (a charge frequently leveled against novel reading);[29] rather, his practice of reading is here portrayed as the need to release the tension of an emotional life *too* intense to experience directly, to escape the psychological devastation that would result from a direct confrontation with his damaged identity. At fault is not an idle disposition in need of discipline, but rather the conditions that reinforce his alienation from himself, his self-contempt, his inability to identify with himself directly. Conditioned by the necessity of coping with these conditions, reading becomes a *need*; seen in this light, even Anton's compulsive reading is not so much a disorder as a survival strategy. The passage quoted at the beginning of this essay comparing Anton's reading to an opium addiction is often cited by modern critics of the novel as evidence of the dangers posed by reading (see n. 3). Placed in context, however, the passage emphasizes the intolerable conditions that have led to the behavior and is critical more of these conditions than of Anton's reading, which is merely the particular manifestation of his need to withdraw in the face of a relentlessly hostile environment:

> Winter came, and no thought was given to heating Reiser's room—he first endured the most bitter cold, and thought that he would finally be given some consideration—until he heard that he was to stay in the servants' room during the day.—
>
> At this point he began to have no more concern whatsoever for his external circumstances.—Slighted and despised by his teachers as well as his schoolmates—and, owing to his continual bad mood and shy manner, endeared to no one, *he gave himself up in regard to human society, so to speak*—and tried to draw back entirely into himself.
>
> He went to a second-hand bookstore and obtained one novel, one comedy after the other, and began now to read with a kind of frenzy.... Reading had now become as much a necessity for him as opium might be for the people of the Orient, by means of which they pleasantly dull their senses.[30]

Like the many concerned pedagogues who characterize reading disorders as a disease, Moritz, in describing Anton's reading as an addiction, establishes a relation between reading and issues of health and vitality. This relation is driven home all the more concretely when Anton, who has lost or abandoned most of the "free tables" that are his only regular source of food, nevertheless spends whatever small amount of money he has not on physical sustenance, but uses it instead to borrow books: "Absorbed in his reading, he had forgotten to go to his free table, and he had used the money intended for his evening meal to borrow [Gerstenberg's play] *Ugolino*, ... in which ... he could experience the *starvation scenes* quite vividly."[31] This self-destructive behavior establishes not that Anton is guilty of an unhealthy disposition, but rather that the conditions of his existence have forced his psychological needs into an unfortunate competition with his physical needs. When the narrator states flatly that, had he not found a way to mediate and deflect the intensity of his feelings towards himself, "they would have ... destroyed his own being" (224), it is clear that Anton has not been left with much choice.

Between disease and addiction there is a crucial distinction that reflects the degree of autonomy in principle accorded the child. Preventing the spread of a disease requires no regard for the patient's (child's) volition, other than to prevent the patient's exposure to the disease, through compulsion if necessary. Exposure is tantamount to infection, regardless of the patient's particular condition. In the case of reading disorders, the concerned pedagogue, in the role of physician, has the responsibility to prevent the child's exposure, that is, to prevent access to books deemed to be dangerous; the child's own exercise of will is irrelevant. An addiction, on the other hand, is a disorder relating precisely to the exercise of the will, and has everything to do with the patient's particular condition. In Anton's case, effective treatment of his reading addiction would entail strengthening his sense of identity, which would in turn entail removing or ameliorating the conditions that enforce his alienation and critically low self-esteem. In short, to describe the disorder of compulsive reading as an addiction endows the child with a degree of responsibility for his behavior; treating it as a disease reduces the child's autonomy and responsibility for himself. In fact, Anton's addiction does begin to subside as the conditions of his existence improve and allow him to engage in a greater degree of reflection.

Even during the period of compulsive reading, one of the bleakest times of Anton's life, his aesthetic judgment continues to develop through his reading: "At that time he had already begun to write down the titles of the books he had read in a notebook specially designated for that purpose, and to add his own judgement, which often turned out quite correct."[32] It is important to note that this development occurs autonomously, as it were; rather than being guided by an adult authority toward the application of the correct criteria, Anton develops, through *his own* reading experience, an ability to distinguish good from bad. When the conditions of Anton's existence take an upward turn, his reading habits change as well, and he begins to experience a more analytical, reflective intellectual development through reading:

> For some time he had again been borrowing books from the used book store; but his taste settled now exclusively on scholarly books.—Since that terrible phase of his life, his reading of novels and plays had completely come to an end. . . . Among other things, he had borrowed Gottsched's *Philosophy* from the used book store, and however dilute the material in this book may be, it gave his intellect an initial impetus, as it were.[33]

The encounter with systematic philosophy brings Anton to grapple with the problem of organizing his thoughts; for the purpose of gaining an overview of what he has read, a perspective from which to see the relation of the parts to the whole, he begins to take notes on his reading. The transition from reading to writing also signals a move away from Anton's more passive mode of reception, and he begins to read more critically. The principle of gaining a wider perspective, and seeing the relation of the parts to the whole, becomes an important one that Anton will later apply to his own life. The metaphors employed by the narrator make clear that Anton's encounter with philosophy has sparked a process of "enlightenment" in him:

> The pressing desire to gain quickly an overview of the whole guided him through all the difficulties of the particulars.—A new creation was brought forth in his intellect.—It seemed to him as though it were only just now growing light in his mind, and the day were gradually breaking, and he could not get enough of this invigorating light ... from this point on [he was] less unhappy, because his intellect had begun to develop.[34]

This development has a lasting positive effect, and the narrator, in a formulation that would no doubt occasion some distress for Wigand, expressly emphasizes the value of this auto-didacticism over any learning that Anton has experienced in school:

> if ever a truancy from public school was put to good use, it was Reiser's, in which, in the space of a few months, he accomplished more, and his understanding was enriched with far more concepts than it had been throughout all his years of schooling.[35]

Anton's intellectual development is not without its peculiar dialectic. The powers of analytical intellect and the growing self-awareness and self-confidence brought about through their exercise are not in themselves enough to enable him to bear the many burdens of his existence. As he pursues his philosophical reflections, he is confronted with the problem of language and its relation to existence, and there he encounters an insurmountable barrier. Thus thwarted in the further development of his intellect, he begins to fall back into depression; the metaphors of light are replaced by those of gloom and darkness:

> *Here he came up against the impenetrable wall that distinguishes human thought from the thought of higher beings: the fundamental necessity of language.* ... Language seemed to him to stand in the way of his thought ... sometimes he tormented himself for hours with the attempt to determine *whether it is possible to think without words.*—And then the concept of *existence* occurred to him as the limit of all human thought—then everything became dark and desolate.[36]

But this relapse into gloom proves short-lived; it is overcome when Anton discovers, in Shakespeare, a different function of language, a whole new world of expression that complements the lack he had begun to feel through his exclusive preoccupation with rationalistic philosophy. Thus the direction of his literary tastes at this point mirrors that of the Storm and Stress authors with whose works he becomes preoccupied in the following phase of his literary and intellectual development. At this point, he resumes an earlier effort at keeping a journal. Unlike the previous effort, however, which had remained at a superficial level, merely recording the external events of the day, he is concerned in this journal with recording his subjective experience. In so doing he takes a step in his development toward the stance of the narrator, who has the overview of Anton's life that Anton is now seeking himself:

> The need to communicate his thoughts and emotions led him to the idea of starting up a kind of diary again, in which, however, he wanted to record not just the insignificant external details of his life, as he had done earlier, but rather the inner life of his mind, and to address it to his friend in the form of a letter.... It was this exercise that first made a writer of Anton Reiser; he began to experience an inexpressible pleasure in finding the appropriate words to clothe his thoughts, in order to communicate them to his friend.... Strangely, whenever he was about to write something down, the words *What is my existence, what is my life?* sprang to his pen.[37]

Despite the apparent irony, in essence, the narrator has only more fully realized the effort that Anton undertakes for himself in his diary. Thus a convergence of the course of Anton's development with the position of the narrator is implied. An appreciation of the complexity of the relationship between author, narrator and protagonist—the potential interrelatedness of their identities—adds another dimension to the positive role played by reading in Anton's life. Reading, and the writing which becomes its natural extension, are not a disease, but rather become a method of treatment for that psychological disorder inflicted on Anton by his disastrously misguided upbringing.

Ironically, the positive function of reading in Anton's life is sometimes overlooked by modern critics who fail to appreciate the complex relationship between author, narrator, and protagonist in the novel. For example, in his otherwise insightful study of *Anton Reiser*, Lothar Müller writes:

> In Anton Reiser and the narrator, two types characteristic of the "reading revolution" of the second half of the eighteenth century confront one another, the reading child and the pedagogically concerned mentor.... The narrator writes the biography of Anton Reiser's readings almost exclusively with a view to the risks, not the emancipatory possibilities that reading might have for the child.[38]

The pedagogically concerned mentor as a "type characteristic of the time" might more readily be found in Campe, who, in *Theophron, the Experienced Counselor for Inexperienced Youth*, warns:

> Beware, my son, of this authorship-pestilence, which is as ridiculous as it is harmful. Take note that the terrible flood of books, and the related *compulsive reading* that is spreading further every day are a result and at the same time a cause of the ever-growing corruption of our morals and of all humanity.[39]

Clearly, the concerns of such a pedagogically concerned mentor have little in common with the narrator of *Anton Reiser*, whose aim is not to pontificate, judge, and condemn, but to analyze, understand, and explain the child's behavior. More often than not, the pathological aspects of this behavior are explained specifically as a response to thoughtless, negligent, or otherwise harmful treatment at the hands of adults. Moreover, the child Anton finds a regenerative power within himself to heal at least partially the wounds of his upbringing. Reading plays a crucial role in this healing process, first in merely helping Anton bear his existence, and later in developing in him the powers of reflection that help him come to terms with this difficult existence begun under such inauspicious circumstances. Thus the apparent incongruity between the two passages quoted at the beginning of this essay, from Moritz's *Logic for Children* and from *Anton Reiser*, was somewhat misleading, for while a deep ambivalence towards the reading child is indeed a feature of the mainstream pedagogy of the time (indicative of a distrust of the child's intrinsic nature), Moritz in fact feels no distrust towards books or their potential influence on children. He reserves his distrust for parents and pedagogues.

In presenting the child's perspective as he does, it could perhaps be said that Moritz delivers on the promise of Rousseau, who is often credited with the "discovery" of the child—the focus of attention on the unique characteristics of childhood—in the eighteenth century. The model of autonomous development presented in *Anton Reiser* contrasts with the educational model of *Emile* at almost every point of comparison. While *Emile* is presented as an idealized upbringing, *Anton Reiser* depicts the disastrous consequences of an (actual) misguided upbringing characterized by indifference and neglect, and so a comparison is of only limited relevance. But it is worthy of note that in the effort to instill a sense of autonomy in Emile, his mentor deprives him of any real autonomy through the compulsive control he deems it necessary to exert over Emile's development. Anton, *in spite of* the extremely unfavorable conditions of his upbringing, develops on his own a measure of intellectual autonomy that enables him to reflect and to develop further. Anton's psychological disorders are not an intrinsic part of his nature, the expression of some corrupt predisposition that was not preempted with sufficient vigilance by his mentors; rather, his problems result directly from the incompetence of his mentors, his parents and teachers. Thus the view of the child implicit in *Anton Reiser* is one that puts much more faith in the child's nature, and in the vitality and regenerative power of this nature, than one encounters in most pedagogues contemporary with Moritz. On the other hand, the compulsion to control and influence every aspect of the child's life, paradigmatically illustrated in the fears and anxieties surrounding the phenomenon of children reading, betrays a distrust in the child's nature. Insofar as this control is exerted in the interest of producing an autonomy whose character is predetermined by the pedagogue, it could be termed the *dialectic of pedagogy*: it risks a reproduction of the very unhealthy mechanisms of maladjustment it seeks to overcome.

Notes

1. This and all following translations from the German are my own. "Ein Buch ist ein großer und erhabener Gegenstand. Es ist eine Erfindung des Menschen, die alles andere übertrifft—Alles was der Kopf des Menschen in sich faßt, das kann auch das Buch in sich fassen. . . . Was für ein Verdienst um das menschliche Geschlecht hat der nicht, der zuerst diese vierundzwanzig kleinen Figuren erfand, wodurch alle Wissenschaften, alle menschlichen Begebenheiten, alle Dinge die am Himmel und auf Erden sind, in dem kleinen Umfange eines Buches dergestalt reden können! . . . Und die Seelen der Menschen können sich nun, in jeder Entfernung durch die Bücher miteinander unterreden, und sich untereinander belehren" (Karl Phillip Moritz, *Versuch einer kleinen praktischen Kinderlogik* 408-10).

2. "Das Lesen war ihm nun einmal so zum Bedürfnis geworden, wie es den Morgenländern das Opium sein mag, wodurch sie ihre Sinne in eine angenehme Betäubung bringen. Wenn es ihm an einem Buche fehlte, so hätte er seinen Rock gegen den Kittel eines Bettlers vertauscht, um nur eins zu bekommen" (Moritz, *Anton Reiser* 201-02).

3. The passage comparing reading to opium is quoted, for instance, by Kreuzer 63, Müller 331, Steinlein 72, Weber 58, and Wuthenow 88, to name just a few. The passage is almost always cited (out of context) in support of the view that Moritz's intentions are to warn against the vices to which uncontrolled reading can lead. As I will show, the context of this passage on Anton's addictive reading supports a quite different conclusion.

4. Leaving aside the question of genre classification for this novel, parts of my argument rely on a knowledge of the autobiographical nature of *Anton Reiser*, which has been acknowledged in Moritz scholarship since Hugo Eybisch's painstaking study corroborating the events related in the novel with all that can be independently verified of Moritz's early life.

5. "Die Lesesucht ist ein thörichter, schädlicher Mißbrauch einer sonst guten Sache, ein wirklich großes Uebel, das so ansteckend ist, wie das gelbe Fieber in Philadelphia; sie ist die Quelle des sittlichen Verderbens für Kinder und Kindes Kinder. Thorheiten und Fehler werden durch sie in das gesellige Leben eingeführt und darin erhalten . . . der Geist verwildert anstatt veredelt zu werden" (J. G. Hoche, *Vertraute Briefe*, qtd. Schenda 60).

6. The reaction against reading that sets in towards the close of the eighteenth century has been extensively documented by Rudolf Schenda. Schenda argues that a concept of "limited enlightenment" was introduced in the wake of the French Revolution; in his view, "compulsive reading" was an imaginary danger trumped up for the purpose of discouraging reading, thought and reflection on the part of the public: "This sudden denunciation of compulsive reading—a result of the general fear of revolution—was part of a program of "limited enlightenment" that was by no means uncritically accepted by reasonable, independent observers of the time" (62). In his treatment of late eighteenth-century attitudes towards compulsive reading, Schenda significantly omits any discussion of *Anton Reiser*; the reflections

on reading in this novel would certainly tend to undermine his thesis that compulsive reading was nothing more than a kind of straw man invoked to discourage all reading and intellectual development among the lower classes. A useful corrective to Schenda's exclusive focus on political repression as the motivation behind the fear of reading is provided by Helmut Kreuzer. Kreuzer points out that much of the concern over children's reading habits was sincere and not motivated by a desire to preserve the status quo.

7. Possibly Karl Samuel Wigand (1744-1805), a pedagogue and newspaper editor in Kassel. The article was published in the *Braunschweigisches Journal*, which was edited throughout its publication by Ernst Christian Trapp, and for several years, in addition, by Campe, Conrad Heusinger, and Johannes Stuve. Ewers refers to the journal as a "politically radical educational journal" (486).

8. "[W]ürde dir deine Zeit nicht zehnfältig mehr Frucht bringen, wenn du, statt der hie und da hergeholten und zerstreuten, vielleicht unbedeutenden Zusammenträge, Nachrichten, Bemerkungen dieses oder jenes Reisenden oder Dilletanten, ein Werk läsest, das die Kunst oder deren Geschichte im Ganzen behandelte, wo du Alles oder Vieles von dem, was du in dergleichen Blättern zerstreut findest, in eine zweckmäßige Ordnung gestellet, im Zusammenhange übersehen könntest" (404).

9. "auch dann schon tue ich mir Schaden, wenn ich das Nützliche dem Nützlichern vorziehe" (404).

10. "Durch diese einzige so oft wiederholte Lektüre [von Ramlers Tod Jesu] bekam sein Geschmack in der Poesie eine gewisse Bildung und Festigkeit, die er seit der Zeit nicht wieder verloren hat; so wie in der Prose durch den Telemach; denn er fühlte bei der schönen Banise und Insel Felsenburg, ohngeachtet des Vergnügens, das er darin fand, doch sehr lebhaft das Abstechende und Unedlere in der Schreibart" (40). K. W. Ramler's cantata *Der Tod Jesu* was set by J. C. F. Bach, Graun, and Telemann. The novels are F. de Salignac de la Mothe-Fénelon, *Aventures de Télémaque* (1689), and two examples of the early novel in Germany: H. A. von Zigler und Kliphausen, *Die Asiatische Banise* (1689) and J. G. Schnabel, *Die Insel Felsenburg* (1731/43).

11. "Wenn nun rund um ihn her nichts als Lärmen und Schelten und häusliche Zwietracht herrschte, oder er sich vergeblich nach einem Gespielen umsah, so eilte er hin zu seinem Buch.

So ward er schon früh aus der natürlichen Kinderwelt in eine unnatürliche idealische Welt verdrängt, wo sein Geist für tausend Freuden des Lebens verstimmt wurde" (16-17).

12. "die unverantwortliche Seelenlähmung durch das zurücksetzende Betragen seiner eigenen Eltern gegen ihn, die er von Kindheit an noch nicht hatte wieder vermindern können" (368).

13. Not all pedagogical theorists of the period are as blithely insensitive as Wigand to the problems of such an uncritical acceptance of the authority of adults. While *Anton Reiser* demonstrates graphically the untenability of a faith in adult authority, Kant, in his lectures "On Education," formulates the theoretical difficulty implied by such a faith as follows: "It is worthy of note that human beings are educated only by fellow human beings, who in turn have themselves been educated. For that reason, a lack of discipline and instruction in some people renders them unfit to instruct their pupils" (699); "therefore pedagogy must become a study, otherwise nothing is to be hoped for from it, and one man whose education has been spoiled will only repeat his own mistakes in trying to educate others" (705).

14. Rutschky has assembled a collection of pedagogical writings from the

eighteenth to the twentieth century that highlight, among other things, the assumed prerogative—and the compulsion—to control all aspects of children's lives.

15. See Schenda 57-66.

16. *Emile* 184-85. Emile's isolation, purportedly maintained for the purpose of protecting him from corrupting influences, but clearly also implemented for the sake of maintaining more effective control, is thereby reinforced threefold: he is isolated from society, isolated from any books that could remind him of society, and then forced to identify with a literary hero whose isolation is even bleaker and more absolute than his own.

17. As Ewers has noted: "In leaving out the beginning and the end [of *Robinson Crusoe*], the moral-religous dimension of the original is lost" ("Aufklärung" 55).

18. Steinlein examines the treatment of reading in *Emile* from the standpoint of Rousseau's concern with the production and regulation of fantasy/imagination: "To forego reading and books is of decisive importance in the prevention of a premature stimulation of the child's imagination. . . . The mentor, however, acts as the decisive agent of prevention" (126-27). Steinlein emphasizes the benevolent intent behind Rousseau's goal of preventing the development of an imbalance between desires and ability in the psyche of the child. Yet he is not unaware of the exercise of power implied in Rousseau's program: "[Trapp's] discourse on the pedagogy of imagination reveals itself to be concerned with the mechanisms of power, which is not to imply that this dimension is fundamentally lacking in Rousseau's work; rather it is just expressed more subtly" (128-29). It might be fair to point out that Rousseau does not necessarily intend for the pedagogical prescriptions in *Emile*, which represents an idealized upbringing, to be followed literally. But it is also fair to consider the rather extreme degree of control and manipulation necessary for Rousseau, even (or especially) in his idealized pedagogical situation, to achieve his desired end, and that the child Emile is consistently valued not for what he is but rather for what kind of adult he is to become.

19. Rutschky writes of this instrumentalization: "Education as a secular bestowal of meaning on human life takes up the legacy of another illusion, religion. . . . [T]he optimistic enlightened pedagogues Campe and Basedow reveal the real intent behind the founding of a new school to be the fundamental improvement of the human race!" (57).

20. "hinter der Edukation steckt das große Geheimnis der Vollkommenheit der menschlichen Natur" (700); "Nicht einzelne Menschen, sondern die Menschengattung soll dahin gelangen" (702).

21. "Auch hier, meine Kinder, . . . findet der Vergleich [der Baumzucht] mit der jugendlichen Erziehung sehr statt. Eure Neigungen und Begierden, die, wenn man sie, ohne sie zu beschneiden oder zu unterdrücken, fortwachsen ließe, würden oft die größten Auswüchse werden, eure moralische Schönheit verderben und keine oder doch schlechte Früchte hervorbringen. Wenn man ihren schwelgerischen Wuchs aber verhindert, und sie in ihren Schranken hält, werden sie oft die herrlichsten Tugenden" (qtd. Rutschky 128).

22. The eroticization of children's reading in pedagogical theory of the eighteenth and nineteenth centuries is dealt with extensively by Steinlein.

23. "Was Wunder, da er an nichts teilnahm, daß man auch wieder an ihm nicht teilnahm, sondern ihn verachtete, hintansetzte und vergaß.
Allein man erwog nicht, daß eben dies Betragen, weswegen man ihn zurücksetzte, selbst eine Folge von vorhergegangner Zurücksetzung war.— Diese Zurücksetzung, welche in einer Reihe von zufälligen Umständen gegründet war, hatte den Anfang zu

seinem Betragen, und nicht sein Betragen, wie man glaubte, den Anfang zur Zurück-setzung gemacht. Möchte dies alle Lehrer und Pädagogen aufmerksamer, und in ihren Urteilen über die Entwickelung der Charaktere junger Leute behutsamer machen, daß sie die Einwirkung unzähliger zufälliger Umstände mit in Anschlag brächten, und von diesen erst die genaueste Erkundigung einzuziehen suchten, ehe sie es wagten, durch ihr Urteil über das Schicksal eines Menschen zu entscheiden, bei dem es vielleicht nur eines aufmunternden Blicks bedurfte, um ihn plötzlich umzuschaffen, weil nicht die Grundlage seines Charakters, sondern eine sonderbare Verkettung von Umständen zu einem schlecht in die Augen fallenden Betragen schuld war" (205, emphasis in original).

24. J. G. Hoche, *Vertraute Briefe*, qtd. Schenda 60.

25. "er [wurde] nun fast ganz vernachlässigt, und hörte sich, sooft man von ihm sprach, mit einer Art von Geringschätzung und Verachtung nennen, die ihm durch die Seele ging" (14).

26. "Durch das Lesen war ihm nun auf einmal eine neue Welt eröffnet, in deren Genuß er sich für alle das unangenehme in seiner wirklichen Welt einigermaßen entschädigen konnte" (17).

27. "Die häufigsten Tränen welche er oft beim Buche, und im Schauspielhause vergoß, flossen im Grunde ebensowohl über sein eignes Schicksal, als über das Schicksal der Personen, an denen er teilnahm, er fand sich immer auf eine nähere oder entferntere Weise in dem unschuldig Unterdrückten, in dem Unzufriednen mit sich und der Welt, in dem Schwermutsvollen, dem Selbsthasser wieder" (221).

28. "denn er war sich selbst so gleichgültig geworden, und hatte so wenige Achtung gegen sich und Mitleid mit sich selber übrigbehalten, daß wenn seine Achtung und Empfindung des Mitleids, und alle die Leidenschaften, wovon sein Herz überströmte, nicht auf Personen aus einer erdichteten Welt gefallen wären, sie notwendig sich alle gegen ihn selbst kehren, und sein eignes Wesen hätten zerstören müssen" (224).

29. For instance, Campe, in denouncing sentimental literature and promoting his own children's novel *Robinson Junior* (*Robinson der Jüngere*), writes in the foreword to this novel of the indolent contemplation ("unthätige Beschauungen") and idle feelings of compassion ("müßige Rührungen") to which the former leads, in contrast to the self-motivated activity ("Selbstätigkeit") encouraged by the latter (8).

30. "Es wurde Winter, und man dachte nicht daran, Reisers Stube zu heizen—er stand erst die bitterste Kälte aus, und glaubte, man würde doch endlich auch an ihn denken—bis er hörte, daß er sich bei Tage in der Gesindestube mit aufhalten sollte.—

Nun fing er an, sich um seine äußern Verhältnisse gar nicht mehr zu bekümmern.—Von seinen Lehrern sowohl als von seinen Mitschülern verachtet, und hintangesetzt—und wegen seines immerwährenden Mißmuts und menschenscheuen Wesens bei niemand beliebt, *gab er sich gleichsam selber in Rücksicht der menschlichen Gesellschaft auf*—und suchte sich nun vollends ganz in sich zurückzuziehen.

Er ging zu einem Antiquarius und holte sich einen Roman, eine Komödie nach der andern, und fing nun mit einer Art von Wut an, zu lesen. . . . Das Lesen war ihm nun einmal so zum Bedürfnis geworden, wie es den Morgenländern das Opium sein mag, wodurch sie ihre Sinne in eine angenehme Betäubung bringen" (201-02, emphasis in original).

31. "seinen Freitisch hatte er über dem Lesen versäumt, und für das Geld, was

zum Abendbrot bestimmt war, hatte er sich den Ugolino geliehen, . . . bei welchem er . . . die *Hungerszenen* recht lebhaft mitempfinden konnte" (202, emphasis in original).

32. "Nun hatte er damals schon angefangen, sich die Titel der Bücher, welche er gelesen hatte, in einem dazu bestimmten Buche niederzuschreiben, und sein Urteil dabei zu setzen, das mehrmalen ziemlich richtig ausfiel" (203).

33. "Er liehe sich seit einiger Zeit wieder Bücher vom Antiquarius; aber sein Geschmack fiel nun auf lauter wissenschaftliche Bücher.—Seine Romanen- und Komödienlektüre hatte seit jener schrecklichen Epoche seines Lebens gänzlich aufgehört. . . . Er hatte sich von dem Bücherantiquarius unter andern *Gottscheds Philosophie* geliehen, und sosehr auch in diesem Buche die Materien durchwässert sind, so gab doch dies seiner Denkkraft gleichsam den ersten Stoß" (252). The reference is to J. G. Gottsched's extremely influential summary of Wolff's philosophy, *Erste Gründe der gesamten Weltweisheit* (1734).

34. "Die immerwährende Begierde, das Ganze bald zu überschauen, leitete ihn durch alle Schwierigkeiten des Einzelnen hindurch.—In seiner Denkkraft ging eine neue Schöpfung hervor.— Es war ihm, als ob es erst in seinem Verstande dämmerte, und nun allmählich der Tag anbräche, und er sich an dem erquickenden Licht nicht satt sehen könnte . . . [er war] von nun an, minder unglücklich, weil seine Denkkraft angefangen hatte, sich zu entwickeln" (253-54).

35. "wenn nun ja eine Versäumnis von öffentlichen Schulstunden gut genutzt worden ist, so war es die seinige—in welcher er in Zeit von ein paar Monaten mehr tat, und sein Verstand mit weit mehr Begriffen, als seine ganzen akademischen Jahre hindurch, bereichert wurde" (256).

36. "*Er stieß hier an die undurchdringliche Scheidewand, welche das menschliche Denken von dem Denken höherer Wesen verschieden macht, an das notwendige Bedürfnis der Sprache.* . . . Die Sprache schien ihm beim Denken im Wege zu stehen . . . manchmal quälte er sich stundenlang, zu versuchen, *ob es möglich sei, ohne Worte zu denken.*—Und dann stieß ihm der Begriff von *Dasein* als die Grenze alles menschlichen Denkens auf—da wurde ihm alles dunkel und öde" (254-55).

37. "Das Bedürfnis, seine Gedanken und Empfindungen mitzuteilen, brachte ihn auf den Einfall, sich wieder eine Art von Tagebuch zu machen, worin er aber nicht sowohl seine äußern geringfügigen Begebenheiten, wie ehemals, sondern die innere Geschichte seines Geistes aufzeichnen, und das, was er aufzeichnete, in Form eines Briefes an seinen Freund richten wollte. . . . Diese Übung bildete Anton Reisern zuerst zum Schriftsteller; er fing an, ein unbeschreibliches Vergnügen daran zu empfinden, Gedanken, die er für sich gedacht hatte, nun in anpassende Worte einzukleiden, um sie seinem Freunde mitteilen zu können. . . . Nun war es sonderbar; wenn er im Anfang etwas niederschreiben wollte, so kamen ihm immer die Worte in die Feder: *Was ist mein Dasein, was mein Leben?*" (268).

38. "In Anton Reiser und seinem Erzähler stehen zwei zeittypische Figuren der 'Leserevolution' in der zweiten Hälfte des 18. Jahrhunderts gegenüber, das lesende Kind und sein pädagogisch besorgter Mentor. . . . Die Lektürebiographie Anton Reisers schreibt der Erzähler fast ausschließlich aus der Perspektive der Risiken, nicht der emanzipativen Chancen des kindlichen Lesens" (322-23).

39. "Hüte dich, mein Sohn, vor dieser eben so lächerlichen als schädlichen Autorseuche. Wisse, daß das fürchterliche Anschwellen der Bücher und die damit verbundene *Lesewuth*, welche täglich weiter um sich greift, eine Folge und zugleich mit eine Ursache der immer größer werdenden Verderbniß unserer Sitten und der ganzen Menschheit ist" (Campe, *Theophron*; Ewers 128).

Works Cited

Campe, Joachim Heinrich. *Robinson der Jüngere: Ein Lesebuch für Kinder.* Braunschweig: Verlag der Schulbuchhandlung, 1812.

Eybisch, Hugo. *Anton Reiser: Untersuchungen zur Lebensgeschichte von K. Ph. Moritz und zur Kritik seiner Autobiographie.* Leipzig: Voigtlander, 1909.

Ewers, Hans-Heino. *Kinder- und Jugendliteratur der Aufklärung: Eine Textsammlung.* Stuttgart: Reclam, 1980.

————. "Aufklärung und Romantik im Spiegel klassischer Kinderbücher." *Jahrbuch der Jean-Paul-Gesellschaft* 19 (1984): 43-63.

Kant, Immanuel. "Über Pädagogik." *Werke in zwölf Bänden.* Frankfurt/M.: Insel, 1964. 12: 691-761.

Kreuzer, Helmut. "Gefährliche Lesesucht? Bemerkungen zu politischer Lektürekritik im ausgehenden 18. Jahrhundert." *Lesen und Leser im 18. Jahrhundert.* Ed. Rainer Gruenter. Heidelberg: Winter, 1977.

Moritz, Karl Philipp. *Versuch einer kleinen praktischen Kinderlogik. Werke in drei Bänden.* Frankfurt/M.: Insel, 1981.

————. *Anton Reiser: Ein psychologischer Roman.* Stuttgart: Reclam, 1972.

Müller, Lothar. *Die kranke Seele und das Licht der Erkenntnis: Karl Philipp Moritz' Anton Reiser.* Frankfurt/M.: Athenäum, 1987.

Rousseau, Jean Jacques. *Emile.* Trans. Allan Bloom. New York: Basic, 1979.

Rutschky, Katharina, ed. *Schwarze Pädagogik: Quellen zur Naturgeschichte der bürgerlichen Erziehung.* Frankfurt/M.: Ullstein, 1987.

Schenda, Rudolf. *Volk ohne Buch: Studien zur Sozialgeschichte der populären Lesestoffe.* Frankfurt/M.: Klostermann, 1970.

Steinlein, Rüdiger. *Die domestizierte Phantasie: Studien zur Kinderliteratur, Kinderlektüre und Literaturpädagogik des 18. und frühen 19. Jahrhunderts.* Heidelberg: Winter, 1987.

Weber, Dietrich. "Lektüre im *Anton Reiser.*" *Lesen und Leser im 18. Jahrhundert.* Ed. Rainer Gruenter. Heidelberg: Winter, 1977.

Wigand, [Karl Samuel?] "Ist angehenden Studirenden das Lesen der Zeitschriften zu empfehlen?" *Braunschweigisches Journal.* 1790. 10. Stück. Klaus Reprint, Nendeln: 1972. 398-432.

Wuthenow, Ralph-Rainer. *Im Buch die Bücher oder Der Held als Leser.* Frankfurt/M.: Europäische Verlagsanstalt, 1980.

CONTRIBUTORS

Dagmar Barnouw, Professor of German and Comparative Literature at the University of Southern California and a recent Getty senior research fellow, has published widely on modern literature and has lately turned her attention to the eighteenth century. Most recently, she is the author of *Weimar Intellectuals and the Threat of Modernity* (1988), *Visible Spaces: Hannah Arendt and the German-Jewish Experience* (1990), and *There and Then: History, Photography and the Critical Realism of Siegfried Kracauer* (1993).

Barbara Becker-Cantarino, Research Professor at Ohio State University, has published extensively on the literature of Early Modern Germany, intellectual history, and women's literature. After books on and/or editions of Opitz, satire, Anna Ovena Hoyers, Sophie von La Roche, and the social history of Early Modern women, she published the pioneering study of women's literature from 1500 to 1800, *Der lange Weg zur Mündigkeit* (1987). A forthcoming book treats patriarchy, gender, and German Romanticism.

Klaus L. Berghahn, Senior Member of the Institute for Research in the Humanities at the University of Wisconsin at Madison, has published extensively in literature of the eighteenth century and Classical period. He has written or edited several books on and by Schiller (most recently a 1986 monograph) and has also edited many volumes of essays, including *Utopian Vision, Technological Innovation, and Poetic Imagination* (with Reinhold Grimm, 1990). He is currently working on a book on antisemitism and tolerance in eighteenth-century literature.

Jeannine Blackwell is Associate Professor of German at the University of Kentucky. She has published numerous articles on German women's literature and culture from 1600 to 1900, and together with Susanne Zantop edited a highly acclaimed collection of German women's literature of the eighteenth and early nineteenth century in English translation, *Bitter Healing* (1990). She is currently writing a book on autobiographical confessions by German women.

Christiane Bohnert is an independent scholar. She wrote a book on Brecht's poetry (1982) and another on the theory and practice of satire in different cultures, with emphasis on the eighteenth century (forthcoming). She is currently writing a reference work on satire, and has published articles on Wieland and Wezel, Kant's

ethics in contemporary Western culture, and on E. T. A. Hoffmann and literature
of the German Democratic Republic.

Sara Friedrichsmeyer is Professor of German at the University of Cincinnati,
Raymond Walters College. Her publications include articles on German Romanticism, feminist theory, forms of autobiographical representation, and various
nineteenth- and twentieth-century women writers as well as a monograph, *The An-
drogyne in Early German Romanticism* (1983). A co-editor of the *Women in German Yearbook*, she is currently writing a book on nature and gender in German literature since the Enlightenment.

Andreas Gailus is a graduate student in the German Department at Columbia
University. He is writing his doctoral thesis on Heinrich von Kleist and the
emergence of the modern German novella.

Robert C. Holub, Professor and Chair of the German Department at the University
of California at Berkeley, has published extensively on German literature, culture,
and intellectual history since the Enlightenment, especially on Heinrich Heine. His
most recent book publications are *Reflections of Realism: Paradox, Norm, and
Ideology in Nineteenth-Century German Prose* (Wayne State, 1991); *Jürgen Habermas: Critic in the Public Sphere* (1991); and *Crossing Borders: Reception Theory,
Poststructuralism, Deconstruction* (1992).

Michael T. Jones is Associate Professor of German at the University of Kentucky.
He has written on idealist aesthetics (Schiller), on E.T.A. Hoffmann, and on
literary theory (Adorno). He is presently at work on a book on the criticism and
aesthetic theory of Friedrich Schlegel.

Volker Kaiser teaches in the German Department of the University of Virginia.
He is the author of articles on Kleist, Rilke, Brecht, and the postmodern, and a
book on Rilke, Benn and Celan, *Das Echo jeder Verschattung* (1993). He is currently working on a book that investigates the literary and political friendship
between Brecht and Benjamin.

Karen Kenkel is a Ph.D. candidate in German Studies at Cornell University. She is
a former Fulbright scholar and is completing a dissertation on the representation
and discussion of "the masses" in drama and film of the Wilhelminian period. She
has published articles on minority culture, pornography, and (together with David
Phillips) on Ronald Reagan.

Todd Kontje, Associate Professor of German at the University of California at San
Diego, has written articles on eighteenth-century and other topics, as well as books
on Schiller's aesthetics (*Constructing Reality*, 1987) and the German Bildungsroman
(*Private Lives in the Public Sphere*, 1992). A volume on the history of Bildungsroman criticism (*The German Bildungsroman: History of a National Genre*)
appeared in the Literary Criticism in Perspective series of Camden House press in
the fall of 1993.

Jill Anne Kowalik is Associate Professor of German at the University of California
at Los Angeles. She has published articles on Lessing, Kleist, Goethe, Nietzsche,

Dilthey, and Thomas Mann, and recently authored a book entitled *The Poetics of Historical Perspectivism: Breitinger's* Critische Dichtkunst *and the Neoclassic Tradition* (1992).

Sigrid Lange received her doctorate in 1979 and her "Habilitation" in 1990 at the University of Jena, where she also teaches; she was one of the few feminist literary critics in the former German Democratic Republic, and has held visiting appointments at Göttingen and Munich. She has published extensively on Goethe, Schiller, Sophie Mereau, Dorothea Veit, and Friedrich Schlegel, as well as twentieth-century topics.

John A. McCarthy, Professor of German at Vanderbilt University, has done research on a wide variety of topics in eighteenth-century culture, concentrating on Wieland, Lessing, Schiller, censorship, and reading habits. After earlier books on Wieland, he has published *Crossing Boundaries: A Theory and History of Essayistic Writing, 1680-1815* (1989), co-authored another book on Wieland (forthcoming, 1993), and co-edited a volume on censorship entitled *Kultur und Zensur: Zwischen Weimarer Klassik und Weimarer Republik* (forthcoming, 1994).

Helga Meise, who teaches at the Universities of Marburg and Frankfurt, has written extensively on women's literature, including a book on the eighteenth-century novel by women: *Die Unschuld und die Schrift: Deutsche Frauenromane im 18. Jahrhundert* (1983). She is preparing a book on autobiographical writing and courtly society in the Early Modern period.

Arnim Polster is writing his dissertation at the University of California at Berkeley on Karl Phillip Moritz and the pedagogy of reading.

David V. Pugh, who earned his Ph.D. from the University of Toronto before teaching at the University of California at Santa Barbara, is Assistant Professor of German at Queen's University in Kingston, Ontario. He has published articles on Goethe, Schiller, and Klopstock, and is working on a book on Schiller and Platonism.

Jochen Schulte-Sasse, one of America's leading Germanists and Professor of German and Comparative Literature at the University of Minnesota, has written extensively on eighteenth-century to contemporary culture and literary theory; among his numerous books are a study of Lessing (1975). His most recent project is entitled *Critique of Aesthetic Culture*. He serves on several editorial boards, including the series "Theory and History of Literature" (University of Minnesota Press), *Cultural Critique*, and *Enclitic*.

Robert Tobin received his Ph.D. in German from Princeton University in 1990 after study in Munich and Freiburg and is Assistant Professor at Whitman College. He has written a number of articles on sexuality and medicine in the literature of such writers as Goethe and Thomas Mann.

W. Daniel Wilson, Professor of German at the University of California at Berkeley, has published widely on eighteenth-century literature and history, especially questions of the writer's relation to power, examining authors from Lessing and Wieland to the Romantics. His most recent book, *Geheimräte gegen Geheimbünde* (1991), uses unpublished documents to detail the importance of secret societies and conspiracy theories for Goethe's relations to other intellectuals. He is currently writing on the dilemma of German intellectuals in "enlightened" absolutism.

Hans-Gerd Winter is Professor of German at the University of Hamburg. He has written many articles on literature of the Enlightenment and particularly the "Storm and Stress" movement, on contemporary German literature and literary theory. He is the author of several books, including two on J.M.R. Lenz (1984—together with Inge Stephan—and 1987), and has edited collections of essays, especially on eighteenth-century topics and on Hamburg literature.

Susanne Zantop is Associate Professor of German and Comparative Literature at Dartmouth College. After writing/editing two books on Heine (*Zeitbilder*, 1988; *Paintings on the Move*, 1989), she has turned her attention to a study of colonial fantasies in pre-colonial Germany. She has published editions of previously neglected novels by eighteenth-century women and (with Jeannine Blackwell) a ground-breaking anthology in English translation, *Bitter Healing: German Women Writers 1700-1830* (1990).

Carsten Zelle teaches German and Comparative Literature at the University of Siegen; in 1987 he published an important study of eighteenth-century aesthetics of pleasurable horror, *Angenehmes Grauen*. He has written numerous articles on eighteenth and nineteenth-century topics, literary theory and aesthetics and the history of German studies, and has published editions of works of Grosse, Lavater and Pyra. He is currently completing a book about the duality of aesthetics in modernity from 1674 to 1915.

INDEX OF NAMES

489

Rosenberg, Hans, 366, 377
Rosmarin, Adena, 223
Rothschuh, Karl Eduard, 243
Rousseau, Jean-Jacques, 110, 112, 135-
   37, 140, 141, 168, 171, 178, 205, 228,
   269, 312, 331, 389-90, 392, 396, 398,
   400, 444-45, 449-50, 454, 456, 469-
   70, 472, 478
Rubin, Gail, 54
Rückert, Josef, 20, 27

Sade,   Donatien-Alphonse-François,
   marquis de, 111
Saint-Pierre, Charles Irénée Castel,
   abbé de, 388-90, 393, 396, 400
Sale, Kirpatrick, 315
Sappho, 245
Sauder, Gerhard, 118, 119, 369
Saurin, Jacques, 431
Schabert, Tilo, 129
Schelle, Karl Gottlob, 314
Schiller, Friedrich, 9, 59, 109, 111, 113,
   118, 137, 142, 146-84, 186, 188, 192,
   193, 195, 223-24, 261, 373-74
Schings, Hans Jürgen, 111, 419
Schlegel, August Wilhelm, 261
Schlegel, Friedrich, 58, 110, 138, 261
Schleiermacher, Friedrich, 426
Schlözer, August Ludwig, 39, 447
Schmidt, Johann Christoph, 371
Schnabel, Johann Gottfried, 468
Schnauß, Christian Friedrich, 371
Schneider, Helmut, 190
Schneider, Karl Ludwig, 368
Schneiders, Werner, 13, 17, 29
Schoefer, Christine, 81
Schönert, Jörg, 460
Schopenhauer, Arthur, 59
Schubart, Christian Friedrich Daniel,
   39
Schuchartin, Anna Marie, 428
Schulte-Sasse, Jochen, 58
Schulz, Gerhard, 332
Schwanitz, Hans Joachim, 246
Seghers, Anna, 69
Selbmann, Rolf, 224
Semler, Johann Salomo, 425-42
Sengle, Friedrich, 166
Sepúlveda, Juan Ginés de, 305

Shaftesbury, Anthony Ashley Cooper,
   Third Earl of, 111
Shakespeare, William, 260, 263-64,
   446, 476
Sidney, Sir Philip, 169-70, 173
Silverman, Kaja, 162
Smith, Adam, 110, 347
Smith, John H., 222, 227
Socrates, 26
Sömmering, Samuel Thomas, 335
Spalding, Johann Joachim, 445
Spener, Philipp, 427
Spinoza, Baruch de, 195
Stahl, Georg Ernst, 243
Steenhuis, Aafke, 81
Stein, Heinrich Friedrich Karl Reichs-
   freiherr vom und zum, 366
Stephan, Inge, 58
Stifter, Adalbert, 222
Strauss, David Friedrich, 426
Strube, Werner, 114
Stutz, Johann Ernst August, 232-33
Sühnel, Rudolf, 112

Taylor, Charles, 19, 29
Theweleit, Klaus, 144
Thomasberger, Andreas, 187, 189
Thomasius, Christian, 21, 428
Tieck, Ludwig, 222
Tietz, Manfred, 309
Tietze, Johann Christian, 425, 428, 429,
   431
Tissot, Samuel, 244, 245
Titel, Britta, 443
Träger, Christine, 209, 210
Tucholsky, Kurt, 460
Twell, 431

Ueding, Gert, 370
Unger, Friederike Helene, 221, 227,
   232-33, 235

Vaget, Hans Rudolf, 267
Vespucci, Amerigo, 305, 307
Vetter, Anna, 427
Virgil, 169
Voit, Friedrich, 453
Voltaire (François-Marie Arouet), 312,
   377, 452